The International Survey of Family Law

2012 Edition

The International Survey of Family Law

Published on behalf of the International Society of Family Law

2012 Edition

General Editor
Bill Atkin
Faculty of Law
Victoria University of Wellington
PO Box 600
Wellington
New Zealand

Associate Editor (Africa)
Fareda Banda
Reader in the Laws of Africa
School of Oriental and African Studies
London

Family Law

Published by Family Law
a publishing imprint of
Jordan Publishing Limited
21 St Thomas Street
Bristol BS1 6JS

British Library Cataloguing-in-Publication Data

A catalogue record for this book is available from the British Library.

ISBN 978 1 84661 331 9

Typeset by Letterpart Ltd, Reigate, Surrey

Printed in Great Britain by CPI Antony Rowe, Chippenham and Eastbourne

MEMBERS OF THE INTERNATIONAL SOCIETY OF FAMILY LAW

ASSOCIATION INTERNATIONALE DE DROIT DE LA FAMILLE

INTERNATIONALE GESELLSCHAFT FÜR FAMILIENRECHT

Website: www.law2.byu.edu/ISFL

Officers and Council Members 2011-2014

PRESIDENT
Professor Patrick Parkinson
Faculty of Law
University of Sydney
SYDNEY 2006
AUSTRALIA
Tel: +61 2 9351 0309
Fax: +61 2 9351 0200
E-mail: patrickp@law.usyd.edu.au

EDITOR OF THE INTERNATIONAL SURVEY
Professor Bill Atkin
Faculty of Law
Victoria University of Wellington
PO Box 600
Wellington
NEW ZEALAND
Tel: +64 04 463 6343
Fax: +64 04 463 6366
E-mail: bill.atkin@vuw.ac.nz

TREASURER
Professor Adriaan van der Linden
Beetslaan 2
3818 VH Aersfoort
THE NETHERLANDS
Tel: +31 33 461 90 97
Fax: +31 33 465 94 29
E-mail: a.vanderlinden@law.uu.nl

SECRETARY-GENERAL
Professor Marsha Garrison
Brooklyn Law School
250 Joralemon Street
Brooklyn, NY 11201
USA
Tel: +1 718 780 7947
Fax: +1 718 780 0375
E-mail: marsha.garrison@brooklaw.edu

EDITOR OF THE NEWSLETTER
Professor Margaret F Brinig
Fritz Duda Family Professor of Law
University of Notre Dame
Box 780, 3157 Eck Hall of Law
Notre Dame, IN 46556
USA
Tel: +1 574 631 2303
Fax: +1 574 631 3595
Email: mbrinig@nd.edu

Immediate past president

Professor Dr Bea Verschraegen LLM, MEM
Abteilung für Rechtsvergleichung
Universität Wien – Juridicum
Schottenbastei 10-16
A-1010 Wien
AUSTRIA
Tel: +43 1 4277 35102
Fax: +43 1 4277 9351
E-mail: bea.verschraegen@univie.ac.at

Vice presidents

Professor Olga Dyuzheva
Law Faculty
Moscow State University (Lomonosov)
Moscow 119991
RUSSIA
Tel: +7 495 939 5153
Fax: +7 495 939 5195
E-mail: odyuzheva@gmail.com

Professor Dominique Goubau
Faculté de droit de l'Université Laval
Québec QUE
G1V 0A6
CANADA
Tel: +1 418 656 2131 (#2384)
Fax: +1 418 656 7230
E-mail: Dominique.goubau@fd.ulaval.ca

Professor Satoshi Minimakata
Faculty of Law
Niigata University
8050 Ikarashi-ninocho
Nishi-ku
Niigata
JAPAN 950-2181
Tel: +25 262 6522 or 6478
Fax: +25 262 5435
E-mail: satoshi@jura.niigata-u.ac.jp

Professor Hugues Fulchiron
Faculté de Droit
Université Jean Moulin
Lyon 3, 15 quai Claude-Bernard
F-69007 Lyon
FRANCE
Tel: +33 4 72 41 05 54
Fax: +33 4 78 78 71 31
E-mail: hugues.fulchiron@online.fr

Professor Giselle Groeninga
Rua Professor Artur Ramos 241 #93
São Paulo SP 01454-030
BRAZIL
Tel: +55 11 30315320
Fax: +55 11 30315320
E-mail: giselle@groeninga.com.br

Professor June D Sinclair
PO Box 651479
Benmore 2010
SOUTH AFRICA
Tel: +27 82 900 8690
E-mail: june.sinclair@up.ac.za

Executive council

Professor Penelope Agallopoulou
University of Piraeus
4 Kyprou Str
154 52 P Psychico
Athens
GREECE
Tel/Fax: +30 210 67 75 404
E-mail: agal@otenet.gr

Professor Dr MV Antokolskaia
VU University Amsterdam
Faculty of Law
De Boelelaan 1105
1081 HV Amsterdam
THE NETHERLANDS
Tel: +31 20 5986294
Fax: +31 20 5986280
E-mail: m.v.antokolskaia@rechten.vu.nl

Associate Professor Datin Noor Aziah Mohd Awal
Faculty of Law
Universiti Kebangsaan Malaysia
43600 Bangi
Selangor
MALAYSIA
Tel: +60 3 89215921
Fax: +60 3 89215117
E-mail: naha@pkrisc.cc.ukm.my

Dr Ursula Cristina Bassett
Faculty of Law
Pontificia Universidad Católica Argentina
Santa María de los Buenos Aires
Alicia Moreau de Justo 1400
Buenos Aires
ARGENTINA
Tel: +54 005411 43490200
E-mail: ubassett@uca.edu.ar

Dr Piotr Fiedorczyk
Faculty of Law
University of Bialystok
15-213 Bialystok
Ul Mickiewicza 1
POLAND
Tel: + 48 85 7457146
E-mail: fiedorczyk@tlen.pl

Professor Olga A Khazova
Institute of State and Law
Russian Academy of Sciences
Znamenka Str 10
119992 Moscow
RUSSIA
Tel: +7 495 691 1709
Fax: +7 495 691 8574
E-mail: o.khazova@gmail.com

Professor Nigel Lowe
Cardiff Law School
University of Wales
PO Box 427
Cardiff CF10 3XJ
UK
Tel: +44 029 20 874365
Fax: +44 029 20 874097
E-mail: lowe@cardiff.ac.uk

Professor Marie-Therese Meulders
29, Chaussee de la verte voie
1300 Wavre
BELGIUM
Tel: +32 10 24 78 92
Fax: +32 10 22 91 60
E-mail: meulders@cfap.ucl.ac.be

Peter Barth
Federal Ministry of Justice
Museumstraße 7
1070 Wien
AUSTRIA
Tel: +43 1 52152 2069
Fax: +43 1 52152 2829
E-Mail: peter.barth@bmj.gv.at

Professor Dr Nina Dethloff LLM
Institut für Deutsches, Europäisches und Internationales Familienrecht
Universität Bonn
Adenauerallee 8a
D 53113 Bonn
GERMANY
Tel: +49 228 739290
Fax: +49 228 733909
E-mail: dethloff@uni-bonn.de

Professor Sanford N Katz
Boston College Law School
885 Centre Street
Newton Centre, Mass 02459
USA
Tel: +1 617 552 437
Fax: +1 617 552 2615
E-mail: sanford.katz@bc.edu

Associate Professor Zdeňka Králíčková
Faculty of Law
Masaryk Univerzity
Veveří 70
611 80 Brno
CZECH REPUBLIC
Tel:+420 723 727 060
Fax:+420 549 49 7926
E-mail: zdenka.kralickova@law.muni.cz

Professor Dr Miquel Martin-Casals
Facultat de Dret
Universitat de Girona
Campus de Montilivi 17071
Girona
SPAIN
Tel: +34 972 41 81 39
Fax: +34 972 41 81 46
E-mail: martin@elaw.udg.edu

Professor Jo Miles
Trinity College
Cambridge
CB2 1TQ
UK
Tel: +44 1223 339922
Fax: +44 1223 338564 [FAO Jo Miles]
E-mail: jkm33@cam.ac.uk

Professor Linda Nielsen
Copenhagen University
Faculty of Law
Studiegården, Studiestræde 6
1455 Copenhagen K
DENMARK
Tel: +45 35 32 31 23
Fax: +45 35 32 32 06
E-mail: Linda.Nielsen@jur.ku.dk

Professor JA Robinson
Faculty of Law
Room 8, Old Main Building
Potchefstroom Campus of the North West
University
Potchefstroom 2520
SOUTH AFRICA
Tel: +27 18 299 1940
Fax: +27 18 299 1933

Professor Anna Singer
Uppsala University
Faculty of Law
PO Box 512
SE-751 20 Uppsala
SWEDEN
Tel: +46 18 471 20 35
Fax: +46 18 15 27 14
E-mail: anna.singer@jur.uu.se

Professor Hazel Thompson-Ahye
Eugene Dupuch Law School
Farrington Road
PO Box SS-6394
Nassau, NP
THE BAHAMAS
Tel: +242-326-8507/8
Fax: +242-326-8504
E-mail: thomahye2000@yahoo.com

Professor Avv Maria Donata Panforti
Dipartimento di Scienze del linguaggio e
della cultura
Largo Sant'Eufemia 19
I-41100 Modena
ITALY
Tel: +39 059 205 5916
Fax: +39 059 205 5933
E-mail: panforti.mariadonata@unimore.it

Professor Carol Rogerson
Faculty of Law
University of Toronto
78 Queen's Park
Toronto M5S 2C5
CANADA
Tel: +1 416 978 2648
Fax: +1 416 978 3715

Professor dr juris Tone Sverdrup
Department of Private Law
Faculty of Law, University of Oslo
PO Box 6706 St Olavs plass
NO-0130 Oslo
NORWAY
Tel: +47 22859781
Fax: +47 22859620
E-mail: tone.sverdrup@jus.uio.no

Professor Paul Vlaardingerbroek
Faculty of Law
Tilburg University
PO Box 90153
5000 LE Tilburg
NETHERLANDS
Tel: +31-013-466-2032/2281
Fax: +31-013-466-2323
E-mail: p.vlaardingerbroek@uvt.nl

Professor Lynn D Wardle
Bruce C Hafen Professor of Law
518 J Reuben Clark Law School
Brigham Young University
Provo, UT 84602
USA
Tel: +1 801 422 2617
Fax: +1 801 422 0391
E-mail: Wardlel@law.byu.edu

Professor Barbara Bennett Woodhouse
LQC Lamar Chair in Law
Co-Director of the Barton Child Law and
Policy Clinic
Emory University
Gambrell Hall
1301 Clifton Road
Atlanta, GA
USA
Tel: +1 404 727 4934
Fax: +1 404 727 6820
E-mail: barbara.woodhouse@emory.edu

Professor Dr Jinsu Yune
School of Law, Seoul National University
599 Gwanak-ro, Gwanak-gu
Seoul, 151-743
Republic of Korea
Tel: +82 2 880 7599
Fax:+82 2 885 7584
E-mail: jsyune@snu.ac.kr

HISTORY OF THE INTERNATIONAL SOCIETY OF FAMILY LAW

A   THE HISTORY OF THE SOCIETY

On the initiative of Professor Zeev Falk, the Society was launched at the University of Birmingham, UK, in April 1973. The Society's first international conference was held in West Berlin in April 1975 on the theme *The Child and the Law*. There were over 200 participants, including representatives of governments and international organisations. The second international conference was held in Montreal in June 1977 on the subject *Violence in the Family*. There were over 300 participants from over 20 countries. A third world conference on the theme *Family Living in a Changing Society* was held in Uppsala, Sweden in June 1979. There were over 270 participants from 26 countries. The fourth world conference was held in June 1982 at Harvard Law School, USA. There were over 180 participants from 23 countries. The fifth world conference was held in July 1985 in Brussels, Belgium on the theme *The Family, The State and Individual Security*, under the patronage of Her Majesty Queen Fabiola of Belgium, the Director-General of UNESCO, the Secretary-General of the Council of Europe and the President of the Commission of the European Communities. The sixth world conference on *Issues of the Ageing in Modern Society* was held in 1988 in Tokyo, Japan, under the patronage of HIH Takahito Mikasa. There were over 450 participants. The seventh world conference was held in May 1991 in Croatia on the theme, *Parenthood: The Legal Significance of Motherhood and Fatherhood in a Changing Society*. There were 187 participants from 37 countries. The eighth world conference took place in Cardiff, Wales in June/July 1994 on the theme *Families Across Frontiers*. The ninth world conference of the Society was held in July 1997 in Durban, South Africa on the theme *Changing Family Forms: World Themes and African Issues*. The Society's tenth world conference was held in July 2000 in Queensland, Australia on the theme *Family Law: Processes, Practices and Pressures*. The eleventh world conference was held in August 2002 in Copenhagen and Oslo on the theme *Family Life and Human Rights*. The Society's twelfth world conference was held in Salt Lake City, Utah in July 2005 on the theme *Family Law: Balancing Interests and Pursuing Priorities*. The Society's thirteenth world conference was held in Vienna in September 2008. The Society has also increasingly held regional conferences including those in Lyon, France (1995); Quebec City, Canada (1996); Seoul, South Korea (1996); Prague, Czech Republic (1998); Albuquerque, New Mexico, USA (June 1999); Oxford, UK (August 1999); and Kingston, Ontario (2001). In 2003, regional conferences took place in Oregon, USA; Tossa de

Mar, Spain; and Lyon, France and, in July 2004, in Beijing, China, on the theme 'Divorce and its Consequences'. In 2005, a regional conference took place in Amsterdam (the Netherlands) and dealt with the centennial anniversary of the establishment of legislation on child protection and the juvenile courts. In 2007 there were regional conferences in Chester (England), entitled 'Family Justice: For Whom and How?' and Vancouver (Canada), entitled 'Making Family Law: Facts, Values and Practicalities'. In 2009 there were conferences in Tel Aviv (Israel), Porto (Portugal) and Sao Paolo (Brazil), and in 2010 Kansas City (USA), Tsukuba University (Japan), the University of Ulster (Northern Ireland) and the Caribbean. There has since been a world conference in Lyon (France) in July 2011 and a regional conference in Iowa City in June 2012. The next world conference will be in Recife, Brazil from 6 to 9 August 2014.

B   ITS NATURE AND OBJECTIVES

The following principles were adopted at the first Annual General Meeting of the Society held in the Kongresshalle of West Berlin on the afternoon of Saturday 12 April 1975.

(1)   The Society's objectives are the study and discussion of problems of family law. To this end the Society sponsors and promotes:

    (a)   International co-operation in research on family law subjects of worldwide interest.

    (b)   Periodic international conferences on family law subjects of worldwide interest.

    (c)   Collection and dissemination of information in the field of family law by the publication of a survey concerning developments in family law throughout the world, and by publication of relevant materials in family law, including papers presented at conferences of the Society.

    (d)   Co-operation with other international, regional or national associations having the same or similar objectives.

    (e)   Interdisciplinary contact and research.

    (f)   The advancement of legal education in family law by all practical means including furtherance of exchanges of teachers, students, judges and practising lawyers.

    (g)   Other objectives in furtherance of or connected with the above objectives.

C   MEMBERSHIP AND DUES

In 2011 the Society had approximately 630 members.

(a)   Membership:

- Ordinary Membership, which is open to any member of the legal or a related profession. The Council may defer or decline any application for membership.

- Institutional Membership, which is open to interested organisations at the discretion of, and on terms approved by, the Council.

- Student Membership, which is open to interested students of law and related disciplines at the discretion of, and on terms approved by, the Council.

- Honorary Membership, which may be offered to distinguished persons by decision of the Executive Council.

(b) Each member shall pay such annual dues as may be established from time to time by the Council. At present, dues for ordinary membership are €50 (or equivalent) for one year, €120 (or equivalent) for 3 years and €180 (or equivalent) for 5 years, plus €12.50 (or equivalent) if cheque is in another currency.

D DIRECTORY OF MEMBERS

A Directory of Members of the Society is available to all members.

E BOOKS

The proceedings of the first world conference were published as *The Child and the Law* (F Bates, ed, Oceana, 1976); the proceedings of the second as *Family Violence* (J Eekelaar and S Katz, eds, Butterworths, Canada, 1978); the proceedings of the third as *Marriage and Cohabitation* (J Eekelaar and S Katz, eds, Butterworths, Canada, 1980); the fourth, *The Resolution of Family Conflict* (J Eekelaar and S Katz, eds, Butterworths, Canada, 1984); the fifth, *Family, State and Individual Economic Security (Vols I & II)* (MT Meulders-Klein and J Eekelaar, eds, Story Scientia and Kluwer, 1988); the sixth, *An Ageing World: Dilemmas and Challenges for Law and Social Policy* (J Eekelaar and D Pearl, eds, Clarendon Press, 1989); the seventh *Parenthood in Modern Society* (J Eekelaar and P Sarcevic, eds, Martinus Nijhoff, 1993); the eighth *Families Across Frontiers* (N Lowe and G Douglas, eds, Martinus Nijhoff, 1996) and the ninth *The Changing Family: Family Forms and Family Law* (J Eekelaar and T Nhlapo, eds, Hart Publishing, 1998). The proceedings of the tenth world conference in Australia were published as *Family Law, Processes, Practices and Pressures* (J Dewar and S Parker, eds, Hart Publishing, 2003). The proceedings of the eleventh world conference in Denmark and Norway were published as *Family Life and Human Rights* (P Lødrup and E Modvar, eds, Gyldendal Akademisk, 2004). The proceedings of the twelfth world conference held in Salt Lake City, Utah have been published as *Family Law: Balancing Interests and Pursuing Priorities* (L Wardle and C Williams, eds, Wm S Hein & Co, 2007). The proceedings of the thirteenth world conference held in Vienna in

2008 have been published as *Family Finances* (B Verschraegen, ed, Jan Sramek Verlag, 2009). These proceedings are commercially marketed but are available to Society members at reduced prices.

F   THE SOCIETY'S PUBLICATIONS

The Society regularly publishes a newsletter, *The Family Letter*, which appears twice a year and which is circulated to the members of the Society and reports on its activities and other matters of interest. *The International Survey of Family Law* provides information on current developments in family law throughout the world and is received free of charge by members of the Society. The editor is currently Bill Atkin, Faculty of Law, Victoria University of Wellington, PO Box 600, Wellington, New Zealand 6140. The Survey is circulated to members or may be obtained on application to the Editor.

INTERNATIONAL SOCIETY OF FAMILY LAW
SUBSCRIPTION FORM

☐ I prefer to communicate in   ☐ English   ☐ French

☐ Please charge my credit card ☐ **MASTERCARD or EUROCARD** ☐ **VISA or JCB**

☐ Subscription for 1 year   €50

☐ Subscription for 3 years   €120

☐ Subscription for 5 years   €180

Name of Card Holder: _____

Card no. | | | | | | | | | | | | | | | | | | | | | | | |

CVC-code (three figures at the back of your card behind the 16 figures): | | | |

Expiry date: ——— / ———

Address of Card Holder: _____
_____

☐ I pay by *postgiro* to **63.18.019** €180[1] for 5 years, €120 for 3 years or €50 for one year,

plus €12.50 **if cheque in another currency** (from)

The International Society of Family Law,
Beetslaan 2
3818 VH Amersfoort
The Netherlands

(We have a bank account at the Postbank, Amsterdam, The Netherlands. The IBAN code is: NL22 PSTB 0006 3180 19; BIC: PSTBNL21)

☐ Payment enclosed *by cheque* to the amount of €180[1] for 5 years, €120 for 3 years or €50

for one year, *plus €12.50* **if cheque in another currency**.

Date: _____   Signature: _____

☐ *New member, or*

☐ *(Change of) name/address:* _____
_____

Tel: _____

Fax: _____

E-mail: _____

Comments: _____
_____

To be sent to the treasurer of the ISFL:
Dr Adriaan van der Linden, International Society of Family Law
Beetslaan 2, 3818 VH Amersfoort
THE NETHERLANDS (or by fax: +31-33-4659429;
E-mail address: a.p.vanderlinden@uu.nl)
Website ISFL: http://www.law2.byu.edu/ISFL

[1] Or its *counter*value in US dollars.

ASSOCIATION INTERNATIONALE DE DROIT DE LA FAMILLE FORMULAIRE DE COTISATION

☐ Je désire de communiquer ☐ en français ☐ en anglais

☐ Je vous prie de charger ma carte de crédit: ☐ **MASTERCARD/EUROCARD** ☐ **VISA/JCB**

☐ Souscription pour une année €50

Souscription pour trois années €120

Souscription pour cinq années €180

Le nom du possesseur de la carte de crédit: _____

Carte no ☐☐☐☐ ☐☐☐☐ ☐☐☐☐ ☐☐☐☐

CVC-code (trois numéros sur l'arrière-coté de votre carte) ☐☐☐

Date d'expiration: ____ / ____

L'adresse du possesseur de la carte de crédit: _____

_____

☐ Je payerai par postgiro à **63.18.019** €180[1] pour 5 ans ou €120 pour 3 ans ou €50 pour 1 an, *plus €12.50* **surcharge si paiement est un autre cours**,

(du) International Society of Family Law
Beetslaan 2
3818 VH Amersfoort
Les Pays-Bas
(Nous avons un crédit au Postbank, Amsterdam, les Pays-Bas. Le *code IBAN* est: *NL22 PSTB 0006 3180 19; BIC: PSTBNL21*)

☐ Paiement est inclus avec un chèque de €180[1] pour 5 ans ou €120 pour 3 ans ou €50 pour 1 an, *plus €12.50* **surcharge si paiement est un autre cours**.

La date: _____ Souscription: _____

☐ *Nouveau membre, ou*

☐ *(Changement de) nom/adresse:* _____

_____

Tel: _____
Fax: _____
E-mail: _____

Remarques: _____

_____

Veuillez envoyer ce formulaire au trésorier de l'Association:
Dr Adriaan van der Linden, International Society of Family Law
Beetslaan 2, 3818 VH Amersfoort
LES PAYS BAS (ou par fax: +31-33-4659429;
E-mail address: a.p.vanderlinden@uu.nl)
Website ISFL: http://www.law2.byu.edu/ISFL

[1] Ou la *contre*valeur en US dollars.

PREFACE

This 2012 edition of the International Survey continues the tradition of a wide range of topics from many different countries around the world.

Not surprisingly, the law relating to children predominates. We have chapters on shared parenting (Australia), missing children (India), adoption law in China, relocation law in England and Wales with the challenging suggestion that the overarching principle of the child's welfare be abandoned, child abduction where Japan is encouraged to come into line with other jurisdictions, corporal punishment (Serbia), foster care (Slovenia) and South African children living in extended families. Serbia also reports on the law relating to surrogacy, while Sweden has changes to its tort liability legislation making parents liable to a limited extent for the harm caused by their children's criminal acts. Countries such as Botswana, Uganda, Malawi and Malaysia continue to wrestle the tensions between custom and notions of human rights, with the added complication of mixed religious legal systems in Malaysia.

Issues to do with unmarried cohabitation are explored in the chapters from Hungary, Ireland, Macedonia and Serbia while Canada, France and the Netherlands deal with various issues relating to same-sex couples. Questions concerning marriage and divorce crop up in Samoa and Sri Lanka. Financial matters are also tackled in Poland and Samoa (property), the United States (premarital agreements), the Netherlands (maintenance) and New Zealand (child support). Procedural changes in Switzerland represent something of a lost opportunity, while in New Zealand a review of the Family Court is mainly about the increasing expenditure of the services provided.

Thanks are owed to many people who have helped this edition of the International Survey to be published. We must start with the authors, some of whom have written before, others contributing for the first time. Dominique Goubau and Hugues Fulchiron's team in Lyon translate the abstracts into French. Our publishers especially Greg Woodgate and Cheryl Prophett, who does the copy-editing, perform a sterling service. I personally am very grateful for the excellent work of my secretary, Angela Funnell, and my former research assistant, David Neild, who is now admitted as a barrister and solicitor and practising in a town called Blenheim in New Zealand's South Island.

Bill Atkin
General Editor
Wellington
June 2012

CONTENTS

Australia

REFLECTIONS ON THE SHARED PARENTING EXPERIENCE

*Lisa Young**

Résumé

Largement motivée par la perception que les enfants souffrent du peu de contacts avec un de leurs parents (généralement le père), l'Australie a légiféré en 2006 pour favoriser la coparentalité en cas de séparation. Même si la recherche montre qu'en réalité les choses sont plus complexes que cela, on peut tout de même affirmer sans se tromper que la promotion d'une saine relation avec le père bénéficiera dans la plupart des cas à l'enfant. Cette fin 2011 est le bon moment pour faire le point sur la coparentalité en Australie. En effet, tant les chercheurs indépendants que ceux qui oeuvrent pour le compte du gouvernement, ont été très actifs dans l'évaluation des réformes. Ces recherches mettent en lumière les points positifs des réformes, mais ils font également quelques constats inquiétants. L'Australie a récemment apporté des modifications législatives en vue de répondre aux préoccupations que soulève l'impact qu'ont certaines lois sur les victimes de la violence familiale. Le présent texte présente brièvement l'historique de ces amendements. Il s'intéresse ensuite aux résultats des recherches évaluatives, particulièrement celle portant sur l'application des dispositions les plus controversées. Le texte s'attarde également aux très récents changements apportés au droit de la famille en matière de violence familiale. En conclusion, il formule quelques commentaires sur ce que l'on peut retenir de l'expérience australienne.

I INTRODUCTION

Legislating to try to increase post-separation shared parenting, as Australia did in 2006, is intuitively attractive; however, as has been noted by commentators, 'empirical support for legislating to prioritise shared time over other parenting arrangements is lacking'.[1] A key driver for this brand of legislative reform is the perception that the well-being of children suffers when they have too little contact with one parent (typically their father). In fact, the research presents a much more complex picture than this. However, it can safely be said that

---

* Associate Professor, School of Law, Murdoch University. The author would like to thank Professor Belinda Fehlberg for her most helpful comments on a draft of this paper; all errors of course remain the responsibility of the author.

[1] B Fehlberg, B Smyth, M Maclean and C Roberts 'Legislating for shared parenting after separation: A research review' (2011) 25(3) *International Journal of Law, Policy and the Family* 318, 332.

promoting high quality father-child relationships post-separation will benefit most children.[2] The end of 2011 presents an opportune time to reflect on Australia's shared parenting experience as other jurisdictions continue to grapple with the question of whether to make similar legislative changes.[3] Interestingly, England has just announced that it is considering heading down the shared parenting legislative path.[4]

Australia presents a particularly interesting example, as Australian researchers have been very active, both independently and at the behest of the government, in assessing the impact of the reforms. Thus, in just 6 years a considerable body of evidence has been accumulated. There are certainly some positives to be drawn from that research, but there have also been some very disturbing findings. So much so, that the English Parliament considered it appropriate to appraise itself of the research with the aim of avoiding the pitfalls that have been identified with the Australian legislation.[5] Indeed, Australia has very recently passed some amendments to address issues to do with how the laws impact on the victims of family violence.

As the Australian shared parenting laws have not been covered in detail in more recent editions of this Survey, this chapter will begin by tracing briefly the history of the introduction of the key amendments. It will then discuss the research findings that provide some insight into the operation of these provisions, and in particular those aspects of the legislation that have raised concern. In looking at the research on the reforms and family violence, the very recent changes to the legislation directed to this issue will be considered. Finally, the chapter will make some comments on what can be learned from the Australian experience.

---

[2]   See B Fehlberg, B Smyth, M Maclean and C Roberts 'Legislating for shared parenting after separation: A research review' (2011) 25(3) *International Journal of Law, Policy and the Family* 318 at 2; J Baxter, R Weston, L Qu 'Family structure, coparental relationship quality, post-separation paternal involvement and children's emotional wellbeing' (2011) 17(2) *Journal of Family Studies* 86, 87–88.

[3]   See e g Minnesota as discussed in J Jeske 'Issues in Joint Custody and Shared Parenting: Lessons from Australia' (2011) available at http://mnbenchbar.com/2011/12/issues-in-joint-custody/ (accessed 2 March 2012). In Canada, pro-shared parenting private member's Bill C-422 was introduced into Parliament some years ago though it has not been debated and the government has not taken a position on it as yet: see http://openparliament.ca/bills/40-3/C-422/ (accessed 3 March 2012). For a review of the laws in different jurisdictions see B Fehlberg, B Smyth, M Maclean and C Roberts *Caring for children after parental separation: would legislation for shared parenting time help children?* (Family Policy Briefing 7, University of Oxford, Department of Social Policy and Intervention, May 2011).

[4]   See Family Justice Review Panel *Family Justice Review: Final Report* (November 2011) available at www.justice.gov.uk/downloads/publications/moj/2011/family-justice-review-final-report.pdf (accessed 2 March 2012); Ministry of Justice and Department of Education *The Government Response to the Family Justice Review: A system with children and families at its heart* (2012) available at www.education.gov.uk/publications/eOrderingDownload/CM-8273. pdf (accessed 2 March 2012); and for further comment see O Bowcott 'Government backs "shared parenting" legislation after separation' *The Guardian*, 6 February 2012, available at www.guardian.co.uk/lifeandstyle/2012/feb/06/government-backs-shared-parenting-legislation (last accessed 2 March 2012).

[5]   See e g Annex G to Family Justice Review Panel, *Family Justice Review: Final Report*, ibid.

II THE AUSTRALIAN SHARED PARENTING LEGISLATIVE REGIME

Prior to the 2006 reforms, Australia's laws on resolving parenting disputes, found in the Family Law Act 1975 (Cth) (FLA), gave judges a very broad discretion, requiring (a) that the paramount consideration in making an order be the best interests of the child, and (b) that in assessing those best interests, they consider a range of matters set out in a checklist provision ('best interests checklist'). The FLA provided no guidance as to the weight to be given to any particular factor.

An attempt was made in 1995[6] to encourage judges to abandon what was, by then, considered to be the standard outcome, namely giving custody to the pre-separation primary caregiver of the child, with access to the other parent set typically for every second weekend and half the school holidays (the '80/20' arrangement). In addition to amendments aimed at promoting more court ordered shared parenting, the terms 'guardianship', 'custody' and 'access' were abandoned in that round of reforms, with a view to minimising the appearance of someone having 'won' and avoiding the unfortunate connotation of children as property. At the time, those reforms were not considered successful by fathers' groups in sufficiently changing outcomes[7] (though it might be fair to say that, if one looked at shared parenting trends post-separation over time, perhaps they were more influential than was then appreciated).[8] Criticism of how parenting disputes were resolved in court continued and the government ultimately undertook a significant review[9] which led to the Family Law Amendment (Shared Parental Responsibility) Act 2006 (Cth).

This Act brought extensive reforms in a number of areas. Insofar as the reforms attempt to promote shared parenting they can be summarised as follows. First, a presumption of 'equal shared parental responsibility' (ESPR) was introduced.[10] While it is not readily apparent from the legislation, in fact this is a presumption of what Australians used to call joint 'guardianship' – that is, joint responsibility for 'major long-term issues' (essentially education, name, religion, medical issues and major changes to living arrangements).[11] In fact, this presumption did not change much in terms of the likely outcome of a decision as to who should have 'guardianship', as there was a de facto

---

[6]   Family Law Reform Act 1995 (Cth).
[7]   See the discussion in R Graycar 'Family Law Reform in Australia, or Frozen Chooks Revisited Again?' (2012) 13(1) *Theoretical Inquiries in Law* 241, 251.
[8]   See the discussion below about the increase in shared parenting in the general community; J Cashmore, P Parkinson, R Weston, R Patulny, G Redmond, L Qu, J Baxter, M Rajkovic, T Sitek and I Katz *Shared care parenting arrangements since the 2006 Family Law Reforms: Report to the Australian Attorney-General's Department* (Sydney: Social Policy Research Centre, University of New South Wales, 2010) x.
[9]   House of Representatives Standing Committee on Family and Community Affairs *Every picture tells a story: Report on the inquiry into child custody arrangements in the event of family separation* (Canberra: CanPrint Communications Pty Ltd, 2003).
[10] FLA, s 61DA(1).
[11] FLA, s 4(1).

presumption in favour of joint guardianship operating prior to the reforms – only the most delinquent or absent parents would have been excluded as guardians of their children. The presumption does not apply where there are plausible violence and abuse concerns.[12] Further, the presumption is rebutted if a court is satisfied that it is not in the best interests of the particular child for the parents to have ESPR.[13] This is consistent with the fact that the child's best interests remain 'the paramount consideration' in the making of any parenting order (the so-called paramountcy principle).[14] The significance of this presumption was, in fact, that the making of an order for ESPR triggered a prescribed process for considering parenting, which is discussed further below.

The second major change was the division of the best interests checklist into two parts, 'primary' and 'additional' considerations. The benefit to the child of a meaningful relationship with both parents and protection of children from violence and abuse are now the two 'primary' considerations, with all other factors relegated to a list of 'additional' considerations. This was underscored by one of the new objects of this Part VII of the legislation being to 'ensure that the best interests of children are met by ensuring that children have the benefit of both of their parents having a meaningful involvement in their lives, to the maximum extent consistent with' that child's best interests.[15]

The third key reform was the introduction of a prescribed process for considering parenting orders. This is only mandatory where an order for ESPR is made – however, given there is a presumption in favour of making that order that will very often be the case. Moreover, even where such an order is not made, the Full Family Court of Australia has indicated that, even where neither parent seeks 50/50 care, the facts of the case may lead the court to consider it.[16] Having identified all the evidence relevant to the mandatory considerations,[17] the court must consider potential parenting arrangements in a specified hierarchical order: first, it must directly consider whether 50/50 shared physical care would be best for the child[18] and, if it is not, it must then consider whether 'substantial and significant time'[19] with both parents would be best.[20] Thereafter it can consider other parenting arrangements.

The introduction of compulsory mediation in parenting disputes was another important aspect of the 2006 shared parenting law reform package. One objective of changes to the FLA in recent times has been to encourage parents to see court proceedings as a last resort. In keeping with this goal, the 1995

---

12   FLA, s 61DA(2).
13   FLA, s 61DA(4).
14   FLA, s 60CA.
15   FLA, s 60B(1)(a).
16   *Goode and Goode* (2006) FLC 93–424 at [82].
17   It is generally accepted that the proper approach is first to identify all evidence as it relates to the various considerations, before applying the provisions that prescribe what orders must be considered: *Taylor and Barker* (2007) 37 Fam LR 461.
18   FLA, s 65DAA(1).
19   See the definition in FLA, s 65DAA(3).
20   FLA, s 65DAA(2).

reforms rebadged alternative dispute resolution 'primary dispute resolution'. In 2006 the term 'family dispute resolution' (FDR) was adopted and a requirement was added that before any application for parenting orders can be made parents must first go through FDR.[21] FDR is delivered by accredited family dispute resolution practitioners, many of whom operate out of Family Dispute Resolution Centres that were set up and funded as part of the 2006 reforms. At the time of the announcement, 65 centres were proposed and $400m allocated by the federal government. These centres provide 3 free hours of mediation.

Given that most parents do not proceed to a judicially determined outcome, mediation is an important consideration when looking at shared parenting. Family dispute resolution practitioners – like lawyers and family consultants[22] – who are advising parents about a parenting plan have, since the 2006 reforms, been obligated to inform the parents that they could consider shared parenting if that is practicable and best for the child.[23] This mediation does not necessarily follow a standard model,[24] and generally focuses on outcomes that will benefit children. In this regard, two particular models of mediation have been developed: child focused mediation and child inclusive mediation.[25] While the former model, as the name suggests, focuses on the needs and interests of the child, the latter model incorporates another mediator who will have spoken to the child and brings the voice of the child into the parents' mediation. This can be used for children as young as 6.

III   RESEARCH FINDINGS ON THE REFORMS

For the purposes of this discussion, one can usefully organise the relevant evidence into three broad categories. First, there is the general data about the impact of the reforms. Second, there is the evidence that relates particularly to the impact of the changes on cases involving family violence. Third, there is the research on children's well-being in shared care arrangements.

(a)   Research evidence on the impact of the reforms

A first and obvious question is to what extent have the reforms promoted post-separation shared parenting. There is evidence that fathers have been encouraged by the reforms to seek shared physical care post-2006.[26] However, having reviewed the available data in relation to the incidence of shared

---

[21]   FLA, ss 60I and 60J. There are, of course, exceptions.

[22]   Family consultants are social scientists attached to the Family Court who assist in a broad range of ways in helping to resolve parenting disputes: see FLA, Pt III.

[23]   FLA, s 63DA.

[24]   The FLA does not require any specific model of mediation.

[25]   See further J McIntosh, C Long and L Moloney 'Child-Focused and Child-Inclusive Mediation: A comparative study of outcomes' (2004) 10(1) *Journal of Family Studies* 87.

[26]   B Fehlberg, C Millward and M Campo 'Shared post-separation parenting in 2009: An empirical snapshot' (2009) 23(3) *Australian Journal of Family Law* 247, 261.

parenting generally,[27] Weston et al[28] (researchers at the Australian Institute of Family Studies, which has done the major government-funded 'Evaluation' of the 2006 reforms) conclude:

- While on the increase, shared care parenting remains a minority arrangement for separated parents.

- Across the general population, the increase in post-separation shared parenting arrangements began in the 1990s, built slowly between 2002 and 2008 but did not spike after the 2006 reforms.

- However, the increase is much greater where there is a court ordered parenting arrangement; shared care orders have increased from 4% before the reforms to 34% post-reform.[29]

- Within that group of court ordered shared care, the incidence of shared care is higher where the order is judicially determined rather than by consent; 10% of consent orders before the reforms reflected shared care as compared to 15% after the reforms.[30]

As one might predict, the frequency of shared care differs according to the age of the child, with 5–11 year olds being the group most likely to experience shared parental care.[31] Nearly three-quarters of children aged 4 and under spent all their nights with their mother, with 12–14 year olds experiencing the most diverse range of parenting patterns.[32]

One cannot conclude, therefore, that the reforms have been responsible for significant increases in shared parenting across the board. Moreover, it is still very much a minority parenting arrangement. However, more shared care is being sought, agreed and ordered. In this climate, it is not surprising that the research evidence suggests that consent to shared parenting may often not be a

---

[27] The relevant definition for shared parenting used in this research, and generally, is where each parent has 35–65% of nights with a child: R Weston, L Qu, M Gray, J De Maio, R Kaspiew, L Moloney and K Hand 'Shared care time: An increasingly common arrangement' (2011) 88 *Family Matters* 51, 52.

[28] R Weston, L Qu, M Gray, J De Maio, R Kaspiew, L Moloney and K Hand 'Shared care time: An increasingly common arrangement' (2011) 88 *Family Matters* 51.

[29] R Kaspiew, M Gray, R Weston, L Moloney, K Hand, L Qu and the Family Law Evaluation Team *Evaluation of the 2006 Family Law Reforms* (Melbourne: Australian Institute of Family Studies, 2009) 133.

[30] Family Court of Australia, Shared parental responsibility statistics – 2008/2009 available at www.familycourt.gov.au/wps/wcm/connect/FCOA/home/about/Court/Admin/Business/ Statistics/SPR/FCOA_SPR_2008 (accessed 6 March 2012); R Kaspiew, M Gray, R Weston, L Moloney, K Hand, L Qu and the Family Law Evaluation Team, *Evaluation of the 2006 Family Law Reforms* (Melbourne: Australian Institute of Family Studies, 2009).

[31] R Kaspiew, M Gray, R Weston, L Moloney, K Hand, L Qu and the Family Law Evaluation Team 'The Australian Institute of Family Studies' Evaluation of the 2006 family law reforms: Key findings' (2010) 24(1) AJFL 5, 22.

[32] Ibid.

product of real agreement, but rather a case of agreement driven by fear of the level of shared care that might be court ordered.[33] In that respect, the legislative prod appears to have succeeded.

Another research focus (building on benchmarking research conducted before the changes)[34] has been identifying families where shared care works for children. Important factors would appear to be:

- residential proximity;

- mutual parental respect;

- child-focused parenting;

- parents adopting flexible approaches to sharing parenting;

- lower conflict levels at the outset of arrangement; and

- paternal confidence in parenting ability.

The research also indicates that, in families where shared care works, mothers and fathers tend to be more educated and have higher incomes. Importantly, in these families it is far more likely that fathers will have played an active parenting role while children were very young and were more emotionally available to their children. The fact many of these families had used other forms of care indicates the likelihood both parents were working. Those families where the mother had played the primary carer role for the children whilst young were far more likely to have sole care post-separation and for the father to lose contact.[35]

While the rationale for moving towards legislative language that reflects parental responsibilities rather than rights is admirable, there has been an unfortunate consequence with the current choice of terminology in the FLA and in particular the introduction of the presumption of ESPR. One consistent and key message coming from the research into these reforms is that parents – and even some professionals working in the family law system – are confused

---

[33] B Fehlberg, C Millward and M Campo 'Shared post-separation parenting in 2009: An empirical snapshot' (2009) 23(3) AJFL 247, 257.

[34] B Smyth, C Caruana and A Ferro 'Fifty-fifty care' in B Smyth (ed) *Parent-child contact and post separation parenting arrangements* (Melbourne: Research Report No 9, Australian Institute of Family Studies, 2004) 18–29.

[35] J McIntosh, B Smyth, M Kelaher, Y Wells, and C Long *Post-separation parenting arrangements and developmental outcomes for infants and children. Collected reports* (2010) available at www.familytransitions.com.au/Family_Transitions/Family_Transitions_files/Post%20 Separation%20parenting%20arrangements%20and%20developmental%20outcomes%20for% 20children%20%26%20infants%202010.pdf (accessed 4 March 2012) at paras 6.3.2–6.3.4. See also R Weston, L Qu, M Gray, R Kaspiew, L Moloney, K Hand and the Family Law Evaluation Team 'Care-time arrangements after the 2006 reforms: Implications for children and their parents' (2011) 86 *Family Matters* 19, 26.

by the shared parenting provisions and there is a common misconception that the law now imposes an obligation to order equal shared time parenting.[36] This is hardly surprising given the complexity of the provisions (especially the link between orders for ESPR and consideration of time sharing) and the change in court outcomes.

The context of the introduction of these reforms cannot be overlooked in this regard. While the official line is always that legislative changes to parenting laws are about maximising the welfare of children, the influence of fathers' rights groups in driving legislative reform is generally accepted.[37] While such groups may well be concerned about the best interests of children, like women's groups, they are also very concerned about perceived bias against them in the family law system. As a result, the 2006 reforms were no doubt welcomed by many fathers. However, as we now know, they were interpreted in a particular way by parents and professionals working in the family law system. The implications of parental confusion over the supposed 'right' to equal time are highlighted by some legal practitioners saying the new provisions hinder the process of securing parental (often father) acceptance of arrangements that are developmentally appropriate for their children.[38] Moreover, amongst lawyers there is a sense that the reforms have shifted the focus to parents' rights rather than children's needs, and favoured fathers over mothers.[39] A majority of lawyers surveyed did not accept that the reforms had benefited most children.[40] A study of parents in 2009 who had shared care arrangements confirmed earlier findings that, when considering the fairness of such arrangements, fathers focused more on the time allocation and fairness to themselves whereas mothers focused more on the interests of their children and the father–child relationship.[41]

There is also now some evidence as to what happens over time to shared parenting arrangements. A study that followed families for 4 years after mediation found that shared care (as opposed to primary care) arrangements were much more likely to change post-mediation, often reverting to the pre-mediation pattern of primary mother care. Interestingly, child inclusive mediation was more likely to result in a primary care arrangement

---

[36] R Chisholm *Family courts violence review: A report by Professor Richard Chisholm* (Australian Government Attorney-General's Department, Canberra, 2009) 120; R Kaspiew, M Gray, R Weston, L Moloney, K Hand, L Qu and the Family Law Evaluation Team 'The AIFS evaluation of the 2006 family law reforms' (2011) 86 *Family Matters* 8, 14.

[37] For a further discussion of this see R Graycar 'Family Law Reform in Australia, or Frozen Chooks Revisited Again?' (2012) 13(1) *Theoretical Inquiries in Law* 241.

[38] R Kaspiew, M Gray, R Weston, L Moloney, K Hand, L Qu and the Family Law Evaluation Team 'The AIFS evaluation of the 2006 family law reforms' (2011) 86 *Family Matters* 8, 14.

[39] R Kaspiew, M Gray, R Weston, L Moloney, K Hand, L Qu and the Family Law Evaluation Team 'The Australian Institute of Family Studies' Evaluation of the 2006 family law reforms: Key findings' (2010) 24(1) AJFL 5, 17.

[40] R Kaspiew, M Gray, R Weston, L Moloney, K Hand, L Qu and the Family Law Evaluation Team 'The Australian Institute of Family Studies' Evaluation of the 2006 family law reforms: Key findings' (2010) 24(1) AJFL 5, 20.

[41] B Fehlberg, C Millward and M Campo 'Shared post-separation parenting in 2009: An empirical snapshot' (2009) 23(3) AJFL 247, (15 in printed version).

post-mediation than other forms of mediation, and the arrangements were more stable than those negotiated through child-focused mediation.[42] Parents who shared care before mediation were more than twice as likely to maintain their arrangement as those who went to shared parenting post-mediation.[43] Fehlberg et al suggest the evidence indicates that 'shared time negotiated without involvement of the family law system appears to be more workable and more long-lasting'.[44] In combination, these results call into question whether shared care arrangements are being ordered or agreed in inappropriate situations. However, one must be mindful that permanence is not necessarily the measure of whether a parenting arrangement was suitable at a particular time.

There are also some indications that there may be financial consequences for parents flowing from these reforms. In the Australian child support scheme, the number of nights a parent cares for a child relates directly to the amount of child support a parent pays/receives; since 2008 reforms to child support legislation, increased levels of care have resulted in greater reductions in child support payments by payers of child support. Research suggests that the motivation for some parents in seeking greater shared care may be the prospect of reduced child support payments.[45] In relation to the sharing of costs of children, the evidence does not suggest that, just because fathers are spending more time with their children, they are providing more financial support for them (however, this is a complex issue that deserves more research attention).[46] The level of shared care of children is also relevant to the way property is divided in Australia. Early indications from surveyed lawyers suggest that the overall share of property mothers receive on separation may be declining due to the reforms.[47]

---

[42] J McIntosh, B Smythe, M Kelaher, Y Wells and C Long 'Post-separation parenting arrangements: Patterns and developmental outcomes. Studies of two risk groups' (2011) 86 *Family Matters* 33, 42. Shared care was also found to be relatively unstable in J Cashmore, P Parkinson, R Weston, R Patulny, G Redmond, L Qu, J Baxter, M Rajkovic, T Sitek and I Katz *Shared care parenting arrangements since the 2006 Family Law Reforms: Report to the Australian Attorney-General's Department* (Sydney: Social Policy Research Centre, University of New South Wales, 2010) x.

[43] Ibid.

[44] B Fehlberg, B Smyth, M Maclean, C Roberts 'Legislating for Shared Time Parenting after Separation: A Research Review' (2011) 25(3) *International Journal of Law, Policy and the Family* 318, 329.

[45] R Kaspiew, M Gray, R Weston, L Moloney, K Hand, L Qu and the Family Law Evaluation Team ' The Australian Institute of Family Studies' Evaluation of the 2006 family law reforms: Key findings' (2010) 24(1) AJFL 5, 17.

[46] B Fehlberg, C Millward and M Campo 'Post-separation parenting arrangements, child support and property settlement: exploring the connections' (2010) 24(2) AJFL 214.

[47] R Kaspiew, M Gray, R Weston, L Moloney, K Hand, L Qu and the Family Law Evaluation Team 'The Australian Institute of Family Studies' Evaluation of the 2006 family law reforms: Key findings' (2010) 24(1) AJFL 5, 17.

(b)   The reforms and family violence

Even before the reforms were enacted, there were concerns expressed that the changes might compromise the protection of women and children from violence.[48] In a general sense, the worry was that an increased emphasis on shared parenting would lead judges to place more weight on this factor than protection from violence. These concerns were tied to particular aspects of the 2006 legislation.

The first, and very obvious, issue was that shared parenting and protection from violence were given equal prominence as 'primary' considerations. That is to say, there was no clear legislative expression that protection from violence took precedence over child–parent contact. The perceived dangers of the way the primary considerations were expressed were arguably even more likely to eventuate, in light of the fact that in most cases there will be ESPR and so mandatory consideration of shared time parenting. That is, the very strong message coming from the prescribed process of considering the division of physical care described above might sway judges to order shared care notwithstanding real concerns about violence.

Then there was concern at the introduction of a new 'additional' consideration, a so-called 'friendly parent' provision. While this section merely reflected the long-standing practice of taking into account the extent to which a parent facilitated contact, there was reason to believe that giving this factor legislative force would discourage parents from disclosing violence for fear of being branded 'unfriendly' in court.[49] Another concern was the introduction of s 117AB, which imposed a mandatory costs order for parents making false allegations. While couched in neutral terms, the clear remit of this provision was to discourage false accusations of violence, despite a lack of evidence that false allegations were in fact a particular problem in the family court.[50] Given the difficulty of proving violence, again it was predicted this would also discourage true allegations.

Within a few years those within the system were starting to express the view that the reforms had, indeed, compromised the safety of victims of violence. To the current government's credit it has acted quickly and commissioned a number of major reports, the results from which are now available. The

---

[48]   C Banks, B Batagol, R Carson, B Fehlberg, M Harrison, R Hunter, R Kaspiew, M MacLean, Z Rathus, H Rhoades, G Sheehan and L Young 'Review of exposure draft of the Family Law Amendment (Shared Parental Responsibility) Bill 2005' (2005) 19(2) AJFL 79; note, however, P Parkinson 'The family law reform pendulum' (2009) 23(3) AJFL 155.

[49]   See the discussion in T de Simone 'The friendly parent provisions in Australian family law: how friendly will you need to be?' (2008) 22(1) AJFL 56.

[50]   D Bagshaw, T Brown, S Wendt, A Campbell, E McInnes, B Tinning, B Bagatol, A Sifris, D Tyson, J Baker and P Arias 'The effect of family violence on post-separation parenting arrangements: The experiences and views of children and adults from families who separated post-1995 and post-2006' (2011) 86 *Family Matters* 49, 54; R Chisholm *Family courts violence review: A report by Professor Richard Chisholm* (Canberra: Australian Government Attorney-General's Department, 2009) 26.

evidence from those reports and other relevant research[51] was largely consistent and confirmed that the legislative provisions had exacerbated the situation for victims of violence and that reform was needed. The particular findings that relate to violence have been described in detail in many publications[52] and each of the legislative issues mentioned above have now been confirmed as problematic. However, it is interesting to note some of the particular findings:

- Cases which come to court commonly include allegations of violence.[53]

- Many of these families use FDR but often victims of violence do not disclose violence; if they do, they are very often not screened out,[54] and these families are just as likely to end up with shared care arrangements as families who disclose no violence concerns.[55]

- Professionals working in the system are sometimes confused as to whether the presumption of ESPR applies when there are grounds to believe violence is an issue.[56]

- Professionals in the family law system need better training in relation to family violence.[57]

---

[51] R Chisholm *Family courts violence review: A report by Professor Richard Chisholm*, (Australian Government Attorney-General's Department, Canberra, 2009); R Kaspiew, M Gray, R Weston, L Moloney, K Hand, L Qu and the Family Law Evaluation Team *Evaluation of the 2006 Family Law Reforms* (Australian Institute of Family Studies, Melbourne, 2009); Family Law Council *Improving responses to family violence in the family law system: An advice on the intersection of family violence and family law issues* (Canberra: Australian Government Attorney-General's Department, 2010); Australian Law Reform Commission and New South Wales Law Reform Commission *Family Violence – A National Legal Response* (Ligare Pty Ltd, 2010) available at www.alrc.gov.au/sites/default/files/pdfs/publications/ALRC114_WholeReport.pdf (accessed 2 March 2012); D Bagshaw, T Brown, S Wendt, A Campbell, E McInnes, B Tinning, B Bagatol, A Sifris, D Tyson, J Baker and P Arias 'The effect of family violence on post-separation parenting arrangements: The experiences and views of children and adults from families who separated post-1995 and post-2006' (2011) 86 *Family Matters* 49.

[52] For a summary of key findings of the major reports, see D Higgins and R Kaspiew *Child protection and family law ... Joining the dots* (National Child Protection Clearinghouse Issues Paper No 34, 2011).

[53] R Kaspiew, M Gray, R Weston, L Moloney, K Hand, L Qu and the Family Law Evaluation Team, *Evaluation of the 2006 Family Law Reforms* (Melbourne: Australian Institute of Family Studies, 2009) 232.

[54] D Bagshaw, T Brown, S Wendt, A Campbell, E McInnes, B Tinning, B Bagatol, A Sifris, D Tyson, J Baker and P Arias 'The effect of family violence on post-separation parenting arrangements: The experiences and views of children and adults from families who separated post-1995 and post-2006' (2011) 86 *Family Matters* 49, 54.

[55] R Kaspiew, M Gray, R Weston, L Moloney, K Hand, L Qu and the Family Law Evaluation Team *Evaluation of the 2006 Family Law Reforms* (Melbourne, Australian Institute of Family Studies, 2009) 165.

[56] D Higgins and R Kaspiew *Child protection and family law ... Joining the dots* (National Child Protection Clearinghouse Issues Paper No 34, 2011) 15–16.

[57] D Bagshaw, T Brown, S Wendt, A Campbell, E McInnes, B Tinning, B Bagatol, A Sifris, D Tyson, J Baker and P Arias *Family Violence and Family Law in Australia: the Experiences and Views of Children and Adults from Families who separated Post-1995 and Post-2006*

- People working in the family law system consider it is better at delivering shared care than protection from violence.[58]

In a general sense it can be said that the research evidence has satisfied the Australian Parliament that victims of family violence were being discouraged from bringing forward their experiences of violence for fear of being labelled an unfriendly parent, or suffering a costs order, and that decision-makers were underplaying the significance of violence in favour of trying to secure shared parenting. Case examples of the latter are not hard to find.[59] The very recent appeal decision *of Green & Graham*[60] highlights the point. The Federal Magistrate who heard this case ordered unsupervised contact between a 2-year-old child and her father in circumstances where the father was found to have engaged in violence towards the mother and where the child had not seen her father for 12–16 months (the precise period was not clear). It was acknowledged the mother had cause to fear for her own safety and so handover was to be at an appropriate centre. Coleman J upheld the appeal on the basis that insufficient reasons for this decision had been provided and it certainly appears that the original decision-maker's primary focus was on re-establishing the father–child relationship and not protection of the child.

In response, the federal Parliament amended the FLA in late 2011; the amendments had not commenced at the time of writing.[61] While, as outlined below, the amended provisions are an improvement on current provisions relevant to the treatment of family violence under the FLA,[62] debate continues about various aspects of these latest reforms and their overall potential to bring about any real change.

The definition of 'abuse' in s 4(1) has been extended. Previously it was limited to something that was either an illegal assault of a child or which involved a child in some sexual activity. The new provision extends to causing a child 'serious psychological harm' including when that arises because the child is subjected or exposed to family violence. As the Explanatory Memorandum notes, this brings the FLA into line with current evidence on the impacts on

---

(Commonwealth Attorney General's Department, Canberra, 2010) 100–101; D Higgins and R Kaspiew *Child protection and family law … Joining the dots* (National Child Protection Clearinghouse Issues Paper No 34, 2011) 16.

[58] R Kaspiew, M Gray, R Weston, L Moloney, K Hand, L Qu and the Family Law Evaluation Team *Evaluation of the 2006 Family Law Reforms* (Melbourne: Australian Institute of Family Studies, 2009) 235–236.

[59] For a discussion of one such example, *Mills v Watson* (2008) 39 FamLR 52, see L Young 'Child Protection Family Law: The Australian Experience' in R Sheehan, H Rhoades and N Stanley (eds) *Vulnerable Children and the Law: International Perspectives on Challenges to Child Welfare, Child Protection, and Children's Rights* (London: Jessica Kingsley, 2002).

[60] [2011] FamCAFC 248.

[61] They are due to commence on 7 June 2012.

[62] Note the comments, however, about the impact of the historical context on the potential for change in H Rhoades, C Frew and S Swain 'Recognition of violence in the Australian family law system: A long journey' (2010) 24(3) AJFL 296.

children of exposure to violence.[63] Section 4AB(3) explains that being 'exposed' to family violence means seeing or hearing family violence or otherwise experiencing its effects.

The definition of 'family violence' has also been amended. The insertion of a new definition of 'family violence' in 2006 was subject to some critique. Under the 2006 version, s 4(1) of the FLA defined family violence as:

> '... conduct, whether actual or threatened ... that causes that or any other member of the person's family reasonably to fear for ... his or her personal wellbeing or safety.'

In particular, critics were concerned because this required value judgments as to whether a victim's fear was 'reasonable'.[64] The very latest reforms have abandoned that formulation and a new and expanded definition for 'family violence' is now found in s 4AB. The definition went through a number of iterations[65] before reaching the final version, which:

- describes family violence as 'violent, threatening or other behaviour by a person that coerces or controls a member of the person's family ... or causes the family member to be fearful';

- provides a non-exhaustive, though extensive, list of examples of behaviour that 'may' amount to family violence; and

- defines when a child is 'exposed' to family violence (such that intent to expose is not required) and again provides a list of examples.

This definition gives legislative recognition to the broader range of conduct that is experienced by victims of family violence, including: stalking, intentional destruction of property, unreasonable denial of financial autonomy and withholding financial support, and preventing a family member from maintaining connections with 'family, friends or culture'.

The 'friendly parent' provision has been removed, as has the mandatory costs order for false allegations. The issue of the relationship between the two 'primary' considerations in the best interests checklist has been addressed by the insertion of s 60CC(2A) which stipulates that 'the court is to give greater weight to' the protection of children from violence when applying the primary considerations. In the first draft this section was only to apply 'if there [was] any inconsistency in applying' the two primary considerations. One obvious criticism of the earlier version was that a judge could decide that, by providing

---

[63] Available at www.austlii.edu.au/au/legis/cth/bill_em/fllavaomb2011623/memo_0.html (accessed 17 February 2012).

[64] For discussion of the critique, see R Chisholm *Family courts violence review: A report by Professor Richard Chisholm* (Canberra: Australian Government Attorney-General's Department, 2009) 144ff.

[65] See R Chisholm 'The Family Law Violence Amendment of 2011: A progress report, featuring the debate about Family Violence Orders' (2011) 25(2) AJFL 79, 79–80.

protective measures, the two provisions were not in conflict and so not be required to put protection ahead of shared care. Advisers (such as lawyers and FDR practitioners) are still required to advise parents about the shared parenting objectives of the FLA, but they must also now tell parents that protection from violence must be given priority (new s 60D).

In the 2006 reforms, the best interests checklist had been amended such that judges were required to take account of family violence orders[66] *only if* the order was a final, or contested, order; thus interim and consent family violence orders were not mandatory considerations. It was proposed that this be changed so that judges must have regard to 'any family violence order' applying to the child or a member of the child's family. Chisholm has chartered the differing views expressed in submissions on this proposed amendment and concluded that the proposed wording suffered from considerable ambiguity.[67] Given that the mere existence of an interim, uncontested, family violence order does not provide good evidence of what, if any, violence occurred, Chisholm queried what 'having regard to it' would achieve, as the proposed section did not require any inference of violence to be drawn. As Chisholm notes, the existence of an order, and the manner in which it was granted, is simply evidence – the relevant consideration is the presence of any family violence and its potential impact on the child and others. Reflecting this commentary, the final version of the new s 60CC(3)(k) requires that, where there is, or has been, a family violence order, the court must give consideration to any inferences that can be drawn therefrom bearing in mind: the nature of the order, the circumstances in which it was made, and evidence admitted to, and findings made by, the court.

(c) Shared parenting and children's well-being

Implicit in the 2006 reforms was an assumption that shared time parenting was, as a general rule, good for *all* children; otherwise, why would a judge be compelled to consider a 50/50 time model first, regardless of the circumstances? However, the research data available that preceded the Australian government's reforms did not, in fact, establish that 50/50 care provided any particular benefits to children. Indeed, there is no evidence to this effect.[68] Further, there

---

[66] This term refers to 'restraining orders', that is, injunctive orders restraining contact due to violence.

[67] R Chisholm 'The Family Law Violence Amendment of 2011: A progress report, featuring the debate about Family Violence Orders' (2011) 25(2) AJFL 79, 82ff.

[68] B Fehlberg, B Smyth, M Maclean, C Roberts 'Legislating for Shared Time Parenting after Separation: A Research Review' (2011) 25(3) Int J Law Policy Family 318, 321.

was evidence to suggest that shared care may not be suitable for very young children.[69] However, there was ample evidence to show that benefits to children were connected to:[70]

> '… the quality of parenting they receive; the quality of the relationship between their parents and practical resources such as adequate housing and income.'

Research has identified three situations in which the risks for children of shared time arrangements outweigh the benefits for them: very young children, children whose parents suffer from entrenched conflict and children whose mothers identify safety concerns.

Shared parenting is not a common arrangement for young children; Kaspiew et al found that children under 3 were represented in about 8% of the shared care cases studied.[71] Nonetheless, a court *must* first consider 50/50 shared care for all children where ESPR is ordered, including very young ones. Post-2006, the federal Attorney-General's Department commissioned two studies, one of which focused on infants and toddlers in separated families.[72] The authors of that study concluded that 'regardless of socio-economic background, parenting or inter-parental cooperation, shared overnight care of children under four years of age had an independent and deleterious impact on several emotional and behavioural regulation outcomes'.[73] They found children under 2 having as little as one regular night away from their primary carer were reported to be 'more irritable and were more watchful and wary of separation from their primary caregiver' than children primarily in one parent's care; children aged 2–3 in shared care exhibited behaviours 'consistent with high levels of attachment distress'.[74] The same outcomes were not found for children aged 4–5.[75]

---

[69] J Solomon and C George 'The development of attachment in separated and divorced families: Effects of overnight visitation, parent and couple variables' (1999) *Attachment and Human Development* 2.

[70] B Fehlberg, B Smyth, M Maclean, C Roberts 'Legislating for Shared Time Parenting after Separation: A Research Review' (2011) 25(3) Int J Law Policy Family 318, 320.

[71] R Kaspiew, M Gray, R Weston, L Moloney, K Hand, L Qu and the Family Law Evaluation Team, *Evaluation of the 2006 Family Law Reforms* (Melbourne: Australian Institute of Family Studies, 2009).

[72] J McIntosh, B Smyth, M Kelaher, Y Wells and C Long *Post-separation parenting arrangements and developmental outcomes for infants and children. Collected reports* (2010) available at www.familytransitions.com.au/Family_Transitions/Family_Transitions_files/Post%20 Separation%20parenting%20arrangements%20and%20developmental%20outcomes%20for% 20children%20%26%20infants%202010.pdf (accessed 4 March 2012) 14.

[73] Ibid 9.

[74] Ibid.

[75] For further discussion of this study, see J Cashmore and P Parkinson 'Parenting arrangements for young children: Messages from research' (2011) 25(3) AJFL 236; B Smyth, J McIntosh and M Kelaher 'Research into parenting arrangements for young children; Comment on Cashmore and Parkinson' (2011) 25(3) AJFL 258; and P Parkinson and J Cashmore 'Parenting arrangements for young children – A reply to Smyth, McIntosh and Kelaher' (2011) 25(3) AJFL 284. See also MK Pruett, R Ebing and G Insabella 'Parenting plans and visitation: Critical aspects of parenting plans for young children interjecting data into the debate about overnights' (2004) 42 *Family Court Review* 39.

The second study was of school aged children and parenting arrangements where the parents were 4 years post-mediation, and in high conflict. The outcomes of this research in relation to stability of mediated parenting arrangements have been discussed above. The study also considered satisfaction of children with their parenting arrangement. Children with shared parenting arrangements were the least satisfied and most likely of the groups of children to want a change to their arrangement and of these children those with rigid and inflexible arrangements were the least satisfied of all. It is notable that, notwithstanding children's levels of satisfaction with shared parenting, fathers of these children in shared care were the most content of all the groups with the parenting regime. At the same time, this group of fathers reported higher levels of conflict and less effective management of disputes.

This research also showed that levels of conflict between parents with shared time arrangements were reported by children to be higher than by children in other parenting arrangements; the level of conflict in shared care cases did not decrease over the period of the study as reported by the children. These children were the most likely to feel 'caught in the middle' and (as discussed earlier) it is in court cases that we have seen the most marked increase in shared time arrangements post-2006.

For many years now the evidence has been mounting that ongoing parental conflict presents risks for the well-being of children of separated parents;[76] this study has provided further evidence to support this. The children in shared care, for whom conflict generally did not decrease, were exhibiting 'greater difficulties in attention, concentration, and task completion by the fourth year of this study'.[77] It seems from this study that inflexible shared parenting regimes are particularly problematic and boys in this group 'were the most likely to have Hyperactivity/Inattention scores in the clinical/borderline range'.[78]

A final and important finding to note is that in this study, after 4 years, '[n]either the nature of a child's living arrangement at any single point in time, nor their pattern of care across time, independently predicted total mental

---

[76] See eg P Amato 'The impact of family formation change on the cognitive, social, and emotional wellbeing of the next generation' (2005) 15(2) *Future of Children* 75; J Grych 'Inter-parental conflict as a risk factor for child maladjustment: Implications for the development of prevention programs' (2005) 43(1) *Family Court Review* 97; and D Potter 'Psychosocial wellbeing and the relationship between divorce and children's academic achievement' (2010) 72(4) *Journal of Marriage and Family* 933.

[77] J McIntosh, B Smyth, M Kelaher, Y Wells and C Long *Post-separation parenting arrangements and developmental outcomes for infants and children. Collected reports* (2010) available at www.familytransitions.com.au/Family_Transitions/Family_Transitions_files/Post%20 Separation%20parenting%20arrangements%20and%20developmental%20outcomes%20for% 20children%20%26%20infants%202010.pdf (accessed 4 March 2012) 14.

[78] Ibid.

health scores' for the children.[79] In terms of the relevance of these findings, it must be remembered that parents who go to court are very likely to experience high levels of conflict.

Another group of children that may not benefit from shared care are those whose mothers report safety concerns. Kaspiew et al[80] found, based on maternal reports, that child well-being of children in shared care was lower (than for children spending more time with their mother) where mothers reported safety concerns as a result of the child spending time with the other parent. Cashmore et al[81] reported similar findings.

IV THE LESSONS OF THE AUSTRALIAN SHARED PARENTING REFORMS

This chapter has focused on where Australia's shared parenting legislation has been found wanting. In that regard, there are a number of clear messages that emerge from the Australian experience. However, it must be stressed, the overriding message is not one that eschews the ultimate goal of promoting shared parenting. Shared care is an arrangement that will benefit many children.[82] However, that does not mean it is appropriate for all children, at all stages in their lives. Rather, the key message to be taken from the evidence, which coincides with common sense, is that this goal cannot be safely achieved simply by changing family law legislation; that is, the research highlights the need for a much broader and more complex approach. There is no reason that appropriate legislation would not be a part of a more holistic approach to achieving better post-separation parenting outcomes. However, in drafting that legislation, a number of key issues need to be kept in mind.

(a) Choose your words carefully

The significance of terminology is not something new to family law reformers, at least in Australia. We have gone from 'custody' to 'residence' to 'live with' orders and from 'access' to 'contact' to 'spend time with' orders all in the name of driving change in the way we think about parenting disputes. With

---

[79] Ibid.

[80] R Kaspiew, M Gray, R Weston, L Moloney, K Hand, L Qu and the Family Law Evaluation Team *Evaluation of the 2006 Family Law Reforms* (Melbourne: Australian Institute of Family Studies, 2009) 273.

[81] J Cashmore, P Parkinson, R Weston, R Patulny, G Redmond, L Qu, J Baxter, M Rajkovic, T Sitek and I Katz *Shared care parenting arrangements since the 2006 Family Law Reforms: Report to the Australian Attorney-General's Department* (Sydney: Social Policy Research Centre, University of New South Wales, 2010) xi.

[82] R Kaspiew, M Gray, R Weston, L Moloney, K Hand, L Qu and the Family Law Evaluation Team, *Evaluation of the 2006 Family Law Reforms* (Melbourne: Australian Institute of Family Studies, 2009) 273.

hindsight, it may seem something of an irony that the committee which coined the phrase 'equal shared parental responsibility'[83] said the following early in its report:

> 'Differences of language used in this debate about similar concepts causes confusion. Concepts need to be clearly defined to avoid misunderstandings.[84]... Legislation can have an educative effect on the separating population outside the context of court decisions, if its messages are clear, it is accessible to the general public and well understood by those who offer assistance under it ...'[85]

The Australian legislation does not clearly define concepts. One striking example is a provision that has not been discussed in detail above, but which is central to the application of Australia's shared parenting laws. As indicated, there are two 'primary' best interests considerations. The first of those is expressed to be 'the benefit to the child of having a meaningful relationship with both of the child's parents' (s 60CC(2)(a)). The concept of a 'meaningful relationship' is not defined in the FLA. One has only to read the section carefully to begin to appreciate the uncertainty such wording might generate and much judicial thought has gone into precisely what this requires of decision-makers. In *McCall v Clark*[86] the Full Family Court came up with three possible interpretations of these words, two of which it said might apply depending on the circumstances.

Another example of problematic phraseology is the concept of ESPR – to work out what this actually means requires a convoluted journey through different provisions of Part VII of the FLA. The inaccessibility of the legislation to the public is highlighted by the fact that even some legal professionals are confused by it. It might even be argued that the phrase ESPR is misleading on its face, as in reality it only relates to a relatively small portion of parental responsibility. However, when one reads the committee's report it is quickly apparent why this occurred; their discussion of sharing parental responsibility suffers from vague and interchangeable use of words[87] and little thought is given to the practical application of provisions that might ultimately implement their recommendations.

---

[83] House of Representatives Standing Committee on Family and Community Affairs *Every picture tells a story: Report on the inquiry into child custody arrangements in the event of family separation* (CanPrint Communications Pty Ltd, 2003) available at www.aph.gov.au/ Parliamentary_Business/Committees/House_of_Representatives_Committees?url=fca/ childcustody/report.htm (accessed 2 March 2011) Recommendation 1.
[84] Ibid para 2.30.
[85] Ibid para 2.74.
[86] (2009) FLC 93–405 at [118]–[122].
[87] House of Representatives Standing Committee on Family and Community Affairs *Every picture tells a story: Report on the inquiry into child custody arrangements in the event of family separation* (CanPrint Communications Pty Ltd, 2003) available at www.aph.gov.au/ Parliamentary_Business/Committees/House_of_Representatives_Committees?url=fca/ childcustody/report.htm (accessed 2 March 2011) Recommendation 1. See e g the discussion at para 2.35.

Having said that, the reality is that the legislation as drafted has sent precisely the message that the Committee hoped it would. For all the Committee made clear it was not recommending a 'one size fits all' legal presumption of 50/50 shared physical care, it was equally clear that 'parents should start with an expectation of equal care'[88] and the legislation and its implementation ought 'set the community standard of substantially shared post separation parenting'.[89] It is little wonder then that many Australian parents might believe they now have a right to shared care, even if the legislation does not actually provide that. We have seen from the research outlined above that when parents focus on their rights this may be a barrier to them negotiating a child-focused agreement. This outcome is not surprising given the committee noted that, notwithstanding wide support for the best interests principle, 'most individuals have come before the committee focused on their own needs. A real child focus is not yet a reality in the system or in the behaviour of separating families'.[90] Thus, we might have predicted that sending a strong message about particular models of shared parenting could exacerbate the tendency to focus on parental rights rather than reduce it.

So, legislation that both is overly complex and vague has the potential to result in confusion and compromise outcomes for children. If parliamentarians want to send a legislative message, they must reflect carefully on what the precise message is, its suitability for a wide range of children, and on how that message is likely to be interpreted by the particular users of the family law system.

(b) Always prioritise protection from violence

We have seen how relatively simple it was to persuade judges to abandon a preference for making sole parenting orders. However, if history has taught us anything, it is how difficult it is to protect women and children anywhere, at any time, from violent men. It is therefore important to keep at the forefront of the law reform agenda an open mind to the ways in which laws can have the effect of undermining the protection of victims of violence. Criticisms of the 2006 reforms in this regard were largely ignored.[91] More recent research indicates that the correct balance was not achieved.

The most recent amendments have some positive aspects and directly address issues raised in the research. In relation to the expanded definition of 'family violence', Rhoades et al note this will 'bring the Family Law Act into line with approach used in state and territory legislation' and reflects research literature on what constitutes family violence. However, they also sound a note of caution:[92]

---

88 Ibid para 2.35.
89 Ibid para 2.78.
90 Ibid para 2.20.
91 And indeed commentators at the time were not all critical of the provisions: see P Parkinson 'The family law reform pendulum' (2009) 23(3) AJFL 155, 157.
92 H Rhoades, C Frew and S Swain 'Recognition of violence in the Australian family law system: A long journey' (2010) 24(3) AJFL 296, 311.

'... it may be that the very breadth of this definition harbours the potential for revival of the mutuality model of family conflict that shaped the system's original design. To counter this possibility, we support the [Australian Law Reform Commission] and [New South Law Reform Commission's] recommendation that the ... (new) definition of family violence be supplemented by a provision that explains the 'nature, features and dynamics' of family violence – including that "while anyone may be a victim of family violence, or may use family violence, it is predominantly committed by men" – to help guide its interpretation by the courts and family law professionals.'

The recommendations in the Australian Law Reform Commission and New South Wales Law Commission Report[93] called for a 'common interpretative framework' and while this has been adopted to the extent of a new definition of family violence, there is nothing further to give context. This shortcoming is echoed in comments by Chisholm, when discussing how the FLA might be reformed to better deal with the persistent problem of family violence. As he notes, we have two primary considerations – shared care and protection from violence. Only shared care, however, is fleshed out in terms of how courts should think about it; there is no equivalent explication of family violence as a primary consideration.[94] Given the difficulties experienced with judicial interpretation of the 2006 reforms, this indicates the need for more direct legislative guidance on the treatment of family violence.

(c)   Mediation v adversarialism

A strong message from the research reflects what common sense tells us to be true: parenting is an organic process and best outcomes are promoted by flexibility and responsiveness to children's needs at different stages in their life. This remains one of the inherent difficulties with court-imposed solutions. By definition a court order leaves little to no room for flexibility. Court orders are made at one point in time and, bar another expensive court action, no process for engaging in an ongoing dialogue about the parenting of their children can realistically be provided to parents.

There is much to be said, therefore, for promoting policies that focus on building parenting skills and in particular the ability of parents to co-operate in a child-focused and flexible way:[95]

'Prevention and early intervention parenting programs for ameliorating the impact of divorce on children have been supported throughout the literature ... with outcomes including the reporting by parents of increased parental cooperation,

---

[93]   Australian Law Reform Commission and New South Wales Law Reform Commission, *Family Violence – A National Legal Response* (Ligare Pty Ltd, 2010) available at www.alrc.gov.au/sites/default/files/pdfs/publications/ALRC114_WholeReport.pdf (accessed 2 March 2012).

[94]   R Chisholm 'The Family Law Violence Amendment of 2011: A progress report, featuring the debate about Family Violence Orders' (2011) 25(2) AJFL 79, 93–4.

[95]   J McIntosh, S Burke, N Dour and H Gridley *Parenting after Separation: A Position Statement prepared for the Australian Psychological Society* (The Australian Psychological Society Ltd, 2009) 7.

restoration of parental alliance, improved children's well-being, and a belief that early attendance at separated parenting programs will prevent or reduce enduring parental conflict. Research comparing collaborative forums for dispute resolution with litigation following separation, found that parents who mediated their dispute had significantly lower conflict with each other, and that both parents were significantly more involved in their children's lives.'

It is for this reason that the move to compulsory pre-filing mediation in Australia is potentially so important. However, one very unfortunate aspect of the FLA is that it does not prescribe any particular model of mediation. Recent evidence would indicate that at the very least child-focused mediation should be statutorily required and indeed child-inclusive mediation should be a goal even where quite young children are involved. Further, the success of mediation will depend very much on the quality of the mediators. While the sums already allocated to FDR in Australia may seem high, it is evident that, for an optimal outcome, funding needs to be increased to permit child-inclusive mediation where appropriate and to increase the amount and availability of free mediation for parents. The research is consistent in pointing us to the conclusion that many parents do not need an agreement as such; they need the skills and capacity to assist them in co-operatively arranging parenting regimes that are responsive to the developmental and other individual needs of their child. They also need to be flexible about those arrangements over time, as the child's needs change. For many parents this would be better achieved by working with parents, on an ongoing basis, rather than by a court order.

This is not to suggest that judicial determinations may not be appropriate in some cases. However, if it truly is to be a last resort, then parents should – ideally – be given a real chance first to build co-operative parenting alliances.

From a policy perspective, there is another aspect that seems to get lost in the shared parenting debate, namely, the significant potential for achieving shared parenting *post*-separation by focusing on *pre*-separation parenting. If the government, and fathers' rights groups, focused their efforts on ways of encouraging men to parent more *during* cohabitation, it seems almost inevitable this would result in more durable post-separation shared parenting than any legislative reform.

(d)   Shared parenting must be considered in its specific context

If the legislative goal is a system that is sensitive to individual families and children, and which promotes a child-focused, negotiated, resolution of parenting disagreements, then legislators must avoid provisions which presuppose a particular solution is appropriate for a generic child. McIntosh et al conclude that research findings do not 'support using shared care ... as the starting point for discussions about parenting arrangements for infants and young children under four years'.[96] We have also seen that shared care works for some groups but that it is a minority of families and while they are not an homogenous group, certain factors are more likely to predict success of shared parenting arrangements. We have also seen too many families where violence is an issue ending up in shared care where the research indicates this can have adverse impacts for the children.

Given this backdrop, serious questions must be asked as to why one would adopt a system that, over all other arrangements, prescribes 50/50 shared parenting as the starting point for discussion. The Australian research is strongly indicating that statutory provisions need to be much more targeted than is presently the case in Australia; however, the target should not be some pre-determined parenting model but rather focusing parents, family consultants, mediators and decision-makers on the matters that are most relevant to assessing what parenting regime will be best for an individual child. At a minimum, such provisions need to reflect that any decision about the parenting arrangements for a child must take account of:

- The age and developmental stage of the child, taking account of the particular needs of younger children. The FLA refers only to the 'maturity' of the child, as an 'additional' consideration in determining a child's best interests, with nothing further.[97]

- The capacity of the family to share care in a way that will result in an emotionally beneficial environment for the child. This would involve looking specifically at those family dynamics identified in the research as relevant to the potential success of a shared parenting regime. In particular, the ability of the parents to respond flexibly to the child's needs should be considered.

- The potential impact on the child of any conflict or violence between the parents or safety concerns held by a primary carer.

(e)   Laws should be evidence based

Graycar, amongst others, has written about the disconcerting tendency for Australian family law reform not to be based on the available research evidence[98] and speculates as to why Australian politicians seem more easily influenced by vocal lobby groups than are their counterparts in other parts of the world. If anything, the last two rounds of family law reform in Australia have shown that relying on legislative 'gut feeling' and the views of the loudest

---

[96] J McIntosh, B Smyth, M Kelaher, Y Wells and C Long 'Post-separation parenting arrangements: Patterns and developmental outcomes. Studies of two risk groups' (2011) 86 *Family Matters* 40, 47.

[97] FLA, s 60CC(3)(g).

[98] R Graycar 'Family Law Reform in Australia, or Frozen Chooks Revisited Again?' (2012) 13(1) *Theoretical Inquiries in Law* 241. See also A Melville and R Hunter '"As Everybody Knows": Countering Myths of Gender Bias in Family Law' (2001) 10 *Griffith Law Review* 124.

critics can be a dangerous experiment for some children. While the latest research on the reforms and family violence has prompted some legislative reconsideration, it is interesting to consider why other aspects of the 2006 shared parenting reforms have not attracted greater parliamentary scrutiny. As early as 2009, Parkinson concluded that '[t]hree years on, the requirement for judges to consider equal time is one area where reconsideration is likely to occur'[99] and, as we have seen, there is considerable evidence which would support that conclusion; and yet that has not happened. As Graycar implies, in Australia at least, the forces which drove the reforms in the first place have the potential to slow what might be seen as obvious reforms based on the research evidence.[100] Thus, it may be that, while recent reforms aimed at addressing concerns about family violence might be politically palatable (just), a broader reconsideration of the shared parenting laws which de-emphasises the focus on 50/50 care is not something either side of Australian politics appears eager to tackle.

(f) Consideration of interrelated financial issues

The way parents physically share care has necessary financial implications. The interests of children are impacted not only by who cares for them, but the financial situation of their carers. A key reason for the introduction of Australia's much celebrated child support system was to ensure that children did not suffer unnecessary poverty after separation. Where there is sole care, or 50/50 care, it is, to an extent, easier to understand how parents should contribute to the financial support of their children. Sole care parents basically meet all of the child's financial needs utilising any contribution from the other parent made by way of child support. The Child Support Agency can collect and enforce that liability. Where there is 50/50 care, in theory the parents *actually* pay one half each of all costs; child support is then used to adjust on the basis that the ultimate result should be parents contributing to total child costs[101] according to their relative share of combined parental income. The payment of child support can be enforced, but the actual payment of expenses – on which the formulation rests – cannot be. Even more complex is a less than equal shared care arrangement, where standard discounts in child support will be given on the assumption of a sharing of overall child expenses; the relevant legislation[102] does not explain, however, how those expenses are to be shared between the parents and, again, enforcement is impossible. The evidence suggests, however, that increased care may not equate to increased sharing of costs. This is an extremely difficult issue to address; however, it seems highly likely that if parents were to be more routinely provided with support to build

---

[99]   P Parkinson 'The family law reform pendulum' (2009) 23(3) AJFL 155, 157.

[100]   R Graycar 'Family Law Reform in Australia, or Frozen Chooks Revisited Again?' (2012) 13(1) *Theoretical Inquiries in Law* 241, 269.

[101]   Which is a notional figure essentially derived from combined parental income and the age of the child.

[102]   Child Support (Assessment) Act 1989 (Cth).

their capacity to parent co-operatively as discussed above, this would increase their ability to resolve issues of financial support more equitably and in a child-focused way.[103]

The other financial consideration raised by the research is the intersection of care decisions and the division of property between separating parents. Reductions in property settlements for mothers based on shared care arrangements that are unlikely to persist over time threaten to exacerbate the financial disadvantage many women face through fulfilling the role of primary carer.[104] The FLA places a premium on achieving financial finality between separating parents, which means that it is always difficult to take account of changes to parenting regimes down the track. Trying to ensure that shared parenting is more routinely agreed or ordered in those circumstances where it is likely to persist might reduce this danger. Having said that, the importance for children of flexible parenting models highlights the fact that stability of parenting arrangements is not the goal as such. Again, this is a complex issue that may need further detailed consideration.

V THE FUTURE

This chapter has focused on an issue that has dominated discourse on Australian family law over the past 2 years. However, there have been other interesting developments on the family law front in Australia. It may be that in 2 years time the Australian chapter will be charting the path to legalisation of same-sex marriage. While much has happened in this regard, same-sex couples do not yet have this option in Australia.[105] Until recently, the federal government has taken whatever steps it can to ensure states and territories do not attempt to legalise same-sex marriage; however, in December 2011 the Labor government changed its policy in favour of same-sex marriage. The government will not go so far as to sponsor a bill itself[106] and has said any vote

---

[103] On options for where parents can discuss financial matters (as this is not part of the family dispute resolution process) see L Moloney, B Smyth and K Fraser 'Beyond the formula: Where can parents go to discuss child support together?' (2010) 16 *Journal of Family Studies* 33; B Fehlberg, B Smyth and K Fraser 'Pre-filing family dispute resolution for financial disputes: Putting the cart before the horse' (2010) 16 *Journal of Family Studies* 197.

[104] For data on the relative financial disadvantage suffered by sole parent mothers, see Australian Bureau of Statistics 'Australian Social Trends 2007' (Cat No 4102.0) 2, 5 available at www.abs.gov.au. (accessed 3 March 2012); P Saunders, Y Naidoo and M Griffiths *Towards New Indicators of Disadvantage: Deprivation and Social Exclusion in Australia* (Social Policy Research Centre, University of New South Wales, 2007); B Smyth and R Weston, *Financial Living Standards After Divorce: A Recent Snapshot* (Research Paper No 23, Australian Institute of Family Studies, 2000).

[105] Though registration of relationships is available to some extent: for a recent discussion of the relationship registration schemes operating in Australia's various jurisdictions see O Rundle 'An examination of relationship registration schemes in Australia' (2011) 25(2) AJFL 25. Queensland has recently passed the Civil Partnerships Act (2011) (Q'ld) which encompasses same-sex unions.

[106] In February 2012 the Australian Greens introduced the Marriage Equality Amendment Bill (Cth) 2012 into the lower house of the federal Parliament. This Bill proposes to alter the

will be one of conscience for Labor parliamentarians. Currently the opposition Liberal party platform opposes same-sex marriage. Thus, while there are moves afoot, it remains to be seen whether the federal politicians can embrace a change it seems the general population would support.[107]

While state-based regimes have existed for some time, the introduction in 2009 of federal laws governing the separation of cohabiting spouses – equating their rights in relation to maintenance and property settlement on separation to those of married spouses – was another significant step in recent years.[108] One would expect in the next few years we will see the Family Court of Australia having to grapple with the complex questions of what amounts to a de facto relationship and when has such a relationship ended.[109] Legislation for prenuptial agreements (called 'binding financial agreements')[110] was introduced in Australia in late 2000 and the courts are now starting to see some interesting questions arising from the application of those provisions. One particular issue that has arisen is the extent to which failures to comply with technicalities of execution should undermine enforceability of the agreement.[111] No doubt as time goes on, we will see more cases dealing with the question of whether they can be undone due to changing circumstances, as provided for in the FLA.[112] As ever, change is the constant in Australian family law.

---

definition of marriage in the Marriage Act (Cth) 1961 to include the union of any two people, 'regardless of their sex, sexual orientation or gender identity': Sch 1, s 1.

[107] Polls indicate public support for same-sex marriage: see J Tovey 'New poll backs same-sex marriage' *Sydney Morning Herald*, 13 February 2012 available at www.smh.com.au/national/new-poll-backs-samesex-marriage-20120213-1t1h4.html (accessed 28 February 2012).

[108] FLA, Pt VIIIAB.

[109] See eg *Ricci & Jones* [2011] FamCAFC 222.

[110] FLA, Pt VIIIA.

[111] See eg *Black v Black* (208) 38 Fam LR 503 and *Senior & Anderson* [2011] FamCAFC 129.

[112] FLA, s 90K.

Botswana

A NEW CHILDREN'S LAW IN BOTSWANA: RESHAPING FAMILY RELATIONS FOR THE TWENTY-FIRST CENTURY

*Julia Sloth-Nielsen**

Résumé

La loi sur l'enfance de 2009 représente une avancée importante pour les droits des enfants en général, notamment grâce à l'incorporation d'une mini déclaration des droits de l'enfant , à l'élaboration du principe de l'intérêt supérieur de l'enfant et à l'attention portée aux enfants dans des situations de vulnérabilité (qui ne seront en grande partie pas traitées dans ce chapitre). La loi affiche des préoccupations nuancés pour les réalités locales, par son assimilation des structures traditionnelles d'autorité à des comités Enfant du village, son attention portée au renforcement de l'égalité des sexes par une large gamme de moyens, et le souci des droits de succession des enfants, qui prend une place importante dans l'ère du VIH/SIDA.

En ce qui concerne la transformation du droit de la famille et de la vie familiale, il y a beaucoup de nouvelles idées, parmi lesquelles l'élaboration soigneuse d'une variété de devoirs parentaux, la reconnaissance des liens de parenté et d'alliance, et par l'affirmation de la préoccupation révolutionnaire pour la promotion de la participation des enfants dans un contexte culturel où la voix des enfants a été rarement mise en évidence. Pour ces raisons, la loi est destinée à devenir un tournant dans la refonte des relations familiales et de la pratique au Botswana.

I INTRODUCTION AND CONTEXT

Botswana is a landlocked country bordered by South Africa, Zimbabwe, Zambia and Namibia. It is sparsely populated – some 2 million citizens – of whom (as elsewhere in Africa) fully half are children. A large part of the country is constituted by the Kalahari desert. Although the population are mainly Tswana speakers, English is the official language. The Botswana Children's Act 2009 was promulgated on 8 June 2009. It was a decade in the making, having first being mooted in 1999. The Act covers an array of topics and purports to domesticate the United Nations Convention on the Rights of the Child (CRC) and the African Charter on the Rights and Welfare of the

---

* BA LLB LLD, Dean Faculty of Law, University of Western Cape. The author was involved in commenting and providing technical assistance on the Regulations to the Children's Act, 2009, discussed in the body of this chapter.

Child (ACRWC) in municipal law in the country. The context within which this takes place is at once similar to the context in neighbouring Southern African Development Community (SADC) countries (such as Swaziland, Namibia and South Africa) and, at the same time, different.

Similarities lie in the percentage of children as a proportion of the total population (around 50%), and in the devastating effects upon children of HIV/Aids. Infection rates in Botswana are second in the world only to Swaziland, and current data has it that 35% of pregnant mothers are testing positive for HIV/Aids.[1] Efforts to address this pandemic, however, have been impressive, with up to 80% of HIV infected citizens now able to obtain antiretroviral drugs for the purposes of treatment. However, the number of children orphaned by HIV was, in 2007, estimated to be over 111,000.[2]

Also, a point of similarity is the underlying Roman Dutch law backdrop against which child and family law reform takes place: as the former protectorate of Bechuanaland, many aspects of Roman Dutch common law that prevailed in neighbouring South Africa also formed the founding basis of the legal system of Botswana (and that of Namibia, Zimbabwe, Lesotho and Swaziland).[3] As is the case in the region, however, a large number of children grow up in an environment in which the applicable law is customary law, as the majority of children still live in rural areas in which customary law plays a central role in community life. According to Botswana custom, which is patriarchal in nature, children were not seen as subjects of rights in their own right.

However, there are elements of the social context in Botswana which set it apart from its Southern African neighbours. The regime is generally thought to be conservative by comparison to neighbouring territories, and Botswana is the only SADC country that retains and uses the death penalty. Indeed, a disappointment in the new Children's Act is the retention of corporal punishment as a penal sanction for convicted juvenile offenders, setting Botswana at odds with neighbours South Africa, Namibia and Zimbabwe, where corporal punishment as a penal sanction has long since been abolished by judicial decisions.[4]

Furthermore, Botswana is regarded as a middle income country due to the wealth accrued from diamond mining which gives it a GDP way above those of her neighbours. Botswana is regarded as a success story of development in

---

[1]   Irin news, 20 January 2012.

[2]   M Tabengwa 'Harmonisation of national and international laws to protect children's Rights: The Botswana case study' (unpublished paper prepared for the African Child Policy Forum composite report on harmonisaton of child laws in Eastern and Southern Africa, 2008) 30 (copy on file with the author, hereafter 'Botswana Harmonisation Report').

[3]   EK Quansah 'Botswana' in R Blanpain (ed) 'Family and Succession Laws' in *International Encyclopaedia of Laws* (Kluwer International, 2002). See also EK Quansah *Introduction to Family Law in Botswana* (Pula Press, 2001) especially chapter 9 ('Aspects of parental power').

[4]   *S v Williams* 1995 (7) BCLR 861 (CC); *Ex parte Attorney General: In Re Corporal Punishment by organs of State* 1991 (3) SALR 76 (NmSc); *S v A Juvenile* 1990 (4) SA 151 (ZS).

Africa, having risen from one of the world's least developed nations to being a middle income country.[5] It has a stable and credible government, and succession has been non-violent and sustained over many years. These successive governments have utilised the diamond and other revenues to effect the social and economic upliftment of the nation, in contrast to African governments who have spent surpluses on elites and military hardware.[6] Nevertheless, it is a largely rural country, with many children growing up under customary law regimes, and a significant minority of children growing up with tribal affiliations to nomadic people, and are Basarwa or San pastoralists.

II   THE SITUATION PRIOR TO THE CHILDREN'S ACT

Family and child law in Botswana were previously to be found in statute (e g the Children Act 1981, the Adoption of Children Act 1951, the Maintenance Orders Enforcement Act 1970), common law derived from Roman Dutch law, and customary law. Botswana has ratified the CRC (in March 1995) and the ACRWC (in 2001), but these were not domesticated in national law. Botswana entered a reservation to art 1 of the CRC upon ratification, due to the multitude of differing definitions of a child prevailing in various statutes.[7] The new Children's Act seeks to harmonise the definition of a child in a manner consistent with international law. Parental authority (or the parent–child relationship) was regulated by Roman Dutch common law. Judicial precedent and the Children's Act 1981 recognised the best interests of the child principle in determining custody, guardianship and maintenance of children. Guardianship under common law was the preserve of married fathers, and equal guardianship of mothers and fathers came about only in 2004 with the enactment of the Abolition of Marital Power Act of that year, which then conferred equal guardianship upon both parents.[8] As will be discussed subsequently, children born out of wedlock had, under common law, a legal relationship with their mother only.[9]

---

[5]   Botswana Harmonisation Report, above n 2, 4.

[6]   African Child Policy Forum *African Report on Child Wellbeing 2008* and *African Report on Child Wellbeing 2011*.

[7]   Botswana Harmonisation Report, above n 2, 13, which records that the subsequent ratification of the ACRWC was not accompanied by any such reservation and therefore provides a higher standard concerning the definition of a child to which the country must adhere.

[8]   In a similar fashion to the South African Guardianship Act of 1993 which conferred guardianship upon mothers for the first time. The Guardianship Act has been repealed by the South African Children's Act of 2005, in force from 1 April 2010. Equality in parental relations is required by the African Women's Protocol (Protocol to the African Charter on Human and People's Rights, 2006, ratified by both Botswana and South Africa).

[9]   Additionally, customary law granted guardianship of children born out of wedlock to their mother's family only, with the male head of the household enjoying the status of guardian. The biological father incurred no duty of support, and his liability was limited to the payment of damages for seduction. The child does not acquire any right to inherit from his biological father, or to take the father's name.

According to Quansah, case-law in Botswana recognised the following general principles prior to the enactment of the new Children's Act:[10]

'1.   Custody of children of tender age should be given to the mother
2.   Custody of a son should be given to a father and that of a daughter to the mother
3.   Custody of a child should not be given to an immoral parent
4.   The wishes of the child may be taken into account
5.   The child's existing association and environment should not be lightly disturbed
6.   The material advantage of one parent over the other should not generally be a consideration.'

The Customary Law Act of 1969, which was an attempt to regulate some aspects of customary law, made some reference to the concept of the best interests of the child under s 6, where it required that 'in any case relating to the custody of children, the welfare of children shall be the paramount consideration irrespective of which law is applied'.

The 1981 Children's Act had the specific purpose to deal with the care and custody of children, to provide for the establishment of children's and juvenile courts, and made maltreatment or neglect of children an offence, but was limited in scope and did not proceed from a rights-based approach. In its 2004 concluding observations to the initial Botswana Country Report, the CRC Committee urged the speedy finalisation of the law review process.

Pre-2009, the Botswana legal system recognised the 'juvenile court' which was established for the trials of young offenders. It had jurisdiction to hear charges against children of 18 years or younger, and juvenile courts were either magistrate's courts or customary courts established for this purpose. Courts were supposed to sit informally (albeit chaired by a magistrate dedicated for that purpose), and attended by a probation officer and/or a social worker concerned with the case. Emphasis was placed on the welfare of the juvenile, and a range of penalties was available for the disposition of the case, including dismissing the charge, discharging the offender on his entering into a recognisance, placing the offender on probation for up to 3 years, sending the offender to a school of industries until the age of 21 years, or ordering the parent or guardian to pay a fine, damages or costs. These powers were to be found in s 29 of the 1981 Children's Act, which excluded imprisonment save as specified in s 29 (where the juvenile fails to comply with a prior order of court or commits another offence whilst on probation).[11] The exclusion of a sentence of imprisonment did not apply equally to a sentence of corporal punishment, which was upheld as competent by courts.[12] Children's courts, in the same fashion as in South Africa and Namibia, were quasi civil courts which dealt with welfare and adoption matters.

---

[10]   Quansah *Introduction to Family Law in Botswana*, above n 3, 67.
[11]   See in general CM Fombad and EK Quansah *The Botswana legal system* (Durban: Lexis Nexis Butterworths, 2006).
[12]   See *Dikgang v S* [1990] BLR 329.

III BACKGROUND TO THE ACT

The 2009 Children's Act is an overt attempt to give effect in domestic law to the CRC and the ACRWC. The Act was developed with reference to recent enactments in the region, such as the South African Children's Act 38 of 2005, and the Lesotho Child Care and Protection Act, passed finally in 2011, but available and widely disseminated in Bill form since 2005. Regulations, which have been drafted but are yet to be approved and promulgated, flesh out the provisions of the principal Act. The Act's objectives are 'to make provision for the promotion and protection of the rights of the child; for the promotion of the physical, emotional, intellectual and social development and general well-being of children; for the protection and care of children; for the establishment of structures to provide for the care, support, protection and rehabilitation of children; and for matters connected therewith'. The various chapters of the Act that will not be covered here include chapters on children in need of protection, offences against children, alternative care of children, foster care, children in conflict with the law, homes and institutions for the reception of children and measures to combat trafficking. The principal focus of this contribution will be the family law dimensions of the Act, which, it is argued, pave the way for a comprehensive overhaul of family relations in the country.

IV RECOGNITION OF CHILD RIGHTS

The Act recognises, for the first time,[13] a series of rights for children. These are found in Pt II and Pt III of the Act. Part II, which covers the objects,[14] guiding principles, child participation and the primacy of the child's best interests, clearly incorporates in the legislation two of the four pillars of the CRC, in addition to laying a framework for the interpretation and application of the Act's provisions. Part III contains a 'mini bill of child rights', spelling out a series of rights spanning civil and political rights (right to a name and nationality, right to life), socio-economic rights (right to health, right to shelter, right to clothing, right to education) and rights critical to underpin a child rights orientation (right to leisure play and recreation, and recognition of the child's right to parental care and guidance, right to protection against harmful labour practices and sexual abuse and exploitation).

---

[13] The Constitution of Botswana contains no provision relating to families or children: Quansah *Introduction to Family Law in Botswana,* above n 3.

[14] The objects of the Act are to: (a) promote the well-being of children, families and communities in Botswana; (b) provide for the protection and care of children where their parents have not provided, or are unable or unlikely to provide, that protection and care; (c) protect children from harm; (d) acknowledge the primary responsibility of parents and families to care for and protect children, and to support and assist them in carrying out that responsibility; (e) acknowledge the role played by communities in promoting and safeguarding the well-being of children and to encourage and support them in carrying out that role; and (f) protect children from unlawful or exploitative labour practices.

The rights contained in the Bill of Child Rights in Pt III are seemingly to a greater or lesser extent justiciable. All are justiciable to the extent that they are laid down in national legislation, and practice or policies which conflict could be challenged. However, some are rather more aspirational, such as the right to freedom of association in s 22:

> 'Every child has the right to freedom of association subject to the child's age, maturity and level of understanding, of parental guidance, national security, public health or morals, and the rights and freedoms of others.'

Other rights are far more directly enforceable, insofar as duty bearers are identified more closely, and in some rights provisions, contraventions are rendered criminal offences for which sanctions are provided. Two examples illustrate this: in s 13 (child's right to know and be cared for by parents), s 13(4) provides that: 'No person shall separate a child from his or her parents, other relatives or guardian unless it is in the child's best interests to do so.' Section 13(5) continues that: 'Subject to a child's age, maturity and level of understanding, any person seeking to separate the child from his or her parents, other relatives or guardian shall seek the child's consent.' Section 13(6) encapsulates the criminal provision: 'Any person who contravenes the provisions of subsection (4) or (5) shall be guilty of an offence and shall be sentenced to a fine of not less than P2,000 but not more than P5,000, or to imprisonment for a term of not less than three months but not more than six years, or both.'[15] A similar level of detail has been provided in respect to child labour in s 24(5) and (6).[16]

V GUIDING PRINCIPLES

Section 7 of the Act contains a set of guiding principles which must be applied in the interpretation of the Act. Some clearly apply in cases of family dissolution or conflict. They include that:

> '(a) no decision or action shall be taken whose result or likelihood is to discriminate against any child on the basis of sex, family, colour, race, ethnicity, place of origin, language, religion, economic status, parents, physical or mental status, or any other status;
>
> (b) every child shall be cared for and protected from harm;
>
> (c) the parents, family and community of a child have the primary responsibility of safeguarding and promoting the child's well-being;

---

[15] P is Pula, the currency of Botswana.

[16] Section 24(5): 'Every person who lawfully employs a child shall submit the records of such employment to the Ministry responsible for labour and if he or she fails to do so, shall be guilty of an offence and shall be sentenced to a fine of P10,000' and s 24(6): 'Any person who unlawfully employs a child shall be guilty of an offence and shall be sentenced to a fine of not less than P10 000 but not more than P30,000, or to imprisonment for a term of not less than 12 months, but not more than five years, or both.'

(*d*) every child shall have stable, secure and safe relationships and living arrangements;

(*e*) a child's parents, other relatives, guardian and any other people who are significant in the child's life shall be given an opportunity and assistance to participate in decision-making processes under this Act that are likely to have a significant impact on the child's life;

(*f*) the people referred to in paragraph (*e*) shall be given adequate information, in a manner and language they understand, regarding–

(i)   decision-making processes under this Act that are likely to have a significant impact on the child's life,

(ii)   the outcome and implications of any decision about the child, including an explanation of the reasons for the decision, and

(iii)   any relevant complaint or review procedure;

(*g*) decisions about a child shall be consistent with cultural, ethnic and religious values and traditions relevant to the child; and

(*h*) decisions about a child shall be made promptly having regard to the age, circumstances and needs of the child.'

These build substantially on equivalent provisions in the South African Children's Act 38 of 2005, and are supplemented by criteria underpinning the application of the best interests of the child (s 6), such as the capacity of the child's parents, other relative, guardian or other person to care for and protect the child; the likely effect on the child of any change in the child's circumstances; the importance of stability and continuity in the child's living arrangements and the likely effect on the child of any change in, or disruption of, those arrangements; and any wishes or views expressed by the child, having regard to the child's age, maturity and level of understanding in determining the weight to be given to those wishes or views (s 6(b), (f), (g) and (h)). Some criteria mirror earlier developments in Botswana case-law. However, the 'tender years doctrine' and the 'gender matching' principle alluded to by Quansah above are implicitly forsaken insofar as the equality of parents to fulfil the caring function is the premise.

VI FAMILY LAW DIMENSIONS OF THE CHILDREN'S ACT

Who are the duty bearers in respect of the parent–child relationship? The Act is insistent that the primary responsibility for children lies with the family, and the way in which this is framed is consistent with the African view on kinship and family care. Examples highlighting this are to be found in Part IV, entitled 'Parental duties and rights', and commencing with an elaboration of the former. ('Duties', rather than responsibilities, echoes the language of the African Charter on Human and People's Rights, 1981). Section 27(1)–(3) sets up the basic position: biological parents are duty bearers in the first instance, as regards care and provision of maintenance. Where parents do not live together, these duties shall be carried out jointly, unless it would not be in the best interests of the child: in effect a presumption of joint custody or shared parenting. Third, s 27(3) establishes a default position:

> 'Where both or one of the biological parents is deceased, or the biological parents do not live together as a nuclear family and the absent parent plays no role in the child's life, the other relatives, guardian, adoptive parent, step-parent or foster parent of the child shall be deemed to have assumed the parental duties associated with the biological parents of the child.'

This provision ensures that the Batswana child is almost always associated with a duty bearer, and that the child does not land in legal limbo upon the death of a parent (eg due to HIV/Aids). It allows for this to take place automatically, without the intervention of a court order. It explicitly recognises the de facto reality of kinship care in African communities. Finally, by providing legal recognition to other relatives, and de facto carers such as step-parents, in instances where the child is being cared for by a (single) biological parent where the other biological parent is absent, the Act provides in essence a legal support circle surrounding the single parent (who is more often than not the child's mother) in respect of the duties provided for in s 27.

From the above it is also apparent that the Act recognises the wider concept of 'family' as prevails in traditional African culture. Reference is made to relatives, other people who are significant in a child's life, and 'relative' is defined (in the definitions section of the Act) as a grandparent, sibling, uncle, aunt or cousin. No definition of family is provided.

The duties which rest upon (primarily) the child's parents are set out in s 27(4), and proceed well beyond the traditional configuration of access and custody rights which prevailed under Roman Dutch common law. They include ensuring that the basis of every decision and action he or she takes concerning the child is in the child's best interests; providing for the physical, emotional, educational and material needs of the child; providing direction and guidance to the child in accordance with the age, maturity and level of understanding of the child; seeking professional advice, including advice from family members and community leaders, and complying with such advice where it is in the best interests of the child to do so; encouraging the child's participation in household decisions and actions subject to the child's age, maturity and level of understanding; raising each child in the household as being of equal dignity as other persons in the household, irrespective of sex; ensuring the child inherits adequately from his or her estate; respecting the child's dignity and refraining from administering discipline which violates such dignity or adversely affects the physical, emotional or psychological well-being of the child or any other child living in the household (although the following subsection contains the caveat that this must not be read to outlaw corporal punishment); bringing up the child to respect and value the family and the institution of marriage; and doing all such other things as are necessary to ensure the good health, safety, educational development and general well-being of the child.

Notable in the above array of duties are those which encourage child participation in family decisions, and the requirement that gender equality in the home setting prevails. These seek to overturn traditional attitudes which ignore children and treat girls as inferior to boys. Child participation as an element of the new Act is accorded more discussion in Part VIII below.

As regards the incidence of guardianship, reference has already been made to the recent changes to the inherited position that only biological fathers were awarded guardianship of their minor children, to the exclusion of mothers. Guardianship was a common law concept which under the Children's Act 2009 now receives a statutory definition: 'guardian' means a person who has the charge of, or control over, a child, or a person appointed according to law to be the guardian of a child. Traditionally, the concept of guardianship involved the totality (umbrella) of capacities to represent the child legally, including in contractual arrangements and in any litigation; by furnishing consent to acts such as marriage or surgical operations; and consenting to adoption.

In the South African Children's Act 38 of 2005, the concept of guardianship has been confined to the capacity to undertake five discrete acts in s 18: consent to adoption, consent to marriage; consent to the application for a passport for the child and the removal of the child from the Republic; consent to the alienation or encumbrance of the child's immovable property. The vesting (incidence) of guardianship as an element of parental responsibilities and rights is clearly set out. Unfortunately the new Botswana Children's Act is lacking in clarity about how guardianship (although defined) relates to parental duties and responsibilities, and the key concepts of 'charge over a child' or 'control over a child' which constitute the definitional underpinnings of the concept of guardianship are (a) not themselves defined and (b) do not 'match' the language relating to the duties of the parents (see s 27(1), which speaks of the 'care and maintenance' of the child). However, s 28(1)(d), which spells out the rights of parents, refers to the right to represent the child in all contractual and other legal matters regarding the child's property and other interests, traditionally part of the functions of a guardian; s 28(1)(e) provides for the parental right to 'participate, in the prescribed manner, in court and other proceedings related to his or her child', similarly a function of guardianship; and s 28(1)(f) grants a parent the right to appoint a guardian or revoke the appointment of a guardian where one has been appointed, subject to the court's approval, which again suggests that all parents are automatically guardians. This means that unmarried fathers automatically qualify as guardians, overturning the previous dispensation under Roman Dutch common law. The position of unmarried fathers is discussed in more detail in the next part.

VII   THE POSITION OF UNMARRIED PARENTS

According to Quansah, a preponderance of children in Botswana are born out of wedlock. The position of fathers of children born out of wedlock is an issue which has recently concerned lawmakers in other countries in the region, and led to very different outcomes in different jurisdictions.[17] The backdrop is the Roman Dutch common law position that the unmarried father enjoyed no automatic parental rights in relation to the child born out of wedlock, although some jurisdictions recognised the father's duty of support (which was therefore not reciprocal in the sense that payment of child support did not give rise to any rights, including access rights). In Botswana, the Affiliation Proceedings Act 1970, as amended in 1999, provided for procedures for single women to access maintenance for their child and for the ascertainment of paternity (this Act has not been repealed).[18] Historically, however, children born out of wedlock had no legal relationship with their father, and, as mentioned, did not take his name or inherit from him.[19] At the same time, regional instruments and international child rights law provided for non-discrimination for the child on the basis of his or her parents marital status, also in the context of the child's right to know and be cared for by both parent's, as well as equality rights for men and women regarding the responsibility for child rearing (in the African Women's Protocol) seems to require that equal responsibilities and rights for married and non-married fathers be provided in law as the starting point.

The Botswana Children's Act does, at first glance, appear to achieve equality between the roles of married and unmarried parents. This can be seen from a variety of provisions. Section 13(2), which falls in Pt III of the Act dealing with the Bill of Child's Rights, provides that:

> 'A child who is born out of wedlock and does not live with both of his or her biological parents has a right to access the absent parent, and to be nurtured, supported and maintained by such absent parent in accordance with the provisions of this and any other Act which deals with the care and maintenance of children.'

The right is (consistent with the CRC provision) that of the child. This right is buttressed by s 13(3) which follows immediately thereafter ('Any parent, other relative or guardian or other person who, without reasonable excuse, refuses the absent parent access to the child shall be guilty of an offence and shall be sentenced to a fine of not less than P2 000 but not more than P5 000, or to imprisonment for a term of not less than three months but not more than six months, or both') and s 12(4) (right to a nationality) which provides that 'the

---

[17]   See N Murungi, J Sloth-Nielsen and L Wakefield 'Does the differential criteria for awarding parental rights and responsibilities violate international law? A legislative and social study of three southern and eastern African countries' (2011) 55(2) *Journal of African Law* 203–229.

[18]   Quansah *Introduction to Family Law in Botswana,* above n 3.

[19]   Quansah *Introduction to Family Law in Botswana,* above n 3.

birth certificate shall indicate the name, citizenship and address of the biological mother and the biological father of the child whether the child is born in or out of wedlock'.

Finally, this right of the child is mirrored by an unequivocal award of duties (or responsibilities) to unmarried fathers in s 27(2): 'The duties of the biological parents of a child shall, where those parents do not live together, be carried out jointly by them unless it would not be in the best interests of the child.'

However, it is submitted that the matter remains somewhat unclear in the scheme of the Act. Following on the detailed section dealing with duties (s 27) is a section (s 28) which deals with parental rights. This section commences with the elaboration of three parental rights, to wit:

> 'Subject to the best interests of the child, and to section 78, every parent shall have the right, in relation to that child, to–
>
> (*a*)   have the child live with him or her;
> (*b*)   control and guide the child's upbringing;
> (*c*)   maintain personal relations with, and have access to, the child if the child does not live with him or her.'

These provisions apply equally to married parents who reside together with the child, and to unmarried parents, who may well live together with the child but who frequently do not. The award of residence rights to the absent father appears to set up the potential for conflict, with struggles (based on claims of rights) over the residence of the child. However, a deadlock breaking mechanism is newly provided for in the form of s 29, which provides for co-parenting agreements. These are reserved for parents who are not married to each other and who do not live together. These must be in writing and registered with the clerk of the children's court, and may contain details as to which parent the child shall reside with; which parent shall determine the child's upbringing; the times the child will spend with the absent parent; the financial and other responsibilities of each parent towards the child; and such other matters as may be prescribed. These are voluntary agreements, and unlike the South African Children's Act 38 of 2005 which also newly introduced co-parenting agreements, no provision for compulsory mediation prior to litigation is included,[20] and it therefore remains the position that unless parties come to an agreement, the spectre of conflict looms.

VIII   CHILD PARTICIPATION AND THE BOTSWANA ACT

The Act transcends custom and tradition by providing expansively for child participation, which is accorded a prominent role. Not only is there a dedicated

---

[20]   Section 21(3) of the Children's Act 38 of 2005.

section on child participation, s 8, comprising three parts, but it is contended that this section goes further than contemporary formulations of the child's right to participate in other recent African children's statutes. The section commences with an overall statement of the right of a child of sufficient age, maturity and level of understanding so as to be able to participate to be able to do so in regard to decisions which have a significant effect on a child's life (s 8(1)). Section 8(3) explains that decisions which might have a significant effect on a child's life include, but are not limited to, decisions about the alternative care of the child, decisions in the course of preparing, modifying or reviewing care or alternative care agreements or plans for the child, decisions about the provision of social services to the child, and decisions about contact with the child's parents, other relatives, guardian or other persons who are significant in the child's life.

Section 8(2) elaborates at a practical level how the child is to be enabled to exercise his or her participation rights, an unusually detailed exposition in domestic law.[21] The subsection spells out that the child, for the purpose of ensuring that the child is able to participate in the decision-making process, shall be given:

'(*a*) adequate information, in a manner and language that the child understands, about–

(i)   the decision to be made,
(ii)   the reasons for the involvement of persons or institutions other than his or her parents, other relatives or guardian,
(iii)   the ways in which the child can participate in the decision-making process, and
(iv)   any relevant complaint or review procedures;

(*b*) the opportunity to express the child's wishes and views freely, according to the child's age, maturity and level of understanding;

(*c*) any assistance that is necessary for the child to express those wishes and views;

(*d*) adequate information regarding how the child's wishes and views will be taken into account;

(*e*) adequate information about the decision made and a full explanation of the reasons for the decision; and

(*f*) an opportunity to respond to the decision made.'

As noted above, s 27, which elaborates the contents of the parental responsibility towards a child, also includes as a principle that parents have the

---

[21]   See, however, the Council of Europe *Guidelines on Child Friendly Justice* (2010) which contain similar provisions, and the draft *Guidelines on Action in the Justice System for Children in Africa* (2011) presented at the Kampala conference on children deprived of their liberty, November 2011, which too echo these underlying principles.

duty to encourage the child's participation in household decisions and actions subject to the child's age, maturity and level of understanding (s 27(4)(e)). Section 51 which provides for care agreements when court ordered alternative care is ordered for a child similarly provides that '[t]he concerned parties shall take the child's views into account in drawing up the care agreement unless the child is unable to form and express a view on account of his or her age and level of maturity or understanding' (s 51(2)).

Section 34 also represents an unusual developing area of law, as it constitutes the first known legislative provision in Africa for what are colloquially known in the region as children's parliaments. The section names this body a 'National Children's Forum', and its composition and functions are set out in Sch 2 to the Act. This schedule explains that the mandate of the forum is to discuss 'issues affecting the education, health, safety or general well-being of children'. The forum is to be comprised of ten child representatives from each district, whose selection is to be facilitated by the local district council, appointed for a term of 2 years. At least one annual meeting of the forum must be held, although more frequent meetings are possible, with the Ministry responsible for children being required to convene and provide secretarial support to the forum. The reporting line is from the forum to the National Children's Council, established in terms of s 35 of the Act. The mandate, functions and composition of the council are set out in Sch 3 to the Act.[22] The legislative formulation addresses one criticism often raised in connection with children's parliaments – that their deliberations find no avenue for expression, as they are not actually linked to formal policy and other processes, parliamentary or otherwise. The Botswana Children's Act provides a clear destination for recommendations and concerns to surface.

Finally, in the context of the discussion of child participation, mention must be made of s 94 ('Access to court') which provides that, except where otherwise provided in this Act, a child affected by or involved in the matter to be adjudicated is one of the identified parties who may bring a matter which falls within the jurisdiction of a children's court before that court. This appears to abolish the child's lack of capacity to litigate in his or her own name, as was the case at common law. A child also has the express capacity to appeal or apply for a review to a High Court should he or she be dissatisfied with any magistrate's court order (s 96).

---

[22] The functions are to coordinate, support, monitor and ensure the implementation of sectoral Ministries' activities relating to children; to guide sectoral Ministries' interventions as they relate to or impact on children; to advocate for a child-centred approach to legislation, policies, strategies and programmes; and to advocate for a substantive share of national resources to be allocated to children-related initiatives and activities. The Council is comprised of both government functionaries, e g from the Ministries of Labour, Education, the Attorney-General etc, and six representatives appointed from amongst persons and non-governmental bodies representing children's interests. According to the Botswana Harmonisation Report, the precursor to the National Council was a National Child Welfare Committee which had not functioned optimally, due to poor attendance at meetings, inconsistent membership and the lack of a statutory mandate (Botswana Harmonisation Report, above n 2, 38).

IX   COMMUNITY INVOLVEMENT AND DEVOLUTION OF FUNCTIONS

Building on the precedent set first in the Lesotho Child Care and Protection Bill 2005 (now as of 2011, Act), the Botswana Act takes a lead in legislating for community involvement in matters of child welfare and child rights. Section 33 and Sch 1 elaborate a system of 'Village Child Committees' to be established at village level and comprising the *kgosi* or *kgosana* (traditional leader) of the community concerned; a social worker; a man and a woman representing parents in that community; a female child representing the female children in that community, and a male child representing the male children in that community. All members of the Village Child Committee, except for the *kgosi* or *kgosana*, shall be elected at a *kgotla* gathering (a traditional clan meeting).

The functions of the Village Child Committee are to educate their respective communities about the neglect, ill-treatment, exploitation or other abuse of children, and to promote, amongst members of those communities, such education; and to monitor the welfare of children in their respective communities. Although serving primarily to form the backbone of a nascent child protection system by serving as the 'eyes and ears' of the community to detect any child maltreatment, neglect or welfare-related issue, it is not inconceivable that individual and family relations might come to the fore at the Village Child Committee meetings from time to time. It is therefore welcome that children themselves will enjoy representation on the Village Child Committee, which has also been set up to ensure gender equality amongst its members, in stark contrast to the patriarchy that prevailed in traditional justice and customary systems. Indeed, it is forecast that the statutory Village Child Committees may well in future usurp completely the role of traditional dispute resolutions structures (*Kgotla* and traditional courts) insofar as they may at present deal with family and child-related disputes.

X   CONCLUSIONS

The Botswana Children's Act 2009 represents a milestone for the country in advancing children's rights generally, through its incorporation of a mini bill of child rights, its elaboration of the best interests principle and the attention to children in vulnerable situations (which were largely not dealt with in this chapter).The Act displays nuanced concern for local realities, through its assimilation of traditional leadership structures into Village Child Committees, its attention to furthering gender equality in a range of ways, as described, and the concern for children's inheritance rights which loom large in the era of HIV/Aids.

As regards the transformation of family law and family life, much new thinking is evident, including the careful elaboration of a variety of parental duties, the recognition of kinship ties and relative care, and by displaying groundbreaking concern for the promotion of child participation in a cultural setting in which children's voices were seldom brought to the fore. The Act is, for these reasons, destined to become a watershed in the reshaping of family relations and practice in Botswana.

Canada

TOURIST MARRIAGES, SEPARATION AGREEMENTS AND POLYGAMY

*Martha Bailey**

Résumé

Le droit de la famille canadien a été marqué en 2011 principalement par trois questions. La première concerne une règle de conflits de lois ayant pour effet de rendre invalides certains mariages célébrés au Canada. Un couple de même sexe qui s'était marié au Canada, l'État respectif des parties ne leur offrant pas cette possibilité, revient au Canada pour y demander le divorce et se voit répondre que ce mariage est invalide et que, dès lors, le tribunal n'a pas la compétence pour prononcer le divorce. En réponse à cette situation, le gouvernement a déposé un projet de loi qui édicte qu'un mariage célébré au Canada et qui serait valide si l'époux était domicilié au Canada, est également valide pour ce qui est du droit canadien, en dépit du fait que le droit national de l'un ou l'autre époux n'autorise pas un tel mariage. Le deuxième élément majeur est une décision de la Cour suprême du Canada qui clarifie les principes en matière de révision des ordonnances qui entérinent une convention sur le soutien alimentaire entre ex-époux. Finalement, la Cour suprême de la Colombie-Britannique a rendu son jugement très attendu sur la constitutionnalité de la disposition du Code criminel qui interdit la polygamie. Le tribunal reconnaît que cette interdiction est, pour l'essentiel, conforme à la Constitution, ce qui pave la voie à de possibles poursuites criminelles, même si pour le moment aucune accusation n'a encore été portée.

I INTRODUCTION

Choice of law rules for marriage rarely capture the public's attention. But this year Canadians were surprised to learn that, under Canada's choice of law rules, some marriages that take place in Canada are not considered valid. A same-sex couple who came to Canada to get married because they were not legally permitted to do so in their home states found, when they returned to Canada to get a divorce, that their marriage was not recognised in Canada and that the Canadian court had no jurisdiction to grant them a divorce. This story was widely reported in the media and gave rise to extensive public criticism of the ruling Conservative government. The government responded quickly with a bill to change the law and assured the public that the same-sex marriage issue would not be reopened. The Supreme Court of Canada handed down an

---

* Professor of Law, Queen's University.

important decision on spousal support agreements. The court ruled that, when a spousal support agreement has been incorporated into a divorce judgment, any subsequent application to vary support should depend on whether there has been a material change in circumstances since the original order was made. The court was divided on the question of the weight to be given to the separation agreement on a variation application.

After a lengthy and expensive hearing on the constitutionality of Canada's criminal prohibition of polygamy, the British Columbia Supreme Court determined that the provision is largely constitutional, clearing the way for possible prosecutions. No polygamy charges have yet been laid, but the British Columbia special prosecutor was assessing whether such charges were appropriate in early 2012 (at the time of writing).

II   TOURIST MARRIAGES

Same-sex marriage became available across Canada in 2005 pursuant to the federal Civil Marriage Act.[1] And even earlier, same-sex marriage was available in Ontario and British Columbia after appellate courts in those provinces ruled that exclusion of same-sex couples from marriage violated the constitutional guarantee of equality.[2] Many of the same-sex marriages that took place after the changes in the law involved non-residents of Canada.[3]

The laws across Canada were very accommodating to 'tourist marriages'. Other countries that had opened up civil marriage to same-sex couples required that at least one of the parties be a citizen or habitual resident (domiciliary) of the country.[4] Canadian provinces imposed no such requirement. And Canada has never had an 'evasion law' that forbids the celebration of a marriage by non-residents if the marriage would be void in their home state.[5] No blood tests were required to marry in Canada. There was no waiting period after obtaining a licence before the marriage can be solemnised. At the time same-sex marriage became available it was easy for non-residents to get married in Canada, and

---

[1]   Civil Marriage Act, SC 2005, c 33.

[2]   *Halpern v Canada* (2003), 225 DLR (4th) 529 (Ont CA); *Eagle v Canada* (2003), 225 DLR (4th) 472 and (2003), 228 DLR (4th) 416 (BCCA).

[3]   More than half of people who entered into the same-sex marriage in British Columbia in 2003 (when same-sex marriage first became available) were non-residents of Canada: Statistics Canada *The Daily*, 17 January 2007.

[4]   Kees Waaldijk 'Others May Follow: The Introduction of marriage, Quasi-marriage, and Semi-marriage for Same-sex couples in European Countries' (2004) 38 *New England Law Review* 569, 576–577 and 582–583.

[5]   The Massachusetts court decision that led to same-sex marriage in that state was handed down in 2003: *Goodrich v Department of Public Health*, 798 NE 2d 941, 948 (Mass 2003). When same-sex couples tried to get married in Massachusetts, they initially had to deal with the state's 'evasion' law. General Laws of Massachusetts, Chapter 207, s 11 read: 'No marriage shall be contracted in this commonwealth by a party residing and intending to continue to reside in another jurisdiction if such marriage would be void if contracted in such other jurisdiction, and every marriage contracted in this commonwealth in violation hereof shall be null and void.' The law was repealed in 2008: 2008, 216, Sec 1.

the same laws are in place today. Parties can cross the border, obtain a marriage licence and 20 minutes later get married.

When opening up civil marriage to same-sex couples, Canada did not concern itself with the portability of the status that non-residents sought by coming to Canada to be married. It was apparent that many non-residents who entered into a same-sex marriage in Canada did so because they were not legally permitted to marry in their home state. Whether they could take home either a new marital status or any of the incidents of marriage depended on the willingness of their home state to recognise the Canadian marriage. It seemed that non-residents placed a value on their Canadian marriage, regardless of whether it was given legal effect in their home state.[6]

Canada also failed to concern itself with whether non-residents who married in Canada would be considered validly married in Canada. As noted above, Canadian provinces do not have 'evasion' laws, and parties seeking marriage licences are not screened to determine whether they have capacity to marry under the law of their home states. All that Canadian provinces require is that applicants for a marriage licence satisfy Canada's rules as to who may marry.

Common law Canada determines the essential validity of marriage according to the law of the domicile of each of the intended spouses at the time of the marriage (the 'dual domicile rule').[7] In Quebec, the rule is that: 'Marriage is governed with respect to its essential validity by the law applicable to the status of each of the intended spouses.'[8] There is also some support for the law of the parties' intended domicile as the appropriate choice of law rule,[9] and this rule has been applied by the Federal Court of Appeal.[10] Formal validity of marriage is governed by the lex loci celebrationis.[11] In Quebec, formal validity 'is governed by the law of the place of its solemnization or by the law of the

---

[6] For further discussion see Martha Bailey, 'Migration of the Same-Sex Family' (2004) Social Science Research Network, online at http://papers.ssrn.com/sol3/papers.cfm?abstract_id= 704748.

[7] *Schwebel v Ungar* [1964] 1 OR 420 (CA), aff'd [1965] SCR 148. The common law rule that the capacity to marry is governed by the lex domicilii was enunciated in *Brook v Brook* (1861) 9 HL Cas 193, where the House of Lords refused recognition of a marriage that was valid under the lex loci celebrationis but was void for being within the prohibited degrees under the law of the putative husband's domicile (England). In *Brook*, Lord Campbell, LC stated: 'It is quite obvious that no civilised state can allow its domiciled subject or citizens, by making a temporary visit to a foreign country to enter into a contract, to be performed in the place of the domicile, if the contract is forbidden by the law of the place of the domicile as contrary to religion, or morality, or to any of its fundamental institutions.'

[8] Civil Code of Québec, SQ 1991, c 64, art 3088.

[9] See e g Adrian Briggs *The Conflict of Laws* (Oxford: OUP, 2002) 226, where the author, adopting a government interest analysis, writes that 'there is much to be said for the view that the law of the society in which the spouses are going to live has the closest interest in whether they have capacity to live as husband and wife'.

[10] *Canada v Narwal* (1990), 26 RFL (3d) 95 (Fed Ct AD) ('*Narwal*').

[11] *Keddie v Currie* (1991), 85 DLR (4th) 342 (BCCA). For the province of Québec, see the Civil Code of Québec, SQ 1991, c 64., art 3088, which provides: 'With respect to formal validity, [marriage] is governed by the law of the place of its solemnization or by the law of the country of domicile or of nationality of one of the spouses.'

country of domicile or of nationality of one of the spouses'.[12] At common law there is a limited judicial discretion to refuse to recognise a foreign judgment on public policy grounds.[13]

It is doubtful whether all same-sex marriages of non-residents would be recognised under existing choice of law rules. The problem most likely to arise is lack of essential validity under the domiciliary law of one or both parties. For example, a same-sex couple domiciled in Alabama, a state that does not permit or recognise same-sex marriage, may get married in Ontario. Because the marriage would be essentially invalid under the lex domicilii, it would not be recognised pursuant to Canada's choice of law rules, unless, perhaps, the parties intended to acquire a matrimonial domicile in Canada and did in fact do so after their marriage.[14] The same result would follow if the parties married in The Netherlands, Belgium or Massachusetts (unless the intended matrimonial domicile rule could be applied). Although the Netherlands and Belgium require that at least one of the parties be a citizen or habitual resident (domiciliary) of the country,[15] it would be possible for a party domiciled in, say, the Netherlands to marry a party domiciled in, say, Alabama. Under existing rules, the marriage would not be recognised in Canada because one of the parties would lack capacity under the lex domicilii.

An argument could be made, however, that, if a party's personal law denies capacity to enter into a same-sex marriage, that incapacity should be ignored on public policy grounds.[16] Although Canadian authority is lacking, there are some common law precedents for this approach. In *Sottomayer v De Barros (No 2)*,[17] an English court refused to give effect to the incapacity of a Portuguese domiciliary to marry in England her first cousin, an English domiciliary, without dispensation from the Pope. The court stated that: 'Numerous examples may be suggested on the injustice which might be caused to our own subjects if a marriage were declared invalid, on the grounds that it was forbidden by the law of the domicile of one of the parties.'[18] Examples cited by the court were US anti-miscegenation laws and laws imposing incapacity to marry at all on members of religious orders.[19] In cases of marriages celebrated in England, English courts have also refused to give effect to an incapacity to remarry imposed on an adulterous wife under the law of Natal,[20] and to an incapacity imposed on a Hindu to marry outside his religion.[21] The exception to the generally applicable dual domicile rule

---

12   Civil Code of Québec, SQ 1991, c 64, art 3088.
13   *Boardwalk Regency Corp v Maalouf* (1992), 6 OR (3d) 737 (CA).
14   *Narwal*, above n 10.
15   Kees Waaldijk 'Others May Follow: The Introduction of marriage, Quasi-marriage, and Semi-marriage for Same-sex couples in European Countries' (2004) 38 *New England Law Review* 569, 576–577 and 582–583.
16   Adrian Briggs makes this suggestion in *The Conflict of Laws* (Oxford: OUP, 2002) 231.
17   [1879] LR 5 PD 94.
18   Ibid at 104.
19   Ibid at 104.
20   *Scott v Att-Gen*, [1886] LR 11 PD 128.
21   *Chetti v Chetti*, [1909] P 67.

expressed in these cases has been criticised, but Graveson points out that the exception is limited in scope – it applies only to marriages that take place in England – and has a very specific purpose, that is, 'to protect Englishmen and Englishwomen on entering into marriages with person domiciled abroad'.[22] This established exception to the dual domicile rule could apply to marriages that took place in Canada between a Canadian domiciliary and a party domiciled in a state that prohibits same-sex marriage. But it would not apply to marriages celebrated abroad or to marriages in Canada of two non-residents.

It may be possible to build on the *Sottomayer* line of cases and to argue for a broader exception to the dual domicile rule in regard to same-sex marriages celebrated abroad or where neither party is a Canadian domiciliary. In light of the values enshrined in international human rights documents and the Charter,[23] it is at least arguable that giving effect to a foreign law prohibiting same-sex marriage would be discriminatory, an unjustifiable interference with the freedom to marry and contrary to public policy.

It was in this context that the federal government caused a storm when it intervened in a divorce proceeding brought in Canada by a non-resident same-sex couple who had married in Canada. One member of the couple was from England, the other from Florida.[24] The federal government opposed the divorce on two grounds. First, under Canada's Divorce Act, one member of a couple must have been ordinarily resident in the province for at least one year immediately preceding the commencement of the proceeding.[25] Although Canada permits tourist marriages, it does not grant tourist divorces. Second, as discussed above, marriages are recognised as essentially valid in Canada only if the dual domicile rule is satisfied. Although the federal government's position was solidly grounded in the law, there were strong expressions of outrage coupled with ill-informed calls for the government to stop its perverse refusal to recognise the non-resident marriages.[26] The government rushed to assure everyone that it did not wish to reopen the same-sex marriage debate,[27] and swiftly introduced Bill C-32, An Act to Amend the Civil Marriage Act.[28]

Bill C-32 was introduced and had its first reading in the House of Commons on 17 February 2012. The most important section of Bill C-32 is s 5, which provides, with retroactive effect, that a marriage 'performed in Canada that would be valid in Canada if the spouses were domiciled in Canada is valid for the purposes of Canadian law even though either or both of the spouses do

---

[22] RH Graveson *The Conflict of Laws* (London: Sweet & Maxwell, 4th edn, 1960) 146–147.

[23] Canadian Charter of Rights and Freedoms, Part I of the Constitution Act, 1982, being Sch B to the Canada Act 1982 (UK), 1982, c 11, s 15.

[24] There was extensive media coverage of this story. See e g Kirk Makin 'Ottawa moves to defuse same-sex controversy' *Globe & Mail*, 12 January 2011.

[25] Divorce Act, RSC 1985, c 3 (2nd Supp), s 3(1) ('Divorce Act').

[26] Jane Taber 'Sudden legal stand against same-sex marriage defies logic, Rae says' *Globe & Mail*, 12 January 2012.

[27] Kirk Makin 'Despite legal about-face, Harper has "no intention" of reopening gay marriage' *Globe & Mail*, 12 January 2012.

[28] Bill C-32 (2012) 41st Parliament, 1st Session ('Bill C-32').

not, at the time of the marriage, have the capacity to enter into it under the law of their respective state of domicile'. So far so good. The controversial provisions in Bill C-32 provide a process for non-residents who married in Canada to get a divorce in Canada on the grounds of separation for one year if 'each of the spouses is residing – and for at least one year immediately before the application is made, has resided – in a state where a divorce cannot be granted because that state does not recognize the validity of the marriage'.[29] The provision only extends to parties who are seeking a divorce on consent, although one party may apply for a divorce without consent of the other if the other is incapable of giving consent or unreasonably withholding consent or cannot be found.[30]

The Divorce Act is explicitly excluded from application to divorces granted under Bill C-32.[31] This means that the corollary relief available to parties under the Divorce Act will not be available to parties seeking a divorce under Bill C-32. No provision is made in Bill C-32 for custody, access, spousal support or child support claims. It also means that those seeking a divorce under Bill C-32 will have to live separate and apart for one year and will not be able to obtain a divorce on the basis of cruelty or adultery as parties applying under the Divorce Act may do.

Bill C-32 has attracted criticism because of the exclusion of the Divorce Act corollary relief provisions and the Divorce Act grounds for divorce and because of the requirement of consent from both spouses.[32] Indeed some experts predicted Charter challenges to the proposed regime on the basis that excluding non-residents from the more favourable Divorce Act regime may violate the constitutional guarantee of equality.[33] It remains to be seen whether the federal government will respond to criticisms by amending Bill C-32.

III SEPARATION AGREEMENTS

At the end of 2011, the Supreme Court of Canada released its decision in *LMP v LS*[34] The case involved a couple who married in 1988 and divorced in 2002. Soon after the parties' marriage, the wife was diagnosed with multiple sclerosis and withdrew from the waged labour force. She looked after the children and household, while the husband worked outside the home. After separation the parties entered into a separation agreement which was then incorporated into the divorce order in 2003. Under the order the wife was to be paid spousal support in the amount of $3,688 per month, indexed. In 2007, the husband applied for a variation of the spousal support order, seeking a reduction and,

---

[29]   Bill C-32, s 7(1)c.
[30]   Bill C-32, s 7(2).
[31]   Bill C-32, s 8.
[32]   Tamara Baluja 'Bill to close loophole in same-sex marriages creates "double standard"' *Globe & Mail*, 17 February 2012.
[33]   Christin Schmitz 'C-32: "It is not a real divorce"' (30 March 2012) *Lawyers Weekly* 4.
[34]   *LMP v LS*, 2011 SCC 64.

ultimately, a cancellation of spousal support. The trial judge found that the wife was able to work outside the home, and therefore reduced and then terminated her support. The Quebec Court of Appeal rejected the wife's appeal, concluding that her failure to become self-sufficient over time gave rise to a material change in circumstances.

The Supreme Court of Canada allowed the wife's appeal and ordered that the original 2003 order be restored. The court was unanimous in the result but split 5 to 2 in its reasoning. The majority distinguished between s 15(2) of the Divorce Act, which authorises courts to make spousal support orders, and s 17, which authorises courts to vary an existing court order. When a party to a spousal support agreement applies for an initial spousal support order that differs from the agreement, the application is made under s 15(2) and the relevant authority is the *Miglin v Miglin*.[35] *Miglin* requires a court to first consider the circumstances at the time of formation of the agreement. The court must consider whether the circumstances relating to the execution of the agreement give rise to any concerns and whether the agreement substantially complied with the objectives of the Divorce Act. The court is then required to consider the circumstances at the time of the application for support. At this stage the court must determine whether the agreement still reflects the original intention of the parties and whether it is still in substantial compliance with the Divorce Act.

The majority said that the *Miglin* test was applicable to applications for support orders under s 15(2) of the Divorce Act, but did not apply to applications to vary existing court orders. The majority's reasons were grounded in the wording of the relevant statutory provisions. Section 17 of the Divorce Act authorises a court to vary, rescind or suspend prior orders, defines the factors allowing for variation, and sets out the objectives such a variation should serve. In contrast with s 15(2), which direct courts to consider 'any order, agreement or arrangement relating to support of either spouse', s 17 makes no reference to agreements. Section 17 simply requires that a court be satisfied 'that a change in the condition, means, needs or other circumstances of either former spouse has occurred' since the making of the prior order or the last variation. The majority stated that, under either s 15(2) or s 17, the parties' spousal support agreement is given attention, but that it is far less significant in an application under s 17.

The majority said applications under s 17 to vary existing orders are governed by *Willick v Willick* and *G (L) v B (G)*.[36] In these decisions from 1994 and 1995, the Supreme Court of Canada held that a court must be satisfied that there has been a material change in circumstances since the making of the prior order or variation, meaning a change that, 'if known at the time, would likely have resulted in different terms'. Applying these authorities to the current case, the majority said that the threshold variation question is whether there has been a material change of circumstances since the making of the order, and this

---

[35] *Miglin v Miglin*, 2003 SCC 24.
[36] *Willick v Willick*, [1994] 3 SCR 670; *G (L) v B (G)*, [1995] 3 SCR 370.

is so regardless of whether a spousal support order incorporates an agreement. A court hearing a variation application must presume that the terms of the prior order were in compliance with the objectives of the Divorce Act at the time the order was made. The court that made the prior order will already have applied the *Miglin* test, and it must be presumed that the test was applied correctly.

The majority stated that an agreement that a specific type of change will (or will not) justify a variation should informs a court's application of the *Willick* test. However, the majority further observed that an agreement containing only a general statement that the agreement is intended to be final would provide little guidance in practice on whether or not a particular event or circumstance was contemplated by the parties or what consequences they would have ascribed to it. After exhaustively considering the material change in circumstances test, the majority then observed that, if the test is met, the variation order should properly reflect that change and the objectives set out in s 17.

The trial judge in this case erred in making a variation order without making a finding that there had been a material change in circumstances. The Court of Appeal erred in determining that the wife had the capacity to work, and that this, coupled with the passage of time, amounted to a material change of circumstances. The record showed that there had been no material change of circumstances since the making of the order and that there was therefore no basis on which to vary it under s 17. At the time of the order, the wife had multiple sclerosis and was not expected to seek employment outside the home. There has been no material change in circumstances since that time.

Chief Justice McLachlin and Cromwell J agreed with the majority that there had been no material change of circumstances justifying a variation. In contrast with the majority, however, they would give significant weight to spousal support agreements and would use the *Miglin* approach for variation applications. The concurring justices took the view that, in order to meet the threshold for variation under s 17 of the Divorce Act, a court must satisfy itself that there has been a material change in the circumstances of either former spouse since the making of the spousal support order. In order to be 'material' a change must: (1) relate to something that was not either expressly addressed by the parties in the agreement or that cannot be taken as having been in their contemplation; and (2) result in the support provision, considered in the context of the entire agreement, no longer being in substantial compliance with the objectives of the Divorce Act.

The majority's approach directs courts hearing variation applications to focus on whether there has been a material change of circumstances. The agreement that was incorporated into the court order will not play a significant role in most cases.

IV POLYGAMY

The Canadian province of British Columbia has long been under pressure to deal with a group of fundamentalist Mormons who practise 'marriage' in an isolated community within the province. Because of uncertainty about the constitutional validity of s 293 of the Criminal Code,[37] Canada's criminal provision outlawing polygamy, prosecutors were reluctant to lay charges. British Columbia's government sought an advisory opinion from its Supreme Court as to the constitutionality of the polygamy provision. The court handed down its decision in November 2011.[38]

The court ruled that s 293 is consistent with the Canadian Charter of Rights and Freedoms, except to the extent that it applies to children between the ages of 12 and 17 who marry into polygamy or a conjugal union with more than one person at the same time. The court ruled that the elements of s 293 are:[39]

'1. 'an identified person, who
2. with the intent to do so
3. practices, enters into, or in any manner agrees to consents to practice or enter into
4. a marriage, whether or not it is by law recognized as a binding form of marriage, with more than one person at the same time.'

Because of the court's ruling that some sort of 'marriage' is a requisite element of the offence, parties who cohabit in polyamorous relationships would not be subject to prosecution. Only those who participate in some 'sanctioning event'[40] and who purport to be married[41] (whether or not they are legally married) are caught by the offence. The court stated that proof of the sanctioning event is not an element of the offence, but '[w]hat is an element of the offence is a "marriage" with more than one person at the same time, and an indicia [sic] of "marriage" … is some form of sanctioning event'.[42] The court acknowledged that there was vagueness as to the meaning of a marriage that is not necessarily legal and that is sanctioned by some undefined event. However, the court considered that it was not so vague as to be unconstitutional.

The distinction drawn by the court between parties whose union is a 'purported form of marriage'[43] and those who live together without a 'sanctioning event' is irrational and unfair. Why should the fact that parties have undergone some sort of sanctioning event and are purporting to be married render otherwise legal behaviour criminal? The fact that it is legal to carry on multiple simultaneous relationships provided those involved do not purport to be married will make it difficult to identify the relationships that engage the

---

[37] *Criminal Code*, RSC 1985, C-46, s 293.
[38] *Reference re: Section 293 of the Criminal Code of Canada*, 2011 BCSC 1588 ('*Reference*').
[39] *Reference*, para 1363.
[40] *Reference*, para 939.
[41] *Reference*, para 1017.
[42] *Reference*, para 1022.
[43] *Reference*, para 1017.

criminal law. Because it is not possible to legally marry more than one person in Canada, most of the 'marriages' will be extra-legal. There will be no marriage licences and no registration of these extra-legal unions. And the plural unions that have given rise to concern in British Columbia have been carried on in an isolated community whose members may not be willing to incriminate themselves or their family and neighbours.

No appeal will be taken from the British Columbia Supreme Court's ruling.[44] The Attorney-General of British Columbia announced in early 2012 that a new special prosecutor in the Bountiful polygamy case would be appointed to determine if charges should be laid and to conduct any prosecutions.[45] Initially the special prosecutor was to focus on charges other than polygamy. Then in March 2012 the Attorney-General confirmed that the province would not refer the issue of the constitutionality of the polygamy provision to British Columbia's Court of Appeal or to the Supreme Court of Canada. Until the Supreme Court of Canada has the opportunity to deal with the polygamy provision, doubts about its constitutionality will remain. The Attorney-General, however, stated that she was satisfied that the British Columbia Supreme Court decision was a strong enough basis on which to proceed, and has broadened the mandate of the special prosecutor to include consideration of polygamy charges.[46]

---

[44] Marc Ellison 'Polygamy Ruling Won't be Appealed' *Globe & Mail*, 21 December 2011.
[45] Wendy Stueck 'Polygamy Special Prosecutor Steps Down' *Globe & Mail*, 9 January 2012.
[46] Jeff Lee 'B.C. won't seek more definitive ruling on polygamy ban' *Vancouver Sun*, 26 March 2012.

China

PRESENT LEGISLATION ON ADOPTION IN CHINA AND ITS REFORM PROPOSALS

*Chen Wei and Shi Lei**

Résumé

Dans de nombreuses juridictions le critère du meilleur intérêt de l'enfant a été la pierre angulaire des réformes législatives en matière d'adoption. À ce chapitre, la législation chinoise est défaillante. Les auteurs plaident donc pour une intégration expresse de ce critère dans la loi, un meilleur encadrement des conditions permettant d'adopter et d'être adopté, de même qu'ils proposent l'instauration d'une période probatoire avant l'adoption et la création d'un système légal de supervision des adoptions en Chine.

Adoption law is an integral part of family law. In the twenty-first century, new problems have arisen in the adoption laws in China. Based on an introduction to the social background of the present adoption law reform and related foreign legislation, the authors analyse the present adoption laws in China and their shortcomings, and offer reform proposals.

I THE GUIDELINES FOR CONTEMPORARY ADOPTION LAW REFORM

(a) Social background of the doctrine of the child's best interests and its legislative concept

In the first half of the twentieth century, international child rights law emerged with the development of international human rights law. Generally speaking, the development of international child rights law can be divided into three parts. In the first phase, the child is recognised as a member of international society and as a subject under the protection of international law. In the second phase, the child is granted rights in substantive laws. The third phase witnessed a new development of granting the child procedural abilities to employ and

---

* Chen Wei (1954–), female, doctoral supervisor, Professor of Law, Southwest University of Political Science and Law, Chongqing, China. E-mail: chenwei5058@163.com.
Shi Lei (1980–), male, Teacher in Applied Law School, PhD Candidate in Civil and Commercial Law School, Southwest University of Political Science and Law, Chongqing, China. E-mail: shilei8311@hotmail.com.

petition for these rights and freedoms while enjoying basic rights.[1] Relevant multinational conventions reached in this period also reflected this trend. After World War II, the concept of child protection was widespread. Based on the Geneva Declaration on the Rights of the Child of 1924 approved by the League of Nations, the United Nations General Assembly adopted the Declaration of the Rights of the Child in November 1959. Principle 2 in this Declaration states:

> 'The child shall enjoy special protection, and shall be given opportunities and facilities, by law and by other means, to enable him to develop physically, mentally, morally, spiritually and socially in a healthy and normal manner and in conditions of freedom and dignity. In the enactment of laws for this purpose, the best interests of the child shall be the paramount consideration.'

This Declaration first expressly stipulated the concept of 'best interests of the child'. Afterwards, the Convention on the Elimination of All Forms of Discrimination against Women (CEDAW), adopted in 1979 by the UN General Assembly,[2] and the Convention on the Rights of the Child, adopted in 1989, continued to stipulate the best interests of the child doctrine. Children's human rights were further laid down in the latter convention. The Adoption and Ratification of the Convention on the Rights of the Child of 1989 is a landmark in establishing the best interests of the child doctrine. Article 3(1) in this Convention expressly stipulates:

> 'In all actions concerning children, whether undertaken by public or private social welfare institutions, courts of law, administrative authorities or legislative bodies, the best interests of the child shall be a primary consideration.'

At present, the best interests of the child doctrine has become a guideline in adoption legislative reforms in many jurisdictions. The value orientation of modern adoption legislation shifts from traditional 'family-oriented', 'parents-oriented' to 'child-oriented' centred on the doctrine of the child's best interests.[3] In modern society, under the guidance of the child's best interests doctrine advocated in international literature, 'giving more respect and protection of the child's interests' has been one of developing trends in the realm of family law.[4]

---

[1] Geraldine van Bueren *The International Law on the Rights of the Child* (Martinus Nijhoff Publishers, 1999) 1. See Wang Xuemei *On the Child's Rights* (Beijing: Social Science Academic Press, 2005) 12.

[2] See CEDAW, Art 5(b), Art 16(1)(d) and (f).

[3] Shi Shangkuan *On Family Law* (Beijing: China University of Political Science and Law Press, 2000) 532–533; Chen Qiyan et al *New Research on the Relatives Section in the Civil Law* (Sanmin Book Company, 1987) 247–248.

[4] See Chen Wei *Researches on the Legislation of Marriage and Family Law in China* (Beiing: Qunzhong Publishing House, 2000) 45–46 and 49.

(b)   Adoption rules in international literature

In the 1960s, as welfare state policies were carried out, the traditional concept of adoption for the purpose of creating a family line was gradually replaced by an emphasis on the child's interests within adoption legislation.[5] This legislative shift is mirrored in relevant international treaties and conventions. For example, in 1986, the UN General Assembly adopted the Declaration on Social and Legal Principles Relating to the Protection and Welfare of Children, with Special Reference to Foster Placement and Adoption Nationally and Internationally. In this Declaration, Art 13 stipulates that the primary aim of adoption is to provide the child who cannot be cared for by his or her own parents with a permanent family. Article 21 in the Convention on the Rights of the Child provides that states parties that recognise and/or permit the system of adoption shall ensure that the best interests of the child shall be the paramount consideration. The Hague Convention of 29 May 1993 on the Protection of Children and Cooperation in Respect of Intercountry Adoption completely embodies the best interests of the child doctrine. Article 1 in the Hague Adoption Convention expressly states the objects of the Convention and stresses 'safeguards to ensure that intercountry adoptions take place in the best interests of the child'. Moreover, Arts 4, 16, 21, 24 and 30 repeat the emphasis on this doctrine and its position. That contemporary international adoption law is oriented to the object of protecting the best interests of the child is mirrored in all of these treaties and regulations.

II   THE PRESENT LEGISLATION ON ADOPTION IN CHINA

In China, the main sources of adoption laws include the Adoption Law of the People's Republic of China (PRC) effective as of 1 April 1992. In 1998, this Act was amended, and the amendment was effective from 1 April 1999. The Supreme People's Court also made relevant judicial explanations on adoptions. Furthermore, the Ministry of Civil Affairs of the PRC promulgated Measures for Registration of the Adoption of Children by Chinese Citizens in 1999. The present legislation and regulations on adoptions contain mainly the following.

(a)   The basic principles of adoption law

The fundamental principles of adoption legislation embody the legislative goals and the guiding ideologies in this field. They also provide basic behaviour models for adoptive parties. Furthermore, they can be used in the explanation and enforcement of adoptive legislation. They are legally binding on common people. As stipulated in the General Provisions of the Adoption Law of the PRC, there are five principles as follows: (a) being beneficial to the upbringing and growth of adopted minors, which mirrors the nurturing role of the

---

[5]   Lin Juzhi *Study on Topics in Family Law* (Taibei: Wu-Nan Book Inc, 1985) 85.

adoption law; (b) protecting legal rights of adopters and adoptees; this principle embodies the legislative concept of balancing the rights of parties concerned. Meanwhile, with society's vicissitudes, pensions become[6] the other key issue in adoption law; (c) complying with the principle of equality and voluntariness; this principle requires that first the parties concerned in an adoption have equal legal status and that secondly they shall negotiate with each other of their own free will, and adoption against one's will cannot be recognised by law; (d) not being in contravention of social morality, which reflects the morality of adoption law; and (e) not being against the laws and regulations on family planning. Since China is populous, family planning is a basic policy to reduce the birth rate and to guarantee the healthy development of her economy and society. Hence, the adoption system concerning a child's change of family necessarily requires that adoption practice be guided by the last principle.

(b) Conditions for establishing adoption

A common adoption is established under the following conditions:[7]

(a) If the adoptee is less than 14 years old and no parent is raising him or her. It includes three situations: ie an orphan bereaved of parents, abandoned infants or children whose parents cannot be ascertained or found, or children whose parents are unable to rear them due to unusual difficulties.

(b) Those who can place children for adoption are the guardians of an orphan; social welfare institutions; or parents unable to rear their children due to unusual difficulties. In order to avoid infringement of minors' interests, two restrictions are imposed on adoption in China pursuant to the present legislation. One is that, if the parents of a minor are both persons without full civil capacity, the guardian(s) of the minor may not place him or her for adoption, except where the parents are likely to do serious harm to the minor. The other is that, where a spouse places a minor child for adoption after the death of the other spouse, the parents of the deceased have priority in rearing the child.[8]

(c) Adopters must have the ability to rear the child, including: being childless; capable of rearing and educating the adoptee; healthy without any diseases which are regarded in medical science as making a person unfit to

---

[6] China's population is aging rapidly; thus, old age problems have been added to the government's agenda. Article 7 in the Adoption Law of the PRC sets looser conditions for the adopter to adopt a child from a collateral relative by blood of the same generation and up to the third degree of kinship. The child to be adopted in this situation can be an adult; and the conditions for the person placing the child are looser too for the law does not require them to have experienced special difficulties in rearing the child. The looser provisions on adoptions between relatives essentially indicate that adoption will favour resolving old age problems for the adopter.

[7] See arts 4, 5, 6 of the Adoption Law of the PRC.

[8] See arts 12, 18 of the Adoption Law of the PRC.

adopt a child; and having reached the age of 30. Also, the adopter may only adopt one child in principle, although some special adoptions are not covered by this rule.[9] Where a male person without a spouse adopts a female child, the age difference between the adopter and the adoptee shall be no less than 40 years.[10] Furthermore, where a person with a spouse adopts a child, the husband and wife must adopt the child in concert.[11]

The conditions to establish a special adoption in this law are looser. Special adoptions mainly refer to the following:

(a)   Adoption of a child belonging to a collateral relative by blood of the same generation and up to the third degree of kinship: in this adoption, the adoptee is not restricted to a child under 14 years old; concerning the people placing out children, irrespective of the biological parents' unusual difficulties in rearing their child, they can place out their own child; in terms of the adopter, an overseas Chinese adopter is not even subject to the restrictions that the adopter must be childless. Furthermore, where the adopter is a bachelor and the adoptee is a daughter of his collateral relative by blood of the same generation, they can establish an adoption relationship irrespective of the requirement of the 40 years age gap.[12]

(b)   Adoption of orphans or disabled children and those brought up by social welfare institutions whose parents cannot be found: these children may be adopted irrespective of the restrictions that the adopter be childless, reached the age of 35 and adopt one child only.[13]

(c)   Adoption of stepchild: a step-father or step-mother may, with the consent of the parents of the stepchild, adopt the stepchild, and such an adoption may be free from such restrictions as that the biological parents have difficulties in raising the child, that the adopters must meet the requirement specified in arts 8, 9, 10 of this law, as well as from the restriction that the adoptee must be under the age of 14.[14]

(d)   Adoption of 'grand-generation': adoption of 'grand-generation' refers to adoption of a grandchild. Where the adopter regards the adoptee as his or her grandchild and there is an established adoptive relationship between the grandparents and grandchildren, such an adoption should be recognised as legal.[15] Thus it is can be dealt with pursuant to the marriage law as regards to the rules on adoptive parent-child relationships.[16]

---

[9]   See art 8(1) of the Adoption Law of the PRC.
[10]   See art 9 of the Adoption Law of the PRC.
[11]   See art 10 of the Adoption Law of the PRC.
[12]   See art 7 of the Adoption Law of the PRC.
[13]   See art 8(2) of the Adoption Law of the PRC.
[14]   See art 14 of the Adoption Law of the PRC.
[15]   See art 29 in Opinions on the Implementation of Civil Law and Policies on Several Issues in 1984 promulgated by the Supreme People's Court of China.
[16]   According to the provision concerning the adoptive effects in the judicial opinions, where the adopter and the adoptee have a huge age gap or they have different seniority in a clan, the

(c) Adoption procedures

Adoption procedures in China can be divided into three steps, ie application, examination and announcement, as well as registration.

(i)   Application

In accordance with provisions in the Measures for Registration for the Adoption of Children by Chinese Citizens, both parties of the adoption shall be present at the registration office so as to complete the adoption registration. If the adopters are married, both shall be present. If one spouse cannot be present, due to legitimate reasons, a power of attorney is required from the absent spouse. The power of attorney shall be notarised by a country/city neighbourhood committee.

(ii)   Examination and announcement

According to the Measures, the registration office shall do a formal examination and verify the authenticity and completion of the adoption application form and relevant supporting documentation. Meanwhile, they shall check in a substantive examination whether such an adoption is compatible with the Adoption Law. The registration office shall complete the examination within 30 days, beginning the day after they receive an application and all supporting documentation. The registration office shall post public announcements in an attempt to locate the biological parents, if the biological parents cannot be ascertained or found, prior to the registration. The announcement lasts at most 60 days. The dates of posting will not be calculated toward the dates of the registration process.

(iii)   Registration

The registration office then issues adoption decrees, provided that the applicants satisfy the requirements of the Adoption Law after the aforesaid examination and announcement.

(d) Termination of adoption

In China, where the parties in an adoption relationship intend to terminate their adoption relationship, they can end it with an agreement or a judgment.

---

adopter may call the adoptee his or her grandchild. As a matter of fact, the adopter does this for himself or herself not for his or her children. Therefore, the judicial opinions stipulated that the adopter and the adoptee in this kind of adoption have the same rights and duties as those of adoptive parent-child relationships, ie the adopter and the adoptee in a 'grand-generation' adoption only have different titles, but the rights and duties between them are identical to those of adoptive parents and children.

As regards to termination with an agreement, the present adoption law provides that the parties concerned may terminate the adoptive relationship before the adoptee reaches adult age on the mutual agreement between the adopter and the biological parents or institutions who placed the child out. If the adopted child involved reaches the age of 10 or more, his or her consent shall be obtained. Where the adoptee is an adult already, the adoptive relationship can be terminated as long as the adopter and the adoptee reach an agreement. The parties shall complete the procedure for registering the termination of the adoptive relationship at a civil affairs department.[17] The registration offices shall process terminations of adoptions within 30 days, beginning the day after they receive the application and all required supporting documentation. The office shall then terminate the relationship, retrace the adoption decrees, and issue certificates for the termination of the adoption, provided the termination requests satisfy the provisions of the Adoption Law.[18]

Concerning termination with a judgment, the present adoption law stipulates that, where an adopter fails to perform the duty of rearing the adoptee or commits maltreatment, abandonment, or other acts of encroachment upon the lawful rights of the minor adopted child, the person having placed the child for adoption shall have the right to demand termination of the adoptive relationship. Where the adopter and the person having placed the child for adoption fail to reach an agreement thereon, a suit may be brought in a people's court. Where the relationship between the adoptive parents and an adult adopted child deteriorates to such a degree that their living together in the same household becomes impossible and they cannot reach an agreement on termination of adoption, either of the parties may petition for a judgment in a people's court.[19]

III THE SHORTCOMINGS IN THE PRESENT ADOPTION LAW IN CHINA

After the Adoption Law in China came into force in 1992 and was amended in 1998, the adoption legislation has generally been suitable for regulating Chinese adoption in real life, with certain achievements. First, in respect of legislative principles, the principle of being beneficial to the upbringing and growth of adopted minors actually conforms to the requirement of the child's best interests doctrine. The principle of protecting the legal rights of adopters and adoptees embodies the fairness and justice of the law. The principle of equality and voluntariness and that of not being in contravention of social morality have the identical goal of protecting legal and effective adoption. And the last principle of not being against the laws and regulations on family planning is in line with the Chinese social reality.

---

[17] See arts 26, 27, 28 of the Adoption Law of the PRC.
[18] See art 10 of Measures for Registration for the Adoption of Children by Chinese Citizens.
[19] See arts 26, 27 of the Adoption Law of the PRC.

Secondly, in terms of the actual requirements of establishing an adoption, such restrictions as the age of the adoptee and the qualifications of the adopter are conducive to realising the harmony and stability of foster families and to protecting adopted minors' rights. Furthermore, considering that adoptions between relatives and adoptions of orphans or disabled children and those brought up by social welfare institutions whose parents cannot be found are different from general adoptions, the requirements for these special adoptions are less strict. The former adoption mentioned above aims at maintaining the relative emotional needs; while the latter are intended to provide a more comfortable and family-like living condition for the minors. The third kind of special adoptions have looser requirements too in pursuit of stable remarried families.

Thirdly, as regards to formal requirements, adoption law before the enactment of the Adoption Law of the PRC in 1992 recognised de facto adoption and household registered adoption. But after the promulgation of this law, de facto adoption was no longer recognised as an effective adoption while registered adoption and consensual adoption were legally binding. After the Adoption Law Amendment 1998, registered adoption became the only legal procedure to establish an adoption. The public supervision over adoption is strengthened to further protect adopted minors' interests.

Finally, concerning termination of adoption, the present legislation provides two means to end the adoptive relationship, either by an agreement or with a judgment. If the parties concerned agree to terminate the adoption, they shall be present at the registration office and register the termination. Thus, the public power intervenes in these two ways to protect the legal rights of parties concerned. Moreover, the present legislation stipulates that, if the adopted child involved reaches the age of 10 or more, his or her consent shall be obtained.[20] From the perspective of the Convention on the Rights of the Child and the child's best interests doctrine, this stipulation represents child's rights of expression and participation, totally in conformity with the international treaty.

However, scrutinising the present adoption legislation in accordance with the Convention on the Rights of the Child and the child's best interests doctrine, we observe that there are some provisions needing improvements.

(a) The shortcomings of the basic principles of the adoption law

At present, scholars have mainly two views in terms of the basic principles of the adoption legislation. Some argue that the enactment of the adoption legislation and its development should, reflecting its human significance, be oriented to safeguarding the best interests of adopted minors. They think that the enactment of the adoption law and its development reflect its human significance and it is now oriented to safeguarding the adopted minors' best

---

[20] See art 26 of the Adoption Law of the PRC.

interests.[21] Moreover, some maintain that if the adoptee is a minor, a restrictive provision should be added to the present legislation that the child's best interest should be prioritised when the adopter and the person placing the child discuss terminating the adoption relationship.[22] By contrast, others hold that the adoption legislation should protect rights of both the adopter and the adoptee.[23]

We maintain the first viewpoint because, pursuant to the child's best interests doctrine advocated by United Nations international literature, the adoption legislation should undoubtedly rank the adopted minors' interests as the top priority. This also conforms to the concepts inherent in our ratification of the Convention on the Rights of the Child. Furthermore, art 2 of the Adoption Law of the PRC expressly stipulates that adoption should be in the interest of the upbringing and growth of the minors adopted. Obviously, this rule already demonstrates the concept of the child's best interests. By comparison, although the principle of safeguarding the adopter and the adoptee indicates equal legal protection for the adopter and the adoptee, it may result in inequality in reality when there are conflicts between adopters' rights and those of the minors adopted. Since the minors adopted are dependent on the adopters for living and education, the adoptee is essentially in a disadvantageous position in adoptive relationships. Thus the principle is incompatible with the child's best interests doctrine. The child's best interests should be the biggest consideration in adoption affairs.

Secondly, adoption legislation in other countries explicitly stipulates the child's best interests doctrine or reflects this concept. Thus, the child's best interests doctrine, instead of the principle of safeguarding the rights of adopters and adoptees, is more represented in adoption legislation. For example, s 1741(1) of Title 7 Adoption in the German Civil Code[24] explicitly provides that 'adoption is admissible if it serves the best interests of the child'. Article 345 of the French Civil Code[25] stipulates that adoption is allowed only in favour of children under 15, who have been received into the home of the adopter for at least 6 months. Article 264 of the Swiss Civil Code[26] stipulates that a child may be adopted if the prospective adoptive parents have raised and cared for the child for at least one year and provided the general circumstances suggest that establishing a parent–child relationship would be in the child's best interests without being inequitable to other children of the adoptive parents.

---

[21] Jiang Xinmiao and Yu Guohua 'Review and Outlook of the Tendency of International Adoption Law' (2001) 1 *China Legal Science* 173–175; Li Gang 'On Legislative Orientation of the Adoption System' (2006) 1 *Journal of Adults Education of Gansu Political Science and Law Institute* 15–17.

[22] See Chen Wei and Xie Jingjie 'On the Establishing of the Paramount Principle of the Best Interests of the Child: the Weaknesses and Improvements of Marriage and Family Law of China' (2005) 5 *Studies in Law and Business* 37–43.

[23] Wang Geya 'Thinking on Improving the Adoption Legislation' (1997) 4 *Legal Application* 15–16.

[24] See www.gesetze-im-internet.de/englisch_bgb/englisch_bgb.html (accessed 12 February 2012).

[25] See http://lexinter.net/ENGLISH/civil_code.htm (accessed 12 February 2012).

[26] See www.admin.ch/ch/e/rs/2/210.en.pdf (accessed 12 February 2012).

(b)   The deficiencies in the conditions for establishing an adoption

The conditions for establishing an adoption directly relate to the legal force of an adoption. The present conditions prescribed in the adoption law are too strict.

(i)   Age limit to be adopted

There is an age limit for those to be adopted. A child over 14 years old cannot be adopted, which is contrary to the doctrine of the child's best interests. Although the present rule on the age limit is devised to more easily establish a stable foster family and to enhance the parent–child relationship when the child is younger, such a limit unfortunately deprives minors aged from 14 to 18 of being adopted. A stable adoption is critical to foster families' relationships; therefore, the present rule seems reasonable in this respect. However, it costs too much in sacrificing some minors' rights to be adopted for a stable foster family.

(ii)   Age limit to adopt

The article concerning the age limit of the adopter in the present adoption legislation sets a stricter restriction. Thus, the scope of qualified adopters is narrowed down. Article 6 in the Marriage Law of the PRC stipulates that no marriage may be contracted before the man has reached 22 years of age and the woman 20 years of age. Late marriage and late childbirth are encouraged. If the man is over 25 years old and the woman is 23 years old, the marriage of the couple is a late marriage. But the age limit for adopters is 30 years old, which is older than the statutory marriage age and the late marriage age. Some scholars argue that adopters aged over 30 generally have a more stable family and a steady income. Thus, they have better resources to bear child support responsibilities.[27] We disagree with this viewpoint. The criteria to decide whether the adopter has the ability to foster a child should be his or her earning capacity rather than his or her age. In fact, to assess the adopter's ability to bring up a child should function as a substantive examination and eliminate those without a steady income or without a fixed abode. Therefore, the age restriction imposed in this article is unnecessary from this perspective. Besides, for those infertile couples, such an age requirement to adopt is not reasonable. Finally, more and more Child Welfare Centres are carrying out family foster care for those children living in these centres. This is a new device to save money and, more significantly, to give the children family-like living surroundings which are more conducive to their development.[28] Arguments indicate that, compared with family foster care and welfare centre support, adoption is a better method in terms of the full development of the child's

---

[27]   Yu Tingman *Original Study on Relatives Law* (Beijing: Law Press, 2007).
[28]   'The Full Implementation of Family Foster Care for Orphans' *Nanfang Daily*, 21 July 2003 available at http://news.sina.com.cn/c/2003-07-21/1229417993s.shtml (accessed 15 December 2011).

physical and psychological health.[29] If there are more families and more people with the necessary abilities willing to adopt, it conforms with the child's interests to let them adopt more children in accordance with the child's best interests doctrine.

(c) Weaknesses in the adoption procedures

The present adoption legislation concerning the establishing procedures has no rules on a 'probationary adoption period'.[30] A probationary adoption period is a concept used in some Western countries whose adoption legislation provides that the adopted minor shall live in the home of the adopter for a statutory period, usually for 6 or 12 months. After this probationary adoption period, the family court shall issue an adoption order to the adopter upon receipt of an application, thus establishing the foster parent–child relationship in law.

As a special legal provision in these countries' adoption legislation, a probationary adoption period has primarily the following functions. First, a probationary adoption period supplies the adopter and the adoptee with an adjustment period to become acquainted with each other and to live together. In reality, before the adopters make a decision to adopt, they usually prepare well both in psychological and material terms. However, the minors to be adopted know this fact only a few days before they are living together, which undoubtedly needs adjustment. Therefore, such a period essentially has a 'cushioning effect' for their life together. Secondly, probationary adoption periods also favour guidance for and surveillance over the quasi-adoptive relationship by the adoption centres and supervisors. On the one hand, these agencies may visit these families and provide services and consultations they need to gradually move into a harmonious relationship. On the other hand, they learn about how the adoptee is living during this period by home visits. If any infringements on the adoptee's rights is found, these centres may file a visit report to the authorities concerned and suggest rejecting such an adoption application so as to protect the child's interests. Thirdly, a probationary adoption period provides a grace period for parties involved in the adoption to withdraw their consent. As long as the adoptive relationship is established, the personal relationship of the parties concerned will undergo a great change. For example, the relationship between the adoptee and his or her biological parents ends in legal terms. Therefore, it is a tough decision for the biological parents and they certainly will be very prudent. If they change their mind during the probationary adoption period, they may take the adoptee home and raise him or her themselves in this period. Living with one's biological parents instead of foster parents without doubt favours the child's development. Thus it is safe to say that this rule is compatible with the child's best interests doctrine.

---

[29]   Bi Lanfeng, Huang Banghan, Zhang Yuxia 'Analysis of Means to Raise the Abandoned Baby' (2010) 3 *China Civil Affairs* 37–38.

[30]   See Chen Wei and Song Yu (eds) *Comparative Studies on Foreign Marriage and Family Law* (Beijing: Qunzhong Publishing House, 2006) 379–380.

As regards to probationary adoption periods, some foreign legislation already has explicit rules. For example, s 1744 of the German Civil Law stipulates that the adoption, as a general rule, should not be pronounced until the adoptive parent has had the child in foster care for a reasonable period. Article 345 of the French Civil Code provides that the probationary period for adoption is 6 months. Article 264 of the Swiss Civil Code[31] stipulates that a child may be adopted if the prospective adoptive parents have raised and cared for the child for at least one year.

(d)   Weak supervision of adoption[32]

In China, public surveillance over the adoption after it is set up and during the termination process is generally not strong. After the adoptive relationship is established, the relationship between foster parents and the adopted child will be presumed to have the same legal effort as the natural parent-child relationship. Therefore, the guardianship system in the General Principles of the Civil Law of PRC can be applied in the supervision over adoptive families. If a guardian does not fulfil his legal duties or infringes upon the lawful rights and interests of his ward, he shall be held responsible; if a guardian causes any property loss for his ward, he shall compensate for such loss. The people's court may disqualify a guardian based on the application of a party or unit concerned.[33] Pursuant to the present legislation, the court's intervention is initiated by a complaint as regards to custody supervision, while the child centres will engage themselves in the supervision of adopted orphans or disabled children. As a matter of fact, the protection of the adopted child provided by the present legislation in real life disappoints us. For example, 'A Network Adventure', which was screened in a TV programme named 'Today to Say' (a law propaganda programme telecasting a documentary each day) on China Central Television (CCTV) on 26 December 2011, tells the experience of Hong Han. Hong is a minor adopted by her parents. In her foster parents' eyes, she is naughty and intractable. When she was about 15 years old, she got pregnant partly because of a failure to accept her adoptive parents' discipline. Hong was forced out of home, led a vagrant life and finally violated the law. Unfairly, her adoptive parents did not bear any liabilities for this. This case fully represents the imperfect aspects of the supervision system of custody in adoptive parent-child relationships. Compared with natural relatives, fictitious relatives generally have a weaker emotional attachment. Hence the adoptive relationship demands much more in terms of measures to protect the child's interests and it also deserves more attention of public authorities. Moreover, under the present legislation on the supervision of negotiated termination of an adoption, the intervention of public powers is weak. Although the adoptee's consent is required in a negotiated termination of an adoption when the

---

[31]   See www.admin.ch/ch/e/rs/2/210.en.pdf (accessed 12 February 2012).
[32]   We have explored supervision before adoption is established; therefore the following discussion focuses on supervision after adoption is set up and supervision of the termination of an adoption.
[33]   See art 18 of the General Principles of the Civil Law of PRC.

adoptee is over 10, the adoptee's opinion usually will be affected by other factors since the adoptee is not mature yet in terms of both the physical and mental aspects. Therefore, it is doubtful whether such a termination will guarantee that there is no infringement of the child's interests. As for those under 10 years old, the only requirement to end the adoption is the agreement reached by the adopter and the donor who placed the child. We still doubt whether this legal requirement fully safeguards the child's interests.

IV   REFORM PROPOSALS FOR ADOPTION LAW IN CHINA

Comparing foreign legislation with the counterpart in China, we put forward the following suggestions to remedy the above-mentioned deficiencies.

(a)   Proposals on the basic principles of adoption law

We conclude from the above analysis that a principle concerning parent-child relationships, ie the child's best interests doctrine, should be added to the fundamental principles in the marriage and family division of the future civil code legislation. We propose that the adoption law explicitly state that an adoption is not permissible unless it is in conformity with the adopted child's best interests under the child's best interests doctrine. Where the adoptee is a minor, the termination of an adoption relationship is not permissible unless it conforms with the adopted child's best interests.

(b)   Proposals on the conditions for establishing adoptions

Concerning the requirements for establishing an adoption, we put forward the following suggestion based on Chinese realities.

As regards to the adoptee, we suggest that the present art 4 be amended as follows: Minors under the age of 18, as enumerated below, may be adopted: (1) orphans bereaved of parents; (2) abandoned infants or children whose parents cannot be ascertained or found; and (3) children whose parents are unable to rear them due to unusual difficulties.

Concerning the adopter, we suggest that the present art 6 be amended as follows: Adopters shall meet simultaneously the following requirements: (1) being childless; (2) being capable of rearing and educating the adoptee; and (3) having reached the age of 28. Those who get a medical certificate of infertility may adopt a child after being married for at least a year.

(c)   Improving the adoption procedures

We hold that, learning from foreign legislation, the probationary adoption period system should be adopted by the Chinese legislature. Before the adoption is established, the adoptee will live in the adopter's home for at least 6 months. In this period, the staff in neighbourhood committees or village committees designated by child welfare centres or civil affairs departments may visit the adopter's home and give a final visitation report, which is a required document to decide whether to register the adoptive relationship or not. If anything against the adopted child's interests is found in a visitation and stated in an urgent report, the probationary adoption period shall be terminated and the adoptee shall be conveyed to the original donor.

(d)   Establishing an adoption supervision system

We advise that an adoption supervision system be established.

(i)   Supervisors

The supervisors will be the civil affairs departments which are in charge of adoption registration or the child welfare centres. They will assign specific visitation tasks to local neighbourhood committees or village committees where the adoptee lives to fulfil the supervision duties.

(ii)   Supervision measures

The law will stipulate a rule on regular visits. Meanwhile, we may learn from foreign regulations to set up an information network in local neighbourhoods or villages so that the neighbourhood committees or village committees can collect information on the adopted child such as being a victim of domestic violence or collect some police records, medical certificates, and reports from schools. If necessary, they shall report to the supervisors.

(iii)   Providing exceptions for negotiated termination of an adoption

The parties concerned in an adoption may make an agreement to end adoption and register it with the relevant authorities, except where the adoptee is a minor. Where the adoptee is a minor, the parties wishing to terminate the adoption will file a petition in a people's court. The people's court shall, after examination, issue a termination order to the parties concerned if the termination is compatible with the adopted minor's interests. Meanwhile, a system of ad litem agents of minors will be established in litigation involving terminating the adoption of a minor. It is up to an independent third party – counsel – acting on their behalf to protect their rights.

(iv)   *Strengthening the accountability mechanism for violation of the minor's rights*

The law enforcement agencies will intensify the enforcement operations where the adopter is negligent in caring for the minor or infringes upon the minor's rights.

England and Wales

I WANT TO GO HOME – PARENT AND CHILD RELOCATION OUTSIDE THE JURISDICTION

*Mary Welstead**

Résumé

Nous vivons dans un monde de familles internationales. La facilité des déplacements et l'augmentation de la mobilité professionelle internationale a conduit à une explosion des relations transfrontalières. Quand ces relations cessent, se pose l'inévitable problème de qui doit vivre où et avec qui. Un parent, presque toujours la mère, peut souhaiter quitter le territoire avec l'enfant issu de la relation et rentrer dans son pays d'origine. Les parents, souvent les pères, qui s'opposent à la délocalisation de leur enfant, le font, la plupart du temps, parce qu'ils veulent avoir un contact régulier avec leur enfant. Ils craignent qu'en raison de cette délocalisation, ils perdent le contact relationnel avec leurs enfants, en terme de qualitatif et quantitatif. Les décisions dans le domaine du déplacement international d'enfant ont toujours eu une connotation très factuelle. Néanmoins, la jurisprudence *Payne vs Payne* a imposé un éclat judiciaire, sous la forme de lignes directrices. Cela a induit des critiques, avec des appels à la réforme lancés par les juges, les praticiens, les universitaires et les parents. Des décisions récentes à propos de la délocalisation international sur le territoire anglais et gallois ont attiré l'attention sur la façon de surmonter ces critiques ou de s'interroger sur leur pertinence. L'auteur suggère qu'une réforme de la loi sur la délocalisation est nécessaire. Une nouvelle loi devrait abandonner le principe fondamentale de la primauté du bien-être de l'enfant et contenir, à défaut d'accord entre les parties, une liste de points de contrôle hiérarchisés pour assurer entre autre le bien être de tous les membres de la famille.

I   THE PROBLEM OF INTERNATIONAL RELOCATION

'I want to go home ... I feel just like I'm living someone else's life ... let me go home.'[1]

The words of this well-known song will resonate with many family lawyers who, regularly, face the despair which parents and children experience as a consequence of international relocation disputes. We live in a world of

---

*   CAP Fellow, Harvard Law School, and Visiting Professor, University of Buckingham.
[1]   See 'Home' composed in 2005 by M Bublé, A Foster-Gillies, A Chang.

international families; the ease of travel and the increase in international careers have led to an explosion of cross-border relationships. When these relationships break down, the inevitable problem arises of who should live where and with whom. One parent, almost always a mother, may wish to leave the jurisdiction with the child of the relationship and return to her country of origin. Relocation is perceived by some mothers as a panacea for the unhappy consequences of a failed relationship. They hope that the support of family and friends in their home country will end their fears of cultural isolation caused by living in a country which is not where they now wish to be. For others relocation holds out the promise of a fresh start, a new career and maybe a relationship. In a small number of cases, a parent may wish to relocate to make a home with a new partner who lives outside of the jurisdiction.

Those parents, usually fathers, who oppose the relocation of their children, do so, for the most part, because they want to have regular contact with their children. They fear that as a consequence of relocation they risk the loss of a relationship with them in both quantitive and qualitative terms. This is not an unrealistic fear; their financial situation or work commitments will often make regular visits to their children impossible. Even where an absent parent can afford such visits, visiting is not an easy option. He may have nowhere appropriate to stay where he can create a temporary home in which he can have meaningful contact with his children. Where children are old enough to visit the parent left behind, they may find it difficult to readjust to his world, a world which they may have forgotten, and which has become culturally alien to them. Some parents, of course, have less honourable motives in their objections to relocation. They may wish to control or punish a partner and prevent her from beginning a new and happier life elsewhere.

There is an important overlap between international relocation and international child abduction. A number of parents who wish to relocate are so fearful that a request will be rejected, they take matters into their own hands and remove their children without seeking the permission of the other parent or the court.[2]

There are no ideal solutions to the problem of international relocation as Mostyn J explained in *Re AR (A Child)*:[3]

> 'Applications for leave to relocate are always difficult for the court and distressing for the parties. They involve a binary decision – either the child stays or goes. There is no scope for any middle way. If the decision is that the child goes, then the

---

[2]   In *Payne v Payne* [2001] 1 FLR 1052 at [28], Thorpe LJ suggested that: 'There is a clear interaction between the approach of courts in abduction cases and in relocation cases. If individual jurisdictions adopt a chauvinistic approach to applications to relocate then there is a risk that the parent affected will resort to flight. Conversely recognition of the respect due to the primary carer's reasonable proposals for relocation encourages applications in place of unilateral removal'; see also *Re H (Leave to Remove)* [2010] 2 FLR 1875, where the mother did abduct the child without permission to the Czech Republic but returned with the child immediately she was ordered to do so.

[3]   [2010] 2 FLR 1577 at [4].

left behind parent inevitably suffers a disruption in his relationship with his child, at the very least in terms of quantum and periodicity of contact. If the decision is that the child stays then the primary carer, if not invariably, then frequently will suffer distress and disappointment in having what will normally be well-reasoned and bona fide plans for the future frustrated. So the decision, whichever way, is bound to cause considerable trauma.'

The decisions in the field of international child relocation have always been very much fact dependent. Nevertheless, in *Payne v Payne*,[4] Thorpe LJ felt the need to impose a judicial gloss, in the form of guidelines, on s 1 of the Children Act 1989 which governs the determination of applications for international relocation (see below). He explained why he thought that this was necessary:[5]

'Where guidelines can be formulated there are obvious benefits. The opportunity for practitioners to give clear and confident advice as to outcome helps to limit the volume of contested litigation. Of the cases that do proceed to a hearing clear guidance from this court simplifies the task of the trial judge and helps to limit the volume of appeals. The opportunity for this court to give guidance capable of general application is plainly circumscribed by the obvious consideration that any exercise of discretion is fact dependent and no two cases are identical. But in relocation cases there are a number of factors that are sufficiently commonplace to enhance the utility of guidelines.'

However useful judicial guidance can be, it can also prove to be unhelpful. Too often, it has been elevated to the level of legal principle, or followed slavishly and inappropriately. When that happens, it has a tendency to drive rather than guide the court's decision. Following the decision in *Payne*, criticism has been made of Thorpe LJ's guidelines and the way in which they have been interpreted in subsequent decisions; calls for reform have been made by judges, practitioners, academics and parents. A number of recent decisions on international relocation in the jurisdiction of England and Wales have drawn attention to, supported, or queried the relevance of, these criticisms. It seems, therefore, to be an appropriate moment to consider these decisions and question whether reform of relocation law is necessary.[6]

II   THE LAW

The Children Act 1989, s 13 provides:

'(1) Where a residence order is in force with respect to a child, no person may

---

4   [2001] 1 FLR 1052.

5   Ibid at [27]; see also *K v K* [2011] EWCA CIV 793, in which Thorpe LJ reiterated the importance of the guidelines: 'In family law principles are scarce and generally the more important function of this court is to state guidance. Guidance that directs the exercise of the welfare discretion is equivalent to a statutory checklist. It is valuable if it renders outcomes more predictable and if it supports judges in reaching and explaining discretionary conclusions in a way that is not open to appellate challenge': at [40].

6   See the discussion in S Gilmore 'The Payne Saga: Precedent and Family Law Cases' [2011] Fam Law 970.

...

 (b) remove him from the United Kingdom;

without either the written consent of every person who has parental responsibility for the child or with leave of the court.'

The only exception to this is that a parent who has a residence order may take the child out of the jurisdiction for a period of no longer than one month.[7]

Section 1 of the Act demands that the child's welfare must be the court's paramount consideration in deciding whether to grant leave to relocate. In making its decision, the court must, in particular, have regard to the rather limited checklist in s 1(3).

Section 1(5) provides that the court must not make any order unless it considers that to do so would be better for the child than making no order at all.

In addition to the provisions of the Children Act,[8] both parents and children have a right to respect for private and family life under the European Convention on Human Rights 1950 (ECHR), Art 8. Article 8 is of relevance in the determination of any relocation application although there is disagreement about its interrelationship with the Children Act.[9] However, Art 8(2) provides that the court may interfere with this right for the protection of the rights and freedoms of others providing it is proportionate to the need demonstrated.

The Court of Appeal decision in *Payne* in 2001 is the leading case on international relocation. It is also the starting point for the current debate and the clamour for reform. The mother had left New Zealand to work and travel in Europe. In 1996, during her time in England, she met and married an Englishman. Their daughter was born in 1997 and one year later, the mother took her to live New Zealand with no intention of returning to England. At the time of her departure, the father was working in Malaysia. He subsequently joined his wife and daughter in New Zealand but soon realised the mother's intentions, and that their relationship was at an end. In custody proceedings in New Zealand, an order was made for the daughter to be returned to England where, by consent of the parents, the court made a residence order in favour of the mother. She was forbidden to remove the child from the jurisdiction and the father was given substantial contact. The daughter began to spend 23 out of every 56 nights with him.

The mother was not happy. She wished to return to New Zealand and applied to the court for leave to take her daughter, who, by then, was aged 4, with her.

---

[7] Children Act 1989, s 13(2).

[8] A child who is the subject of a relocation request also has a right to have his or her best interests taken into account as the primary consideration under the United Nations Convention on the Rights of the Child 1989, Art 3(1).

[9] See n 37 below.

The father objected and applied for a residence order in his favour. The court found that the mother was living in less than ideal conditions in a poor and crime-ridden area of London. She dropped her daughter at a day nursery each morning and then had a difficult journey to work. She felt isolated and depressed, had no friends close by, and missed her New Zealand family. The father's application for a residence order was refused and the mother was allowed to relocate to New Zealand.

The father appealed unsuccessfully. Thorpe LJ, after reviewing some 30 years of decisions, concluded that in all of them two propositions had been applied. First, the welfare of the child was paramount and, second, a refusal of the primary carer's reasonable proposal to relocate was likely to be detrimental to the welfare of her dependent children. Thorpe LJ explained that:[10]

> 'In a broad sense the health and well-being of a child depends upon emotional and psychological stability and security. Both security and stability come from the child's emotional and psychological dependency upon the primary carer.'

He added that:[11]

> 'The extent of that dependency will depend upon many factors including its duration and the extent to which it is tempered by or shared with other dependencies. For instance is the absent parent an important figure in the child's life? What is the child's relationship with siblings and/or grandparents and/or a step-parent? In most relocation cases the judge will need to make some evaluation of these factors.'

As a consequence of the application of these two propositions, Thorpe LJ maintained that a primary carer's request to relocate her family will be granted unless the court concludes that it will be detrimental to the welfare of the children. He rejected the idea that this approach would elevate the acceptance of a parent's reasonable proposals to relocate to the status of an automatic presumption in her favour. To do so would risk a breach of the ECHR, Art 8, and also of Art 6, the right to a fair trial.[12]

To ensure that relocation was compatible with the child's welfare, Thorpe LJ suggested the following guidelines in the form of questions which the courts should pose:

- Is the mother's application genuine or is it motivated by some selfish desire to exclude the father from the child's life?

- Is her proposal realistic and practical, based on well-researched information?

---

[10] [2001] 1 FLR 1052 at [30].

[11] Ibid.

[12] See J Herring and R Taylor 'Relocating Relocation' (2006) 18 CFLQ 517.

If her application fails either of these tests, refusal to relocate will inevitably follow. If her application passes these tests, the court must consider the reasons for the father's opposition and ask further questions:

- Is it motivated by a genuine concern for the child's future welfare or is it driven by some ulterior motive?

- What would be the extent of the detriment to him and his future relationship with his child if the application were granted?

- To what extent would that be offset by extension of the child's relationships with the mother's family maternal family and home country?

- What would be the impact on the mother, either as a single parent or as a new wife, of a refusal of her realistic proposal?

The answers to this second group of questions should then be considered, where appropriate, alongside the checklist in the Children Act 1989, s 1(3).

Finally, Thorpe LJ emphasised that great weight must continue to be given to emotional and psychological well-being of the primary carer in evaluating the welfare of the child.[13]

III   RECENT DECISIONS ON RELOCATION

Following *Payne,* the decisions on relocation have vacillated between attempts to limit Thorpe LJ's guidelines, or treat them as rigid principles. His hope that the guidelines would give rise to clarity and predictability has been so dashed that he must sometimes regret having ever proposed them. The debate continues; the proponents of the emotional well-being of the mother see it as the lodestar of relocation decisions. They are at war with those who wish to see more emphasis placed on fathers' rights often disguised as the need for a child to have contact with both parents. Each group maintains that its view does not negate, but rather conforms with, the paramountcy principle.

In *Re H (Leave to Remove),*[14] the mother came to England, from the Czech Republic in 2000, where she met and married an Englishman who was 17 years older than her. One year later, their daughter was born, and in 2004, the family moved to the Czech Republic because the mother was miserable in England. The mother was a nurse and found work easily but the father, who did not speak Czech, was less successful. In 2007, he insisted that the family return to England. The mother was unhappy at the move and the marriage broke down. In 2009, the mother removed the child back to the Czech Republic without the father's permission. He immediately applied for an order for the child's return

---

[13]   [2001] 1 FLR 1052 at [41].
[14]   [2010] 2 FLR 1875.

and the mother complied with it. Soon after the parents were granted a joint residence order but the actual living arrangements for the child were such that she spent the majority of time with the mother.

In 2010, the mother, who had begun a relationship with a new man in the Czech Republic, applied to relocate the 7-year-old daughter, who was bilingual and had a good relationship with her mother's new partner. The judge granted the application. He found that both parents were good and caring. He accepted that the father would be devastated if permission to relocate were given, but if permission were not granted, the mother's distress, and the fact that her new relationship would be unlikely to thrive, would affect the daughter. If the daughter were to become unhappy, it could even have adverse consequences on her relationship with her father.

The father was given staying contact of 4 or 5 weeks in England, and a further week in the Czech Republic each year. He was also given frequent indirect contact with her, and both parents were encouraged to agree between themselves further periods of direct contact.

The father appealed on the basis that the judge had not considered the child's wishes and that he had viewed the mother's application only through the prism constructed by the decision in *Payne* which he argued ought to be reviewed.

Wilson LJ dismissed the father's appeal and accepted that the decision would be devastating and heartbreaking for the father. He acknowledged that there was a respectable argument for the proposition that *Payne* inappropriately relegates the harm done to children by a permanent breach in their relationship with the absent parent below that of the harm likely to be sustained by a child through the negative impact upon the applicant of a refusal of the application.[15] However, regardless of the guidelines in *Payne*, Wilson LJ thought that this was a clear case for the grant of permission to relocate based on the paramountcy of the child's welfare. He took into account the following factors in favour of relocation:

- The mother is a Czech national and would be returning home to an extensive supportive family and could make excellent practical arrangements for the child's life in the Republic, in terms of accommodation and education and in emotional terms by contact with the wider family.

- The parents and child had lived there for almost half of the child's life.

- The child had dual Czech and British nationality and was bilingual.

---

[15]   Ibid at [23].

- Even when the marriage was intact, the mother never felt able to settle down to life in England and it was natural that, after the breakdown of the marriage, she would wish to return home.

- The mother has developed a relationship with a Czech man which, if it were to develop, would very likely benefit the child.

- The mother is a wonderful mother who is well aware of the importance of the father in the child's life and is likely to do all that she can to preserve and develop the contact and relationship between the child and father.

- The mother would be devastated by the refusal of her application and it would be impossible for her to remain in England because of her sense of isolation from her family.

The factors in favour of the mother's relocation were balanced with those against it. The father had an excellent relationship with his daughter which would be seriously limited if relocation were to take place. The mother had offered to provide a fund for the daughter to visit the father but the father had insufficient income to fund his own visits to the Czech Republic to visit his daughter there.

It is interesting to note that, although Wilson LJ found that the case could be decided solely on the child's welfare, three of the seven points in favour of relocation centred on the welfare of the mother without reference to the child.

In his judgment Wilson LJ referred to the recent Washington Declaration on International Relocation (see below). He accepted that it might ultimately become the foundation for some reform of English law. However, he suggested that, even if the present law placed undue emphasis on the effect of a refusal to permit relocation on the emotional well-being of the primary carer, the Washington Declaration placed insufficient weight upon it.[16]

In *Re AR (A Child: Relocation)*,[17] Mostyn J made a direct attack on *Payne* although he accepted the binding nature of the decision. He maintained, *per curiam*, that there was a strong view that:[18]

> '... it represents an illegitimate gloss on the purity of the paramountcy principle. Moreover, some argue that it promotes selfishness and detracts from the importance of co-parenting. Some argue that on the birth of children parents are indentured to sacrifice throughout their minority, but that the one word that is missing from *Payne* is, in fact, sacrifice.'

---

[16]	Ibid at [27].
[17]	[2010] 2 FLR 1577.
[18]	Ibid at [8], Mostyn J, made clear that they were also his own personal conviction. As counsel in *Re G (Leave to Remove)* [2008] 1 FLR 1587, he had put forward these criticisms; they were rejected by Thorpe LJ at [13].

Mostyn J also drew attention to the Washington Declaration which he thought would provide a more balanced, non-presumptive, and neutral approach to relocation applications. He felt that it reflected the process in many other jurisdictions. It would require the court, in a very real way, to take into account the impact on both the child and the parent who was left behind of the disruption of the existing contact arrangements. In his view, Mostyn J thought that the Declaration quite rightly relegated the psychological impact on what he referred to as 'the thwarted primary carer' to a minor role. He believed that the psychological impact deserved its due weight, but no more, and no less. The problem with the attribution of great weight to this latter factor appeared:[19]

> '... to penalise selflessness and virtue, while rewarding selfishness and uncontrolled emotions. The core question of the putative relocator is always "how would you react if leave were refused?" The parent who stoically accepts that she would accept the decision, make the most of it, move on and work to promote contact with the other parent is far more likely to be refused leave than the parent who states that she will collapse emotionally and psychologically. This is the reverse of the Judgment of Solomon, where of course selflessness and sacrifice received their due reward.'

The mother in *Re AR* was French and the father an unemployed Englishman living on welfare benefits. They had never married and did not live together. Their child was born in London and had both British and French nationality. The mother applied to return to France; it was her second relocation application. Her previous application had been granted, when the child was aged 3, and she had moved with him to France. At that time, the judge was unaware that she had an ongoing sexual relationship with the child's father and was pregnant by him. She had actually miscarried during the hearing. The judge was also ignorant of the mother's decision to retain the tenancy of her flat in London. Soon after the move to France, the mother expressed her concerns to the father about the child whom she believed had not settled happily in France. Nor would it appear had she. Six months after arriving in France, she returned to London where she began a one-year postgraduate course. The father applied to have the relocation order set aside and for the grant of a residence order in his favour. By this time the child was aged 5.

Mostyn J felt able to decide the child's future without recourse to what he termed the presumptive approach in favour of mothers in *Payne*. He believed that the mother had had no intention of permanently relocating to France when her first application to relocate was granted. Since her return to London to begin her course there, she appeared to be content and had not travelled back to France although she had applied to work there as well as in London. She had engaged in discussions with the father as to where the child should go to school in London if her application to relocate was turned down. Her plans, if she were permitted to live in France with her son, were vague. She had siblings in Paris who had children but she thought that she and the child might live with her grandmother near Troyes where her aunt and cousins also lived.

---

[19]   Ibid at [12].

The mother's own mother was a manic depressive and lived permanently in England. Her father, with whom she had a troubled relationship, lived in Bénin in West Africa.

The mother maintained that, of all foreign jurisdictions, France, by virtue of its close proximity to England, was a place to which relocation should be readily granted. However, Mostyn J turned this argument on its head and suggested that the mother could just as easily visit France were her application to relocate be declined.

The father claimed that the relationship he had with the child would be severely disrupted if he went back to France. He maintained that he would not be able to afford to visit the child in France.

Mostyn J drew attention to the fact that the mother:[20]

> '... did not make a mountain out of the disappointment she would experience were her relocation application to be refused. This is to her credit, but then credit should hardly need to be given to authenticity and a disinclination to dissimulate. I gained the strong impression that were leave to be refused M would make the most of her situation here; would seek to obtain employment and a better home; and would cooperate with F in co-parenting A.'

Mostyn J concluded that he should reject the father's application for a residence order. The mother had always been the child's primary carer, and it was in the child's best interests that she should continue in that role. However, he decided to make a shared residence order even though the care of the child would be divided very unequally between the parents. Such an order, he thought, would avoid the psychological baggage of one parent being in control which was inherent in a sole residence order.

Mostyn J also rejected the mother's relocation application. He put a gloss on Art 8 of the ECHR and suggested that if one were to draw up a hierarchy of those human rights protected by Art 8:[21]

> '... very near to the top would be the right of a child, while he or she is growing up, to have a meaningful participation by both of his parents in his upbringing. Although this is (strangely) not explicitly spelt out in the text it must be implicit in the notion of the right to a family life. Recognition of the existence of this very obvious and critically important right is sometimes, so it seems to me, lost in the relocation cases.'

The decision in *Re AR* draws attention to the fact that women who wish to relocate for reasons of self-determination, which will also benefit their children, are likely to receive a less sympathetic hearing than women who plead emotional distress if they are denied permission to relocate.

---

[20]   [2010] 2 FLR 1577 at [54].
[21]   Ibid at [53].

By contrast with the facts in *Re AR*, those in *J v S (Leave to Remove)*[22] provide an extreme example of the relocation application of an emotionally fragile mother. Such was her emotional fragility, that it is questionable question whether the court's decision to allow her to relocate with the two children did in fact satisfy the paramountcy principle.

The mother was Japanese and the father Swedish. They had met in Japan, and moved to England where they decided to settle. Both worked in the financial sector. Ten years after their move, their first child was born. Three years later a second child was born. The mother gave up her work, apart from occasional translating and some signing for deaf people, to care for the children. The parents' relationship broke down and the children lived with the mother. The father saw the children on alternate weekends and during the school holidays. The children who were bilingual in English and Japanese regularly visited Sweden with their father and Japan with their mother.

When the father was made redundant, he decided to set up his own business which would give him the opportunity to spend more time with the children. He and the mother reached an agreement to increase his contact with them. Soon after, the father told her that he would have to decrease his child maintenance from £26,000 per annum per child to £12,000 per annum per child because of the change in his circumstances. At this point, the mother told the father that she wished to move to Japan with the children who were aged 10 and 8. She maintained that she felt isolated, lonely and unhappy in England. She was concerned about her parents. Her father had suffered a stroke, and her mother was no longer able to come to England from Japan to spend 6 to 8 months a year with her, as she had done in the past. Furthermore, she believed that she had a better chance of finding a job in Japan than in England. The father objected to the children being moved and immediately applied for a shared residence order. The mother applied to the court for leave to relocate them. Medical evidence was given that she suffered from a long-term gastrointestinal illness, which was associated with stress and depression. In 2 months she had lost 8.6% of her body weight and was at risk of severely compromising her immune system. She was on multiple medications including anti-depressants.

On granting the mother's application, the court imposed an order for security of £100,000 because Japan was not a signatory to the Hague Convention on International Child Abduction 1980. It accepted that, in conducting the balancing exercise to determine the children's future, it was bound by *Payne*. However, it held that the health of the mother was only one of the factors to be taken into account. It was only relevant to her ability as the children's primary carer to provide them with the best possible care, and not directly to her own needs or wishes. The loss of frequent contact between the father and children must also be considered. The mother's relocation application was genuine and realistic. It was not motivated by a selfish desire to exclude the father from the

---

[22]   [2011] 1 FLR 1694.

children's lives. She had tried hard to make life in England work, but could no longer cope. Her illness and consequent distress would continue if she were to remain in England. This would be damaging to the children who were all too aware of her fragile emotional state. The court was satisfied that the mother would ensure that the children's contact with their father would be maintained.

In *W (Relocation: Removal outside Jurisdiction),*[23] a mother appealed successfully against the lower court's decision to deny her request to relocate with her children to Australia where her family lived. Given the facts, the lower court's approach was rather surprising. The mother had never been married to, or lived with, the father of their two children who were aged 12 and 8 at the time of the appeal. The father did not have parental responsibility for them and, although he lived close by, had played a minimal part in their lives. He and the mother had argued frequently about contact. She was concerned about his heavy social drinking and recreational drug use. He had no fixed abode and lived in a van. His first real contact with the children had only begun after the mother had applied to relocate. The Cafcass officer thought that the father should try to build a relationship with them which would survive if they were allowed to relocate with their mother to Australia. The judge considered the mother's plans to be well thought out and well intentioned and that a refusal would devastate her. However, he thought that the father's embryonic relationship with the children should be allowed to develop and not be jeopardised by their removal to Australia.

On the mother's appeal, Sir Nicolas Wall, President of the Family Division, concluded that the judge had erred to such an extent that his decision was plainly wrong. In doing so, he upheld totally the approach of Thorpe LJ in *Payne.*[24] He held that the lower court judge had failed to consider specifically all of the criteria in *Payne*. In particular, he had failed to give sufficient weight to the mother's well-being and its in effect on the children's welfare; he had failed to make any reference to statements from the mother's health visitor and doctor; he had failed to consider the loss to the children of their relationship with the mother's side of the family, and he had failed to consider that the court could make orders about indirect contact with the father to enable him to continue his new found relationship with the children.

Father's applications to relocate are rare. Few fathers are primary carers and although many fathers have significant contact with their children, joint

---

[23] [2011] 2 FLR 409.

[24] Ibid at [128], the President made clear that undue prominence had been accorded to his own words in the case of *Re D (Leave to Remove: Appeal)* [2010] 2 FLR 1605, in which he had appeared to support criticism of *Payne*. In any event *Re D* was a case where leave to appeal was not granted and was not therefore a precedent. He drew attention to Marilyn Freeman 'Relocation Research: Where Are We Now?' [2011] IFL 131 and accepted that more research is needed on the effects of relocation, and until Parliament imposes a new test the courts are bound by *Payne*.

residence orders are not the norm.[25] In *Re S (Relocation: Interests of Siblings)*,[26] a Canadian father without a residence order did make a relocation application. The father and the English mother had met in Canada, married and lived there for 6 years. After the birth of their first child, they moved to England where their second child was born. Their relationship broke down and they separated. Since the separation, the mother had lived with a new partner, and was the primary carer of the boys. She had obtained a residence order in her favour. The father, who lived nearby, continued to have regular contact with the children. Four years after the separation, the father applied to remove the children, who were aged 16 and 12, to Canada. The mother believed that his request was an act of retribution because of her new relationship. She was prepared to compromise and accept that the older child could spend a year in Canada at the end of his secondary education and, perhaps, ultimately go to university there.

The Cafcass officer had recommended that the children's future, wherever that might be, should be together. The boys had a very close relationship with each other. The judge accepted the recommendation. He met with the older boy and read a letter which purported to come from both children. The boy expressed a strong desire to live in Canada and suggested that his younger brother also wanted to go there and that he would not want to leave England without him. The judge never met with the younger child. The judge described the father's proposals as a lifestyle choice and not based on malicious motives. He then balanced the factors for and against relocation and ruled in its favour. He believed that to deny the father's request might adversely affect the children's relationship with their mother because they would resent the fact that she had prevented them from going to Canada. Immediately after the court's decision, the 16-year-old left for Canada on his own. The mother accepted that she could do nothing about his departure but appealed against the order to allow his younger brother to relocate too.

The Appeal Court found that the judge had erred in not considering the welfare principle for each child separately and granted the mother's appeal. Whilst the older boy clearly wished to go to Canada, the younger boy did not. He lacked the maturity to make up his own mind about where he wanted to live and did not want such a responsibility to be imposed on him. He was happy and satisfactorily settled with his mother in England and did not seem to significantly miss his older brother. This meant that there was a heavy onus on the father to establish that the welfare of the child would be served by uprooting him to live in Canada. The father was still working in England and did not appear to have any reason for going to live in Canada other than a personal wish to do so. There was no suggestion that he or the boys would suffer emotionally as a consequence of the refusal to permit him to relocate with the younger child.

---

[25]   A recent national survey, 'Understanding Society', puts the proportion of equal shared care at 3.1% of the total, see *K v K (Relocation: Shared Care Arrangement)* [2011] EWCA Civ 793 at [59].

[26]   [2011] 2 FLR 678.

The court in *C v C (International Relocation: Shared Care Arrangement)*[27] was faced with determining a mother's application to relocate in a situation where she and the father did genuinely share the care of their children between them, albeit not equally. The family was a perfect example of a truly international family. The mother was Australian and had met her French husband when they were both living in the United States where their first child was born. They subsequently moved to England before the birth of their second child. Both parents ran successful international businesses. They were sufficiently wealthy to move around the world regularly, for both business and pleasure, often in private aeroplanes. The children often travelled with them. After their relationship broke down, the couple agreed to share the care of their children aided by household staff. At first, the children spent equal amounts of time with each parent and moved back and forth between the parents' homes. The father subsequently became engaged to a woman living in the United States, and wanted to change these arrangements. He proposed that during term time each parent would have a 2 week block of time with the children in England, and holidays would continue to be shared equally. The mother rejected this proposal but was prepared to compromise to help him with his new life. She offered to divide term time into 30 day blocks; she would have the children with her for the first 20 days and the father would have them for the next 10 days. He agreed to try out this new arrangement.

The mother eventually began a new relationship with a man who lived in Florida but who also travelled extensively, often piloting his own aeroplane to visit his children who lived in Colorado. The mother explained to the court that she wanted to relocate because she and her new partner wished to have more than a visiting romantic relationship with each other; they wanted to properly integrate their two families into one.

By the time the mother made her application to relocate the children, the father's engagement had ended. Not only did he oppose the relocation, but he also sought to return to the equal sharing arrangement which he had abandoned for his own benefit. The court dismissed the mother's application and also dismissed the father's application to revert to an equal division of time. The court held that there was no clear primary carer. Therefore, a modification to the approach of Thorpe LJ in *Payne* was necessary. The President, Dame Elizabeth Butler-Sloss, in that case, had suggested that a different proposition might be necessary where the parents shared the care of the children. Her suggestion was followed by Hedley J in *Re Y (Leave to Remove from Jurisdiction)*.[28] He explained that:[29]

> 'Now, the court clearly contemplates two different states of affairs. The one, the more common and in some ways the more obvious, is where the child is clearly living with one parent, and it is that parent that wishes to leave the jurisdiction, for whatever reason. The other, and much less common state of affairs, is where that

---

27   [2011] 2 FLR 701.
28   [2004] 2 FLR 330.
29   Ibid at [14].

does not exist and either there is a real issue about where the child should live, or there is in place an arrangement which demonstrates that the child's home is equally with both parents. In those circumstances, which are the ones that apply in this case, many of the factors to which the court drew attention in *Payne* whilst relevant may carry less weight than otherwise they commonly do.'

The court also considered the views expressed by Thorpe LJ in *Payne* and *Re B (Removal from Jurisdiction); Re S (Removal from Jurisdiction)*[30] where the prime carer wishes to move to begin a new relationship. The judge accepted that if the mother were permitted to relocate, there might be a price to pay in welfare terms because the children would be likely to have less contact with their father but he made the very valid point that:[31]

'... the court's powers to ensure the children's continuing contact with both parents after separation or divorce is necessarily circumscribed. The court has the power to support the father who seeks to maintain or extend his relationship with his children through contact. However, if in the aftermath of separation the father takes employment abroad or marries a woman whose employment takes her abroad or who marries a woman whose every connection is with another jurisdiction, the father will accompany her there and the consequential loss or diminution in his contact with the children of the prior relationship cannot be surveyed or controlled by the court. These are the tides of chance and life and in the exercise of its paternalistic jurisdiction it is important that the court should recognise the force of these movements and not frustrate them unless they are shown to be contrary to the welfare of the child.'

These dicta are important and could well have led the court in *C v C* to reach a different conclusion and allow the mother to relocate. After all, the father had been very ready to explore a new relationship in another jurisdiction and had asked to alter the caring arrangements with the children to suit his changed circumstances. When the relationship did not work out, he immediately tried to revert to the original plans. In the context of his international lifestyle, it might be that he could well relocate himself in the future and, thereby, affect the children's so-called rights to contact with him.

In the most recent relocation case to be considered by the Court of Appeal, *K v K (Relocation: Shared Care Arrangement)*,[32] the court attempted to clarify its decision in *Payne* and expand on Hedley J's decision in *Re Y*. The Polish father and the Canadian mother had met at university in Canada in 1992, were married in London in July 2004 and subsequently their two children were born there. The parents were bankers. The marriage broke down and in 2010 the couple were divorced. They agreed an arrangement that the children would spend 5 nights a fortnight with the father and 9 nights with the mother. The father had persuaded his employer to allow him to organise his working schedule so that he could take care of the children for 6 full days at a time. The

---

[30] [2003] 2 FLR 1043.
[31] Ibid at [12].
[32] [2011] EWCA Civ 793; see also D Eaton QC and M Reardon 'Relocation after *K v K*' [2011] Fam Law 1093.

mother's work schedule was such that she was free to care for the children one day a week and at weekends. Her nanny took care of them for the remainder of the time.

The mother applied for leave to relocate to Canada. She wanted to live near her family and believed that the benefits of living in Canada would be better for the children. However, her overwhelming reason for wishing to leave England was that she felt isolated and lonely; her mental health had suffered to such an extent that she was prescribed medication for stress and depression. She saw herself as the primary carer of the children and was concerned that, despite her best efforts to conceal her distress from them, it would have a harmful effect on them. The husband objected to the application on the grounds that there was not only a shared residence order but that he actually shared the care of the children equally with the mother. He argued that these circumstances meant that the approach in *Payne* was inappropriate.

The Cafcass officer thought that the decision as a finely balanced one. Her view was that relocation might be appropriate for the children in a few years' time but she recommended that the current application be refused. The lower court judge rejected the officer's recommendations and, on the basis of *Payne,* decided to allow the mother to relocate. The father appealed.

The Court of Appeal allowed the father's appeal on the grounds, inter alia, that the lower court judge had only considered the decision in *Payne* and not *Re Y;* had failed to consider all the particular facts of the case; had not given sufficient weight to the Cafcass report nor given sufficient reasons for rejecting its recommendation, and finally, had failed to take into account properly the father's emotional relationship with the children and their right to enjoy family life with each other. The court declined to substitute its judgment for that of the lower court. It thought that it would be impossible for it to exercise its discretion and decide the family's future in a case which depended so much upon oral evidence and the assessment of the witnesses. It, therefore, urged the parents to consider mediation to explore the possibilities for the children's future in England and a possible planned move to Canada at some point. It also suggested that the ideal situation might be for both parents to move to Canada in the future. The children and parents all held Canadian and British citizenship. If the parents were not able to reach a compromise between them, a retrial would have to be held.

The court took the opportunity to leave no room for future doubt that the decision in *Payne* is binding only to the extent of the single legal principle contained within it – the paramountcy of the child's welfare is the lodestar for determining relocation applications. The guidelines in *Payne* are not legal principles but merely factors for a judge to freely weigh up, where relevant, in deciding whether relocation would best serve the child's welfare. The court also reiterated that it was inappropriate to isolate individual sentences from *Payne,* relating to the weight to be given to the emotional and psychological well-being of the primary carer in evaluating the welfare of the child, and raise them to the level of a determinative presumption. The court was, however, divided on the precise relevance of the guidelines. The three separate judgments of Thorpe LJ, Moore-Bick LJ and Black LJ all centred on this issue.

Thorpe LJ held that the decision in *Re Y*, which had not been cited in the lower court, provided good authority that the guidelines only applied to circumstances in which one parent cared for the children and not to those where the parents shared the care between them. Once there was co-parenting, the children were not so dependent upon the stability and well-being of one parent and the role of each parent might be equally important for them. Furthermore, the court should look at the actual practical arrangements for the children rather than the actual nature of the residence order. Some parents share the care of their children without a joint residence order. Other parents may have a joint residence order but one parent remains the primary carer of the children. Moore-Bick LJ maintained that the guidelines were important and:[33]

> '... judges at all levels must pay heed to that guidance and depart from it only after careful deliberation and when it is clear that the particular circumstances of the case require them to do so in order to give effect to fundamental principles. I am conscious that any views I express on this subject will be seen as coming from one who has little familiarity with family law and practice ...'

He thought that difficulties had arisen because the guidelines had been treated as if they:

> '... contained principles of law from which no departure is permitted. Guidance of the kind provided in *Payne* is, of course, very valuable both in ensuring that judges identify what are likely to be the most important factors to be taken into account and the weight that should generally be attached to them. It also plays a valuable role in promoting consistency in decision-making. However, the circumstances in which these difficult decisions have to be made vary infinitely and the judge in each case must be free to weigh up the individual factors and make whatever decision he or she considers to be in the best interests of the child.'

For Black LJ, *Re Y* was not a different line of authority from *Payne* but one which stood squarely within its framework. It demonstrated how the weight to be attached to the guidelines by the court depended entirely on the facts of the case. Black LJ was anxious to avoid yet another gloss on the welfare principle. She maintained that cases should not become bogged down with arguments as to whether they could be labelled as a shared care case or a primary carer case and the label then used to determine the outcome of the relocation application.

---

[33]   [2011] EWCA Civ 793 at [86].

IV   REFORM OF THE LAW

In the light of the decision in *K v K,* were the criticisms of *Payne* justified? Even prior to *K v K,* a detailed reading of *Payne* does not support the critics' view that Thorpe LJ, in his imposition of guidelines, was trying to usurp the legal principle of the paramountcy of the child's welfare. It is possible that the proponents on either side of the relocation debate have tended to elevate the guidelines to the level of legal principles to strengthen their own standpoint. Those sympathetic to the dilemma faced by mothers, if they have to remain within the jurisdiction, may have done so to permit mothers to leave and determine their own future unencumbered by the unrealistic demands of a former partner. Their opponents, who have maintained that the guidelines favour mothers over fathers who, as a consequence, risk the loss of contact with their children, may have also overemphasised the importance given to the guidelines. They may have done so to decry their illegal existence, to demand that they be abandoned and that a complete overhaul of relocation law be undertaken.

The question in the minds of all those involved in the relocation debate is where do we go after *K v K*? It seems readily understandable that, as long as the guidelines remain in place, they will be used and not necessarily in a judicious manner. They, undoubtedly, make the task of judges a little easier in an area of law which is inevitably discretionary in that they provide a framework for the resolution of relocation disputes. The downside of retaining the guidelines is that mothers who wish to relocate will be encouraged to present themselves as emotionally disturbed victims whose lives will fall apart, and, thereby, adversely affect their children, if they are not allowed to do so. Women who refuse to play the victim role will be penalised. Fathers who wish to object to relocation will be encouraged to present themselves as equal carers in their children's lives even when sociological evidence reveals that the majority of them are not.[34]

It is not merely the guidelines in *Payne* which are problematic in this morass, but the law itself. The provisions of the Children Act 1989 are inappropriate for the resolution of relocation disputes between two parents who both care about their children. It is too easy for the principle of the paramountcy of the child's welfare to be used, ex post facto, to justify a relocation decision. The principle has become elided with the concept of children's rights,[35] in particular the so-called right of the child to have contact with both parents. If one parent chooses to leave the jurisdiction alone, or even relocate within the jurisdiction to a place which is at a considerable distance from the child, there are no means by which the child can enforce contact with this absent parent. Is this 'child's right to contact', which is often used as a weapon by the parent who wishes to object to relocation, merely a thinly veiled disguise of what is, in reality, nothing more than a parental wish to ensure that the status quo remains intact.

---

[34]   See n 25 above.
[35]   Cf U Kilkelly 'Relocation: a Children's Rights Perspective' (2010) 1 J Family Law and Practice 23.

The relocation debate is not about children's welfare, or children's rights, even though it is couched in these terms. It is, in reality, about the rights of parents to self-determination and a relationship with their children. On the one hand, there are mothers who wish to make a new life for themselves, with their children, outside of the jurisdiction, and on the other hand, there are fathers who wish to remain within the jurisdiction, continuing a lifestyle which is satisfying to them, and sharing in the care of their children or having significant contact with them. It is not possible to please both parents. Relationship breakdown in the international context will always leave one parent unhappy whatever decision the court makes about relocation. At the risk of being branded a heretic, the question must be asked whether the welfare of the child should remain the lodestar for decision making in this field or whether it should finally be abandoned and a new law backed up with new legal guidelines put in its place?

Any proposed reform of the law of international relocation must recognise the complexity of the lives of international families even before relationship breakdown. One or both parents often face, inter alia: homesickness; cultural conflict; career clashes; difficulties in remaining in real, and not merely virtual, contact with their extended families (Skype, e-mail, telephones, although helpful, are not a substitute for real contact), and language problems. After relationship breakdown, these problems are inevitably exacerbated. Arrangements which worked during the currency of the relationship become impossible to sustain when the relationship ends; it is unrealistic to assume otherwise. Primary carers (usually mothers) may be prepared to sacrifice their own desire for self-determination whilst a relationship is working but not after its breakdown. Once the relationship ends, mothers may have to confront the fact that fathers suddenly discover the desire to co-parent, or to have substantial contact with, their children, in order to keep the children within the jurisdiction. If fathers succeed, mothers risk being trapped and denied the possibility of creating a new and, often, economically secure life for themselves and their children in a place of their choosing. How many of those fathers who object to relocation are capable or willing to take genuine joint responsibility for their children? How many of them are prepared to sacrifice a future career move or the possibility of a new relationship outside of the jurisdiction for the sake of contact with their children?[36] If they are not, why should they be permitted to object to a mother's relocation?

Even if the law of international relocation is reformed, the child's welfare will still remain an important element but one which cannot be viewed in isolation from the well-being, in every sense of the word, of the parents. The two are interdependent. Parental well-being after relationship breakdown includes, in addition to contact with their children, self-determination, mobility, career

---

[36] See 'Relocation and the Case for Reform' published by the lobbying group for father's rights with respect to their children, available at www.thecustodyminefield.com/Reports/FamilyLaw-Relocation_The_Need_For_Reform.pdf (accessed June 2012).

satisfaction, financial security, contact with the wider family, participation in the culture of the country of origin, and the potential for new friendships and emotional relationships.

Article 8 of the ECHR, the right to respect for private and family life, has been raised as an argument by parents who are opposed to the relocation of their children, although there has been insufficient discussion of it in the case-law.[37] Art 8 does not place the rights of children over and above the rights of their parents; rather, every member of the family should have his or her right under Art 8 taken into account. There must be a balancing exercise.[38] The provisions of Art 2 of Protocol 4 of the ECHR have been overlooked in the relocation debate. Article 2 specifically recognises the right of mobility both within and outside of the jurisdiction. The United Kingdom is a signatory to the protocol but has not yet ratified it.[39]

In 2010, family law experts from a cross-section of jurisdictions met in Washington DC to discuss the problem of international family relocation and formulate recommendations. Thorpe LJ represented the jurisdiction of England and Wales. At the end of the discussions, The Washington Declaration on International Relocation was drawn up. The participants agreed that, in all applications concerning international relocation, the best interests of the child should be the paramount consideration. Therefore, determinations should be made without any presumptions for or against relocation. The exercise of judicial discretion should be guided in particular, but not exclusively, by a number factors listed in no order of priority. The weight to be given to any one of them would be fact dependent and would obviously vary from case to case. The factors are listed in s 4 of the Declaration:

'i.   the right of the child separated from one parent to maintain personal relations and direct contact with both parents on a regular basis in a manner consistent with the child's development, except if the contact is contrary to the child's best interest;

ii.   the views of the child having regard to the child's age and maturity;

iii.   the parties' proposals for the practical arrangements for relocation, including accommodation, schooling and employment;

---

[37]   Dame Elizabeth Butler-Sloss in *Payne*, above n 2 at [21] did consider the impact of Art 8 but concluded that the right of the child took first place.

[38]   Cf *Re AR* above n 3. Article 8(2) provides that: 'There shall be no interference by a public authority with the essence of this right except ... for the protection of the rights and freedoms of others.' See the view presented by S Choudhry and H Fenwick 'Taking the Rights of Parents and Children Seriously: Confronting the Welfare Principle under the Human Rights Act' (2005) 25 Oxford J Legal Studies 453.

[39]   Article 2 of Protocol 4:
'1. Everyone lawfully within the territory of a state shall, within that territory, have the right to liberty of movement and freedom to choose his residence.
2. Everybody shall be free to leave any country, including his own.
3. No restrictions shall be placed on the exercise of these rights other than such as are in accordance with law and are necessary in a democratic society in the interests of national security or public safety, for the maintenance of public order, for the prevention of crime, for the protection of health and morals, or for the protection of the rights and freedom of others.'

iv.   where relevant to the determination of the outcome, the reasons for seeking or opposing the relocation;

v.   any history of family violence or abuse, whether physical or psychological;

vi.   the history of the family and particularly the continuity and quality of past and current care and contact arrangements;

vii. pre-existing custody and access determinations;

viii. the impact of grant or refusal on the child, in the context of his or her extended family, education and social life, and on the parties;

ix.   the nature of the inter-parental relationship and the commitment of the applicant to support and facilitate the relationship between the child and the respondent after the relocation;

x.   whether the parties' proposals for contact after relocation are realistic, having particular regard to the cost to the family and the burden to the child;

xi.   the enforceability of contact provisions ordered as a condition of relocation in the State of destination;

xii. issues of mobility for family members;

xiii. any other circumstances deemed to be relevant by the judge.'

The Declaration maintains that the major goal should be for parents to voluntarily settle relocation disputes themselves. Mediation and similar services should be promoted and made available both within, and outside of, court proceedings to encourage parents to agree. The Declaration has no legal force in England and Wales.

No matter how many factors one takes into account in determining the outcome of relocation applications, and the Washington Declaration lists a significant number of factors, the Declaration does not meet the concerns expressed above. Two specific criticisms may be made of its recommendations. First, yet again, the welfare of the child has been given its own place ahead of the list of factors which should be taken into consideration. Second, minimal attention has been given to the effect, on the future life of a parent who is the primary carer, of a refusal to allow her to relocate.

The Washington Declaration also recommended that additional research in the area of relocation is necessary to analyse trends and outcomes in relocation cases. If research is to be undertaken, it should, perhaps, also look at how children in intact families cope with international relocation which, so often, is for career purposes which will involve one parent spending significant periods of time away from the children.

In conclusion, it would seem that parents must face the fact that life post-separation inevitably has adverse consequences. Encouragement and practical help should be given to them so that they might agree relocation and contact arrangements rather than have the court impose its view on them. In default of agreement, any new law of relocation should abandon the overarching principle of the paramountcy of the child's welfare, and draw up a hierarchical checklist, which relates, inter alia, to the well-being of *all* members of the family, and to which the court should refer in making its determination. It is suggested that unless, having had regard to the checklist, there are overwhelming reasons to decide otherwise, the primary carer should be allowed to relocate. This does, unfortunately, mean that the other parent will have to bear the consequences. By contrast, if both parents genuinely share in the every day practical care of the child, and this will be a comparatively rare event, the parent who wishes to relocate may have to bear the consequences of being denied permission to do so.

Those who contemplate child rearing in an international context may well wish to consider very seriously the possible consequences of relationship breakdown before they embark upon it.

France

A CHRONICLE OF FAMILY LAW IN 2011

Centre de droit de la famille (Université Jean Moulin)*

Résumé

L'année 2011 n'a pas été marquée par de profonds bouleversements en droit français de la famille. Toutefois, le législateur et surtout la jurisprudence internes ont apporté ici et là différentes précisions et retouches qui seront peut-être les prémisses d'une évolution ultérieure. La poursuite du rapprochement des modes de conjugalité et l'omniprésence du contentieux lié à la revendication de la coparentalité et de la coparenté dans les familles homosexuelles, ajoutées aux récents changements politiques français pourraient bien donner lieu à de véritables réformes dans les années à venir …

I ESTABLISHING THE 'PRIORITY QUESTION OF CONSTITUTIONALITY' IN FRENCH LAW AND ITS APPLICATION TO FAMILY LAW

Established by the constitutional reform of 23 July 2008 and effective as of 1 March 2010, the 'priority question of constitutionality' (referred to as QPC) has deeply changed the very conception of checking the constitutionality of laws. This reform, the terms of implementation of which are laid out in the organic law number 2009–1523 of 10 December 2009,[1] and two decrees of 16 February 2010,[2] constitutes a major legal upheaval since it introduces the retrospective checking of the constitutionality of French law. Previously, the checking of the constitutionality of a law had only been possible upstream, ie before it took effect, and could not be reverted to by just anyone subject to trial.

In the future, within the meaning of art 61–1, first paragraph of the Constitution:

---

* This chronicle was collectively written by the academic staff, PhD holders and PhD candidates at the Centre for Family Law at Jean Moulin University Lyon 3 (research team on private law – EA3707) aimed at presenting recent developments in family law in France. It was written under the direction of Hugues Fulchiron and Christine Bidaud-Garon by Younès Bernand, Benoît de Boysson, Jézabel Jannot, Aurélien Molière, Amélie Panet, Stessy Tetard and Fabrice Toulieux.

[1] *Journal Officiel*, 11 December 2009.
[2] Decree nos 2010–148 and 2010–149.

'If, during proceedings in progress before a court of law, it is claimed that a legislative provision infringes the rights and freedoms guaranteed by the Constitution, the matter may be referred by the Conseil d'État or by the Cour de Cassation to the Constitutional Council which shall rule within a determined period.'

In other words, during a court case irrespective of its nature (civil, criminal, administrative, tax-related, social, electoral, commercial, etc) the priority question of constitutionality allows anyone subject to trial to contest the constitutionality of the law applicable to the case in which that person is a party. Today, the Constitutional Council may therefore de facto set aside the enforcement of a law, *following its promulgation*, as soon as it deems it in non-compliance with the Constitution. To raise a priority question of constitutionality, the person subject to law must claim that a legislative measure being opposed or applied to him or her impedes upon fundamental rights guaranteed by the Constitution. On the other hand, administrative acts, ie decrees, bylaws and individual rulings, cannot be made subject to a priority question of constitutionality.

In concrete terms, the subject of law must be able to demonstrate that a law or a ruling ratified by Parliament represents a breach of a *basic right* (guaranteed by the Constitution of 4 October 1958, by the Declaration of the rights of man and the citizen of 1789 or by the preamble of the Constitution of 1946 to which the preamble of the Constitution of 4 October 1958 refers) or on the other hand the *basic principles* recognised by the laws of the Republic and the Charter of the environment of 2004.

In the field of family law, referring a QPC was the occasion for the Constitutional Council to recall clear principles such as the *prohibition of the adoption of the other partner's child within a homosexual couple* and the *ban on homosexual marriage*. As regards rights claimed by homosexual couples, the Constitutional Council refers to the legislative power, as it is of the opinion that it is up to the legislator to take decisions on the controversial issues of society (1). Other questions related to the right of persons and the family raised QPCs. We shall mention two here, one related to the *right to levy*, and the other to *genetic certifications on a deceased person* (2).

(1) Having been appealed to on a QPC on the constitutionality of art 365 of the Civil Code[3] which prohibits adoption by homosexual couples, the

---

[3] 'The adopting parent is, with regard to the adopted child, the only person to be vested with all the rights of parental authority, including that of consenting to the marriage of the adopted child, unless s/he is the spouse of the father or mother of the adopted child; in this case, the adopting parent shares parental authority with his or her spouse, who alone maintains exercise of that authority provided that a joint declaration has been made with the adopting parent at the head clerk at the Tribunal de Grande Instance or district courts with the aim of the joint exercise of said authority. The rights of parental authority are exercised by the adopting parent(s) under conditions laid down in chapter 1 of Title IX of this book. The rules of legal administration and supervision of minors apply to the adopted child.'

Constitutional Council concluded with its ruling of 6 October 2010[4] that the decision to authorise adoption for couples consisting of persons of the same sex or not was incumbent upon the legislator. According to the Constitutional Council, 'restricting adoption to married couples (is) constitutional'.

As it happens, what was at stake was the sensitive matter of the simple adoption of the child by the other member of a couple. Now in the case of a simple adoption, the adopted child maintains ties with the original family while becoming the child of the adoptive parent and the parental authority is transferred to the adopting parent. According to the plaintiffs, art 365 of the Civil Code ran contrary to:

> '... the rights to have a normal family life, to the principle of the protection of the greater interest of the child, to that of non-discrimination between children, to the rights of the partners or common law partner to found a family and have a normal family life and to the principle of non-discrimination on the basis of sexual orientation.'

Put differently, they claim that the provisions of art 365 of the Civil Code set up a system of discrimination inasmuch as this article makes a 'distinction between children regarding parental authority depending on whether they are adopted by the spouse or common law partner of their biological parent'. By judging art 365 of the Civil Code as complying with the rights and freedoms guaranteed by the Constitution, the Constitutional Council implicitly deems that prohibiting adoption by a member of a homosexual couple is in conformity with the Constitution. Some people are of the opinion that the Constitutional Council refused to decide on the question.

In a ruling of 16 November 2010,[5] the Cour de cassation referred a priority question of constitutionality to the Constitutional Council asking it to rule on compliance of arts 75[6] and 144[7] of the Civil Code, which stipulates that

---

4   Constitutional Council of 6 October 2010, no 2010/39 QPC.
5   Cass, civ 1re (First civil chamber of the Cour de cassation), QPC, 16 November 2010, F-P-D, no 10–40.042.
6   'The day designated by the parties following the deadline for publication, the registrar at the town hall, in the presence of at least two or at the most four witnesses who may or not be related to the parties shall read articles 212, 213 (paragraphs 1 and 2), 214 (paragraph 1), 215 (paragraph 1) and 220 of the present code to the future spouses. Article 371–1 shall also be read. Nevertheless, in the event of a serious inconvenience, the public prosecutor of the place of the marriage may require that the registrar go to the domicile or residence of one of the parties to celebrate the marriage. If the death of one of the future spouses appears imminent, the registrar may go prior to any requirement or authorisation from the public prosecutor, to whom he must then explain the need for celebrating this marriage outside the usual venue as quickly as possible. Mention of this is made in the marriage deed. The registrar shall ask the future spouses, and if they are minors, their ascendants who are present at the wedding and authorise the marriage, whether a marriage contract has been drawn up and if so, the date of the contract as well as the name and place of residence of the notary who received it. If the documents produced by one of the future spouses are not in agreement as regards the first names or their spellings, he will call those who are concerned by them and if s/he is a minor his or her closest ascendants present at the celebration to declare that the discrepancy is the result of an omission or an error. He will receive the declaration that they do take the other party as

marriage can only be celebrated between two persons one of whom is female and the other male with constitutionally guaranteed rights and freedoms.

In this case, the plaintiffs, Corinne C and Sophie H who are a homosexual couple, wish to marry. At the Cour de cassation appellate court, they raised a priority question of constitutionality related to the compliance of arts 74 and 144 of the Civil Code with the rights and freedoms guaranteed by the Constitution. The interested parties raised the question of whether these articles in their implementation run contrary to the provisions of art 66 of the Constitution as well as to the preambles of the Constitutions of 1946 and of 1958, which enshrine the principles of the individual freedom of a French citizen, among which is the freedom to marry. Moreover, the non-profit organisations which took part in the hearings maintained that arts 144 and 75 of the Civil Code do not recognise the right to lead a normal family life and equality before the law.

Two questions were thus put to the Constitutional Council. First, it had to rule on the constitutionality of the prohibition of contracting a marriage between two persons of the same sex given the various texts guaranteeing the individual freedom of citizens. Then it was up to the Council to rule on the forbidding judges from allowing a marriage between two persons of the same sex with regard to art 66 of the Constitution. In its ruling of 28 January 2011,[8] the Constitutional Council opined that the forbidding of marriage between two persons of the same sex resulting from the application of the provisions of the Civil Code, which reserves marriage to a man and a woman, is compliant with constitutionally guaranteed rights.

By these two rulings, through which both the prohibition of adoption by an unmarried couple[9] and the prohibition of homosexual marriage[10] are deemed to be in conformity with the principle of equality, the Constitutional Council took care to preserve the prerogatives of members of parliament and more generally the political authorities. The Constitutional Council deemed that it was up to the legislator alone to create law and not to the claims of the defenders of the subjectivising of marriage, both in its formation and in its effects, and notably with a view to descent or offspring.

(2) In the same vein, in its ruling of 30 September 2011,[11] the Constitutional Council ruled that genetic certification carried out on a deceased person was constitutional. What was at stake were the provisions of art 16–11, para 2, in fine, of the Civil Code, which states that, without the explicit agreement of the person expressed during his or her lifetime, no identification through genetic

---

husband and wife from each party, one after the other, and shall, in the name of the law, pronounce them married and draw up a deed on the spot.'
7   'A man and a woman can only contract marriage after reaching eighteen years of age.'
8   No 2010–92 QPC.
9   Ruling no 2010–39 QPC of 6 October 2010.
10   Ruling no 2010–92 QPC of 28 January 2011.
11   Ruling no 2011–173 QPC.

fingerprints can be carried out after his or her death. On 6 July 2011, the Constitutional Council had had the matter referred to it by the Cour de cassation,[12] of a priority question of the constitutionality of the last sentence of the fifth paragraph of art 16–11 of the Civil Code[13] with regard to the rights and freedoms guaranteed by the Constitution. The claimants felt that prohibiting identification of a deceased person by genetic fingerprints in a civil procedure concerning paternity was a breach of the respect of private life and the right to have a normal family life, and that moreover the provisions that were being contested established a difference of treatment between men and women that ran contrary to the principle of equality before the law. According to the Constitutional Council, by providing that deceased persons are presumed not to have consented to identification by genetic fingerprints, the legislator intended to create obstacles to exhumations so as to ensure the respect due to the deceased persons. As it had done with regard to questions related to claims staked by homosexual couples, the Constitutional Council emphasised that it was not in its purview to substitute its view for that of the legislator as regards taking account of the respect due to the human body. As for the grievance related to the difference of treatment between men and women, the Constitutional Council recalled that, in the application of art 325 of the Civil Code, paternity is mainly proved by genetics and maternity by gestation. Consequently, the difference in treatment corresponds to a difference in situation and can therefore not be deemed contrary to the principle of equality before the law.

In succession law, the break in equality before the law allowed the Constitutional Council to deem the right to levy unconstitutional, as provided for in art 2 of the law of 14 July 1819.[14] This text protects French heirs from discriminatory effects due to foreign succession law: it institutes a right to levy, allowing any French citizen to claim any assets situated in France to which French law would give him or her a right and which he or she was deprived of through the application of foreign law.

The Constitutional Council emphasised that this French rule of substance is aimed at being applied when at least one co-heir is French and the succession includes assets situated on French territory. According to the Council, such criteria are directly related to the object of the law, and do not per se ignore the principle of equality. Moreover, the Constitutional Council deems that, so as to re-establish equality between the heirs guaranteed by French law, the legislator

---

[12]   First civil chamber, ruling no 866 of 6 July 2011.
[13]   This article foresees cases in which the identification of a person through genetic fingerprinting may be sought; the fifth paragraph indicates that in civil cases, this identification can only be sought through the execution of a measure ordered by the judge to whom a case has been referred aiming at establishing or contesting a tie of descendent or obtaining or eliminating allowances. Moreover, it specifies that the consent of the person concerned must be obtained in advance and explicitly. Finally, according to the last sentence of the fifth paragraph: 'Without the explicit agreement of the person manifested during his or her lifetime, no identification by genetic fingerprints may be carried out after his or her death.'
[14]   Constitutional Council ruling no 2011–159 QPC of 5 August 2011.

can found a difference in treatment on the basis that the foreign law privileges the foreign heir against the French heir.

On the other hand, by reserving the right to levy from the succession to the French heir alone, the Constitutional Council deems that the measure at issue establishes a difference in treatment between heirs who also come to the succession according to French law and who are not privileged by foreign law. Nevertheless, according to the Council, this difference in treatment is not directly related to the object of the law, which tends notably to protect the hereditary reserve and the equality among heirs guaranteed by French law. Upon this basis, art 2 of the law of 14 July 1819 establishing the right to levy runs contrary to the constitutional principle of equality before the law.

In the years to come, it is certain that the priority question of constitutionality will allow the Constitutional Council to rule on the constitutionality of numerous measures of family law. Regarding the aforementioned decisions, it is nevertheless clear that in this matter those subject to justice will have to await normative developments through the legislator rather than through the constitutional judge, in conformity with the principle of the separation of powers, of which the Constitutional Council is moreover a guardian.

II PACS (CIVIL UNIONS), MARRIAGES AND FORMS OF CONJUGALITY

First, the year 2011 was full of important international news for French law on conjugality, with the effectiveness and adoption of important international instruments.

The beginning of 2011 followed on the heels of the adoption of an unprecedented instrument for reinforced co-operation within the European Union on 20 December 2010: the so-called 'Rome III' regulation on the law applicable to divorce and physical separation which on 21 June 2012 became effective in 14 member states,[15] among which is France. This regulation, with its universal evocation, provides for a complete legal framework and allows for the expression of the autonomy of will regarding the law applicable to divorce: its principle is that of optio juris (a choice of the spouses among the various laws at hand), completed, in the event that no choice is made, by a sequence of applicable national laws.

The effectiveness of the European 'alimony' regulation[16] on 18 June 2011 should also be noted, as it has become French common law in the field of

---

[15]   At the time of writing, Germany, Austria, Belgium, Bulgaria, Spain, France, Hungary, Italy, Latvia, Luxembourg, Malta, Portugal, Romania and Slovenia are participants in the instrument of reinforced co-operation.

[16]   Regulation (EC) 4/2009 on competence, the applicable law, the recognition and the execution of decisions and co-operation in terms of alimony obligations.

judicial purview and the law applicable to alimony, which also includes questions of compensation following a divorce.

For its part, French domestic law on conjugality has not been marked by far-reaching reforms in 2011. It only saw minor developments, restricted to three fields: minor alterations to the marriage law, a further narrowing of the gap between PACS or civil unions on the one hand and marriage on the other and an emphasis upon the procedural character of the law of conjugality.

Marriage law is first marked by a more protected entry into marital union. Since 1 May 2011, the Law[17] provides that during the marriage ceremony the civil status officer read the measures of the Civil Code regarding legal solidarity among the spouses regarding household debts, which should ensure that they are better informed.

The conditions for celebrating a posthumous marriage, ie a marriage between two persons, one of whom is deceased, have been simplified: the accomplishment of the first 'official formalities' for matrimonial union is no longer required, but simply a 'sufficient gathering of facts' which establish unambiguously the consent of the deceased. These changes have no effect on marriage between two living people, and, given the low number of posthumous marriages that are authorised every year by the President of the Republic, it in no way constitutes a legal upheaval.

The debate on the question of same-sex marriages continued to rage during the year 2011. The first occasion concerned the celebration of a marriage between a woman and a transsexual whose civil status had not been rectified in June 2011. From the point of view of the acts of the registrar, the two partners were indeed of differing sexes. However, in appearance, it was a homosexual marriage. This legal difference of their sexes made it possible to celebrate the marriage.

The Constitutional Council provided the second occasion by judging that opening marriage to homosexual couples was not within its competence: the law's reserving marriage to couples only of differing sexes was not deemed to run contrary to the rights and freedoms guaranteed by the Constitution.

Finally, the Cour de cassation went back on the content of public order in the field of marriage in the month of November 2011:[18] it affirmed that the conclusion of a marriage brokerage contract by a man undergoing a divorce did not run contrary to common decency and public order. For the court deemed that meeting someone with a view to marriage was not the same thing as carrying out the marriage.

---

[17] Law no 2010–737 of 1 July 2010 reforming consumer loans, effective as of 1 May 2011.
[18] Cass civ 1ère, ruling no 10–20.114 of 4 November 2011.

The year 2011 also saw that the *various forms of conjugality* were brought closer together. Thus, just as the identity of the surviving spouse is mentioned on the death certificate of the deceased spouse, that of the surviving partner is mentioned on his or her companion's death certificate.[19]

Nevertheless, one must not believe that the attraction of marriage excludes other forms of conjugality: it is sometimes the rules of PACS or civil partnership which are extended. Treatment of couples for tax purposes has become harmonised: the French finance law of 2011 amended art 6 of the General Tax Code, which provides that in the future married couples, like partners in a civil union, can choose between a single declaration or two separate declarations during the first year of their marriage.

The advantage they used to have of submitting three declarations (one for each spouse followed by a joint declaration for the period following the wedding) has been abolished.

Nevertheless, this harmonisation has not led to complete assimilation: the Constitutional Council asserted[20] that measures in the Code for military pensions reserving the benefits of pensions only to widowed spouses are in conformity with the rights and freedoms guaranteed by the Constitution. Thus, French law seems to maintain a certain special place for marriage.

Finally, one should note an increase in the *procedural character of the law of conjugality*, which has become tangible in three forms.

First, the possibility of concluding a participative procedure conference 'with the aim of finding a consensual solution regarding divorce or physical separation' has been available for spouses since 1 September 2011. The law[21] now makes it possible for parties to a dispute which has not yet been referred to a judge or an arbitrator to commit themselves to working jointly and in good faith towards an amiable resolution. This procedure makes all recourse to the judge inadmissible (except for non-execution of the conference) and is possible regarding both divorce and physical separation. This said, divorce remains necessarily a legal matter, and this means that the judge alone can pronounce a divorce. However this participative procedure allows the spouses to find an agreement upstream, and particularly regarding the consequences of their divorce for their finances, and to envisage a divorce procedure directly by mutual consent. Any partial agreement of the spouses during this participative procedure can be certified by the judge, thereby binding the parties from the moment of certification.

---

[19]   Law no 2011–525 of 17 May 2011 for simplifying and improving family law.
[20]   Constitutional Council ruling no 2011–155 QPC of 29 July 2011.
[21]   Law no 2010–1609 of 22 December 2010 on the enforcement of judicial rulings, the conditions of the exercise of certain regulated professions and of legal experts.

Then, a modernisation law[22] of the judicial and regulated legal professions, definitively adopted on 15 March 2011, created the 'act of the lawyer'. This new type of act is subject to recording and is given higher conclusive force than simple acts of private agreement. Questioning its validity has also become more complicated. It is possible to think that lawyers will use this new form of act in family matters, notably to support engagement agreements, nuptial contracts or civil unions. These acts may also concern common-law marriage so as to adapt the organisation of property or pecuniary arrangements for the couple, or to cope with particular difficulties or crises. This law also gave notaries public a monopoly to officially register the partnership agreements (PACS) they would have written.

III THE EXERCISE OF PARENTAL AUTHORITY IN THE EVENT OF THE SEPARATION OF A COUPLE

The law of 4 March 2002 stipulates the principle of the joint exercise of parental authority, irrespective of whether the couple is together or separated. Article 373–2 of the Civil Code states that the separation of the parents has no impact on the exercise of parental authority. The principle of the indifference of separation was symbolically expressed in the Civil Code by abrogating provisions on parental authority in the part devoted to divorce. The rules on parental authority thus transcend the rules of conjugality.

The exercise of parental authority during the separation of a married couple can be treated from three different vantages, from the perspective of current events. Here, we propose to address the issues of the place of the will in the post-conjugal exercise of parental authority, of the increasing trend to alternative residence and of the situation of shared delegation in the case of separation.

(a) The place of the will in determining the modalities of post-conjugal exercise of parental authority

French law on parental authority accords broad scope to parental agreements. Article 373–2–7 of the Civil Code thus allows parents 'to refer their case to the judge for family matters so as to have the agreement through which they organise the modalities for exercising parental authority certified'. In the absence of an agreement concluded by both parents, can the judge nevertheless say that parental authority will be exercised through a joint agreement between them? The Cour de cassation deemed that, in the absence of parental agreement, it is incumbent upon the judge to establish the modalities for exercising the visiting rights of the parent with whom the child does not

---

[22] Law no 2011–331 of 28 March 2011 for modernising judicial or legal professions and certain regulated professions.

reside.[23] Certain authors analysed this decision as a limit on contract formation with regard to parental authority. One can certainly see an invitation to the parents to take a position on the ways parental authority will be exercised at the moment of the break-up, and thus ultimately a promotion of parental agreements.

(b)   An increase in alternating residence

Article 373–2–9 of the Civil Code stipulates that:

> '... upon the request of one of the parents or in case of disagreement between them on the form of residence, the judge can provisionally order alternating residence for a period the judge determines. At the end of it, the judge takes a definitive decision on the child's residence – either alternating or in the home of either parent.'

The legislator thus seems to give preference to alternating residence. The Minister of justice recently drew attention to the increase in alternating residence: 20% of arrangements were the sharing of parent time in 2010, whereas up until 2007, the figure had stagnated at around 10%.[24] This rise is partially due to the substantial share of divorce procedures by mutual consent in which the parents decide by joint agreement to set up alternating residence for their children. While this was very much decried when the measure was adopted, alternating residence gradually gained ground in parenthood cases. In situations in which its implementation is possible (depending on the age of the child, the understanding between the parents, the proximity of the homes, etc), judges for the most part seem open to such a measure. The latter seems to constitute the preferred way of restoring the position of fathers and guaranteeing the continuity of the relations between the parents and the child.

(c)   Maintaining the delegation of parental authority despite conjugal separation

The impact of the exercise of parental authority during conjugal separation is not only the prerogative of heterosexual couples. The question of parenthood is also raised during the deconstitution of the 'homosexual family', created by the delegation of authority through sharing. Can the parent to whom authority is delegated be allowed to maintain the ties of parenthood created with the child despite the break-up of the couple? Jurisdictions to which this problem has been referred seem to indicate that they can. The principle of co-parenthood is expressed through the delegation of parental authority and the separation of

---

[23]   Civ 1ère, 23 November 2011.
[24]   *Rép min no 125239*, JOAN Q, 20 March 2012, p 2476.

the conjugal couple then has no effect on the modalities of the exercise of the parental authority. A right to visit and to stay[25] or alternating residence[26] can be decided by the judge.

IV DELEGATION OF PARENTAL AUTHORITY IN SAME-SEX COUPLES

French legislation is as follows: the child can only have a father and a mother as parents, thus implying a difference of sex in a parental couple. This rule is as important for establishing descent as for the legal devolution of parental authority. Nevertheless, it is not out of the question that the matter be referred to the judge so as to organise the exercise of the latter. It is then possible for the judge to decide the total or partial delegation to a third party (art 377 of the Civil Code), or to carry out the sharing of said delegation (art 377–1 of the Civil Code). Consequently, same-sex couples to whom the law does not give joint parental authority rapidly tried to make use of this power. The judge does not make favourable rulings *unless the circumstances require it*, ie mainly when in the given situation it is not otherwise possible to satisfy the various purposes of parental authority based upon the child's interest.

It is in reference to this requirement of law that the Cour de cassation rules, when it is called upon to check a ruling for such a delegation by the judges who rule on the substance.[27] Nevertheless, the formula is ambiguous and thus open to interpretation. One can, moreover, wonder whether the legislator really had the will to provide for such a delegation for same-sex couples. But in the absence of clarity, the text may constitute the basis for what French authors refer to as *homoparentalité* (homosexual parenthood), ie parental authority exercised jointly be persons of the same sex. A series of rulings given high media coverage passed down by courts has recently demonstrated this.

First of all, a ruling by the Tribunal de Grande Instance or District Court of Bayonne authorised the *general and shared delegation of parental authority* to a same-sex couple.[28] The solution is not per se innovative because it only confirms the application of delegation to all types of couples. However, it is

[25] TGI (district court) Briey, 21 October 2010, no 09/00482; TGI Nanterre, 14 December 2010, no 10/02107.

[26] TGI Annecy, 1 July 2010, no 09/02356.

[27] Cass civ 1ère, February 24, 2006, *Bull civ* I, no 105; *GAJC*, 12th edn, no 53–55; *D* 2006.897, n D VIGNEAU; *AJF* 2006.159, obs F CHENEDE; *JCP G* 2006.I.199, no 16, obs M REBOURG. More recently, Cass civ 1ère, 8 July 2010, *Bull civ* I, no 158; *JCP G* 2010.994, n A GOUTTENOIRE; *AJF* 2010.394, obs F CHENEDE; *RDSS* 2010.1128, n C NEIRINCK. The result of these two rulings may be a standard reason: 'If article 377, paragraph 1 of the Civil Code is not opposed to a mother who is the only holder of parental authority delegating all or part of the exercise to the woman with whom she lives in a stable and continued union, it is on the condition that the circumstances require it and that the measure corresponds to the higher interest of the child.'

[28] TGI Bayonne, 26 October 2011, no 11/00950; *Dr Famille 2011*, no 12, comm 179, C NEIRINCK.

striking through the absence of reasons, since the judge did not justify the ruling. For at no time are particular circumstances referred to. Nevertheless, reasons were more necessary in the event of a total shared delegation. This ruling is clearly marginal with regard to the position of the legislator and the Cour de cassation.

The Paris Appeals Court also ruled on this point. But it did so in a different situation, since the issue was shared delegation in a separated same-sex couple.[29] Initially, the decision was supported by reasons. The judges especially underlined the need to ensure the stability of the situation, presented as a necessary condition for the healthy development of the two young children. Going more deeply, we note that the decision essentially takes account of the desire of both partners to raise the children of one of the partners jointly, and that the interest of the children is prioritised without being particularly justified. In the end, the reasoning is more apparent than real and does not mention the existence of particular circumstances, which is a condition that has been misused by the courts and appeal courts. What is unique about the ruling is the situation in which the decision was made. For it is the first time a judge has allowed for the shared delegation of parental authority between two people of the same sex who are no longer living as a couple. One might thus think that the judge's intention was to extend solutions resulting from the law of 4 March 2002 to same-sex couples, and more particularly the principle that the separation of the couple *has no effect on the rules of devolution of the exercise of parental authority* (art 373–2).

Given these decisions, one must remain prudent and avoid interpretations, conclusions and hasty predictions. It is not possible for the time being to talk about the enshrining of *homoparentalité*. One must acknowledge the existence of recognition through case-law. What many present as an innovation is in fact merely the reiteration in the media of a position that had previously been adopted by a few judges, particularly by those of the Paris Appeals Court,[30] which reduce *particular circumstances* to a two-fold observation: the child is being raised in the context of homosexual parents and has an established relationship of biological descent only with regard to his or her mother. If these are circumstances, one may doubt that they are really particular. What is more, although the rulings presented here have not been appealed, and thus have not been submitted for consideration by the Cour de cassation, it is possible to suppose that they would have been overruled.

Nevertheless, one must not ignore the fact that these few signs, if they grow to a trend, may create a tension between case-law and legislation. Thus, these rulings should give food for thought but also give rise to patience, while waiting for a ruling from the highest jurisdictions to clarify the rule or new legislation, which will be more or less the direct consequence of the national elections.

---

[29]   CA (appeals court) Paris, 1 December 2011, no 11/06495; *AJF* 2011.146, obs C SIFFREIN-BLANC.

[30]   With no claim to exhaustiveness, CA Paris, 16 June 2011, no 10/22338; 20 October 2011, nos 11/04042 and 10/11743.

V THE IMPOSSIBILITY OF ADOPTING THE OTHER PARTNER'S CHILD IN A SAME-SEX COUPLE

In French law, homosexual parenthood is at the core of concerns related to the law on descent. If our law forbids establishing a dual tie of descent within a same-sex couple, it does, on the other hand, allow for sharing parental authority through the shared delegation of authority.[31] Nevertheless, this delegation must not be a means of circumventing the aforesaid prohibition. It is nonetheless what some believed, when they tried to circumvent art 365 of the Civil Code. This text on simple adoption only allows for sharing parental authority between the adoptive parent and the biological parent under condition that they be married. Since the French conception of marriage is founded on the difference of sex,[32] this rule precludes the joint exercise of parental authority in same-sex couples in the case of simple adoption.

So as to circumvent this rule, a two-stage legal scheme was imagined. The biological parent of the child first allowed the other member of the couple to carry out a simple adoption. Contrary to fully fledged adoption, this type of adoption makes it possible for parenthood by blood to co-exist with adoptive parenthood. Nonetheless, the adoptive parent, just as in a fully fledged adoption, is the only parent to enjoy parental prerogatives. Simple adoption thus makes it possible to create a dual tie of descent, however without sharing parental authority. Then the second stage of the legal scheme enters effect: the adoptive parent carries out a shared delegation of parental authority on behalf of the biological parent. The effects of art 365 of the Civil Code are thus neutralised, since both members of the couple, the biological parent and the adoptive parent, exercise parental authority jointly, even though they are not married.

If this initiative appears to be judicious, it was not welcomed by the Cour de cassation. For in two rulings of 20 February 2007,[33] it condemned this practice since the shared delegation of parental authority was, 'towards the adoption, antinomic and contradictory, since the adoption of a child is aimed at conferring parental authority on the adoptive parent alone'. The formula taken from the Appeals Court is laconic and leaves little room for interpretation: the Cour de cassation expressly prohibits same-sex couples from instrumentalising the shared delegation of parental authority so as to neutralise certain effects of simple adoption. Thus, the highest instance of the legal order ruled that the clarity with which the rule laid down in art 365 of the Civil Code was expressed

---

[31] See the discussion in Part IV.

[32] The Cour de cassation reasserted the traditional conception of marriage in a ruling of 13 March 2007 (Cass civ 1ère, 13 March 2007 *Bull civ* I, no 113). As for the Constitutional Council, it deemed that arts 77 and 144 of the Civil Code did not run contrary to the Constitution (CC, 28 January 2011, DC no 2010–92 QPC). Finally, the ECtHR refused to oblige member states to allow same-sex couples to get married. For in the absence of a European consensus, it refers this to the judgement of the member states (*Schalk and Kopf v Austria*, ECtHR, Gde Ch, 24 June 2010, App no 30141/04).

[33] Cass civ 1ère, 20 February 2007, *Bull civ* I, no 70.

did not allow for such derogations. This solution, which is in favour of the rigorous application of the text, is nevertheless not preserved from criticism, because it seems that its very foundation is open to a debate of substance. For this provision links parenthood to blood relationship by deeming that simple adoption, which modifies parenthood, allows the spouse of the adopting person to exercise parental authority, and thus parenthood. This rule is unfortunate inasmuch as French law allows for a disconnection between the status of the parent and the state of the parent, for instance through the delegation of parental authority.

Following rulings from the Cour de cassation, the Constitutional Council, to whom the matter was referred on the occasion of a priority question of constitutionality, was called upon to rule on the constitutionality of art 365. The plaintiffs maintained that the text was unconstitutional, as they believed that it ran contrary to the possibility of having a normal family life and the principle of the equality of citizens before the law, thus referring to the different treatment of same-sex couples and couples of different sexes with regard to parenthood. The ruling again leaves no room for doubt: art 365 of the Civil Code is not unconstitutional.[34] The Constitutional Council moreover cleverly places the ball in the court of the legislator, who alone has the remit to change rules related to adoption.[35] Through this expert opinion, same-sex couples were thus confronted with a new setback.

Since the rulings of French domestic jurisdictions pose obstacles to questioning the effects of simple adoption, it was up to the judges in Strasbourg to rule on the issue. Thus, with the ruling on *Gas and Dubois*,[36] which was awaited with great expectations the European Court of Human Rights (ECtHR) acknowledged that art 365 of the Civil Code was in compliance with the European Convention on Human Rights (ECHR). In other words, prohibiting adoption by a same-sex couple does not run contrary to the rights protected by the Convention.

The two plaintiffs, who had lived together since 1989, took recourse to medically assisted procreation in Belgium. After giving birth to a little girl on 21 September 2000, Ms Dubois entered into a civil union (*pacte civil de solidarity*) with Ms Gas on 15 April 2002. Since they wished to establish a double link of descent with the child, the couple tried to appeal to the French courts using the legal scheme described previously: the adoption of the child by Ms Gas followed by the sharing of parental authority by Ms Dubois. Since this approach was illegal because of art 365 of the Civil Code, their request proved unfruitful. Since then, they reproached the French state with being the author of a discrimination based upon their sexual orientation, thus constituting a breach of their right to the respect of their private and family life. For this reason, they invoked a breach of art 14 of the ECHR combined with art 8. The

---

[34] *Mmes Isabelle D et Isabelle B* Constitutional Council ruling no 2010–39 QPC of 6 October 2010.

[35] See above Part I on priority questions of constitutionality.

[36] *Gas and Dubois v France* (ECtHR), App no 25951/07, 15 March 2012.

ECtHR rejected the petition submitted by Ms Gas and Ms Dubois for the reason that there was no discrimination based upon their sexual orientation to the extent that they were not in a legal situation comparable to that of married couples.[37]

One must nevertheless regret that the Court did not rule on the possible analogy between same-sex couples and couples of different sexes regarding parenthood. Nevertheless, thanks to its conclusion, it ipso facto resolves the question of shared parental authority within the same-sex couple: it is a matrimonial privilege from which one cannot benefit without being able to get married. One can see that it decides on the litigation without directly confronting the issue of homosexual parenthood (*homoparentalité*).

This approach, which seems motivated by a strict compliance with the principle of subsidiarity in the absence of a European consensus, leaves the reader sceptical. On the one hand, the findings of the Court may be hailed inasmuch as the ruling is in perfect continuity with rulings passed down in domestic law and thus contributes to a necessary consistency between French law and European law. But on the other hand, the reasoning is disappointing since the Court simply sets aside the question of homosexual parenthood without providing those legal justifications which would be necessary to understand its position.

Nonetheless, this ruling has been the outcome, at least temporary, of questions related to the effect of the simple adoption of a child within a same-sex couple, demonstrating that art 365 of the Civil Code is in compliance with both domestic and European law.

VI   LAW ON BIOETHICS: REVISED BY THE LAW OF 7 JULY 2011

French law on bioethics was revised through Law number 2011–814 of 7 July 2011; this text marks the end to a process that started more than 3 years previously; like preceding laws (1994 and 2004), numerous reports and opinions from various instances fed into the reflection during this period of legislative gestation. But for the first time, there was also a public consultation of the citizens, the conclusions of whom were established in the framework of *états généraux* or a general conference on bioethics; 'participative experimentation' was thus initiated. A rich and varied method for creating law was thus implemented, resulting, however, in a text which did not present any major developments.

---

[37]   The ECtHR first observes (§ 65) that 'article 365 of the Civil Code provides for the sharing of parental authority when the adopting parent is the spouse of the biological parent of the adopted child, which the petitioners cannot benefit from given that French law prohibits that they get married', and then (§ 68) that 'marriage confers a particular status to those who are engaged in it' and consequently 'we cannot deem, as regards adoption by the second parent, that the petitioners are in a legal situation comparable to that of married couples'.

(a) A law of adaptation

As regards the most controversial issues in society (research on the human embryo, medically assisted procreation, the anonymity of gamete donations), none of the developments put forward by certain movements during the national consultation or even during parliamentary debates was ultimately accepted. This is why many people refer to it as a 'minor text'. However, it was not the status quo; the law of 7 July 2011 is far from being useless as a text, since it includes various innovations. However, the scope of those innovations remains limited. In short, it is a law of simple adaptation, since the innovations made have an impact only *within* the existing framework, which was established by the laws on bioethics of 1994 and 2004; nothing goes beyond this apart from the authorisation, at last, of the ratification of the convention of the Council of Europe for the protection of human rights and the dignity of the human being regarding applications of biology and medicine.[38] The principle of a periodic revision has been maintained; the text of 2011 shall be subject to a new overall examination by the Parliament within at most 7 years from the date it takes effect. Recourse to consulting citizens has been rubber stamped, so a public discussion through a general conference shall in the future precede any draft reform.

In the framework of the present review, we cannot provide an exhaustive analysis of the revised law of bioethics. These are only a few aspects which are of interest to cardinal notions of the law of persons and the family – the person, the human being, the family, the couple, biological descent and the child – which we shall touch upon.

(b) Information on the family in the event of a serious genetic anomaly

The law of 2011 organises information on relations in the event of the diagnosis of a grave genetic anomaly established when examining the genetic characteristics of a person, when preventive measures or care may be offered to members of the family. For art 2 makes it possible to implement the measure of 'medical information of a family character' provided for by the law of 6 August 2004 which, however, remained unenforced, since the decree of enforcement was not passed due to the complexity of the procedure that was envisaged. The new law thus simplifies the system for conveying information; as the explanation of the reasons for the law explains:

> 'The person in question will be accompanied from the first genetic consultations as early as possible, even prior to the genetic examination so as to prepare as early as possible the conditions for conveying the information to the members of his or her family. The principle, which at present is implicit, according to which it is left to the person to advise them himself or herself is made explicit.'

---

[38] Convention on human rights and biomedicine, signed in Oviedo on 4 April 1997 – ratified by France on 13 December 2011 and effective as of 1 April 2012.

Thus, the law of 2011 obliges the patient to inform his or her family, but leaves him or her the possibility of entrusting the doctor with the task; if the person in question does not wish to convey the information directly, he or she may, according to the new art L 1131–1–2 of the Public Health Code, request:

> '... the prescribing doctor by a written document, who certifies this request, to carry out the informing of the relatives. He or she gives the doctor the addresses of those concerned persons that he or she disposes of. The doctor then advises them that there is medical information of a family character which may concern them and invites them to go to a genetic consultation, without revealing either the name of the person who was examined or the genetic anomaly or the associated risks. The doctor consulted by the related person is informed by the prescribing doctor of the genetic anomaly in question.'

This is how the legislator chose to resolve the ethical and legal conflict between the maintenance of medical confidentiality and the relationship between the doctor and the patient on the one hand, and the divulging by the doctor to interested third parties of medical information from which they may gain direct therapeutic benefit on the other. The law also provides that children coming from a gamete donor which was diagnosed as having a serious genetic anomaly potentially giving rise to preventative measures or health care be informed, since this person *could* (since the obligation to inform is optional) authorise the prescribing doctor to refer the matter to the centre of medical assistance for procreation so that the concerned parties can be informed. Strictly speaking, it is thus an obligation to inform 'relatives', and not just the 'family'.

(c)   Organ donations: the broadening of the circle of living donors

As regards organ donations in vivo, the circle of donors has been expanded in two respects: on the one hand it now includes 'any person who can prove a close and stable affective tie with the receiver for at least two years', while it was previously limited only to parents, grandparents, brothers and sisters, sons or daughters and spouses. On the other hand, it is now possible to 'cross' donate organs: it is nothing less than an exchange, albeit a 'masked' exchange through the principle of anonymity. A 'crossed' donation makes it possible to find a remedy for the incompatibility of the transplant between two members of the same family (for instance donor A is incompatible with receiver A; the same applies to the donor-receiver couple in family B. On the other hand, donor A and receiver B are compatible, just as are donor B and receiver A. The organ of the donor of family A is transplanted in the receiver of the family B, while the organ of the donor of family B is transplanted in the receiver of family A). These developments are welcome, given the shortage of organs, but change the nature of the donation carried out by a living person; it is no longer a donation carried out exclusively within the *family* in the strict sense of the term. Above all, the 'crossed donation' introduces the logics of exchange.

(d)   Gamete and embryo donations: maintaining the principle of anonymity

In the interest of the child to know his or her origins, the government wishes to remove anonymity on behalf of a child conceived through a gamete or embryo donation; the draft legislation thus provides that these children, 'once they have attained majority, have the possibility of getting to know the donor's identity'. In reality, a 'dual window' system has been proposed: the text offered the possibility for the child, who has attained majority and makes the request, to get non-identifying information (such as age, socio-professional category, or motive for the donation). The child could also find out the identity of the donor if and only if the latter had consented; removal of anonymity could only be voluntary. These possibilities were suspended after intense debate and the definitive text maintains the principle of anonymity as it stands, excepting the slight breach allowed for so as to inform those who are 'related' in case of a serious genetic anomaly as described above and which does not provide identifying elements.

(e)   Opening up of gamete donation

The law of 2011 now authorises persons who have not yet procreated to carry out a donation. In this case, the donor has the possibility of conserving part of his or her gametes for the subsequent carrying out of medically assisted procreation on his or her behalf. This opening should help to reduce the shortage of oocyte donations and also to reduce procreation tourism in relation to such a shortage.

(f)   Medically assisted procreation (MAP): no liberalisation

The opening of MAP to homosexual couples and single women, otherwise referred to as 'social' infertility, was one of the most important social issues in the context of the revision of the law on bioethics. The proposal put forward by the Senate during the first reading was ultimately rejected: recourse to MAP according to the law of 2011 remains reserved for a couple who are still of an age to procreate, the infertility of which has been *medically* diagnosed (so it can only be a heterosexual couple) or to avoid the transmission of an illness of a certain gravity. The only additional flexibility is that a marriage or life as a couple for at least 2 years is no longer required to be given access to MAP. One of the motivations behind this restriction of access to MAP is to avoid the legal organisation of the deliberate conception of a child who would be deprived of a father. A negative answer was also given to another question which was hotly debated, namely that of *post mortem* embryo transfers: the National Assembly wanted to make this possible, provided that the father had provided prior consent. Even if strict conditions were laid down, the opposition of the Senate was stronger, based notably upon the 'interest of the child not to be born without a father' and on the fact that such an authorisation would challenge the founding principles of bioethics, family law and the law of succession. The lot of embryos in excess remains unchanged: their destruction, research or use by another couple – but in the 2011 version of the law, such use is no longer 'exceptional'.

The question of post mortem embryo transfer must also be related to that of the very practice of an excessive number of embryos: authorising post mortem transfer incurs the risk of making the practice perpetual. Yet one of the objectives of the law of 2011 was to the contrary to limit the number of excessive embryos. To these ends, the new law stipulates that the number of oocytes must be limited to what is strictly required for the success of medical assistance; the legislator nevertheless refused to set a maximum number. Moreover, it explicitly authorised the procedure of vitrifying oocytes; this extremely fast freezing technique should make it possible to conserve more oocytes alone rather than embryos.

(g) Surrogate pregnancy: the status quo

The law of 2011 thus implicitly allows a conventional acceptance of ideas of the couple and procreation to emerge; medically assisted procreation must be inspired by the laws of nature, and a 'right to a child' does not exist. This paradigm of the laws of nature is to be found in surrogate pregnancy, another 'technique' of 'assisted' procreation: the law of 2011 remains silent on this procedure, which thus remains prohibited. The genetic origin is of little importance: the prohibition of surrogate pregnancy remains general, including when the child comes from two 'intentional' parents. It is transparently a traditional acceptance of motherhood that comes into play; in French law, and outside adoption, the mother is the person who gives birth, and the genetic truth, which in other fields is the queen of proof, is incapable of shaking this dogma: *Mater semper certa est* ...

(h) Research on the embryo: maintaining the principle of forbidding it and arrangements for exceptions

After a lively debate as to the expediency of opening up research on the human embryo, the legislator repeated the choice of prudence adopted in 2004 and consisting, in principle, of forbidding experiments, with a few exceptions. Within this framework, important amendments were nonetheless undertaken. The prohibition now explicitly includes embryo stem cells and stem cell lines. The creation of transgenic or chimerical embryos is prohibited. Research is still allowed exceptionally, but while in 2004 its authorisation was subject to the requirement of a major 'therapeutic' end, a major 'medical' end takes its place in the 2011 version of the law. Moreover, they are provided for without limiting the period, while the 2004 law provided for their use for experiments. On the other hand, while in 2004, research could be authorised 'under the condition that it could not be pursued using an alternative method which was comparably effective', one must now explicitly establish the *impossibility* of achieving the result using another method and that the scientific pertinence of the research project be proved. Finally, the law introduces a clause of conscience:

> 'No researcher, no engineer, technician or research assistant, irrespective of who, no doctor or medical assistant shall be obliged to participate in any capacity in research on human embryos or on embryo stem cells.'

The law of 2011 does therefore not introduce any fundamental developments to French law on bioethics, the architecture of which remains structured by the major principles established in 1994 and reasserted by the new law. Change is not to take place just yet! But is not the main thing that it was possible to create genuine debate around those controversial questions in society that are seen as most important?

VII THE PROTECTION OF VULNERABLE ADULTS AND THE *BETTENCOURT* CASE

The main objectives of the law of 5 March 2007 on the protection of adults were to centre protection on vulnerable persons, to respect their will, their rights and their dignity, and to reassert the essential role of their family and those close to them. In order to do so, the French legislator set up a system based upon three major principles: necessity, subsidiarity and the proportionality of the protection (art 428 of the Civil Code) To these ends, the legislator encouraged the personalisation of the measure so that the protection which is set up corresponds to the needs of each and every one; the legislator asserts the need to respect the person and his or her rights (art 415 of the Civil Code), notably by reinforcing the procedural rights of the protected adult and redefining the regime of personal acts; the legislator gave more freedom to the interested parties by allowing them to choose those in advance who would take charge of their protection and by creating the mandate for future protection; the legislator made the rules of the various schemes of protection more flexible while reinforcing the guarantees offered to a protected adult (with an improved supervision of the most dangerous acts, the reorganisation of the supervision of the management of accounts, the creation of a status for a legal mandate for protecting the adult for third parties in charge of carrying out legal protection measures) and by giving new remits to the supervisory judge and the public prosecutor.

However, what is to be done when the vulnerable person refuses the protection he or she needs? How can one ensure compliance with his or her will or freedom to choose, while at the same time guaranteeing that his or her vulnerability not render that will or freedom too fragile? These are the issues that the famous *Bettencourt* case put in the limelight of current events. We know that Ms Liliane Bettencourt, who holds one of the world's greatest fortunes, was in conflict with her daughter, who accused those close to the old lady of wishing to cut her off from her family so as to despoil her wealth. The case was all the more spectacular since the sums in question were several hundred million euros and that soon political and media ramifications were revealed, linked to the funding of French presidential elections. But at the heart of a plot worthy of the best soap operas, the most sensitive legal and human problems were raised: how can one set up a measure of protection that the interested party categorically rejects?

The French judge was obliged to respond to two series of questions.

(1) Can a person's refusal to submit to a medical examination prevent the setting up of a protective measure?

In their concern not to set up a protective measure unless it is necessary, the French legislators in 2007 reasserted the need for a medical certificate for all measures of legal protection. When legal guardianship (assistance) or tutelage (representation) are being called for, the request must be accompanied by a medical certificate which describes the alteration of the faculties of the adult who is to be protected and which provides all useful information on the development and consequences of this alteration (art 431 of the Civil Code). In the absence thereof, the request is inadmissible. This rule applies whoever the person is who formulates the request. A medical certificate is also necessary for setting up a measure for temporary judicial protection (*mesure de sauvegarde de justice*) (such a measure does not declare that the interested party no longer has legal capacity, but makes the party's acts easier to challenge, art 433 et seq of the Civil Code); it is also required for a mandate for future protection to be activated (art 477 et seq of the Civil Code). But what happens if the person to be protected refuses to undergo any examination, as in the *Bettencourt* case?

Prior to 2007, it was easy to surmount the obstacle. The supervisory judge was able to take up the matter of his or her own accord and designate an expert to draw up a report on the concerned person's state of health. However, this right to take up a case was abolished in 2007, since it seemed to run contrary to a right to due process: the same judge would look into the case, take the measure and guarantee its execution and follow-up.

What is more, case-law had established two rules for setting aside the refusal of the person to be protected. On the one hand, the requirement of a certificate to support the petition was not necessary when the public minister made the request. The former disappeared with the law of 2007, which made producing the certificate a condition for the petition to be admissible, irrespective of the identity of the petitioner.

On the other hand, the courts deemed that the person subject to a protection measure could not use in argument the absence of a medical observation of the alteration of his or her faculties when the person had made this observation impossible by refusing to submit to a medical examination. In practice, the doctor establishes a certificate of deficiency observing that it was impossible to examine the patient: it is up to the judge to evaluate the need for the measure on the basis of items in the file. This case-law ran too contrary to the letter and the spirit of the law of 2007 to be upheld. In a case comparable to the *Bettencourt* case (without the billions and media hue and cry), the first Civil Chamber of the Cour de cassation dropped it.[39]

In the context of the *Bettencourt* case, this turn-around in case-law became particularly striking. But did the ruling prohibit setting up a measure for protection in the absence of a medical certificate resulting from the personal examination of the person to be protected, which would amount to saying that the person could paralyse the procedure by getting out of the examination? Such a requirement would obviously have unacceptable consequences. In point of fact, it would seem that the Cour de cassation simply wanted to condemn the practice of a certificate of deficiency through which the doctor is content to observe that examining the ill person is impossible and through which the judge can draw all the consequences of this refusal and decide the consequences for the matter upon the basis of the evidence collected. The request is therefore only admissible if it is accompanied by a detailed medical certificate which bears witness to the state of the person in question and the need for protective measures. It is no doubt difficult for a doctor to establish a certificate without personally examining the patient. If reduced to doing so, the doctor might nevertheless rely upon other elements: previous certificates, previous notifications or reports, witnesses, the opinions of the person's general practitioner, etc. If this data is deemed insufficient, the judge can always order an expert's report.

The Cour de cassation thus attempts to reconcile personal freedom and the need for the person's protection.

(2) Can an agreement between the person who is to be protected and those close to the person paralyse the judge's action?

Since they were aware of the scandal caused by the relentless turns of events in the case, Mrs. Bettencourt and her family put an end to it by making an agreement: in exchange for dropping all requests for enforced guardianship by law, Mrs Bettencourt accepted the setting up of a mandate for future protection; parallel to this, the parties committed themselves to putting an end to all civil and penal procedures they had undertaken against those close to them. A mandate for future protection was concluded at a notary public in December 2010, and on the basis of a medical certificate for which Mrs Bettencourt had allowed herself to be examined, was implemented in January 2011. A few weeks later, Mrs Bettencourt's daughter and her two sons dropped their petition, and this was immediately accepted by Mrs Bettencourt who withdrew.

Given the concerted manoeuvre by the vulnerable person and her family, the supervisory judge whose investigations had established Mrs Bettencourt's fragility and the need to place her under a measure of legal protection

---

[39]   Civ 1ère, 29 June 2011.

undertook a final counterattack. He referred the matter to the Cour de cassation with a request for an opinion while pointing to two difficulties: what impact does the implementation of a mandate for future protection have upon the procedure for setting up a measure of legal protection? Does the withdrawal of a case by the vulnerable person put an end to the case?

In its opinion of 20 June 2011, the Cour de cassation responded to the second point in the affirmative: in keeping with the common law of procedure, withdrawing a case by the petitioner puts an end to the case as soon as it is accepted by the defendant. The judge can do nothing to change this. One might have suspected that, since the procedure is aimed at guaranteeing the protection of a vulnerable person, it is not an instance just like any other; does the mission of protection with which the judge is entrusted not impose particular duties, which would be expressed in specific powers? But no such provision has been made in the law: *ubi lex non distinguit* ... One might at any rate regret that the application of common law may leave the vulnerable person with no protection.

Since the Cour de cassation had asserted that the withdrawal by the petitioner as accepted by the vulnerable person puts an end to the instance, the first question is no longer of relevance. It nevertheless deserves to be looked at in greater depth: does the principle of subsidiarity lead to preferring a mandate which has been freely chosen by the constituent leaving him in full capacity to a measure of supervision or legal guardianship ordered by the judge? The issue was all the more sensitive since in the *Bettencourt* case the mandate was concluded and triggered during the procedure in an operation aimed at putting an end to the procedure.

As regards the adopting of the mandate, the fact that a procedure aimed at legal protection had been opened does not forbid the vulnerable person from contracting: for the person maintains full capacity. The mandate may only be cancelled for reasons of insanity or be rendered fragile if a measure of supervision or legal guardianship is set up subsequently.[40] As for the effects of the mandate, its implementation does not prevent the judge from continuing to investigate the case. If needed, the judge may decide upon a measure for temporary legal protection (*mesure de sauvegarde de justice*) for the duration of the instance, but in the name of the principle of subsidiarity will have to explain why this measure is necessary despite the existence of a mandate for future protection. Under these circumstances, the judge can appoint a special representative whose powers shall limit those of the proxy chosen by the vulnerable person. If the judge deems that the execution of the mandate compromises the constituent's interests, he or she can, upon the request of any interested party, revoke it (art 483(4) of the Civil Code) or suspend its execution throughout the instance (art 483 final paragraph). If subsequently the judge decides to set up a measure for supervision or legal guardianship, he or she will have to ensure that the principles of necessity and subsidiarity are

---

[40]   Cf art 464 of the Civil Code.

complied with: the measure of legal protection can only be taken if it is necessary and cannot be sufficiently provided in the interest of the person to be protected through the mandate for future protection. In another case, the Cour de cassation reasserted these various principles by its ruling of 12 January 2011.[41]

In the *Bettencourt* case, the feeling of frustration that the judge no doubt felt after being forced to drop the case because of withdrawal from the instance was only passing. The agreement made between Mrs Bettencourt and her family was soon shattered. Mrs Bettencourt's daughter requested the revocation of the mandate, the execution of which seemed in many respects contestable. At the same time, she requested that the judge take all measures that seemed necessary so as to guarantee the protection of her mother. Thanks to a procedural sleight of hand (since the request for the revocation of a mandate is not subject to the requirements of the request to open a measure of legal protection and notably to that of producing a medical certificate, and in this case the judge may exceptionally refer the matter to him or herself so as – in the event of revoking the mandate – to guarantee the protection of the vulnerable person), it was possible to set up a measure of supervision. This measure was contested by Mrs Bettencourt, but confirmed in the appeals, and we await a possible ruling from the Cour de cassation.

During this period, the 'affair' has continued and further revelations may yet blow it out of proportion to a real affair of state.

---

[41]   Civ 1ère, 12 January 2011.

Hungary

PARTNERSHIPS IN HUNGARY IN THE BLIGHT OF THE NEW LEGAL DEVELOPMENTS: STATUS OR CONTRACT?

*Orsolya Szeibert**

Résumé

Trois formes d'union existent dans la loi Hongroise depuis 2009, à savoir le mariage, le partenariat enregistré et le concubinage. Alors que le mariage et le partenariat enregistré sont des statuts, le concubinage est un contrat, malgré le fait que la majorité des personnes accepte ce type d'union. Cette contribution analyse brièvement si les dernières modifications législatives hongroises ont des conséquences sur cette conception de chacun des modes de conjugalité. Trois questions spécifiques sont envisagées: les conséquences de la pratique judiciaire relative à la propriété des biens sur les régimes matrimoniaux, les accords matrimoniaux en matière de propriété et les rapports de propriété entre les concubins; la dernière réforme hongroise, qui est une loi fondamentale de Hongrie, et l'Acte de protection de la famille qui entrera en vigueur en 2012; et enfin, le dernier projet de Code de la famille qui serait une partie du Code civil. A certains égards, il y a une convergence, à d'autres le législateur maintient des divergences entre les différents types d'union.

I   INTRODUCTION

Three forms of partnership are available now in Hungary: a man and a woman can marry or live together as cohabitants; same-sex persons can choose registered partnership or cohabitation. Marriage is regulated in the independent Family Act;[1] registered partnership is a relatively new legal solution regulated in Act No XXIX 2009;[2] rules of cohabitation have been found in the Civil Code since 1977.[3]

---

*   PhD, Assistant Professor, Department of Civil Law, Law Faculty, Eötvös Loránd University, Budapest, Hungary. This paper was supported by the János Bolyai Research Scholarship of the Hungarian Academy of Sciences.

[1]   Act No IV 1952, Hungarian Family Act on marriage, family and guardianship.

[2]   Act No XXIX 2009 on Registered Partnership and the Modification of Legal Rules in Connection with Registered Partnership and the Facilitation of the Proof of Cohabitation.

[3]   More on cohabitation and same-sex partnerships in Hungary see Orsolya Szeibert-Erdős 'Unmarried Partnerships in Hungary' in Katharina Boele-Woelki (ed) *Common Core and*

Marriage gives status for the spouses and registered partnership has the same result. Cohabitation, on the other hand, is rather a contract between the partners. Albeit the context of partnerships nowadays seems to be clear, some changes have happened lately and are happening even now (early 2012) and prospectively in the next months. These changes make us think about the Hungarian attitude towards the different partnerships. Three changes are going to be discussed, in a nutshell: judicial practice, especially in property issues; the latest Hungarian regulations affecting the notions of family and marriage and the position of marriage; and the latest Draft of our Civil Code which is planned to contain the Family Law Book.

II JUDICIAL PRACTICE IN PROPERTY CASES AND THE ROLE OF CONTRACT

(a) Marriage

The Hungarian default property regime is the community of property regime which was introduced in 1952.[4] At that time there was no opportunity at all to enter into a matrimonial property agreement which could exclude the community of property as the legislator endeavoured to protect the weaker party. This measure was in harmony with the approach that marriage is a bond of solidarity between spouses and not a contract. Under the community of property regime the spouses have separate property, which is listed, although not exclusively, in the Family Act and primarily common property.[5] Objects of common property are not listed in the Family Act at all as there is a main rule that the property which spouses acquire during the matrimonial community of life is common property if it is not separate property. In a judicial case it is often debated whether a moveable belongs to the common property or to the separate property of one spouse. This problem is solved in judicial practice by presumption: the debatable property is presumed to be a common property and the spouse who claims it can prove the opposite.

The community of property regime functions in judicial practice in a really strict way. According to judicial attitudes, common property really comes into

---

Better Law in European Family Law (Intersentia, 2005) 313–330; Orsolya Szeibert-Erdős 'Same-Sex Partners in Hungary. Cohabitation and Registered Partnership' in Katharina Boele-Woelki (ed) *Debates in Family Law around the Globe at the Dawn of the 21st Century* (Intersentia, 2009) 305–318; Orsolya Szeibert 'Cohabitation, Registered Partnership and their Financial Consequences in Hungary' in Bill Atkin (ed) *International Survey of Family Law, 2009 Edition* (Jordan Publishing Limited, 2009) 203–213; Orsolya Szeibert 'How Cohabitants and Registered Partners Can or Cannot be a Child's Legal Parents in Hungary with a Special View to the "Pater Est" Principle for Cohabitants' in Bill Atkin (ed) *International Survey of Family Law, 2011 Edition* (Jordan Publishing Limited, 2011) 211–220.

4   For more on Hungarian matrimonial property regime, see the answers given in the Hungarian national report from Emilia Weiss and Orsolya Szeibert in Katharina Boele-Woelki, Bente Braat and Ian Curry-Sumner (eds) *European Family Law in Action* Volume IV: 'Property Relations Between Spouses' (Intersentia, 2009).

5   Article 27 and following of the Family Act.

being at the time of acquisition and not only at termination of marriage. This concept strengthens the solidarity between the partners. Although marriage establishes a bond of solidarity by the strict perception of the community of property regime between the spouses, self-determination also plays a role. Since 1986, spouses can enter into a matrimonial property agreement and can choose another property regime. As no alternative matrimonial property regime is regulated in the Family Act, these classic matrimonial property agreements do not occur too often. Nevertheless, spousal agreements on the division of common property and on the use of the common dwelling are part of everyday legal life.

There is another point which weakens the solidarity and protective character of the community of property regime. According to the legal rules, neither spouse can enter into a transaction with a third party without the consent of the other spouse. As occurs often, there is a need to balance the interest of the other, non-consenting spouse and the bona fide third party who acquired the property from the spouse for an equivalent price. This interest of the bona fide third party is fully protected partly by the legal rule and partly by the approach of judicial practice, even causing drawbacks for the non-consenting spouse. Although the community of property regime is a strong one, which protects the spouses and, especially the weaker, usually homemaker spouse, the third party's interest can be privileged for the sake of the trade safety.

The same property rules are to be applied for registered partners and their property relations.

(b) Cohabitation

Although it is unambiguous that property relations of cohabitants cannot be equal to those of spouses, the legal regulation itself seems to create a special community of property regime for cohabitants. In the last decade both this approach and another approach were applied in judicial practice. The latter one looks at cohabitation as a pure contract. The Supreme Court (the name of which has changed since January 2012 and is called now the Curia) has applied this contractual approach lately and it strengthened the contractual character of cohabitation.

The contractual character has several sources and these are underlined in the latest judgments of the Supreme Court. The first is that cohabitation itself does not create status but a contract, which follows from the fact that the property relations of cohabitation are regulated in the Civil Code. Besides, the property relations of cohabitants are located just after the rules concerning *civil law companionship*. In the sixties and seventies, the legislator's aim was to distinguish sharply between marriage and cohabitation: marriage creates family law status, cohabitants live together like the contractual and co-operative partners of a civil law companionship. Albeit civil law companionship is not a pure joint ownership, this companionship is based on agreement and not on a bond of solidarity.

Cohabitants acquire common property in proportion to the contribution they have made in acquiring that property according to the Civil Code.[6] As the common property comes into being at the time of its acquisition, the main difference between the spouses' community of property regime and the special community of property regime of cohabitants seemed to be the fact that, while the extent of contribution is not relevant in marriage, it is relevant when dividing the common property between the cohabitants. On that point, however, divergent judicial practice could be observed over the years. According to one concept, the presumption of common property has to be applied in the case of cohabitants, as between spouses. Another and nowadays dominant practice is based upon the fact that the cohabitants' pure community of life cannot serve as a legal basis for acquiring joint property. Common property comes into existence only when there is an agreement between the cohabitants, if their intention aims at acquiring together. As there is no formal requirement for that intention, it can be an explicit or an implicit one. The contractual character comes into the foreground if one cohabitant has to prove that their asset during the community of life was intended to be common property.

The last mentioned source of the contractual nature emerges from the fact that cohabitants can change from the special community of property regime by contract. Although spouses also can do that and enter into a matrimonial property agreement, there are strict formal requirements in the Family Act. No such requirement can be found in the laconic regulations for cohabitation. The easy alteration from the property regulations of the Civil Code is strengthened by the fact that there is no status but only a contract. Even an oral agreement or implied conduct is enough for an agreement which leads usually to a separate property regime.

## III	FUNDAMENTAL LAW OF HUNGARY AND FAMILY PROTECTION ACT

Two new and basic legal regulations entered into force in Hungary in January 2012, namely the new Fundamental Law of Hungary (April 2011) and Act No CCXI 2011 on family protection (Family Protection Act). Both sources of law contain some regulations on family and marriage.

### (a)	Fundamental Law of Hungary

The rules of the Fundamental Law of Hungary will be stated here according to both the official translation[7] and an alternative translation[8] in case of

---

6	Article 578/G(1) of the Civil Code.
7	www.kormany.hu/download/2/ab/30000/Alap_angol.pdf (accessed April 2012).
8	http://tasz.hu/files/tasz/imce/alternative_translation_of_the_draft_constituion.pdf	(accessed April 2012).

differences between the two texts (the alternative translation in brackets). The text even in Hungarian is a really new one, the interpretation of which is going to be the task of the coming years.

The Fundamental Law of Hungary begins with the National Avowal (National Avowal of Faith). This avowal (or national commitment) says the following:

> 'We hold that the family and the nation constitute the principal framework of our coexistence, and that our fundamental cohesive values are fidelity, faith and love. (We proclaim that the family and the nation provide the fundamental framework for community, in which the pre-eminent values are loyalty, faith and love.)'

The Fundamentals follow the Avowal. Article L of the Fundamentals makes a definite and unambiguous commitment towards marriage between a man and a woman. According to the official motivation of the Fundamental Law it undertakes the obligation of protecting the institution of marriage. The heterosexuality of marriage seems to be unquestionable; and, besides, the Fundamental Law protects marriage in contrast to cohabitation between a man and a woman. Article L(1) states that:

> 'Hungary shall protect the institution of marriage as the union of a man and a woman established by voluntary decision, and the family as the basis of the nation's survival. (Hungary shall protect the institution of marriage, understood to be the conjugal union of a man and a woman based on their independent consent; Hungary shall also protect the institution of the family, which it recognises as the basis for survival of the nation.)'

Paragraphs (2) and (3) of the same article contain an obligation on the state of Hungary to encourage the commitment to have children; and they also refer to the Family Protection Act, mentioned already ('The protection of families shall be regulated by a cardinal Act').

(b)   Family Protection Act

The Family Protection Act, which is a cardinal one and refers to Art L(3) of the Fundamental Law of Hungary, protects the institution of family and marriage.[9] According to its preamble, the family is based upon morality, and besides, it is the main national human resource in Hungary and the guarantee of national subsistence. The preamble emphasises the importance of being raised up in family as it gives the safest framework for a child. The preamble enlightens the legislator's motives and objectives with the following sentences: the secure basis of the family is marriage as a union based upon mutual love and respect and deserving privileged appreciation. The family performs its task if the partnership is stable and children are raised up in this unit.

Although the Act is intended to give rules for the child–parent relationship, this contribution focuses on the definition of family and that of marriage. The Act

---

[9]   Article 1(1).

concentrates on family but neither the same-sex relationship as registered partnership nor cohabitation is ranked as family or as the basis of family.

Article 7 gives the definition of family. Although the decisions of the Constitutional Court contributed to the approaches to family and family life upon the basis of the Hungarian Constitution being in force until 31 December 2011, neither the Constitution nor any law made an effort to define and specify the family. The cardinal Family Protection Act gives the theoretical framework for the proper interpretation when applying this Act. It says that family is the relationship of natural persons living in emotional and economical community upon the basis of the marriage of a man and a woman or lineal descent or family-creating guardianship. Lineal descent is established by filiation or adoption.[10] Family-creating guardianship is a new name. The Act endeavours to encourage adoption.

There is one more independent chapter in the Act concerning the approach to family and family members. Albeit the Act primarily regulates the parent–child relationship, the parents' rights and obligations and the state's obligations towards the families, children and parents in the different spheres of life, it gives some basic legal points to an issue which definitely belongs to the civil law, namely inheritance. Statutory succession is possible between the lineal and collateral relatives (the degree of relationship is determined by law), those who are connected by adoption and the statutory inheritor who is the spouse (widow). The state and any other person can be the statutory successor only in absence of the above-mentioned circle.[11] Neither the heterosexual cohabitant nor the same-sex partner (registered partner or cohabitant) is mentioned.

IV   DRAFT OF THE FAMILY LAW BOOK AS PART OF THE NEW CIVIL CODE

The Draft of the new Civil Code was published by the government in February 2012.[12] The codification proceedings began in 1998. During the different stages of preparation, the ideas of regulating marriage and cohabitation (and from 2009 also registered partnership) have not changed either at all, or at least not profoundly.

The Draft provides regulation for all the three forms of partnership. This means that, according to the members of the committees and legal experts taking part in preparing this document, not only marriage but also cohabitation and registered partnership deserve to be regulated in the framework of family law. While nowadays marriage is the only institution of family law as officially interpreted, the Family Law Book is planned to contain

---

[10]   Article 7(1)–(2).
[11]   Article 8(1)–(2).
[12]   www.kormany.hu/download/e/2c/70000/Megkezd%C5%91d%C3%B6tt%20a%20Ptk%20k%
        C3%B6zigazgat%C3%A1si%20eygeztet%C3%A9sev.pdf#!DocumentBrowse (accessed April
        2012).

regulation concerning other partnerships. These forms (primarily marriage, then cohabitation and lastly registered partnership) are regulated in different depths, distinctive manners and in different chapters, but they are in the Family Law Book.

The principles of the Family Law Book protect the family and marriage in harmony with the earlier Constitution and the new Fundamental Law of Hungary. Principles, which emphasise, among others, children's rights, the protection of the weaker party and the requirement of equitable adjudication in family issues, are followed by an independent part (Part 2) concerning spouses. The next part (Part 3) regulates cohabitation and then comes the regulation of registered partnership (Part 4).

The Draft of Family Law Book makes 'cautious progress'.[13] The intention has been to modify the effective law if there is a real need of change, to build in the crystallised judicial practice if there is a need to govern and unify judicial practice, and to abstain from changing if there is already a good law, a well-established practice and well-satisfied claims.

Matrimonial property law receives a great emphasis in the new Draft, trying to answer the challenges of today. While the effective Family Act regulates property law briefly, the new regulations give complex rules. Albeit it is planned to maintain the well-known community of property regime, the matrimonial property agreement seems to given major importance. The Draft regulates alternative regimes, namely the regime of participation in acquisitions (which was the mandatory regime before 1952 in Hungary) and the separation of property regime (which was also better known in Hungary before 1945). The same property rules are planned to apply to registered partners (as now). A new regime would be introduced for cohabitants, a special kind of regime of participation in acquisitions. The possibility of entering into contract and arranging property relations by agreement is underlined also for those who live together as cohabitants.

V CONCLUSION

Marriage is a privileged partnership in Hungary. Although this position was provided by the earlier Constitution and strengthened by the judgments of the Constitutional Court, the new Fundamental Law and the cardinal Family Protection Act make marriage not only the first but maybe the only form of partnership and the only form which can serve as a basis for family. The Family Protection Act sets high value not only on heterosexual marriage but also on relatives, adoptive families and family-creating guardianship families. Neither

---

13   'Cautious progress' was the title of a series which published the planned new family law regulations in the periodical *Family Law* in 2005–2007, the author of the series being András Kőrös. See also András Kőrös 'New Features of Hungarian Matrimonial Property Law in the Draft of a New Civil Code' in Bea Verschraegen (ed) *Family Finances* (Jan Sramek Verlag, 2009) 675–681.

cohabitation nor registered partnership is mentioned in the Family Protection Act. When applying that law, one parent and this parent's child will be recognised as family, which is correct and an existing type of family (also) in Hungary, but cohabiting partners with their common child (which is also an existing type of family) seem to create a family only towards that child but not towards each other.

The Draft of the Civil Code in this form shows a different attitude, namely the attitude which has evolved in legal thinking for decades in Hungary. According to this approach marriage is the privileged institution but besides marriage there are other forms of partnerships which create family. At the same time contracts by spouses are clearly encouraged, in spite of the fact that Hungarian social attitudes lack confidence in matrimonial property agreements.

Judicial practice proceeds in its own way, as its aim is not theoretical thinking but the solution of real problems between spouses and cohabitants. Nevertheless, there are also convergences and divergences. In the case of cohabitants judicial practice maintains a growing distance between marriage and cohabitation, which supports the privileged rank of marriage and it seems as if there is n effort to keep people from pure (de facto) cohabitation. (It has to be remarked that the majority of Hungarian society accepts cohabitation and would even propose to young partners that they should live together before marrying.) However, in the case of spouses solidarity is not always strengthened as judicial practice recognises contracts and agreements between spouses and abstains from intervening in the contractual relations of spouses in the name of solidarity.

India

MISSING CHILDREN IN INDIA: SUGGESTIONS, REMEDIES AND SOLUTIONS

*Anil Malhotra and Ranjit Malhotra**

Résumé

L'augmentation du nombre d'enfants disparus est devenue une question préoccupante en Inde. Une enquête appropriée est nécessaire pour appréhender la disparition d'enfants car, en raison de leur âge et de leur sexe, ils sont particulièrement vulnérables et exposés aux crimes. Plusieurs pétitions ont d'ailleurs été déposées devant différentes juridictions supérieures du pays, afin de militer pour la formation de cellules d'enquête distinctes, spécialisées dans la recherche d'enfants disparus et regroupant pour cela des agents ayant une connaissance aiguë de la matière. Ce chapitre contient quelques statistiques récentes. Il énonce ensuite un certain nombre de mesures, prévues dans le cadre de la loi, pour aider à la recherche d'enfants disparus. Il est notamment question du renforcement du rôle de la police et des médias, et de la mise en place de systèmes d'information efficaces. Il suggère également la mise en œuvre des dispositions de la *Commission for Protection of Child Rights Act, 2005.*

I INTRODUCTION

The Constitution of India enacted on the 26 November 1949 resolved to constitute India as a Union of States and a sovereign, socialist, secular, democratic republic. Today, a population of over 1.1 billion Indians live in 28 states and 7 union territories within India besides about 30 million Indians who reside in foreign jurisdictions and are called non-resident Indians. Within the territory of India spread over an area of 3.28 million sq kms, the large Indian population comprised of multicultural societies professing and practising different religions and speaking different local languages coexist in harmony in one of the largest democracies in the world.

The Indian Parliament at the helm of affairs legislates on central subjects in the Union and concurrent lists, and state legislatures enact laws pertaining to state subjects as per the state and concurrent lists with regard to the subjects

---

* Anil Malhotra LLM (London), Advocate, Chandigarh.
  Ranjit Malhotra LLM (London), Advocate, Chandigarh.

enumerated in the Constitution of India. Likewise, pertaining to the judiciary, under art 214 of the Indian Constitution there is a High Court for each state and under art 124 there is a Supreme Court of India. Under art 41 of the Constitution, the law declared by the Supreme Court is binding on all courts within the territory of India. However, the Supreme Court may not be bound by its own earlier views and can render new decisions.

Part III of the Constitution of India secures for its citizens 'Fundamental Rights' which can be enforced directly in the respective High Courts of the states or directly in the Supreme Court of India by issue of prerogative writs under arts 226 and 32 respectively of the Constitution of India. Under the constitutional scheme, amongst others, freedom of religion and the right to freely profess, practise and propagate religion is sacrosanct and is thus enforceable in the extraordinary writ jurisdiction.

Simultaneously Part IV of the Indian Constitution lays down 'Directive Principles of State Policy' which are not enforceable by any court but are nevertheless fundamental in the governance of the country and it is the duty of the state to apply these principles while making laws. Under art 44 of the Constitution in this Part, the state shall endeavour to secure for the citizens a Uniform Civil Code throughout the territory of India. However, realistically speaking, to date a Uniform Civil Code remains an aspiration which India has yet to achieve and enact.

The Indian Penal Code, 1860 is a general penal code for India and extends to the whole of India. Chapter XVI of the Indian Penal Code (IPC) relates to 'Offences Affecting the Human Body' which include not merely culpable homicide (including one amounting to murder) but also 'hurt' (simple or grievous) and involves within its sweep cases of wrongful restraint, wrongful confinement, use of criminal force, assault simpliciter, kidnapping or abduction or trafficking in human beings and sexual offences including rape and unnatural offence. It is plain that the expression 'hurt', as defined in s 319 of the IPC includes causing of 'bodily pain, disease or infirmity' to any person. The offence of dowry death (s 304B) was added in 1986, along with the offence of cruelty by husband or relatives of husband (s 498A) in the wake of outrage felt by the civil society due to increased incidents of cases where women had been subjected to domestic violence and harassment soon after marriage.

The increase in the number of missing children in India and the need for a proper investigation in such cases of missing children, who due to their age and gender are more vulnerable to crimes, has become an alarming and a startling issue at the present time in India. A number of petitions have been filed before different High Courts in the country seeking formation of separate investigation cells for the search of missing children, involving officers having special knowledge and expertise in the matter. A news item appeared on 25 December 2011 in the *Indian Express* (*Chandigarh Newsline*) titled, '943 missing since 2000, no sign of 54 abducted'. The news item was based on the data furnished by the police department of the union territory of Chandigarh. The statistics reveal that 943 persons from Chandigarh have been missing since 2000 and 54 persons who have been kidnapped since 2000 are yet to be traced. It has become a prime concern for the entire country that certain guidelines and measures are laid down in order to trace the missing children and to prevent an increase in the number of children missing or abducted in future. Before doing so, it may be useful to quote relevant extracts from synopsis of the book entitled *Missing Children of India*,[1] a pioneering study by the Bachpan Bachao Andolan (BBA) which is a leading child rights organisation in New Delhi. This book was released in December 2011 by BBA. Furthermore, the National Human Rights Commission report on missing children[2] released in 2007 is also an authentic, detailed and wholesome study on the subject of missing children all over India. Both these studies are the basis of the present chapter to suggest remedies and solutions which can possibly be utilised and implemented as a measure for resolving this malady.

II   CRIMINAL OFFENCES AND PROCESS IN CRIMINAL MATTERS IN INDIA

The substantive law of crimes in India is contained in the Indian Penal Code (Act XLV of 1860) (IPC) which is governed by the procedure enacted in the Code of Criminal Procedure, 1973 (CrPC). Both are federal laws and apply uniformly throughout the territory of India.

Section 2(c) of the CrPC defines a 'cognizable offence' as an offence for which, and defines a 'cognizable case' as a case in which, a police officer may, in accordance with the First Schedule or under any other law for the time being in force, arrest without warrant.

Section 2(l) of the CrPC defines a 'non-cognizable offence' as an offence for which, and defines a 'non-cognizable case' as a case in which, a police officer has no authority to arrest without warrant.

An aggrieved person can approach a police station which falls in the jurisdiction of the area where the offence has been allegedly committed and can get his or her grievance recorded. The police are under a duty to record the complaint in the form of a Daily Diary Report (DDR).

(i)   If upon inquiry, the police are of the opinion that a cognisable offence is made out in terms of the Indian Penal Code or any other law in force in India, then the DDR can be converted to a First Information Report (hereinafter referred to as FIR) under s 154 of the CrPC. An FIR is recorded by the police officer on duty upon information given either by

---

[1]   Bachpan Bachao Andolan *Missing Children of India* (Delhi: Vitasta Publishing Pvt Ltd, 2011).
[2]   *Report of the NHRC Committee on Missing Children* (New Delhi: National Human Rights Commission, 2007).

the aggrieved person or any other person about the commission of an alleged offence and is followed by an investigation into the offence.

(ii) If, upon inquiry, the police are of the opinion that a non-cognisable offence is made out in terms of the IPC or any other law in force in India, then according to s 155 of the CrPC, the police officer shall enter or cause to be entered the substance of the information in a book to be kept by such officer in such form as may be prescribed by the state government from time to time (DDR). He shall then refer the informant to the magistrate.

(iii) According to s 155(2) of the CrPC, a police officer does not have the power to investigate a non-cognisable case without an order of a magistrate having power to try such a case or commit the case for trial.

Therefore, any person who is aggrieved on account of a criminal wrong having been committed against her or him on account of any offence having been made out in terms of the IPC or any other law in force in India has an option of making a grievance in three possible ways which are briefly explained here:

First, the aggrieved person can give the information relating to the commission of a cognisable/non-cognisable offence to an officer in charge of a police station as mentioned under ss 154 and 155 of the CrPC.

Section 154 of the CrPC is reproduced here for ready reference:

'154. Information in cognizable cases.

(1) Every information relating to the commission of a cognizable offence, if given orally to an officer in charge of a police station, shall be reduced to writing by him or under his direction, and be read over to the informant; and every such information, whether given in writing or reduced to writing as aforesaid, shall be signed by the person giving it, and the substance thereof shall be entered in a book to be kept by such officer in such form as the State Government may prescribe in this behalf.

(2) A copy of the information as recorded under sub-section (1) shall be given forthwith, free of cost, to the informant.

(3) Any person, aggrieved by a refusal on the part of an officer in charge of a police station to record the information referred to in sub-section (1) may send the substance of such information, in writing and by post, to the Superintendent of Police concerned who, if satisfied that such information discloses the commission of a cognizable offence, shall either investigate the case himself or direct an investigation to be made by any police officer subordinate to him, in the manner provided by this Code, and such officer shall have all the powers of an officer in charge of the police station in relation to that offence.'

Secondly, if a person has a grievance that the police station is not registering the FIR under s 154 of CrPC, then that person can approach the superintendent of police under s 154(3) of the CrPC by an application in writing as stated above.

Thirdly, if the FIR is not registered in any way as mentioned above, then it is open to the aggrieved person to file an application under s 156(3) of the CrPC before the magistrate concerned. If such an application under s 156(3) is filed, the magistrate can direct the FIR to be registered.

The Supreme Court of India in *Sakiri Vasu v State of UP* has ruled at p 908 as follows:[3]

> '... if a person has a grievance that the police station is not registering his FIR under Section 154, CrPC, then he can approach the Superintendent of Police under Section 154(3), CrPC, by an application in writing. Even if that does not yield any satisfactory result in the sense that either the FIR is still not registered, or that even after registering it no proper investigation is held, it is open to the aggrieved person to file an application under Section 156(3), CrPC before the learned Magistrate concerned. If such an application under Section 156(3) is filed before the Magistrate, the Magistrate can direct the FIR to be registered and also can direct a proper investigation to be made, in a case where, according to the aggrieved person, no proper investigation was made. The Magistrate can also under the same provision monitor the investigation to ensure a proper investigation.'

Once the FIR has been registered, the investigation in the case commences. Investigation includes all the proceedings of the collection of evidence conducted by a police officer or by any person who is authorised by the magistrate on his behalf.

Section 156 of the CrPC in this regard which gives the powers to the police to investigate the cognizable offences is reproduced here:

'156. Police officer's power to investigate cognizable cases

(1) Any officer in charge of a police station may, without the order of a Magistrate, investigate any cognizable case which a Court having jurisdiction over the local area within the limits of such station would have power to inquire into or try under the provisions of Chapter XIII.

(2) No proceeding of a police officer in any such case shall at any stage be called in question on the ground that the case was one which such officer was not empowered under this section to investigate.

(3) Any Magistrate empowered under section 190 may order such an investigation as above-mentioned.'

---

[3] *Sakiri Vasu v State of UP* All India Reporter 2008, 907 at 908, para 11.

According to the judgment of the Indian Supreme Court (above), even if after registering the FIR no proper investigation is conducted, it is open to the aggrieved person to file an application under s 156(3) of the CrPC before the magistrate concerned. If such an application under s 156(3) is filed before the magistrate, the magistrate can direct a proper investigation to be made. It may be added here that the magistrate can also under the same provision monitor the investigation to ensure a proper investigation.

The police while conducting the investigation of the case records the statements of the witnesses under s 161 of the CrPC. Section 157 of the CrPC casts a duty upon the investigating police officer to forthwith send the report of the cognisable offence, prepared under s 173 of the CrPC, to the concerned magistrate. The police officer is also under a duty to follow the procedure laid down in s 157 of the CrPC as follows:

'157. Procedure for investigation.

(1) If, from information received or otherwise, an officer in charge of a police station has reason to suspect the commission of an offence which he is empowered under section 156 to investigate, he shall forthwith send a report of the same to a Magistrate empowered to take cognizance of such offence upon a police report and shall proceed in person, or shall depute one of his subordinate officers not being below such rank as the State Government may, by general or special order, prescribe in this behalf, to proceed, to the spot, to investigate the facts and circumstances of the case, and, if necessary, to take measures for the discovery and arrest of the offender:

Provided that–

(a) when information as to the commission of any such offence is given against any person by name and the case is not of a serious nature, the officer in charge of a police station need not proceed in person or depute a subordinate officer to make an investigation on the spot;

(b) if it appears to the officer in charge of a police station that there is no sufficient ground for entering on an investigation, he shall not investigate the case.

(2) In each of the cases mentioned in clauses (a) and (b) of the proviso to sub-section (1), the officer in charge of the police station shall state in his report his reasons for not fully complying with the requirements to that sub-section, and, in the case mentioned in clause (b) of the said proviso, the officer shall also forthwith notify to the informant, if any, in such manner as may be prescribed by the State Government, the fact that he will not investigate the case or cause it to be investigated.'

Thereupon, after all the evidence has been collected by the police, a report (called 'Challan') is filed in the court before a competent magistrate and thereafter, as prescribed in the CrPC, charges are framed by the court against the accused under s 211 of the CrPC. The court under s 211 of the CrPC has the power to alter the charges at any time during the trial but before the judgment.

Besides the procedural provisions quoted above, s 482 of the CrPC is also reproduced for ready reference:

'482. Saving of inherent power of High Court

Nothing in this Code shall be deemed to limit or affect the inherent powers of the High Court to make such orders as may be necessary to give effect to any order under this Code, or to prevent abuse of the process of any Court or otherwise to secure the ends of justice.'

It may be commented that, if there is any lacuna in the criminal process or there is failure to comply with the provisions of law or there is any apprehension to any party in any criminal litigation of any threat to life or personal liberty, the person can invoke the jurisdiction of the High Court directly in a petition under s 482 of the CrPC for seeking appropriate orders to secure the ends of justice.

III   EXTRACT FROM BACHPAN BACHAO ANDOLAN'S SYNOPSIS OF THE BOOK TITLED *MISSING CHILDREN OF INDIA* (2011)

The book *Missing Children of India*[4] is a compilation of information collected on missing children by Bachpan Bachao Andolan during the period from January 2008 to January 2010. This book gives the following findings and figures which are extracted for ready reference.

'The recent official figures (of Census 2011) related to children are yet to be published, but, figures regarding missing children (as per RTI[5] applications) show that 117,480 children were reported missing, 74,209 were traced and 41,546 remained untraced in two years between 2008 and 2010.'

A tabulated extract of the numbers of missing children state/union territory wise in the country for the period January 2008 to January 2010 follows:

---

[4]   Above n 1.
[5]   RTI stands for Right to Information under the Right to Information Act 2005.

Status of missing children (national)

Jan 2008–Jan 2010

S No	State/UTs	Re-ported	Traced	Un-traced	NCRB[6] (200820010)
1	A&N	115	112	3	22
2	Andhra Pradesh	3,555	2,939	616	1,146
3	Arunachal Pradesh	243	152	91	30
4	Assam	2,686	551	410	12
5	Bihar	3,345	1,752	1,593	1,321
6	Chandigarh	156	116	40	63
7	Chhatisgarh	5,594	4,252	1342	226
8	Dadra & Nagar Haveli	48	39	9	19
9	Delhi	13,570	11,870	1,700	3,459
10	Goa	238	206	32	45
11	Haryana	185	146	39	253
12	HP	113	72	41	158
13	Jharkhand	320	178	142	45
14	Karnataka	9,956	6,522	3,434	175
15	Kerala	2116	1900	216	197
16	MP	12,777	9,537	3,240	713
17	Maharashtra	26,211	18,706	7,505	1,244
18	Meghalaya	178	112	66	33
19	Mizoram	0	0	0	3
20	Nagaland	457	226	231	3
21	Sikkim	342	279	63	9
22	UP	9,482	7,586	1,896	3,759
23	Uttarakhand	380	303	77	36
24	W Bengal	25,413	6,653	18,760	583
	TOTAL	117,480	74,209	41,546	13,554

---

[6]   National Crimes Record Bureau.

In the synopsis of the book, the following findings have been attributed to the large number of missing children:

'Findings:

Some of the most significant findings of this study are:

- No clear-cut definition of missing children as per legal system, which leads to confusion as to how the cases should be treated.
- No provision on addressing the issue of missing children in the Indian legal system.
- No comprehensive SOPs/Protocol for addressing the issue of missing children at the national level, involving all states/UTs and other stakeholders.
- No proper mechanism to document and update the database and information on the number of registered, traced and untraced cases of missing children.
- Lack of coordination between the agencies dealing with the missing children for example police, NCRB/SCRB/DCRB and NGOs/CSOs.
- Urban centres have high number of children reported missing.
- Areas with better connectivity and facility of transport and communications have high number of missing children.
- States and districts with international borders also have large number of children registered missing.
- Regions with migratory population, including slums, are registering more missing children.
- Children and families from socially and economically poorer background formed the majority of victims.'[7]

In the light of the findings given in the book, Bachpan Bachao Andolan has made its recommendations and suggests a plan of action that needs to be followed in order to deal with the disturbing issue of the rise in the cases of the missing children all over the country.

IV   EXTRACT FROM THE NHRC REPORT (2007)

It is further pertinent to analyse the approximate number of missing children complaints that are increasing over the years. For this purpose, the National Human Rights Commission (NHRC) Report[8] may be the most relevant document. The NHRC was constituted in India under the protection of Human Rights Act, 1993, for better protection of human rights and for matters connected therewith or incidental thereto. The NHRC Report is based on an

---

[7]   Abbreviations used: SOP – Standing Operating Procedure, NCRB – National Crime Records Bureau, SCRB – State Crime Records Bureau, DCRB – District Crime Records Bureau, NGOs – Non-Government Organisations, CSOs – Civil Society Organisations.

[8]   Above n 2.

exhaustive study on the subject of missing children in India. For purposes of ready reference, an extract from Executive Summary of the NHRC Report follows:[9]

'India is home to more than 400 million children below the age of 18 years, and is considered one of the countries in which youth and children comprise more than 55% of the population. These children represent diverse cultures, religions, castes, communities & social and economic groups. The Government is undoubtedly committed to doing its best for children. However, despite its best efforts, there are innumerable children who are subjected to exploitation and atrocities of various kinds. Moreover, countless children go "missing" every year. These cases of missing children represent a conglomeration of a number of problems, including abductions/kidnappings by family members, abductions/kidnappings carried out by non-family members or strangers, children who run away on their own or are forced to run away due to compelling circumstances in their families and extended surroundings, children who face unfriendly and hostile environment and are asked to leave home or who are abandoned, children who are trafficked or smuggled or exploited for various purposes, and children who are lost or injured. Undoubtedly, each of these groups of children exemplifies different social problems. Since, as a group, missing children – are so heterogeneous, there is no adequate data or consistently applied set of definitions to describe them. In addition, many cases of missing children are not reported to the police at all for various reasons, and police involvement in the resolution of different kinds of cases varies widely across the country. All this poses a serious problem. The NHRC Action Research on Trafficking, published by Orient Longman in 2005, has shown that in any given year, an average of 44000 children are reported missing; of them, as many as 11000 remain untraced.

The revelations at Nithari exemplify that missing children may end up in a variety of places and situations – killed and buried in a neighbour's backyard, working as cheap forced labour in illegal factories/establishments/homes, exploited as sex slaves or forced into the child porn industry, as camel jockeys in the Gulf countries, as child beggars in begging rackets, as victims of illegal adoptions or forced marriages, or perhaps worse than any of these as victims of organ trade and even grotesque cannibalism as reported at Nithari.

The Committee observed that there are some studies conducted by both governmental and non-governmental organizations which bear testimony to the fact that a large number of girls and boys who run away from their homes or are said to have run away from their homes are mainly school dropouts or children get fed up with domestic conditions. The glamour and lure of big cities often make them blind to the stark realities of urban life. Being vulnerable, they often fall prey to promises of jobs or careers in films or modeling and eventually end up as sex workers or as domestic help/labourers in homes, small hotels/restaurants, tea shops/stalls and unorganized establishments, many of them hazardous. Many of the run away boys and girls become victims of the organized begging rackets or pickpocketing/drug peddling racket etc. Most of these children are also trafficked and further abused, physically or sexually, and their cases are not even brought to

---

[9]   Above n 2, 9–12 (from chapter 2 entitled 'Situational Analysis of Missing Children in India').

the knowledge of the police. Many of these children come from indigent families who either do not have access to authorities or whose complaints are not treated with due diligence.

The Action Research Study on Trafficking by NHRC has brought out several case studies to establish this linkage between "trafficking" and "persons reported missing".

The Committee observed that the juvenile justice system too has failed to provide due care and protection to children. Despite the specific provisions made in the Juvenile Justice (Care and Protection of Children) Act, 2000, many State Governments/Union Territories are yet to frame Rules under the principal Act. In a majority of places, Special Juvenile Police Units had not been set up. All this has eroded the confidence of the people in the system.

When a child goes missing, nobody, except the perpetrator, knows the real intent behind it. It could be quite possible that the child for various reasons has run away on his or her own from home, a relative's home, or an institution which the child's parents/caretakers construe as "missing". On the other hand, it is also possible that the child may have gone missing from the scene for a different reason altogether, which could be sexual gratification, sexual exploitation, labour exploitation, profit-making, or personal vengeance etc. In these cases the person(s) directly or indirectly involved in the incident may resort to crimes of various kinds ranging from kidnapping, abduction, grievous hurt, assault, rape, unnatural offences, and even murder of the child. In fact, even a child who has run away on purpose is also susceptible to being kidnapped, abducted, abused or assaulted. This raises the question as to why reports of missing children are not treated as cognizable offence.'

Later the Report states:[10]

'The NCRB, under the TALASH Information System, maintains a national level database of missing persons under the following broad categories – "missing", "kidnapped", "arrested", "deserted", "escaped", "proclaimed offender", "wanted", "unidentified dead body", "unidentified person" and "traced/found". Earlier, data on missing children under the broad category of "missing" was not available. However, this is now available for both the sexes under the age group 0–12 and 13–18. The NCRB, by and large, functions as a "Documentation Centre" or at best a "Transfer Desk"' because as of today the NCRB neither investigates, nor does it monitor or facilitates the recovery of missing children as a pro-active organization. The Police Stations, too, generally do not give any feed back to the NCRB when the missing child is rescued, traced or returned. Hence the data lacks accuracy. Thus, despite being the national repository of "crime data", the NCRB is unaware both of children who are traced or of those who remain untraced.

Interestingly enough, though the category of missing children has come to be reflected in the TALASH Information System, there is no mention or analysis of it to date in the Crime in India Report being published by the NCRB. This is in spite of the fact that Chapter Six therein titled "Crime Against Children" categorically

---

[10]   Ibid 13–15.

affirms that "Generally, the offences committed against children or the crimes in which children are the victims are considered as Crime Against Children". It then goes on to highlight crimes committed against children that are punishable under the Indian Penal Code 1860 and crimes committed against children that are punishable under the Special and Local Laws.

As per the latest Crime in India Report – 2005, a total of 14,975 cases of crimes against children were reported in the country during 2005 as compared to 14,423 cases during 2004, signifying an increase of 3.8 per cent. The highest crime rate was reported from Delhi (6.5) followed by Chandigarh (5.7) and Madhya Pradesh (5.6) as compared to the national average of 1.4. A total of 4026 cases of child rape were reported in the country during 2005 as compared to 3542 in 2004 accounting for a significant increase of 13.7 % during the year. The State of Madhya Pradesh reported the highest number of cases (870) followed by Maharashtra (634). These two States together accounted for 37.3% of the total child rape cases reported in the country. Highlighting cases related to kidnapping and abduction, the Report mentions that a total of 3518 cases were reported during the year as compared to 3196 cases reported in the previous year accounting for an increase of 10.1%. Delhi reported the highest percentage of such cases among children up to 15 years. The analysis of data clearly reveals the increase of number of crimes against children in the country.

The aforesaid data reveals the predicament of missing children in many ways. Apart from the NCRB, there are some regional police websites like the Zonal Integrated Police Network (ZIPNET) and a few State police websites, which provide data on missing persons, including data on missing children. But the information provided therein remains largely incomplete. Since awareness about these databases – particularly, among police personnel – is low, it has not drawn adequate attention in the investigation and tracing of missing children.'

From a reading of these extracts, it transpires that thousands of cases are registered in various police stations regarding children and adults who go missing every year in India. The list of reasons for which such children are kidnapped is unending. Children and women specifically are the worst sufferers of such situations where they are either forced into begging or prostitution. It is in the context of seeking the proper investigation of such cases of missing children reported all over India that the following suggestions are mooted.

V   SUGGESTIONS IN THE EXISTING FRAMEWORK OF INDIAN LAWS

(a)   Suggestions for tracing missing children and preventing future incidents in India

The suggestions given here are based on the 2011 report of the BBA, the 2007 report of the NHRC and the guidelines given by the Supreme Court in *Horilal v Commissioner of Police, Delhi and others*,[11] as well as a study of subsequent judgments of different High Courts in India on the subject of tracing missing children. Accordingly, the following suggestions can take the shape of guidelines in order to trace the missing children effectively in a lesser period of time. These suggestions are a compilation of the collective study of all the above reports on the subject with our various independent inputs. The guidelines are laid down in the following steps:

(i)   Compulsory registration and investigation of all cases of missing children

The first and the foremost step with a view to starting the investigation and to moving a step closer to finding the missing child is the prompt and compulsory registration of the case with the police. The earlier the case gets reported/registered and the police start their investigation, the better the chances that the missing child is located in a short period of time. Police have to promptly and compulsorily register the case of missing children and initiate actions on all fronts to trace the missing child. A centralised system is to be established by which any one aggrieved by non-registration at the police station can, through this centralised system, forward their petition to senior police officers for appropriate intervention. An acknowledgement has to be provided to the aggrieved person. Once the case gets registered and the investigation starts soon after the crime is committed, it is possible that the missing child is found before being removed from the territorial limits of India or any state within the territory of India.

(ii)   Immediate action to be taken to secure any evidence that might be of help

Immediate action is to be taken to secure evidence necessary to compare and conclusively establish the identity of the missing child through DNA/DMA analysis, in case only the mortal remains of the missing person were to be located. This would aid and assist in establishing the identity of the missing child as well as giving suitable clues to detect the identity of persons responsible for abduction if the missing child has been kidnapped or removed by force.

Subjecting the suspects to further narco-analysis may be of further help in eliciting finer details pertaining to the revelations already made and the activities that took place at the alleged time of disappearance so that the field verification of the revelations made is possible. Subjecting some key witnesses also to narco-analysis will help in checking and verifying their statements made earlier to the police.

---

[11]   *Horilal v Commissioner of Police, Delhi and others* Writ Petition (Criminal) No 610 of 1996, decided on 14 November 2002.

(iii)   Speeding up the investigation

A senior police officer in every state in India has to be entrusted with the investigation. Regular reviews at periodic intervals with respect to the progress should be taken by the police officers in the state. The officer should also get the details with regard to pending cases of children missing and in identifying dead bodies. Special squads if needed should be appointed to pursue further investigation. The state should issue strict instructions directing all police officers to treat matters of missing children as high priority cases.

Further, police investigation cells can be made in the police stations in a state to look immediately into the matters of missing children. The cells, however, should have an adequate number of police officials to work on a case immediately and the police officials included in the police investigation cell should be qualified to do the job successfully. Introduction of these special cells will speed up the investigation process considering the fact that the team of such officers will look only into the matter of missing children and with time and experience will get better in the field.

(iv)   Setting up a police information network or a national database for quick information on missing children in India

It is very important that the present methods of collecting information about missing children be modified by way of a centralised network in India. It is necessary that the network is web-enabled, maintained and most importantly updated. A national tracking system that would encompass the grass roots in locating and tracing missing children should be introduced. There should be prompt reporting of not only missing children cases, but also return, rescue or recovery. All instances where children are rescued from places of exploitation including places of sexual exploitation and also exploitative labour should be updated in the national database. The database should be updated on a regular and systematic basis. This would help the investigating authorities to know the complete details of the children missing and those found, and keep themselves updated on the pending cases as well. The details of previous missing children and the places and the way they were found would help the authorities to track the culprit very soon in the future.

The government of India should establish a centre for such missing children at the national level. The centre if established should be the repository of all the data on the missing children including the collection, analysis, interpretation and documentation of data. However, it is very important that the centre for missing children is adopted and implemented by the government of India without any delay.

Another step that might be taken is to have a separate website for all the state police authorities like the Delhi Police web-based Zipnet programme to upload all the details of the cases regarding missing children and to update it with the latest details on the case to help the family of the missing children to know more about the case.

(v) Improvement in the mechanism of publishing details of missing children and the role of media

Publication of look-out notices in local dailies, TV and cable networks including private TV channels/Doordarshan government programme, vernacular newspapers and other electronic media agencies needs to be devised. Improved arrangements are required to instantly communicate the disseminated details of missing children to important hospitals, mortuaries, all police stations, outposts, entry and exit points in every state to help them to correlate and give feedback of any information of relevance in tracing the missing child. Such details should also be made available to officials in charge of temples, churches, mosques, marriage registration offices as well as hospitals etc automatically, with photographs of missing children for any useful feedback and intervention as required.

In view of the current alarming situation, the media can play an important role in increasing public awareness of missing children and the plight of the thousands of hapless families whose family members/children are listed as untraced. This could be achieved by taking the following steps:

(a) At the newsroom level, crime reporters and metro editors need to include the category of missing children as a regular beat and as part of their daily news grind. Regular follow-up news reports and look-out notices in the media would help a lot.

(b) These stories need to be followed up and tracked regularly just like other stories of murder, human trafficking, abduction and kidnapping.

(c) Newspapers can make a separate section in their classified sections on missing children. The notices and advertisements on missing children need to have a better display and be given more prominence and space in newspapers and TV bulletins. TV channels should have a repetitive telecast on missing children details.

The above suggested measures will help to a great extent to create awareness among the citizens of India and also to be careful and cautious and help prevention of any further increase in the number of missing children.

(vi) Speedy communication of information by the police personnel

One of the important aspects of a police investigation in such cases is communication of the crime to other states or places where the missing children are likely to be taken and further to communicate important messages during the continuation of the investigation. However, the communication between police personnel in India is not very prompt resulting in losing the chances of finding the missing children. Therefore, it is very important that the communication techniques between police personnel for transfer of important information are modified. Police personnel should be able to communicate and pass on information promptly. It is suggested that e-communications and Skype contact must be promoted for use by state police and police personnel must be educated/updated with using latest technology communication methods for tracing missing children. This would greatly facilitate faster communication by the police forces in India.

(vii) Collection of forensic evidence for establishing identity of unidentified dead bodies

No unidentified dead body should be permitted to be disposed of without ensuring collection of all possible evidence that will enable conclusive identity to be established by comparison of necessary forensic samples. A mandate must be issued to all police stations not to cremate the body of any missing/unclaimed child/person till a conclusive effort has been made to consolidate all evidence necessary which may lead to establishing the identity of the missing unclaimed child's remains.

Finger and palm prints, DNA comparison and skull superimposition techniques are being used now to conclusively establish the identity of a person. Since these techniques require some control samples for the purpose of comparison, immediately after a person goes missing, it is necessary to arrange for collection and preservation of control samples of the finger/palm print, DNA specimen, good photographs of the face, etc of the missing person. Some of these can be collected from the already available personal effects or through samples taken from parents, siblings etc.

The photograph of an unidentified dead body should be taken in such a manner that it assists in identification of facial features, personal items, any personal identification marks, shoes, watches, jewellery, tattoo marks, finger prints/palm print, DNA finger print, etc. Dental records must be preserved to establish the identity.

(viii) Introduction of a child tracking system

Children who go missing are likely to be unwary victims of exploitation and trafficking. A child tracking system should be part of the national database to prevent trafficking and exploitation of the person missing. It is extremely important that both at state and central level a missing children database should be established which facilitates countrywide exchange of information for locating/tracing missing children. Compilation of data of missing children and the mode/methods utilised for their location and search will help to resolve future cases of missing children and aid in the compilation of statistics for future reference. Exchange of data state-wide will greatly help police authorities to resolve cases of missing children.

(ix)   Public co-operation

Police help centres should be established in the jurisdiction of all the police stations in a state or union territory (UT) as well as in public places such as malls, public amusement places, bus stations, railway stations, etc so that the information on the missing children and unnatural and unidentified bodies may be disseminated to the public for possible clues or information exchange. These centres should be integrated with closed circuit television systems to be put at all public places covering the ports of entry/exit, malls, prominent public amusement places, eateries, etc to facilitate public-spirited persons to assist the police in tracing missing persons.

(b)   Further suggestions to help in prevention of abduction, kidnapping and forcible removal of children in future

(i)   Necessity of defining the term 'missing children'

Defining a 'missing child' is very important to help investigating agencies to deal with the problem. It is important to have a clear mandate on definitions of 'human trafficking' and 'missing children'. The reason for the need of a clear and specific definition lies in the fact that, because the term 'missing children' is not specifically defined in Indian penal laws, many cases are not registered by the police authorities in the state claiming that the matter is not of a 'missing child'. The special operating procedure developed by the Delhi Police has defined a missing child in the following words:

> 'A child (a person who is below 18 years of the age) whose whereabouts are not known to the parents, legal guardians or any other person who may be legally entrusted with knowing whereabouts/well being of the child whatever may be the circumstances/causes of disappearance. The child in need of care and protection will be considered missing until located and/or his/her safety/well-being is established.'

Once, the term 'missing persons' is defined exhaustively, it will be much easier for the family members of such a child to get the case registered and the investigation can be started at the earliest without any ambiguity or uncertainty.

(ii)   Missing children squad or children's desk in police stations

Creation of a skilled investigation and rapid response squad on missing children is a necessity. One of the recommendations is that every police station across the respective states should have a special squad/missing persons desk to trace missing children. This squad/desk should have a registering officer who should be made responsible for registering complaints of missing children. The officer should maintain complete records of efforts made by them to trace missing children as well as by the special squad. The registering officer should also work as an enquiry officer, responsible for following up the entire procedure of tracing/tracking the missing child. The squad should also be regularly updated with the small details they have about the missing persons so that the families of the missing persons are well aware of the steps being taken by the authorities in finding their lost family members. The records should also be updated with the information of the missing persons who have been traced and returned back to their respective families at least in the past 6 months.

(iii)   Involving Panchayati Raj Institutions (PRIs) (village bodies) etc

In order to make the investigative procedures concerning missing children more transparent and user-friendly, it would be preferable for the police investigating team to involve the community at large, such as representatives of Panchayati Raj Institutions (village level bodies), municipal committees, neighbourhood committees, resident welfare associations, in addition to existing helplines. This will enable the community to get fully involved along with the police in tracing missing children and also if these institutions at a lower level are involved, it is easy to pass on the information of the missing children to more and more people making the search of such children or adults easier and faster. The Director-General of Police (DGP) in every state and UT in India should seriously consider taking full advantage of these agencies in the task of not only investigating crimes relating to children but also tracking down missing children. The role of Panchayats and such bodies should be extended to:

- prompt reporting of missing children;

- prompt dissemination of intelligence, if any, to the law enforcement agencies;

- rendering assistance to law enforcement agencies for tracing children;

- provide timely feedback to the law enforcement agencies about the return of the child.

This would not only help in finding missing children whose complaints have been registered but, because of the involvement of the agencies at a lower level, also help people in villages and the surrounding areas to report more cases of missing children, making them more aware in their daily lives and thus preventing the increase of crime at such a fast rate.

(iv)   Involving non-government organisations (NGOs)/state legal services authorities and setting up of advisory boards

In places where vulnerable groups of children are found in large numbers, there is need for enforcement agencies to evolve some kind of a mechanism in partnership with non-governmental organisations and social workers, whereby apart from rendering counselling to them, awareness raising activities are also carried out. The involvement of the state legal services authority and its district level units can be extremely useful in this regard. This would not only instil confidence in the general public but also empower people and give them special protection so that they are in no way lured by external agencies/factors. This initiative could be taken by the missing children squad/cell in the districts. The DGPs need to ensure action on this initiative of public–private partnership.

Each state government in India should set up an advisory body including all government departments concerned as well as appropriate NGOs working in the field of missing children, trafficked children, child labour, etc. The body should be given statutory powers to ensure monitoring of the enforcement of child welfare legislative provisions.

(v) Establishing helplines

There is a need to establish a child helpline through NGOs and other agencies with adequate support from the government in all districts in India. The Department of Women and Child Development, Government of India, may take the initiative to set up such a national network. Such a helpline helps in immediate registration or providing the police with the information of missing children immediately, thereby improving the chances of finding the missing children or persons sooner.

(vi) Importance of registration of the cases of 'missing children' as a cognisable offence

It should be made mandatory for the police to promptly register without any delay all complaints of missing children as a First Information Report (FIR). At the moment the issue of missing children is not a cognisable offence and the very fact that a child is missing does not convey occurrence of a crime. However, some states like Andhra Pradesh, Tamil Nadu and New Delhi allow police to register FIRs and take up investigation. In order to facilitate proper enquiry/investigation, it is advisable that a FIR is registered by the police with respect to the issue of missing children at the very inception without awaiting initial police preliminary inquiries. However, experience shows that in many cases a child may not have gone missing and the panic reaction of the parents or wards leads to such reporting. Therefore, all such issues may not warrant registration of an FIR immediately. Nevertheless, it is advisable to register a FIR if a missing child does not come back or is not traced within a reasonable time. State governments are advised to consider the issue of appropriate directions to law enforcement agencies to set a time-limit of 15 days from the date of reporting, that if a missing child is not traced back within that time, a presumption may be made of some mala fides and a FIR must be registered with respect to all such issues of missing children. Filing of a FIR greatly assists in finding missing children in a country like India, where the population is large and the criminal rate is very high. Registering a FIR makes it incumbent on the police authorities to look into the matter and they become responsible to the family of the missing child or person, thereby leading to good chances of finding the missing children or persons.

(vii)   Mandatory intimation of missing children FIRs to state legal services authorities

It should be mandatory for police authorities in all states and UTs in India to forward both by e-mail and by post a copy of each FIR registered with regard to missing children to the respective state legal services authority or its district level chapters. In turn the legal services authority should provide all possible legal aid to parents and families of missing children and act as an interface between the parents of the missing children and the police authorities. This will help in keeping a vigil on any large scale kidnapping by organised gangs and provide a monitoring avenue whereby the police authorities can be asked to give regular feedback on the FIR so lodged.

(viii)   Attention to transit points of trafficking

There is a need to keep special vigils at railway stations, bus stands, airports, seaports and such other places, which act as transit points for missing children, including children who run away or are made to run away. In this context, the government railway police, the Railway Protection Force, airport and seaport authorities need to be oriented about the issue of missing children. It is important that, as soon as the information about a missing child or person is received, authorities and police posts at all the nearest airports, railway stations, bus stands and seaports are informed about them and photographs/details are displayed at such places.

(ix)   Nodal officers

Nodal officers on missing children in every district should be appointed. The officer should be notified by the respective state governments and should be made accountable to take all steps to trace/give care and protection to the missing child. Adequate legal administrative and financial support should be provided by the state government. The family members of the missing child would have another option to get the complaint registered if it is refused by the police officers.

(x)   Cross-border missing children

This is a grey area, which largely remains unaddressed. It has been reported that several foreign children who have been trafficked into India have been punished as illegal immigrants and are made to suffer. In this regard the National Human Rights Commission (NHRC) has already recommended that state governments undertake a review of all such cases and provide relief to such children, as all trafficked children, irrespective of their nationality, are children in need of care and attention. Moreover, there is a need of developing a protocol on this issue. It is learnt that United Nations Office on Drugs and Crime (UNODC) in its anti-human trafficking project can provide the required technical assistance. In this regard the Ministry of Women and Child Development can utilise the technical assistance of UNODC and, in close coordination with the Ministry of External Affairs (MEA), develop a protocol on this topic.

(xi)   Interparental child abduction issues

Interparental child removal both within India and across international borders (both inbound and outbound) is a common phenomenon today. Parental child removal is neither defined in any law as an offence nor is it taken cognisance of by the police unless there is court intervention. India is not a signatory to the Hague Convention on Civil Aspects of International Child Abduction, 1980 and children forcibly brought to India or taken out of India by estranged parents do not fall within the ambit of any penal law. This grey area seriously needs legislation. Until that is done, the state/district legal services authorities and/or the mediation cells at the High Court/District Court levels must be associated or involved by police authorities and the courts to whom these matters get reported. Alternative dispute resolution and mediation in such cases can play a major role in the return of children to the place/country of their habitual and permanent residence. Return of children, their forcible removal and/or abduction by parents must be stopped forthwith.

(xii)   Procedure after return of the child

The duty of the police authorities should not end with the child returning back home. Rather, whenever a missing child is traced or comes back on his or her own, the police or investigating officer should make sure that all relevant angles such as involvement of organised gangs, application of provisions of Bonded Labour Act and such other relevant Acts applicable in India are looked into as probable causes of the child going missing.

If the involvement of an organised gang is found, it is the responsibility of the police or investigating officer to refer the matter to the Crime Branch of the respective state police or the special cell constituted by the Central Bureau of Investigation (CBI) in this regard to prevent future recurrence.

(xiii)   Comprehensive plan for the rehabilitation of the missing child

Another very important step that should be kept in mind once the missing child comes back to the family or is found by the police is their rehabilitation. So, to achieve this purpose it is important that the government of India or of the respective state takes steps for creation of a comprehensive plan for rehabilitation of the rescued children who need rehabilitation or any other assistance to come back to the mainstream of life.

Hence, the above-mentioned steps for protection and prevention of cases of missing children in future, and for tracing the already missing minor children all over the country, if followed diligently, can help solve the problem of kidnapping and abduction of innocent minor children. It is further stated that, if the guidelines are strictly looked into and followed by the concerned state departments, it can be an important step in saving lives of many children in the future.

VI   SUGGESTIONS IN THE ALTERNATIVE FRAMEWORK – THE COMMISSION FOR PROTECTION OF CHILD RIGHTS ACT, 2005

(a)   Introduction

Besides the above steps that can be taken in the framework of existing statutory laws, another suggestion can be mooted within the framework of the Commission for Protection of Child Rights Act, 2005 (CPCRA). In this context, it is relevant to quote the Preamble of the CPCRA:

> 'An Act to provide for the constitution of a National Commission and State Commissions for Protection of Child Rights and Children's Courts for providing speedy trial of offences against children or of violation of child rights and for matters connected therewith or incidental thereto.
>
> WHEREAS India participated in the United Nations (UN) General Assembly Summit in 1990, which adopted a Declaration on Survival, Protection and Development of Children;
>
> AND WHEREAS India has also acceded to the Convention on the Rights of the Child (CRC) on the 11th December, 1992;
>
> AND WHEREAS CRC is an international treaty that makes it incumbent upon the signatory States to take all necessary steps to protect children's rights enumerated in the Convention;
>
> AND WHEREAS in order to ensure protection of rights of children one of the recent initiatives that the Government have taken for Children is the adoption of National Charter for Children, 2003;
>
> AND WHEREAS the UN General Assembly Special Session on Children held in May, 2002 adopted an Outcome Document titled "A World Fit for Children" containing the goals, objectives, strategies and activities to be undertaken by the member countries for the current decade;
>
> AND WHEREAS it is expedient to enact a law relating to children to give effect to the policies adopted by the Government in this regard, standards prescribed in the CRC, and all other relevant international instruments.'

(b)   Sections 13, 17, 24, 25 and 26 of the CPCRA.

It may now be useful to quote ss 13, 17, 24, 25 and 26 of the CPCRA which are extracted for ready reference.

'13. Functions of Commission.

(1) The Commission shall perform all or any of the following functions, namely:–

(a)   examine and review the safeguards provided by or under any law for the time being in force for the protection of child rights and recommend measures for their effective implementation;

(b)   present to the Central Government, annually and at such other intervals, as the Commission may deem fit, reports upon the working of those safeguards;

(c)   inquire into violation of child rights and recommend initiation of proceedings in such cases;

(d)   examine all factors that inhibit the enjoyment of rights of children affected by terrorism, communal violence, riots, natural disaster, domestic violence, HIV/AIDS, trafficking, maltreatment, torture and exploitation, pornography and prostitution and recommend appropriate remedial measures;

(e)   look into the matters relating to children in need of special care and protection including children in distress, marginalized and disadvantaged children, children in conflict with law, juveniles, children without family and children of prisoners and recommend appropriate remedial measures;

(f)   study treaties and other international instruments and undertake periodical review of existing policies, programmes and other activities on child rights and make recommendations for their effective implementation in the best interest of children;

(g)   undertake and promote research in the field of child rights;

(h)   spread child rights literacy among various sections of the society and promote awareness of the safeguards available for protection of these rights through publications, the media, seminars and other available means;

(i)   inspect or cause to be inspected any juvenile custodial home, or any other place of residence or institution meant for children, under the control of the Central Government or any State Government or any other authority, including any institution run by a social organisation; where children are detained or lodged for the purpose of treatment, reformation or protection and take up with these authorities for remedial action, if found necessary;

(j)   inquire into complaints and take suo motu notice of matters relating to,–
   (i)   deprivation and violation of child rights;
   (ii)   non-implementation of laws providing for protection and development of children;
   (iii)   non-compliance of policy decisions, guidelines or instructions aimed at mitigating hardships to and ensuring welfare of the children and to provide relief to such children, or take up the issues arising out of such matters with appropriate authorities; and

(k)   such other functions as it may consider necessary for the promotion of child rights and any other matter incidental to the above functions.

(2) The Commission shall not inquire into any matter which is pending before a State Commission or any other Commission duly constituted under any law for the time being in force.'

'17. Constitution of State Commission for Protection of Child Rights.

(1) A State Government may constitute a body to be known as the (name of the State) Commission for Protection of Child Rights to exercise the powers conferred upon, and to perform the functions assigned to, a State Commission under this Chapter.

(2) The State Commission shall consist of the following Members, namely: –

(a)   a Chairperson who is a person of eminence and has done outstanding work for promoting the welfare of children; and
(b)   six Members, out of which at least two shall be women, from the following fields, to be appointed by the State Government from amongst persons of eminence, ability, integrity, standing and experience in,–
    (i)   education;
    (ii)   child health, care, welfare or child development;
    (iii)   juvenile justice or care of neglected or marginalized children or children with disabilities;
    (iv)   elimination of child labour or children in distress;
    (v)   child psychology or sociology; and
    (vi)   laws relating to children.

(3) The headquarter of the State Commission shall be at such place as the State Government may, by notification, specify.'

'24. Application of certain provisions relating to National Commission for Protection of Child Rights to State Commissions.

The provisions of sections 7, 8, 9, 10, sub-section (1) of section 13 and sections 14 and 15 shall apply to a State Commission and shall have effect, subject to the following modifications, namely:–

(a)   references to "Commission" shall be construed as references to "State Commission";
(b)   references to "Central Government" shall be construed as references to "State Government"; and
(c)   references to "Member-Secretary" shall be construed as references to "Secretary".

25. Children's Courts.

For the purpose of providing speedy trial of offences against children or of violation of child rights, the State Government may, with the concurrence of the Chief Justice of the High Court, by notification, specify at least a court in the State or specify, for each district, a Court of Session to be a Children's Court to try the said offences:

Provided that nothing in this section shall apply if –

(a)   a Court of Session is already specified as a special court; or
(b)   a special court is already constituted,

for such offences under any other law for the time being in force.

26. Special Public Prosecutor.

For every Children's Court, the State Government shall, by notification, specify a Public Prosecutor or appoint an advocate who has been in practice as an advocate for not less than seven years, as a Special Public Prosecutor for the purpose of conducting cases in that Court.'

(c)   Suggested measures under CPCRA

In the light of the above provisions of the CPCRA, it is incumbent on governments of all states and UTs of the country to take all necessary steps to protect children's rights enumerated in the Convention on the Rights of the Child (CRC). Sections 13 and 24 of the CPCRA provide ample powers both to the national commission and the state commissions for inter alia taking necessary steps and recommending appropriate remedial measures with regard to issues pertaining to missing children and all children in distress. These can be enforced in all states and UTs by setting up and/or constituting state commissions for protection of child rights under s 17 of the CPCRA in the respective territories of the individual governments. Hence, as a starting point, states and UTs should forthwith set up such state commissions so that the entire machinery can be galvanised under their regime.

It is suggested that any averment by state or UT governments against setting up state commissions for protection of child rights in their territories should not be entertained due to the sensitivity and magnitude of the problems relating to missing children. This is supported by the following contentions. A news report in the *English Tribune* dated 29 December 2011, quoting the Bureau of Police Research and Development (BPRD) of the Union Home Ministry which organised a workshop to study the problem of disappearance of children in the northern states showed the concern in this matter. The news report quotes that over 200 of the 800 missing persons in Haryana in the last 6 months are minors. 72 of these 200 missing children are girls, which indicates the direct bearing on the safety of children. Likewise, a news report in *The Pioneer* dated 3 October 2010 indicates that:

'Child protection continues to be the last priority of the city administration. Even after the recent study of the UT Health Department, which stated that child abuse is rampant in the city of Chandigarh, the Chandigarh Administration continues to overlook the need to implement the Integrated Child Protection Scheme (ICPS) here.'

Hence, all states and UTs in India need to set up state commissions as a priority.

To complete the setting up of a fully operational system under the CPCRA, children's courts can be constituted in the said respective territories under s 25 of the CPCRA and special public prosecutors can be appointed in these territories under s 26 of the CPCRA. Thus, independent of other statutory enactments dealing with criminal laws or other penal provisions in general, CPCRA can be very effectively utilised for individually setting up a statutory system for enforcement of child rights specifically and particularly in the larger interest of children. This will create a special, exclusive and individual forum to redress breachers of children's rights and will provide effective, speedy and timely relief in the case of any individual incident of missing or distressed children.

The issues pertaining to missing children and children in distress can be exclusively looked into by the respective state commissions in their individual territories in view of the powers vested in them under ss 13 and 24 of the CPCRA. Clearly, if the state commission concerned suo motu or upon inquiry into complaints regarding missing children or children in distress comes to a conclusion that there is a violation of child rights, there is non-implementation of laws relating to children or there is non-compliance of decisions, guidelines or instructions pertaining to the welfare of children, such commission under s 15 of the CPCRA can approach the Supreme Court or High Court for issuance of directions, orders or writs as may be deemed necessary by the court, besides recommending that concerned governments grant interim relief as deemed necessary. Thus, any individual case of missing children or children in distress can be immediately remedied by the state commission by enforcing the above provisions of the CPCRA.

The composition of the state commission with its six members, out of which at least two should be women specialising in child health, care, welfare or child development, juvenile justice, child psychology, laws related to children and/or having knowledge of children in distress will give adequate opportunity to the state commission to receive complaints or act suo moto whenever there is any issue of kidnapping or removal of children and deprivation or violation of child rights. The commission is vastly empowered to examine all factors affecting children and relating to trafficking, torture, exploitation, pornography and prostitution and to recommend appropriate remedial measures. The commission has mandatory powers to forward cases to any magistrate and hear them as complaints. Independently, the commission upon inquiry can recommend initiation of proceedings for prosecution or such other action as deemed fit. Hence, all cases of trafficking of children particularly for exploitation, begging, prostitution and pornography can be monitored and future recurrence can be checked. All organised child mafias can therefore be attempted to be eliminated.

(d)　Conclusion of suggested measures under CPCRA

A reading of the provisions, remedies and suggestions made above under the CPCRA indicates that a separate and independent machinery can be set into motion under the auspices of the CPCRA to specifically look into all issues related to child rights while the process of the criminal law moves in the mainstream.

The menace of missing children in large numbers can be curbed with a heavy hand only if the issues relating to children are segregated and dealt with under separate parameters under the watchful eye of child specialists, ie qualified members of the state commissions for protection of child rights. Only if qualified, trained and experienced persons sensitive to child rights are empowered to handle the problems of missing children can the process and machinery of the criminal law work in tandem.

Once offenders are apprehended, speedy trials of offences against children or of violation of child rights can be ensured in children's courts which can be set up under the CPCRA. This can prevent recurrence of organised children-related offences.

A vigilant state commission for protection of child rights both as a watch dog and as an investigator can serve a very significant role in the removal of problems of missing children. Hence, only if the issue of missing children is taken out of the general stream of treatment and handed over to child specialists to monitor it from the outside can the necessary attention, time and energy be devoted to this highly sensitive issue of missing children.

VII　CONCLUSION

In the backdrop of the above study, all missing children whose whereabouts are not known even after years of investigations and all the new cases registered every day in the police stations across the country can benefit and be traced if the above suggestions and recommendations are taken into account by the police or the investigating authorities while searching for the missing children. It may be suggested that not only should the police or the investigating authorities be responsible for finding the missing children whose cases have been reported in the police stations but the public bodies, NGOs/state legal services authorities should also be made a part of the support services. That would help and speed up the investigation process making it possible for missing children to come back home. If all authorities at all levels, ie village, district, state and centre, as well as public bodies, work together to find missing children, it will not be very difficult to find the missing children. Therefore, keeping in mind the above guidelines and suggestions it is possible to efficiently investigate and find the missing children besides preventing future instances of kidnapping of children. Considering that India is a large nation geographically with vast territories housing a multicultural society and a huge population of over 1.1 billion people, resolving critical issues like missing children is not an easy task. However, keeping in view that this vulnerable section of society is at a very high risk rate, every effort, step and endeavour should be made to adapt means and methods to protect the future of the nation's children. Therefore, it should be the endeavour of every official body of the system to contribute and do whatever is possible for the plight of missing children who must be helped. Resolving their problems should be the top priority in all walks of life.

Ireland

A SOFTENING OF THE MARITAL FAMILY PARADIGM?

*Maebh Harding**

Résumé

Ces dernières années, le droit irlandais a connu une importante évolution, créant des structures familiales alternatives à la famille traditionnelle fondée sur le mariage. Le *Civil Partnership and Certains Rights and Obligations of Cohabitants Act 2010* (Loi de 2010 pour le Partenariat Civil & Certains Droits aux Concubins) est entré en vigueur le 1er janvier 2011. Cette loi a créé la nouvelle institution du partenariat civil et a instauré une protection légale pour les couples en concubinage. Les tribunaux ont montré leur soutien aux structures familiales alternatives et la Commission de Réforme du Droit Irlandais a proposé une réforme du droit privé de l'enfance afin qu'il soit plus facile pour les pères non mariés, les beaux-parents ou les partenaires civils de prendre soin de leurs enfants. Cependant, la loi irlandaise conserve tout de même une préférence constitution-nelle pour la famille traditionnelle.

Ce chapitre traite des dispositions légales concernant les structures familiales alternatives et évalue dans quelle mesure le mariage conserve son importance en tant que paradigme des relations familiales en Irlande. Il est soutenu que les effets de cette préférence constitutionnelle pour le mariage se ressentent à travers l'ensemble du droit de la famille irlandais et ceci au détriment des enfants. Les réformes proposées pour protéger les droits des enfants restent limitées par la protection constitutionnelle de la famille traditionnelle.

I   INTRODUCTION

The last couple of years have seen several developments in Irish law providing for alternative family structures to the traditional married family. The Civil Partnership and Certain Rights and Obligations of Cohabitants Act 2010 came into force on 1 January 2011.[1] This Act created a new institution of civil partnership and provided statutory protection for cohabiting couples. The courts have shown support for alternative family structures in the high profile

---

*   BCL (UCD), PhD (UCD), Senior Lecturer, University of Portsmouth.
[1]   Civil Partnership and Certain Rights and Obligations of Cohabitants Act 2010 (Commencement) Order 2010, SI 648/2010.

case of *McD v L*[2] and the Irish Law Reform Commission has suggested reform to private child law to make it easier for unmarried fathers, step-parents and civil partners to care for their children.[3]

However, Irish law still retains a constitution preference for the marital family. Articles 41[4] and 42[5] of the Irish Constitution expressly protect the institution of marriage and the marital family. The marital family is given inalienable rights superior to all positive law and the autonomy of married parents to make decisions for their children is given heavy weight in child law cases.

This chapter will discuss the legal provision of alternative family structures and assess to what extent marriage retains its importance as the paradigm for family relationships in Ireland. It will be argued that the effects of constitutional preference for marriage are still felt throughout the Irish family law system and have the greatest detrimental effect on children. Proposed reforms to protect children's rights remain limited by the constitutional protection of the marital family.

II   CONSTITUTIONAL PROBLEMS OVERCOME?

In art 41 of the Irish Constitution the state pledges to protect the institution of marriage from attack. Duncan concluded that the law discriminated against the non-marital family, partly because of factual difference in the quality of the relationship but more especially because of a moral and social preference for marital families.[6] Judicial interpretation of this article has created some constitutional problems for the recognition of alternative family structures in Irish law. The state cannot introduce legislation that discriminates against the marital family.[7] The courts have held that such discrimination is unconstitutional if it causes disadvantage to the marital family over other family forms when all the privileges and disadvantages accorded by the state to the marital family are taken into account. Thus preferential taxation of single parent families could be justified as the state had not made it more advantageous to be an unmarried mother than to be married with children, all

---

[2]   [2010] 2 IR 199.

[3]   Law Reform Commission *Report on Legal Aspects of Family* Relationships (LRC 101 – 2010).

[4]   Article 41.1.1: 'The State recognises the Family as the natural primary and fundamental unit group of Society, and as a moral institution possessing inalienable and imprescriptible rights, antecedent and superior to all positive law.'
       Article 41.3.1: 'The State pledges itself to guard with special care the institution of Marriage, on which the Family is founded, and to protect it against attack.'

[5]   Article 42.1: 'The State acknowledges that the primary and natural educator of the child is the Family and guarantees to respect the inalienable right and duty of parents to provide, according to their means, for the religious and moral, intellectual, physical and social education of their children.'

[6]   W Duncan 'Supporting the Institution of Marriage in Ireland' [1978] *The Irish Jurist* 215, 230–231.

[7]   *Murphy v Attorney General* [1982] IR 241 (IESC); *Muckley v Ireland* [1985] IR 472, [1986] ILRM 364 (IESC); *Hyland v Minister for Social Welfare* [1989] IR 624, [1990] ILRM 213 (IESC); *Greene v Minister for Agriculture* [1990] 2 IR 17, [1990] ILRM 364 (IEHC).

things considered.[8] The state is permitted to make policies that discriminate in favour of the marital family over other family forms.[9]

It is not possible for the non-marital family to enjoy the protections conferred on the marital family. In *Nicolaou* it was held that art 41 precluded the state from conferring equal constitutional protection on a family based on a non-marital union.[10] To do so would constitute an 'attack on marriage' eroding marriage as a status and discouraging couples from entering into marriage.

In *Ennis v Butterly*,[11] two parties who were married but not to each other, entered into a contract to live together as man and wife until such a time as they could legally marry.[12] In consideration of this agreement, the plaintiff discontinued her business and lived as a full-time homemaker. When the relationship broke down she sought damages for breach of contract. Following *Nicolaou*, Kelly J held that non-marital cohabitation did not and could not have the same constitutional status as marriage.[13] To enforce an express cohabitation contract would give that cohabitation a similar status in law to a marriage contract.

Ennis v Butterly and *Nicolaou* suggested that, rather than just allowing positive discrimination in favour of the marital family, art 41 created a duty to promote the marital family over any other type of family. This meant that, if the state decided to introduce civil partnership or statutory relief for cohabiting couples, this would be subject to constitutional challenge as an 'attack on marriage'.[14]

Carolan argued that *Ennis v Butterly* was inconsistent with the case-law that allowed some unfavourable legislative treatment to be justified as long as marriage came out as being treated with parity or better than other family forms.[15] It could also be argued that it is impossible for statutory protection of people who cannot marry under the rules of the state – same-sex couples and individuals who have previously married but are not yet divorced – to constitute an attack on marriage.

The 2006 Review of the Constitution took the view that legislation providing for other family forms could be introduced without the need to amend the

---

[8]   *MhicMathúna v Ireland* [1989] IR 504 (IEHC), 511–512.

[9]   *O'B v S* [1984] IR 316 (IESC).

[10] For the state to award equal constitutional protection to the family founded on marriage and the 'family' founded on an extramarital union would in effect be a disregard of the pledge which the state gives in art 41.3.1, 'to guard with special care the institution of marriage' *State (Nicolaou) v An Bord Uchtála* [1966] IR 567, 622.

[11] *Ennis v Butterly* [1996] 1 IR 426, [1997] 1 ILRM 28 (IEHC).

[12] A case that preceded the introduction of divorce in Ireland in 1996.

[13] Above n 11, 438.

[14] J Mee 'Cohabitation, Civil partnership and the Constitution' in W Binchy and O Doyle (eds) *Committed Relationships and the Law* (Dublin: Four Courts Press, 2007) 210.

[15] E Carolan 'Committed non-marital couples and the Irish Constitution' in W Binchy and O Doyle (eds) *Committed Relationships and the Law* (Dublin: Four Courts Press, 2007) 257.

Constitution.[16] 'Marriage-like' privileges can be extended to cohabiting heterosexual couples, provided they do not exceed those of the family based on marriage so as to act as an inducement not to marry.[17] The group concluded that the introduction of same-sex marriage would require a constitutional referendum to change the definition of the family. However, legislation could be used to extend marriage-like rights to same-sex couples.[18] Both the *Options Paper on Domestic Partnership*[19] and the Law Reform Commission's *Report on the Rights and Duties of Cohabitants*[20] agreed with these conclusions on the perceived constitutional barriers to reform.

The legitimacy of excluding same-sex partners from the institution of marriage was challenged in *Zappone v Revenue Commissioners* as an unconstitutional restriction on the right to marry.[21] The Irish Constitution protects both the institution of marriage itself[22] and the right to marry as part of the unenumerated rights doctrine.[23] The exclusion of same-sex couples was justified, as protecting the traditional understanding of the institution of marriage.[24] Dunne J located the right to marry as implicitly stemming from art 41 rather than art 40.3.1 as had been the case in previous case-law.[25] As a right that is identified in the text of the Constitution itself, the definition marriage could not be changed in light of prevailing norms.[26]

It is submitted that Dunne J's approach was simply incorrect. Article 41 refers to the protection of marriage as an institution. Rights under art 41 are accorded to individuals due to their status as part of the constitutional family. Those seeking the right to marry are, by definition, not part of the constitutional family as it currently stands and so there is no possibility that the right to marry could be located in this article. Previous and subsequent case-law has very clearly based the right to marry in art 40.3.1,[27] making it part of the unenumerated rights jurisprudence to which the living document approach is applicable.[28] Following *Zappone,* any extension to the right to marry should be curtailed by the express protection of marriage in art 41 where it would change the institution of marriage as it was understood in 1937. Protecting marriage under this interpretation seems to mean excluding those who have never been

---

[16]   The All-Party Oireachtas Committee on the Constitution *Tenth Progress Report: The Family* (Dublin: Stationery Office, 2006) 76.

[17]   Ibid 122.

[18]   Ibid 86.

[19]   Department of Justice *Options Paper presented by the Working Group on Domestic Partnership* (Dublin 2006) 51.

[20]   Law Reform Commission *Rights and Duties of Cohabitants* (LRC 82–2006, Dublin 2006).

[21]   *Zappone & Anor v Revenue Commissioners & Ors* [2006] IEHC 404 (HC).

[22]   Article 41.

[23]   Unenumerated rights are personal rights stemming from art 40.3.1.

[24]   *Zappone & Anor v Revenue Commissioners & Ors* [2006] IEHC 404 at [129].

[25]   Ibid at [127].

[26]   Ibid at [123].

[27]   *Ryan v The Attorney General* [1965] IR 294; *O'Shea v Ireland* [2007] 2 IR 313; *TF v Ireland* [1995] 1 IR 321.

[28]   See further Ennis 'Marriage: Redefined and Realigned with Bunreacht na hÉireann' [2010] *Irish Journal of Legal Studies* 29.

allowed to marry before, and would seem to indicate cases such as *O'Shea*,[29] which extended eligibility for marriage, were incorrectly decided.

Gilligan and Zappone were refused an appeal to the Supreme Court in October 2011, but the possibility of further constitutional challenge remains open.[30] Tobin has suggested that the introduction of civil partnership may mean the end of the same-sex marriage debate. The Supreme Court could refuse to expand the current constitutional understanding of marriage as same-sex couples are now able to enjoy most of the benefits of the institution.[31]

The Civil Partnership and Certain Rights and Obligations of Cohabitants Act 2010 (2010 Act) provides cohabiting couples with statutory rights and creates a new institution of civil partnership. The statutory provisions remain subject to constitutional challenge in light of the unresolved question of whether art 41 creates a duty to promote the marital family over any other type of family.[32]

III   CIVIL PARTNERSHIP

The institution of civil partnership mirrors civil marriage and most of the practical legislative protections given to married couples have been extended to civil partners. The institution of civil partnership is not defined within the 2010 Act. Some idea of what the institution represents can be gleaned from s 5 which lays down the criteria for recognising a foreign relationship as civil partnership. The relationship must be between two members of the same sex who are not within the prohibited degrees of relationship. It must also be exclusive in nature and registered publicly in the foreign jurisdiction. It must also create a certain level of rights and obligations in order to be treated as an Irish civil partnership.

In Ireland, a marriage with legally recognised consequences can be entered into through either a civil or religious ceremony. In contrast, civil partnership can only be entered into through a civil ceremony.[33] Declarations must be made in the presence of a registrar and witnesses and the partners must sign a civil partnership form.[34]

---

[29]   [2007] 2 IR 313, 334.
[30]   www.marriagequality.ie/justlove/aboutcase/updates/2011/10/24/statement-from-dr-ann-louise-gilligan-and-senator-katherine-zappone-regarding-their-court-case/ (accessed 10 March 2012).
[31]   B Tobin 'Same-Sex Couples and the Law: Recent Developments in the British Isles' (2009) 23 *International Journal of Law Policy and the Family* 309.
[32]   It would have been possible to refer the 2010 Act to the Supreme Court for a declaration of its constitutionality under art 26 of the Constitution. However, such a ruling might have precluded the possibility in the future of providing further equality for same-sex couples.
[33]   2010 Act, Part 3.
[34]   Civil Registration Act 2004, s 59D.

The grounds for nullity of civil partnership[35] differ slightly to those of marriage which are governed by the common law.[36] As a result the threshold for entering a civil partnership could be seen as somewhat lower than that in place in relation to marriage.[37] A decree of nullity will be granted where the parties lack capacity, where formalities were not respected and where consent is considered invalid by reason of mental incapacity, duress or undue influence. The prohibited degrees for civil partnership are limited to a much smaller category than those outlined for marriage[38] reflecting a statutory desire to reduce the prohibited degrees for marriage in light of the ruling in *O'Shea v Ireland*.[39] A civil partnership is considered void where the parties are not of the same sex. This mirrors the rule that a marriage is considered void where both parties are of the same sex.[40]

Dissolution of civil partnership is obtained in a similar way to an Irish divorce although some of the obligations are not as onerous.[41] Dissolution is no-fault. Parties must live apart for 2 years out of the previous 3 rather than the 4-year period imposed for marriage.[42] Before dissolution can be granted the courts must ensure that proper provision is made for each civil partner.[43]

Most of the legal protections given to the married couple under Irish law have been extended to civil partners. Part 4 of the 2010 Act gives civil partners a right to remain in their shared home regardless of legal ownership. This is equivalent to the protection given to spouses under the Family Home Protection Act 1976. Civil partners also have the same entitlements to protected tenancies as spouses and are subject to the same maintenance obligations in respect of their civil partners.[44] Part 8 of the 2010 Act amends the Succession Act 1965 to grant civil partners the same rights on intestacy as spouses. Civil partners are also given a right to challenge their partner's will.[45] Part 9 of the 2010 Act extends the same level of protection to civil partners as that granted to spouses under the Domestic Violence Act 1996.

---

[35] 2010 Act, Part 11.

[36] M Harding 'Religion and Family Law in Ireland: from a Catholic protection of marriage to a "catholic" approach nullity' in E Orucu and Mair (eds) *The Place of Religion in Family Law: A Comparative Search* (Antwerp: Intersentia, 2011) 161–183.

[37] F Ryan 'The General Scheme of the Civil Partnership Bill 2008: Brave New Dawn or Missed Opportunity?' (2008) 11 *Irish Journal of Family Law* 51, 55.

[38] Third Schedule to the 2004 Act.

[39] See further M Harding 'The curious incident of the Marriage Act (No 2) 1537 and the Irish Statute Book' (2012) 32 *Legal Studies* 78–108: J Mee 'Marriage, Civil Partnership and the Prohibited Degrees of Relationship' (2009) 27 *Irish Law Times* 259–264.

[40] *Foy v An t-Ard Chláraitheoir* [2007] IEHC 470.

[41] 2010 Act, Part 12.

[42] 2010 Act, s 110.

[43] 2010 Act, s 110b.

[44] 2010 Act, Part 5.

[45] Succession Act 1965, s 11A. This is not an absolute right. See L Mee 'Succession and the Civil Partnership Bill 2009' 14 *Conveyancing and Property Law Journal* 86–88.

The Finance (No 3) Act 2011 now allows registered civil partners to receive the same tax treatment as married couples in respect of income tax, stamp duty, capital acquisitions tax, capital gains tax and VAT.

Unlike married couples, civil partners enjoy no presumption of parenthood in relation to any child born during the civil partnership and they cannot jointly adopt.[46] Where civil partners raise children together they will not enjoy the same level of autonomy given to married parents to care for their children. The Act has been criticised as missing an opportunity to regulate the legal position of children living with same-sex couples.[47]

IV   COHABITATION

Part 15 of the 2010 Act provides protective measures for cohabitants. Such protections apply to relationships where both cohabitants are ordinarily resident in the state for a one-year period prior to the end of the relationship and at least one of the cohabitants is domiciled or ordinarily resident in Ireland for the year preceding the application.[48]

A cohabitant is defined as one of two adults who live together as a couple in an intimate and committed relationship.[49] Such adults cannot be related to each other or within the prohibited degrees of relationship. Married couples or civil partners cannot be treated as cohabitants. The court is given discretion in determining whether two adults are in an 'intimate and committed relationship'. The court must consider a number of factors outlined in s 172 including the basis on which the couple live together, their degree of financial dependence, whether or not the couple care for children together and the extent to which the couple present themselves as a couple to the world. The legislation presumes that the relationship will have been sexual at one point, but even where the sexual relationship has ceased the couple may still be considered to be in an intimate relationship.[50]

The Act allows qualified cohabitants to apply for a number of different orders to redress financial unfairness caused by the relationship. Cohabitants who have been in a relationship of 5 years duration or who have been together for 2 years and have a child together are treated as 'qualified cohabitants'.[51]

---

[46]   Section 11 of the 1952 Adoption Act allows married couples to adopt jointly. This is only situation in which Irish adoption law permits the adoption of a child by more than one person. Section 33 of the Adoption Act 2010 applies the same preference to the recognition of international adoption.

[47]   F Ryan 'The General Scheme of the Civil Partnership Bill 2008: Brave New Dawn or Missed Opportunity?' (2008) 11 *Irish Journal of Family Law* 51.

[48]   2010 Act, s 196(3).

[49]   2010 Act, s 172.

[50]   2010 Act, s 172(3).

[51]   2010 Act, s 172(5).

It is not possible to become a qualified cohabitant if, during the prescribed time for living together, either partner was married and the ground for divorce has not been satisfied.[52] The purpose of this exception is to ensure that if an application for relief is made against a cohabitant who is married to a third party the cohabitant's spouse will not be precluded from seeking a divorce and applying for ancillary relief.[53] This means that the cohabitation protection cannot be seen as an unconstitutional 'attack on marriage'. No such exception is made for a civil partner. Mee criticises this provision as unnecessary as other provisions of the 2010 Act protect the cohabitant's spouse.[54] The exception excludes a whole class of cohabitants from legal protection.

A qualified cohabitant can make an application for redress,[55] an application for a property adjustment order,[56] an application for compulsory maintenance[57] and a pension adjustment order.[58] A qualified cohabitant can also apply for provision from the estate of deceased cohabitant.[59]

In order to be eligible for an order of redress, a property adjustment or a pension adjustment order, the qualified cohabitant must satisfy the court that he is financially dependent on the other cohabitant and this dependence has been caused by the relationship or the ending of the relationship. The court may make an order only if it considers it to be fair and equitable to do so in the circumstances.[60]

The court must consider the financial needs and obligations of each cohabitant, the rights and entitlements of the spouses and civil partners or former spouses and former civil partners of each cohabitant. It must also consider the needs of any dependent child. In determining what is just and equitable the court must also consider the duration of the relationship and the degree of commitment shown. The court also considers the contributions of each cohabitant, the effect the relationship has had on their future earning capacity and the conduct of the cohabitants.[61]

The requirement for financial dependency reflects the fact that a cohabitant is under no duty to maintain the other cohabitant. Instead the legislation creates a safety net for those who have become economically dependent. The scheme provides no remedy for claimants who have suffered major financial losses during the relationship but remain financially independent and so provides a

---

[52] Ie living apart for 4 years out of the previous 5 years: art 41.3.2 of the Constitution.
[53] J Mee 'Cohabitation Law Reform in Ireland' (2011) 23 *Child and Family Law Quarterly* 323–343, 332.
[54] 2010 Act, ss 173(3)(b), s 173(5), s 201 and s 208.
[55] 2010 Act, s 173.
[56] 2010 Act, s 174.
[57] 2010 Act, s 175.
[58] 2010 Act, s 187.
[59] 2010 Act, s 194.
[60] 2010 Act, s 173(2).
[61] 2010 Act, s 173.

very basic level of protection.[62] Mee argues that the scheme may give cohabitants a false sense of security that the law will look after them which will prevent individuals from seeking to protect their individual property rights and may lead to very serious financial losses.[63]

Part 15 of the 2010 Act allows all cohabitants to regulate their own financial affairs and opt out of the statutory protection. It also removes any non-constitutional impediments to the enforcement of cohabitation agreements.[64] Section 202 requires such agreements to comply with the general law of contract. Such agreements are also subject to rather onerous formalities; they must be in writing and both cohabitants must have received legal advice. Such agreements can be set aside by the courts in exceptional circumstances where enforcement would cause serious injustice.[65]

V REMAINING INEQUALITIES OF STATUS

Cohabitation and civil partnership remain inferior statuses to marriage in the constitutional hierarchy. While marital families are constitutionally protected, civil partnerships and cohabiting families are not. This difference in treatment has created inequality between how the state treats the children born to marital families and those raised in same-sex or cohabiting families. This interferes with children's rights to be cared for by loving parents and to be protected within the family unit.

VI MARITAL STATUS AND LEGAL PARENTHOOD

Ireland has not passed legislation to regulate assisted reproduction in spite of repeated calls for reform.[66] As a result, the marital presumptions of parenthood are often relied on to ensure that intentional parents have legal rights to care for children conceived using donor gametes. Such options are not open to civil partners or cohabitants. Where cohabitants or civil partners do not hold the status of parent their legal rights to care for any child of the relationship are quite limited.

Fatherhood is based on a series of rebuttable presumptions found in the Status of Children Act 1987. A father's position is dependent on his relationship with

---

[62]   J Mee 'Cohabitation Law Reform in Ireland'(2011) 23 *Child and Family Law Quarterly* 323–343, 335.

[63]   Ibid 339.

[64]   Ibid 341.

[65]   2010 Act, s 202(4).

[66]   See Collins *Seanad Debates* Wednesday 14 October 1987. Law Reform Commission *Report on Illegitimacy* (LRC 4 – 1982), [387]. See Henry *Seanad Debates* Wednesday 7 July 1999. Commission on Assisted Human Reproduction *Report of the Commission on Assisted Human Reproduction* (2005) available online at www.dohc.ie/publications/cahr.html (accessed June 2012).

the child's 'natural mother' unless he asserts his rights in court.[67] Where the 'natural mother' is married, her husband will be presumed to be the father of the child.[68] Where a child is born to a married mother, either spouse can register the birth with both spouses listed as parents regardless of the genetic relationship.[69] A married father also has automatic guardianship rights which he cannot lose.[70]

Where a man is named on a birth certificate he is presumed to be the legal father and must be treated as such for all notification purposes unless a statutory declaration of parentage is made stating that he is not the father.[71] Opposite-sex cohabitants can rely on this presumption but it is unlikely that a same-sex partner would be able do so.

If the father is not named on the birth certificate, he will have to go to court to prove his status. A court declaration of parentage creates a binding legal relationship that cannot be rebutted.[72] This method is of little use where the child has been donor-conceived and the father has no biological relationship. Section 38 of the Status of Children Act 1987 allows the court to order blood tests to assist it in determining whether or not a named person is the parent of a child.[73]

The status of 'legal parent' is vital in establishing nationality, immigration rights, appropriate taxation regimes, rights on intestacy and obligations to pay maintenance.[74] The status of parent also determines the eligibility of an individual to apply for guardianship, custody and access.

The unmarried 'natural mother' is deemed automatically to be the sole guardian of the child and given exclusive control and decision-making authority.[75] Irish law grants the natural mother of a child a further constitutional right to the custody of her child under art 40.3 of the Constitution[76] although she and her child are not recognised as a family for the purposes of protection under art 41.[77] Married parents have automatic joint guardianship and a constitutional right to the custody of their children. It is

---

[67]   *K v W* [1990] 2 IR 437; *W'O'R v EH* [1996] 2 IR 248.
[68]   No such presumption exists if the married woman is living apart from her husband under a deed of separation or judicial separation: s 46 of the Status of Children Act 1987.
[69]   A valid marriage certificate must be presented to the Registrar.
[70]   Family Law (Divorce) Act 1996, s 10(2).
[71]   *FP v SP and the Attorney General*, unreported judgment Smith J, HC 31 July 1999.
[72]   Unless there is new evidence.
[73]   Status of Children Act 1987, s 38; *JPD v MG* [1991] ILRM 217.
[74]   Section 11(2)(B) of the Guardianship of Infants Act allows the court to make an order requiring either the *father* or the *mother* to make such maintenance payments as it considers reasonable. Applications for the maintenance of a child under the Guardianship of Infants Act 1964 can be made only by parents who are married to one another or by a guardian: *E Mc E v J O'S* unreported High court Sheehan J, 5 February 2009.
[75]   Guardianship of Infants Act 1964, s 6(4).
[76]   *G v An Bord Uchtála* [1980] IR 32, 55.
[77]   *State (Nicolaou) v An Bord Uchtála* [1966] IR 567.

not possible to strip a natural mother or married parents of their guardianship rights unless an adoption order is made.[78]

The unmarried father does not have automatic guardianship rights. In order to obtain the status of guardian the natural father must be registered as father on the child's birth certificate and have completed a joint statutory declaration with the legal mother.[79] Where no such agreement can be reached, the father has to apply to court under s 6A of the 1964 Guardianship of Infants Act to have the status of guardian conferred upon him.[80]

A civil partner of a birth parent cannot rely on the marital presumption of parenthood to give him or her the status of legal parent or automatic guardianship. This leaves civil partners who have had children together using surrogacy or assisted reproduction in a vulnerable position if the relationship breaks down.

Without the status of father/parent, guardianship cannot be obtained by agreement with the mother[81] or from the court.[82] Same-sex partners cannot become guardians of donor-conceived children or their partner's children from a previous relationship. Thus without the status of legal parent, essential for guardianship, a non-parent will be limited to an application for mere access rights. There is currently no right for unrelated individuals to apply to the court for custody.

VII   THE AUTONOMY OF THE MARITAL FAMILY UNIT

Articles 41 and 42 accord the marital family inalienable and imprescriptible constitutional rights, superior to all positive law.[83] The 2006 Constitutional Review surmised that the intention behind arts 41 and 42 was to defend the family against unwarranted interference by the state.[84] The state cannot interfere with the marital family unit except in exceptional cases, where the parents have failed in their duty towards a child, for physical or moral reasons, a power given by art 42.5.[85]

---

[78]   Guardianship of Infants Act 1964, s 8(4).
[79]   In the form prescribed by the Guardianship of Children (Statutory Declaration) Regulations 1998.
[80]   *K v W* [1990] ILRM 121.
[81]   Guardianship of Infants Act 1964, s 2(4).
[82]   Guardianship of Infants Act 1964, s 6A.
[83]   *In re Doyle, an Infant* [1956] IR 213 (IEHC).
[84]   The All-Party Oireachtas Committee on the Constitution, *Tenth Progress Report: The Family* (Dublin: Stationery Office, 2006) 37.
[85]   'In exceptional cases, where the parents, for physical or moral reasons fail in their duty towards their children, the State as guardian of the common good, by appropriate means shall endeavour to supply the place of the parents, but always with due regard for the natural and imprescriptible rights of the child.'

Marital children can only be adopted if their parents have failed in their duty of care towards them.[86] This has proved an onerous burden of proof to discharge.[87] The same limitation does not apply in respect of unmarried parents.[88]

The deference given to the married family is not limited to public law cases. The protection of the marital family limits the court's ability to interfere with parental decisions and resolve custody in the child's best interest. For example, in *North Western Health Board v HW*,[89] the Supreme Court refused to grant an order permitting the Health Board to carry out a PKU test on an infant in defiance of the wishes of the child's parents. Irish statutory law requires the courts to apply a welfare test to any such question over the upbringing of a child where the child's best interests are paramount.[90] Both sides in the dispute argued that their position best protected the rights and interests of the child. Instead of weighing up the merits of each argument the court assumed that the welfare of the child is properly protected within the marital family unit unless the contrary is shown. In order to interfere with the decisions of the family unit, the test under art 42.5 would have to be satisfied. This focuses on parental failure of duty rather than the best interest of the child.[91] The constitutional protection of the marital family has led to a parent-centred welfare test in Irish private law cases.

This effect is felt in custody cases.[92] Where the court decides that the parent has abandoned or deserted the child to the care of another individual, the court can refuse to enforce the parental right to custody of the child.[93] In early cases this decision was made using a child-focused welfare test.[94] In more recent cases, the courts have assumed that the best interest of a marital child means leaving them with their parents except in compelling circumstances.[95] For example, in *N v HSE and others*,[96] Geoghan J held that where married parents are caught up in a custody dispute with third parties there is a constitutional presumption that it is in the best interests of the child to be with the natural parents within a

---

86   Adoption Act 1988, s 3.
87   *FO'D v An Bord Uchtála* [200] 1 IR 165.
88   *State (Nicolaou) v An Bord Uchtála* [1966] IR 567, (1968) 102 ILTR 1 (IEHC); *G v An Bord Uchtála* [1980] IR 32 (IRSC) and *Keegan v Ireland* (1994) 18 EHRR 342 (ECtHR).
89   *North Western Health Board v HW* [2001] 3 IR 622 (IESC).
90   Guardianship of Infants Act 1964, s 3: 'Where in any proceedings before any court the custody, guardianship or upbringing of an infant, or the administration of any property belonging to or held on trust for an infant, or the application of the income thereof, is in question, the court, in deciding that question, shall regard the welfare of the infant as the first and paramount consideration.'
91   G Shannon *Child Law* (Dublin: Round Hall Ltd, 2nd edn, 2010) [1-20]–[1-21].
92   Article 42.5.
93   Guardianship of Infants Act 1964, s 14.
94   *In the matter of Derek Joseph Williams* [1939] IR 421; *In re M* [1946] IR 334.
95   *Re JH (an Infant) aka KC and AC v An Bord Uchtala* [1985] IR 375. G Shannon *Child* (Dublin: Round Hall Ltd, 2nd edn, 2010) [12–30].
96   [2006] 4 IR 374 IESC 60 (*Baby Ann* case).

family founded on marriage unless there are either compelling reasons why such a result cannot be achieved or there is a failure of duty of the kind envisaged by art 42.5.[97]

The result of this case-law means that parents are treated differently by the Irish child law system depending on whether they are married or unmarried. More worryingly, how the court determines what is in the best interests of the child depends on their parents' marital status.[98] Welfare is subject to the institutional protection of the marital family and does not necessarily reflect what is in fact in the best interests of the child.

VIII   THE POTENTIAL EXTENSION OF MARITAL FAMILY AUTONOMY TO OTHER FAMILY UNITS

The case of *McD v L*[99] demonstrates the relative positions of different types of parents in private child law disputes. This case concerned a dispute between two lesbian partners (PL and BN) and McD who was the genetic father of their son. PL and BM had been in a committed relationship for some time and wished to have a child. They decided against anonymous sperm donation as they wanted their child to know and have a relationship with his genetic father. They entered into an agreement with McD to have a child together. Both women were very clear that McD was to be a father but not a 'parent'. The child would be raised in a two-parent nuclear family unit; McD's role was limited to that of a 'favourite uncle'. Legally PL was the natural mother with constitutional rights, McD was the father who enjoyed limited statutory rights[100] and BM was a non-parent with no legal rights to even apply for custody.

Relationships between the parties soured after the child was born and McD's access to his son ceased in 2007. McD wanted access and to make sure he could not be cut out of the child's life by securing guardianship. When deciding whether to grant guardianship to an unmarried father, the court uses an unvarnished welfare test under s 3 of the Guardianship of Infants Act.[101]

In the High Court, it was decided that McD should have no guardianship or access rights. The judge held that the two lesbian women and the child constituted a de facto family with rights under Art 8 of the European Convention on Human Rights (ECHR).[102] As such they should have a similar autonomy to that of a marital family under Irish law and this right to autonomy took precedence over a pure welfare test. The legal integrity of this

---

[97]   Ibid at [543].

[98]   Irish Council of Civil Liberties *Equality for All Families* (Dublin, 2006) 20.

[99]   [2010] 2 IR 199.

[100]   A right to apply for guardianship under s 6A of the Guardianship of Infants Act 1964 and apply for custody or access under s 11(4) 1964 without guardianship being awarded.

[101]   *JK v VW* [1990] 2 IR 437.

[102]   Above n 99 at [122].

family would be broken by any order of guardianship or access to the father.[103] This seemingly progressive statement about same-sex families erodes a child-centred approach to access.

The Supreme Court refused to recognise the same-sex family as a de facto family with comparable rights to the marital family. They held that it was not open to the High Court to reinterpret the silence in Irish law regarding de facto families in light of Art 8.[104] And even if it were open to him to do so, the ECHR had yet to establish that two lesbians and a child were a de facto family in the meaning of Art 8.[105]

The Supreme Court found that the High Court was entitled to find that the disruption caused by giving McD the status of guardian would not be in the best interest of the child on a purely child-centred approach. However, access should be granted to McD on the best interests of the child basis.[106] It was held that insufficient weight had been given to the blood relationship between father and child.[107]

The position of non-biological second mother was not considered in *McD* except in her capacity to provide a stable family home with her partner.[108] If the relationship had broken down, her position would be even weaker than McD's. Under s 9 of the Children Act 1997 she would be able to apply for access as a person in loco parentis.

Some commentators saw the High Court decision as a huge step forward for same-sex rights and the recognition of the same-sex family and criticised the Supreme Court decision as a return to a conservative approach to the family.[109] Others saw the Supreme Court decision as an inappropriate elevation of the mere sperm donor and campaigned for Ireland to regulate its assisted reproduction.[110]

It is argued that *McD* demonstrates the inequality that exists in giving different types of parents different types of status in childcare proceedings. The best interest test works out differently for the child depending on the constitutional status of each parent. The answer is not to give stable same-sex family units the same autonomy as marital units on the basis of equality, but to question why we have accorded such autonomy to the marital unit in the first place,

---

[103] Ibid at [143].

[104] Ibid at [66].

[105] Ibid at [168].

[106] *B v B* unreported July 1974 Kenny J.

[107] Above n 99 at [207].

[108] Ibid at [65].

[109] D Thornton 'Gay Irish sperm donor wins visiting rights to lesbian couple's child: Supreme Court says lesbians are not a valid family unit' *Irish Times* 11 December 2009; Connor O'Mahony 'Irreconcilable differences? Article 8 ECHR and Irish Law on non-Traditional Families' (2012) 26 *International Journal of Law, Policy and the Family* 31–61.

[110] C Hogan 'JMcD v PL and BM Sperm Donor Fathers and De Facto Families' (2010) 13 *Irish Journal of Family Law* 83.

particularly where it conflicts with the best interests of the child. When it comes to childcare disputes presumptions of welfare based on marital status are something to be abolished, not emulated for other types of family under the banner of equality. If there is any real benefit on the facts for the child being raised by the parents in a more stable relationship, then this can be encompassed in the welfare test itself.

IX   FUTURE REFORMS

The marital family remains the constitutionally protected paradigm in Irish law. The most worrying effect of this protection is the difference in treatment of parent–child relationships by the courts depending on marital status. The Law Reform Commission has proposed legislative changes to grant automatic parental responsibility to non-marital parents and make it easier for non-parents (such as civil partners) to care for children. An amendment to the constitution has been proposed to ensure that children's rights are adequately considered when the state has to interfere with the decisions of any type of family unit.

(a)   The Law Reform Commission proposals

The 2010 Law Reform Commission *Report on Legal Aspects of Family Relationships* has recommended that automatic guardianship should attach to both parents of a child on compulsory joint registration of the birth of the child.[111] This would ensure that the non-marital father would have guardianship in the vast majority of cases and put him on the same footing as the married father.[112]

The Commission has also proposed the extension of guardianship to step-parents and civil partners by way of an agreement with the other guardians of the child or by application to court.[113] This extension would not remove parental responsibility from the biological parents of the child, but reflect the reality that in some circumstances a child may have more than two adults fulfilling parental roles.[114]

A cohabitant who is not a parent will not be able to apply for guardianship by itself, but could be granted guardianship where an order for custody is made. This guardianship is limited. The cohabitant would not be permitted to make

---

[111] Law Reform Commission *Report on Legal Aspects of Family Relationships* (LRC 101 – 2010) at [11].
[112] Ibid at [2.08], [2.26]. The Commission recommends that the Civil Registration Act 2004 be amended to provide that where a non-marital mother (a) honestly does not know the identity of the father, or (b) honestly does not know the whereabouts of the father, or (c) where she fears for her safety and/or the safety of the child if the father were to be contacted in relation to the registration of the birth of the child, she shall make a statutory declaration to that effect.
[113] Ibid at [3.24].
[114] Ibid at [3.20].

any decisions in relation to the adoption of a child or to appoint a testamentary guardian to care for the child.[115]

The ability to apply for custody is to be extended to relatives of a child, persons in loco parentis and persons with a bona fide interest in the child in circumstances where the parents are unable or unwilling to exercise guardianship.[116]

The report does not tackle the definition of 'parent' or the advantage given to married couples in this regard.[117] Neither do the proposals address the gloss in the favour of marital parents inherent in the welfare principle. While the proposals will be of great practical benefit to the families involved, they work around the constitutional protection of the marital family rather than questioning its utility in modern Ireland.

(b)   The Children's Rights Amendments

In 2007 in response to the *Baby Ann*[118] case, the government published the Twenty-eighth Amendment to the Constitution Bill 2007.[119] This Bill would have inserted a statement into art 42 to the effect that all children should have the same rights. Article 42.5 was to be removed and replaced with a section limiting state involvement in any family to exceptional cases 'where the parents of any child for physical or moral reasons fail in their duty towards such child'.[120] Where the state did take action it should do so 'with due regard for the natural and imprescriptible rights of the child'. A constitutional statement to the effect that the court should endeavour to secure the best interests of the child in any private child law dispute if required to by law was proposed.[121] The Bill fell, due to the general election in May 2007.

As the amendment made no changes to the art 41 pledge to defend the institution of marriage from attack it could be argued that it would have made little difference in practice; the deference to the marital family unit would have remained. It was tacitly accepted by most campaigners for children's rights that strengthening the position of children's rights under the Constitution should not be at the expense of the family.[122] This meant that children's rights would necessarily remain subordinate to the stability of the family unit based on marriage.[123]

---

[115]   Ibid at [3.35].
[116]   Ibid at [3.33].
[117]   These are to be addressed in Project 31 of the Third Programme of Law Reform 2008–2014 (LRC 86 – 2007); Legal Aspects of Assisted Human Reproduction.
[118]   Above n 96.
[119]   No 14 of 2007.
[120]   Proposed art 42A.2.1
[121]   Proposed art 42A.4.
[122]   A Nolan 'The Battle(s) over Children's Rights in the Irish Constitution' (2007) 22(4) *Irish Political Studies* 495, 508.
[123]   Ibid 511.

A new proposal for a children's rights referendum has been published.[124] Much like the 2007 amendment this version declares that all children will be treated equally[125] but does not dismantle the constitutional definition of the family as one based on marriage.

The new proposal gives children a natural and imprescriptible right to have their welfare regarded as a *primary consideration*[126] and further elaborates that in guardianship, adoption, custody, care or upbringing of a child, the welfare and best interests of the child shall be the *first and paramount consideration.*[127] However, the new amendment also bolsters parental rights in every type of family. Article 42.3 acknowledges parents as primary and natural carers and protectors of children's welfare. This seems to give parental autonomy a strong position in determining what is in the child's best interest. As the respect for the marital family as the natural primary and fundamental unit group of society is retained, there is no guarantee that the assumption that the best interests of the child are preserved by following the wishes of the marital unit will be changed.

The proposed amendments lay out the same test for state interference into the family regardless of marital status. However, the threshold is set at, 'where the parents of any child fail in their responsibility towards such child'.[128] As seen from the case-law above, marital parents are considered to have stronger rights and duties towards their children than non-married parents.

The amendment has been criticised as poorly identifying the circumstances in which the state can impose an objective understanding of the best interests of the child in place of the parents' understanding of the child's best interests.[129]

The current deference for the wishes of marital parents has developed out of the combined effect of the state's obligation to define the family based on marriage,[130] recognise the family as the natural primary and fundamental unit group of society possessing inalienable and imprescriptible rights as a unit,[131] recognise the family as best placed to look after the family[132] and leaving them to their own decision except in exceptional circumstances.[133] By inserting children's rights and adult rights concerns into art 42 without changing art 41 to remove the institutional protection given to the marital family as a unit, inequality will continue to exist between categories of children and parents. As

---

[124] www.oireachtas.ie/parliament/mediazone/proposalforanamendmenttotheconstitution/#d.en. 1552 (accessed 10 March 2012).
[125] Proposed art 42.1: '1 The State shall cherish all the children of the State equally.'
[126] Proposed art 42.1.2.
[127] Proposed art 42.1.3.
[128] Proposed art 42.4.
[129] O Doyle 'Referendum must address best interests of children' *The Irish Times*, 21 February 2012.
[130] Article 41.3.3.
[131] Article 41.1.1.
[132] Article 42.1.
[133] Article 42.5.

held by Hardiman J in the *Baby Ann* case: 'The provisions of the Constitution provide for the family unit, and its autonomy over and above the individual members of the family itself.'[134]

The possibility of redefining the constitutional family has been considered by Constitutional Reform Groups in the past, although no action has been taken. The 1996 Constitution Review Group recommended that the protection of marriage should remain, but that a further amendment should be made so as to make it clear that this pledge would not prevent the Oireachtas from providing protection for the benefit of families based on a relationship other than marriage.[135] They also recommended that the definition of the family as a purely marriage-based institution should be removed, as it no longer accorded with the social structure of Ireland. However, in 2006, the Constitutional Review Group recommended that there be no change to the definition of the family as it would be too divisive to Irish society.[136] The Irish Council of Civil Liberties has suggested that the best way to ensure equality for all families would be to remove the constitutional protection of the marital family.[137]

X   CONCLUSION

Irish law has come a long way in recent years in recognising different family forms but the marital family remains the constitutionally protected paradigm in Irish law. The constitutional protection of marriage in Irish law guarantees autonomy to the marital family which puts children at risk and perpetuates the traditional institution of marriage which potentially prevents the introduction of same-sex marriage by statute. The children's rights amendments aim to secure equal treatment for all children but fail to tackle the underlying question. If the protection of children requires the state to achieve a balance between adult rights and children's interests, should institutional rights be given to a family unit at all? Surely any benefit to a child in being part of a marital or non-marital unit can be assessed by the court on the facts using a welfare test.

Articles 41 and 42 no longer give any real tangible benefit to adults in a marital relationship. The courts have established that the institutional protection of marriage is subject to the common good.[138] Other constitutional rights can affect the constitutional protection of marriage such as those under art 40.3.1.[139] The favourable treatment of marriage is not mandated by the Constitution and the state has shown that rights can be accorded to other family forms by statute alone.

---

[134]   *Baby Ann*, above n 96 at [259].
[135]   Constitution Review Group *Report of the Constitution Review Group* (Dublin: Stationery Office, 1996) 332.
[136]   The All-Party Oireachtas Committee on the Constitution *Tenth Progress Report: The Family* (Dublin: Stationery Office, 2006) 122.
[137]   Irish Council of Civil Liberties *Equality for All Families* (Dublin 2006) 16.
[138]   *TF v Ireland* [1995] 1 IR 321, [1995] 2 ILRM 321 (IESC).
[139]   *O'Shea v Ireland* [2007] 2 IR 313.

The combined effect of arts 41 and 42 of the Constitution has come under strain. The articles have been criticised as 'an embarrassing irrelevance; at best naively aspirational; at worst a hopelessly outdated impediment to reform'.[140] It is argued that the goals of Irish family law have shifted towards a plurality of family forms and a balancing of parental and children's rights with a priority given to children's rights. The constitutional protection of the traditional marital family remains as a troublesome relic of 1930's societal norms.

---

[140] E Carolan 'Committed non-marital couples and the Irish Constitution' in W Binchy and O Doyle (eds) *Committed Relationships and the Law* (Dublin: Four Courts Press, 2007) 240.

Japan

CHILD CUSTODY ISSUES AT THE TIME OF DIVORCE – FROM THE POINT OF VIEW OF JAPANESE FAMILY LAW

*Tomiyuki Ogawa**

Résumé

Le Japon est critiqué pour le nombre d'enlèvements internationaux d'enfants. L'auteur du présent texte soutient que les différences entre le Japon et les autres pays occidentaux industrialisés expliquent ce phénomène. Par exemple, le droit actuel japonais prévoit que seul un parent peut obtenir l'autorité parentale et que ce dernier a le pouvoir de restreindre les droits d'accès de l'autre parent. Le Japon ne peut dès lors être partie à la Convention de La Haye sur les aspects civils de l'enlèvement international d'enfants. Les tribunaux japonais de la famille avaient l'habitude de rejeter les demandes de retour d'enfants vers les autres pays mais cela est en train de changer et la jurisprudence est de plus en plus encline à ordonner de tels retours. Afin de combattre l'enlèvement international d'enfants par des parents japonais, l'auteur fait deux recommandations: d'une part, le droit japonais devrait s'harmoniser avec celui des pays industrialisés et d'autre part, le gouvernement devrait sensibiliser la population au caractère illégal de ces déplacements internationaux d'enfants.

I INTRODUCTION – PROBLEMS RELATING TO CHILDREN AS A RESULT OF INTERNATIONAL DIVERSITY WITHIN A FAMILY

In late 1990s, the writer attended an international conference in Australia. During the conference, the writer received complaints concerning a Japanese mother who took her child back to Japan without the consent of her Australian husband after the divorce proceedings. Since then, the writer has received many more similar complaints from the international community. The writer has since attempted to learn the causes of 'international child abduction' and devised possible solutions to prevent further incidents of international child abduction.

The writer has written several academic opinions on the topic upon requests from legal practitioners around the world. The writer acknowledges practical

---

* Professor, Faculty of Law, Kindai University, Osaka.

difficulties in resolving the disputes involving 'international child abductions' as it often involves conflict of laws between jurisdictions. The writer further acknowledges that it is often impossible to resolve the disputes harmoniously as the resolution will always be a 'win-lose' situation.

This chapter will examine some of the differences between Japan and other Western industrialised countries that create 'international child abduction'. It will also propose possible solutions to prevent further incidents of 'international child abduction'.

II   HISTORY AND THE CURRENT DIVORCE LAW

(a)   Western countries

(i)   *History*

In Western countries, jurisdiction in family matters originally resided with the Christian Church. This jurisdiction was later transferred to the government; however, the Christian Church retained significant influence over family matters. Thus, divorces were prohibited. Gradually, the governments of the Western countries allowed divorces only on certain fault grounds such as adultery and desertion.

(ii)   *Current law*

Most of the Western industrialised countries have now abandoned the fault-based divorce system and adopted the no-fault divorce system, where the only ground to obtain a divorce order is irretrievable breakdown of marriage.[1]

Who may apply for a divorce order?

Most of Western industrialised countries allow either party to apply for a divorce order irrespective of fault (eg Australia). Only some Western industrialised countries retain the restriction that only the party whom the court considers to be innocent may apply for a divorce order (ie if the marriage has broken down irretrievably due to adultery committed by one party, only the other party may apply for a divorce order).

What is an irretrievable breakdown of marriage?

A court may decide that there has been an irretrievable breakdown of marriage between the parties to the marriage:

(1)   where the parties have lived apart and separately for a certain period of time (*set period method*); or

---

[1]   For example Australia; s 48(1) of the Family Law Act 1975 (Cth).

(2)   where in the court's opinion, after examination of the facts, there has been irretrievable breakdown of marriage (*substance method*).

Most of the Western industrialised countries are currently using the set period method to determine whether there has been irretrievable breakdown of marriage.[2]

Custody of the child aka parental responsibility

In Western industrialised countries, parental responsibility or custody of the child is generally shared between the parents after the divorce proceedings.[3]

Benefit of no-fault divorce system

No-fault divorce system makes it possible for the divorced couples to have joint custody of their children as it significantly reduces the hostility between them.

(b)   Japanese family law crash course

(i)   *Divorce*

In Japan, there are five main ways a married couple may divorce:

(1)   Divorce by consent under art 763 of the Civil Code (*Minpo*): the parties in these circumstances agree to divorce by making a divorce notification and filing the divorce notification in the Registry of Family Relation. The Family Court of Japan is not involved in this process.

(2)   Divorce through Family Court Mediation under art 17 of the Family Affairs Law (*Kajishinpanho*): if an agreement cannot be made by consent, the parties must apply for the mediation procedure through the Family Court where divorce by mediation is rendered only when the mediation committee establishes an agreement in writing between the parties.

(3)   Divorce after obtaining a Family Court Judicial Decree under art 24 of the Family Affairs Law (*Kajishinpanho*): A Family Court Judicial Decree is available only when a Family Court Adjudicator is satisfied that the parties are unable to reach an agreement due only to a property and custody dispute. An Adjudicator may render a Decree to resolve the dispute after accepting arguments and evidence from the parties and making its own enquiries.

(4)   Divorce after obtaining a Court Judgment under art 770 of the Civil Code (*Minpo*): the parties decide to go through a hearing for divorce after mediation has failed. A judgment for divorce can only be given by the court after careful examination of the evidence.

---

2   Eg Australia; s 48(2) of the Family Law Act 1975 (Cth).
3   Eg Australia; s 61DA of the Family Law Act 1975 (Cth).

(5) Settlement Agreement during the divorce proceedings under art 37 of the Family Procedure Law (*Jinjisoshouho*): the parties agree to settle during the proceedings and the Family Court renders a judgment in accordance to the agreement.

90% of all divorces in Japan are obtained by consent, 9% are obtained by Family Court Mediation and only 1% are obtained by a Family Court Judgment. Thus, 99% of divorces in Japan occur without the need of showing grounds for divorce to the court. However, while only 1% of all divorces are obtained through a Family Court Judgment, the rationale behind these judgments significantly influences all of the divorce matters as the parties usually consider the possible outcome of court proceedings during their negotiation.

Grounds for divorce

Article 770 of the Civil Code (*Minpo*) provides that:

> 'only in the cases stated in the following items may either husband or wife file a suit for divorce:
>
> (1) If a spouse has committed an act of unchastity;
> (2) If abandoned by a spouse in bad faith;
> (3) If it is not clear whether a spouse is dead or alive for not less than three years;
> (4) If a spouse is suffering from severe mental illness and there is no prospect of recovery; or
> (5) If there is any other grave cause making it difficult to continue the marriage.'

As is apparent from the article, the Japanese grounds for divorce are a mixture of fault, neutral and no-fault grounds. The majority of plaintiffs bring an application for a divorce judgment under the fault grounds. The writer submits that the reasons for that tendency are:

(1) it is often easier for a spouse to prove that his or her partner is committing a fault rather than proving there is irretrievable marriage breakdown; and

(2) a spouse may obtain compensation for his or her suffering as a result of a fault committed by his or her spouse.

Who may apply for a divorce judgment?

Traditionally, only the innocent party may apply for a divorce order (ie if the marriage has broken down irretrievably due to adultery committed by one party, only the other party may apply for a divorce order).[4]

---

4   19 February 1952, *Minshu* Vol 6 No 2 page 110.

In 1987, the Supreme Court of Japan changed its view.[5] A party at fault can now file an application for a divorce judgment on the basis of the following requirements:

(1) there has been a long-term separation (in that particular case 36 years of separation);

(2) there are no infants between them; and

(3) the divorce does not cause severe circumstances for the other spouse, mentally, socially and economically.

The most common example of 'other grave cause making it difficult to continue the marriage'

The most common example of 'other grave cause making it difficult to continue the marriage' is irretrievable breakdown of marriage. The Japanese Family Court uses the substance method in determining whether a marriage between a couple has broken down irretrievably (see Part II(a)(ii) under the heading 'What is an irretrievable breakdown of marriage?').

(ii)   Property settlement

Article 768(1) of the Civil Code (*Minpo*) provides 'one party to a divorce by agreement may claim a distribution of property from the other party'. Article 768(2) of the Civil Code (*Minpo*) provides 'if the parties do not, or cannot, settle on agreement … either party may make a claim to the family court for … distribution of property'.

The court may take into consideration the following factors in property settlement matters:

(1) the contributions of each of the parties to the assets of the household;

(2) the necessity of each of the parties for financial support; and

(3) whether a party committing a fault should compensate the other party for his or her suffering.

The third factor has created controversies as it blurs the distinction between tort law and family law. The writer argues that the Family Court should only deal with the first two factors as the third factor falls under tort law.

The Supreme Court has held that the plaintiff has an option to claim property distribution under the first two factors and compensation under the third factor either separately or together. If the plaintiff has not received any

---

[5]   2 September 1987, *Minshu* Vol 41 No 6 page 1423.

property distribution from the defendant, the plaintiff may claim compensation under the third factor within the same Family Court proceedings.[6] If the plaintiff has received a property distribution from the defendant which does not sufficiently compensate the plaintiff under the third factor, the plaintiff may commence other proceedings against the defendant in the Local Court to obtain additional compensation.[7]

The writer submits that these judgments further blur the distinction between the family property distribution law and tort law.

(iii)   Custody of the children

If parties to a marriage wish to divorce by consent, they must agree upon which parent shall have sole parental authority.[8] If the parties are unable to agree, then the court shall determine which parent shall have parental authority.[9]

A parent who has parental authority has:

(1)   the right and duty to care for and educate the child;[10]

(2)   the right to determine the residence of the child;[11]

(3)   the right to discipline the child to the extent necessary;[12]

(4)   the right to decide whether to allow the child to have an occupation;[13] and

(5)   the right to administer the property of the child and represent the child in any legal matters.[14]

The parties may agree or the court may make a determination of who will have authority over the personal matters of the child (the first four authorities of the parental authority).[15] Generally, a person who has authority over the personal matters of the child will have the physical custody of the child. In practice, it is quite rare for the parties to make an agreement under this provision.

Consequently, in most cases, the parties will only have an agreement about which parent shall have sole parental authority under art 819 of the Civil Code (*Minpo*). A parent who has sole parental authority will have both physical

---

6   The Supreme Court Judgment, 21 February 1956, *Minshu* Vol 10 No 2 page 124.
7   The Supreme Court Judgment, 23 July 1971, *Minshu* Vol 25 No 5 page 805.
8   Article 819(1) of the Civil Code (*Minpo*).
9   Article 819(2) of the Civil Code (*Minpo*).
10   Article 820 of the Civil Code (*Minpo*).
11   Article 821 of the Civil Code (*Minpo*).
12   Article 822 of the Civil Code (*Minpo*).
13   Article 823 of the Civil Code (*Minpo*).
14   Article 824 of the Civil Code (*Minpo*).
15   Article 766 of the Civil Code (*Minpo*).

custody of the child and sole parental responsibility (ie the other parent has no rights in relation to the child apart from visitation rights as agreed between the parties).

Before the 1960s, it was the fathers who usually obtained the sole parental authority over the children. At present, in over 80% of the divorces matters, the mothers obtain sole parental authority over the child. In most of the cases, the mothers will obtain sole parental authority over the children if the children are infants. Hence, it is a common understanding among Japanese mothers who have infants that they will obtain the sole parental authority. This seems to be the case even if the Japanese mother reside outside Japan.

III   MAIN CAUSES OF INTERNATIONAL CHILD ABDUCTIONS INVOLVING JAPANESE PARENTS

The majority of Japanese people fail to understand that taking children away back to Japan without the consent of their overseas spouses after the divorce proceedings constitutes child abduction in many countries. They also fail to appreciate that 'international child abduction' is a substantial issue within the international community. The writer submits that these failures are caused by the differences between Japan and other Western industrialised countries, such as differences in legal systems, culture and customs. The writer understands that 'international child abductions' also occur in other countries that have similar systems to the Japanese family law.

(a)   Differences in legal systems

As mentioned previously, in Japan, the parties usually only have an agreement about which parent shall have sole parental authority under art 819 of the Civil Code (*Minpo*). A parent who has sole parental authority will have both physical custody of the child and sole parental responsibility. There is no concept of shared parental responsibility in the Japanese legal system. Shared parental responsibility after divorce does not exist in Japan since it is often easier for a spouse to prove that his or her partner is committing a fault rather than proving there is irretrievable marriage breakdown. As such, there is often hostility between the divorcing couple which makes it impossible for the divorcing couple to have joint custody of children after the divorce proceedings.

Conversely, the majority of Western industrialised countries have abandoned the fault-based divorce system and adopted no-fault divorce system. No-fault divorce system makes it possible for the divorced couples to have joint custody of their children as it significantly reduces the hostility between them.

Most Japanese mothers who reside outside Japan have significant difficulties in understanding the concept of joint parental responsibility as there is no such concept in the Japanese legal system. Most Japanese mothers consider that the court's decision which grants shared parental responsibility to the other party is preposterous. As a result, some Japanese mothers decide to take the children back to Japan where they will obtain 'justice'.

(b) Differences in culture and customs

Most Japanese mothers believe that the sole custody system is better than the shared custody system. There are two reasons for this belief:

(1) the shared custody system does not exist in the Japanese legal system and thus, the Family Court has always handed down sole custody to one of the parents; and

(2) there are often hostilities between the parties during the divorce proceedings in Japan which makes it very difficult to have shared custody of the child between the parties.

Japanese mothers are often acting on this belief when they decide to defy the shared custody order of a foreign country. Most Japanese mothers also believe that it is better to raise their children in Japan under Japanese traditions. Japanese mothers believe that they are acting in the best interest of the children when they decide to take the children to Japan in defiance of court orders. Japanese fathers are often pressured by their family to bring the children back to Japan to continue the family name. This pressure often contributes to the fathers' decision to commit international child abduction.

IV PROPOSED SOLUTIONS TO PREVENT FURTHER INCIDENTS OF INTERNATIONAL CHILD ABDUCTION

(a) Alterations of the Japanese legal system to make it more harmonious with other Western industrialised countries

Abandonment of the fault-based divorce system

As mentioned previously, the fault-based divorce system often introduces hostility between the divorcing couple which makes it impossible for the divorcing couple to have joint custody of children after the divorce proceedings. Japan needs to abandon this fault-based divorce system in favour of a no-fault divorce system to reduce the hostility during the divorce proceedings.

Introduction of 'set period method' to determine whether the marriage between the parties has broken down irretrievably

Any party should be allowed to file an application for a divorce judgment irrespective of fault. This is to ensure the parties can obtain a divorce when there has been an irretrievable marriage breakdown. Irretrievable marriage breakdown should then be determined using the set period method (ie a court will deem that the marriage has broken down irretrievably after the parties have lived apart and separate for a certain period of time). The writer submits that the above steps will further ameliorate hostility between the divorcing couples during the divorce proceedings.

Introduction of a joint custody system in Japan

The abandonment of a fault-based divorce system and the introduction of the set period system will significantly reduce the tension and hostility between the divorcing couples. The reduction of hostility between the divorcing couples will make it possible for the divorcing couples to have a discussion regarding long-term decisions in relation to the child. The Japanese government should introduce a joint custody system in Japan after the reduction of hostility and establishment of harmonious conversations between the divorcing couple.

(b) Community education

The Japanese government should educate the community:

(1)   about the advantages of the no-fault divorce system, such as:

    (a)   it reduces tension and hostility between the parties; and
    (b)   it increases expediency in divorce matters by simplifying the process;

(2)   the benefit of the joint custody system of the child, such as:

    (a)   it allows the child to have a meaningful relationship with both parents;
    (b)   it allows both parents to be directly involved with decisions concerning the child; and
    (c)   it reduces economic tension for single mothers as the fathers are more likely to pay child support as a result of direct involvement with the child;

(3)   that it is illegal for Japanese citizens to take their children from foreign countries to Japan without the consent of their spouse.

V   CONCLUSION

Japan has received numerous criticisms concerning 'international child abductions'. The writer submits that international child abductions are caused by the differences between Japan and other Western industrialised countries, such as differences in legal systems, culture and customs.

Differences in legal systems between Japan and other Western industrialised countries are the main cause of 'international child abductions'. Under the current Japanese legal system, only one of the parents will obtain sole parental authority. The parent who obtains sole parental authority may prevent the other parent from contacting the child. As such, under the current legal system, Japan cannot become a party to the Hague Convention on the Civil Aspects of International Child Abduction due to inconsistencies between the current Japanese legal system (sole parental authority) and the Convention.

The Japanese Family Court used to refuse applications from overseas parents to allow them to take their children back to their original countries. The Family Court generally refused the applications because the court considered that it would be inappropriate to allow the child to be returned to the original country when the child is well settled in his or her current environment. This view is changing and the Family Court is now a lot more willing to allow the applications from overseas parents. The Family Court now considers 'international child abductions' to be illegal. The Family Court cannot allow Japanese citizens to retain children because to do so would mean the court is condoning the citizens' illegal behaviour.

The writer proposes that to prevent further incidents of international child abduction by Japanese parents:

(1) the current Japanese legal system should be altered so it is more harmonious with other Western industrialised countries; and

(2) the Japanese government should conduct community education to improve Japanese parents' understanding of the illegality of international child abductions.

The writer submits that the proposed solutions to prevent further incidents of international child abductions may also work for other countries that have similar legal systems to Japan.

Macedonia

THE LEGAL REGULATION OF NONMARITAL COHABITATION IN MACEDONIAN FAMILY LAW

Dejan Mickovikj and Angel Ristov*

Résumé

Les changements rapides qui se produisent dans la famille et dans les relations familiales ont contribué à l'essor de la conjugalité hors mariage dans presque toutes les sociétés modernes. Bien que légèrement en retard par rapport à d'autres juridictions, la loi macédonienne de la famille prévoit la cohabitation basée sur le concept de 'mariage non enregistré'. Selon le droit familial macédonien, la cohabitation est définie comme l'union de l'homme et de la femme qui a duré au moins un an. La cohabitation est assimilée au mariage mais uniquement pour ce qui est des biens acquis pendant la vie commune ainsi que de l'obligation alimentaire. Les conjoints n'ont pas de droits successoraux, ni de droits dans les domaines de l'assurance maladie, des retraites ou de la sécurité sociale. Ils ont, par contre, accès à la procréation médicalement assistée ainsi qu'à la procréation à titre posthume.

L'analyse de la législation nationale permet de constater qu'il existe de nombreuses lacunes dans l'encadrement des relations hors mariage, ce qui crée des problèmes au niveau des recours judiciaires. Ces lacunes devraient être corrigées dans les futures réformes de droit de la famille, qui seront intégrées dans le nouveau Code Civil qui est actuellement en chantier. À cet égard, il conviendra d'appliquer à la cohabitation les obstacles du mariage, de même qu'il faudra prévoir un meilleur arrimage entre le mariage et la cohabitation au chapitre du droit patrimonial. La prochaine reforme devrait reconnaître aux cohabitants certains droit successoraux, introduire un système d'enregistrement volontaire et accorder le statut d'héritier à l'enfant né après le décès d'un parent.

---

*   Dejan Mickovikj, Associate Professor at Faculty of Law 'Iustinianus Primus', University 'Saints Cyril and Methodius', Skopje, Republic of Macedonia.
Angel Ristov, lecturer at Faculty of Law 'Iustinianus Primus', University 'Saints Cyril and Methodius', Skopje, Republic of Macedonia.

I INTRODUCTION

In modern Western societies the famous saying of Napoleon 'Les concubins ignore le loi, le loi les ignore'[1] is obviously no longer valid. The statistical data for marital and family relations of Western countries clearly shows that marriage does not represent a unique form to start a family.[2] This dramatic increase in nonmarital cohabitation confronts the legislators with the dilemma 'whether legal policy should take an adverse attitude, to ignore or to accept the evolution in the sphere of the custom'.[3] This is a relatively new phenomenon, because, as Mary Ann Glendon states: '[a]s late as the 1960s, informal cohabitation was not considered a legal subject ... It was as though jurists everywhere had agreed to pretend the phenomenon did not exist.'[4] The number

---

[1] Marie-Thérèse Meulders-Klein 'Mariage et concubinage ou les sens et contresens de l'histoire' in *La Personne, La Famille et le Droit 1968–1998, Trois décennies de mutations en occident* (Brussels: Bruylant, Paris: LGDJ, 1999) 23.

[2] In New Zealand with a total population of a little over 4 million, according to the 2006 census, 428,130 people lived in nonmarital unions, compared with 87,960 in 1981 when figures were first collected. Two in five people between 15 and 44 years were in de facto relationships. Also according to the 2006 census there were 6,171 couples living in same-sex relationships, 2,655 male couples and 3,516 female couples. See Bill Atkin 'The Legal World of Nonmarital Couples: Reflections on "De Facto Relationships" in recent New Zealand Legislation' (2009) 39 VUWLR 793–812. According to the 2006 Census 28.8% of all families in Quebec were nonmarital. See further on cohabitation in Canada Martha Bailey 'Polygamy and Nonmarital Cohabitation' Canada in Bill Atkin (ed) *International Survey of Family Law, 2011 Edition* (Jordan Publishing Limited, 2011) 139–145. According to Judith A Seltzer in the USA in 1960 there were 400,000 nonmarital couples, and in 2004 the number of nonmarital couples was 4.6 million. See Judith A Seltzer 'Cohabitation in the United States and Britain: Demography, Kinship and the Future' (2004) 66 *Journal of Marriage and Family* 922. According to Popenoe the percentage of nonmarital couples compared to all couples in Australia, for the period 1996–2006, increased from 10.1% to 15%. In France for the period 1995–2001 the percentage of nonmarital couples increased from 13.6% to 17.2%. In Great Britain for the period 1995–2004 the percentage of nonmarital couples increased from 10.1% to 15.4%. See David Popenoe *Cohabitation, Marriage and Child Wellbeing* (The National Marriage Project, 2008) 2. For the increase of the number of nonmarital communities see: François Boulanger *Droit Civil de la Famille* 3 édition, tom I, 'Aspects comparatives et internationaux' (Paris: Economica, 1998) 355–356.

[3] Marie-Thérèse Meulders-Klein, above n 1, 14. In this sense, Bill Atkin states: 'The Western phenomenon of increasing cohabitation outside marriage hardly needs documenting. From a legal point of view, it cannot be ignored. There are several approaches that can be taken into account, for example: laissez faire, leaving the parties to rely on the general law for any remedy; an 'opt-in' scheme, which enables parties to jointly sign up to a legislatively determined regime (or perhaps to choose from more than one option).' Bill Atkin, above n 2, 793. According to Sarah Bulloch and Debbie Headrick: 'Approaches to legal recognition of cohabitants can be broadly separated into: the *registration approach* (Netherlands, France), the *presumptive approach*, (Australia, New South Wales, New Zealand) and the *contractual approach*'. See Sarah Bulloch and Debbie Headrick *Cross-jurisdictional Comparison of Legal Provisions for Nonmarital Cohabiting Couples* (Legal Studies Research Team, Scottish Executive, No 55, 2005) 2.

[4] Mary Ann Glendon *The Transformation of Family Law* (Chicago and London: The University of Chicago Press, 1989) 252.

of European legislators that allow spouses to choose whether they will contract a marriage or will enter into another legally regulated form of cohabitation is growing.[5]

The increase in nonmarital cohabitation does not only pose a dilemma for the legislators, but also represents a huge challenge for legal and social theory, in which there is an enormous increase of published texts in peer-reviewed social science journals.[6] Nonmarital cohabitation, according to many authors, is not only a first step towards marriage, as before, but in contemporary society it is an actual alternative to marriage. This leads to a change in attitude by the courts when they resolve disputes related to nonmarital cohabitation.[7]

In Macedonian family legislation, nonmarital cohabitation was regulated, for the first time, in the Family Law Act[8] of 1992. The basis for this change was the

---

[5]   See further: Jacqueline Rubellin-Devichi *Des concubinages dans le monde* (Paris: Centre de droit de la famille, Editions du Centre National de la Recherche Scientifique, 1990).

[6]   According to Pamela Smock, Lynne Casper and Jessica Wyse the number of published texts that analyse nonmarital unions in peer-reviewed social science journals for the period 1988–1993 was 88, for the period 1994–1999 was 196, and for the period 2000–2005 was 436. See Pamela Smock, Lynne Casper and Jessica Wyse *Nonmarital Cohabitation: Current Knowledge and Future Direction for Research* Report 08–648 (University of Michigan, Population Studies Center, July 2008) 2.

[7]   According to Katherine O'Donovan: 'Where a man and a woman have lived together for some 20 years it has nevertheless been held as follows: "To say two people masquerading, as these two were, as husband and wife there being no children to complicate the picture, that they were members of the same family, seems to be an abuse of the English language" and the court therefore denied the status of family membership to the survivor' (*Gammans v Ekins* [1950] 2 KB 328). However, in a later case, 21 years of heterosexual cohabitation sufficed to enable the tenancy to pass to surviving cohabitee. The word 'family' was 'not restricted to blood relationships and those created by the marriage ceremony', but must be considered in common parlance or the 'popular meaning or concept of the word' (*Dyson Holdings v Fox* [1976] QB 503 (CA)). See Katherine O'Donovan *Family Law Matters* (London: Pluto Press, 1993) 34. According to Katz, in 1976, the California Supreme Court decided the case of *Marvin v Marvin*, and the court in this case basically recognised a social reality. Katz points out that the decision by the Supreme Court of California is important for recognising that there can be legal consequences for two adults living together in a nonmarital relationship. In particular, the court specifically allows nonmarital couples who live together the power to arrange their lives using contract principles. In addition, the court also permits the judicial application of equitable remedies if facts permit it. In the case *Marvin v Marvin* 18 Cal 3d 660 (1976) the Supreme Court of California recognised the rights of nonmarital couples to sue each other for compensation if the facts support either contract or some equitable doctrine. In the case *Wilcox v Trautz* 427 Mass 326 (1998), Justice Greany wrote: 'Social mores regarding cohabitation between nonmarital parties have changed dramatically in recent years and living arrangements that were once criticized are now relatively common and accepted. With the prevalence of nonmarital relationships today, a considerable number of persons live together without benefit of the rules of law that govern property, financial, and other matters in a marital relationship ... Thus, we do well to recognize the benefits to be gained by encouraging nonmarital cohabitants to enter into written agreements respecting these matters, as the consequences for each partner may be considerable on termination of the relationship or, in particular in the event of the death of one of the partners.' See Sanford N Katz 'New Directions for Family Law in the United States' in *Dret revista para el analisis del derecho* (Barcelona, April 2007).

[8]   *Official Gazette of Republic of Macedonia* nos 80/92, 9/96, 38/2004, 33/06, 84/08 and 157/08.

new Constitution of the Republic of Macedonia[9] of 1991. Article 40(2) states: 'Marriage, the family, and *nonmarital cohabitation* are regulated by Law.' The legal regulation of the status of nonmarital cohabitation was one of the more significant innovations introduced in Macedonian family legislation.[10] In the Republic of Macedonia, the greatest reform since the independence of the country in the sphere of civil law recently started.[11] The government of the Republic of Macedonia adopted a decision in December 2010 to establish a Commission for drafting a Civil Code of the Republic of Macedonia. This will represent the most serious reform in the sphere of civil law. With the drafting of the Civil Code, the expectation is that a new quality in the regulation of civil law can be achieved. Following the example of the European Civil Codes, the new Macedonian Civil Code will consist of the general part, property law, the law of obligations, inheritance law and family law. The Commission accepted this concept, unlike other post-socialist family legislation, such as the Russian Federation, where family law is not an integral part of the Civil Code, but is regulated in a specific family code of the Russian Federation.[12]

The legal recognition and regulation of nonmarital cohabitation represents one of the novel developments in contemporary family law systems, following the enhancement of the legal status of children born out of wedlock. Nonmarital cohabitation is becoming a more prevalent and important basis for the creation of a family.[13] Having this in mind, as well as other transformations in the family that are taking place in Macedonian society, it is obvious that there is a need to introduce more significant reforms in family legislation, including reform regarding nonmarital cohabitation. It is expected that these changes will be incorporated in the new Civil Code.[14] Therefore, this paper will provide an analysis of the legal regulation of nonmarital cohabitation, in order to answer

---

[9]   *Official Gazette of Republic of Macedonia* no 52/91.

[10] See more: Ljiljana Spirovikj-Trpenovska *Characteristics of Family Law in Republic of Macedonia, Family legislation in Republic of Macedonia* Essays on the National Consultation (Skopje: Supreme Court of the Republic of Macedonia, 1994) 11–12; Hadji Lega Kocho 'Nonmarital Cohabitation: Occurrence, Termination, Property Relations and Maintenance of Non-marital Couples' in *Family Legislation of Republic of Macedonia* Essays on the National Consultation (Skopje: Supreme Court of the Republic of Macedonia, 1994) 214–221.

[11] See more: *Codification of Macedonian Civil and Trade Law,* Miscellany on the scientific debate held in Skopje on 18 June 2008, Macedonian Academy of Sciences and Arts.

[12] For more information see: Alexandra Matveevna Nechaeva, *Family Law* (Moscow: Yurait, 2011). For the reforms in the family law systems in post-soviet states see further: Olga A Khazova 'Family Law on Post-Soviet European Territory: A Comparative Overview of Some Recent Trends' (2010) 14(1) *Electronic Journal of Comparative Law.*

[13] Regarding the question of a specific number of nonmarital communities in Macedonian society, there are no official figures. However, compared to Scandinavian countries and other countries in Europe, nonmarital communities in the Republic of Macedonia are insignificant. This is due to patriarchal values, still dominant and present in our society.

[14] See: Dejan Mickovikj and Angel Ristov 'The Changes within Family and Family Law Reforms in European Countries' in *Collection of articles in honour of Prof Naum Grizo* (Skopje: Law Faculty 'Iustinianus Primus', 2011); Dejan Mickovikj and Ristov Angel 'Reforms in Family and Inheritance Law and Competencies of Notaries' (2011) *Notarius* (Skopje: professional magazine).

the question whether it is necessary to revise certain remedies and introduce changes and reforms to the legal status of nonmarital cohabitation in the Republic of Macedonia.

II LEGAL REGULATION OF NONMARITAL COHABITATION

Macedonian family law did not regulate nonmarital cohabitation until the adoption of the Family Law Act (FLA) in 1992.[15] In the preceding period, nonmarital cohabitation was not regulated and did not enjoy legal protection.[16] Nonetheless, in judicial practice there were a few cases where the nonmarital cohabitation partner had certain property rights.[17] Regarding the attitude of society towards this phenomenon, we can see fluctuations that depended on the development of social relations, but in general the attitude towards nonmarital cohabitation was negative.

In Macedonian family law theory, nonmarital cohabitation is defined as 'the community of life between man and woman, which, according to the content of the actual relations between the nonmarital partners, is no different than the marriage community'.[18] According to another opinion, nonmarital cohabitation represents 'a community of life of two people of different sex who did not enter into marriage, based on their intention that this relation was to be permanent'.[19] In other words, nonmarital cohabitation represents community of life with a permanent character of a man and woman, which did not conclude in a valid marriage.

---

[15] Unlike Macedonia, the other republics and provinces, members of the former Federation, in their legislation started to regulate nonmarital cohabitation after the adoption of the Constitution of Yugoslavia (SFRJ) in 1974: Kosovo (1974), Slovenia (1976), Croatia (1978), Bosnia and Herzegovina (1979) and Serbia (1980). See Mile Hadji Vasilev 'Family Law' (1990) *Student's Word* (Skopje) 225–226.

[16] Macedonia's Constitutions from 1946, 1963 and 1974 did not contain provisions for nonmarital cohabitation: ibid.

[17] For judicial practice see: Hadji Lega Kocho, above n 10, 215; Kiril Chavdar *The Law on Family and other Regulations* (Skopje: *Official Gazette of Republic of Macedonia*, 1993). According to the decision of the Supreme Court of Macedonia, where the plaintiff suffered from the beginning of the nonmarital cohabitation with the defendant, after she was promised that they would enter into marriage and the defendant hid the fact that he had child born out of wedlock and that he lived in a nonmarital union with another woman – the defendant was responsible for the damage, because he deluded the plaintiff. Without this the plaintiff would not have entered into nonmarital cohabitation relations with the defendant (*VSM Gz 366/72,Zb.VM I odl. 169*).

[18] Mile Hadji Vasilev, above n 15, 223.

[19] Kocho Hadji Lega, above n 10, 215.

In the FLA, even though during the drafting period, the idea of introducing 'registered' nonmarital cohabitation was present, the concept of unregistered nonmarital cohabitation was accepted.[20] In art 13 of the FLA nonmarital cohabitation is defined as:

> 'The living community of a man and woman, which has not been established according to the provisions of this law (nonmarital cohabitation) and has endured at least one year, is equal to marriage in the right of mutual maintenance and the property acquired during the time of existence of that cohabitation.'

It can be noticed that the essential conditions for the existence and validity of nonmarital cohabitation are: (1) the existence of community between a man and woman; and (2) the endurance of this cohabitation for at least one year.

(1) With regard to the *first condition* – diversity of sexes, it can be ascertained that Macedonian family law legislation envisages and permits only heterosexual nonmarital cohabitation. For the recognition of nonmarital cohabitation, the totality of the relations between spouses, its quality and a real intention for joint living are essential.[21] Therefore, it is rightly pointed out that 'temporary, short-term, and often "accidental" relations between man and woman cannot be called nonmarital cohabitation'.[22]

(2) *The second condition* envisaged by the FLA is that nonmarital cohabitation should last at least one year. Bearing in mind that in Macedonia law the concept of 'unregistered' nonmarital cohabitation is accepted, the necessity to prove the existence and the duration of nonmarital cohabitation is essential when nonmarital cohabitation is terminated. This problem is often present in judicial practice and manifested in long and difficult judicial processes. Thus, one of the more important principles, the principle of legal security in property relations, is endangered.

From the legal definition of nonmarital cohabitation and conditions envisaged for its validity, it can be noticed that the legislator did not envisage legal impediments for nonmarital cohabitation partners. In family law theory, even before the adoption of the FLA, a number of authors wrote that there should be marriage impediments if nonmarital cohabitation is to produce legal consequences.[23] This attitude has not changed even today, and some authors are of the opinion that this omission should be remedied.[24] Thus, the legislator

---

[20] See: Ljiljana Spirovikj-Trpenovska *Characteristics of Family Law in Republic of Macedonia,* above n 10, 11–12.

[21] See: Ljiljana Spirovikj-Trpenovska *Family Law* (Skopje: Law Faculty 'Iustinianus Primus', 2008) 252.

[22] Mile Hadji Vasilev, above n 15, 224.

[23] On this view Mile Hadzi Vasilev considers that nonmarital cohabitation communities where there are no marriage obstacles are rightfully permitted. According to Mile Hadzi Vasilev, nonmarital cohabitation communities where there are certain obstacles, envisaged by law, are to be considered illegal and immoral communities: ibid.

[24] See: Dejan Mickovikj, Lidija Stojkova 'Non-marital Cohabitation in Contemporary Families'

should envisage that, in order to equalise the legal effects of marriage and nonmarital cohabitation, with regard to the right to maintenance and division of property acquired during the community, *there should be no marriage impediments between the individual nonmarital cohabitation partners.*[25]

In comparative law, most of the European legislation envisages that individual nonmarital cohabitation partners should have no marriage impediments between them,[26] but Macedonia is the rare country where, according to the current solution envisaged in the FLA, marriage impediments are not envisaged at all for nonmarital partners.[27] As a result of this omission of the legislator in Macedonia, in reality there are cases where a man or a woman can have simultaneously marital and nonmarital partners, which represents a rare case in comparative law.[28]

This kind of omission by the legislator causes legal inconsistencies and troubles in practice. In Macedonia the nonmarital cohabitation community might create legal consequences, even though one or both nonmarital partners are in a marriage or are closely related, for example they are first cousins etc. The legal regulation of nonmarital cohabitation in Macedonia produces a lot of dilemmas and problems in judicial practice.[29]

(1999) 15 *Student's Word* (Skopje: Eurodialogue) 99; Ljiljana Spirovikj-Trpenovska *Analogy between Non-marital Cohabitation and Marriage* Collection of articles in honour of Prof Borislav Blagoev (Skopje, 2007); Dejan Mickovikj 'Legal Regulation of Non-marital Cohabitation' (2008) 195–196 *Lawyer* (Lawyers Association of Republic of Macedonia, magazine) 8; Angel Ristov *Non-marital Cohabitation and the Status of Non-marital partners due to the Law on Inheritance* (Strumica: Association Iuridica, 2010); Ljiljana Spirovikj-Trpenovska, Dejan Mickovikj and Angel Ristov, *Succession Law in Republic of Macedonia* (Skopje: Institution of culture 'Shine', 2010); Ljiljana Spirovikj-Trpenovska, Dejan Mickovikj and Angel Ristov, 'Does the Law on Inheritance in Republic of Macedonia Require Changes?' in *Collection of articles in honour of Prof Ganzovski* (Skopje: Law Faculty 'Iustinianus Primus', 2011).

[25] Ljiljana Spirovikj-Trpenovska, Dejan Mickovikj and Angel Ristov *Inheritance in Europe* (Skopje: Institution of Culture 'Shine', 2011).

[26] See: Ljiljana Spirovikj-Trpenovska, Dejan Mickovikj and Angel Ristov, ibid 164–169.

[27] In the Family Law Acts and judicial practice in the former Yugoslav republics, the view was that there should be no marriage impediments between nonmarital partners. Nonmarital cohabitation does not produce legal consequences, if during the existence of the community, one of the partners was married (Decision of District Court Kragujevac Gzh *169/92, 23.02.1993, ISP – 7*). See: Ilija Babik *Comments on the Law on Marriage and Family matters* (Belgrade: *Official Gazette of SRJ*, 1999) 15.

[28] See Angel Ristov 'Nonmarital Cohabitation Community', Scientific Conference on the occasion of the 20th anniversary of the establishment of Faculty of Law in Veliko Trnovo, *Ius est ars boni et aequi,* Republic of Bulgaria, 14–16 April 2011.

[29] In the case 17 P-927/10 од 30.11.2010, the Primary Court Skopje 2 determined that the plaintiff SA on the basis of joint acquisition of property in nonmarital cohabitation with the deceased SA obtained the right of mutual ownership of real estate in Skopje. In the appeal against the first instance decision the defendant stated that the existence of marriage represented a marital impediment for the existence of nonmarital cohabitation. The Primary Court provided the following answer: 'Pursuant to Article 13 from the Family Law Act, the community of living between man and woman that is not based on the provisions of this law (nonmarital cohabitation) and which lasts for at least one year is equal with marriage, regarding the right to mutual maintenance and acquired property during the common life. The higher court in the

III   THE BEGINNING OF NONMARITAL COHABITATION

One of the most significant differences between marriage and nonmarital cohabitation is in the informal character of the beginning of the nonmarital community. In order to conclude a valid marriage certain essential conditions are necessary to be fulfilled. Essential conditions for a valid marriage according to the Macedonian FLA are: (1) different sexes of the partners; (2) free will to conclude a marriage from both partners; and (3) fulfillment of the formal requirements to conclude a marriage. To conclude a valid marriage there should not be any marital impediments. Marriage is concluded with a specific written and official form (*ad solemnitatem*) in the presence of the future marital partners, two witnesses and an official registry officer. Unlike marriage, nonmarital cohabitation is informal, and based on the free will of the nonmarital partners to live together. For its establishment there is no need for participation of a competent state authority, witnesses or other persons. In Macedonian legislation the marital impediments are not prescribed as a condition for the validity of the nonmarital community. In order to produce legal consequences, the legislator has prescribed only two conditions for nonmarital community: differences of sex of the nonmarital partners and a common life that should last at least one year.

Macedonian family law has accepted the concept of unregistered nonmarital cohabitation, so there is no need for a written statement, or for registration of the nonmarital community in front of any competent state authority. For its establishment a common life between the man and women for at least one year is sufficient. The exact moment of the establishment of nonmarital cohabitation is known only to the nonmarital partners, but not to the wider public. Because nonmarital cohabitation is not registered and no public document is issued, after its termination it is necessary to prove the beginning and the cessation of community, so that the rights in the FLA can be applied correctly.

In comparative law, there are only a few countries (Croatia, Slovenia, Monte Negro and Kosovo) which approve legally unregistered nonmarital cohabitation.[30] Therefore, we consider that the legislator should provide a solution for nonmarital partners who want to avoid possible difficulties in the exercising of their rights, enabling them to formalise their union with a

---

first judgment stated that nonmarital cohabitation cannot produce legal consequences, if there are marital impediments. After the second judgment of the Primary Court, the Skopje Court of Appeal reached a verdict by which the appeal of the co-defendant E.A. was rejected as groundless, and the verdict of the Primary Court Skopje was confirmed. In the explanation of the verdict, the Court of Appeal stated that the formal existence of marriage as an impediment for the actual existence of nonmarital cohabitation cannot be an obstacle for nonmarital cohabitation to create legal consequences.' For more information see Dejan Mickovikj and Angel Ristov 'Reforms in Family and Inheritance Law and Competencies of Notaries' (2011) *Notarius* (Skopje: professional magazine) 70–83.

[30]   See: Ljiljana Spirovikj-Trpenovska, Dejan Mickovikj and Angel Ristov, above n 25, 203–212.

two-sided statement. The statement could be certified and deposited to a notary. Nonmarital cohabitation will produce legal consequences from the day of certification of the statement. Under this proposal, the termination of a nonmarital community will be either with a joint statement or with a statement of the will expressed by one of the partners. Nonmarital partners who do not want to register their nonmarital union will be exposed to more severe consequences and problems in the proving of the existence of the nonmarital life and in exercising their rights.

IV THE LEGAL CONSEQUENCES OF NONMARITAL COHABITATION

Nonmarital cohabitation in the Macedonian FLA is equalised to marriage in regard to *the right of jointly acquired property and the right of maintenance*.[31] In comparative law there is legislation which prescribes the same legal effects for nonmarital cohabitation as for marriage. Nonetheless, as a result of conservative and the traditional values, there are still some countries that do not regulate nonmarital cohabitation.[32]

According to the provisions of the FLA (art 13), it can be concluded that nonmarital partners do not enjoy other rights and duties. In that sense, nonmarital partners, unlike spouses, do not enjoy certain rights in the area of the social security, health and pension insurance.[33] In the Macedonian FLA there is a difference between the legal position of marital and nonmarital partners towards their children. The paternity of children born in marriage is not subject to assessment, whereas the paternity of the children born out of wedlock is subject to assessment through the procedure prescribed by the FLA (arts 51–64).[34] Pursuant to the FLA the marital spouse of the mother is

---

[31] For more details see: Ljiljana Spirovikj-Trpenovska, *Family Law,* above n 21, 252, Ljiljana Spirovikj-Trpenovska *Analogy between Non-marital Cohabitation and Marriage,* above n 24; Dejan Mickovikj 'The Law on Biomedical Assisted Fertilization – Dilemmas' (2009) 203 *Lawyer* (Lawyers Association of Republic of Macedonia, Skopje) 45.

[32] In Bulgarian law nonmarital cohabitation is not regulated, even though nonmarital cohabitation is widely present, which can be seen by the huge number of children born out of wedlock (over 50%). Although, the regulation of nonmarital cohabitation was hinted at as a significant innovation in the draft Family Code, it was omitted during the adoption of the Family Code, due to influence of the church and traditional values. See Ekaterina Mateeva *Family Law of Republic of Bulgaria* (Sofia, 2009); Canka Cankova, Metodi Markov, Anna Staneva and Velina Todorova *Comment on the New Family Code* (Sofia: IK Labour and Law, 2009); Hristo Tasev *Bulgarian Law on Inheritance* new editorial, Georgi Petkanov, Simeon Tasev (Sofia: Siela, 8th edn, 2006); Metodi Markov *Family Law and Inheritance Law* (Sofia: Sibi, 2009).

[33] According to the decision of the Supreme Court of Macedonia: 'The beneficiary of permanent social assistance cannot be a person who lives in nonmarital cohabitation' *(VSM У 1139/82, 36. VSM III dec. 93)*.

[34] The court practice of the European Court of Human Rights was essential for improving the legal position of children born out of wedlock (for example, the case of *Marchx v Belgium* (1979) 2 EHRR 330). The systematic and continuous adoption of judgments for the benefit of the children born of out of wedlock by the Court is proven by the recent decision of

considered to be father of the child born during the marriage or within 300 days after the termination of the marriage (art 50). The father of the child born out of wedlock is considered to be the person who recognises the child. Paternity can be recognised in front of a registrar officer, Centre for Social Work and the court. Recognition of paternity can be made via will, as well.

## (a)	The right of nonmarital partners to joint property

Macedonian family law envisages two marital regimes: the legal marital regime and the conventional marital regime. The legal marital regime is dominant,[35] because, in the sphere of the conventional property regime, the Law on Property and Other Real Rights (LPORR)[36] from 2001 envisages only the contract with which marital partners regulate the management and use of their joint and individual property.[37] Nevertheless, this contract represents only a small part of the conventional regime of property. The legal marital property regime foresees that the property of the marital spouses can be individual property or joint property, and the same applies to nonmarital spouses.

With the adoption of the LPORR (arts 203–218), the provisions that regulate the marital property of spouses and nonmarital spouses were taken from the FLA. These provisions in the LPORR were incorporated in the part that regulates joint ownership (arts 59–94). Article 81 of the law that regulates the acquisition of property in nonmarital cohabitation stipulates that: 'The property that the nonmarital partners acquired in a nonmarital community is considered their joint property.'

### (i)	*Joint property of nonmarital partners*

Joint property shall be considered the property acquired by the nonmarital partners during their nonmarital cohabitation (LPORR, art 67). Therefore, in order to have joint property, a nonmarital partner must live in a nonmarital community for at least one year and the property should be acquired during the

---

Zaunagger v Germany (2009) 50 EHRR 38. In this case the plaintiff, a nonmarital father, submitted to the European Court of Human Rights that the decision of the German court, where his demand for mutual parenthood was overruled, represented an infringement of his right under Art 8 and Art 14 of the ECHR. The European Court of Human Rights in *Zaunagger v Germany* decided that Arts 14 and 8 from the ECHR were infringed. In the judgment, the Court underlined that the term 'family' envisaged in Art 8 refers not only to marital relations, but entails other de facto family relations, when persons live in nonmarital cohabitation. The child born in this kind of relationship ipso iure is part of the family from the moment of birth. See Elaine O'Callaghan 'Annual Review of International Family Law 2009' in Bill Atkin (ed) *International Survey of Family Law, 2011 Edition* (Jordan Publishing Limited, 2011) 13.

35	For more on the regulation of property relations of spouses see: Ljiljana Spirovikj-Trpenovska, *Family Law*, above n 21, 240–252; Bozidar Kochov 'Property relations of spouses' (Skopje: Family legislation of the Republic of Macedonia Supreme Court of the Republic of Macedonia, 1994) 197–214.

36	*Official Gazette of Republic of Macedonia*, nos 18/01 and 92/08.

37	'This kind of agreement can be concluded by spouses regarding their individual, as well as the joint property': Ljiljana Spirovikj-Trpenovska, *Family Law*, above n 21, 250–251.

common life. Apart from these conditions, judicial practice states that it is necessary to have a mutual consensus between the partners that the acquired property would be mutual.[38] Unlike individual property, for joint property, the law does not provide a clear definition of how the property can be acquired. The most significant basis for the creation of joint property is the work and the income of the nonmarital partners. According to judicial practice, contributions to the joint property are considered work, which does not create property directly, but includes raising children, domestic work, etc. Besides work, the joint property of the nonmarital partners can be gained with gifts, in favour of both nonmarital partners, by inheritance, as well as other gift rights, where both nonmarital partners are included. If the property of one of the partners is acquired after the termination of the nonmarital cohabitation, this property shall not be considered as mutual, but as individual property.[39]

The nonmarital partners have joint responsibility for the debts that one of the partners has incurred for the fulfillment of the current needs of the community (LPORR, art 79(2)). The partner who has fulfilled a joint obligation from individual property has the right to request compensation from the other partner (LPORR, art 79(3)).

The ownership right of the nonmarital partners over real estate that is their joint property is registered in the public register in the name of the two partners as their joint property (LPORR, art 69(1)). If in the public register only one of the partners is registered as the owner of the joint property, it will be considered that the registering is carried out in the name of the two partners (LPORR, art 69(2)). If the interests in the joint property are determined, then the nonmarital partners are registered as co-owners.

(ii) Individual property of nonmarital partners

Individual property, according to Macedonian law, is the property that a partner possessed before the conclusion of the marriage,[40] as well as the property obtained on the basis of inheritance, legacy and gift after the wedding. Basically, individual property is not acquired by mutual work of both nonmarital partners.[41] Apart from these provisions, the legislator omitted to regulate certain contentious issues pointed out by the courts and legal theory.[42] Contentious is the issue of the revenues from the rights of intellectual property

---

[38] According to the decision of the Supreme Court of Macedonia: 'Property acquired in a nonmarital cohabitation belongs to the nonmarital partners, if according to their behaviour there is a will for it to be considered as mutual.' (*VSM 249/85,* 3Б. *VSM IV dec. 55*).

[39] According to the decision of the Supreme Court of Macedonia: 'The funds of the partners acquired by one of the partners after the termination of cohabitation are not considered as joint property.' (*VSM rev 174/82ZB VSM III dec. 17*).

[40] According to the decision of the Supreme Court of Macedonia: 'By entering into marriage and repaying the due instalments during the marriage, a marital spouse does not acquire a right to mutual ownership of the flat, which before entering into marriage was bought by one of the spouses.' (*VSM rev 675/83* 36 *VSM dec. 18*).

[41] Bozidar Kochov, above n 35, 199–200.

[42] Ibid 200–201.

created before the beginning of the nonmarital community, and entering into effect during the period of the community, as well as the status of the property acquired on the basis of revenues from individual property of one of the nonmarital partners during the nonmarital cohabitation. Also, in Macedonian legislation there is no provision that regulates the property acquired on the basis of a game of chance. Thus, it is necessary for the legislator to envisage a provision, according to which the property acquired through a game of chance shall represent joint property, except in cases when one of the partners invested funds from his or her individual property.

The other partner is not responsible for the obligations which one of the partners had before the marriage or cohabitation, nor the personal obligations contracted after the beginning of the community (LPORR, art 79(1)).

(iii)   Management and use of the nonmarital partners' property

With regard to the management and use of the joint property, the nonmarital partners can decide by agreement (LPORR, art 70(1)).[43] A spouse while alive cannot independently use or burden with legal action his or her part in the joint property before it is divided (LPORR, art 70(2)). During the sale of a certain part of the joint property, the nonmarital partners have priority of purchasing. The partners can agree in written form for the management and use of the joint property or part of it to be carried out by one of them (LPORR, art 71(1)). The agreement can refer to all works of management and use of the property or just to the regular management or to exactly specified matters. The agreement can be broken at any time, except where obvious damage is inflicted on the other partner with the breaking of the agreement (LPORR, art 71(4)). For carrying out matters which pass the boundaries of regular management or use of property, the consent of the other partner is required, expressed in a form required for appropriate legal action (LPORR, art 72). If the partners cannot agree on the management of the property, then it is determined by a competent court (LPORR, art 73). With regard to the management and use of separate property, each partner independently manages and uses it, if they do not otherwise agree in written form (LPORR, art 68(3)).

(iv)   Necessity to regulate the agreement

Macedonian family legislation, unlike other modern legislation, does not regulate the marital agreement.[44] Nevertheless, even though in the FLA the marital agreement is not legally regulated, it is present in practice on the basis

---

[43]   'There are no legal consequences when one of the marital spouses, without the permission of the other marital spouse, has alienated and burdened the property acquired during the marriage before its division among the marital spouses.' (Supreme Court of Macedonia *rev 282/86* 36. *VSM IV dec. 3*).

[44]   Angel Ristov 'Marital contract – Obscurity, Reality or Necessity in Modern Macedonian Family Law' in *Collection of articles in honour of Prof. Ljiljana Spirovikj-Trpenovska* (Skopje: Faculty 'Iustinianus Primus', 2012).

of the principle of freedom of contract. Apart from marital spouses, in Macedonian law this kind of agreement can be stipulated between nonmarital partners as well.[45]

In Macedonian family legislation the legal marital property regime dominates.[46] This is due to the fact that the legislator envisages only one agreement, which can be used by spouses or nonmarital partners, for the regulation and the use of the separate and joint property (LPORR, arts 68(3) and 71). However, this agreement is rarely used in practice, and therefore it represents an insignificant part of the conventional regime of property of spouses and nonmarital partners.

There have passed 2 decades since the independence of the Republic of Macedonia and the establishment of the new social and legal system. During this period, it can be noted that, in the area of property relations of marital and nonmarital partners, the legislator did not foresee any changes and has adopted, almost in its entirety, the same solutions from the previous legal system.[47] Taking into account that the new social, legal and economic systems are based upon the principle of freedom of the market and entrepreneurship, it is high time for the revision of the provisions that regulate the property of marital spouses.

In comparative law the marital agreement is widely accepted.[48] Marital agreements are accepted in many of the post-socialist countries (Croatia,[49] Serbia,[50] Russia,[51] Bulgaria,[52] Monte Negro, Republika Srpska, Hungary, etc).[53] In Macedonia, the marital agreement, as an unnamed agreement, can be

---

[45] Ibid.

[46] For more details see Ljiljana Spirovikj-Trpenovska, *Family Law,* above n 21, 240–252; See also Bozidar Kochov, above n 35, 197–214.

[47] In the Positive Law as well as the Primary Law on marriage from 1946, the following models for the marital regime are accepted: (1) legal property regime in which there is a regime of joint property of the marital spouses and regime of individual property of the marital spouses, and (2) conventional property regime. Ljiljana Spirovikj-Trpenovska, *Family Law,* above n 21, 240.

[48] Marital agreements are accepted in France, Germany, Austria, Switzerland and other countries.

[49] For the Croatian Law see: Mira Alinčić, Dubravka Hrabar, Dijana Jakovac-Lozić and Aleksandra Korać-Graovac *Family Law* (Zagreb: National Newspapers, 2007) 514–518.

[50] For the marital agreement in Serbian Law see: Slobodan Panev *Family Law* (Belrade: Faculty of Law at the University in Belgrade, 2010) 356–368; Gordana Kovachek Stanikj *Family Law: Law on Partners, Law on Children and Custodian Law,* (Novi Sad: Faculty of Law in Novi Sad, 2007) 125–129; Marija Drashkikj *Family Law and Law on Children* (Belgrade: *JP Official Gazette,* 2009) 408–412; Milan Pochucha *Family Law* (Novi Sad: University Business Academy, 2010) 324–326.

[51] For the amendments in the Russian Law see: Aleksandra Matveevna Nechaeva, above n 12, 77–78.

[52] According to Mateeva: 'The introduction of the institution of the marital agreement can be determined as the essence of the reform in the new Family Code in the area of marital and property relations', above n 32, 164. For more in depth see: Canka Canova, Metodi Markov, Anna Staneva and Velina Todorova, above n 32, 105–133; Metodi Markov, above n 32, 58–63.

[53] For the marital agreement in comparative law see: Gordana Kovachek Stanikj *Comparative Family Law* (Novi Sad: University in Novi Sad, Faculty of Law, 2002) 62–72.

concluded only on the basis of the principles of the Law of Obligations. Based on the advantages of marital agreements for spouses and nonmarital partners and the experiences from comparative law, we can expect that, in the future reform of family legislation in Macedonia, marital agreements will be accepted and regulated by the FLA.

(v)   *Division of joint property of nonmarital partners*

During the duration and following the end of the community, the nonmarital partners can agree to divide the joint property (LPORR, art 74(1)). If an agreement cannot be reached, the division of the joint property is carried out by the court, and the basic principle is that the joint property of nonmarital partners is divided into equal parts (LPORR, art 75(1) and (2)). Nevertheless, at the request of one of the spouses, the court can award a larger part of the joint property, if that spouse can prove that his or her contribution to the joint property is obviously and significantly larger than the contribution of the other spouse. The same principles for the division of joint property are applied for the nonmarital partners as well.

During the division of the joint property, the items that belong exclusively for the personal use of the nonmarital spouses are separated (LPORR, art 76(2)). Each nonmarital spouse has the right to acquire the items from the joint property that serve for carrying out this activity. (LPORR, art 76(1)). If the value of the items from paragraphs 1 and 2 of this article is disproportionately large compared to the value of the joint property, division of those items will also be carried out, unless the spouse who should receive these items does not compensate the other spouse with the appropriate value or give other items to the other spouse with that spouse's consent (LPORR, art 76(3)).

The spouse who is entrusted to raise and educate the joint children is also awarded the ownership of items that serve for the children or are intended solely for their direct use (LPORR, art 77(1)). The spouse who is awarded custody of the joint children is also awarded those objects where there is an obvious interest in their remaining in the property and to be owned by the spouse with the custody of the children (LPORR, art 77(2)). Gifts that the spouses had given to each other before or during the nonmarital cohabitation are not to be returned (LPORR, art 80).[54]

V   RIGHT TO MAINTENANCE OF UNSUPPORTED PARTNER

Nonmarital partners, apart from the right of joint property, have the right to maintenance. According to the provisions of the FLA, when the court is

---

[54]   'The relatives of the fiancé who gave gifts to the fiancée during the betrothal have no right to ask to have the gifts returned, if a marriage is concluded, or in cases where the marriage has been terminated.' (Supreme Court of Macedonia *rev 347/85* 36 *VSM IV dec. 13*).

'deciding on the maintenance of a nonmarital partner, a provision which refers to the maintenance of spouses shall be applied appropriately' (art 193). On the basis of this, the same provisions for spouses are applied to nonmarital partners to regulate the conditions for obtaining maintenance, the moment when the right to maintenance occurs, the limitation period for requesting maintenance, the duration of maintenance and termination of maintenance (FLA, arts 185–202).

(a) Conditions for obtaining maintenance for the nonmarital partner

The first condition for obtaining maintenance for a nonmarital partner is the termination of a nonmarital community. With this the need for maintenance of the unsupported partner arises. The *second condition* is the duration of the nonmarital union: at least one year from its beginning. The *third condition* for maintenance is that the nonmarital partner does not have enough estate for maintenance and is incapable of work or does not have work through no fault of their own. In this sense the nonmarital partner is entitled to maintenance from his or her nonmarital partner proportionately to the latter's abilities (FLA, art 185(1)). The court must take into account all the circumstances of the case, and reject the request for maintenance, if maintenance is required by a nonmarital partner who maliciously or without justified reasons has left the other partner (FLA, art 185(2)). *The fourth condition* is the nonexistence of circumstances on the basis of which the court can reject the request for maintenance of the other nonmarital partner. In that case, the court can reject the maintenance request, if the nonmarital partner without serious provocation by the other nonmarital partner, behaved cruelly during the nonmarital cohabitation or if the request for maintenance represents an obvious injustice for the other partner (FLA, art 187). Furthermore, the court can reject the maintenance request if the nonmarital partners live separated for a long period, fully independently, and each of them is providing assets for his or her maintenance. The court will reject the maintenance request if the circumstances of the case determine that the nonmarital partner who requests maintenance is not put in a more difficult position than the one in which he or she was in at the moment of the beginning of the nonmarital cohabitation (FLA, art 188).

(b) Determination of maintenance

In determining the need for maintenance of the nonmarital partner, the court shall take into consideration the status of the estate of the nonmarital partner, working ability, employment possibilities, health status as well as other circumstances on which the assessment of needs depends (FLA, art 194(1)). In determining the position of the nonmarital partner who is obliged to pay maintenance, the court must take into account all the income and the real possibilities for earning, as well as his or her own needs and legal obligations to maintain other persons (FLA, art 194(3)). The amount of maintenance the court can determine can be a certain sum of money or a percentage of the realised personal income, realised from the revenues and incomes of other types of activity (FLA, art 196). If the circumstances on which the order was based change, a nonmarital partner may request the court to increase, to decrease or to abolish the maintenance (FLA, art 201).

(c) Time limitation for submission of a request for maintenance

If all conditions for acquiring maintenance are fulfilled, the unsupported nonmarital partner has the right to make a special complaint at the moment when the nonmarital cohabitation ceased. On the basis of this complaint the court can determine the amount of maintenance to be paid to the unsupported nonmarital partner (FLA, art 186(1)). The right to maintenance of the unsupported nonmarital partner can be exercised within one year after the termination of the nonmarital life (FLA, art 186(2)).

(d) Duration of the maintenance

Pursuant to the legal provisions of the FLA, the right to maintenance of the unsupported former nonmarital partner shall endure no more than 5 years from the termination of the nonmarital community (art 189(1)). Nevertheless, if the nonmarital partner requires, the court may prolong the maintenance even after this period if there are justifiable reasons, and particularly if the unsupported nonmarital partner is incapable of maintaining (supporting) him or herself (FLA, art 189(2)). Nonetheless, the court can determine that the maintenance is to last less than 5 years, when there is a presumption that the nonmarital partner will be capable of providing means and estate for his or her own maintenance in the future. In those cases where the nonmarital union lasted for a short period of time, the court may decide that the maintenance is to last for a determined period of time, or to completely reject the request for maintenance if the nonmarital partner who requests maintenance can provide his or her own means for maintenance in a foreseeable time frame. In some cases, the court can prolong the payment of maintenance for an undetermined period (FLA, art 190(3)). In this case, the application for prolonging maintenance can be submitted solely after the termination of the period for maintenance (FLA, art 190(4)).

(e) Termination of the maintenance

The right to maintenance of an unsupported nonmarital partner can be terminated on the basis of several reasons. Thus, the right to maintenance of the former nonmarital partner ceases when the conditions for maintenance envisaged by the law cease to exist. The right to maintenance of the former nonmarital partner shall cease with the end of the time determined in the order for maintenance and when the former nonmarital partner enters a new marriage or begins a new nonmarital union (FLA, art 191).

VI   RIGHT TO BIOMEDICAL ASSISTED REPRODUCTION

With the adoption of the Law on Biomedical Assisted Reproduction (LBAR) in 2008,[55] nonmarital partners obtained a right to biomedical assisted reproduction.[56] According to the legal provisions of this Law, the procedure of biomedical assisted reproduction (BAR) shall be implemented if prior treatment for infertility is unsuccessful and in cases where a severe hereditary disease can be transmitted to the offspring.[57] The Law envisages priority being given to the use of personal reproductive cells, or an embryo of the marital and nonmarital partners, on whom the procedure is performed.[58] Donated sperm, ovum or embryo of other persons can be used only in cases when it is not possible to use personal cells or if they are not used to prevent the transmission of a severe hereditary disease to the child.[59] According to the provisions of the Law on BAR, when prior treatment is unsuccessful, the right to use the procedure of BAR resides with adult men and women, who are capable of performing parental care and who are married or live in *nonmarital cohabitation*, as well as single women, who are not married or who do not have a nonmarital partner (art 9). This provision of the Law, that regulates subjects of BAR, causes two problems. The first one is related to the determination of the existence of nonmarital cohabitation. Unlike other European countries, where nonmarital partners who live in nonmarital cohabitation have the duty to register their nonmarital union (usually with a notary) in order for this union to produce legal consequences, in Macedonia this is not the case. Nevertheless, it is not stated how the existence of cohabitation will be proved. Thus, organisations that carry out the procedure of BAR must simply trust the man and woman who are submitting the application that they live in nonmarital cohabitation.[60] In the Law on BAR of the Republic of Macedonia, as well as most European countries, choosing the sex of the child is banned, as well as the combination of male or female reproduction cells, that is, that originate from the spermatozoids of two or more men or ova from two or more women. In Macedonian BAR the reproductive cloning of human beings and surrogate motherhood are also not permitted.

VII   RIGHT TO POSTHUMOUS REPRODUCTION

The Republic of Macedonia is one of the countries in Europe where posthumous reproduction is allowed and regulated by the law. The Law on

---

[55]   *Official Gazette of Republic of Macedonia*, no 37/2008.
[56]   For more details see: Dejan Mickovikj 'Law on Biomedical Assisted Fertilization – Dilemmas' (2009) 203 *Lawyer*, (Lawyers Association of Republic of Macedonia, Skopje).
[57]   Article 3 of LBAR.
[58]   Article 6 of LBAR.
[59]   Article 7 of LBAR.
[60]   Ibid.

BAR, besides spouses, extends the right to posthumous reproduction to nonmarital partners.[61] In art 33 of the Law on BAR it is stated that:

> 'A man and woman, who on the basis of medical examinations and the experience from the medical sciences face the danger of infertility due to health reasons, can keep their spermatozoids, ova, tissue from the ovaries or testes, for their personal use in an authorized medical institution. In the case of death of the man, a posthumous BAR is allowed upon his prior written consent during the period of one year after his death.'

In this sense under the Macedonian Law on BAR it is envisaged that the child should be conceived within one year of the death of the donor. We consider that this deadline is too short. After the death of the spouse, the woman should have a reasonable time for grieving and time to consider whether she wants to start the procedure of posthumous reproduction. Immediately after the death of the partner she finds herself in a difficult emotional condition, when she has to face the loss of the beloved and close person, and during this period she is not capable of making such a serious decision as to conceive a child who shall not have a father, and whom she will have to take care of alone.[62] Therefore, we consider that the deadline for posthumous reproduction should be at least 2 or 3 years, having also in mind that the procedure is not always successful the first time. The decision of the woman whether she is going to use the process of posthumous reproduction or not depends only on her. She has no legal or moral obligations to bear a child with the sperm of her deceased nonmarital partner. For that reason she should have a reasonable period of time at her disposal in order to be able to make a serious and meaningful decision, and not a decision based on stress, grief or distraction caused by the death of the nonmarital partner.

According to the provisions of the Law on BAR the right to posthumous reproduction is envisaged for nonmarital partners. This solution is contradictory to most contemporary legislation. The comparative legal analysis of the legal solutions in European countries and in the United States shows that, in most cases, posthumous reproduction is allowed only for married couples.

If posthumous reproduction occurs and if the child is born after the death of the husband who gave his consent to posthumous reproduction (during a period longer than 300 days), then the child will be considered as illegitimate, due to the fact that the marriage of his or her parents ceased to exist after the death of one of the spouses.[63] The same applies when the partners are not married. For these reasons, in order to determine paternity it is necessary to

---

[61]   *Official Gazette of Republic of Macedonia*, no 37/2008.

[62]   See also J Greenfield, 'Dad Was Born a Thousand Years Ago? An Examination of Post-Mortem Conception and Inheritance, with a Focus on the Rule Against Perpetuities' (2007) 8(1) Minn J L Sci & Tech 292.

[63]   Article 50 of the FLA envisages that the spouse of the mother shall be considered the father of the child born during the marriage, or within 300 days after the termination of the marriage.

follow the procedure envisaged by the law.[64] The paternity of a child born out of wedlock (with posthumous reproduction it will always be the case, because the biological father is already dead before the conception of the child) can be recognised even before the birth of the child.[65] Determination of paternity has very great significance for the identity of the child and for the establishment of relations between the child and the relatives of the father.

In compliance with Macedonian inheritance law, the conceived child has no right of inheritance. Namely, in art 122 of the Law on Inheritance[66] of 1996, it is envisaged that an heir can be a person who is alive at the moment of the death of the decedent, or a person who is conceived during the life of the decedent. Having regard to the fact that in posthumous reproduction the child is conceived after the death of the decedent, the posthumously conceived children should be recognised as legal heirs.[67]

VIII   RIGHT TO INHERITANCE OF NONMARITAL PARTNERS

In the Macedonian inheritance law, nonmarital partners do not have a right to an intestate inheritance.[68] Therefore, in the Law on Inheritance nonmarital partners are not considered as legal heirs. According to the provision from art 13 of this Law: 'the bequest of the deceased is inherited by his children and his spouse. They inherit equal shares'. However, there are no obstacles, as with any other third person, for a nonmarital partner to become an heir by will of the other nonmarital partner.

---

[64] Article 51 of the FLA predicts that the father of the child born out of wedlock will be considered the person who will acknowledge the child as his own. Paternity may be acknowledged in front of the registry officer, the Centre for Social Work and the court. The authority to whom this acknowledgement has been given has the duty to deliver the acknowledgment of paternity to the registry officer authorised for the registration of the child in the register of births, without delay. Acknowledgment of paternity may be also made by will.

[65] Article 53 of the FLA prescribes that the declaration for acknowledgment of paternity for a child born out of wedlock may be also made prior to the birth of the child. A declaration made before the birth of the child shall have legal consequences provided that the child has been born alive.

[66] *Official Gazette of Republic of Macedonia*, no 47/96.

[67] In the Macedonian legal system children born out of wedlock have the same hereditary right as the children born in marriage. In art 4 of the Law on Inheritance it is envisaged that, in respect of inheritance, nonmarital children are equal to marital children.

[68] For more details see: Dejan Mickovikj and Angel Ristov *Civil Applied Law – Succession Law,* (Skopje: Institution of Culture 'Shine', 2011) 72; Angel Ristov 'Hereditary Rows' in *Collection of articles in honour of Prof. Ganzovski* (Skopje, Faculty of Law 'Iustinianus Primus', 2011); Ljiljana Spirovikj-Trpenovska, Dejan Mickovikj and Angel Ristov *Succession Law in Republic of Macedonia*, above n 24, 76–81; Ljiljana Spirovikj-Trpenovska *Succession Law* (Skopje: 2 August 2009) 109–112; Kiril Chavdar *Comment on the Law on Inheritance* (Skopje: Academic, 1996).

With regard to the issue of whether nonmarital partners should have a right to inheritance, legal theory in Macedonia for quite some time has been striving to recognise the hereditary and legal status of nonmarital partners.[69] This proposal is completely justifiable, because nonmarital unions occur more and more in contemporary societies. The proposal is justified given the fact that the Macedonian legislator envisages the possibility for certain persons who lived in a permanent community with the deceased, uninterruptedly for 5 years until death, to appear as heirs under the conditions prescribed by the Law on Inheritance (art 29). In this sense, it is more than necessary to anticipate a provision according to which nonmarital partners will have a right to intestate inheritance. Nonmarital cohabitation should be envisaged as a basis for intestate inheritance if it lasted for more than a specifically determined period prescribed by the Law on the condition that there is no matrimonial impediment between the nonmarital partners. Thus, a solution is needed according to which, if nonmarital cohabitation lasted for at least 5 years until the death of the deceased, the nonmarital partner would have a right to inheritance, subsequent to provision for the spouse, within the intestate inheritance rules.[70] In cases where during nonmarital cohabitation there were mutual children, the term should be shorter, ie nonmarital cohabitation should have lasted for at least 3 years until the death of the deceased. Under this proposal, this will be the period necessary for the nonmarital partner to obtain a right to inheritance.[71]

---

[69] See more: Ljiljana Spirovikj-Trpenovska *Analogy between Non-marital Cohabitation and Marriage,* above n 24, 8–9; Dejan Mickovikj *Legal Regulation of Non-marital Cohabitation,* above n 24, 8; Ljiljana Spirovikj-Trpenovska, Dejan Mickovikj and Angel Ristov *Succession Law in Republic of Macedonia,* above n 24, 76–81.

[70] See Dejan Mickovikj *Legal Regulation of Non-marital Cohabitation,* above n 24, 8.

[71] Norway adopted a law which entered into force on 1 July 2009, according to which nonmarital partners who have mutual children have legal rights to inheritance. See more: John Aslan and Peter Hambro, 'New Developments and Expansion of Relationships Covered by Norwegian Law' in Bill Atkin (ed) *International Survey of Family Law, 2009 Edition* (Jordan Publishing Limited, 2009) 381.

Malawi

CHILD CARE, PROTECTION AND JUSTICE ACT: MERGING CUSTOMARY FAMILY LAW?

Lea Mwambene[*]

Résumé

Les règles et les pratiques coutumières ont été longtemps perçues comme des d'obstacles à la mise en œuvre complète des droits de l'enfant au Malawi. La raison en est que certaines coutumes et croyances sont considérées comme incompatibles avec les droits fondamentaux de la personne. La Loi sur la justice et la protection des enfants de 2010 (Children's Act) qui a donné effet à l'article 23 de la constitution du Malawi, à la Convention internationale sur les droits de l'enfant et à la Charte africaine des droits et du bien-être des enfants, a directement ou indirectement incorporé certaines règles et pratiques coutumières dans le système de protection de la jeunesse et dans la promotion des droits de l'enfant. Le présent article examine les interactions entre cette loi, les principes des droits de l'enfant et le respect des coutumes. L'objectif est de vérifier dans quelle mesure la nouvelle loi permet de prendre en considération le contexte culturel dans la protection et la promotion des droits de l'enfant. Cet article démontre que même si la loi reconnaît la coutume, le fait d'avoir exclu certaines règles coutumières qui représentent pourtant une réponse adéquate aux violations des droits de l'enfant, est d'autant plus regrettable que la situation de la plupart des enfants au Malawi est gouvernée par les règles coutumières. En raison de ces exclusions, la loi pourrait bien rester lettre morte.

I INTRODUCTION

The Child Care, Protection and Justice Act of 2010 (Children's Act) was enacted by the Malawi government in June 2010.[1] The Children's Act 'consolidates the law relating to children by making provision for the child care and protection and for child justice; and for matters of social development of the child and for connected matters'.[2] It is therefore now the principal

---

[*] LLB (Hons), LLM, LLD, Senior Lecturer at the University of the Western Cape, Cape Town. This chapter is a revised version of the paper the author presented at the UWC/Miller DuToit International Conference, Cape Town, April 2011.
[1] Act 22 of 2010.
[2] See title of the Children's Act.

Children's Act[3] that gives effect to s 23[4] of the Malawi Constitution, the United Nations Convention of the Rights of the Child (CRC) and the African Children's Charter on the Rights and Welfare of the Child (the Charter) provisions.[5] However, in the protection and promotion of children's rights, the Children's Act, inspired by the CRC and the Charter, has directly or indirectly incorporated African customary rules and practices.[6] Customary rules and practices have long been perceived as obstacles to the full realisation of the enjoyment of children's rights.[7] This is so because some customs and beliefs are felt to be inconsistent with human rights.

In light of the Children's Act focus on children's rights principles as well as respect for some African tradition and practices, this chapter examines the manner in which the Children's Act addresses this interaction. The aim is to assess the extent to which the Children's Act allows for considerations of cultural context in the protection and promotion of children's rights in Malawi. The background to the Children's Act approach to customary law and practices is the recognition of customary law by international treaties such as the CRC and the Charter[8] as well as the constitutional protection of the right to culture.[9] The provisions of the CRC and the Charter will therefore be outlined in the first part of the chapter to show how they have addressed the interaction between customary law and children's rights at the international level. Thereafter, the law on children in Malawi leading up to the current Children's Act will be outlined. This is followed by an account of the legislature's approach on the interaction between customary rules and practices and children's rights as set out in the Children's Act. The focus will be on how specific customary rules and practices regulating the welfare of the child have been addressed in the Children's Act. In particular, we consider child marriages, proof of parentage (customary damages), parental responsibilities, custody, guardianship and dispute resolution mechanisms. The last part is a conclusion.

---

[3] According to its memorandum, the Children's Act abrogates the provisions of the Affiliation Act and provisions contained in Part III of the Children and Young Persons Act.

[4] Section 23 of the Malawi Constitution provides that: '(1) All children, regardless of the circumstances of their birth, are entitled to equal treatment before the law; (2) All children shall have the right to a given name and family name and the right to a nationality; (3) Children have the right to know, and to be raised by their parents; (4) Children are entitled to be protected from economic exploitation or any treatment, work or punishment that is, or likely to– (a) be hazardous; (b) interfere with their education; or (c) be harmful to their health or to their physical, mental or spiritual or social development. (5) For purposes of this section, children shall be persons under sixteen years of age.'

[5] Malawi ratified the CRC in 1991 and the Charter in 1999. Both these instruments lay down normative and substantive standards for the protection of children's rights at the international and regional level.

[6] See for example s 57 which provides that 'a child to be placed with a foster parent who has the same cultural background as the child's parents and who originates from the same area in Malawi as the parents of the child'.

[7] Himonga 'Implementing the rights of the child in African legal system: The *Mthembu* journey in search of justice'(2006) 9 *The International Journal of Children's Rights* 90.

[8] Himonga 'African Customary Law and Children's Rights: Intersections and Domains in a New Era' in J Sloth-Nielsen (ed) *Children's Rights in Africa* (England: Ashgate Publishing, 2008) 74.

[9] Section 26 of the Malawi Constitution provides: 'Every person shall have the right to use the language and to participate in the cultural life of his or her choice.'

II INTERNATIONAL LAW CONTEXT

Malawi is party to the CRC and the Charter, having ratified the instruments on 2 January 1991 and 10 September 1999, respectively.[10] Both instruments are intentionally polite to cultural rights.[11] The preamble to the CRC recognises the significance of culture: emphasising 'taking due account of the importance of the traditions and cultural values of each people for the protection and harmonious development of the child'. In addition, the CRC recognises one of the core values of the African culture when in art 5 it places the rights of the child in the context of the community and the extended family as provided by local custom.[12] Further, art 30 of the CRC provides for the child's right to enjoy her culture in community with other members of his or her group.[13]

However, the CRC envisages the incorporation of customary laws that protect and promote children's rights only. This position is demonstrated in art 24(3) of the CRC where states parties are required 'to take all effective and appropriate measures with a view to abolishing traditional practices that are prejudicial to the health of children'.

In a similar fashion, the Charter has many provisions that recognise the importance of culture in the protection of children's rights in Africa. For instance, the Preamble stresses the African cultural context for the implementation of children's rights on the continent.[14] Just like the CRC, the Charter also provides that appropriate measures must be taken by states parties to eliminate harmful, social and cultural practices affecting the welfare, dignity, normal growth and development of the child.[15] Article 1(3) of the Charter provides that 'any custom, tradition, cultural or religious practice that is

---

[10]   'The CRC was ratified by the Malawi government at a time when the State was ruled by Dr Banda who had no respect for human rights. This position led to zero implementation of the provisions of the CRC.' Chirwa and Kaime 'The CRC and the African Children's Charter in Malawi's Law and Policy'(2008) *Malawi Law Journal* 86.

[11]   Other international instruments that also recognise the right to culture are: arts 22 and 27(1) of the Universal Declaration of Human Rights (UDHR); art 15(1)(a) of the International Covenant on Economic, Social and Cultural Rights (ICESCR); and art 27 of the International Covenant on Civil and Political Rights (ICCPR). Malawi ratified both the ICESCR and ICCPR in1993. See also art 3 of the Convention on the Elimination of All Forms of Discrimination against Women (CEDAW), ratified by Malawi in 1987.

[12]   Section 5 provides: 'States Parties shall respect the responsibilities, rights and duties of parents or, where applicable, the members of the extended family or community as provided for by local custom, legal guardians or other persons legally responsible for the child.' See also arts 14(2) and 18(1) of the CRC.

[13]   Article 30 reads: 'In those States in which ethnic, religious or linguistic minorities or persons of indigenous origin exist, a child belonging to such a minority or who is indigenous shall not be denied the right, in community with other members of his or her group, to enjoy his or her own culture, to profess and practice his or her own religion, or to use his or her own language.' See also art 29(c) and (d) of the CRC.

[14]   See the Preamble to the Charter. See also L Mwambene and J Sloth Nielsen 'Benign accommodation? *Ukuthwala* and the Children's Act' (2011) AHRJ, 1; and Himonga, above n 8 on detailed discussion on how the Charter recognises the importance of culture in the protection and promotion of children's rights in the African context.

[15]   See arts 1(3) and 21(1) of the Charter.

inconsistent with the rights, duties and obligations contained in the present Charter shall to the extent of such inconsistency be discouraged'. Article 21(1) provides:

> 'State Parties to the present Charter shall take all appropriate measures to eliminate harmful social and cultural practices affecting the welfare, dignity, normal growth and development of the child and in particular: (a) those customs and practices prejudicial to the health or life of the child; and (b) those customs and practices discriminatory to the child on the grounds of sex or other status.'

From the above discussion, both the CRC and the Charter clearly envisage that states parties will incorporate customary values and practices that are aimed at the protection and promotion of children's rights only.[16] At the same time, they send a very strong message that they ensure that harmful cultural practices are eliminated.[17] In the following section we examine the national legal position.

III   THE MALAWIAN LEGAL FRAMEWORK

Malawi's legal system is still characterised by a mixture of pre- and post-independence[18] laws, including, British common law, statutory law, customary law[19] and the constitution based on human rights.[20] Before 2010, the law relating to children in Malawi was found in several statutes; primarily in the Children and Young Person's Act,[21] Adoption Act[22] and the Affiliation Act.[23] The Children and Young Person's Act, enacted in 1969, was the primary legislation on matters related to child justice, child care and protection.[24] The Adoption Act, enacted in 1949, was intended for non-Malawians employed in the colonial government intending to adopt children. The Affiliation Act, enacted in 1948, was the law that provided for proof of parentage where it is not known or it is disputed so as to make provision for the affected children.[25]

---

[16] See Himonga, above n 8, 76.

[17] See also Himonga, above n 8, 73–74, argues that 'the recognition of customary by human rights legal frameworks constitutes the broad level at which customary law intersects with children's rights. This intersection anticipates the incorporation of "harmless" customary law norms into domestic laws for the promotion and protection of the rights of children'.

[18] Malawi became independent from the colonial rule in 1964.

[19] According to s 200 of the Malawi Constitution, customary law remains a legal system for those who wish to be governed by them. The rules of customary law may not, however, conflict with the provisions of the Constitution (s 5 of the Malawi Constitution).

[20] The Republic of Malawi Constitution, 1994.

[21] Chapter 26:03, Laws of Malawi.

[22] Chapter 26:01, Laws of Malawi.

[23] Chapter 26:02, Laws of Malawi. The provisions for maintenance of illegitimate children provided under the Affiliation Act.

[24] This Act, however, focused on child justice and had no provisions on the protection of the child in the family environment.

[25] However, the provisions for maintenance of illegitimate children provided under the Affiliation Act are less favourable than those that apply to children who are legitimate. It obviously discriminates against children on the basis of their birth, contrary to s 23 of the Malawi Constitution.

Customary rules and practices applicable to children were dependent on whether children were born in matrilineal or patrilineal marriage systems.[26]

On 16 May 1994, the Malawi Parliament adopted a draft constitution which provisionally came into force on 18 May 1994 (Malawi Constitution).[27] The Malawi Constitution contains a viable Bill of Rights. The Bill of Rights contains some rights afforded to children, in contrast to the 1966 Constitution, its predecessor, which contained no substantial recognition of or respect for human rights.[28] Section 23 of the Malawi Constitution is a provision dedicated towards children's rights. At the same time, s 26 of the Malawi Constitution recognises the right to culture. However, the protection of children's rights in the Malawi Constitution as well as the ratification of the CRC and the Charter meant that all laws applicable to children (including, customary law) have to meet constitutional and international children's rights standards. As earlier mentioned, the CRC and the Charter both impose general obligations on states parties to adopt legislation and implement other measures to realise children's rights.[29]

After 1994, in part as a measure to meet its obligations, the Malawi government appointed a special ministry for women and children and tasked the Malawi Law Commission to deal with comprehensive law reform. In 2001, a Special Law Commission was appointed to deal with reform relating to children. The result is the Child Care, Protection and Justice Act, 2010. It is against the enactment of the Children's Act that the interaction between customary law and children's rights is examined.

IV   CUSTOMARY LAW AND CHILDREN'S RIGHTS IN THE CHILDREN'S ACT

The preamble to the Children's Act shows a human rights motivation for its enactment. It proclaims to be 'new legislation that seeks to modernize law relating to children by incorporating provisions aimed at protecting and upholding the best interests of the child'. However, as noted in the introduction, the Children's Act has directly or indirectly incorporated customary rules and practices. This approach, it has been argued, echoes the

---

[26] For a discussion on the specific rules applicable in the patrilineal and matrilineal systems, see Mwambene 'African customary law and children in Malawi: Adaptability to change?' (Unpublished) presented at the International Family Law Conference on Intergenerational Solidarity, Lyon, France 19–23 July 2011.

[27] The Republic of Malawi (Constitution) Act No 20 of 1994 came provisionally into force on 18 May1994, and was fully in force on 18 May 1995, as Act No 7 of 1995.

[28] See s 5 of the Malawi Constitution on the supremacy of the constitution.

[29] Article 4 of the CRC provides: 'States Parties shall undertake all appropriate legislative, administrative and other measures for the implementation of the rights recognised in the Convention.' Article 1(1) of the Charter provides: 'Members ... shall undertake the necessary steps, in accordance with their Constitutional processes ... to adopt such legislative or other measures as may be necessary to give effect to the provisions of this Charter.'

cultural orientation of the CRC and the Charter.[30] The legal position of customary law is highlighted in the Malawi Constitution.[31] Section 200 of the Malawi Constitution provides:[32]

> 'Except in so far as they are inconsistent with this Constitution, all Acts of Parliament, common law and customary law in force on the appointed day shall continue to have force of law, as if they had been made in accordance with and in pursuance of this Constitution: Provided that any laws currently in force may be amended or repealed by an Act of Parliament or be declared unconstitutional by a competent court.'

However, it is important to emphasise that the discussion which follows is that of the interaction between customary law and children's rights in the Children's Act. The focus is in the areas of child marriages (definition of the child), parental responsibilities, harmful cultural practices' dispute resolution, proof of parentage (customary damages), custody and guardianship.

(a)   Child marriages

Under customary marriage laws there is no precise age at which one is allowed to enter into marriage. Entry into marriage is determined by the age of puberty and initiation ceremonies.[33] Thus Bennett[34] rightly observed: 'the absence of any precise method for determining status can work to the disadvantage of children, because it allows guardians to manipulate the duration of childhood to their own advantage'. Obviously, this position leads to many children, especially girls, being married young. In Malawi there are so many cultural practices that encourage child marriages and support Bennett's observation.[35] According to the Malawi Human Rights Commission study (MHRC),[36] some of the practices that are still prevalent include: *chimeta masisi* (replacement of deceased wife by her young sister or niece); *mbirigha* (a young sister or niece given to a husband as a bonus wife); *kupawila* (paying off a debt by marrying a daughter); *kupimbira* (asking loans in exchange for a daughter); *kuhaha* (an arrangement by a man with the girl's parents to take care of the girl and marry her upon that girl reaching puberty).

In line with the approach adopted by the Charter, s 81of the Children's Act unequivocally prohibits child marriages or betrothal of children in the

---

30   Himonga, above n 8, 77.

31   Sections 5 and 200 of the Malawi Constitution.

32   According to s 212(1) of the Malawi Constitution, 18 May 1994 is the appointed day when the Malawi Constitution, as earlier mentioned, came provisionally into force.

33   See also Bennett *Customary Law in South Africa* (Cape Town: Juta, 2004) 304 for a similar discussion.

34   Ibid 304.

35   See a discussion by L Mwambene 'Marriage under African customary law in the face of the Bill of Rights and international human rights standards in Malawi' (2010) *African Human Rights Law Journal* 100–103.

36   MHRC *Cultural practices and their impact on the enjoyment of human rights, particularly women and children* (2005) as cited by Mwambene, ibid 100–103.

following fashion: 'No person shall – (a) force a child into marriage; or (b) force a child to be betrothed.' Moreover, s 82 of the Children's Act directly addresses cultural practices such as *kupawila*.[37] This section provides that: 'No person shall – (a) sell a child or use a child as a pledge to obtain credit; (b) use a child as surety for a debt or mortgage; or force a child into providing labour for the income of parent, guardian or any other person.' Anyone who contravenes these provisions commits an offence and shall be liable for 10 years.[38]

Furthermore, the Children's Act has banned harmful cultural practices outright.[39] Section 80 of the Act provides that '[no] person shall subject a child to a social or customary practice that is harmful to the health or general development of the child'. Sloth-Nielsen,[40] commenting on art 24 of the CRC, which is similar to s 80 of the Children's Act, observed, 'no specific practices are mentioned in this provision which obviously leaves out any harmful cultural practices which may violate equality rights, dignity, or invade children's rights'.[41] This observation could also be applicable to s 80 of the Children's Act.[42] The Children's Act therefore prohibits all harmful cultural practices that violate children's rights. No doubt, in the Malawian context banning all harmful cultural practices sends a very strong message that any cultural practice that is harmful to children cannot be in the best interests of the child. The opposite is also true; the Children's Act allows harmless customary practices that are in the best interests of the child.

Closely linked to the issue of child marriages is the definition of the child. According to the Children's Act,[43] a child 'means a person below the age of sixteen years'.[44] This definition highlights its significance in addressing children's rights in the following ways.[45] First, according to this definition, the Children's Act applies to every child under the age of 16, irrespective of sex. This is important because customary rules and practices discriminate against mostly girl children. Secondly, the definition, arguably, goes to the root of

---

[37] This is a customary practice where a parent enters into an agreement with his creditors whereby he will be allowed paying off a debt by marrying his daughter.

[38] Section 83 of the Children's Act.

[39] Section 80 of the Act.

[40] Sloth-Nielsen 'A foreskin too far? Religious, medical and customary circumcision and the Children's Act 38 of 2005 in the context of HIV Aids' (unpublished) presented at the Jubilee Congress of the Commission on Legal Pluralism, Cape Town, 8–10 September 2011.

[41] See also Himonga, above n 8, 84.

[42] See Mwambene 'Marriage under African customary law in the face of the Bill of Rights and international human rights standards in Malawi (2010) *African Human Rights Law Journal* 100–103 for a discussion of some of the harmful cultural practices that affect children's rights in Malawi. See also Ntata and Sinoya *Customary law and the UN Conventions on women and children* (unpublished) 1999.

[43] According to s 23(5) of the Malawi Constitution, children are persons below the age of 16.

[44] Section 2 of the Children's Act.

[45] This significance is appreciated when the definition of a child under the Charter is contrasted with the definition of a child provided by the CRC. The CRC defines a child as 'every human being below the age of 18 years unless, under the laws applicable to the child, majority is attained earlier'.

addressing the cultural practice of marrying girls determined by age of puberty. However, this definition is inconsistent with the Charter and the CRC. According to the CRC[46] and the Charter[47] a child is defined to be a person who is below the age of 18 years.[48] Indeed neither the CRC nor the Charter requires states parties to enact laws specifying an age of majority. The age limit, it has been argued, is only for the purposes of enjoying rights enshrined in the CRC and the Charter.[49] However, countries that are party to these instruments would be expected to comply with the CRC and the Charter's age limit and therefore enact laws to reflect this.[50] This line of thinking is buttressed in the recommendation by the CRC Committee on the report submitted by Malawi in 2002.[51]

(b)   Parental responsibilities

Under Malawian customary law, just like other African societies, the concept of parental rights and responsibilities is loose; a child belongs to a community, layered into various levels.[52] The various levels are: where a child belongs to a particular household. A household is basically a unit attached to and arising out of the customary marriage of each woman.[53] At the same time, a number of such households may constitute the family head's family home and be subject to his guardianship and control.[54] A child may also belong to a clan.[55] With such a structure, responsibilities are placed in various layers; some may accrue to the mother, some to the family head or to the clan at large depending on whether the family is matrilineal or patrilineal.[56] Thus, the ranges of persons who may be entitled to have parental responsibilities over children are not limited to the father and mother. The extended family members may be

---

[46]   The CRC was ratified by Malawi on 2 January 1991.

[47]   The Charter was ratified by Malawi on 16 September 1999.

[48]   See arts 1 and 2 of the CRC and the Charter respectively.

[49]   Bennett, above n 33, 304–305.

[50]   The basis of this argument is that state parties to these Conventions will be expected to implement the rights contained therein.

[51]   See www1.umn.edu/humanrts/crc/malawi2002.html (accessed June 2012), where the Committee recommended that state parties take the necessary legislative measures to establish a clear definition of 'child' in accordance with art 1 of the CRC and other related principles and provisions of the Convention.

[52]   This position is contrasted to common law where a child belongs to individual parents, father and mother.

[53]   Households under customary law are centres of day to day domestic activity. The traditional model of household implied a nuclear unit, extended to include polygynous wives and their offspring, together with grandchildren, siblings and any other people who became attached to this household (Bennett, above n 33, 181).

[54]   Ibid 181.

[55]   The term 'clan' according to Bennett, above n 33, 180 denotes a group of people who believe themselves to be related through a common ancestor, although their exact genealogical links cannot be traced.

[56]   Under the matrilineal system a child belongs to the mother and her family; and in the patrilineal system, provided *lobola* obligations have been complied with, a child belong to the father and his family.

obligated to take care of a child.[57] It is therefore submitted that in the African traditional order, the concept of parental responsibilities is not only a phenomenon complex, but, may also not have regard to the best interests of the child.

The duties and responsibilities of parents towards their children and its legal occurrences are addressed in Part II of the Children's Act. Section 3 of the Children Act provides:

> 'In addition to the duties and responsibilities imposed by section 23 of the constitution, a parent or guardian; (a) shall not deprive a child of his or her welfare; (b) has responsibilities whether imposed by law or otherwise towards the child which include the responsibility to – (i) Protect the child from neglect, discrimination, violence, abuse, exploitation, oppression and to exposure to physical, mental, social and moral hazards; (ii) Provide proper guidance, care, assistance and maintenance for the child to ensure his or her survival and development, including in particular adequate diet, clothing, shelter and medical attention; (iii) ensure that during the temporary absence of the parent or guardian, the child shall be cared for by a competent person; (iv) exercise joint primary responsibility for raising their children, except where the parent or guardian has forfeited or surrendered his or her rights and responsibilities in accordance with the law ...'

From the above provision, the Children's Act assigns full duties and responsibilities to both parents and whose rights include care, guardianship and maintenance, custody and contact.[58] Thus, there is no distinction between the incidences of parental responsibilities between married and unmarried parents or between fathers and mothers.[59] Parental responsibility includes protection from neglect and all harm such as abuse and exploitation. In addition, the Children's Act allocates the right to care to any person who does not have parental responsibility for a particular child but has care of the child.[60] Furthermore, more than one person may hold parental responsibilities and rights in respect of the same child, and in such a scenario, each of them may act alone and without the other or others in meeting that responsibility.[61] However, the Children's Act provides that 'nothing in the *Division* shall affect the operation of any law which requires the consent of more than one person in a matter affecting the child'.

Section 3 of the Children's Act has thus incorporated the importance of the various layers as recognised under customary law in the protection and promotion of the children's rights by allocating parental rights and

---

[57] Sloth-Nielsen, above n 40.
[58] Section 3(1) of the Children's Act.
[59] This position is distinguished to the Kenyan Children's Act 2001 and South African Children's Act 2005 where these statutes make distinctions between incidences of parental responsibility for fathers of children born in and out of wedlock.
[60] Section 3(3) of the Children's Act.
[61] Section 3(5) of the Children's Act.

responsibilities in different layers of people. This position 'intersects with a number of rights of the child particularly the right to parental care'.[62]

(c) Guardianship

Customary rules and practices regulating guardianship and custody of the child are as follows: if *lobola* requirements were met, the father of the child becomes the legal guardian of his minor children in the patrilineal marriage systems. The opposite is also true; if *lobola* requirements were not met, the mother of the child becomes the legal guardian.[63] In the matrilineal customary system, the legal guardian of children is at all times the mother. However, the constitutional protection of children's rights and the principle of the best interests of the child contained in the CRC and the Charter apply to customary law as well.[64] These have been used to determine issues of custody and guardianship without consideration of *lobola*. For example, in *Nyirenda v Mwenda*,[65] on the issue of custody of the children it was stated: 'according to the patrilineal custom, where *lobola* has not been paid, the custody of the child goes to the mother. However, in line with the Constitution, the issue of custody has to be decided in the best interests of the child'.[66]

Guardianship is covered in Part II, Division 3 of the Children's Act.[67] According to s 2 of the Children's Act 'guardian' 'means a person who has lawful or legitimate custody, care or control of a child in place of a parent'.[68] The appointment of a guardian may be by: the testamentary will or choice of parent; an order of the court; and the family of the child to take parental responsibility over the child upon the death of the parent.[69] The guardian may act alone or jointly with the surviving parent.[70] The Children's Act further provides that the guardian need not be the custodian of the child where only appointed only over the estate of the child.[71] It also provides for rules of termination of guardianship.[72]

---

[62] Himonga, above n 8, 77.

[63] See also Bennett, above n 33, 308–309.

[64] See art 3 and 4 of the CRC and the Charter, respectively.

[65] Civil Case No 118 of 2003, Mzuzu Magistrate Court (Unreported).

[66] See also *Katimba v Katimba* Matrimonial Cause No 6 of 2008 in which custody of the child was granted to the mother after the court had discussed the applicable customary matrilineal rules but mentioned that the decision was based on s 23 of the Malawi Constitution which provides that a child has the right to know and be raised by both parents. Similarly, in the South African case of *Hlope v Mahlalele* 1998 (1) SA 449 (T) it was held that in accordance with the Republic of South African Constitution, 1996, the best interests of the child rather than the payment or nonpayment of *lobola* are paramount in matters concerning the guardianship of the child.

[67] It should be noted that the Children and Young Person's Act (Part III now repealed by the Children's Act) was silent on the issue of guardianship.

[68] Section 2 defines a parent to 'include adoptive parent, foster parent or any person acting in whatever way as parent'.

[69] Section 38(1) of the Children's Act.

[70] Section 40(2) of the Children's Act.

[71] Section 38(4) of the Children's Act.

[72] Sections 43, 44 and 45 of the Children's Act.

The Children's Act is to be commended for not making it explicit that should a child not have parents, the determination of guardianship should prefer the next of kin in the extended family.

(d) Custody

In many African communities, custody of children is largely determined by predetermined rules of African customary family law.[73] The best interests of the child principle does not play a part in custody issues. In Malawi, children born out of a matrilineal marriage are affiliated to the clan of the wife.[74] In the patrilineal system, provided *lobola* obligations have been complied with, children born out of a patrilineal marriage are affiliated to the clan of the husband.[75] The 1994 Malawi Constitution alters these customary rules in that it gives both spouses equal rights to custody over their children irrespective of whether they were married under customary law or not.[76] At the international level, both the CRC and the Charter dictate that the principle of the best interests of the child must guide whoever is in the decision-making process concerning custody of children.[77]

Section 8 of the Children's Act provides:

> '(1) A parent, a family member or any other appropriate person may apply to a child justice court for custody of a child. (2) A family member or any other appropriate person may apply to a child justice court for periodic access to the child. (3) The child justice court shall consider the best interests of the child and the importance of the child, on account of age, being with his mother when making an order for custody or access.'

The above provision effectively follows the customary rules where a range of persons related to a child can have custody of the child. 'Parent' in the Children's Act has been defined widely to include adoptive parent, foster parent or any person acting in whatever way as parent.[78] Therefore, apart from the child's parents (father or mother), the Children's Act affords other members of the family to apply for custody of a child.[79] This position is significant considering that most Malawians live in circumstances where the extended family is still in place and play a crucial role in the upbringing of a child.[80] As rightly observed by Himonga,[81] the extended family system intersects with many rights of the child and therefore is to be encouraged. The Children's Act is therefore commended for the inclusion of the extended family as this

---

[73] L Mwambene 'Custody disputes under African customary family law in Malawi: Adaptability to change?' *International Journal of Law, Policy and the Family* (forthcoming 2012).
[74] In Malawi, the majority of the tribes are governed by matrilineal customary law.
[75] See also similar position for South Africa as discussed by Bennett, above n 33, 307.
[76] Section 24 of the Malawi Constitution.
[77] Articles 3 and 4 of the CRC and the Charter respectively.
[78] Section 2 of the Children's Act.
[79] See also Ghana's Children's Act (s 111).
[80] Himonga, above n 8, 77.
[81] Ibid.

institution intersects with rights of children, including the right to parental care, right to grow up with parents, among others.[82]

However, the Children's Act has, whilst maintaining the importance of the extended family in the protection of children's rights, incorporated the best interests of the child principle in custody and access matters under s 8(3) of the Children's Act. By incorporating the best interests of the child principle in all matters of custody and access of the child, the Children's Act is clearly intended to institute a uniform legal system in all matters, including guardianship and custody of children and leaves no room for the application of customary law to dictate what is in the best interests of the child.[83] This is a clear indication that in matters of custody of children the predetermined customary rules will no longer determine custody of the child.

(e)   Proof of parentage (customary damages)

In most systems of customary law, a man who impregnates a woman out of wedlock is liable to pay damages to the woman's family.[84] This rule is also part of the rules for the affiliation of children born out of wedlock.[85]

Section 6(1)(b) of the Children's Act provides: 'The following shall be considered by a child justice court as evidence of parentage – performance of a customary ceremony[86] towards the child by the purported father of the child.'

The incorporation of this customary practice ensures that the child's right to the father's care is achieved by giving the father full parental responsibilities and rights as provided under s 3 of the Children's Act.[87] It is also significant in that it can facilitate the realisation of the rights of the child to know and be raised by his or her parents.[88] In this particular instance, this customary practice and children's rights are in tandem.[89]

---

[82]   Ibid.

[83]   See also Du Bois (ed) (2007) *Wille's Principles of South African Law* (Cape Town: Juta, 9th edn, 2007) with respect to South African Children's Act 38 of 2005, 208.

[84]   Himonga, above n 8, 82.

[85]   Bennett, above n 33, 310.

[86]   Customary ceremony would, in my opinion include the payment of customary damages.

[87]   Section 3 of the Children's Act provides: '(1) In addition to the duties and responsibilities imposed by section 23 of the constitution, a parent or guardian;
(a)   Shall not deprive a child of his or her welfare
(b)   Has responsibilities whether imposed by law or otherwise towards the child which include the responsibility to–
(i)   Protect the child from neglect ... and to exposure to physical, mental, social and moral hazards
(ii)   Provide proper guidance, care, assistance and maintenance for the child to ensure his or her survival and development, including in particular adequate diet ....'

[88]   See s 23(2) of the Constitution.

[89]   See also Mwambene 'Reconciling African customary law with women's rights in Malawi: The Proposed Marriage, Divorce and Family Relations Bill' (2007) *Malawi Law Journal* 113–122.

(f) Dispute resolution

In Malawi most children live in rural areas where access to the formal courts is limited. The role of traditional forums in the enforcement of children's rights cannot therefore be overemphasised. Thus, Himonga has observed, 'legislation will merely be paper law if it cannot be enforced by court'.[90] The Children's Act does not explicitly mention the role of traditional leaders in court processes aimed at enforcing and promoting the rights of children.[91] Section 70(1)(b) of the Act provides:

> '... it is the general duty of every local government authority within its area of jurisdiction to mediate in any situation where the rights of a child are infringed, especially the child's right to succeed to property of his parents and all the rights accorded to the child by this Act.'

In addition, s 132[92] provides that a child justice court shall be subordinate to the High Court and shall be presided over by the professional magistrate or a magistrate of the first grade. Just like s 70, this provision essentially excludes other forums to adjudicate over children matters. In Malawi, just like most African communities, children living under customary family law reside in rural communities where access to formal courts is difficult. The fact that s 132 of the Children's Act seems to be limited to child justice courts presided by magistrates is very unfortunate.[93] Most disputes, in Malawi, are resolved by traditional leaders who have not been recognised by the formal court system. The effect of ss 132 and 70(1)(b) of the Children's Act, it is submitted, limits the application of the Children's Act to those forums that are adjudicated by magistrates and local government authorities, respectively.

V CONCLUSION

This chapter has given an overview of the interaction between customary law and children's rights in the Children's Act. The focus is on the manner in which the Children's Act addresses this interface. It has pointed out provisions in the Children's Act that incorporate customary practices which constitute a part of the child's rights framework in the Malawian context. Examples include s 57 of the Children's Act that requires 'a child to be placed with a foster parent who

---

[90] Himonga, above n 8, 85.

[91] Similarly, s 11(2)(b) of the Malawi Constitution excludes informal forums to promote the objects of the Bill of Rights. It provides: 'in interpreting the provisions of this Constitution a court of law shall take full account of the provisions of Chapter 3 and Chapter 4'. Section 11(2)(b) of the Malawi Constitution excludes any forum to promote the objects of the Bill of Rights.

[92] Section 132 of the Children's Act provides: 'there shall be established child justice courts, which shall be subordinate to the High Court and shall exercise jurisdiction conferred on them by this Act or any other written law'.

[93] It is however, observed that some children's legislation marks out a role of traditional forums in the enforcement of children's rights, for example Act 38 of 2005 Children's Act of South Africa.

has the same cultural background as the child's parents and who originates from the same area in Malawi as the parents of the child'.[94] At the same time, the chapter has highlighted areas of concern in the Children's Act where some customary practices that would promote children's rights have been left out. For example, there is no provision for the recognition of the role that customary forums play in the enforcement of children's rights. This exclusion is a regrettable oversight as most children in Malawi live in rural areas where access to a child justice court will be impossible.[95] In addition, provisions aimed at protecting children from child marriages and harmful cultural practices fall short of fully complying with international standards on the rights of the child on a number of issues, including the definition of a child.

---

[94] See s 57 of the Children's Act. See also similarly s 184(1)(a) of the South African Children's Act 38 of 2005.

[95] In Malawi, the majority of people live in rural areas.

Malaysia

RIGHTS OF CHILDREN: FUTURE CHALLENGES IN MALAYSIA

*Datin Noor Aziah Mohd Awal**

Résumé

Les droits de l'enfant sont devenus une question importante depuis que la Malaisie a signé et ratifié, en 1995, la Convention internationale des droits de l'enfant. Cela signifie que les enfants malaisiens bénéficient des droits contenus dans la Convention et que l'Etat doit en assurer la protection. Nation multiethnique et multiconfessionnelle, la Malaisie doit trouver un juste milieu entre les droits des enfants musulmans et non musulmans. Les parents jouant un rôle prépondérant dans l'éducation et le choix de la religion de l'enfant, cela peut entrer en conflit avec les droits de celui-ci à effectuer ses propres choix et définir ses conditions de vie. Lorsqu'un litige s'élève, le tribunal ou la médiation doit proposer l'issue la plus favorable à l'intérêt de l'enfant et à la sauvegarde des droits de ce dernier.

I INTRODUCTION

The rights of children have been a topical issue since Malaysia signed and ratified the United Nations Convention on the Rights of the Child (CRC) in 1995. This means that children in Malaysia have rights in accordance with the CRC and the government shall comply with the convention. The CRC has 54 articles which carry more than 40 rights which can be divided as follows:

(i)   right to protection and special assistance;

(ii) right to access to services like education and health;

(iii) rights to development of personality, capacity and talents;

(iv) rights to a serene living environment, with love and understanding; and

(v)   a right to be informed and to take part in the discussion of all issues involving children's rights.

---

*   Associate Professor, Faculty of Law, University Kebangsaan Malaysia.

This chapter discusses the future challenges of the rights of children in Malaysia after the ratification of the CRC and analyses how far those rights which have been promised and not reserved have been enforced or fulfilled by Malaysia. This chapter will also look into current issues involving children in Malaysia.

II   CRC RESERVATIONS

When Malaysia signed the CRC, it made 12 reservations and later it was reduced to 8 reservations namely arts 1, 2, 7, 13, 14, 15, 28(1)(a) and 37. Recently Malaysia announced the withdrawal of the reservation on arts 1 (definition), 13 (freedom of speech) and 15 (freedom of association and assembly).[1] With this commitment, can Malaysia claim that it has fulfilled all obligations under the CRC? It is important to note that Malaysia still have the following reservations:

(a)   art 2 – non-discrimination;

(b)   art 7 – nationality;

(c)   art 14 – freedom of conscience and religion;

(d)   art 28(1)(a) – free and compulsory primary education; and

(e)   art 37 – torture.

Reservation on art 2 is maintained due to the fact that Malaysia still has a number of written laws that discriminate against children. In Malaysia children are divided into Muslim and non-Muslim children and also Bumiputera or son of the soils and non-Bumiputera. It is true that the Court for Children was established to adjudicate on matters relating to children. However, most cases that were taken to the Court for Children were cases involving young offenders, children who need care and protection, children who need care and rehabilitation and adoption. Cases involving guardianship and custody, maintenance, legal status such as legitimacy will be heard in the Syariah Court for Muslim children and the High Court of Malaya or better known as the civil High court for non-Muslims children. The two laws have different sources and different jurisprudence and it is not unexpected that the application and effect will be totally different. As such, children may be seen to be discriminated against because there are no uniform laws that apply to a class of children except in cases of child offenders[2] as well as where children are victims of abuse.[3]

---

[1]   Ministry of Women, Family and Community Development in its media release on 6 July 2010.
[2]   Child Act 2001 (Act 611), Part IV.
[3]   Child Act 2001 (Act 611), Part V.

The Federal Constitution makes special provision for Malays or Bumiputera under art 153[4] which means that children of different origin will not be treated

---

[4] Art 153 provides that:
'(1) It shall be the responsibility of the Yang di-Pertuan Agong to safeguard the special position of the Malays and natives of any of the States of Sabah and Sarawak and the legitimate interests of other communities in accordance with the provisions of this Article.
(2) Notwithstanding anything in this Constitution, but subject to the provisions of Article 40 and of this Article, the Yang di-Pertuan Agong shall exercise his functions under this Constitutions and federal law in such manner as may be necessary to safeguard the special position of the Malays and natives of any of the States of Sabah and Sarawak and to ensure the reservation for Malays and natives of any of the States of Sabah and Sarawak of such proportion as he may deem reasonable of positions in the public service (other than the public service of a State) and of scholarships, exhibitions and other similar educational or training privileges or special facilities given or accorded by the Federal Government and, when any permit or license for the operation of any trade or business is required by federal law, then, subject to the provisions of that law and this Article, of such permits and licenses.
(3) The Yang di-Pertuan Agong may, in order to ensure in accordance with Clause (2) the reservation to Malays and natives of any of the States of Sabah and Sarawak of positions in the public service and of scholarships, exhibitions and other educational or training privileges or special facilities, give such general directions as may be required for that purpose to any Commission to which Part X applies or to any authority charged with responsibility for the grant of such scholarships, exhibitions or other educational or training privileges or special facilities; and the Commission or authority shall duly comply with the directions.
(4) In exercising his functions under this Constitution and federal law in accordance with Clauses (1) to (3) the Yang di-Pertuan Agong shall not deprive any person of any public office held by him or of the continuance of any scholarship, exhibition or other educational or training privileges or special facilities enjoyed by him.
(5) This Article does not derogate from the provisions of Article 136.
(6) Where by existing federal law a permit or license is required for the operation of any trade or business the Yang di-Pertuan Agong may exercise his functions under that law in such manner, or give such general directions to any authority charged under that law with the grant of such permits or licenses, as may be required to ensure the reservation of such proportion of such permits or licenses for Malays and natives of any of the States of Sabah and Sarawak as the Yang di-Pertuan Agong may deem reasonably; and the authority shall duly comply with the directions.
(7) Nothing in this Article shall operate to deprive or authorize the deprivation of any person of any right, privilege, permit or license accrued to or enjoyed or held by him or to authorize a refusal to renew to any person any such permit or license or a refusal to grant to the heirs, successors or assigns of a person any permit or license when the renewal or grant might reasonably be expected in the ordinary course of events.
(8) Notwithstanding anything in this Constitution, where by any federal law any permit or license is required for the operation of any trade or business, that law may provide for the reservation of a proportion of such permits or licenses for Malays and natives of any of the States of Sabah and Sarawak; but no such law shall for the purpose of ensuring such a reservation—
(a) deprive or authorize the deprivation of any person of any right, privilege, permit or license accrued to or enjoyed or held by him; or
(b) authorize a refusal to renew to any person any such permit or license or a refusal to grant to the heirs, successors or assigns of any person any permit or license when the renewal or grant might in accordance with the other provisions of the law reasonably be expected in the ordinary course of events, or prevent any person from transferring together with his business any transferable license to operate that business; or
(c) where no permit or license was previously required for the operation of the trade or business, authorize a refusal to grant a permit or license to any person for the operation of any trade or business which immediately before the coming into force of the law he had been bona fide carrying on, or authorize a refusal subsequently to renew to any such person any permit or

equally. It is understandable why such provisions were made 55 years ago when Malaysia became independent. It must also be pointed out the children have equal rights to education and the same limited rights to freedom of religion as provided by art 11 of the Federal Constitution.[5] Malaysia's *1 Malaysia Policy* which was introduced by the 5th Prime Minister of Malaysia is certainly a transformation of policies towards a more equal opportunity society for all Malaysians.

Another article which is still reserved is art 7 on nationality. Malaysian nationality laws are governed by Part III of the Federal Constitution.[6] It is unfortunate that citizenship of a child will depend upon his father's citizenship. If a Malaysian woman married a non-Malaysian and lives abroad and a child is born abroad, unless the mother registers the birth at a Malaysian Embassy, the child shall not be a Malaysian. The situation is the same for many Malaysian women who decide to marry foreigners and live abroad. A worse scenario is, if a male Malaysian marries a foreign woman, lives in Malaysia after the marriage and all the children of the marriage are born in Malaysia, the foreign wife may be granted permanent residence after 5 years but many husbands do not bother to apply for his wife's permanent residency. Should the marriage end in divorce, a foreign wife without a permanent residence permit has to leave Malaysia and will be denied the right to see her children. The children will be denied access to their mother. Despite its discriminatory nature the Federal Constitution maintains the status quo in the national interest.

Malaysia also reserved art 14 of the CRC on freedom of conscience and religion. Malaysia is a multireligious nation where Islam is the religion of the Federation as provided by art 3 of the Federal Constitution.[7] However, other

---

license, or a refusal to grant to the heirs, successors or assigns of any such person any such permit or license when the renewal or grant might in accordance with the other provisions of that law reasonably be expected in the ordinary course of events.

(8A) Notwithstanding anything in this Constitution, where in any University, College and other educational institution providing education after Malaysian Certificate of Education or its equivalent, the number of places offered by the authority responsible for the management of the University, College or such educational institution to candidates for any course of study is less than the number of candidates qualified for such places, it shall be lawful for the Yang di-Pertuan Agong by virtue of this Article to give such directions to the authority as may be required to ensure the reservation of such proportion of such places for Malays and natives of any of the States of Sabah and Sarawak as the Yang di-Pertuan Agong may deem reasonable; and the authority shall duly comply with the directions.

(9) Nothing in this Article shall empower Parliament to restrict business or trade solely for the purpose of reservations for Malays and natives of any of the States of Sabah and Sarawak.

(9A) In this Article the expression "natives" in relation to the State of Sabah or Sarawak shall have the meaning assigned to it in Article 161A.

(10) The Constitution of the State of any Ruler may make provision corresponding (with the necessary modifications) to the provisions of this Article.'

5   Set out below.
6   Federal Constitution, arts 14–22 where a person may become a citizen by operation of law, by registration and by naturalisation.
7   *In Che Omar bin Che Soh* [1988] 2 MLJ 55 the court held that the meaning of Islam in art 3 was relating to official functions and ceremonials matters. However, in *Meor Atiqulrahman bin Ishak & Ors v Fatimah bte Sihi & Ors* [2000] 5 MLJ 375, the High Court held that the meaning

religions are allowed to be practised in harmony. Freedom of religion is guaranteed under art 11 of the Federal Constitution where it states:

'(1) Every person has the right to profess and practise his religion and, subject to Clause (4), to propagate it.

(2) No person shall be compelled to pay any tax the proceeds of which are specially allocated in whole or in part for the purposes of a religion other than his own.

(3) Every religious group has the right—

(a)   To manage its own religious affairs;
(b)   To establish and maintain institutions for religious or charitable purposes; and
(c)   To acquire and own property and hold and administer it in accordance with law.

(4) State law and in respect of the Federal Territories of Kuala Lumpur, Labuan and Putrajaya, federal law may control or restrict the propagation of any religious doctrine or belief among persons professing the religion of Islam.

(5) This Article does not authorize any act contrary to any general law relating to public order, public health or morality.'

The provision guaranteed freedom of religion for every citizen. However a child is further subjected to another restriction where art 12(4) of the Federal Constitution provides that:

'For the purposes of Clause (3) the religion of a person under the age of eighteen years shall be decided by his parent or guardian.'[8]

Hence a child in Malaysia has no right to change religion from the religion he or she was born with until reaching 18 years of age. However, Muslims, adult or child, do not have the same freedom to convert from Islam, since matters relating to Muslims and Islamic law come under the preview of the state legislature. Hence Muslim whether children or adult may have to face certain

---

of Islam in art 3 should extend beyond rituals. In fact the learned judge went on to say that Islam is a way of life and should take priority over other religions in Malaysia. The same was concluded by the Court of Appeal in *Kamariah Ali v Kerajaan Negeri Kelantan, Malaysia & Satu Lagi dan Rayuan Yang Lain* [2002] 3 CL 7.

[8]   In the case of *Teoh Eng Huat v Kadhi Pasir Mas & Anor* [1986] 2 MLJ 228, the High Court held that the religion of an infant under the age of 18 is guaranteed by art 11 of the Federal Constitution like any other citizen in Malaysia. However, on appeal the Supreme Court [1990] 2 MLJ 300 held that the religion of a child under the age of 18 shall be determined by her parents. See also Noor Aziah Mohd Awal 'A Child's Right To Religion In Malaysia: An Overview' [2005] IKIM Law Journal 289.

repercussions if they convert from Islam. It is unlikely that Malaysia will withdraw its reservation on art 14 as it is one of the most controversial areas of law in Malaysia.[9]

Another article which is still reserved is art 28(1)(a) on free and compulsory primary education. Malaysia made primary education compulsory by amending the Education Act 1961 in 2002[10] and parents who fail to send their children to school commit a crime and, if found guilty, may face a RM5,000 fine or 6 months jail sentence or both. In the 2007 Budget, the 4th Prime Minister of Malaysia announced that all primary school would be made free. However, many schools insisted on charging special fees including the parents and teachers association fees at the beginning of the school term. In the 2012 Budget the 5th Prime Minister once again made another announcement that both primary and secondary education would be free and abolished all forms of school fees. In fact the government also distributed a RM100 voucher per child to assist parents with the new school term in January 2012. School books are free in all schools and all children are entitled to free books. Students in higher education are also given a RM200 book voucher per student. Hence the reservation on art 28(1)(a) can now be withdrawn as both primary and secondary schools are almost free.

On the subject of education, Malaysia needs to look at education for handicapped children as this is an area which is still very much in need of improvement. Handicapped children have limited access to education as the number of schools is limited. The most popular schools are for the blind and deaf but Malaysia still needs special schools for autistic children as well as children with physical and mental disabilities.

Article 37 of the CRC on torture is still reserved in Malaysia even though the Child Act 2001 governed all matters relating to children who commit any offence. This is because a number of statutes like the Dangerous Drugs Act 1952,[11] Internal Security Act 1960[12] and the Fire Arms Act 1960[13] still impose the death penalty on children. Under the Child Act 2001, children cannot be sentenced to death but may be detained at the pleasure of the *Yang di-Pertuan Agong* or the King. There is no doubt that children detained at the pleasure of the King may be released with the recommendation of the Board of Visiting Justices[14] but it is open to a wide discretion and a child may be detained longer than an adult offender having to serve a life sentence.

The reservation on art 37 means that children in Malaysia may still be subjected to torture or other cruel, inhuman or degrading treatment or

---

[9]   Noor Aziah Mohd Awal 'A Child's Right To Religion In Malaysia: An Overview' [2005] IKIM Law Journal 289.
[10] Education Act (Amendment) 2002, s 29A.
[11] Act 234.
[12] Act 82.
[13] Act 206.
[14] The Board is appointed under s 64 of the Prison Act 1995 (Act 537).

punishment and may be detained unlawfully or arbitrarily. The Child Act 2001 provides that a child shall be brought before a Court for Children within 24 hours of being arrested. Act 611 has special provisions on arrest, detention, punishments and places of detention. Even the manner in which a child should be charged in a court is also provided for in great detail. However, the Act makes it possible for a child from the age of 16 to be sent to prison, if necessary, and also to be caned. This certainly goes against the whole concept of the CRC and the Child Act 2001 itself.

III RIGHTS OF CHILDREN IN MALAYSIA: FUTURE CHALLENGES

Malaysia may have reserved five articles of the CRC but does that means that Malaysia has fulfilled all the obligations in the articles which it has not reserved? Its first step was to pass the Child Act 2001[15] where the preamble of the Act highlighted its intention to implement the CRC. After 10 years of its application, the Act is being reviewed and amendments of various provisions are being drafted based on various criticisms made. Apart from the Child Act, other areas of law which are related to the rights of children need to be looked at and these are the real challenges for the future. The immediate challenges are as follows.

(a) Right to medical treatment and family planning

Article 24 gives children the right to the enjoyment of the highest attainable standard of health and to facilities for the treatment of illness and rehabilitation of health. States have the responsibilities to ensure that no child is deprived of the right of access to such health care services. States parties must take the appropriate measures to diminish infant and child mortality. In Malaysia one of the most worrying issues are the incidents of abandoned babies, many of whom were found dead. This is due to the fact that in Malaysia unwanted pregnancy, in particular the birth of illegitimate children, is a taboo and controversial. Consequently unwed mothers, who are not allowed to have an abortion,[16] abandon their babies as soon as they are born.[17] Many of the unwed mothers are themselves children as they are under the age of 18 years old. It is very difficult to ensure appropriate pre-natal and post-natal health care for mothers as most of them run away from home and have not been to the

---

[15] Act 611.

[16] Abortion is illegal according to ss 312 to 315 of the Penal Code. The law protects the right of the unborn whereby its right to be born alive must be safeguarded. It is unfortunate that no specific definition is given to the words woman with child or quick with child and no limits were also set in terms of the stages of the pregnancy where abortion may be permissible. It seems that, if it could be proved that it is done in good faith and to save the life of the mother, it does not matter how long she has been pregnant. Because of the prohibition, abortion is still done quietly and mostly by private practitioners.

[17] According to the Malaysian police, from 2005 to 2010 there were 472 cases of abandoned babies, 241 were rescued and 258 babies were found dead.

hospital for pre-natal care. Many deliver their babies in dreadful circumstances because of shame and fear. They are afraid that they will be arrested and punished. This is particularly true if these unwed mothers are Muslims. Under Islamic criminal law, it is an offence to be pregnant out of wedlock, unless she can prove that she has been raped.[18]

Many abandoned babies are assumed to be illegitimate and as such, under the present laws in Malaysia, are treated differently. For non-Muslims, illegitimate children are governed by the common law. They can be legitimated by the Legitimacy Act 1961.[19] Under Islamic law, an illegitimate child has only a right against his or her mother. The child can never be legitimised by subsequent marriage as Islam does not recognise such a relationship. An illegitimate child shall remain illegitimate and shall not be entitled to use his or her father's name. The child's lineage remains his or her mother's. Nor can the child be adopted by the biological father as Islam does not recognise adoption. Hence, it is very difficult for Malaysia to fulfil its obligation under arts 7 and 8 of the CRC. That is also the reason why Malaysia still reserves art 7. Many illegitimate children do not have a birth certificate as they were not registered. Many do not know their origins as when they were abandoned without any documents. According to the National Registration Department, the numbers of children who do not have their fathers' information and therefore were not able to record them are as follows:

Year	Malay	Chinese	Indian	Others	Total
2005	4,773	778	530	3,748	9,829
2006	7,090	885	694	5,450	14,119
2007	12,082	1,047	916	8,541	22,586
2008	15,652	1,218	1,150	10,839	28,859

---

[18] The Syariah Criminal Offences Act (Federal Territory) 1997 (Act 559) provides in s 23:
'(1) Any man who performs sexual intercourse with a woman who is not his lawful wife shall be guilty of an offence and shall on conviction be liable to a fine not exceeding five thousand ringgit or to imprisonment for a term not exceeding three years or to whipping not exceeding six strokes or to any combination thereof.
(2) Any woman who performs sexual intercourse with a man who is not her lawful husband shall be guilty of an offence and shall on conviction be liable to a fine not exceeding five thousand ringgit or to imprisonment for a term not exceeding three years or to whipping not exceeding six strokes or to any combination thereof.
(3) The fact that a woman is pregnant out of wedlock as a result of sexual intercourse performed with her consent shall be prima facie evidence of the commission of an offence under subsection (2) by that woman.
(4) For the purpose of subsection (3), any woman who gives birth to a fully developed child within a period of six qamariah months from the date of her marriage shall be deemed to have been pregnant out of wedlock.'
Section 24 of the Act states that '[a]ny person who does an act preparatory to sexual intercourse out of wedlock shall be guilty of an offence and shall on conviction be liable to a fine not exceeding three thousand ringgit or to imprisonment for a term not exceeding two years or to both'.
[19] Act 60.

Year	Malay	Chinese	Indian	Others	Total
2009	14,504	1,266	1,294	12,377	29,441
Total	54,101	5,194	4,584	40,955	104,834

Source: National Registration Department

The number of illegitimate children born in Malaysia during the past 5 years has also increased as can been seen below:

Year	Malay	Chinese	Indian	Others	Total
2005	6,461	3,993	3,911	8,147	22,512
2006	6,455	3,854	3,927	9,903	24,139
2007	4,018	4,064	3,902	9,664	21,648
2008	889	3,725	3,622	9,727	17,963
2009	2,799	2,862	3,750	13,526	22,937
Total	20,622	18,498	19,112	50,967	109,199

Source: National Registration Department

Hence, at present it is very difficult for Malaysia to lift its reservation on art 7 and it has not fully satisfied the requirements of art 24. Another area of art 24 that needs attention is art 24(3) which states that:

> 'States Parties shall take all effective and appropriate measures with a view to abolishing traditional practices prejudicial to the health of children.'

Malaysia is multiracial and multireligious and hence, it has many customary and religious practices which may be looked upon as 'traditional practices prejudicial to ...'. One of the main concerns is female circumcision. The Public Health Department, Ministry of Health has formed a special committee to look into this matter.[20] Female circumcision in Malaysia is not female genital mutilation as practised in many parts of the world. The procedure has been described as a mere 'pricking' and harmless to female children. Furthermore, the *Majlis Fatwa* or the *Fatwa* Council has decided that female circumcision is compulsory and shall be imposed on all female babies as soon as they are born. At present the Public Health Department, Ministry of Health is finalising the guidelines for female circumcision to make sure that it is done in a manner that will not harm female genitals and cause hurt to female infants.

Under art 24, states parties also need to develop preventive health care, guidance for parents and family planning education and services. Preventive health care includes making sure children do not get HIV or AIDS or any other

---

[20] The author is one of the experts appointed to advise the Department on various issues involving children such as female circumcision and children's rights to family planning advice and medication.

communicable diseases. According to the Ministry of Health nearly 80,000 people are currently living with HIV/AIDS in Malaysia.[21] Most HIV and AIDS sufferers are drug addicts and acquired the disease through sexual intercourse or sharing of needles. In 2009, out of the average nine new HIV cases recorded every day, six would have contracted HIV through injecting drug use, and three via sexual transmission.[22] The Malaysian government has seriously started various preventive measures in order to prevent the spread of HIV and AIDS. These are:

(1)   needle and syringe programmes (NSPs);

(2)   opioid substitution therapy (OST) and other drug dependence treatment;

(3)   HIV testing and counselling;

(4)   antiretroviral therapy (ART);

(5)   prevention and treatment of sexually transmitted infections (STIs);

(6)   condom programmes for persons who inject drugs (PWID) and their sexual partners;

(7)   targeted information, education and communication for PWID and their sexual partners;

(8)   vaccination for and diagnosis and treatment of viral hepatitis; and

(9)   prevention, diagnosis and treatment of tuberculosis (TB).

Children get infected with HIV or AIDS through their mothers. One of the ways in which the government could prevent them from getting HIV and AIDS is to make blood tests compulsory for all Muslims who wish to marry. If the blood test proved to be positive, both parties to the marriage may be counselled or may wish to change their minds about the impending marriage. However, blood tests are not compulsory for non-Muslims.

Another area of concern under art 24 is the state responsibility to provide guidance for parents and family planning education and services. Family planning education would mean that parents must be able to give children information on family planning and services. Family planning includes information about contraceptives, abortion and sex education in general.

Contraception is one of the methods used for family planning and only available to married women. This includes the use of condoms, pills or injection. A woman may be prescribed pills or injection after being examined

[21]   Ministry of Health *Malaysia UNGASS country progress report* (Kuala Lumpur: MOH, 2010).
[22]   Ministry of Health *National strategic plan on HIV/AIDS 2006–2010* (Kuala Lumpur: MOH, 2005).

by a medical practitioner. A doctor must obtain parental consent before a child is examined unless the child is brought to the hospital under s 20 of the Child Act 2001.[23] This area of law is underdeveloped and as such reference is made to English cases as Malaysia's legal system is based on the English common law legal system.

For a very long time in England, the father was the sole guardian where he had the power over his children's religion, education, medical care, choice of partners and property. In relation to custody, women or mothers had a long history of fighting for their rights to custody of their children. If parental rights conflict with the rights of others, then the concept of 'unimpeachable parents' is invoked. However, in *J v C*[24] the House of Lords held that the welfare of children takes priority over 'unimpeachable parents' rights and this decision was upheld in *S (BD) v S (DJ) (Children: Care and Control)*[25] where Ormrod LJ commented on the concept of 'unimpeachable parents':

> 'I have never known and still do not know what it means. It cannot mean a parent who is above criticism because there is no such thing. It might mean a parent against whom no matrimonial offence has been proved. If so, it adds nothing to the record which is before the court and in any event is now outmoded. I think it is really an advocate's phrase.'

J v C was in the context of guardianship and custody but it can be seen that the highest court in England was willing to set aside the 'unimpeachable parents' concept where it involved parental consent for an operation.

In relation to contraceptives, in England the most relevant case to discuss is *Gillick v West Norfolk and Wisbech Area Health Authority*.[26] In this case Lord Scarman said:

> 'It is not enough that she should understand the advice which is being given: she must also have sufficient maturity to understand what is involved. There are moral and family questions, especially her relationship with her parents, long-term problems associated with the emotional impact of pregnancy and its termination;

---

[23] Section 20 states that:
'(1) If a Protector or police officer who takes a child into temporary custody under section 18 (neglect or abuse or abandon) is of the opinion that the child is in need of medical examination or treatment, the Protector or police officer may, instead of bringing the child before a Court For Children or Magistrate, as the case may be, present the child before a medical officer;
(2) If at the time of being taken into custody a child is a patient in a hospital, the Protector or police officer who takes the child into custody may leave the child in the hospital;
(3) If a Protector or police officer does not take a child into temporary custody under section 18 but he is satisfied on reasonable grounds that the child is in need of medical examination or treatment, he may direct in writing the person who appears to him to have the care of the child for the time being to immediately take the child to a medical officer;
(4) If the person referred to in subsection (3) fails to comply within forty-eight hours with a direction made under that subsection, a Protector or police officer may take the child into temporary custody for the purpose of presenting the child before a medical officer.'

[24] [1970] AC 668.
[25] [1977] Fam 109.
[26] [1986] AC 112.

and there are risks to health of sexual intercourse at her age, risks which contraception may diminish but cannot eliminate.'

It looks as if Lord Scarman was trying to include 'informed consent' in the relationship between children and parents but many rejected this[27] and the focus is whether a child has achieved sufficient maturity and understanding in order to receive advice. Gillick established the 'Gillick competency test' to be applied to children under 16 years old. Children aged 16 years and above have the right to receive medical treatment including the right to receive advice on contraception and taking contraception without parental knowledge or consent. However, the English courts were reluctant to recognise that children 16 years and above have the right to decide on their medical treatment.[28]

In Malaysia there is no decided case on contraception. In relation to Muslim children, reference can be made to the 8th National Fatwa Council Committee Conference decision that family planning including contraception is generally prohibited but excusable in certain circumstances.[29] A *Fatwa*[30] in Malaysia is made by a council consisting of Muslim scholars appointed by the King. A National Fatwa is only applicable to Muslims if it is adopted by the State Fatwa Council. A National Fatwa serves as a guideline to the State Fatwa Council. Family planning including contraception is permissible only in certain extraneous circumstances, for an adult female and with her husband's permission. As Islam prohibits any sexual relations before marriage, use of contraception before marriage does not arise. However, as research has shown, children start to have sexual intercourse as young as 12 years old.[31] This means that children are open to the danger of sexually transmitted diseases as well as being pregnant out of wedlock. If they are not given or allowed information on family planning or contraception, Malaysia is not fulfilling its obligation under art 24. For non-Muslim children, there is no data to support the allegation that they are already using contraception as they may have obtained it from private hospitals or clinics. As the law stands, medical practitioners are put in a dilemma whether or not to give children family planning advice or medication or even to give them medical treatment for any sexual diseases as they are required to inform parents and seek parental consent but the children that came for assistance do not wish their parents to be informed.

---

[27] N Lowe and G Douglas *Bromley's Family Law* (Oxford: Oxford University Press, 10th edn, 2007) 363–364.

[28] In *Re R (A Minor) (Wardship: Medical Treatment)* [1992] Fam 11, the court held that parents can veto their child's medical treatment even though the child passed the Gillick competency test. In *Re W (A Minor) (Medical Treatment: Court's Jurisdiction)* [1993] Fam 64, the Court of Appeal held that a 16-year-old has the right to decide whether or not to have a medical treatment but the court and parents can still veto that right.

[29] The Fatwa was made on 23 November 1973. See www.e-fatwa.gov.my/fatwa-kebangsaan/rancangan-keluarga (accessed June 2012).

[30] A Fatwa is a juristic ruling concerning Islamic law issued by Islamic scholars.

[31] Noor Aziah Mohd Awal et al *Kajian Modul Pembentukan Akhlak (Ta'dib) Untuk Pesalah Kanak-kanak di Sekolah Henry Gurney* [*Formation of the Ta'dib Modul for Child Offenders at the Henry Gurney School*], UKM-11KH-05-FRGS0086–2009 and Noor Aziah Mohd Awal et al *Hak Anak tak Sah Taraf di Malaysia* [*Rights of Illegitimate Children in Malaysia*], UKM-UU-04-FRGS0006–2006.

Apart from family planning advice and contraception, children have no right to have an abortion unless pregnancy threatens the mother's life. Under Islamic law, abortion is *haram* or strictly prohibited and can only be performed if there is a reasonable cause to do it.[32] According to Dr Yusuf al Qardawi abortion performed after 120 days is *haram* or prohibited and, if committed, is the same as killing a living person.[33] Only the *Hanafi* school thought that termination of pregnancy can only be done before 4 months of pregnancy. The other three schools of thought concluded that abortion is *haram*. Hence abortion is *haram* for female Muslim adult and children.

Under the civil law, abortion is governed by the Penal Code where it is a criminal offence which carries a jail sentence of 3 to 7 years.[34] The provision is not applicable in cases where a registered medical practitioner terminated the pregnancy in good faith believing that, if it continues, it will cause a high risk to the life of the pregnant woman or cause mental and physical injury to the pregnant mother.[35] The problem with this provision is that it is open to abuse.

A very topical question in this area is whether a child who is a victim of rape can have her pregnancy terminated? Both civil and Islamic laws do not permit abortion unless it can be shown that continuation may cause a high risk to the mother's life.

Sterilisation is also prohibited under Islamic law. Under civil law, there are no decided cases and reference has been made to English authority such as *Re B (A Minor) (Wardship: Sterilization)*[36] and *Re D (Minor) Wardship: Sterilization)*.[37] However, in Malaysia it is a known fact that many sterilisation operations have been performed on handicapped children in government hospitals at the request of the child's parents. This is highly disturbing as handicapped children have the right to enjoy life like any normal children.

(b)   Rights to identity, nationality and name and family

Article 8(1) states that: 'States Parties undertake to respect the right of the child to preserve his or her identity, including nationality, name and family relations as recognized by law without unlawful interference' and art 8(2) states that where a child is illegally deprived of some or all of the elements of his or her identity, states parties shall provide appropriate assistance and protection, with a view to re-establishing speedily his or her identity. One of the main problems that arise in fulfilling this article has been discussed above under art 24. Many

---

[32]   Mohammed Mekki Naciri 'A View of Family Planning in Islamic Legislation' in Olivia Schieffelin (ed) *Muslims' Attitudes Towards Family Planning* (New York: The Population Council, 1973) 144 as taken from Abul Fadl Mohsin Ebrahim *Abortion, Birth Control and Surrogate Parenting, An Islamic Perspective* (American Trust Publication, 1989) 89.

[33]   Yusuf al Qardawi *Halal and Haram in Islam* (translated) (Cairo, 14th edn, 1980) 169.

[34]   Penal Code, s 312.

[35]   Act A 727/89, s 9(a) in force from 5 May1989.

[36]   [1988] AC 199.

[37]   [1967] 1 All ER 326.

illegitimate children were not registered as the unwed mothers were afraid that legal action would be taken against them. Under Islamic law, an illegitimate child can only take his or her mother's name and not his or her father's. Even if the biological father marries the mother some years later after the child is born, the child is still an illegitimate child. An illegitimate child can only inherit from his or her mother, and only the mother is responsible for the upbringing, maintenance, education and religion of the child. This is also the reason why Malaysia still reserves art 2 as Malaysia still has discriminatory laws relating to children. However, it must be pointed out that, under Islamic law, an illegitimate child whose mother is unable to support him or her due to poverty or any other reason, shall be supported by the state. Non-Muslim illegitimate children can be legitimised by subsequent marriage of their parents under the Legitimacy Act 1961. They can also be adopted under the Adoption Act 1952 where the rights of an adopted child are the same as a child born within wedlock.

In relation to nationality, if the mother of the illegitimate child is a foreigner, the child will have the status of a foreign child. If a child is born in Malaysia and the mother's legal status is doubtful, the child will also be a foreign child. If the child is not a Malaysian national, he or she will lose the rights to education and maintenance by the government. This is also the reason why Malaysia has still reserved art 7 of the CRC.

(c)   Rights to maintenance

Children have a right to be maintained. However, there are many cases where children's maintenance has been neglected.[38] Article 27 states that:

> 'Parties shall take all appropriate measures to secure the recovery of maintenance for the child from the parents or other persons having financial responsibility for the child, both within the State Party and from abroad.'

In order to fulfil its obligation under the article, the Department of Islamic Judiciary has set up the Family Support Section, better known as BSK. The objectives of this unit or section are as follows:

(i)   To ensure that all maintenance orders are fully enforced.

(ii)   To ensure that no wives or children face any problem in enforcing their maintenance order.

(iii) To ensure that syariah court orders are respected and obeyed.

(iv)   To give all kinds of assistance relating to family matters.

---

[38]   Noor Aziah Mohd Awal *Perlaksanaan Perintah Nafkah Isteri dan Anak di Malaysia* [*Enforcement of Wives and children Maintenance in Malaysia*] UKM UU/002/2004 (June 2004–June 2005).

In Malaysia, the *Syariah* legal system is state-based and each state has its own syariah courts. The decision of a syariah court in state A does not bind state B nor can it be enforced out of jurisdiction.[39] The syariah court does not follow precedent like the civil courts. Since Islam and Islamic law are within state jurisdiction, there are states which have not accepted the establishment of BSK. Furthermore BSK income comes from the federal government as well as states *Baitul Mal*. If states decide not to contribute, there will be no money to pay maintenance in advance.

For non-Muslims, there is no equivalent of BSK. Many non-Muslim children who have obtained a maintenance order from the Session or High Court can only proceed for an enforcement order or committal for non-compliance. Many non-Muslim wives decide not to enforce the maintenance order for non-compliance because it is expensive.[40]

(d) Child's right to rest and leisure, to engage in play and recreational activities

Malaysia has not reserved art 31 which states that states parties must recognise the right of the child to rest and leisure, to engage in play and recreational activities appropriate to the age of the child and to participate freely in cultural life and the arts. States Parties shall also respect and promote the right of the child to participate fully in cultural and artistic life and shall encourage the provision of appropriate and equal opportunities for cultural, artistic, recreational and leisure activity. This is another challenge for Malaysia, a developing nation and hoping to be a developed nation by 2020. With such development many Malaysian parents are over-zealous about education and making sure that their children are able to achieve excellent examination results. Hence the majority of children today do not have the opportunity to play and rest as most of their time is spent studying. Children no longer play sports or have other extracurricular activities as they are not counted as part of the examinations. The Ministry of Education has made a change of policy whereby those who wish to join tertiary education must have 10% in co-curriculum or sports.[41] Hence, it is true that all work and no play make Jack a dull boy. What is more worrying is the number of students who are diagnosed with stress and obesity in Malaysia due to overemphasis on examinations and lack of sports.

---

[39] Only seven states have accepted the unification under the federal system, these are Selangor, Negeri Sembilan, Malacca, Penang, Perlis, Sabah and Federal Territory. A syariah court order in these states is enforceable in these seven states. Otherwise, one needs to apply for an enforcement order.

[40] Noor Aziah Mohd Awal *Perlaksanaan Perintah Nafkah Isteri dan Anak di Malaysia* [*Enforcement of Wives and children Maintenance in Malaysia*] UKM UU/002/2004 (June 2004–June 2005).

[41] Ministry of Education announcement in May 2008.

(e) Rights to education

The government has taken very serious actions in relation to children's rights to education. Amongst the actions taken are as follows:

(a) making primary education compulsory and free;

(b) establishing the Integrity School in prison and at the Henry Gurney School;

(c) making co-curriculum part of the requirements to join tertiary education;

(d) making sport compulsory; and

(e) improving education for children with special needs or handicaps.

However, one of the greatest hurdles in this area is the unwillingness of schools not to charge parents anything when school term begins. Schools still charge parents a number of fees such as parents and teachers association fees, special motivational programmes for students who are taking major examinations and computer class fees. At present, all books are given free without discrimination and also a RM100 voucher to help children with school shoes and uniform. If schools abide by the Ministry's no fees rule, all primary and secondary government school in Malaysia should have been free since 2008.

The Integrity schools established in prison and Henry Gurney for young offenders certainly have given them a better second opportunity. Many younger offenders who were interviewed showed their willingness to study and appreciated the second chance given to them.[42] Schools for children with special needs have been set up but it is not enough. Many of these children are not able go to these schools because one of the requirements is that they must be able to manage themselves independently. Many of these children are very dependent on their parents. The Person with Disabilities Act 2002 was to enhance education and care for the handicapped. It is very slow moving but it is hoped it will achieve its target soon.

(f) Children's sexual rights

Sex education has been discussed quite often[43] in a number of conferences especially when discussing the issue of illegitimate birth. On 23 May 2010, the Minister for Women, Family and Community Development announced the

---

[42] Noor Aziah Mohd Awal, Fariza Md Sham and Mohd Al Adib Samuri *Kajian Modul Pembentukan Akhlak(Ta'dib) Untuk Pesalah di Sekolah Henry Gurney [A Study on the ta'dib Module for Young Offenders in Henry Gurney School]* UKM-11KH-05-FRGS0086–2009.

[43] The author was one of the invited panel to discuss the National Policy on Children as well as the National Policy on Women under the Ministry of Women, Family and Community Development.

importance of sex education at school. This was to ensure that children do not get wrong information about it. On 11 October 2010 the Deputy Minister of Education announced that sex education was to be taught at school beginning 1 January 2011 and has been renamed as Health and Social Reproductive Education. However, this policy has received many criticisms from various quarters where it is seen as 'encouraging children to experiment on sex'.

Many of the critics come from various religious groups and Muslim groups. The question is whether sex education is prohibited by Islam. In Islam, parents have the responsibility to educate their children and according to Abdullah Nasir Ulwan in his book,[44] there are seven levels of education and one of them is sex education. The author classified children into three groups:

(i)   7–10 year olds who should be taught the ways and ethics of asking for permission and what they should be able to witness or see;

(ii) 10–14 year olds who should be taught to avoid things or matters that could arouse them;

(iii) 14–16 year olds who should be taught of the ways of having sexual intercourse and as an adult, how to behave and build self-respect. They must be taught not to have sex before marriage as it is haram.

Islam is a comprehensive religion and it gives guidelines in all matters including how to mix with others or how to behave in certain circumstances. Sexual rights include not only rights to have sex whenever a person decides, with whom to have it and also the number of children to have and with whom. The question is should a child be given his or her sexual rights? This could also means that a child should never be forced to marry someone she did not know or like, or not be allowed to marry someone she or he likes.

Again this is a great challenge in Malaysia as, under Islamic law, a female can only marry with the permission of her father as the *wali* or guardian. Marriage solemnised without the consent of the guardian is void and can be annulled.[45] Sex out of wedlock is strictly prohibited.[46] Many young girls whose father refused to consent to her marriage have eloped to Thailand and got married there. Many such marriages are unregistered and, if she has a child, the child may be deemed to be illegitimate. On the other hand there are cases where the father had married his daughter to a man of his choice and she had no way of objecting the marriage. This often involves girls who are very young or child marriage. On many occasions these girls were forced into marriage without their consent.[47] The law is clear that no marriage can be solemnised without the

---

[44]   Quoted by Siti Fatimah Abdul Rahman. See www.ikim.gov.my/v5/index.php?lg=1&opt=com_article&grp=2&sec=&key=684&cmd=resetall (accessed June 2012).

[45]   Malaysian rules are from the *Shafie* school of thought.

[46]   Selangor Criminal Syariah Enactment 1995, No 9 of 1995 – the relevant sections are 22–31 on fornication, incest and indecent behaviour.

[47]   *Utusan Online* (11 May 2010) reported that a father from Jelawang, Kuala Krai solemnised the

consent of both parties to the marriage as well as the *wali*. If the *wali* refuses to consent, the bride can sue her father in the syariah court and the court may give permission for her to marry if consent was unreasonably refused.[48]

The power of the *wali* or guardian to give consent to marriage often comes into conflict with the right of a child or woman to choose her own partner and marry. It is also related to child marriage which happens in many parts of the Muslim world.[49] The main problem here is the difficulty in differentiating between religious practices and culture. Even in Malaysia, the multicultural society often mixes up religious practices with culture in particular where Indian Muslims are involved. Culturally, child brides are common in the Indian community irrespective of religion. In the Malay community, young girls were married off because they were not sent to school but were prepared for marriage. However, after independence, many girls were sent to school and started to have a career of their own and the practice of child brides diminished. The recent cases of child brides were heavily criticised.[50] Statistics from 1 January to 2005 to 12 January 2006 showed that 115 applications to marry under the age of 16 were made in Kelantan, 102 in Sabah and 100 cases in Sarawak. Of these applications, 81 were approved in Kelantan, 92 in Sarawak and 60 in Sabah. Many of these young girls had to stop schooling as soon as they were married.[51]

For non-Muslim children, the Law Reform (Marriage and Divorce) Act 1976[52] provides that the consent of both parties to a marriage must be obtained, otherwise the marriage is voidable.[53] Parental consents must also be obtained if parties to a marriage are under 21 years of age.[54] Furthermore, parties to a marriage must reach 16 years of age for females and 18 years for males. Any marriage solemnised below this age shall be void.[55] All these provisions are made to keep control of marriages solemnised and registered under the Act. They also safeguard the rights of parties to a marriage. However, in relation to

---

marriage of his 11-year-old daughter with a 41-year-old. In another incident, Siti Mariam aged 14 was married to Abdul Amna Othman, 23 years old on 23 July 2010. In this later case, it was a teacher–student relationship and the marriage was consensual and not forced.

[48]   Islamic Family Law Enactment (Negeri Melaka) 2002, s 13(b).

[49]   A UNICEF study in Niger found that 44% of girls aged 20–24 were married under the age of 15. A UNESCO study found that: in Bangladesh 47% girls are married before the age of 15; 50% of girls are married by the time they are 18 in Africa; in Nepal 40% of girls under 14 and 62% of girls between the ages of 15 and 19 are married; in Rajasthan 56% girls are married before 15; and in Latin America and Eastern Europe it is not unusual for girls between 16 and 18 to be married.

[50]   Zaleha Kamarudin 'Kahwinan Bawah Umor: Galak Belajar v Galak Kahwin' (2011) IKIM online available at www.ikim.gov.my/v5/index.php?lg=1&opt=com_article&grp=2&sec= &key=2266&cmd=resetall (accessed June 2012).

[51]   http://ms.wikipedia.org/wiki/Perkahwinan_bawah_umur (accessed June 2012). In 2010, a 10-year-old was married to a 40-year-old man in Pasir Mas, Kelantan. In March 2010, Siti Nur Zubaidah Hussin (11 years old) was married to Shamsuddin Che Derahman at Sudin Ajaib by her father, in Kuala Krai, Kelantan. She was later left at a mosque by her husband.

[52]   Act 164.

[53]   Act 164, s 70(c).

[54]   Act 164, s 12.

[55]   Act 164, s 69(b).

consents, s 12 focuses only on the father's right to give consent whereas a mother has an equal right to do so. It is recommended that, in relation to consent to marry, both parents should give consent if they are living together and in case of divorce, the parent with whom the child is staying.

IV CONCLUSION

Children have basic rights as human beings. In fact their rights are entrenched under the Federal Constitution of Malaysia and the ratification of the CRC has enhanced such rights. As a multiracial and multireligious nation, the greatest challenge for Malaysia in fulfilling its obligation under the CRC is to strike a balance between the rights of Muslim and non-Muslim children. Parents still play a bigger role in the upbringing, education and religion of their children and such a role could come into conflict with the child's right to determine his or her life. When such conflict happens, the court or mediation should play the role of solving and settling such issues so as to ensure the best interests of the children are safeguarded.

The Netherlands

SOMETHING OLD, SOMETHING NEW, SOMETHING INTERNATIONAL AND SOMETHING ASKEW

*Ian Curry-Sumner and Machteld Vonk**

Résumé

Le droit néerlandais de la famille a bien connu quelques développements en 2011, mais aucune réforme importante n'est à signaler. Le Parlement fut saisi de nouveaux projets de lois, dont celui reconnaissant à deux épouses la filiation maternelle ex lege et les droits parentaux à l'égard d'un enfant conçu par donneur anonyme pendant le mariage. Des projets plus anciens ont finalement été adoptés, notamment celui concernant les droits et obligations des époux en matière de droit patrimonial. Sur le plan international, trois nouveaux instruments ont apporté d'importants changements en matière de recouvrement des pensions alimentaires. Deux sont entrés en vigueur aux Pays-Bas le 18 juin 2011, le Règlement communautaire sur les obligations alimentaires et le Protocole de La Haye sur la loi applicable aux obligations alimentaires. Le présent article expose les principaux effets de ces textes sur le droit interne. Par ailleurs, la Cour européenne des droits de l'homme a critiqué les façons de faire de la Cour Suprême néerlandaise dans le traitement d'une affaire dont l'avait saisi un mineur ayant fait l'objet d'un placement en milieu fermé. Cela a immédiatement amené la Cour Suprême à modifier son approche.

I INTRODUCTION

It has been a rather uneventful year in Dutch family law (2011). There have been new developments, but nothing on a large scale. Nevertheless, it is interesting to provide a short overview of the important case-law and (proposed) legislative changes relating to family law. New legislative proposals were introduced in the Dutch Parliament, including a Bill to vest both female spouses parents ex lege with parentage rights over any child conceived with the sperm of an unknown donor born during their marriage, and old legislative

---

* Ian Curry-Sumner, Freelance Lecturer, Researcher and Legal Consultant, Voorts Legal Services (www.voorts.com). Previously Senior Lecturer and Researcher, Utrecht Centre for European Research into Family Law, Molengraaff Institute for Private Law, Utrecht University.
Machteld Vonk, University Lecturer and Researcher, Utrecht Centre for European Research into Family Law, Molengraaff Institute for Private Law, Utrecht University.

proposals were finally adopted, including a Bill relating to the rights and responsibility of spouses regarding their marital property.

At the international level the international recovery of maintenance has undergone enormous changes, with three new instruments having been drafted in the past few years. Two of these new instruments, the European Maintenance Regulation and the Hague Maintenance Protocol entered into force in the Netherlands on 18 June 2011. In this contribution, the major changes for Dutch law will be reviewed. Furthermore, the European Court of Human Rights held that the Dutch Supreme Court had not been efficient when hearing a case brought by a minor who had been placed in a confined institution on a custodial placement. This led to an immediate change in the Supreme Court approach to this issue.

This contribution will, therefore, review some of these judicial and legislative developments providing a brief overview of the major changes to Dutch family law. The *Amsterdam Stories* by Nescio (1882–1961) one of the treasures of Dutch literature, which has finally been translated into English is a perhaps the best example of something old, new, and something quite possibly askew.[1]

II OLD THINGS

(a) Surrogacy arrangements

With respect to surrogacy arrangements the Parliamentary State Secretary to the Minister of Justice has considered the matter in 2011 on the basis of the report discussed in last year's International Survey,[2] as well as other information gathered. In December 2011, he informed Parliament of his intentions regarding the issues of domestic and cross-border surrogacy.[3] Regarding cross-border surrogacy the intention is to accept the Dutch intentional parents as legal parents if one of the intentional parents is genetically related to the child (one of them has either contributed the egg or the sperm). The State Secretary stressed that the rights of the child to know his or her origins as expressed in art 7 of the United Nations Convention on the Rights of the Child also need to be taken into account in cases of surrogacy. In practice, this would mean that the identity of the egg and/or sperm donors involved in the surrogacy will need to be traceable for the child. Presumably, this would also apply to the surrogate mother who does not supply the egg.

---

[1] 'No one has written more feelingly and more beautifully than Nescio about the madness and sadness, courage and vulnerability of youth: its big plans and vague longings, not to mention the binges, crashes, and marathon walks and talks. No one, for that matter, has written with such pristine clarity about the radiating canals of Amsterdam and the cloud-swept landscape of the Netherlands.' See: www.nybooks.com/books/imprints/classics/amsterdam-stories/ (accessed June 2012).

[2] I Curry-Sumner and Machteld Vonk 'National and International Surrogacy: An Odyssey' in B Atkin (ed) *International Survey of Family Law, 2011 Edition* (Jordan Publishing Ltd, 2011).

[3] Letter to the Dutch Second Chamber of 16th December 2011 concerning surrogacy, Dutch Second Chamber, 2011–2012, 33 000 VI, no 69.

Regarding the domestic surrogacy situation, the Minister of Health has promised to review the guidelines for IVF surrogacy that were drawn up in 1999 by the Dutch Society for Obstetrics and Gynecology, and report back to Parliament answering the question whether there are possibilities to expand the eligibility criteria for IVF surrogacy treatment.[4] These guidelines limit the accessibility to surrogacy services in Dutch hospitals to a very specific group, which may result in prospective parents going abroad to access legal or illegal surrogacy services.[5]

(b) Child protection

On 18 July 2009 a Bill was introduced in Parliament to improve the present Child Protection System.[6] There has been a lot of discussion on the question at what point the authorities are allowed/compelled to intervene in order to protect the child from harm. In the original version of the proposal, the threshold for intervention was substantially lowered, but after intensive discussion a middle road was chosen and the main aim is to clarify when authorities can intervene. Moreover, the Bill also aims to introduce a new 'lighter' measure of child protection, 'growing-up support' (*opgroeiondersteuning*). On 15 March 2011 the amended version of the Bill was accepted with general acclaim in the Dutch Second Chamber and sent to the Dutch First Chamber for approval. Again questions were raised with respect to these provisions. Very recently members of the First Chamber sent a letter to the Minister of Justice complaining that their questions have as yet remained unanswered (it has almost been a year since their report was submitted to the Minister of Justice).

(c) Matrimonial property reform

(i) *Legislative amendments*

The Bill on the reform of the matrimonial property system was accepted in 2011 and was implemented on the 1 January 2012. Despite grander ideas at the first submission of the Bill on 7 May 2003,[7] the structure of the Dutch matrimonial property regime remains largely in place. The ultimate changes concern issues within the system and not the system as such. The main change

---

[4] Hoogtechnologisch draagmoederschap Richtlijn Nederlands Vereniging voor Obstetrie en Gynaecologie, no 18, January 1999, available online in Dutch at www.nvog-documenten.nl/uploaded/docs/richtlijnen_pdf/18_hoog_draagmoeder.pdf (accessed June 2012).

[5] For more information on surrogacy in the Netherlands see I Curry-Sumner and M Vonk 'National and International Surrogacy: an Odyssey' in B Atkin (ed) *International Survey of Family Law, 2011 Edition* (Jordan Publishing Ltd, 2011) and I Curry-Sumner and M Vonk 'Surrogacy according to Dutch law' in K Trimmings and P Beaumont (eds) *International Surrogacy Arrangements: Legal Regulation at the International Level* (Hart Publishers, forthcoming November 2012).

[6] Second Chamber 2009–2010, 32015 no 1–3.

[7] See for instance I Curry-Sumner and C Forder 'Proposed Revision of Matrimonial Property Law ...' in A Bainham (ed) *International Survey of Family Law, 2004 Edition* (Jordan Publishing Ltd, 2004).

concerns the fact that reimbursements between the various assets (*vermogens*) in the property regime no longer occur on a nominal basis, but the increase or decrease in value of the object that was financed with the money needs to be taken into account. Parties can have communal assets and private assets alongside each other. If the wife finances part of the house out of her private assets, but the ownership of the house falls into the community of assets, she needs to be reimbursed. Until 1 January 2012, this occurred on a nominal basis, even where the value of the house had increased over time. However, as of 1 January 2012, the increase of the house's value will be taken into account.

(ii)   Absolute separation of property[8]

On 3 March 2011 the research report on the consequences of unfair marital property agreements after the dissolution of marriage and the problems of distributing property after factual separation was presented to the Dutch Second Chamber.[9]

> 'The general conclusion of this research is that total separation of property does lead to financial problems and unfair effects – both in cases where total separation results from a contract between the partners in a formal relationship and from the absence of the legal regulation of the property relationship of partners in informal relationships.'[10]

The report contains a number of suggestions to remedy the unfair effect of the described (lack) of regulation, for instance:[11]

> 'to extrapolate partner maintenance to all informal marriage like relationships. This instrument would allow the temporary mitigation of the reduction of the earning capacity of the child-caring partner, taking into consideration both the needs of the receiving partner and the financial capacity of the paying partner.'

The Parliamentary State Secretary to the Minister of Justice has discussed this proposal with various interested parties working in the field, and has concluded that bringing cohabiting couples into the partner maintenance scheme is not broadly supported in practice.[12]

---

[8]   Absolute separation of property (*koude uitsluiting*) refers to a marital agreement where there is no community of property during the marriage and no system is in place to amend the possible unfair consequences of such an agreement.

[9]   See www.wodc.nl/onderzoeksdatabase/koude-uitsluiting.aspx?cp=44&cs=6780 for an English summary of the report (accessed June 2012).

[10]   Summary of the report p 4: www.wodc.nl/onderzoeksdatabase/koude-uitsluiting.aspx?cp=44&cs=6780.

[11]   Summary of the report p 7: www.wodc.nl/onderzoeksdatabase/koude-uitsluiting.aspx?cp=44&cs=6780.

[12]   Dutch Second Chamber 2001–2012, 28867, no 29.

III NEW THINGS

Lesbian motherhood

On 13 October 2011 a Bill to regulate the parenthood of female same-sex couples was introduced in the Dutch Parliament.[13] There has been ongoing discussion on this topic since the introduction of registered partnership in 1998, and now finally a Bill to regulate the legal status of the birth mother's partner other than through adoption has been introduced.[14] The Bill proposes to attribute parenthood to the female partner on the basis of a combination of two criteria. One the one hand the Bill makes a distinction between female couples who are married and female couples who are unmarried or have entered into a registered partnership. And on the other hand the Bill makes a distinction between couples who have used a known donor and couples who have used an unknown donor.[15] Together these criteria result in the following:

(1) Both spouses in a female marriage will be granted the status of parent ex lege with regard to any child born during marriage, provided the couple have used the sperm of an *unknown donor*. To prove that they have used sperm from an unknown donor but not an anonymous donor, they need to submit a declaration to this end issued by the Donor Registration Foundation (*Stichting donorregistratie kunstmatige voortplanting*).

(2) Female couples that have used a *known donor* (friend, brother, neighbour, internet contact, etc) or have entered into a registered partnership, are cohabiting or living apart will not fall under this scheme. The female partner who has not given birth to the child will be given the opportunity to register her parenthood with the birth mother's consent (recognition).[16]

If the birth mother refuses to give consent for the registration of her female partner's parenthood, the female partner will not be protected by the law as proposed in the Bill. This is and should be a point of discussion in Parliament. If the government chooses not to grant the female partner the option to become a parent without the consent of the birth mother, this choice should be based on clear and convincing arguments.[17] The known donor (friend, brother, neighbour, internet contact etc), however, will be given the possibility to apply

---

[13] Dutch Second Chamber 2011–2012, 33032, no 1–3.

[14] For an extensive discussion of what came before see I Curry-Sumner and M Vonk 'It All Depends on Who You Ask: Dutch Parentage and Adoption Law in Four Acts' in B Atkin (ed) *International Survey of Family Law, 2009 Edition* (Jordan Publishing Ltd, 2009).

[15] An unknown donor is not an anonymous donor. The distinction is made on the question whether the women acquired sperm through a clinic, or whether the women themselves procured sperm. Dutch clinics must register donor data with the Donor Data Foundation, so the child can have access to this information at a later stage. For more information see M Vonk, *Children and their parent: A comparative study of the legal position of children with regard to their intentional and biological parents in* English *and* Dutch *law* (Antwerp: Intersentia, 2007).

[16] This possibility is currently only open to unmarried males (art 1:203 and 204 of the Dutch Civil Code).

[17] Dutch Second Chamber 2011–2012, 33032, no 5.

for fatherhood without the birth mother's consent, provided the child has only one parent and there is family life between the known donor and the child. This suggests a preference for the genetic father over the social mother on the part of the government in cases where conflicts over legal parenthood arise.

IV   SOMETHING INTERNATIONAL

(a)   Introduction

Since 18 June 2011, the international maintenance landscape has changed drastically. Two international organisations, namely the European Union and the Hague Conference for Private International Law, have been working hard over the last decade to draft new instruments to better regulate the international recovery of maintenance payments. These endeavours have culminated in three new instruments, the European Maintenance Regulation (emanating from the European Union), the Hague Maintenance Protocol and the Hague Maintenance Convention (both stemming from the Hague Conference). At present, only the Hague Maintenance Protocol and the European Maintenance Regulation are in force in the Netherlands. Accordingly, four major areas within international maintenance law have been affected, namely jurisdiction, applicable law, recognition and enforcement, and the system of administrative co-operation.

(b)   Jurisdiction

Of the new instruments, only the European Maintenance Regulation contains direct rules of jurisdiction. The rules themselves closely resemble those of the Brussels I Regulation. There are, however, a number of salient differences.[18] First, the Regulation is universally applicable. This means that reference to national rules of jurisdiction is no longer possible. In the Netherlands this thus means that references to arts 1–14 of the Dutch Code of Civil Procedure are banished to the past. The Regulation also introduces a number of interesting novelties with respect to the ability for parties to choose the competent forum. Parties have always had the ability to choose the competent forum in maintenance cases on the basis of art 23 of the Brussels I Regulation. That ability is continued in art 4 of the Maintenance Regulation. However, instead of an unfettered ability to choose the competent forum, parties are now restricted in the courts they are able to choose. Although in theory this would appear to be a huge restriction in party autonomy, in practice this will often not pose much of a restriction. The vast majority of choices made still fall within the boundaries of art 4(1) of the Maintenance Regulation.

---

[18]   For a good overview of the interaction of the various instruments in this field, see T de Boer 'Nieuwe regels voor de internationale alimentatie' (2011) FJR 356–362 and P Vlas 'Alimentatie uit Brussel met een Haags randje' (2009) WPNR 293–295.

Together arts 6 and 7 of the Maintenance Regulation form the result of a political compromise made in June 2008. Since the Regulation is universally applicable and thus excludes reference to national rules of jurisdiction, it was agreed that subsidiary rules of jurisdiction would need to be included in the Regulation. Reference is first made to the common nationality of the parties (art 6), and in the absence of such a factor to a forum necessitatis (art 7). Article 7 can only be consulted if no court is competent on the basis of the arts 3, 4, 5 or 6. Accordingly, this provision should be applied with great restraint. In the Netherlands, such a ground for jurisdiction is not entirely new, since art 9 of the Dutch Code of Civil Procedure contains a similar provision.

(c) Applicable law

Both the European Maintenance Regulation and the Hague Maintenance Protocol contain provisions with regard to the applicable law in maintenance cases. It is with respect to the creation of uniform choice of law rules that the common law–civil law divide is perhaps easiest to witness.[19] From the outset of international negotiations, it was clear that common law countries would not participate in any form of international instrument containing uniform choice of law rules. The application of the law of the forum, or the lex fori, is so ingrained in the fabric of these countries that participation in such an instrument was excluded. As a result, a novel method was created to ensure that these countries were provided the flexibility required to ensure that they were not obliged to participate, whilst at the same time providing them with the possibility to adopt the other rules with respect to jurisdiction, recognition and enforcement and most importantly administrative co-operation.

Consequently, the European Maintenance Regulation does not contain any independent choice of law rules. Instead reference is made to the Hague Maintenance Protocol.[20] In turn, the Hague Maintenance Protocol is a separate instrument to the Hague Maintenance Convention, therefore allowing countries to ratify these instruments independently of each other (the Netherlands has signed both instruments). As a result, the United Kingdom has been able to participate in both the European Maintenance Regulation and the Hague Maintenance Convention, without being obliged to adopt uniform choice of law rules. However, this ingenious way of ensuring that common law countries are able to sign up to the individual international instruments has complicated the European Maintenance Regulation with respect to the recognition and enforcement rules (see Part IV(d)).

The Hague Maintenance Protocol introduces a number of new approaches in comparison to the Hague Maintenance Conventions of 1956 and 1973. First, the Protocol allows for parties to choose the law applicable to their

---

[19] For a good overview of the applicable law provisions, see D van Iterson 'IPR-aspecten van de nieuwe mondiale en Europese regelgeving op het gebied van alimentatie' (2009) FJR 246–263.
[20] For information regarding the interaction between these two provisions see I Curry-Sumner '… Acht, Negen, Tien! Ik kom! Boek 10 BW is in werking getreden' (2012) REP 81–84.

maintenance obligations. Article 7 provides for a choice of law in specific proceedings, even in the case of child maintenance. Article 8 provides for a more general option, but is not permitted in child maintenance cases. A second departure from the previous maintenance conventions arises with respect to the choice of law rules relating to spousal maintenance. According to art 8 of the Hague Maintenance Convention 1973, the law applicable to spousal maintenance was coupled to the law applicable to the divorce proceedings. This link caused many unjust results in practice and led in the Netherlands to the judicial acceptance of a choice of law possibility.[21]

(d)   Recognition and enforcement

Since the Hague Maintenance Convention has not yet entered into force, this section will only discuss the recognition and enforcement rules originating from the European Maintenance Regulation.[22] The main goal of the European Union in this field was to ensure a more efficient and effective recognition procedure. The rules in this field should therefore be seen in light of the trend towards abolition of exequatur procedures. After the simplification of the exequatur procedure under the Brussels I Regulation, the European Enforcement Order Regulation ensured the total abolition of exequatur proceedings for non-contentious decisions. The Maintenance Regulation takes this trend one step further by ensuring the abolition of exequatur for all maintenance decisions, whether contentious or non-contentious.

As already stated, these rules have been strongly affected by the fact that the common law countries required the option of not adopting uniform choice of law rules. During the European negotiations, it was strongly felt (although not by the Dutch delegation) that the abolition of exequatur had to be dependent upon the application of uniform choice of law rules. As a result, a compromise solution was adopted leading to the rather cumbersome rules relating to recognition and enforcement of maintenance decisions. According to art 16 of the Maintenance Regulation, a distinction is drawn between decisions originating from states that have implemented the Hague Maintenance Protocol (Section 1) and those decisions originating from states that have not implemented the Hague Maintenance Protocol (Section 2). In effect this provision means that all decisions from EU member states will fall within Section 1, with the exception of decisions from the United Kingdom and Denmark, which will squarely fall within the ambit of Section 2.

This difference is crucial, since the abolition of exequatur is restricted to those decisions falling within the scope of Section 1. The distinction is also crucial when trying to understand the practical operation of these provisions. Section 1

---

[21]   Dutch Supreme Court, 27 February 1997, RvdW 1997, 56.

[22]   In the forthcoming edition of MJC Koens and APJ Vonken *Tekst en Commentaar Personen en Familierecht* (Devnter: Kluwer, 2012) commentary has been provided on each article of the European Maintenance Regulation. Each analysis begins with a reference to the corresponding provisions of the 1968 Brussels Convention, Brussels I Regulation or the European Enforcement Order Regulation.

is predominantly based upon similar provisions in the European Enforcement Order Regulation, which had already abolished exequatur proceedings for non-contentious monetary claims. Section 2, on the other hand, is based upon the recognition and enforcement provisions of Brussels I.

(e) Administrative co-operation

During the negotiations to the Hague Maintenance Convention and the European Maintenance Regulation, all parties recognised the necessity of an effective and efficient system of administrative co-operation. The fact that the provisions on administrative co-operation form the cornerstone of the new rules is reflected in art 1(a) of the Hague Maintenance Convention; one of the aims of the Convention is to establish 'a comprehensive system of co-operation between the authorities of the Contracting States'.[23] Space restrictions negate an extensive discussion of the functions of these central authorities. In this chapter attention will therefore only be paid to the designation of the authorities (Part IV(e)(i)) and the functions of these authorities (Part IV(e)(ii)).

(i) Designation of Central Authorities

Both the Hague Maintenance Convention and the Maintenance Regulation presume that an efficient and effective administrative co-operation system could be best achieved by establishing a network of Central Authorities.[24] A system of Central Authorities has proven to be successful in the field of adoption (1993 Hague Adoption Convention) and child abduction (1980 Hague Abduction Convention).[25] Furthermore, such a network has also been used in four other Hague Conventions, as well as four European Regulations.[26] Whether the unique nature of maintenance cases, ie the large volume of cases, the ongoing nature of the claims and the constant need for modification of the claim, will be factors that necessitate a different administrative co-operation system will only be answered over the course of time.[27]

A Central Authority is a public authority designated by a contracting or member state to discharge or carry out the duties of administrative

---

[23] This is supported in Preamble 10 of the Maintenance Regulation.

[24] Hague Maintenance Convention, art 4(1) and Maintenance Regulation, art 49(1).

[25] Convention of 25 October 1980 on the civil aspects of international child abduction, Convention of 29 March 1993 on the protection of children and co-operation in respect of inter-country adoption. See also Hague Conference *Draft Explanatory Report* (2007) Preliminary Document No 32, 20–21, § 73.

[26] 1965 Hague Service Convention, 1970 Hague Evidence Convention, 1996 Hague Child Protection Convention and 2000 Hague Adult Protection Convention. At EU level, 2001 EU Evidence Regulation, Brussels IIbis, 2006 EU Consumer Regulation and 2007 EU Service Regulation.

[27] See further, I Curry-Sumner 'International Recovery of Child Support: Are central authorities the way forward?' in B Verschraegen (ed) *Family Finances* (Vienna: Jan Sramek Verlag, 2009) 176–184 and 191–193 and I Curry-Sumner 'International Recovery of Child Maintenance Administrative co-operation in incoming child maintenance cases' in UCERF *Actuele Ontwikkelingen in het Familierecht: Reeks 3* (Nijmegen: Ars Aequi, 2009) 53–58.

co-operation and assistance under the international instruments.[28] Every contracting or member state is, however, free to determine the designation of its Central Authority. As a result, the current variety in transmitting and receiving authorities under the 1956 New York Convention will more-than-likely continue under these new instruments.[29] The variety of these agencies, bureaus and departments is as numerous as the number of agencies themselves. It could take the form of:

- a social insurance agency as in Sweden (*Försäkringskassan*);[30]

- an independent public maintenance enforcing organ as in the Netherlands (*Landelijk Bureau Inning Onderhoudsbijdragen*);[31]

- a specially dedicated ministerial department as in the Czech Republic (*Úřad pro mezianárodně právní ochranu dětí*),[32] or England and Wales (*Reciprocal Enforcement of Maintenance Obligations Office*);[33] or

- a ministerial department as in Austria (*Bundesministerium für Justiz*).[34]

One difference between the Hague Maintenance Convention and the Maintenance Regulation, on the one hand, and the current system of administrative co-operation, on the other, is that countries will be obliged in the future to designate *one* authority for both incoming and outgoing cases.[35] At present, although many countries have indeed fused the streams of incoming and outgoing cases into one agency (eg Austria, Czech Republic, England and Wales, the Netherlands and Sweden),[36] other countries operate two entirely different systems for incoming and outgoing cases (eg Denmark).[37] Despite this

---

[28]   Eg Hague Conference *Draft Explanatory Report* (2007) Preliminary Document No 32, 21, § 76.

[29]   I Curry-Sumner 'International Recovery of Child Support: Are central authorities the way forward?' in B Verschraegen (ed) *Family Finances* (Vienna: Jan Sramek Verlag, 2009) 176–184.

[30]   Translation: Social Insurance Agency.

[31]   Translation: National Maintenance Collection Agency.

[32]   Translation: Office for International Legal Protection of Children.

[33]   REMO is a unit of the International Litigation Section within the Litigation Services Department of the Office of Court Funds, Official Solicitor and Public Trustee. This Office is, in turn, an associated and independent office of the newly formed Ministry of Justice. As such, and in this way, REMO operates under the delegated authority of the British Secretary of State for Justice. More information on the Official Solicitor's Office can be found at www.justice.gov.uk/about/ospt (accessed June 2012). See also I Curry-Sumner 'International Recovery of Child Maintenance Administrative co-operation in incoming child maintenance cases' in UCERF *Actuele Ontwikkelingen in het Familierecht: Reeks 3* (Nijmegen: Ars Aequi, 2009) 53–58.

[34]   Translation: Federal Ministry of Justice.

[35]   This proposal received widespread report in the First Special Commission, Hague Conference *Report on the First Meeting of the Special Commission on the International Recovery of Child Support and Other Forms of Family Maintenance* (2003) Preliminary Document No 5, 14, § 14.

[36]   See for more information with regard to the English system: I Curry-Sumner 'International Recovery of Child Maintenance Administrative co-operation in incoming child maintenance cases' in UCERF *Actuele Ontwikkelingen in het Familierecht: Reeks 3* (Nijmegen: Ars Aequi, 2009) 53–58 and the Dutch system: 59–63 of the same publication.

[37]   See for more information with regard to the Danish system: I Curry-Sumner 'International

difference, both the Hague Maintenance Convention and the Maintenance Regulation provide for the possibility to delegate the duty to transmit and receive applications.[38] How these organisational and structural amendments will affect the practical operation of international maintenance claims is as yet unclear.

The inclusion of a specific duty in the Maintenance Regulation imposed on a Central Authority that receives a request despite not being competent must be regarded as the specification of a rather self-evident obligation.[39] It is to be expected that Central Authorities operating under the authority of the Hague Convention will also apply the same obligation. Furthermore, the requirement to inform the relevant authorities of changes is included in both instruments, albeit in vastly different places within the instrument.[40]

(ii) Functions of Central Authorities

Both instruments permit applicants to pursue claims without using the Central Authority system,[41] and ensure that the use of this system is highly encouraged by providing for free legal assistance/aid if an applicant applies through the Central Authority in the state of his or her residence.[42] An interesting difference between the two instruments surfaces with respect to the interpretation of the term 'residence'. The Hague Maintenance Convention notes that the term 'residence' for the purposes of an application through a Central Authority is to be regarded as excluding mere presence.[43] An equivalent provision in the Maintenance Regulation is noteworthy in its absence. Nevertheless, a similar reference is made in Recital 32 to the Maintenance Regulation. The question must, however, be asked why this explanation has been downgraded to a reference in the preamble. Due to the lack of parliamentary proceedings or explanatory notes to the Maintenance Regulation, the exact significance of the placement of this reference will ultimately have to be determined by the European Court of Justice (ECJ). It is nevertheless to be expected that the reference in the preamble coupled with the original version of the Maintenance Regulation[44] should lead to the conclusion that art 55 of the Maintenance Regulation has the same scope as the equivalent provision in art 9 of the Hague Maintenance Convention.

Recovery of Child Maintenance Administrative co-operation in incoming child maintenance cases' in UCERF *Actuele Ontwikkelingen in het Familierecht: Reeks 3* (Nijmegen: Ars Aequi, 2009) 46–51.

[38] Article 6(1)(a), in conjunction with art 6(3) of the Hague Maintenance Convention and art 51(1)(a), in conjunction with art 51(3) of the Maintenance Regulation.

[39] An obligation is namely imposed on the Central Authority that receives the request whilst not being competent to forward the request to the competent Central Authority, art 49(2) of the Maintenance Regulation.

[40] Hague Maintenance Convention, art 4(3) and Maintenance Regulation, art 71(1).

[41] See eg Hague Maintenance Convention, art 37.

[42] Hague Maintenance Convention, art 9 and Maintenance Regulation, art 55.

[43] A Borrás et al *Explanatory Report* (Hague Conference, November 2009) 52, § 228.

[44] COM (2005) 649 final, art 42(1). The original version obliged the applicant to apply to the Central Authority of his or her habitual residence, whereas the final text of art 55 of the Maintenance Regulation only refers to the term residence.

Both the Hague Maintenance Convention and the Maintenance Regulation draw a threefold distinction between:

- general, mandatory, non-delegable functions;[45]

- specific, mandatory, delegable functions;[46] and

- specific, discretionary, delegable functions.[47]

General, mandatory, non-delegable functions

Central Authorities will be under a general duty to co-operate with each other and promote co-operation amongst all internal competent authorities. The Maintenance Regulation specifically emphasises the obligation to exchange information. This inclusion is at first glance slightly unusual. However, this is linked to the inclusion of provisions in the Maintenance Regulation pursuant to the access of information and the holding of meetings.[48] Accordingly, attention has been explicitly drawn to the express obligation imposed on Central Authorities to exchange information.

Although explicit reference to the provision of information to the Permanent Bureau was made in earlier drafts of the Hague Maintenance Convention,[49] it was stated on numerous occasions that express reference in art 5 to the provision of information was not required if art 57 was accepted.[50] Ultimately, the text of art 57 was accepted and thus express reference to the provision of information in art 5 was deleted. Accordingly, the specific inclusion of this reference in the Maintenance Regulation should not be regarded as an omission in or a narrowing in the scope of the Hague Maintenance Convention. The exchange of information is obviously an integral part of any

---

[45] Hague Maintenance Convention, art 5 and Maintenance Regulation, art 50.

[46] Hague Maintenance Convention, art 6(1) and Maintenance Regulation, art 51(1).

[47] Hague Maintenance Convention, art 6(2) and Maintenance Regulation, art 51(2).

[48] See I Curry-Sumner 'Administrative co-operation and free legal aid in international child maintenance recovery. What is the added value of the European Maintenance Regulation?' (2010) NIPR 161–171.

[49] Hague Conference *Working Draft of a Convention* (2004) Preliminary Document No 7, 5, art 7(2)(a); Hague Conference *Working Draft of a Convention* (2005) Preliminary Document No 13, 5, art 5(b); Hague Conference *Tentative Draft Convention* (2005) Preliminary Document No 16, 5, art 5(b); Hague Conference *Report of the Administrative Co-operation Working Group* (2006) Preliminary Document No 19, 13, art 5(b) suggested language change; Hague Conference *Preliminary Draft Convention* (2007) Preliminary Document No 25, 5, art 5(b); Hague Conference *Revised Preliminary Draft Convention* (2007) Preliminary Document No 29, 5, art 5(b).

[50] See e g the comments made by Australia and the USA: Hague Conference *Consolidated list of comments on revised Preliminary Draft Convention* (2007) Preliminary Document No 36, 13. Article 57 expressly refers to the obligation to provide the Permanent Bureau of the Hague Conference with information describing its laws and procedures with regards maintenance obligations.

administrative network and, therefore, should also be regarded as necessary, according to the Hague Maintenance Convention.[51]

Specific, mandatory, delegable functions

Extensive debate focused not only on the wording of the various articles in these new instruments, but also on their (relative) placement. In the original draft of the Hague Maintenance Convention, no distinction was drawn between different types of specific functions.[52] After deliberations during the Second Special Commission, it was decided that two duties in particular should be set apart from the other duties due to their mandatory nature, namely the duty to 'transmit and receive applications' and the duty to 'initiate or facilitate the institution of proceedings'. In discharging these duties, a Central Authority is denied from taking 'all appropriate measures', and instead must discharge these duties comprehensively. The same distinction is also manifest in the Maintenance Regulation.

It is also worth noting that the Central Authorities are obliged 'in particular' to perform the tasks listed in art 6(1) of the Hague Maintenance Convention and art 51(1) of the Maintenance Regulation. Accordingly, and perhaps rather peculiarly, the mandatory obligations listed are non-exhaustive.[53] On a critical note, it must be stated that the very essence of mandatory obligations is that one is aware of the nature of these obligations prior to discharging the duty. If a Central Authority is not aware that it is obliged to discharge a mandatory duty, can it later be held not to have satisfied this responsibility? Regardless of the nature of the duties listed, the mandatory duties listed in these articles may be delegated and thus may be performed by other public bodies.

Specific, discretionary, delegable functions

With respect to all the discretionary functions listed in art 6(2) of the Hague Maintenance Convention and art 51(2) of the Maintenance Regulation, the Central Authority must take 'all appropriate measures' in ensuring that these obligations are satisfied.[54] This phrase obliges states to do all that is possible

---

[51] This is supported with reference to the *Draft Explanatory Report*, see Hague Conference *Draft Explanatory Report* (2007) Preliminary Document No 32, 24, § 91. Furthermore, the wording of art 5(1) of the Hague Maintenance Convention ensured coherence with the equivalent texts in art 30 of the 1980 Hague Abduction Convention and art 29 of the 2000 Hague Adult Protection Convention.

[52] Hague Convention *Working Draft of a Convention* (2004) Preliminary Document No 7, 5, art 8; Hague Conference *Working Draft of a Convention* (2005) Preliminary Document No 13, 5, art 6.

[53] Hague Conference *Draft Explanatory Report* (2007) Preliminary Document No 32, 26, § 108.

[54] At an earlier stage, reference was made to 'the most effective measures available'. However, this was not acceptable because not all measures taken will eventually be effective. Often measures may well have to be taken regardless of the outcome of success: Hague Conference *Tentative Draft Convention* (2005) Preliminary Document No 16, 5, art 6(2).

within their power with the available resources and within the legal restraints.[55] Moreover, the use of the word 'shall' indicates that Central Authorities are obliged to take all appropriate measures. However, the measures that need to be taken are subsequently left to the discretion of the requested Central Authority.

Differing from the current system of administrative co-operation, both new instruments explicitly list some of the core roles and duties of the administrative authorities. The imposition of specific duties and the inclusion of such duties in international instruments ensured that these provisions were some of the most extensively discussed during the negotiations of both instruments. A delicate balance needed to be drawn between creating a minimum set of standards according to which all states must operate, on the one hand, and overburdening states with inflexible duties and functions, on the other. Furthermore, as was already mentioned previously, the nature and legal position of the Central Authority in any given legal system is crucial to its functioning. As a result, flexible functions needed to be laid down which catered for this diversity in organisational structure. This flexible approach is no more apparent than with respect to the specific, discretionary, delegable functions.

In reaching agreement on the functions, tasks, roles and duties of the Central Authorities careful attention was paid to the balancing of two interests, namely the costs for applicants who often have limited means versus the increased costs for the state. In reaching consensus, delegates attempted to ensure that, although a state may indeed incur more costs, these costs were not disproportionate to the resulting benefits.

(a) *The whereabouts of the debtor*: In the first working draft of the Hague Maintenance Convention, the functions of the Central Authority were defined in rather restrictive terms. For example, authorities were under a duty to 'discover the whereabouts of the debtor'.[56] However, this duty was subsequently weakened so as to impose the duty to 'help locate the debtor'. In this way, flexible verbs such as help, encourage and facilitate have been used to limit the overburdening of authorities with these duties. Furthermore, in the original convention drafts, reference was only made to the assistance needed in locating the debtor; in the preliminary draft of January 2007 this was extended to include locating the creditor.[57] The text

---

[55] Hague Conference *Draft Explanatory Report* (2007) Preliminary Document No 32, 27–28, § 119.

[56] Hague Conference *Working Draft of a Convention* (2003) Preliminary Document No 7, art 8(d).

[57] Hague Conference *Preliminary Draft Convention* (2007) Preliminary Document No 25, 5, art 6(2)(b). Australia was the only state to comment on this inclusion: Hague *Conference Consolidated list of comments on revised Preliminary Draft Convention* (2007) Preliminary Document No 36, 14.

is identical to the relevant provision in the Maintenance Regulation, save for the cross-reference to arts 61, 62 and 63 in the Maintenance Regulation.[58]

(b) *Obtaining relevant information concerning income and assets*: Once again the choice of flexible verbs here is noticeable with a change from 'seek out relevant information' to 'help obtain relevant information'.[59] The only difference between the Maintenance Regulation and the Hague Maintenance Convention here relates to the cross-reference in the Maintenance Regulation to arts 61, 62 and 63.

(c) *Encouraging amicable solutions*: In the earlier drafts of the Hague Maintenance Convention, references to mediation and conciliation had been included in separate provisions.[60] In the end it was felt that these duties would only arise in seeking amicable solutions and therefore were better suited in the same provision. Once again, there are no differences on this point between the Hague Maintenance Convention and the Maintenance Regulation.[61]

(d) *Facilitation of maintenance payments*: In the original drafts of the Hague Maintenance Convention reference was also made to the obligation to monitor payment of maintenance. This phrase was eventually removed. Although the reasons for this removal are not provided in the preliminary documents to the Hague Maintenance Convention, discussions with the Central Authorities reveal a reluctance to burden Central Authorities with case management tasks. In many countries, for example Sweden, Denmark and England and Wales, the payment of maintenance occurs completely outside the oversight of the Central Authority. To change this system would involve major structural change, which would in turn entail associated costs. Again, there are no differences in wording between the Hague Maintenance Convention and the Maintenance Regulation.[62]

(e) *Other obligations*: Both the Hague Maintenance Convention and the Maintenance Regulation also oblige the Central Authorities to facilitate the collection and transfer of payments,[63] facilitate the obtaining of

---

[58] Maintenance Regulation, art 51(2)(b).
[59] Hague Conference *Working Draft Convention* (2007) Preliminary Document No 7, 5, art 8(e) compared with the final text in art 6(2)(c) of the 2007 Hague Convention.
[60] Hague Conference *Draft Explanatory Report* (2007) Preliminary Document No 32, 33, § 153.
[61] Hague Maintenance Convention, art 6(2)(d) and Maintenance Regulation, art 51(2)(d).
[62] Hague Maintenance Convention, art 6(2)(e) and Maintenance Regulation, art 51(2)(e).
[63] Maintenance Regulation, arts 6(2)(f) and 51(2)(f).

evidence,[64] provide assistance in establishing parentage,[65] initiate or facilitate proceedings to obtain provisional measures[66] and the service of documents.[67]

(f) Conclusion

The landscape of the international recovery of maintenance both in European terms as well as globally has undergone a paradigm shift in the last year. Although the progress that has been made cannot be overestimated (for example the abolition of exequatur within the European context and the simplification of administrative co-operation procedures in a global context), problems will arise with respect to the interaction between these instruments and the interpretation of certain provisions.[68]

V THINGS ASKEW

On 7 June 2011 in the judgment in the cases *STS v The Netherlands*[69] the European Court of Human Rights (ECtHR) unanimously held that the Dutch government had violated the rights of STS (a minor) under art 5(4) of the European Convention on Human Rights (right to liberty and security). The case concerned the length and ineffectiveness of STS's appeal against custodial placement in a confined institution. STS was born in 1988. By the time he was in his early teens the Dutch Child Care and Protection Board was made aware of the fact that he had dropped out of school and was committing crimes. On 9 October 2002 he was placed under supervision of a Youth Care Foundation and sent to a confined institution for treatment and observation on the authorisation of the Groningen District Court.

The ECtHR concluded there were two violations. One concerned the time it took the Dutch Supreme Court to rule on the appeal filed by STS (294 days). The ECtHR states that all states that have ratified the European Convention on Human Rights are required to organise their legal system in such a manner that urgent matters can be dealt with speedily. In this case the Court judged that the time it took the Leeuwarden Court of Appeal to judge on the matter (63 days) was acceptable given the fact that the court needed to gather information, but

---

[64] Maintenance Regulation, arts 6(2)(g) and 51(2)(g). The only distinction between the provisions here is that the Maintenance Regulation cross-references with the provisions of the European Evidence Regulation (No 1206/2001).

[65] Hague Maintenance Convention, art 6(2)(h) and Maintenance Regulation, art 51(2)(h).

[66] Hague Maintenance Convention, art 6(2)(i) and Maintenance Regulation, art 51(2)(i).

[67] Hague Maintenance Convention, art 6(2)(j) and Maintenance Regulation, art 51(2)(j). The only distinction between the provisions here is that the Maintenance Regulation cross-references with the provisions of the European Service Regulation (No 1393/2007).

[68] For a critical analysis of the interaction between the administrative co-operation provisions of the Regulation and the Convention, See I Curry-Sumner 'Administrative co-operation and free legal aid in international child maintenance recovery. What is the added value of the European Maintenance Regulation?' (2010) NIPR 161–171.

[69] *STS v The Netherlands*, ECtHR, no 277/05, 7 June 2011.

that the 294 days it took the Supreme Court to judge on the case was not acceptable. Moreover, by the time the Supreme Court came to judge STS's appeal, STS was no longer in custody. The Supreme Court therefore declared STS's appeal on points of law inadmissible for lack of legal interest, since he was no longer in custody. This is the second violation. STS may have a legal interest in the determination of the lawfulness of his or her custodial placement confined institution after liberation, for example if he or she wants to claim compensation for having been subject of an unlawful order for custodial placement in a confined institution. In a subsequent judgment the Dutch Supreme Court[70] reassessed its previous attitude and decided in line with the ECtHR judgment that, even where the detention against which the minor has appealed is no longer there, that in itself is not reason enough for the court not to judge on the facts.

VI   CONCLUSION

The year 2011 was pretty uneventful for Dutch family law. Perhaps that is not such a bad thing after all. The rapid development of family law rules in the past few years has left many feeling that the rate at which family law legislation is drafted and implemented sometimes reduces the quality of the provisions. Overall coherency between the various provisions of Dutch family law is becoming increasingly difficult to grasp. Perhaps years such as 2011 will provide the legislature with the much needed time to assess the current state of affairs and undertake fundamental research into the redevelopment of family law en masse instead of the piecemeal approach that has typified legislative developments over the last few years.

---

[70]   Dutch Supreme Court, LJN BQ2292, 24 June 2011.

New Zealand

THE CHANGING POLITICS OF FAMILY LAW IN NEW ZEALAND

*Mark Henaghan**

Résumé

Cette contribution expose les liens entre la politique et le droit de la famille à la lumière des quatre réformes du droit de la famille récemment proposées en Nouvelle-Zélande. Les réformes envisagées sont les suivantes: une révision gouvernementale approfondie du fonctionnement de la Cour de la Famille néozélandaise, notamment en considération de l'augmentation de ses dépenses; un Livre Vert du gouvernement, contenant des solutions envisageables pour améliorer la situation des enfants vulnérables en Nouvelle-Zélande, sans augmenter les dépenses; une révision détaillée du régime de la pension alimentaire pour les enfants (comprenant l'introduction du Child Support Amendment Bill) dans le but de fournir un système plus juste et plus moderne; et, sur proposition de la Commission des Lois néozélandaises, une révision de la loi sur les trusts, basée sur le fait qu'ils souffrent des réclamations fondées sur le Property (Relationships) Act de 1976. La conclusion de cette contribution est que les réformes du droit de la famille ne doivent pas être uniquement basées sur des préoccupations budgétaires et politiques, mais plutôt sur la recherche de la meilleure façon d'aider les familles en crise, c'est-à-dire de la manière la plus efficace et la plus efficiente.

I INTRODUCTION

Family law always has been, and always will be, an extremely political subject. Even defining what constitutes a family is a political decision.[1] As Laurence Houlgate states:[2]

'... the family itself is political, that is, law and social policy together determine which groups of persons count as a family and which do not, who is a parent

---

*   Professor and Dean of Law, University of Otago, Dunedin, New Zealand. I would like to thank my research assistant Ruth Ballantyne LLB, BA (Hons) for her invaluable contribution.

[1]   See Mark Henaghan 'Legally Defining the Family' in Mark Henaghan and Bill Atkin (eds) *Family Law Policy in New Zealand* (Wellington: LexisNexis, 3rd edn, 2007) 10–11.

[2]   Laurence Houlgate 'Must the Personal be Political? Family Law and the Concept of Family' (1998) 12 *International Journal of Law, Policy and the Family* 107, 109. For more detailed information about the connection between family law and politics see Brenda Almond *The Fragmenting Family* (Oxford: Oxford University Press, 2006).

(mother, father) and who is not, who is a child and who is not, and what specific rights and duties people have within those groups designated as families.'

Since family law disputes are also intensely personal in nature, there is frequent debate as to what extent law, policy and the government should intrude into family life. As the New Zealand Ministry of Justice explains:[3]

'The State has an interest in protecting children and vulnerable adults, however, there is less certainty about where the boundary lies between the role of the State and the role of the individual in regard to some private law disputes (eg, care arrangements for children when parents separate, relationship property or claims against an estate).'

Inevitably, many people have strong opinions (based on their own personal experiences, or on other people's experiences) about how New Zealand's family law system should work.[4] People with personal experience of family law disputes are often dissatisfied with the legal processes and/or the results. Those who have family law determinations made against them are often the most disgruntled. Disappointment with New Zealand family law is often caused by systemic failures such as excessive time delays, repetitive court applications, inappropriate affidavits and overly complex court processes, which can cause significant uncertainty and stress. Frequently, dissatisfaction with family law disputes is also caused by the parties themselves, who make simple resolution impossible.[5]

New Zealand family law is currently facing significant changes. There are four areas targeted for potential reform:

(1)   A substantial governmental review of the New Zealand Family Court seeks to address perceived problems, including the 'increasing expenditure on Family Court services', 'insufficient support' to resolve matters out of court, 'complex and uncertain court processes', parties 'losing sight of the needs of children', questions about the 'best way to resolve disputes', and 'limited responsiveness' to cultural needs.[6]

(2)   The New Zealand government released the Green Paper for Vulnerable Children because it was concerned 'about the number of children who

---

3   Ministry of Justice *Reviewing the Family Court: A Public Consultation Paper* (Wellington: Ministry of Justice, 2011) 12.

4   For example, see Masculinist Evolution New Zealand 'MENZ Issues: News and Discussion About New Zealand Men, Fathers, Family Law, Divorce, Courts, Protests, Gender Politics, and Male Health' (2004) http://menz.org.nz/ (accessed 16 April 2012).

5   As the LexisNexis Family Law Service states: 'Legal practice in family matters is also complicated by the factor of client irrationality. This calls for particular personal qualities and sensitivity on the part of the practitioner, especially tolerance, patience and the ability to take people as one finds them.' See Mark Henaghan et al (eds) *Family Law in New Zealand* (Wellington: LexisNexis NZ Limited,15th edn, 2011) cxiii.

6   Ministry of Justice *Reviewing the Family Court: A Public Consultation Paper* (Wellington: Ministry of Justice, 2011).

have childhoods that make it unlikely that they will thrive, belong and achieve', and consequently the 'long term outcomes and costs to these children and to everyone'.[7]

(3) A detailed overhaul of the New Zealand child support regime (including the introduction of the Child Support Amendment Bill) is intended to provide a fairer and more up-to-date scheme to ensure that parents meet their child support obligations. This proposed reform is based on claims that the current child support scheme does not take account of the parent's 'particular circumstances', concerns about the current costs of raising children in New Zealand, the 'instability of payments', and the way child support is calculated.[8]

(4) The New Zealand Law Commission has undertaken an independent review of the law of trusts, which is likely to have implications for relationship property law. The Law Commission is concerned 'about the modern use of trusts and invited a response as to whether there are any purposes for which trusts should not be used and whether limits should be placed on the effects of trusts'.[9]

Underpinning most of these proposals for change is an economic imperative that less government money should be spent on family law. The political goal is to privatise family law and make families and the community more responsible for resolving family law issues.

II FAMILY COURT REVIEW

(a) Background

New Zealand has had a specialist Family Court since 1 October 1981.[10] The Family Court was introduced as a specialist court, 'with its own atmosphere, specialised services, specialist personnel and specialist Judges to deal with family cases'.[11] The Family Court was intended to encourage 'counselling,

---

[7] Ministry of Social Development *Every Child Thrives, Belongs, Achieves: The Green Paper for Vulnerable Children* (Wellington: Ministry of Social Development, 2011) 1.

[8] Hon Peter Dunne *Supporting Children: A Government Discussion Document on Updating the Child Support Scheme* (Wellington: Policy Advice Division of Inland Revenue, 2010) 1–2.

[9] Nicola Peart, Mark Henaghan and Greg Kelly 'Trusts and Relationship Property in New Zealand' (2011) 17 *Trusts & Trustees* 866, 880.

[10] Mark Henaghan et al (eds) *Family Law in New Zealand* (Wellington: LexisNexis NZ Limited, 15th edn, 2011) ci. The New Zealand Family Court was introduced in 1981, the same year New Zealand as a country was greatly divided by the 1981 South African rugby union tour of New Zealand (known as the Springbok Tour) and the corresponding apartheid in South Africa. For more information about the effects of the Springbok Tour on New Zealand, see Richard Shears and Isobelle Gidley *Storm out of Africa: The* 1981 Springbok Tour *of New Zealand* (Auckland: Macmillan, 1981); and Geoff Chapple *1981: The* Tour (Wellington: Reed, 1984).

[11] Mark Henaghan et al (eds) *Family Law in New Zealand* (15th edition, LexisNexis NZ Limited, Wellington, 2011) c. Over the last 30 years the New Zealand Family Court has built up a strong specialist bench and bar.

conciliation and mediation' so that parties with a family law problem could talk through their differences and work towards their own solution.[12] Litigation was envisioned to be a last resort.

(b)   Perceived problems with the Family Court

The Family Court has long been the subject of political criticism and public attack. Dissatisfied court users of both genders have attacked the Family Court because of its alleged gender bias,[13] and the Family Court is a favourite target of New Zealand talkback radio.[14]

In 2011 the national government decided to formally review the New Zealand Family Court. The primary thrust of the review is fiscal. As the Family Court Review Public Consultation Paper ('the consultation paper') states:[15]

> 'The Court is not financially sustainable and rising costs must be addressed. There has been a rapid increase in government expenditure in the Family Court in recent years ... Family Court costs have increased by 63 percent from \$84 million in 2004/05 to \$137 million in 2009/10. [Judicial costs] have increased by 49 percent from \$9 million to \$13 million over the same period. There is little evidence that increased expenditure since 2004/05 has resulted in improved outcomes for parties, for example, by disposing cases more quickly or by reducing repeat applications.'

However, the consultation paper does not provide a detailed breakdown of how and why these costs have increased. Bald figures frequently gain political attention, but they are a particularly unhelpful way to begin a constructive dialogue about a complex subject. In their submission to the consultation paper the New Zealand Family Court Judges ('the Judges') point out that there are some statistical errors 'which might indicate that caution is needed before placing too much reliance on what is provided'.[16] For example the Judges state:[17]

> 'Another area where context is required to understand the data presented in the paper is Judicial Resourcing. Reference is made ... to "judicial costs" but it is not clear what this comprises; information subsequently provided by the Ministry does not assist ... It is unclear whether the 49% figure [for increased judicial costs] takes

---

[12]   Mark Henaghan et al (eds) *Family Law in New Zealand* (Wellington: LexisNexis NZ Limited, 15th edn, 2011) c.

[13]   For example, see Masculinist Evolution New Zealand 'MENZ Issues: News and Discussion About New Zealand Men, Fathers, Family Law, Divorce, Courts, Protests, Gender Politics, and Male Health' (2004) http://menz.org.nz/ (accessed 16 April 2012).

[14]   Mark Henaghan 'Legally Rearranging Families: Parents and Children After Break-up' in Mark Henaghan and Bill Atkin (eds) *Family Law Policy in New Zealand* (Wellington: LexisNexis, 3rd edn, 2007) 344.

[15]   Ministry of Justice *Reviewing the Family Court: A Public Consultation Paper* (Wellington: Ministry of Justice, 2011) 11.

[16]   Judges of the Family Court of New Zealand *Submissions of the Judges of the Family Court of New Zealand on 'Reviewing the Family Court – A Public Consultation Paper'* (2012) 1.

[17]   Judges of the Family Court of New Zealand *Submissions of the Judges of the Family Court of New Zealand on 'Reviewing the Family Court – A Public Consultation Paper'* (2012) 2.

account of the fact that most Family Court Judges spend 25% of their time presiding in the general jurisdiction of the District Court. If the 49% includes the Ministry's costs of supporting the judges (including the provision of support staff and Chambers as well as library and computer facilities), the percentage figure is further distorted.'

The Judges also express concern that the statistics in the consultation paper do not take account of how statutory and policy changes have affected family legal aid (including increased payment rates and eligibility extensions).[18] Without providing a breakdown of the changes and how they may have directly impacted on Family Court expenditure, the figures do not accurately portray what is actually happening in the Family Court. All systems are capable of becoming uneconomical and inefficient, as work can expand to meet the time and resources available.[19] The only way to address systemic failure is to examine each aspect of the system and decide whether or not it is necessary. An analysis of priorities will reveal where savings can be made, though the system must be considered both as a whole, and in its context, in order to do this properly.

The consultation paper provides a series of selected case samples, which show protracted family law proceedings over several years that become extremely costly and stressful.[20] The cases selected by the consultation paper focus on high levels of conflict between parents, allegations of family violence, drug and alcohol abuse and mental illness. These cases do not represent the entire caseload of the Family Court; they represent a small fraction of the reality of Family Court cases. All Family Court systems (whether due to difficult parties, repeat applications, a need for specialist reports or increased mobility in modern society) have some cases that do take up significant amounts of court time and result in protracted litigation. However, these cases are by no means representative of the majority of cases that are resolved in an effective and efficient manner.

Delays are a significant problem, not just in the Family Courts, but also in the civil and criminal courts. Delays are well known to increase parties' stress levels.[21] The consultation paper sampled 173 Care of Children Act 2004 cases and found a total of 2,312 adjournments.[22] The large number of adjournments was due to obtaining specialist reports, appointing expert counsel, filing of cross-applications, reviewing and monitoring judicial decisions and updating

---

18 Judges of the Family Court of New Zealand *Submissions of the Judges of the Family Court of New Zealand on 'Reviewing the Family Court – A Public Consultation Paper'* (2012) 2–3.

19 C Northcote Parkinson *Parkinson's Law* (New York: Buccaneer Books, 1957) 2.

20 See Ministry of Justice *Reviewing the Family Court: A Public Consultation Paper* (Wellington: Ministry of Justice, 2011) 10, 46 and 53–54.

21 See Saskia Righarts and Mark Henaghan 'Delays in the New Zealand Civil Justice System? Opinion v Fact' (2011) 12 *Otago Law Review* 455.

22 See Ministry of Justice *Reviewing the Family Court: A Public Consultation Paper* (Wellington: Ministry of Justice, 2011) 12.

specialist reports.[23] These kinds of adjournments are a reality for a court that is trying to make the best possible decisions for the families and children concerned. Simplifying legal procedures for cases with more straightforward issues could offset costs and delays. The nature of the dispute is of crucial importance. For example, a dispute over a parent's contact times with their child could usually be resolved more quickly than a relocation case. The contact dispute is much more likely to be able to be resolved by the parents themselves, with some assistance from a counsellor or mediator, whereas, the relocation dispute is more likely to require more significant judicial intervention and the filing of specialist reports.

The consultation paper questions whether the state can place obligations on families to resolve their own disputes privately and at their own expense. As the consultation paper states:[24]

> 'The appropriate role of the State in some family law matters is discussed throughout this paper and includes consideration of the following issues:
>
> - what the State should expect from families in the resolution of their disputes, such as whether there should be obligations on families to attempt to resolve matters themselves where appropriate, and to contribute to costs when they receive assistance from the State
> - whether the State should continue to provide a range of free or subsidised services to assist families to resolve disputes, or if parties should contribute to or pay for these services
> - whether services should be provided in partnership with other government agencies and non-government organisations.'

The thrust of these considerations is that some aspects of family law should be privatised and resolved solely by the parties themselves, without state resources. This essentially cuts some families adrift from the Family Court and leaves them to their own devices. The public/private distinction in family law is not as simple as the consultation paper would suggest. Major personal issues are at stake in family law disputes such as the parties' continuing parental relationships with their children and future property and income issues. Parties come to the Family Court only when they are already unable to resolve these disputes themselves. The parties are frequently in bitter disputes over their children and can be in an extremely distressed state. Power imbalances between parties are common. If the matter was left purely to private resolution then we may be 'governed by the law of the jungle'.[25] This can put vulnerable parties and the children involved at significant risk. It is good for parties to be given information about what they may be able to do to resolve the dispute between themselves. However, do-it-yourself style solutions only work when both parties are fully informed of their rights and responsibilities and are on an

---

[23]   See Ministry of Justice *Reviewing the Family Court: A Public Consultation Paper* (Wellington: Ministry of Justice, 2011) 12.

[24]   See Ministry of Justice *Reviewing the Family Court: A Public Consultation Paper* (Wellington: Ministry of Justice, 2011) 12–13.

[25]   Katherine O'Donovan *Sexual Divisions in Law* (London: Weidenfeld and Nicolson, 1985) 198.

equal footing. Parties of unequal power, who are enmeshed in bitter conflicts, distressed about a relationship breakdown, or concerned about their children's safety are not in a good position to resolve their own disputes.

The consultation paper assumes that if we remove lawyers and legal proceedings from family law there will be considerable cost savings. However, this is not necessarily the case. There is considerable evidence that people without legal advice and legal representation are more likely to litigate, rather than negotiate a settlement.[26] Mavis Maclean and John Eekelaar's research indicates that family lawyers are not purely adversarial and are much more likely to save public funds by working with the parties towards a resolution based on their legal entitlements, by ensuring the parties understand the processes they may have to go through.[27] The selected case samples in the consultation paper involve conflict, allegations of family violence, mental health problems and drug and alcohol abuse.[28] Such cases inevitably require the authority and accountability of a court process and access to a lawyer to ensure protection of each parties' interests. Australian evidence illustrates that when vulnerable parties are diverted away from legal processes to alternative services they have trouble expressing their fears and protecting their interests and those of their children.[29]

Mediation is not necessarily a better alternative to Family Court processes. In the United Kingdom Gywn Davis interviewed consumers of both mediation interviews and lawyer interviews to compare consumers' experiences.[30] As Davis states:[31]

'The study showed that lawyers were regarded more positively than mediators. Sixty per cent of those mediating disputes over their children found their lawyer

---

[26] See Rosemary Hunter 'Adversarial Mythologies: Policy Assumptions and Research Evidence in Family Law' (2003) 30(1) *Journal of Law and Society* 169; Helen Barwick, Alison Gray and Roger Mackay *Characteristics Associated with the Early Identification of Complex Family Court Custody Cases* (Wellington: Ministry of Justice, 2003) 4.2.1.

[27] Mavis Maclean and John Eekelaar *Family Law Advocacy: How Barristers Help the Victims of Family Failure* (Oxford: Hart Publishing, 2009); John Eekelaar, Mavis Maclean and Sarah Beinart *Family Lawyers: The Divorce Work of Solicitors* (Oxford: Oxford University Press, 2000).

[28] See Ministry of Justice *Reviewing the Family Court: A Public Consultation Paper* (Wellington: Ministry of Justice, 2011) 10, 46 and 53–54.

[29] See Rae Kaspiew et al 'Family Violence: Key Findings from the Evaluation of the 2006 Family Law Reforms' (2010) 85 *Family Matters* 38, 45–46; Dale Bagshaw et al *Family Violence and Family Law: The Experiences and Views of Children and Adults from Families Who Separated Post-1995 and Post-2006 Volume 1* (Canberra: Australian Attorney-General's Department, April 2010).

[30] See Gwyn Davis 'Reflections in the Aftermath of the Family Mediation Pilot' (2001) 13 *Child and Family Law Quarterly* 371. Davis carried out 1055 interviews with mediation interview consumers and 646 lawyer interview consumers between 1997 and 2001 to test the effectiveness of a policy promoted by the UK Family Law Act 1996 to discourage the use of lawyers in family separations and to provide a cheaper process via mediation.

[31] Quoted in Mark Henaghan 'Legally Rearranging Families: Parents and Children After Break-up' in Mark Henaghan and Bill Atkin (eds) *Family Law Policy in New Zealand* (Wellington: LexisNexis, 3rd edn, 2007) 292.

"very helpful" with only 35 per cent giving the same rating to their mediator. Sixty-nine per cent said their lawyer understood their problems "very well" with only 51 per cent saying the same about the mediators. Eighty-one per cent said they would recommend that others in their situation of family separation should use a lawyer. The study shows that mediation services did not reduce the need for lawyers and thereby did not reduce the expenditure on lawyers. Mediation was not seen as an alternative to lawyers by the consumers of the system. The research showed that people in family conflict and separation rely on lawyers because they offer the knowledge, authority, and resources which the parties feel they need to achieve a fair outcome. Lawyers were particularly valued for the protection and countering strategies they could provide when the other party is using unreasonable tactics such as lying, threats, evasion or violence.'

(c)   Room for improvement

There are some Family Court processes that could be improved for the benefit of its users. For example, currently the Family Court 'may receive any evidence that it thinks fit, whether or not it is otherwise admissible in a Court of law'.[32] This protracts proceedings and potentially allows for long-winded affidavits based on hearsay rather than appropriate court evidence. Such affidavits can become extremely distressing and costly for the parties, and may fuel further conflict. A tightening of the rules of evidence would focus both the parties' and the lawyers' minds on the most relevant facts and evidence.[33] The creation of a standardised family law affidavit that set out the required relevant information for the Family Court hearing would also be very effective in reducing the ability for parties to draw out proceedings by continuously filing inappropriate and irrelevant affidavits. Repeated unnecessary applications filed on a whim of one party should also be discouraged because they can cause stress and uncertainty for the other party and the children. Section 141 of the Care of Children Act 2004 allows the Family Court to stay vexatious proceedings, but it is rarely used.

In disputes over children the elephant in the room is the welfare principle itself.[34] By its very nature the welfare principle is open-ended and is designed to be flexible enough to adapt to the needs of each different child before the Family Court. The considerable downside to the broadness of the welfare principle is that it provides no certainty of outcome, nor any clarity as to what the Family Court may or may not consider relevant. Given such flexibility, thorough lawyers want to cover all potential angles and are reluctant to leave

---

[32]   Care of Children Act 2004, s 128. See David Burns 'Marshalling the Evidence – Beyond the "Any Evidence Rule"' in *Family Law Conference 2011* (Wellington: New Zealand Law Society, 2011).

[33]   See Pauline Tapp et al *Submission to the Ministry of Justice – Reviewing the Family Court: A Public Consultation Paper* (21 February 2012) 19–20.

[34]   Section 4 of the Care of Children Act 2004 states that the 'welfare and best interests of the child must be the first and paramount consideration' and that the 'welfare and best interests of the particular child in his or her particular circumstances must be considered'. Section 5 of the Care of Children Act 2004 provides a list of principles relevant to a child's welfare and best interests.

anything out. This leads to long affidavits containing every possible permutation of information that could be considered under the welfare principle. Providing the Family Court with more direction as to what to consider when determining what is in the welfare and bests interests of a particular child will increase the predictability of outcomes, appropriately narrow the factual matters to be considered and expedite proceedings.[35]

The outcome of the Family Court Review will not be known until late 2012.

III   THE GREEN PAPER FOR VULNERABLE CHILDREN

(a)   Background

New Zealand has a deplorable child abuse problem. During the 1990s, New Zealand had the third highest child death from maltreatment rate of Organisation for Economic Co-operation and Development countries.[36] New Zealand's sad record of child abuse continues into the twenty-first century, as evinced by the killing of 38 children under the age of 15 by family members between 2002 and 2006.[37] Based on New Zealand's significant child abuse problem, the government released the Green Paper for Vulnerable Children ('the Green Paper').[38] The Green Paper 'outlines a number of ideas on how to improve leadership for vulnerable children, some policy changes, and some changes to how services are delivered'.[39]

The Green Paper begins with some further sad statistics for New Zealand children:[40]

- '• Child, Youth and Family confirmed 21,000 cases of abuse and neglect in 2009/10
- • Over 30,000 students are truant from schools on any given day

---

[35] For a proposed 'checklist' intended to emphasise the crucial issues for determination and to provide more consistency in relocation decisions see Mark Henaghan 'Relocation Cases – The Rhetoric and Reality of a Child's Best Interests – A View from the Bottom of the World' (2011) 23 *Child and Family Law Quarterly* 155. For other proposals to reduce costs see Simon Jefferson 'A Review of the Family Court 2011: Sorry, Snow White Can't Afford Dwarves This Year' in *Family Law Section Symposium 2011: Review of the Family Court* (Wellington: New Zealand Law Society, 2011).

[36] United Nations Children's Fund Innocenti Research Centre *Innocenti Report Card No 5: A League Table of Child Maltreatment Deaths in Rich Nations* (2003) 4.

[37] Jennifer Martin and Rhonda Pritchard *Learning from Tragedy: Homicide within Families in New Zealand 2002–2006* (Working Paper, Centre for Social Research and Evaluation, New Zealand Ministry of Social Development, April 2010) 46.

[38] A government Green Paper is traditionally 'a discussion document that outlines ideas a Government wants to test with the public before making decisions'. See Ministry of Social Development *Every Child Thrives, Belongs, Achieves: The Green Paper for Vulnerable Children* (Wellington: Ministry of Social Development, 2011) vi.

[39] Ministry of Social Development *Every Child Thrives, Belongs, Achieves: The Green Paper for Vulnerable Children* (Wellington: Ministry of Social Development, 2011) vi.

[40] Ministry of Social Development *Every Child Thrives, Belongs, Achieves: The Green Paper for Vulnerable Children* (Wellington: Ministry of Social Development, 2011) 2.

- 7,342 school leavers left with no qualifications in 2009
- 13,351 hospital admissions in 2008/09 were for children under five that could have been avoided. In the same year, 1,286 admissions for all children were as a result of assault, neglect or maltreatment
- 47,374 children (aged 0–16) were present, or usually residing with the victim, at an incident of family violence reported to the Police in 2010.'

The children represented in the above statistics are described as vulnerable children, with approximately 15% of New Zealand's children (163,000) being vulnerable at any given time.[41] The reasons for these children being vulnerable is complex. The Green Paper acknowledges that growing up in poverty and having a significant disability or health problem can be a 'specific risk factor' that increases the likelihood of vulnerability.[42]

The Green Paper ultimately seeks the public's response to changes the government is considering implementing to reduce New Zealand's vulnerable child problem.[43] The possible solutions provided by the Green Paper include:

- sharing responsibility for vulnerable children with families and communities;[44]

- creating a Vulnerable Children's Action Plan;[45]

- making child-centred policy changes (such as working from an evidence base, targeting services and programmes to vulnerable children, increasing spending on early intervention and monitoring vulnerable children);[46]

---

[41] Ministry of Social Development *Every Child Thrives, Belongs, Achieves: The Green Paper for Vulnerable Children* (Wellington: Ministry of Social Development, 2011) 4.

[42] Ministry of Social Development *Every Child Thrives, Belongs, Achieves: The Green Paper for Vulnerable Children* (Wellington: Ministry of Social Development, 2011) 4.

[43] Submission on the Green Paper closed on 28 February 2012. Ministry of Social Development *Every Child Thrives, Belongs, Achieves: The Green Paper for Vulnerable Children* (Wellington: Ministry of Social Development, 2011) 32.

[44] The Green Paper states: 'Responsibility first lies with parents and caregivers. Communities also have an important role. Government alone cannot protect vulnerable children or prevent more children becoming vulnerable.' Ministry of Social Development *Every Child Thrives, Belongs, Achieves: The Green Paper for Vulnerable Children* (Wellington: Ministry of Social Development, 2011) 9–12.

[45] A Vulnerable Children's Action Plan could be 'a long-term, cross-sector and evidence-based plan for children across the stages of their development'. The Vulnerable Children's Action Plan would aim to reduce both the risks faced by vulnerable children, and the number of vulnerable children, by working with families and communities, taking account of what children want and need, providing clear governmental accountabilities, and ensuring ongoing research and education. The Green Paper also proposes that the Vulnerable Children's Action Plan could require the creation of new legislation that would set out the Vulnerable Children's Action Plan and its purposes, create 'cross-agency accountability for implementing the Plan', and make necessary policy and practice changes. Ministry of Social Development *Every Child Thrives, Belongs, Achieves: The Green Paper for Vulnerable Children* (Wellington: Ministry of Social Development, 2011) 13–16.

[46] Ministry of Social Development *Every Child Thrives, Belongs, Achieves: The Green Paper for Vulnerable Children* (Wellington: Ministry of Social Development, 2011) 18–25.

- increased information sharing between agencies;[47] and

- better connecting vulnerable children to services, and improving the delivery of those services.[48]

(b)   Responsibility for vulnerable children

The Green Paper accepts that the government has:[49]

> 'a key role to play – demonstrating leadership, making policy decisions and delivering services to support vulnerable children. This includes delivering effective education and health services, and working with parents, families, and whanau, and communities to make a difference for vulnerable children.'

However, the government does not take complete responsibility for New Zealand's vulnerable children. The Green Paper states that the 'Government is only one player. Many things impact on what happens to children that are beyond the reach of Government'.[50] The Green Paper strongly emphasises that the government will not be allocating more public resources to address this problem. As the New Zealand Prime Minister, the Rt Hon John Key, states: 'Just throwing more money around will not improve the lives of these children.'[51]

The Prime Minister is right that merely throwing money at a situation is not a solution in itself. However, significant resources (both financial and non-financial) are required to help families out of deprivation and poverty cycles. The assistance provided to impoverished families needs to be based on the best available evidence of what works and what does not work, and all members of society should contribute financially to this assistance according to their means. As Rebecca Blank said, 'the greater the moral importance one attaches to reducing poverty and economic need among disadvantaged populations, the more risks one might be willing to take in pursuit of this'.[52] On this basis, the moral importance of reducing child poverty and abuse should oblige the government to provide as many resources as possible. Merely shifting the same amount of money around will not suffice. The Green Paper's

---

[47]   Ministry of Social Development *Every Child Thrives, Belongs, Achieves: The Green Paper for Vulnerable Children* (Wellington: Ministry of Social Development, 2011) 24–25.

[48]   Ministry of Social Development *Every Child Thrives, Belongs, Achieves: The Green Paper for Vulnerable Children* (Wellington: Ministry of Social Development, 2011) 26–31.

[49]   Ministry of Social Development *Every Child Thrives, Belongs, Achieves: The Green Paper for Vulnerable Children* (Wellington: Ministry of Social Development, 2011) 7. 'Whanau' is the Maori word for 'family'.

[50]   Ministry of Social Development *Every Child Thrives, Belongs, Achieves: The Green Paper for Vulnerable Children* (Ministry of Social Development, Wellington, 2011) 1.

[51]   Ministry of Social Development *Every Child Thrives, Belongs, Achieves: The Green Paper for Vulnerable Children* (Wellington: Ministry of Social Development, 2011) Frontispiece.

[52]   Rebecca Blank 'Selecting Among Anti-Poverty Policies: Can an Economist be Both Critical and Caring?' (2003) 61 *Review of Social Economy* 447, 469.

suggestion of spending less on vulnerable older children in order to spend more
on vulnerable young children is completely untenable.[53] As the Salvation Army
report *The Growing Divide* states:[54]

> 'We have two clear choices here: one is to continue the path we have been on more
> or less continuously for the past three decades, concentrating wealth and influence,
> and driving the marginalised further into the shadows with yet [more] restrictive
> welfare entitlements and a yet more punitive criminal justice system. The other is
> to act more inclusively and to work consciously and deliberately at ways of
> ensuring that the most marginalised New Zealanders, and in particular, many
> poor families and unemployed young people, feel as though they are valued and
> valuable members of our society.'

(c)   Mandatory reporting

We do not currently have a mandatory requirement to report child abuse or
neglect. However, the Green Paper has asked the community to consider
mandatory reporting.[55] There is no doubt that New Zealand children are being
abused and neglected.[56] Those in frequent contact with children such as
doctors, nurses and teachers need to be alert to possible child abuse and
neglect. However, a mandatory reporting system will not automatically protect
the children involved. Nothing will change unless sufficient resources are
provided by the government to thoroughly investigate all reports of child abuse
and neglect, and then to provide the help required in the situation. All the
investigations after family members have killed children illustrate that the
appropriate agencies were aware the children were at risk, but were unable to
adequately protect the children due to a lack of resources, staffing and
support.[57] Previous inquiries into the operation of the New Zealand Children,
Young Persons, and Their Families Act 1989 found that in many cases very
little investigation occurred because of lack of resources.[58] In the 1980s (before
the introduction of the Children, Young Persons, and Their Families Act 1989)

---

[53]   Ministry of Social Development *Every Child Thrives, Belongs, Achieves: The Green Paper for
       Vulnerable Children* (Wellington: Ministry of Social Development, 2011) 21.
[54]   The Salvation Army *The Growing Divide: A State of the Nation Report from the Salvation
       Army 2012* (Manukau City: The Salvation Army Social Policy and Parliamentary Unit, 2012)
       Foreword.
[55]   Ministry of Social Development *Every Child Thrives, Belongs, Achieves: The Green Paper for
       Vulnerable Children* (Wellington: Ministry of Social Development, 2011) 24.
[56]   Ministry of Social Development *Every Child Thrives, Belongs, Achieves: The Green Paper for
       Vulnerable Children* (Wellington: Ministry of Social Development, 2011) 2.
[57]   See Department of Social Welfare *Dangerous Situations: The Report of the Independent Inquiry
       Team Reporting on the Circumstances of the Death of a Child* (Wellington: Department of
       Social Welfare, 1989); Ian Hassall *Report to the Minister of Social Welfare on the New Zealand
       Children and Young Persons Service's Review of Practice in Relation to* Craig Manukau *and his
       Family* (Wellington: Commissioner for Children, 1993); and Office of the Commissioner for
       Children *Final Report on the Investigation into the Death of Riri-o-te-Rangi (James)
       Whakaruru* (Wellington: Ministry of Social Policy, 2000).
[58]   See Judge Michael Brown *Care and Protection is About Adult Behaviour, Ministerial Review of
       the Department of Child, Youth and Family: Report to the Minister of Social Services and
       Employment, Hon Steve Maharey* (Wellington: Ministry of Social Policy, 2000). See also Ian

New Zealand had child protection teams made up of health professionals, lawyers and social workers who assessed each report of abuse and/or neglect from the perspective of their different disciplines.[59] Despite the success of such child protection teams, they were seen as too resource intensive and are not funded any more.[60]

(d) Possible solutions

The work done by Michael Wald, J Merrill Carlsmith and P Herbert Leiderman in the United States shows that the single most important consideration is not simply whether the child should be removed from their family or not.[61] What is crucial is whether there is at least one adult in the child's life who can provide the love and nurturing that the child needs: one competent caring adult.[62] Wald, Carlsmith and Leiderman also found that when children had been abused and neglected they needed a great deal of counselling and support to help them back to normality.[63] If we are going to take protecting vulnerable children seriously, then at the very least we must provide the necessary resources to investigate each child abuse report properly, and provide the required assistance afterwards to ensure the child is safe and given every opportunity to recover.

The New Zealand Law Society's submission on the Green Paper also rightly argued:[64]

'A new statute (a Children's Protection Act) is needed, to provide for information-sharing, mandatory reporting, and a statutory duty for collaboration between the "workforce for children". There should be a statutory duty on identified ministries (as part of the workforce for children) to set targets against the Plan and implement strategies to achieve those targets. The Chief Executive of each identified Ministry should report annually to Parliament on its progress to achieve these goals. The Office of the Children's Commissioner (OCC) (or other agency as appropriate) should provide an annual independent report on progress. An impact statement should also be required for any new legislation that has the

---

Hassall *Report to the Minister of Social Welfare on the New Zealand Children and Young Persons Service's Review of Practice in Relation to Craig Manukau and his Family* (Wellington: Commissioner for Children, 1993).

[59] Pauline Tapp and Nicola Taylor 'Protecting the Family' in Mark Henaghan and Bill Atkin (eds) *Family Law Policy in New Zealand* (Wellington: LexisNexis, 3rd edn, 2007) 93.

[60] Pauline Tapp and Nicola Taylor 'Protecting the Family' in Mark Henaghan and Bill Atkin (eds) *Family Law Policy in New Zealand* (Wellington: LexisNexis, 3rd edn, 2007) 94.

[61] Michael Wald, J Merrill Carlsmith and P Herbert Leiderman *Protecting Abused and Neglected Children* (Palo Alto: Stanford University Press, 1988).

[62] Michael Wald, J Merrill Carlsmith and P Herbert Leiderman *Protecting Abused and Neglected Children* (Palo Alto: Stanford University Press, 1988).

[63] Michael Wald, J Merrill Carlsmith and P Herbert Leiderman *Protecting Abused and Neglected Children* (Palo Alto: Stanford University Press, 1988).

[64] New Zealand Law Society *Submission on Every Child Thrives, Belongs, Achieves – A Government Green Paper for Vulnerable Children* (Wellington: New Zealand Law Society, 2012) 2.

potential to impact on vulnerable children. The new Act should make it clear that child protection takes precedence over confidentiality or an individual's privacy.'

Without clear accountability from the government, nothing will change. In the long term New Zealand needs to work towards a more equal and inclusive society.[65] Richard Wilkinson and Kate Pickett's book *The Spirit Level* plainly illustrates that the greater the economic inequality in a society, the more abuse and neglect there is of children in that society.[66]

IV   PROPOSED CHILD SUPPORT SYSTEM REFORMS

(a)   Background

In New Zealand parents with children under the age of 19, who do not live with them for more than 40% of the time, are legally required to pay child support.[67] The amount of child support payable is currently based on the absent parent's taxable income and is either paid to the government (if the other parent is on a government benefit), or to the other parent who is raising the child on a daily basis. Child support is designed to be a financial contribution to the cost of raising their children and to ensure that 'parents take financial responsibility for their children when marriages and relationships end'.[68]

The New Zealand child support system has come under significant political scrutiny in recent years. In September 2010 the government released a discussion paper about the New Zealand child support system.[69] The discussion paper *Supporting Children* ('the discussion paper') found that the current child support system was considered to be out of date which 'if true, could undermine parents' incentives to meet their child support obligations. This could be detrimental to the wellbeing of their children'.[70] The discussion paper also raised concerns about the current child support system on the basis of unfairness in how parents' incomes are measured, increasing numbers of parents in shared care arrangements, significant amounts of unpaid child support, and increased inefficiency.[71] The discussion paper included options to

---

[65]   See Mark Henaghan and Ruth Ballantyne 'Legal Responses to Violence in the Home in New Zealand' (2010) 33 *University of New South Wales Law Journal* 870.

[66]   See Richard Wilkinson and Kate Pickett *The Spirit Level: Why Equality is Better for Everyone* (London: Penguin Books Ltd, 2010).

[67]   Inland Revenue 'Child Support' (2008) www.ird.govt.nz/childsupport/background/ (accessed 16 April 2012).

[68]   Inland Revenue 'Child Support' (2008) www.ird.govt.nz/childsupport/background/ (accessed 16 April 2012).

[69]   Hon Peter Dunne *Supporting Children: A Government Discussion Document on Updating the Child Support Scheme* (Wellington: Policy Advice Division of Inland Revenue, 2010).

[70]   Hon Peter Dunne *Supporting Children: Summary Version* (Wellington: Policy Advice Division of Inland Revenue, 2010) 1.

[71]   Hon Peter Dunne *Supporting Children: A Government Discussion Document on Updating the Child Support Scheme* (Wellington: Policy Advice Division of Inland Revenue, 2010).

revise the current child support system and invited public submissions on how best to improve the current system. More than 2,000 submissions were received in response to the discussion paper.[72]

On 5 October 2011, as a result of the discussion paper and the submissions received, the Minister of Revenue the Hon Peter Dunne, introduced the Child Support Amendment Bill ('the Bill') to Parliament.[73] The Bill will (if passed) amend the current New Zealand child support legislation – the Child Support Act 1991.

(b) Proposed changes

The main changes include the introduction of a 'comprehensive new child support formula' that is intended to 'provide a more equitable system of financial support'.[74] The new formula bases child support payments on three main factors:[75]

- ' • a wider recognition of shared care; and
- • the income of both parents; and
- • the estimated average expenditures for raising children in New Zealand.'

(i) Shared care

Currently, under the Child Support Act 1991 a parent has 'substantially equal sharing of care of child' only if their child spends at least 40% of their nights in their care.[76] This rule puts significant pressure on parents to obtain a minimum of 40% of the child's care (even if that is inappropriate for the child) to reduce the amount of child support they had to pay the other parent. This makes the parenting arrangements a financial dispute, rather than a question of what is best for the particular child. The new child support formula will incorporate lower levels of shared care via 'tiered thresholds'.[77] The lowest tier will recognise shared care commencing from a parent consistently providing 28% of their child's daily care.[78]

(ii) Income of both parents

Currently, under the Child Support Act 1991, only the child support payer's income is examined.[79] The child support receiver's income is not considered.

---

[72] Danya Levy 'Dads Scorn Child Support Timing' *The Dominion Post* (New Zealand, 23 August 2011).

[73] The Child Support Amendment Bill had its first reading on 8 May 2012. See New Zealand Parliament 'Progress of Legislation' for updates on this Bill. Available at www.parliament.nz/en-NZ/PB/Legislation/Bills (accessed June 2012).

[74] Explanatory Note of Child Support Amendment Bill 2011 (337–1) 2.

[75] Explanatory Note of Child Support Amendment Bill 2011 (337–1) 3.

[76] Child Support Act 1991, s 13.

[77] Explanatory Note of Child Support Amendment Bill 2011 (337–1) 3.

[78] Explanatory Note of Child Support Amendment Bill 2011 (337–1) 3.

[79] Child Support Act 1991, Part Two.

This has been a bone of contention between parents where the parent caring for the children is significantly wealthier than the parent paying child support. The Bill will alter the Child Support Act 1991 so that 'both parents' income (less a living allowance for each parent) will be included in the formula, with the costs of raising children being apportioned according to each parent's share of total net income'.[80]

(iii)   Expenditures for raising children

The proposed new formula will take into account more realistic and up-to-date information about the costs of raising children in New Zealand.[81] These are expressed as 'income percentages' and vary according to the number of children, the age of the children, and the total income of the parents.[82] The present formula takes no account of the fact that, as children become older, they become more costly.

(iv)   Other proposed changes

Other changes include: allowing the Inland Revenue Department (IRD) to rely on parenting orders when ascertaining who is caring for the child,[83] implementing compulsory deductions of child support from employment wages,[84] and reducing the age of the child whose support is paid for from 19 years old to under 18 years old (unless the child is 18 and enrolled in a school).[85] New Zealand parents currently owe the IRD child support payments to the sum of $2.3 billion.[86] Thus, there will be a reduction in non-payment penalties to encourage and facilitate 'parents to make timely payments of child support'.[87]

V   TRUSTS

It is not just the government that is currently reviewing aspects of family law in New Zealand. The New Zealand Law Commission (NZLC)[88] is currently

---

[80] Explanatory Note of Child Support Amendment Bill 2011 (337–1) 3.
[81] Explanatory Note of Child Support Amendment Bill 2011 (337–1) 3–4.
[82] Explanatory Note of Child Support Amendment Bill 2011 (337–1) 3–4.
[83] Explanatory Note of Child Support Amendment Bill 2011 (337–1) 4.
[84] Explanatory Note of Child Support Amendment Bill 2011 (337–1) 5.
[85] Explanatory Note of Child Support Amendment Bill 2011 (337–1) 4.
[86] Imogen Neale 'Parents $2.3b in Debt for Support' *Stuff.co.nz* (New Zealand, 23 October 2011).
[87] Explanatory Note of Child Support Amendment Bill 2011 (337–1) 4–5.
[88] In its own words, the NZLC is 'an independent, publicly funded, central advisory board established by statute to undertake the systematic review, reform and development of the law of New Zealand. Its purpose is to help achieve law that is just, principled, and accessible, and that reflects the heritage and aspirations of the peoples of New Zealand'. See NZLC *Some Issues With the Use of Trusts in New Zealand: Review of the Law of Trusts Second Issues Paper* (Wellington: NZLC, December 2010) II.

reviewing the law of trusts.[89] The NZLC outlines concerns about the modern use of trusts and invites a response from 'trust practitioners, people with trusts, settlors, trustees, beneficiaries, and anyone else' as to the legitimate purposes of trusts and whether limits should be placed on the effects of trusts.[90]

Trusts are a major industry in New Zealand. There are at least 245,800 trusts in New Zealand – one for every 17 people.[91] New Zealand trusts are used primarily to protect assets against creditors, for tax advantages, to reduce child support obligations, and to take property out of the pool of relationship property that would otherwise have to be shared equally. The Property (Relationships) Act 1976, which applies to married, civil union and de facto (including same-sex civil union and de facto) couples upon separation and death, provides an entitlement of 50/50 sharing of the property acquired during the relationship once a period of 3 years has passed.[92] If either or both of the parties do not beneficially own the property (for example if the property is held in trust) it falls outside the jurisdiction of the legislation. In some circumstances property held in trust can be clawed back at the end of a relationship.[93] However, these exceptions do not operate evenly across all couples. For example, one exception applies only to marriage and civil unions and not to de facto relationships.[94]

The purposes of the Property (Relationships) Act 1976 are expressly to 'recognise the equal contribution of husband and wife to the marriage partnership, of civil union partners to the civil union, and of de facto partners to the de facto relationship partnership' in order to 'provide for a just division of the relationship property between the spouses or partners'.[95] However, these purposes are currently being destabilised by trusts, which can take property out of reach of one of the parties. This entirely undermines any sense of equality and fairness when one partner may end up with very little in the way of relationship property because it is all held in trust by the other partner. Put more simply, '[w]hy should spouses or partners who put in the same effort get much less at the end, simply because in one case the assets are in trust and in

---

[89] NZLC 'Review of the Law of Trusts' (2009) www.lawcom.govt.nz/project/review-law-trusts (accessed June 2012).

[90] NZLC *Some Issues With the Use of Trusts in New Zealand: Review of the Law of Trusts Second Issues Paper* (Wellington: NZLC, December 2010) 5.

[91] This is based on the number of trust tax returns filed for the 2008–2009 financial year. See Nicola Peart, Mark Henaghan and Greg Kelly 'Trusts and Relationship Property in New Zealand' (2011) 17 *Trusts & Trustees* 866, 866.

[92] Property (Relationships) Act 1976, s 11. For exceptions to the general 3-year rule see the Property (Relationships) Act 1976, ss 2E (where a relationship of longer than 3 years may be deemed to be less than 3 years by the court) and 14A (where relationship property from a short term de facto couple who have a child can be divided based on each parties' contribution to the de facto relationship).

[93] See Property (Relationships) Act 1976, s 44 and Family Proceedings Act 1980, s 182. See also Nicola Peart, Mark Henaghan and Greg Kelly 'Trusts and Relationship Property in New Zealand' (2011) 17 *Trusts & Trustees* 866, 868–873.

[94] Family Proceedings Act 1980, s 182. See also Nicola Peart, Mark Henaghan and Greg Kelly 'Trusts and Relationship Property in New Zealand' (2011) 17 *Trusts & Trustees* 866, 871.

[95] Property (Relationships) Act 1976, s 1M(b) and (c).

the other they are not'.[96] Parliament should create new legislation that counts relationship property held in trust eligible for relationship property division where it has been produced or has increased in value by the efforts of the spouses.[97]

VI   CONCLUSION

The Family Court needs some reform to render it more efficient. However, families should not be cut off from legal processes and left to resolve their own family law disputes privately and at their own expense. Mediation should not be seen as a comprehensive alternative to Family Court processes. There are a number of more positive reforms to be made in this area. Standardised affidavits based solely on relevant material should be introduced. Vulnerable children and their families need significant state resources and intervention to protect vulnerable children and assist impoverished families. Mandatory reporting will not better protect vulnerable children. Rather, providing sufficient financial and staff resources to fully investigate all reports of child abuse and neglect is the best way to protect children. Merely moving funding around to prioritise certain vulnerable children over others will not suffice: more money is required. Making child support fairer is likely to lead to better outcomes, and cost savings in the long term. It should reduce unnecessary applications for more time with a parent purely to reduce child support obligations. Parliament should introduce new legislation allowing relationship property held in trust to be divided under the Property (Relationships) Act 1976. This would lead to a fairer and improved economic outcome for the more financially insecure party and any children they may have in their care.

Political changes and family law reforms often go hand in hand. Thus, it is no surprise that in challenging economic times the New Zealand government should bring a monetary focus to family law. However, the underlying principle of any proposed family law reforms should be how best to assist families in crisis in the most effective and efficient manner, while minimising as much distress as possible. The primary focus of any family law reform should be expansive and forward looking, rather than making expedient, immediate changes. It is easy to cut costs and remove resources under the guises of increased efficiency, but this may ultimately increase long-term costs if decisions about children are not made in a careful and considered manner.

---

[96]   Nicola Peart, Mark Henaghan and Greg Kelly 'Trusts and Relationship Property in New Zealand' (2011) 17 *Trusts & Trustees* 866, 881–882.

[97]   Nicola Peart, Mark Henaghan and Greg Kelly 'Trusts and Relationship Property in New Zealand' (2011) 17 *Trusts & Trustees* 866, 882.

Poland

THE RULES ON THE ADMINISTRATION OF COMMUNITY PROPERTY IN POLAND

*Dr Anna Stępień-Sporek, Paweł Stoppa and Margaret Ryznar**

Résumé

Les règles sur l'administration des biens communs ont connu d'importants changements en Pologne en 2005. Les règles antérieures, qui puisaient leurs racines dans la Pologne communiste d'avant 1989, apparaissaient inadéquates dans le nouveau contexte d'une économie capitaliste et d'un développement dynamique. Les anciennes règles, basées sur une distinction floue entre les actes ordinaires et les actes extraordinaires, engendraient des problèmes pratiques et minaient la stabilité des actes passés sans le consentement de l'autre époux. Les nouvelles règles qui sont basées sur le principe de l'administration personnelle et autonome de chaque époux, sauf pour certains actes particulièrement importants, semblent plus adéquates, même si elles ne sont pas parfaites et si elles nécessiteront des modifications périodiques. Le présent texte décrit les différences les plus notables entre les anciennes et les nouvelles règles et fournit un exposé sommaire du nouveau système de l'administration des biens communs.

I   INTRODUCTION

The most popular marital property regime in Europe is typically some form of community property.[1] Poland is an example of limited community of property, which was introduced in 1965 by the Family and Guardianship Code (KRO)[2] and was intended to benefit socialist marriage.[3] Although there have been

---

*   Dr Anna Stępień-Sporek, Assistant Professor of Law at University of Gdańsk (Poland) and attorney-at-law (barrister) in Stępień-Sporek, Pawelski, Stoppa Law Office (Poland).
Paweł Stoppa, attorney-at-law (barrister) in Stępień-Sporek, Pawelski, Stoppa Law Office (Poland).
Margaret Ryznar, attorney in Washington DC (United States).
[1]   This is the default matrimonial property regime in countries including France, Italy, Spain (excepting Catalonia) and the Netherlands. The Netherlands is a particularly interesting example because, according to Dutch law, the default regime is complete community of property, which is a unique approach in Europe. As Katherina Boele-Woelki suggested, the question is whether such a matrimonial property regime is in harmony with the views on the equal and independent positions of husband and wife (K Boele-Woelki 'The Road Towards a European Family Law' vol 1.1 *Electronic Journal of Comparative Law* (November 1997) available at www.ejcl.org/11/art11-1.html, p 12 (accessed June 2012)).
[2]   Act of 25 February 1964 (JL No 9, item 59 with amendments) (hereinafter KRO).
[3]   D Lasok *Polish Family Law* (Leyden: AW Sijthoff, 1968) 89.

significant societal and legal changes since then – including the disappearance
of socialist marriage into the darkness of history – community property
remains the default property regime by which spouses hold property in Poland,
unless there is a premarital agreement. However, given both the limited
contractual freedom in premarital agreements[4] and their relative unpopularity
despite their increasing numbers,[5] most marriages remain in the statutorily
mandated community property system.[6] When spouses do contract for a
different marital property regime, the trend across Europe favours the regime of
separation of property.[7]

The Polish Family and Guardianship Code, which introduced limited
community of property, finally underwent significant change in 2005. At the
time, scholars debated whether separation of property or a separation of
property with equalisation of surpluses[8] should replace community property as
the default marital property regime, but Polish society was unprepared for the
change and remained strongly attached to community of property.[9] The model
of the family in Poland was another important reason for the continuation of
community property as the default regime. Although the number of working
mothers continues to grow and fathers increasingly share caretaking
responsibilities, such trends are predominant mostly among young and
educated people and do not represent the majority of households, which
remain similar to the households of the recent past.[10] The traditional family
arrangement inevitably leads to the conclusion that community of property is a

---

4   Spouses can choose among only four contractual regimes and are able to make only minor
     changes to them, within the limits imposed by law. Pursuant to art 47 of the KRO, spouses
     may limit or expand the community of property or establish a separation of property or a
     separation of property with equalisation of surpluses. The marital agreement should be
     concluded in a notarial deed.

5   See E Holewińska-Łapińska 'Ochrona wierzyciela jednego z małżonków pozostających w
     umownym ustroju majątkowym' in K Ślebzak and W Wróbel (eds) *Studia i Analizy Sądu
     Najwyższego*, Tom II, (Warszawa: Wolters Kluwer Polska, 2008) 79–80. In Europe, the term
     'marital agreement' is used to describe both premarital agreements and marital agreements. See
     M Ryznar, A Stępień-Sporek 'To Have and to Hold, for Richer or Richer: Premarital
     Agreements in the Comparative Context' (2009) 13 *Chapman Law Review* 42.

6   E Skowrońska-Bocian 'Family and Succession Law' in S Frankowski and A Bodnar (eds)
     Introduction to Polish Family Law (Kluwer Law International, 2005) 96.

7   The reasons for introducing separation of property vary, with the main reason being that this
     regime is the most simple one during marriage, as well as upon divorce. People who have
     decided to start a commercial activity or have notable property want to make their property
     relations as simple as possible without any complications, particularly in regard to the
     co-operation of the spouses in property management or subsequent problems with classifying
     the property as separate or common.

8   The other name for this type of regime is the 'sharing of accruals'. See A Stępień-Sporek
     'Sharing of Accruals as the Best Solution for Marriage' in B Verschraegen (ed) *Family Finances*
     (Vienna: Jan Stramek Verlag, 2009) 371.

9   T Smyczyński 'Reforma małżeńskiego prawa majątkowego' (2004) 18 *Monitor Prawniczy* 827.

10   Polish women have a lower rate of employment than other women in the European Union,
     especially when compared to countries such as Denmark, the Netherlands, Sweden, Germany,
     Finland, Austria and Great Britain. In the last decade, there has been a systematic increase of
     the number of working women, but the rate of working women is still lower than that of
     working men. See www.stat.gov.pl/cps/rde/xbcr/gus/PUBL_f_kob_mez_na_ryn_prac_2010.pdf
     (accessed June 2012).

good marital property regime for families by providing wives the same rights to property as husbands.[11] As long as the dominant model of the family does not change, it is difficult to justify the introduction of a new default marital property regime.[12]

The first part of this chapter reviews the regime of community of property in Poland. The second part introduces readers to the field of the administration of common property – which forms the bulk of the spouses' assets – so as to illustrate the rules of management. Finally, the last part offers concluding observations regarding preferable approaches to the administration of common property.

II COMMUNITY OF PROPERTY

The community of property system seeks to guarantee equal property rights for both spouses, especially useful for women in the traditional family model. The community of property begins from the moment a couple marries and ends with the termination of the marriage, the conclusion of a marital property agreement, the decision of the court to impose a separation of property, or a compulsory property regime of separation of property triggered by operation of law (for example, legal incapacitation or declaration of insolvency).[13]

All of the spouses' property is divided into three types,[14] each addressed by the Family and Guardianship Code: the separate property of the wife, the separate property of the husband and common property. There is a presumption that all property not deemed separate property is common property. Article 31 of the KRO also provides a list of common property, which includes earnings received for work or other personal services performed by either spouse, income from both common and separate property and amounts collected in an account or an employee pension fund for either of the spouses.[15]

On the other hand, there is a numerus clausus of items that constitute the spouses' separate property, which includes chattels acquired before marriage, chattels acquired by inheritance or donation record (unless the testator or donor determined otherwise),[16] joint property rights that are fully covered under separate provisions, inalienable rights that may be exercised only by one person, property that is used exclusively to satisfy the personal needs of one

---

[11]   See also B Rešetar 'Matrimonial Property in Europe: A Link between Sociology and Family Law' (2008) 12 *Electronic Journal of Comparative Law* 9–13.

[12]   Ibid 17–18.

[13]   Articles 52–54 of the KRO.

[14]   E Skowrońska-Bocian 'Family and Succession Law' in S Frankowski and A Bodnar (eds) *Introduction to Polish Family Law* (The Hague: Kluwer Law International, 2005) 97–98.

[15]   The Polish approach is similar to the French one, but different from the Italian one. In Italy, income from separate property belongs to the separate property of each spouse. See W Pintens 'Europeanisation of Family Law' in K Boele-Woelki (ed) *Perspectives for the Unification and Harmonisation of Family Law in Europe* (Oxford/New York/Antwerp: Intersentia, 2003) 10.

[16]   See the decision of the Supreme Court of 11 March 2011 (II CSK 405/10, LEX nr 794576).

spouse, compensation for personal injury (except a pension for complete or partial loss of earning capacity), debts concerning remuneration of one of the spouses, prizes for personal achievements of one of the spouses, royalties for literary or industrial work or inventions, and finally, property acquired in exchange for elements of personal assets, unless particular provisions permit otherwise.

Common property is a species of co-ownership different from the type of co-ownership governed by property law.[17] Common property co-ownership is created by operation of law and is applied exclusively to marriages. Its key characteristic is that neither spouse has a definite share in the common property, but each has equal rights to the whole property. Neither spouse can apply to divide the common property, but each spouse is entitled to apply for a court order that introduces separation of property, by which the common property is divided and each spouse has separate property.[18] The rules on the spouses' management of common property are strictly prescribed by law. Spouses cannot change the rules, even through marital agreements.[19]

III THE OLD VERSUS NEW RULES

The basic rule of Polish family law is equality between a husband and a wife[20] who are to have the same rights to common property. Pursuant to art 36(1) of the KRO, spouses should co-operate in the management of common property, but this is a general rule that does not require all actions regarding common property to be taken by both spouses.

Before 2005, all actions of the spouses were divided into two groups: ordinary actions and extraordinary actions.[21] Ordinary actions, which each spouse was entitled to undertake, were defined as 'transactions of an everyday occurrence involving no risk to the household and to which no reasonable spouse would object'.[22] Extraordinary actions, which demanded strict co-operation of both spouses,[23] were 'ones involving a certain amount of risk'.[24] Extraordinary

---

[17] The law of property is regulated by the Civil Code – Act of 23 April 1964.

[18] See art 52 of the KRO.

[19] On the contrary, in the Netherlands where the system of total community of property exists, spouses are able to change the general rule of administration in a marriage contract (K Boele-Woelki, F Schonewille and W Schrama 'Dutch report concerning the CEFL questioner on property relations between spouses in' K Boele-Woelki, B Braat and I Curry-Sumner (eds) *European Family Law in Action* (Antwerp/Oxford/Portland: Intersentia, 2009) 438).

[20] Pursuant to art 23 of the KRO, spouses have equal rights and obligations in marriage.

[21] Compare to art 180 of the Italian Civil Code, which permits each spouse to act solely as regard to ordinary administration, but to act jointly as regard to extraordinary administration. Actions of ordinary administration concern regular enjoyment of property and its maintenance. Meanwhile, extraordinary actions include a modification of the composition of the patrimonial estate. See S Patti, C Caricato, C Irti, MA Iannicelli, MF Serra, P Di Stefano, Z Csenge Pető and T Bortolu in K Boele-Woelki, B Braat and I Curry-Sumner (eds) *European Family Law in Action* (Antwerp/Oxford/Portland: Intersentia, 2009) 436.

[22] D Lasok *Polish Family Law* (Leyden: AW Sijthoff, 1968) 94.

[23] Compare Portuguese Law. See G de Oliveira, R Martins and P Vitor 'Portuguese report

actions done without the consent of the other spouse were void. Although consent could be given after the transaction, the validity of the transaction depended upon the ratification by the other spouse. When consent was not forthcoming, the third party might set a time-limit by which the other spouse had to decide whether to consent to the action. If no consent was given, the third party was no longer contractually obliged after the expiration of the time-limit.

The main problem with the old rules was their failure to clearly define ordinary actions and extraordinary actions. For example, an extraordinary action for one marriage might be an ordinary one for another marriage. The lack of objective statutory criteria for distinguishing between these two types of actions made it impossible to clearly and explicitly classify each action of the spouses, thereby jeopardising legal certainty.[25] In its various decisions, the Polish Supreme Court explained the actions to be considered ordinary and those to be considered extraordinary. Jurisprudence and doctrine therefore tried to develop a catalogue of criteria that was taken into account when characterising an action as either ordinary or extraordinary, such as the size of common property,[26] the relation between the value of debts or claims and the value of common property,[27] the earning capacity of each spouse and the security of legal transactions. It was suggested that the higher the economic activity of the spouses and the higher the level of their affluence from the activity, the wider the scope of ordinary actions imputed to the spouses ought to be.[28] However, the problem in practice was that the same action could be classified differently. Furthermore, the court characterised each action ex post, which was good for neither the spouses nor the creditors: spouses did not know the limits of their sole management, while creditors were unsure whether an action was valid and effective.[29] This situation created a constant state of uncertainty that negatively impacted on the security of legal transactions.

---

concerning CEFL questionnaire on property relations between spouses' in K Boele-Woelki, B Braat and I Curry-Sumner (eds) *European Family Law in Action* (Antwerp/Oxford/Portland: Intersentia, 2009) 438.

[24]   Ibid 94.

[25]   J Ignaczewski *Małżeńskie ustroje majątkowe. Art. 31–54 of the KRO. Komentarz* (Warsaw: Wydawnictwo CH Beck, 2006) 70.

[26]   See the Decision of the Supreme Court of 21 January 2009, LEX 562977. The Supreme Court classified a spouse's sale of shares for the price of 265.900 PLN as an ordinary action because the common property of the spouses was worth about 2.000.000 PLN.

[27]   See the Decision of the Supreme Court of 10 January 2001, LEX 52417. For example, a guaranty assuring payment of a loan of 35.00 USD granted in Poland in 1992 was treated in that specific case as an extraordinary action – see: Decision of the Supreme Court of 28 July 1998, LEX 376146. A guaranty of 20.000 PLN (about 7.500 USD) granted in Poland in 1996 was classified in another case as an extraordinary action as well – see: Decision of the Supreme Court of 28 November 2002, LEX 75343. However, the Supreme Court stated that a guaranty of a bank loan of 9.000.000 PLN did not predetermine that the action had been an extraordinary one because the person who incurred the debt had been one of the richest men in Poland (Decision of the Supreme Court of 14 February 2008, LEX 457863).

[28]   See the Resolution of the Supreme Court of 25 March 1994, LEX 4025.

[29]   J Ignaczewski *Małżeńskie ustroje majątkowe. Art. 31–54 of the KRO. Komentarz* (Warsaw: Wydawnictwo CH Beck, 2006) 71.

This situation changed in 2005, with the main goal being the adjustment of matrimonial property relations to the new social-economic realities, which had started to significantly change after 1989.[30] According to the new rules on the topic, each spouse could solely administer common property with the exception of several actions, which were explicitly listed in art 37 of the KRO and required the consent of the other spouse, without which the actions were null and void. Importantly, this legal reform included a definition of the administration of common property, which resolved certain practical problems.[31] Pursuant to art 36(2) of the KRO, the administration of common property encompasses actions as to assets included in common property.[32]

IV SPOUSAL POWER TO MANAGE PROPERTY SEPARATELY UNDER THE NEW RULES

As discussed, the property of the spouses is divided into their common property and the separate property of each the wife and the husband. There are no limits on the spouses' actions regarding their separate property because each spouse is the sole owner of his or her separate property. Surprisingly, a spouse is therefore able to dispose of his or her home if it is separate property, even if it is the family home.[33] Of course, such a disposal can be contrary to the non-pecuniary obligations of spouses,[34] but this does not automatically mean that the action of the spouse is void or can be annulled.

A key issue in the new rules, however, is the autonomy and independence of the spouses in administering common property. According to art 36(2) of the KRO, each spouse can solely manage the assets of common property, unless

---

[30] T Mróz Teresa *Zgoda małżonka na dokonanie czynności prawnej w ustroju majątkowej wspólności ustawowej*, LEX 2011, no 132317.

[31] For example, there had been a debate prior to the legal reform on whether increasing a loan is an ordinary or extraordinary action. This debate is now moot because such an action does not currently belong to the administration of common property as it does not concern assets from common property. See M Olczyk [in:] Komentarz do ustawy z dnia 17 czerwca 2004 r. o zmianie ustawy – Kodeks rodzinny i opiekuńczy oraz niektórych innych ustaw (Dz.U.04.162.1691), w zakresie zmian do ustawy z dnia 25 lutego 1964 r. – Kodeks rodzinny i opiekuńczy (Dz.U.64.9.59), LEX 2005, no 79767.

[32] A Mączyński in K Boele-Woelki, B Braat and I Curry-Sumner (eds) *European Family Law in Action* (Antwerp/Oxford/Portland: Intersentia, 2009) 438.

[33] There is only one rule when a single spouse is entitled to the residential premises: the other spouse has the right to use the premises to cater for family needs (art 28(1) of the KRO). Another provision concerns the spouses' rights to residential premises leased during the marriage to accommodate the family (see art 680(1) of the Polish Civil Code). Meanwhile, art 1320 of the Spanish Civil Code states that disposal of the principal residence, even if it belongs only to one spouse, requires the other spouse's consent or judicial permission. Although the action concerns private property of the spouse, the other spouse can demand annulment of the act (see art 1322 of the Spanish Civil Code).

[34] For example, the obligation of spouses to work together for the good of the family that the marriage has created (art 23 of the KRO) and to contribute to meeting the needs of the family founded by the marriage (art 27 of the KRO).

otherwise provided in special rules.[35] Irrespective of this rule, art 36(3) of the KRO guarantees that property used by one spouse for professional or commercial activities can be solely administered by that spouse – only in the case of transient obstacles can the other spouse object.

Sole management of common property by one spouse is limited by the objection of the other spouse. The objection need not take any particular form, but a written one more easily proves the objection.[36] A spouse may object to an envisaged act of the other spouse, and this objection is valid to third parties if they knew about the objection before the act was performed.[37] If the act is performed despite the objection, it is null and void.[38] However, the objection cannot regard minor acts done in everyday life, actions aimed at fulfilling the ordinary needs of the family or acts connected to a commercial activity of a spouse. This last group of actions is noteworthy because the regime of common property with the co-operation of both spouses can be seen as an obstacle to entrepreneurship. However, the impossibility of spousal objections related to commercial activities confirms that it is possible to start a commercial activity without the need for a premarital agreement that introduces the separation of property as the marital property regime.

There is also another limit on a spouse's ability to solely manage common property under the new rules. At the request of one spouse, a court may deny the other spouse the independent right of administration. Such a decision can be made for important reasons pursuant to art 40 of the KRO, which occur when a spouse is unable to undertake, in accordance with the good of the family, decisions concerning the management of common property, exposing the property to substantial harm. Such reasons could include a spouse's alcoholism, stupefaction, improper administration due to carelessness or incompetence or actions such as hiding components of common property, the lack of co-operation in management of common property, or the actual separation of the spouses.[39]

---

[35] This regulation is similar to French law. According to art 1421 of the French Civil Code, each spouse has in principle a power to individually administer and dispose of common assets. See F Ferrand and B Bratt 'French report covering the CEFL questionnaire on property relations between spouses' in K Boele-Woelki, B Braat and I Curry-Sumner (eds) *European Family Law in Action* (Antwerp/Oxford/Portland: Intersentia, 2009) 433.

[36] See the decision of the Appeal Court in Katowice of 20 February 2009, LEX no 508515.

[37] A Mączyński in K Boele-Woelki, B Braat and I Curry-Sumner (eds) *European Family Law in Action* (Antwerp/Oxford/Portland: Intersentia, 2009) 438.

[38] Although the result of such objection was not explicitly mentioned in art 36(1) of the KRO, the opinion that such an act is null and void seems to be currently dominant in Polish jurisprudence. See: T Smyczyński *System Prawa Prywatnego*, vol 11, (Warsaw: Wydawnictwo CH Beck, 2009) 487.

[39] See A Lutkiewicz-Rucińska in Dolecki Henryk, Sokołowski Tomasz, Andrzejewski Marek, Lutkiewicz-Rucińska Anita, Olejniczak Adam, Sylwestrzak Anna and Zielonacki Andrzej (eds) *Kodeks Rodzinny i Opiekuńczy. Komentarz* (Warsaw: LexisNexis, 2010) 86542.

V ACTIONS REQUIRING SPOUSAL CO-OPERATION UNDER THE NEW RULES

The new rules on the administration of common property have introduced a group of actions that require the co-operation of both spouses.[40] In other words, the spouse who wants to act needs to receive the consent of the other spouse. The list of actions is in art 37 of the KRO, and includes:

(1) actions leading to the disposal of, indebting or acquisition of immovable property for payment, providing immovable property for use or usufruct;

(2) actions leading to the disposal of, indebting or acquisition of property for payment regarding a building or living premises;

(3) actions leading to the disposal of, indebting or acquisition of property for payment or leasing of a farm or an enterprise; and

(4) donations, apart from minor donations.[41]

The validity of a contract concluded by one spouse without the required consent of the other depends on the other spouse's affirmation of the contract. The contractual party of one spouse may impose a deadline by which the other spouse, whose consent is required, affirms the contract. The contracting party becomes free after the deadline's expiration and the contract becomes void. A unilateral act performed without the required consent of the other spouse is invalid without the possibility of reformation. The best practice for a contracting party, therefore, is to obtain the consent of the non-contracting spouse before the agreement is concluded. The main goal of obligatory consent is to protect the common property that is a base for the family.[42]

Finally, it is noteworthy that the court may determine that, to carry out the actions listed in art 37(1) of the KRO, judicial permission can be a substitute for the spouse's permission. In these cases, instead of seeking the consent of the spouse, a person needs to obtain the permission of the court. Similarly, if one spouse refuses to provide the consent required by law, or if it is difficult to compromise with that spouse,[43] the other spouse may apply to the court for permission to carry out operations. The court will grant the authorisation if the action is good for the family, pursuant to art 39 of the KRO.[44]

---

[40] A similar rule can be found in French law, which offers a list of transactions that are subject to the joint administration of spouses. See arts 1424–1425.

[41] A Mączyński in K Boele-Woelki, B Braat and I Curry-Sumner (eds) *European Family Law in Action* (Antwerp/Oxford/Portland: Intersentia, 2009) 453.

[42] See M Sychowicz in H Ciepła, B Czech, T Domińczyk, S Kalus, K Piasecki and M Sychowicz *Kodeks rodzinny i opiekuńczy. Komentarz* (Warsaw: LexisNexis, 2006) 206.

[43] For example, due to sickness or lack of contact with the other spouse.

[44] A similar rule can be found in Spanish law. See art 1376 of the Spanish Civil Code.

VI   CONCLUSION

It is difficult to create statutory rules governing the administration of common property that would sufficiently secure the common property of the spouses and also take into account the interests of the creditors who enter into legal relationships with one of the spouses. In considering the preferable model of the administration of common property, one possibility is to allow joint management limited to ordinary actions and require the consent of a spouse in other actions. Another approach is to introduce the principle of self-management of property provided, however, there is a group of particularly important actions that require the consent of the other spouse for their validity. This latter approach is employed today in Poland, while the former was in force prior to 2005.

Neither of these approaches is free from shortcomings. Having indeterminate actions that are extraordinary and in excess of ordinary management activities may raise doubt as to the legal certainty of transactions – it seems difficult to establish general and objective criteria that could be applied in the process of distinguishing extraordinary actions from ordinary ones. Previous jurisprudence and doctrine include several guidelines that were helpful in this regard but were very general, increasing the importance of the judge's role because whether or not an action was valid depended on judicial decision. On the other hand, clearly outlining a directory of actions requiring the consent of the other spouse carries the risk of insufficiency.

With the introduction of art 37(1) of the KRO, lawmakers seemed to have taken into account the most important components of the assets of spouses. At the same time, however, it seems that they have not recognised that the current composition of spousal property includes items other than those included a few decades ago. For example, shares and bonds are currently included in common property. Separate administration means that each spouse can sell them without the consent of the other, even though they are a very important component of common property.[45] Such spousal action will be valid even if not in accordance with the interests of the family. On the other hand, if a spouse decides to sell a small piece of real estate, the consent of the other spouse is indispensable. This is a consequence of the statutory presumption that the type of action determines its legal efficiency, depending on the way the administration of common property is being performed (separately or jointly) instead of the value of the action. On the other hand, the introduction of thresholds based on the value of a specific action seems to be impractical because it would require determining the value of the transaction, which could lead to disagreement and preclude sufficient legal certainty of transactions. Parties to such transactions can also avoid the necessity of the other spouse's

---

[45]   Compare the list of transactions included in common property to those in the French Civil Code. Transactions concerning non-negotiable securities (partnership share) are subject to joint administration.

consent by dividing transactions into several smaller ones[46] or underrating their value. In conclusion, value-based criteria would not be much better than the previous regulation based on an individual assessment of spousal action as ordinary or extraordinary.

However, the new rules governing the administration of property seem to be preferable to the more flexible but occasionally ambiguous rules based on the dichotomy between ordinary and extraordinary actions. The most important advantages resulting from the current regulations are the higher level of stability for legal relationships based on one spouse's actions and the easier identification of actions requiring joint management.

Nonetheless, the new rules do not eliminate all of the practical problems with the administration of common property. This prompts the question of whether it is even possible to eliminate all of the problems concerning the administration of common property: guaranteeing the spouses relative autonomy in the management of common property while guaranteeing creditors certainty in transactions. It is also the choice between, on the one hand, formulating an expansive and detailed list of actions requiring a spouse's consent that can lead to extensive regulation despite drawbacks and, on the other hand, formulating a short list that takes into account the most popular actions that are typically most important for families. The second solution seems preferable, but the introduction of such a list should be preceded by detailed analysis and the resulting list should be reviewed at least once every decade, if not more frequently. Unfortunately, after 7 years of the binding force of the new rules on the topic, there are still few relevant court decisions and resolutions of the Supreme Court that could provide guidelines. This increases the importance of analysing foreign regulations limiting the separate administration of common property.

It seems that in the creation of a revised list of actions requiring the other spouse's consent, the following additional actions should be considered:

(1)   actions leading to the disposal of, indebting or acquisition of a registered ship or a ship under construction for payment, as well as those actions leading to the ship being given for use or for usufruct;[47] and

(2)   actions leading to the disposal of, indebting or acquisition of entire common property for payment, as well as those actions leading to the entire common property being given for use or for usufruct.[48]

There are already Polish regulations that treat a registered ship or a ship under construction similarly to real estate (eg regulations concerning the sale of

---

[46]   If a component of common property could be partially disposed, eg shares.

[47]   Compare to art 1424 of the German Civil Code. The disposal of registered ships and ships under construction is treated the same as the disposal of real estate.

[48]   Compare art 1423 of the German Civil Code, which requires the consent of the other spouse if the entire common property is to be disposed.

property in insolvency proceedings).[49] The value of such ships is usually higher than typical residential property, and there is no logic in classifying the sale of a small flat worth, for example, 100.000 PLN as a potentially more dangerous action for common property than the sale of a ship worth 1.000.000 PLN.

Introducing a higher level of protection for the entire common property should also be considered. Article 37 of the KRO protects the most important components of such property, but the protection does not cover the entire property. This could be particularly significant for marriages where the spouses do not own any real estate, farm or enterprise: one spouse's sale of whole common property – unless real estate, farm or enterprise – would be valid even when not in accordance with the good of the family.

Apart from possible amendments concerning the administration of common property, it might be necessary to introduce a regulation that limits spousal actions over the separate property of each spouse. For example, if a spouse is the sole owner of the principal residence of the family, disposal of the residence ought to be approved by the other spouse. Otherwise, the spouse who did not grant consent would be able to demand the judicial annulment of the action. To achieve the balance between the good of the family and the security of legal transactions, there ought to be a deadline by which to annul such an action; for example, a spouse could have a limit of 2 years to institute relevant legal proceedings. The good faith of the other party to the transaction, however, should be protected as well.

Finally, it should be noted that the harmonisation of certain aspects of family law is currently being discussed in the European Union. Any resulting developments in European regulations on common property could therefore influence Polish law. Nonetheless, the extent to which harmonisation can standardise the rules on the administration of marital property is unclear. Certain specific legal approaches to common property law that result from different historic and economic conditions, as well as different cultural and religious traditions, could properly exist in one country without a realistic chance of adoption in another.

---

[49] See arts 316–324 of the Polish Bankruptcy and Rehabilitation Law dated 28 February 2003.

Samoa

REFORM OF MAINTENANCE AND DIVORCE LAWS IN SAMOA: APPROPRIATE FOR THE 'AIGA'?

Lalotoa Mulitalo and Jennifer Corrin[*]

Résumé

Le droit samoan contient nombre de lois relatives au droit de la famille, notamment l'Ordonnance de 1961 sur le divorce et les régimes matrimoniaux et la loi de 1967 sur la filiation et le devoir solidarité. En 2010, ces deux textes ont été modifiés. Les amendements apportés à la loi relative au divorce ont fait de Samoa l'une des deux petites nations insulaires du Pacifique à avoir institué une procédure de divorce sans faute, l'autre étant Fidji. Par ailleurs, les juridictions ont été autorisées à modifier les droits des époux sur leur propriété. Les nouveaux textes relatifs à la filiation et aux aliments ont aussi donné de nouveaux droits à la Cour fédérale pour modifier les modalités de garde de l'enfant et le montant de la pension alimentaire. Cette contribution commence par un résumé du droit avant les réformes. Ensuite, elle analyse les changements intervenus en droit du divorce et des aliments et apprécie la portée de ces évolutions à la lumière du contexte culturel et social de Samoa.

I INTRODUCTION

The formal, written laws in Samoa include a number of statutes relating to family law,[1] including the Divorce and Matrimonial Causes Ordinance 1961 and the Maintenance and Affiliation Act 1967. In 2010, both these Acts were amended.[2] The amendments to the divorce legislation made Samoa one of the only two small Pacific island nations to have introduced a purely no-fault

---

[*] Lalotoa Mulitalo is former Parliamentary Counsel of Samoa and former Maintenance Officer under the Maintenance and Affiliation laws in Samoa. She is currently a PhD student at the University of Queensland.
Jennifer Corrin is Director of the Centre for International, Public and Comparative Law and Professor in the TC Beirne School of Law at the University of Queensland.
[1] Marriage Act 1961 (Samoa); Marriage Ordinance 1961 (Samoa), Maintenance and Affiliation Act 1967 (Samoa); Divorce and Matrimonial Causes Ordinance 1961 (Samoa).
[2] Divorce and Matrimonial Causes Amendment Act 2010; Maintenance and Affiliation Amendment Act 2010.

system of divorce, the other being Fiji.[3] Neighbouring countries have either fault-based systems[4] or 'mixed' systems, where divorce may be fault-based or based on a no-fault ground.[5] The amendments also introduce a much needed reform which allows the courts to alter property rights. Formerly, the courts had been faced with a choice of denying a remedy to a party whose name was not on the title, or using elaborate devices to supplement the existing law.[6] The changes to the law on maintenance and affiliation give new powers to the District Court to make custody orders and set out guidelines on the amount and payment of maintenance. The court may also require financial information, the execution of necessary instruments to secure payment, and the provision of security for the obedience of a maintenance order. The court may also order parties to go undergo mediation. This chapter commences with a summary of existing law. It then looks at the recent changes to divorce and maintenance legislation and discusses their efficacy in the light of the cultural and social background of Samoa.

II FAMILY LAW IN SAMOA

Family law in Samoa is governed by legislation, common law and customary law.[7] Statutes governing family matters[8] include the Divorce and Matrimonial Causes Ordinance 1961, and the Maintenance and Affiliation Act 1967. This legislation, dating from just before independence, is foreign to the local setting and had become very outdated. For example, the legal capacity and status of women is still governed by the Samoa Act 1921 (NZ).[9] In response to the need for reform, the Divorce and Matrimonial Causes Amendment Act 2010 and the Maintenance and Affiliation Amendment Act 2010 introduced significant

---

3   Family Law Act 2003 (Fiji), s 30(1); Divorce and Matrimonial Causes Ordinance 1961 (Samoa), s 7 as amended by the Divorce and Matrimonial Causes Amendment Act 2010 (Samoa), s 6.

4   Matrimonial Causes Act, Cap 192, s 5 (Vanuatu); Matrimonial Causes Act 1950 (UK), s 4 (applying in Kiribati to divorces between expatriates only); Matrimonial Causes Act 1950 (UK) (applying in Solomon Islands to divorces between expatriates only).

5   Matrimonial Proceedings Act 1963 (NZ, now repealed), s 21(1) (Cook Islands); Matrimonial Causes Act 1973, ss 8, 9 (Nauru); Niue Act 1966 (NZ), s 534(3); Islanders' Divorce Act, Cap 170 (Solomon Islands), ss 2, 3; Divorce Regulations 1987(Tokelau), reg 3; Divorce Act, Cap 29 (Tonga) s 3 (for a detailed examination of Tongan divorce law see Corrin J 'For better or worse: Marriage and divorce laws in the Kingdom of Tonga' in Bill Atkin (ed) *International Survey of Family Law, 2007 Edition* (Jordan Publishing Ltd, 2007) 291; Matrimonial Proceedings Act, Cap 21 (Tuvalu) ss 8, 9; Native Divorce Ordinance, Cap 60 (Kiribati), s 4.

6   See further, Corrin J 'Getting a Fair Share: Financial Relief on Breakdown of Marriage in Samoa' in Bill Atkin (ed) *International Survey of Family Law, 2008 Edition* (Jordan Publishing Ltd, 2008) 297.

7   See further, Corrin J 'Getting a Fair Share: Financial Relief on Breakdown of Marriage in Samoa' in Bill Atkin (ed) *International Survey of Family Law, 2008 Edition* (Jordan Publishing Ltd, 2008) 297.

8   Marriage Act 1961 (Samoa); Marriage Ordinance 1961 (Samoa), Maintenance and Affiliation Act 1967 (Samoa); Divorce and Matrimonial Causes Ordinance 1961 (Samoa).

9   Section 360. This appears to be the only reason this Act is still on Samoa's statute book.

changes. Whilst these reforms constitute a significant improvement, the legislation still does not constitute a coherent regime; nor does it take account of local culture or realities.

Common law and equity also form an important part of family law, particularly in relation to matrimonial property.[10] Lack of legislative provision, particularly in relation to property division, has left the courts to try to find ways of doing justice without blatantly making new law.[11] Customary law in Samoa is particularly strong in relation to family matters. As stated by Powles:[12]

> 'Whole areas of personal relationships – such as kinship, marriage, children, and land-holding groups – may be nationwide spheres largely covered by customary law, where the state intervenes little, if at all.'

This gives rise to tensions between customary and state laws. These problems are discussed by the authors of this chapter in an earlier issue of the *International Survey of Family Law*.[13]

Jurisdiction in family matters is not allocated to one court, but is divided between the Supreme Court, which deals with nullity,[14] termination of marriages and ancillary matters, and the District Courts which deal with maintenance and affiliation,[15] legitimation[16] and adoption orders.[17] Both courts have jurisdiction in relation to guardianship and custody,[18] and provision for destitute or delinquent children.[19]

III DIVORCE AND MATRIMONIAL CAUSES AMENDMENT ACT 2010

(a) Introduction

The Divorce and Matrimonial Causes Ordinance 1961 is a piece of colonial legislation which continued in force at Independence.[20] The purpose of the

---

[10] Jennifer Corrin and Don Paterson *Introduction to South Pacific Law* (Palgrave MacMillan, 2011) chapter 7.

[11] See *Arp v Arp* (unreported, Supreme Court Samoa, Sapolu CJ, 13 June 2008), available via www.paclii.org at [2008] WSSC 35; *Hadley v Hadley* (unreported, Supreme Court Samoa, Nelson J, 19 March 2010), available via www.paclii.org at [2010] WSSC 61.

[12] G Powles 'The Challenge of Law Reform in Pacific Island States' in Weisbrot and Opeskin (eds) *The Promise of Law Reform* (Federation Press, 2005) 411.

[13] Jennifer Corrin and Lalotoa Mulitalo 'Adoption and "Vae Tama" in Samoa' in Bill Atkin (ed) *International Survey of Family Law, 2011 Edition* (Jordan Publishing Ltd, 2011) 313–314.

[14] Divorce and Matrimonial Causes Ordinance 1961, ss 2 and 3.

[15] Maintenance and Affiliation Act 1967, s 3.

[16] Infants Ordinance 1961, ss 24–27.

[17] Infants Ordinance 1961, ss 7–11.

[18] Infants Ordinance 1961, ss 3–6.

[19] Infants Ordinance 1961, ss 15–20.

[20] Constitution of Samoa 1962, Art 111(1).

Ordinance is to make provision for divorce and related matrimonial matters. Jurisdiction to deal with matrimonial disputes is bestowed by the Act on the Supreme Court, with appeal to the Court of Appeal.[21] The court is empowered to grant a decree of judicial separation on the grounds of cruelty, adultery or desertion (2 years).[22] It may also grant a divorce. Before amendment, proof of fault was required in the form of adultery; wilful desertion (3 years); habitual drunkenness or cruelty of a husband (3 years);[23] the habitual drunkenness or habitual neglect of domestic duties of a wife (3 years); conviction for murder, attempted murder, wounding, actual bodily harm, discharge of a firearm at the petitioner or a child; being of unsound mind or confinement in a mental institution for at least 5 years; or separation pursuant to agreement for at least 3 years. Further grounds were provided for petitioners who had been resident in Samoa for at least 2 years, including living apart for at least 5 years; imposition of a prison sentence of at least 7 years; or, in the case of the husband, conviction for rape, sodomy or bestiality.

The court also had power to annul a marriage on the grounds of bigamy; absence of consent; contravention of consanguinity and affinity rules;[24] or lack of form.[25] Further, a marriage was voidable if the respondent was unable or unwilling to consummate; mentally disabled;[26] suffering from venereal disease; or pregnant by someone other than the petitioner at the time of the marriage.

On grant of a divorce, the court was empowered to make a maintenance order in favour of the wife in the form of a lump sum or annuity. The amount to be awarded was such as the court deemed reasonable, having regard to the wife's means, the ability of the husband to pay, and the conduct of the parties. What the legislation did not provide was for property division, and, as discussed below and elsewhere,[27] this left the courts to resort to its equitable jurisdiction to try to find a just solution.[28] In any proceeding for the termination of marriage or judicial separation, the court is also empowered to make orders regarding wardship, custody, maintenance and education of the children of the marriage.[29]

---

[21] Section 36.
[22] Section 4.
[23] See e g *Lauofo v Croker* (unreported, Supreme Court, Samoa, Sapolu CJ, 29 November 1993), available via www.paclii.org at [1993] WSSC 5.
[24] Divorce and Matrimonial Causes Ordinance 1961, s 9(2)(c) and Marriage Ordinance 1961, s 7.
[25] Divorce and Matrimonial Causes Ordinance 1961, s 9(2)(d).
[26] Divorce and Matrimonial Causes Ordinance 1961, s 9(3)(b).
[27] Corrin J 'Getting a Fair Share: Financial Relief on Breakdown of Marriage in Samoa' in Bill Atkin (ed) *International Survey of Family Law, 2008 Edition* (Jordan Publishing Ltd, 2008) 297.
[28] See *Arp v Arp* (unreported, Supreme Court Samoa, Sapolu CJ, 13 June 2008), available via www.paclii.org at [2008] WSSC 35; *Hadley v Hadley* (unreported, Supreme Court Samoa, Nelson J, 19 March 2010), available via www.paclii.org at [2010] WSSC 61.
[29] Section 24.

(b) Overview of changes to the law

In 2010, the Divorce and Matrimonial Causes Amendment Act 2010 was passed with a view to introducing no-fault divorce. The fault-based grounds for divorce or judicial separation were replaced by irretrievable breakdown of marriage as the ground for judicial separation and divorce. As part of a general reform of the court process designed to reduce a backlog of cases awaiting hearing,[30] the amending Act empowers the Registrar to carry out some of the procedural functions of the court. For example, the Registrar may now grant adjournments, set hearing dates, and deal with mentions. Finally, the amending Act makes amendments designed to accommodate new domestic violence legislation, which has yet to be enacted.

(c) Changes to divorce law

As mentioned above, the 2010 amendments replace fault-based grounds with irretrievable breakdown of the marriage, which is now the only basis on which a divorce may be granted.[31] In the absence of domestic violence,[32] the parties must also prove that they have been separated for a continuous period of at least 12 months.[33] The parties may be regarded as living separately notwithstanding that they have continued to reside under the same roof or that either party has rendered some household services to the other.[34] Where, the parties resume cohabitation for a period of up to 3 months, the period of separation before and after this cohabitation may be combined to calculate the 12 months separation.[35] Where the court considers that there may be a possibility of reconciliation it may not grant a decree,[36] and it may require the parties to undergo marriage counselling.[37]

A divorce decree takes effect one month after the making of the decree,[38] or, where an appeal is instituted against the making of a decree, one month from the day the appeal is determined or discontinued, if this is later.[39] Whilst this provision has obviously been drafted on the basis that a right to appeal exists, s 36 states there is no right of appeal against a decree terminating a marriage. On the application of the parties, the court may rescind the divorce order at any time before it takes effect on the ground that the parties have become

---

[30] For example, Draft Supreme Court (Civil Procedure) Amendment Rules 2009, which are yet to be enacted.
[31] Section 7(1).
[32] Section 7(3). Under this subsection, the waiting period is not necessary where there is domestic violence.
[33] Section 7(2).
[34] Section 7A(2).
[35] Section 7B.
[36] Section 7(4).
[37] Section 7E(2).
[38] Section 7C(1)(a).
[39] Section 7C(2).

reconciled.[40] A divorce decree cannot take effect unless proper arrangements have been made for the care, welfare and development of any children of the marriage under 18.[41]

Under the new law, a divorce decree may be granted by the Registrar if the petition is undefended or both parties consent in writing. However, at any time before this decree takes effect the respondent may apply to a District Court judge to have the decree set aside and replaced by such orders as the judge considers appropriate.[42] The grounds for such an application are not stated in the Act.

(d)   Changes to the law on matrimonial property

The amending Act makes a dramatic change to the law in relation to matrimonial property. In applications for financial relief under the Act, the court may now make an order altering property rights[43] if it is satisfied that, in all the circumstances, it is just and equitable to do so.[44] The new provision lists the matters to be taken into account by the court in considering the appropriate property orders. These are:

(a)   the income, financial contribution and commitments of parties;

(b)   the financial or other contribution made by or on behalf of a party to the acquisition or improvement of the property;

(c)   the contribution made by a party to the welfare of the family, including any contribution made in the capacity of homemaker or parent; and

(d)   any special circumstances which, if not taken into account, would result in injustice or undue hardship.

The starting point in the case of marriages of more than 3 years is that both parties have contributed equally, but the presumption may be rebutted if a court considers a finding of equal contribution inappropriate.[45] Matrimonial property does not include property brought into the marriage by a party, unless it would be inequitable to exclude it.

The settlement or transfer order may be made for the benefit of either or both of the parties or their children. The court may vary or set aside the order on proof of fraud, duress, suppression of evidence, the giving of false evidence or any other circumstance amounting to a miscarriage of justice.[46]

---

[40]   Section 7F.
[41]   Section 7D.
[42]   Section 7G.
[43]   Section 22B and C.
[44]   Section 22C.
[45]   Section 2C(3).
[46]   Section 22D.

Whilst this provision is a vast improvement on the old law, which left the court to resort to elaborate devices to alter property rights,[47] it takes no account of local realities. 80% of land is customary land, which is inalienable, except in certain limited circumstances. The need to make sui generis provision in this area of law was recognised by Sapolu CJ in *Arp v Arp*[48] where he stated that the principles he has applied in that case, which were derived from a mixture of the statute and common law of England, Australia and New Zealand, might have to be adjusted to take account of Samoa's 'own unique circumstances'. His Honour specifically stated that he had in mind, 'for example, matrimonial property disputes which involve customary land'.[49]

(e) New provisions on domestic violence

The other major change introduced by the Divorce and Matrimonial Causes Amendment Act 2010 is provision for domestic violence orders. These orders are designed to accommodate new domestic violence legislation, which has yet to be enacted. The new Part IIIA provides for restraining orders to be made on proof of domestic violence. Domestic violence is defined broadly as including not only conduct that causes physical injury, but also extends to psychological damage and damage to property. Threats of violence or damage and harassing or offensive conduct are also covered.[50]

The primary consideration on an application for an order is the need to protect the victim, and any child at risk of exposure to domestic violence.[51] A restraining order remains in force for up to 2 years.[52] A restraining order may be issued by the Registrar,[53] as well as the court, but the Registrar's order remains in force for 7 days only.[54]

(f) Changes to law on alimony and maintenance

The amending Act inserts a new s 22A, listing the matters to be considered by the court when considering alimony and maintenance, to bring it into line with the new s 18A of the Maintenance and Affiliation Act. These detailed provisions will no doubt be of assistance to the court, but they are very general and make no attempt to take account of cultural factors. As ss 22A and 18A are identical, the new provision is discussed below. Strangely, the opportunity has not been taken to get rid of the archaic term 'alimony', which was the word

---

[47] See further, Corrin J 'Getting a Fair Share: Financial Relief on Breakdown of Marriage in Samoa' in Bill Atkin (ed) *International Survey of Family Law, 2008 Edition* (Jordan Publishing Ltd, 2008) 297.

[48] (Unreported, Supreme Court Samoa, Sapolu CJ, 13 June 2008), available via www.paclii.org at [2008] WSSC 35.

[49] *Arp v Arp* (unreported, Supreme Court Samoa, Sapolu CJ, 13 June 2008), 19–20.

[50] Section 26A.

[51] Section 26B.

[52] Section 26D.

[53] Section 26B(1).

[54] Section 26D(2).

used to describe the allowance to a married woman when she was living apart from her husband. The term no longer appears in modern legislation dealing with matrimonial causes in England, Australia or New Zealand.

IV MAINTENANCE AND AFFILIATION AMENDMENT ACT 2010

(a) Introduction

The Maintenance and Affiliation Act 1967 empowers the District Court[55] to make a maintenance order in favour of a spouse or child.[56] Until 2010, the Act gave no legislative guidance on how the judicial discretion to award maintenance should be exercised, other than a provision that such an order should be the amount that the court considered reasonable in all the circumstances[57] and that it should only be made against a person with 'sufficient ability' to pay. In fact, the Chief Justice had acted to fill this gap by setting out guidelines in case-law.[58] There was also a legislative cap on the amount of 'past maintenance', which did not take into account inflation or reflect contemporary realities.[59] As stated by Nelson J in *SV v SV*,[60] '$100 may have been a significant sum in 1967 but today it is grossly antiquated'. The Maintenance Act also makes provision for maintenance of a destitute person by a near relative if that relative has sufficient means to pay.[61] In practice, however, this provision does not appear to have been used. This is probably due to the fact that the customary system in Samoa involves communal living and sharing on a voluntary basis, rather than by virtue of a court order.

Where a maintenance order was made, the court was also empowered to make a custody order for the term of the maintenance order. The person awarded custody had the same powers as a court appointed guardian.[62] The court is also empowered to make an affiliation and maintenance order against the father of an illegitimate child under the age of 16.[63]

---

[55] Section 3.
[56] Maintenance and Affiliation Act 1967, Parts V and VI.
[57] Section 18.
[58] *Soavele v Lilii* (unreported, Supreme Court, Sapolu CJ, 11 March 1993) available via www.paclii.org at [1993] WSSC 22.
[59] Section 20.
[60] (Unreported, District Court, Nelson J, 23 December 2004), available via www.paclii.org at [2004] WSDC 11. Section 20.
[61] Section 5 and 6.
[62] Section 23.
[63] Sections 9 and 11.

(b)   Overview of changes to the law

In 2010, the Maintenance and Affiliation Amendment Act 2010 was passed.[64] The Act lays down specific guidelines for awarding maintenance. It also expands the jurisdiction of the District Court by empowering it to make a custody order in favour of a child, whether or not it also makes a maintenance order relating to the child. In the same way as under the Divorce and Matrimonial Causes Amendment Act, the powers of the Registrar are increased in line with general court process reforms, designed to reduce the backlog of cases awaiting hearing.

(c)   Changes to the law on maintenance

Unlike the original Act,[65] the amending Act provides a list of matters to be taken into account by the court in determining a reasonable amount of maintenance.[66] These appear to be based on the Family Proceedings Act 1980 (NZ)[67] and can be summarised as:

(a)   the needs of the applicant having regard to their age and any special needs;

(b)   the financial resources of the applicant, disregarding the financial resources of any other person unless the court considers this relevant in the special circumstances of the case;

(c)   the financial resources of the defendant;

(d)   the commitments of the defendant for their own support or the support of any other person that the defendant has a duty to maintain; and

(e)   any special circumstances which would result in injustice or undue hardship to any person.

The amending Act also addresses the other criticism that had been made of the existing law, in that it increases the cap on an award of past maintenance from $100 to $1,000.[68] This is a much more realistic limit. There is also provision for the amount to be increased by means of delegated legislation.[69]

A new s 18(1B) provides that a maintenance order may direct how the money payable under that order is to be paid and s 18(1C) specifically empowers the

---

64   The Act commenced on 6 August 2010.
65   See criticism above and in *Soavele v Lilii* (unreported, Supreme Court, Sapolu CJ, 11 March 1993) available via www.paclii.org at [1993] WSSC 22.
66   Section 18(1A).
67   Section 65.
68   Section 8, amending s 20 of the principal Act.
69   The Act does not state who has the power to make such legislation, but it is presumably the Head of State on the advice of Cabinet: s 89.

court to direct maintenance for the benefit of a named child. However, the point of these subsections is hard to discern as these powers already existed under s 18(2). A new s 18A(2) provides that a court may make more than one maintenance order in respect of a child. Whilst the power to vary a maintenance order already existed under s 30, the new section makes it clear that a subsequent order may be made, even where an earlier order has expired.

A new s 18A, which also appears to be based on the Family Proceedings Act 1980 (NZ),[70] specifies the orders that the court may make in respect of maintenance. These may be summarised as:

(a) payment of a lump sum, by instalments or by a single payment;

(b) payment of periodic maintenance;

(c) transfer or settlement of property;

(d) security for the whole or part of the amount to be paid;

(e) execution of any necessary instrument (eg deed of conveyance), production of title deeds and anything else necessary to enable an order to be carried out, or provision of security for the due performance of an order;

(f) any other order that the court considers appropriate.

Paragraph (b) specifically states that court may order 'a weekly, monthly, yearly or other periodic amount' of maintenance, whereas the old law specified a maximum period of one month for periodic payments.[71] The security for obedience to the maintenance order, referred to in para (d) is increased from $400 to $1000 or such higher amount as is prescribed.[72] Also, if the defendant intends to live outside Samoa for a period greater than 3 months, the court may order the defendant to give security of such amount and in such form as it thinks appropriate.[73] The court may also direct either party to provide such further information as it considers necessary.[74] This may include information on the income, earning capacity, including bank statements; employment records; property records, financial resources and other assets of a party; and the commitments of the parties that are necessary to enable them to support themselves or any other person that they have a duty to maintain.

---

[70] Section 69.
[71] Section 19(1), now repealed.
[72] Maintenance and Affiliation Amendment Act 2010, s 10(b), amending s 32(2) in the Principal Act.
[73] Maintenance and Affiliation Amendment Act 2010, s 10(c), inserting s 32(5A) in the Principal Act.
[74] Section 56A.

The amendments also provide for arrears of maintenance to be regarded as a judgment debt for the purposes of s 6 of the Judgment Summonses Act 1965.[75] This means that the court may imprison a defaulting party for up to 6 months.[76] A new s 30A allows parties to vary a maintenance order by a written agreement permitting one party to leave Samoa. Presumably this agreement does not have to be registered with the court in order to be recognised as binding, as registration of consent orders results in their being deemed to be court orders, in which case recognition is not an issue.

(d) Changes to the law on custody

The 2010 Act allows the District Court to make a custody order as principal relief, whereas formerly it was only allowed as an ancillary order in maintenance proceedings.[77] The new s 12A states explicitly that the court may make a custody order. The new section also empowers the Registrar to make an interim custody order of up to 7 days with respect to a child under 16.[78] Prior to this amendment, the practice of the Ministry of Justice and Courts Administration was to return children to the mother's custody in pending proceedings only if they were being breastfed. The amendment does not specify the grounds on which a Registrar may make an interim order. This makes an interim custody order issued by the Registrar hard to challenge, leaving the person from whom the child is taken in a difficult position.

(e) Procedural changes

Under the amendments, the Registrar is empowered to set a hearing date and to grant an adjournment. As mentioned above, these changes were made as part of the broader reform of court processes designed to reduce the backlog of cases. The amending Act also empowers the court to require the parties to the proceeding to undergo mediation.[79]

V FURTHER COMMENTARY

(a) Empirical data

At present, the legislation discussed above is only being used by a small sector of Samoan society. Of the 16 cases decided prior to the reforms, being the only decisions publically available, 87% of applications for maintenance, custody and or property division were from parties living a more Western lifestyle. These parties were part of nuclear families, living on freehold land in a matrimonial home built by one or both parties. The parties were either

---

[75] Section 33(3).
[76] Judgment Summonses Act 1965, s 6.
[77] Section 12A.
[78] Section 12A(3) and (4).
[79] Section 46A.

employed in the commercial sector or engaged in business, and consequently in receipt of salaries or business income. In such circumstances, ascertaining 'financial resources', as required by the legislation, is relatively easy. Incomes and expenditure can be stated in monetary terms and real and personal property is ascertainable and alienable.

(b)   Relevance to customary setting

The empirical evidence discussed above gives rise to the question of whether the statute law is relevant to the majority of the population.[80] Most people live in a communal setting on customary land. The inapplicability of the laws to the majority of the Samoan population is illustrated by two cases: *Soavele v Lilii*[81] and *Maintenance Officer v Fuimaono.*[82] In both these cases, the parties lived in remote rural villages in Savaii and Upolu with their extended families. They were not business people and, except for one party, they were not represented by qualified lawyers, but by maintenance officers from the Ministry of Justice and Courts Administration.

In *Soavele v Lilii*,[83] the applicant was applying for a maintenance order against her husband. In order to qualify for an order under s 16 of the Maintenance and Affiliation Act 1967 she had to prove that she was a 'destitute person'. This is defined in the Act as 'any person unable, whether permanently or temporarily, to support himself or herself by his or her own means of labour'.[84] The only evidence before the court was that the 'respondent was looking after her mother's shop which sometimes made a profit of $30 but sometimes made no profit when there [were] too many faalavelave' (family activities incurring costs). Although it was unclear whether or not the respondent was paid wages for looking after her mother's shop, the court ruled that the respondent wife did not satisfy the definition of 'destitute person'. There was no evidence before the court that the applicant was able to support herself 'by her own means of labour'.

---

[80]   Some 140,000 live in the rural regions, outside of the urban area, on the bigger island of Savaii. The Total Preliminary Population Count 2011 for Samoa by regions showed that some 37,708 of the total population of 180,741 resided in urban Apia region: Samoa Bureau Statistics *2011 Census of Population and Housing* (2011) www.sbs.gov.ws/Portals/138/PDF/census%20survey/ Census%202011/Preliminary%20Count.pdf (accessed June 2012). Most of the freehold land, which accounts for 8% of the total land area, is located in that urban region: Land Equity International and the Ministry of Natural Resources, Environment and Meteorology (MNREM) *Customary Land Tenure Review* (2006) www.mnre.gov.ws/projects/siam-2/ documents/C5/Customary%20LandTenure%20Review%20(Jan%2006).pdf   (accessed   June 2012).

[81]   (Unreported, Supreme Court of Samoa, Sapolu CJ,11 March 1993), available via www.paclii.org at [1993] WSSC 22.

[82]   (Unreported, District Court Samoa, Nelson J, 23 August 2003), available via www.paclii.org at [2003] WSDC 3.

[83]   (Unreported, Supreme Court of Samoa, Sapolu CJ,11 March 1993), available via www.paclii.org at [1993] WSSC 22.

[84]   Section 2.

On whether the respondent was in a position to maintain the applicant, the court was unsure how this could be measured. The respondent was a carpenter and builder by trade, but did not earn a regular income, as the call for his work was irregular. There was also evidence that the appellant was running a plantation,[85] although not as a formal business. Sapolu CJ acknowledged that there was no adequate means of ascertaining profits from such a plantation, particularly as food crops are seasonal.

The second case, *Maintenance Officer v Fuimaono*,[86] was a claim for custody and maintenance. With respect to maintenance, again plantation proceeds were an issue. The court noted that the respondent looked after the family plantation for which he did not receive any set remuneration. The parties were represented by maintenance officers rather than qualified lawyers. The officers lacked knowledge of court procedures and substantive laws relevant to the maintenance proceedings. The court found this unhelpful in trying to resolve the issues according to law.

On the other hand, there have been a number of cases where the courts have found inventive ways of applying state law in a way which takes account of the traditional setting. Whilst there are no reported cases on point, the court has taken account of the fact that every Samoan person has land to work on through their parents, including in-laws, grandparents and the extended family. The fact that the new law replaces the very general provision allowing the court to make a maintenance order 'for such sum as [it] thinks reasonable in the circumstances',[87] with a list of more specific orders[88] might be regarded as preventing the court from making such orders. However, in addition to the specific orders permitted by the amendment, para (f) of the new s 18A permits the court any other order that it considers appropriate. Accordingly, there is no reason why the current practice of making orders more appropriate to those living a subsistence lifestyle should not continue.

VI SUGGESTIONS FOR REFORM

(a) Introduction

Whilst the 2010 amendments have introduced a number of welcome changes they do not take account of Samoan customary law or culture. From a traditional perspective, therefore, there is a need to 'Samoanise' the law, taking into account the cultural setting of family matters prevailing in most cases. For the majority of the population, customary land, which forms about 80% of

---

[85]   In Samoa, the word 'plantation' ('maumaga' in Samoan) usually refers to a place where food is grown for the family, although it can mean a plantation run as a business.

[86]   (Unreported, District Court Samoa, Nelson J, 23 August 2003), available via www.paclii.org at [2003] WSDC 3.

[87]   Section 18.

[88]   Section 18A.

land in Samoa and is inalienable,[89] is a family's most valuable asset. Accordingly, these provisions, based on overseas models of property division,[90] are only suitable to apply in the, mostly urban, areas where land has been alienated and individually registered. This assertion is backed up by the relative dearth of case-law on the legislative provisions. Unless account is taken of traditional law and applicable culture, particularly in rural areas, the law in Samoa will continue to be unhelpful to the majority of the population.

Further, even from a state perspective, the amendments have not resulted in a streamlined regime. Suggestions for reforms which might be given consideration are discussed in the following sections.

(b) A family division

As mentioned above, matrimonial and family disputes are dealt with in the District Court and the Supreme Court, with an appeal to the Court of Appeal in some cases. This results in some overlap and unnecessary duplication of administrative work, including registration of Supreme Court and District Court orders and agreements in the registries of both the District and the Supreme Court. Conferring exclusive first instance jurisdiction in family law matters on one forum would avoid the confusions that result from this. Given the size of Samoa's population and its resources, a dedicated family court is perhaps an unrealistic proposition. However, a family division of the Supreme Court, with a separate registry to deal with all family matters might be a viable solution. The delegation of further matters to the Registrar might also be considered. If the Registrar was a lawyer, well trained in family law, this could go beyond the procedural jurisdiction provided for in the 2010 amending legislation and extend to hearing matters currently within the jurisdiction of the District Court. This would be in accord with many other small Pacific jurisdictions where legally qualified Registrars are permitted to deal with interlocutory hearings and make some final orders.[91]

Reform is also necessary at the support level. A family law database, with records of registered agreements, court orders and decisions, and pending proceedings, would be helpful. Further, the Maintenance and Affiliation Division of the Ministry of Justice and Courts Administration is the only family related legal service available to the public. It does not currently have any legal officers, but ideally it would include a qualified lawyer to give legal advice and assistance to parties unable to afford private legal representation in maintenance and custody cases. This would also assist the court and avoid the type of frustrations which occurred in *Maintenance Officer v Fuimaono*,[92] discussed above. Where maintenance and custody were in issue, this division

---

[89]   Constitution of Samoa 1962, art 102.
[90]   See in particular the Family Proceedings Act 1980.
[91]   See eg powers of the Registrar under the Solomon Islands Courts (Civil Procedure) Rules 2007, chs 17.45 and 19.
[92]   (Unreported, District Court Samoa, Nelson J, 23 August 2003), available via www.paclii.org at [2003] WSDC 3.

might be tasked with the preparation of reports on existing arrangements taking into account culture and local realities, to assist the court with decision making. This would result in a more practical application of the courts powers under the Maintenance and Affiliation Act.

(c) Terminology and concepts

The language of the legislation is also in need of attention. In addition to the archaic term 'alimony', referred to above, some of the terminology does not resonate locally. For example, the concept of 'destitute person' in the Maintenance and Affiliation Act does not fit in with a society founded on a communal philosophy and values. Interestingly, the sign on the door of the office used by the Maintenance and Affiliation Division of the Ministry of Justice and Courts Administration says 'Ofisa o Tausiga o Tina ma Fan', which literally translated means 'Maintenance of Mothers and Children'. There is no mention of the 'destitute person' because no such applications are being instituted. Rural Samoans refer to it only as 'Ofisa o Tausiga o Tina ma Fanau' and it is commonly regarded by men as being biased against them and a body to be held in fear. This is a case where the terminology seems to have had a tangible effect on local attitudes to the office.

(d) Determination of needs and means

As mentioned in the discussion of the new law, the court is now required to look at the financial resources of parties, including income, earning capacity, assets and property, to determine what is a reasonable amount of maintenance.[93] As illustrated in the two cases discussed above, this may be problematic for the majority of Samoans, who do not have a regular income or individually owned assets. In 2008, a household income and expenditure survey carried out in Samoa reported that only 27% of people aged 15 and over were formally employed.[94] This leaves 73% of the population in a position where there is unlikely to be documentary evidence of the matters required to be proved under the legislation.

Under s 18(1A)(d), the court is also required to take account of the defendant's commitments to support other people whom he or she has a duty to maintain. On a liberal interpretation, in the context of Samoa, this includes customary obligations to the extended family, the broader community and the church. This may not have been the intention of the amendment, and this provision requires clarification.

---

[93] Section 18(1A).
[94] Household Income and Expenditure Survey Tabulation Report of the Samoan Statistics Bureau 2008, 17.

(e)   More culturally appropriate orders

As discussed above, the new law replaces the very general provision allowing the court to make a maintenance order 'for such sum as [it] thinks reasonable in the circumstances',[95] with a list of more specific orders.[96] Whilst the new s 18A(f) permits the court to make any other order that it considers appropriate, and therefore leaves room for the court to continue the current practice of making orders appropriate to the Samoan lifestyle, such as planting and fishing, the specific orders set out in the amendment are all aimed at the formal sector. Given that the vast majority of the population will not find these specific orders useful, it would be more appropriate to specifically outline more locally relevant orders.

VII   CONCLUSION

The 2010 amendments to family law in Samoa introduced a number of important changes. In particular, Samoa became the second small Pacific island nation to have a no-fault system of divorce. The amendments also empowered the courts to alter property rights, a reform which means that it is no longer necessary for the courts to resort to elaborate devices to divide real property on the breakdown of a marriage. The amendments to the law on maintenance lay down specific guidelines for awards and give new powers to the District Court to make custody orders, whether or not it also awards maintenance. The courts may also order the parties to go through a mediation process. Further, as part of a general reform of the court process designed to reduce a backlog of cases awaiting hearing, the amending Act empowers the Registrar to carry out some of the procedural functions of the Supreme and District Courts.[97] Amendments designed to accommodate new domestic violence legislation, which has yet to be enacted, were also introduced.

The Divorce and Matrimonial Causes Amendment Act 2010 and the Maintenance and Affiliation Amendment Act 2010 have made some worthwhile changes which have yet to be tested in the courts. In the meantime, there is clearly room for further, more culturally appropriate, changes. These include not just changes in terminology, but also substantive changes, such as introduction of a Family Law Division, more appropriate provisions regarding proof of needs and means, and a more resonant choice of orders. Finding the right path in a legally plural system is no easy task, but a goal that is well worth pursuing.

---

[95]   Section 18.
[96]   Section 18A.
[97]   Eg Supreme Court (Civil Procedure) Amendment Rules 2009 which are yet to be enacted.

Serbia

CHALLENGES OF THE MODERN FAMILY – DRAFT CIVIL CODE OF SERBIA RELATING TO FAMILY LAW RELATIONS

Olga Cvejić Jančić*

Résumé

Ce chapitre traite des innovations en droit de la famille, introduites par le Projet de Code civil serbe. Ce projet modifie les conditions de reconnaissance de la cohabitation hétérosexuelle dans la mesure où le mariage et la parenté biologique empêchent désormais ce type de cohabitation de produire des effets juridiques. Concernant la cohabitation des couples de même sexe, le projet prévoit que cette question sera réglée par une loi spéciale. Une autre disposition nouvelle traite de la maternité de substitution; celle-ci sera autorisée sous réserve qu'il n'existe pas d'autre moyen de devenir parent, autrement dit: (a) en cas d'impossibilité médicale de procéder à une procréation naturelle ou assistée; ou (b) en présence de maladies génétiquement transmissibles. Le projet prévoit ensuite que les châtiments corporels envers les enfants sont prohibés. La Commission pour la rédaction d'un Code civil considère effectivement que la violence doit être exclue des relations familiales, car les parents disposent d'autres mesures éducatives. Il est également prévu qu'un enfant qui a atteint l'âge de 15 ans puisse donner son consentement à un acte médical. Il ne peut en revanche refuser seul, le consentement d'une autorité de tutelle étant alors nécessaire. Parmi les autres innovations les plus importantes figure la création d'un Fonds de pension alimentaire pour le paiement des pensions qu'un parent débiteur n'acquitterait pas. D'autres innovations sont remarquables, comme l'introduction de l'adoption simple, la modification du régime matrimonial, ainsi qu'une réglementation plus détaillée du contrat de mariage.

I INTRODUCTORY REMARKS

The government-appointed Commission for the Drafting of a Civil Code of Serbia ('the Commission') has so far published four volumes. The first volume is dedicated to the open questions that the Commission considered paramount

---

*   Professor, University Singidunum Belgrade, Faculty of Legal and Political Studies – Novi Sad, Department of Private Law, Narodnog fronta 53, 21000 Novi Sad; e-mail: olgacvejic@gmail. com web: www.fepps.edu.rs.
    A similar paper was presented at the 24th Annual International Symposium 'Kopaonik School of Natural Law' in December 2011 and published in the Serbian language in the Special Issue of *Pravni Život* [Legal Life], No 9/2011, 917–930.

to discuss before the actual preparation of the Draft Civil Code (Draft). The second volume encompasses the law of obligations, the third one contains provisions on family law and the fourth one has provisions regulating inheritance law. The fifth book will include property law and the general provisions.

Serbia had a Civil Code in force from its enactment on 24 March 1844 until the end of the Second World War, when the post-war communist revolutionary forces invalidated the entire pre-war legal system. This was effected by means of the Act on the Invalidity of the Legal Regulations Issued Before April 6, 1941 and During Enemy Occupation.[1] However, as life continued after the war and people entered into civil law relations, difficulties of resolving disputes quickly surfaced. The judges needed a legal basis for resolving these disputes. The solution was found as follows: a judgment would be based on the pre-war legal rules without making an explicit reference to the invalidated Civil Code. In the period spanning the end of the Second World War and the present day, Serbia did not have a Civil Code, but merely separate statutes that regulated different fields of law.

II   THE MOST SIGNIFICANT INNOVATIONS

The third volume of the Draft Civil Code[2] encompasses family law relations and it is mostly based on the currently applicable Family Act, which was enacted in 2005. The Family Act served as a base for the codification project, since it already incorporates the most important legal solutions contained in European and international instruments on family law relations. Hence, the third volume of the Draft includes the innovations that seek to improve the current law.

First of all, the Draft has redefined cohabitation in order to protect the vulnerable partner in this relationship, such as the underage extramarital partner, the extramarital partner who is not mentally competent and the ward. The Family Act defines cohabitation as a more permanent[3] community of life between a man and a woman (cohabiting partners or extramarital partners), between whom there are no marriage impediments[4] and who have the same rights and obligations as do spouses under the conditions laid down by the Family Act. This means that cohabitation will not produce any legal consequences that the Family Act provides in the case of spouses, if between extramarital partners there are marital impediments that would preclude them

---

[1]   The Act on the Invalidity of the Legal Regulations Issued Before April 6, 1941 and During Enemy Occupation was published in the *Official Gazette of the Federal People's Republic of Yugoslavia* Nos 86/46, 105/46 and 96/47.

[2]   The third volume was published in June 2011 by the General Secretariat of the government of the Republic of Serbia.

[3]   The Family Act does not specify a time period that should elapse for cohabitation to be considered 'more permanent'.

[4]   Article 4(1) of the Family Act.

from concluding a valid marriage. These impediments are: an existing marriage; blood, in-law and adoptive kinship; minority; incapability for reasoning; lack of will (coercion, threat, error); and guardianship (marriage between guardian and ward). Yet if marriage is concluded with an underage person without the permission of the competent court, with a person incapable of reasoning or between guardian and ward, or despite the existence of other marital impediments, such a marriage will produce the same effects as a valid marriage not only for its duration but also in the event of its termination. It is important to underline, however, that the marriage would then be either voidable (due to the spouse's minority, incapacity to reason that has not terminated during marriage[5] and flaws of will) or null and void (due to all other impediments). This will not happen with cohabiting partners. If the conditions for the so-called 'legal cohabitation' are not met, no family law effects will be produced and this will especially affect the vulnerable cohabiting partners, such as the minor partner, partner incapable of reasoning and the ward. In order to protect their rights, since there are many possibilities to influence them to enter into cohabitation, and they might not even be completely aware of what cohabitation indeed means, the Draft prescribes only existing marriage and blood kinship as obstacles for 'legal cohabitation' which is to say that other marital obstacles will not prevent the consequences which family law provides for 'legal cohabitation' from arising.[6]

The consequences recognised for cohabiting partners in a 'legal cohabitation' are the right to common property and mutual maintenance as well as the right to conclude a '(pre)nuptial contract', ie a contract by which they regulate mutual property rights and obligations during or after the cessation of cohabitation (property contract).

The Commission for the Draft Civil Code is still deliberating on whether cohabitation should be registered or whether it is better for it to remain a factual community without any formalities, which is currently the case under the Family Act. To wit, the registration of cohabitation would facilitate proving its existence, but it is not certain how this would be received among cohabiting partners. It is difficult to assess whether they would be ready and willing to register their community or whether by requiring such registration we would create legal uncertainty by introducing two types of cohabitation: a factual one and a registered one.

The Draft Code does not regulate relations between same-sex partners. Instead, it provides that the life community between persons of the same sex will be regulated by a separate statute.[7] As a member of the Council of Europe, Serbia is obliged to respect the human rights guaranteed by the 1950 Convention for the Protection of Human Rights and Fundamental Freedoms as well as the

---

[5]   If incapacity to reason which had existed at the time of celebration of marriage still exists, such a marriage is null and void. When incapacity to reason no longer exists (the unhealthy spouse heals) a marriage is no longer null and void but voidable.

[6]   Article 4(1) of the Draft Civil Code.

[7]   Article 4(3) of the Draft Civil Code.

decisions and judgments of the European Court of Human Rights (ECtHR), which is set up in order 'to ensure the observance of the engagements undertaken by the High Contracting Parties in the Convention and the Protocols thereto'.[8] The case-law of the ECtHR on the legal status of homosexuals is very clear: treating homosexuals differently from heterosexuals is a breach of the prohibition of discrimination enshrined in art 14 of the Convention and of the right to respect for private and family life enshrined in art 8 thereof.[9]

The Draft furthermore contains a definition of guardianship as a form of protection of minors without parental care, then of adult persons deprived of legal capacity and of persons who for other reasons are incapable of protecting their rights and interests (art 12 of the Draft). Guardianship is not defined in the currently applicable law. The Code emphasises that guardianship shall be based on the respect for human rights, fundamental freedoms and the dignity of the person under guardianship (the ward). This is particularly important since persons under guardianship are not always treated appropriately and because of that the Commission attempted to improve their legal position by amending the provisions of the Draft concerning guardianship. For example, art 153 of the Draft lays down that the ward who has attained the age of 10 and who is capable for reasoning has the right to suggest that some person should or should not be appointed his or her guardian. The ward's proposal must be taken into account as much as possible and if it is in his or her best interest (art 153(2)). The guardianship authority is in charge of explaining its decision if the ward's proposal has not been accepted (art 153(3)). In addition,

---

[8]	Article 19 of the Convention for the Protection of Human Rights and Fundamental Freedoms.
[9]	Among many other examples, this view is expressed for example in *Salgueiro da Silva Mouta v Portugal* (App no 33290/96), where the ECtHR in para 28 states: 'The Court is accordingly forced to conclude that there was a difference of treatment between the applicant and M.'s mother which was based on the applicant's sexual orientation, a concept which is undoubtedly covered by Article 14 of the Convention.' In para 29, it is further decided that 'in accordance with the case law of the Convention institutions, a difference of treatment is discriminatory within the meaning of Article 14 if it has no objective and reasonable justification, that is if it does not pursue a legitimate aim or if there is not a reasonable relationship of proportionity between the means employed and the aim sought to be realized'. Similar discrimination based on sexual orientation has been detected also in *Karner v Austria* (App no 40016/98). The ECtHR's decision in paras 38–40 reads: 'In the present case, after Mr W.'s death, the applicant sought to avail himself of the right under section 14(3) of the Rent Act, which he asserted entitled him as a surviving partner to succeed to the tenancy. The court of first instance dismissed an action by the landlord for termination of the tenancy and the Vienna Regional Court dismissed the appeal. It found that the provision in issue protected persons who had been living together for a long time without being married against sudden homelessness and applied to homosexuals as well as to heterosexuals. The Supreme Court, which ultimately granted the landlord's action for termination of the tenancy, did not argue that there were important reasons for restricting the right to succeed to a tenancy to heterosexual couples. It stated instead that it had not been the intention of the legislature when enacting section 14(3) of the Rent Act in 1974 to include protection for couples of the same sex. The Government now submit that the aim of the provision in issue was the protection of the traditional family unit. The Court can accept that protection of the family in the traditional sense is, in principle, a weighty and legitimate reason which might justify a difference in treatment.' Similar is also the case *Lustig-Prean and Beckett v UK* (App nos 31417/96 and 32377/96).

in the part of the Draft that relates to the obligation of the guardian to take care of the personality of the ward, it is provided that the guardian shall take all necessary measures in order to include the ward in daily life and leisure activities in accordance with his or her health status, affections, preferences, desires and abilities (art 162(3)). The guardian should not be passive and uninterested in the progress of the ward regarding his or her health, recovery, education, wishes, talents and personal development in general.

Another very important provision is the one that imposes an obligation on the guardian to visit the person under guardianship once a month (if they do not live together, which itself is not a requirement) in order to have direct insight and information about the conditions in which the person under guardianship lives. This provides better protection of the interests of the ward, because it is not uncommon in practice that the guardian does not visit the ward at all or does that very rarely, which deprives the ward of the opportunity to talk about the conditions in which he or she lives and to complain, if need be, about the actions of the persons employed in the institutions in charge of taking care of wards (art 162(4)).

Having in mind the basic provision of the Draft that guardianship should be based on respect for human rights, fundamental freedoms and dignity of persons under guardianship, art 163 provides for the duty of the guardian, before undertaking important measures relating to personal and property interests of wards, to obtain his or her opinion and consider his or her views and wishes, if the ward is older than 10 years and able to express them.

The improved legal position of the ward is reflected in many other provisions of the Draft. As an example, we can cite the provision under which the guardian shall notify the ward about the administration of his or her property, unless the ward is in such a condition that he or she cannot understand it (art 167). The aim of this provision is to keep the ward up to date with the legal activities that the guardian has undertaken with respect to the ward's property and to leave sufficient room for the ward to object to these activities where he or she disagrees with them. If the ward is not satisfied with the guardian's work and is capable of understanding, then the ward has the right to file a complaint against the guardian with the guardianship authority (art 375). Certainly, it goes without saying that the ward should have a legal interest in submitting such a complaint. Although the provision on the right of the ward to file a complaint against the guardian is not new in itself, a significant innovation is the obligation of the guardian to keep the ward up to date with the activities concerning the administration of his or her property, because without such a provision the ward would not know what is going on with the property and would therefore be unable to protect those property interests.

Thereupon, the Draft provides that the guardianship authority shall deliver the decision on placement under guardianship not only to the guardian but also to the ward, who, if capable of reasoning, is granted the right to appeal this decision before the ministry responsible for family protection (art 373(1) and

(5)). Under the same condition (ie that the ward is capable of reasoning), the ward may also appeal the decision on dismissal of the guardian before the ministry responsible for family protection (art 377(2)). The Commission has indeed striven to secure a more active legal position and thus better protection of the rights and interests of the ward who is capable of reasoning than is case under the current law.

All these improvements of the legal position of the ward are in fact the implementation of the UN Convention on the Rights of Persons with Disabilities,[10] art 1 of which reads:

> 'The purpose of the present Convention is to promote, protect and ensure the full and equal enjoyment of all human rights and fundamental freedoms by all persons with disabilities, and to promote respect for their inherent dignity. Persons with disabilities include those who have long-term physical, mental, intellectual or sensory impairments which in interaction with various barriers may hinder their full and effective participation in society on an equal basis with others.'

Although the Convention refers to persons with disabilities and gives a definition of such persons, the same rules apply to minor persons who remain without parental care and who are placed under guardianship due to their immaturity. Such minors are also vulnerable and need additional legal protection.

Yet another innovation envisaged by the Draft Civil Code refers to the right to family planning. Under the current Family Act this right is granted only to women,[11] whereas the Draft recognises this right in both parents. In other words, both the woman and man have the right to freely decide on the birth of a child (art 5). A man can also be the holder of certain family planning rights, such as the right to contraception or the right to sterilisation (under certain conditions). The only family planning right a man cannot realise is the right to decide on the artificial interruption of pregnancy, because this is an independent right of the woman. The right to (artificial) interruption of pregnancy is not regulated by the Family Act but by a separate statute – the Act on the Proceeding of the Interruption of Pregnancy in Health Institutions of 1995.[12]

The next innovation in the Draft Civil Code concerns the provision on the measures aimed at stimulating child birth (art 6). The Draft lays down the obligation of the state to stimulate the birth of children by financial, tax law, labour law, economic, social and other measures and activities. These measures should be regulated by a separate statute. The Draft further introduces the so-called 'demographic allowance'. The right to this allowance is given to each mother who has given birth to a third child. This right lasts until the child

---

[10]   The UN Convention on the Rights of Persons with Disabilities was adopted by UN General Assembly on 6 December 2006.
[11]   Women shall have the right to freely decide on birth.
[12]   This Act was published in the *Official Herald of the Republic of Serbia* nos 16/95 and 101/2005.

reaches majority. The amount of the allowance should be determined by the Ministry of Finance on a yearly basis in accordance with the financial capabilities of the state.

Including this provision the Commission was guided by the need to undertake concrete action to encourage procreation, but it has done so very cautiously by proposing an allowance only for the third child and not for more than three children. The intention was not to encourage women to leave their employment in order to rear and bring the children up and thus neglect their job and social promotion. Instead, the intention was to financially stimulate those families that would like to have a third child but hesitate to do so for lack of means to support a new family member. The appropriation of budgetary funds for the promotion of birth should be a top priority for the state, since the birth rate has been very low with the mortality rate exceeding it for years.[13]

The Draft furthermore clearly defines who should be deemed a child. This is also missing in the current Family Act, even though such a provision is crucial considering that the child enjoys special legal protection by means of the provision requiring that 'everyone is obliged to be guided by the best interest of the child in all matters relating to the child'.[14] To wit, the Draft defines that a child is every human being below the age of 18 (art 7(2) of the Draft), as this is regulated by the Convention on the Rights of the Child (CRC).

The innovation that has provoked a lot of comments and misunderstandings refers to the prohibition of physical punishment of children (art 7(7) of the Draft). The Family Act provides that parents may not subject their child to humiliating actions and punishments that insult the human dignity of the child. Instead, they are obliged to protect the child from such actions of other persons (art 69(2) of the Family Act). However, this provision does not explicitly prohibit physical punishment of the child. Yet it is entirely understandable to prohibit physical punishment of the child within the family since the CRC[15] provides that:[16]

> 'States Parties shall take all appropriate legislative, administrative, social and educational measures to protect the child from all forms of physical or mental violence, injury or abuse, neglect or negligent treatment, maltreatment or exploitation, including sexual abuse, while in the care of parent(s), legal guardian(s) or any other person who has the care of the child.'

Hence, each state party shall take all measures to protect the child from all forms of physical violence. The traditional (patriarchal) relationship towards the child, both in Serbia as well as worldwide, was for a long time based on the fact that the child is the object of parental authority and parental rights. The

---

[13]   In 1991 the population of Serbia was 7,548,987; in 2002 it was 7,479,437; in 2008 7,350,222; in 2009 7,320,807; and finally in 2010 7,291,463. Available at: http://webrzs.stat.gov.rs/WebSite/ Public/PageView.aspx?pKey=163 (accessed 1 March 2012).

[14]   This is envisaged in art 6 of the Family Act.

[15]   The Republic of Serbia has been a member of the said Convention since 12 March 2001.

[16]   This is governed by art 19(1) of the CRC.

Convention has changed this by turning the child into a holder of rights. The Committee on the Rights of the Child, as the supervisory body for the implementation of the Convention, has taken a clear stance that corporal punishment is not allowed.

The provision of the Draft that prohibits physical punishment of the child seeks to promote new standards of behaviour within the family, standards of behaviour without violence. First, the child should learn in his or her family that violence is unacceptable and that violence should not be exerted by the parents either among themselves or against their children. Second, children should neither perform violence towards other children and their mates nor accept or tolerate violence performed by someone else. The Draft promotes a new concept of mutual relations in the family – the concept of mutual respect – which does not entail that the child should obey a parent but that the parent should understand the child and bring him or her up properly, ie without violence, insults, humiliation and the like. We want children in their families not to receive any example of approval for performing acts of violence.

The phenomenon of bullying among children, school mates and even preschool children is not negligible[17] and the Commission's proposal takes another direction by resorting to other, non-violent educational measures and measures of disciplining children within the family. This in turn does not mean that the child should be spoiled and that every child's whim should be satisfied.

Parental authority over children can be neither built nor acquired by beating them or by exerting violence against them, but above all by giving a positive personal example, patience, understanding and greater commitment to the child and the child's needs. We are aware that the construction of such family relationships is a lengthy process that requires time and commitment and also that, despite the introduction of this provision in the Draft Code, further breaches of this provision and physical punishments of children will occur. However, this does not mean that we should not take a first step towards changing these unacceptable practices in the family. As mentioned in the English literature, 'a useful analogy could be made with speeding while driving. Clearly not all speeding is punished, and most people do break the speeding laws, yet the laws are still generally accepted'.[18]

The next improvement of the legal status of the child is envisaged in the provision that requires the exercise of parental rights to be in the best interest of the child (art 8 of the Draft). In this way the provision on the protection of the best interests of the child from the CRC has been extended, since it is focused on the extra familial care, ie on the protection of the best interests of the child 'in all actions concerning children whether undertaken by public or

---

[17]   The results of the research on violence among preschool children are presented in the Master's thesis of candidate Halas Izabela 'Vršnjačko nasilje na predškolskom uzrastu' [Violence among children of preschool age] which was defended at the University of Novi Sad in March 2011 (mentor Prof Dr Olga Cvejić Jančić).

[18]   J Herring *Family Law* (Pearson Education, 4th edn, 2009) 481.

private social welfare institutions, courts, administrative authorities, legislative bodies' and the like (art 3 of the CRC). However, the Model Family Law[19] goes further by providing that 'in all matters relating to parents and children, most attention should be given to the best interests of the child' (art 3(1)). Similar is what is prescribed in the 'Principles of European Family Law regarding Parental Responsibility',[20] which states that 'in all matters concerning parental responsibilities the best interest of the child should be the primary consideration' (art 3(3)), which means that the domain of the application of the principle of best interests of the child is not restricted only to extrafamilial processes and actions, but encompasses also those occurring within the family. Thus, the Draft strives to emphasise that the special status and welfare of the child in the family are the centre not only of social care and concern but primarily of the family.

Among other innovations envisaged by the Draft is the legal recognition of the religious form of marriage (art 24 of the Draft). Currently, the religious form of marriage is allowed but not legally recognised. The fiancées may celebrate a religious marriage before or after the civil marriage, but the celebration of the religious marriage only (ie without celebrating the civil marriage) does not produce any legal consequences.[21] The introduction of the religious form of marriage promotes the right of believers to celebrate marriage in their church or religious community without having to enter into civil marriage, which under current law is the only recognised form of marriage. There is, however, one legal obstacle for this amendment to be accepted because the Serbian Constitution provides that marriage shall be concluded before the competent state body (art 62(2)). The competent body is the Registrar. The Draft therefore suggests an amendment of the Constitution in order to meet the needs of believers to have their religiously celebrated marriage legally recognised.

If the Constitution were changed to allow the religious form of marriage, it would then suffice to conclude either of the two types of marriage, because the religious marriage would become a matter of free choice of the future spouses. In that case, the head of the church or religious community before whom the marriage was celebrated would be obliged to deliver to the Registrar, within a very short period of time (no longer than a week), the marital documents signed by the spouses, witnesses and the head of the church or religious community. In turn, the material conditions, particularly marital impediments for the validity of religious marriage as well as the rights and obligations of spouses, would be governed by civil and not canon law. The religious law would be relevant only for the form of marriage.

---

[19] I Schwenzer and M Dimsey *Model Family Code: From a Global Perspective* (Intersentia, 2006) 92.

[20] K Boele-Woelki et al *Principles of European Family Law regarding Parental Responsibilities* (Intersentia, 2007) 38.

[21] Until the amendment of the Criminal Code in 1994, the celebration of the religious marriage before the civil one was a criminal offence. As a consequence, the head of the religious community who allowed the celebration of such a marriage was held responsible and subjected to criminal prosecution.

An essential further innovation in the Draft Code is the regulation of surrogate motherhood. The 2009 Act on the Treatment of Infertility by Biomedical Assistance (Infertility Treatment Act)[22] does not permit gestation for another. However, this Act is inconsistent with the Constitution, which stipulates that everyone has the right to freely decide on procreation and that the state encourages parents to have children and assists them in this matter (art 63 of the Constitution). The Constitution does not foresee the possibility of restricting this right, but rather provides that 'human and minority rights guaranteed by the Constitution may be restricted by statute if the Constitution permits such restriction and for the purpose allowed by the Constitution, to the extent necessary to meet the constitutional purpose of restriction in a democratic society and without encroaching upon the substance of the relevant guaranteed right' (art 20). Any such restriction is not envisaged for the freedom to procreate. Besides, surrogate motherhood may be considered as a method of treatment of female infertility and it should therefore receive legal support, as in the event of male infertility. Prohibition of surrogate motherhood violates not only the constitutional freedom of procreation but also the constitutional principles of gender equality[23] and the prohibition of discrimination, which itself includes the prohibition of discrimination based on sex.[24] Thus, if it comes to treating male infertility, the Infertility Treatment Act allows the use of all known and available medical treatment methods, ie it regulates both homologous insemination (insemination by seed cells of husband or common law partner) and heterologous insemination (insemination by seed cells of another man, a donor) by either in vivo procedures (inserting sperm into a woman's body) or those performed in vitro (outside a woman's body by mixing sperm with an ovum in a test tube).[25] Hence, although scientific progress has enabled the treatment of all forms of female infertility depending on the cause of infertility, including surrogacy procedures, the current Serbian law does not allow it. Surrogate motherhood is thus not the only method of treatment of female infertility. If the cause of infertility is that a woman cannot produce an ovum but can carry a child and give birth, the Infertility Treatment Act permits insemination of a donated ovum, ie that of another woman – woman donor (art 40). The same is permitted if the use of a donated ovum or sperm is needed due to the fact that the other infertility treatment procedures have failed or when it is necessary to prevent transmission of a serious genetic disease to the child. Surrogate motherhood would therefore be the only way for a woman who can produce an ovum but cannot carry and give a birth to a child to become a

---

[22] The Act on the Treatment of Infertility by Biomedical Assistance is published in the *Official Herald of the Republic of Serbia* no 79/2009.

[23] The state shall guarantee the equality of women and men and develop an equal opportunities policy (art 15 of the Constitution).

[24] All *direct or indirect discrimination* based on any grounds, particularly on race, *sex*, national origin, social origin, birth, religion, political or other opinion, property status, culture, language, age, mental or physical disability shall be prohibited (art 21(3) of the Constitution, emphasis added).

[25] See more on surrogate motherhood in: O Cvejić Jančić *Gestation Pour Autrui: Surrogate Motherhood* Académie Internationale de Droit Comparé, Collection Colloques, Vol 14, Société de législation comparée (General Editor Françoise Monéger, Paris, 2011) 231–242.

genetic, biological mother with the help of other women who will carry and give birth to her child (full or gestational surrogacy).

Allowing surrogate motherhood achieves several important goals:

(a) it secures a more complete protection of the right to found a family, which is guaranteed both by the Serbian Constitution and by the Convention for the Protection of Human Rights and Fundamental Freedoms (art 12);

(b) it contributes to the alleviation of personal and family problems and traumas that shake many couples who cannot have children otherwise; and

(c) it saves significant costs for those couples who cannot find a solution to their problems in Serbia and who are, for that reason, forced to seek help in other countries with more flexible solutions to this issue.

The Draft Civil Code stipulates that surrogate motherhood (art 61) may be used only as a method of treatment of infertility and where for health reasons, such as to prevent the transmission of severe hereditary diseases on children, it is not recommended to conceive naturally or through other forms of bio-medically assisted conception. Further, it is required that surrogacy be performed with the reproductive cells of at least one of the future legal parents (intended parents). Agreement on surrogate motherhood may be concluded only between a woman who will carry and give birth to the child (surrogate mother) and the spouses or cohabiting partners who are entitled to infertility treatment (art 61 of the Draft). Exceptionally, the possibility is envisaged for a woman who lives alone (ie without a spouse or cohabiting partner) to conclude this contract if there are particularly justified reasons for it and if the competent court finds that such reasons exist. In this case, the fertilisation of the surrogate mother must be carried out with the fertilising cells of the intended mother and not of the woman who will carry and give birth to the child (art 63(2) and (3) of the Draft). The same opportunity should also be foreseen for a man who lives alone under the same conditions laid down for a woman who lives alone, which the Draft omitted to include.

As regards the surrogate mother, it is envisaged that this can be a woman who is not related to the intended parents by blood or adoptive kinship in a straight line indefinitely and to the fourth degree of collateral lines, or a woman who is not related to the intended parents by in-law kinship in the first degree of the straight line. However, an alternative is envisaged that in the event of full surrogacy, a contract may be concluded with the close relatives, which is also provided for in certain other countries.[26] Otherwise, surrogacy is allowed in

---

26 The flaw in this solution is, for example, that a close relative could be forced by the members of the family to accept, against her free will, to be a surrogate mother for other relatives (eg for her infertile sister). The advantage of this solution, on the other hand, is that one normally has more trust in a relative that she will comply with all the rules of healthy life during pregnancy, if the relative voluntarily agreed to a contract.

Greece, Israel, Russia, Ukraine, Georgia, Belgium, Britain, India, the Netherlands, Australia (in the states of Victoria and Queensland), in certain states of the United States and other countries.

Further, the part of the Draft Code relating to the rights of the child provides that a child cannot refuse consent to medical treatment without the approval of the guardianship authority, if, according to state of the art of medical science, the medical treatment is necessary in order to save life or prevent impairment of the child's health.

The current Family Act provides that a child who has attained the age of 15 and who is capable of reasoning may give medical consent independently but that does not say anything about refusal of consent. Despite this ambiguity, this provision can be interpreted as meaning that a child may not only give but also refuse consent independently. The Commission considered that the child should not be granted the right to refuse medical consent, since that could expose the child to the danger of death or impairment of his or her health. At the same time, it should be taken into account that a 15-year-old child may easily succumb to the influence of others in making decisions that can be very risky for life or health. The refusal of medical consent should therefore be approved by the guardianship authority.

Another innovation is the reintroduction of simple, breakable adoption. The Draft Code reinstated this legal institution because, besides full, unbreakable adoption, certain people might be interested to opt for simple adoption.[27] Moreover, it is in accordance with the revised 2008 Convention on Adoption of the Council of Europe, which permits other forms of adoption beyond the full, unbreakable adoption (art 11(4)).

A further vital innovation relates to the establishment of an alimony fund, which should serve to cover the payment of maintenance established by a final court decision in favour of the child, in the event that a parent debtor does not comply with his or her obligation.

The fund will take the burden of enforced collection of maintenance from the parent debtor, whereupon the fund will pursue the parent debtor for the remuneration of the amount paid, increased by 10–15% as compensation for enforced collection. Eligibility conditions for the payment of maintenance from the alimony fund would be that the debtor does not duly fulfil the child support obligation for a period of 3 consecutive months or does fulfil it but with interruptions that occur within a period of 6 months. The child-creditor of the maintenance must submit proof that enforcement remains without effect. If the

---

[27]   The commentary on art 11 (point 63) of the explanatory report to the European Convention on the Adoption of Children of 2008 reads: 'The revised Convention mainly deals with "full" adoption (which is an adoption that severs all ties with the family of origin) without preventing those States that have "simple" adoption (which is an adoption that does not sever the relationship with the family of origin so that the adopted child is not entirely integrated into his or her adoptive family) from continuing to use this form of adoption.'

Serbian Parliament accepts the provisions regarding the establishment of the alimony fund, this would represent a very significant help for the parent and child who live together but cannot realise the child maintenance from the other parent-debtor of maintenance. It is not so rare a phenomenon that, despite the existence of a final and enforceable court decision to that effect, the parent-debtor avoids his or her obligation and does not pay the contributions towards the child's maintenance. This way the entire burden of rearing and educating children falls on one parent, most often the mother, while the other parent remains free of any obligation towards their children. The establishment of the fund should bring about considerably better protection of children and family, since the fund would regularly pay child support and prosecute parent–debtors to recover the contributions paid.

Another of the many innovations of the Draft Civil Code relates to the property relations of spouses. The current law provides that the joint property of the spouses includes income from separate property that arises from work of either spouse or from their joint work. It also provides that income from separate property that does not arise from work falls under the separate property of the spouse who is the owner of such property. However, with the socio-economic changes it occurs more frequently than used to be the case that people acquire considerable separate property, so it may happen that one spouse brings into marriage significant separate property that allows him or her to lease it and collect rent. Such a spouse may therefore choose not to work as that spouse will have sufficient funds to sustain himself or herself. As a corollary, the common property will be formed only by the property acquired by the work of the spouse who is employed, while the other spouse will not only retain the income from separate property but will even participate in the division of the joint property arising from of work of the other spouse. To address this matter, the Draft provides (art 201) that the common property is formed not only by the assets acquired by work of the spouses during marriage but also by the assets of separate property, whether resulting from work or other activity, unless the spouses' (pre)nuptial contract stipulates otherwise. Since the conclusion of a (pre)nuptial contract is not widespread, the Commission considered that the legal regime of common property should be supplemented by this new provision, which would be a fairer way to protect the interests of both spouses.

In addition, the provisions regarding things intended for the child have also been changed. In this respect, the Family Act lays down that things intended for the child that are purchased from the spouses' common property shall be part of the exclusive property of the spouse who exercises parental rights without these things being calculated as part of his or her share in the common property. If the spouses have joint custody, then things intended for the child shall be a part of their common property. Since things intended for the child can be of substantial value – such as a piano, computer, motorbike and so on – the parent who independently exercises parental rights may freely dispose of these things, because they enter into that parent's exclusive property. Nobody is entitled to prevent him or her from selling them or from using them contrary to the interests of the child. It is obvious that this is not a good solution, because such a provision allows such a parent to dispose of things intended for the child thoughtlessly. The Draft therefore envisages that the things intended for the child shall only be assigned to the parent who exercises parental rights, whereas they remain the spouses' common property regardless of whether parental rights are exercised by one of them and whether the parents have joint custody. Thus, the spouse to whom the things intended for the child are assigned may not freely and independently dispose of these things, because any act of disposal of common property cannot be done without the consent of both parents who hold common property. This provision furnishes much better protection of the interests of the child and prevents the potentially unscrupulous parent from neglecting the child's interests and welfare.

In the part of the Draft devoted to the (pre)marital contract (arts 218–230), the innovation is that the judge is granted the right to refuse to certify (pre)nuptial contracts that do not protect the interests of both contractual parties. Just as under the current law, the Draft provides that the spouses can exclude the common property regime in their (pre)nuptial contract, but the Draft provides also that the judge shall warn both spouses that the unemployed spouse or the spouse who becomes unemployed during marriage will not be entitled to a share of the assets acquired during marriage, which would not happen under the common property regime. Bearing in mind the rather difficult economic situation, aggravated by the economic and financial crises that will not be easy to overcome, it is important that the judge warns the spouses of the effects of their contract, because the spouses or one of them might not know what their contract actually means and what can consequently happen in the event of dissolution of their marriage. This role of the judge is equally significant not only where one of the spouses is unemployed at the time of the commencement of the marriage but also where both spouses are indeed employed; first, because employment is quite an uncertain category and, second, because at the time of the commencement of marriage the fiancées usually do not think about divorcing or getting fired. It is, hence, essential that the judge warns them about the potential outcomes of their contract before certification.

The Draft offers several possible models of marital contract clauses that spouses may use, but prospective spouses may agree on their own clauses. Thus, (pre)nuptial contracts may encompass clauses on the spouses' shares in the common property, on the right of choice of things that are going to belong to each of them in the event of division of the common property, on deferred community, on the universal (general) community property, on the covering of the costs of the family household and the like.

III   CONCLUSION

The above-mentioned innovations represent some of the most significant changes to the Serbian Family Act. Other innovations include a more detailed regulation of property relations between members of the family community, which exists when spouses or cohabiting partners live in the family household together with their children and other blood, in-law or adoptive relatives, and when they work on a farm or do other activities together or otherwise earn income jointly. The Draft also amends the provisions on protection against domestic violence, providing that the family member who perpetrates domestic violence may be referred to a relevant institution for treatment of alcoholism, drug addiction or another addiction. The Draft also innovates with a provision that gives authority to the judge to hand down one or more provisional measures against the perpetrator of domestic violence with effect until the end of the court proceedings.

Slovenia

CRITICAL VIEWS ON THE PERFORMANCE OF FOSTER CARE IN SLOVENIA

Suzana Kraljić and Iva Gajšek[*]

Résumé

Les familles d'accueil représentent une solution subsidiaire de protection des enfants dont les parents ne peuvent ou ne veulent pas s'occuper. Par l'intermédiaire de ces agences, l'État a l'obligation de garantir la meilleure protection des enfants ainsi placés. Même si la Slovénie a une longue tradition d'accueil des enfants au sein de telles familles, ce n'est qu'en 2002 qu'une loi est venue encadrer ce secteur de la protection de l'enfance. Après dix années d'application, certains aspects de la loi méritent d'être revus. Dans l'article qui suit, les auteurs présentent une analyse critique des règles en matière d'accueil des enfants, ainsi qu'une réflexion à propos d'une éventuelle réforme.

I INTRODUCTION

Nelson Mandela said:[1]

> 'There can be no keener revelation of a society's soul than the way in which it treats its children.'

Children are one of the most vulnerable groups of each society, and therefore special care has to be dedicated and special protection offered to them, in order to provide for the realisation of their rights. In 1989, when the United Nations adopted the Convention on the Rights of the Child (CRC),[2] they were aware of their vulnerability. Article 9(1) provides that states parties shall ensure that a child shall not be separated from his or her parents against their will, except when competent authorities subject to judicial review determine, in accordance with applicable law and procedures, that such separation is necessary for the best interests of the child. The continuation of this is given in art 20 of the

---

[*] Suzana Kraljić, Assistant Professor, Faculty of Law, University of Maribor.
    Iva Gajšek, PhD Candidate, Faculty of Law, University of Maribor.
[1] www.nelsonmandelaonline.net (accessed 18 February 2012).
[2] Adopted and opened for signature, ratification and accession by General Assembly resolution 44/25 of 20 November 1989. Entry into force 2 September 1990. In Slovenia published in Uradni list RS-MP, no 9/1992.

CRC. A child temporarily or permanently deprived of his or her family environment, or in whose own best interests cannot be allowed to remain in that environment, shall be entitled to special protection and assistance provided by the state. States shall in accordance with their national laws ensure alternative care for such a child and foster care is, also in Slovenian law, one of such possibilities which should ensure the fulfilment of the child's best interests.

Foster care is an old institution that was used in the medieval era with the intention of guaranteeing alternative protection for children who are not taken care of by their parents. Today, foster care represents a form of social parenthood. In spite of the fact that today, in Slovenia at least, foster care is talked about in a very open way, there is still a stigmatisation of children placed in foster care. The traditional family based on blood relations is still put in the foreground. But, according to Slovenian regulations, since 2002 the Act expressively defines a foster family also as family. In 2002 the Act Concerning the Pursuit of Foster Care (ACPFC)[3] defined foster family as a family, where foster care is carried out and that is composed of the foster parent and all persons who live together with the foster carer (ACPFC, art 2(4)). Thus, the living community between the foster carer and the foster child enjoys the status of a family and by this a certain constitutional protection (Constitution of the Republic of Slovenia (CRS), art 53(3)).[4] Now, one step further was also made by the new Family Code (FC), giving a new definition of family and encompassing also the foster family.[5] An essential novelty introduced by FC is also the change of decision-making power. At present, according to the still valid regulation, the placement of a child in foster care and the nomination of the foster carer is within the power of the Centre for Social Work (CSW), while after the FC this power is transferred to the courts of justice that can provide better protection for the child's rights. Therefore, in what follows, the present regulation will be outlined, and at certain places, essential changes brought in by the new FC will be explained.

In spite of its long tradition in Slovenia and the number of children in foster care at the moment,[6] foster care calls for changes. Empirical research proves that it is a field demanding fundamental changes. Instead of formal placements and follow-ups, specialised professional knowledge on psychological processes, trauma theory, theory of affection, the child perspective, theories of violence

---

[3] Uradni list RS, nos 110/2002; 56/2006; 114/2006; 5/2007.

[4] Uradni list RS, nos 33I/1991; 42/1997, 66/2000, 24/2003, 69/2004, 69/2004, 69/2004, 68/2006.

[5] In art 2, the new Family Code (FC) defines the family as a living community of a child with one or both parents or another adult, if he or she takes care of the child and has certain obligations and rights towards the child according to this Act. For the benefit of the child, the family enjoys special protection of the state. The FC in this way gave a broader definition than the regulation up to now. The definition provides that a family can also be a living community of a child and an adult not being a parent or adopter. There is a condition that this living community is long-lasting and similar to a family community between parents and a child. A person living with the child must have certain rights and duties towards the child.

[6] In May 2012, 1097 children were in foster care (www.mddsz.gov.si/si/uveljavljanje_pravic/statistika/rejnistvo/ (accessed 21 June 2012)).

and systematic approaches to working with two or more families are needed.[7] Further, the regulation of conditions to be met by future foster parents is extraordinarily lacking in some fields, which consequently also influences the benefits to the child in foster care.

II   ESSENTIAL CHARACTERISTICS OF THE LEGAL REGULATION OF FOSTER CARE IN SLOVENIA

According to art 2 of ACPFC, foster care is a special form of protection and upbringing of a child placed in a foster family based on the law regulating family relations or any other law and meant for children who cannot live in their biological family for a certain period of time.[8] Foster care is designed to provide a stable, nurturing, non-institutional environment for the child while the parent or caretaker attempts to remedy the problem which precipitated the child's removal or, if parental rights have been terminated, until suitable adoptive parents are found.[9]

Based on the constitutional protection of the child, the state is obliged to look into the execution of parental rights and to protect the benefits of the child. This duty is especially increased in cases where the parents do not take care of their children and minors, or children and minors do not have parents or are without any proper family care.[10] So, these children enjoy special protection from the state (CRS, art 56(3)). And, foster care is one of the secondary forms of protection of the child who is not taken care of by the parents for any reason.

A child in foster care is a child with two families. It has the original family, where the child cannot live for the moment, where the child has contacts and where the parents still have partial care for the child, except if they were deprived of their parental rights. On the other hand, the child has a foster parent and a foster family, where the child lives for the moment and that

---

[7]   Darja Zaviršek 'Na otroka se ne smete preveč navezati!: od rejništva do posvojitve – tabu socialnega dela' in Vesna Leskošek and Borut Petrović Jesenovec (eds) *Od revščine in socialne izključenosti k enakosti, socialni pravičnosti in solidarnosti: zbornik povzetkov* (Ljubljana: Fakulteta za socialno delo, 2010) 110.

[8]   The authors are of the opinion that the legal term 'biological family' does not fit, as in the case of an adopted child, with foster care: we cannot speak of a 'biological family'. It would be more appropriate to use the expression 'original family', which will be used by the authors in continuation of this chapter.

[9]   Daniel Pollack and Gary L Popham '"Wrongful Death" of Children in Foster Care' (2009) 31 U La Verne L Rev 25, 32.

[10]   MFRA (art 157) determines the conditions regarding the child being in foster care. A child without his or her own family or a child who cannot live with his or her parents for various reasons, or a child, whose physical and mental development are threatened in the home living environment, can be sent into foster care. Disregarding this, the Centre for Social Work can also send to foster care a child in need for training in line with obligatory provisions, i e mainly children with handicaps in physical and mental development – Geč Korošec Miroslava and Kraljić Suzana, *Družinsko pravo*, III. spremenjena in dopolnjena izdaja (III. revised edn) (Maribor: Pravna fakulteta, 2000) 245.

enables the child to have a healthy growing up, upbringing, education, a harmonious personal development and the capacity of independent living and work (FC, art 235). Except as mentioned, a foster parent also has the duty to help the foster child in the maintenance of contacts with the original family.

In the foster relationship, an important role is also played by the CSW, which has the duty to choose a proper foster parent in each concrete case of foster care, and to choose a foster family that fits best with the needs of the child. Further, the CSW has to co-operate in the selection of proper candidates for foster care, as well as to monitor the proper fulfilment of foster care. The new FC also expressly determined that the CSW must strive to overcome the reasons why the child was placed into foster care (FC, art 239).

The ACPFC of 2002 determined the process of selecting foster parents, where it divides foster parents into two sorts, ie the 'usual' foster parent and the foster parent executing foster care as a profession. Next, the essential characteristics of the Slovenian legal regulation of foster care will be set out.

(a)   'Usual' foster parent

A person wishing to undertake foster care applies with proper proof at the local competent CSW, depending on the person's permanent residence (ACPFC, art 8). Then, the CSW establishes whether the candidate fulfils the prescribed conditions, and they are:

(a)   a permanent residence in the Republic of Slovenia;

(b)   completed professional or vocational education – in exceptional cases, this condition might be waived and foster care can be performed also by a person with a lower education, if this is for the benefit of the child. This condition is mainly waived in a case where the foster parent is a relative of the child, as the benefits to the child are in the foreground, and they show in the acquaintance with the foster parent and frequently also the personal affection to that person (eg a grandparent); and

(c)   full age (so-called *positive preconditions* – they have to be met) (ACPFC, art 5).

A person cannot be a foster parent:

(a)   if he or she is deprived of parental rights;

(b)   if he or she is living with a person deprived of parental rights;

(c)   if he or she is living with person without business capacity (these are so-called *negative preconditions* – these must answered in the negative) (ACPFC, art 6). The ACPFC does not demand a clean criminal record as a condition,[11] neither the foster parent nor the members of the foster family. One of the essential changes that should be strived for is the adoption of conditions on the side of the foster parent, that the foster parent must not have been punished for a crime from the group of crimes against marriage, family and children (chapter 21 of the Criminal Code RS (CC-1 RS)), crimes against sexual integrity (CC-1 RS, chapter 19) and crimes against life and body (CC-1 RS, chapter 15).[12]

After the verification of the conditions, CSW works out an assessment of the suitability of a candidate and his or her family. The selected candidates are then sent to training. After the training is successfully finished, the Ministry for Labour, Family and Social Matters (MLFSM) files permissions for the foster parents to undertake foster care and enters them into the register of filed permissions (ACPFC, art 13). The permission to undertake foster care ends if:

(a)   a foster parent declares the ending of the performance of foster care;

(b)   a foster parent does not start to undertake foster care within 3 years from the obtaining the permission; or

(c)   the foster parent dies.

The permission can also be taken from the foster parent if:

(a)   the CSW files a proposal for the deprivation of the permission because the foster parent performs the foster care contrary to the benefit of the child;

(b)   it shows that one of the negative preconditions for foster care happens; or

(c)   the foster parent does not undertake the obligatory prescribed additional training (ACPFC, art 16).

---

[11]   In the case of *Adams v Arizona* (916 P 2d 1156 (Arizona App 1995) sisters sued the Arizona child protection agency (DES) and its employees for sexual abuse they experienced from their adoptive father. The abuse started shortly after the sisters were placed in the foster family. Mr Crossman (foster and later adoptive father) had oral, anal and vaginal intercourse with them. After the sisters were removed, they sued alleging that the state was negligent in its investigation of Mr Crossman, because the DES did not learn that Crossman had been sexually abused as a child; did not contact Crossman's adult stepdaughter (they even had her name and address) who could have told them that during her teenage years she had been sexually abused by her stepfather – Lynn D Wardle 'Adult Sexuality, the Best Interests of Children, and Placement Liability of Foster Care and Adoption Agencies' (2004) 6 J L Fam Stud 59, 90.

[12]   The condition of a clean criminal record for the foster parent has to be given in Serbia (Marija Draškić *Porodično pravo i prava deteta* (Belgrade: Čigoja štampa, 2005) 324) and Greece (Penelope Agallopoulou 'The Institution of Foster Care for Minors in Greece' in Bill Atkin (ed) *International Survey of Family Law, 2010 Edition* (Jordan Publishing Limited, 2010) 154).

(b) 'Professional' foster parent

The foster parent may undertake foster care as a profession only, but, as well as the positive and negative pre-conditions already mentioned, he or she also has to meet following conditions:

(a)   he or she has to be entered into the foster care register;

(b)   he or she has to have a permission; and

(c)   he or she must not be employed, be an associate of a private company or institution in the Republic of Slovenia being at the same time also a directing staff member, undertake other activities as the person's only or main profession, based on which he or she is included in obligatory pension and invalidity insurance scheme according to provisions regulating pension and invalidity insurance (ACPFC, art 18).

A candidate has to apply to be a professional foster carer at the CSW that sends this application to be a professional foster carer to the MLFSW. Foster parents fulfilling the conditions are entered into the register of professional foster carers by MLFSW and granted a confirmation on entry.

Erasing from the register occurs if:

(a)   the foster parent no longer wishes to be a professional foster carer, from the last day when he or she performs foster care as a profession;

(b)   the foster parent gets employed, becomes an associate of a private company or institution in the Republic of Slovenia being a directing staff member, starts an activity based on which he or she is included in an obligatory pension and invalidity insurance scheme according to the provisions regulating pension and invalidity insurance, from the day before the beginning of employment or undertaking of the other activity; or

(c)   the foster parent does not meet the norms (ACPFC, art 21).[13]

---

[13]   Norms represent also one of the essential differences between both sorts of foster parents. A 'usual' foster parent may have a maximum of three foster children at the same time. Exceptionally, he or she may have a higher number of foster children, if it is about a placement of brothers and sisters or if the placement of a child with a foster parent is for special benefit for the child (ACPFC, art 23). A foster parent executing foster care as a profession must have three foster children at the same time. This norm may be lowered if a child has specific needs (e g a severely sick child, a child with disturbances in physical and mental development, abused, tortured, behaviourally or personally disturbed children) (ACPFC, art 24).

(c)   Decision on foster care and foster contract

Foster care may start in two ways, ie:

(a)   based on a decision by the CSW; or

(b)   based on a decision by the parents.

As a rule, the CSW sends a child into foster care only with the consent of the parents. Consent by the parents is not needed if the child was taken from the parents or if the parents were deprived of parental rights or contractual capacity, or their residence is not known (Marriage and Family Relations Act (MFRA), art 158).[14]

We can notice inadequacies in the existing legislation, as we cannot find any provision determining the cases and conditions relating to the consent of the parents giving a child into foster care. This is especially important in cases when the child was taken away from the parents, but they were not deprived of parental rights.

Neither MFRA nor ACPFC nor FC contains provisions expressly determining that the child has such a right. But, from art 12 of the CRC[15] and art 3 of the European Convention on the Exercise of Children's Rights[16] (ECECR)[17] we can derive that a capable child should have the possibility of expressing his or her views.

As foster care frequently lasts until the foster child reaches the age of 26, determined by the ACPFC as the absolute limitation period for the duration of foster care, the child's consent is needed, for the first and only time, after the age of 18 to determine the continuation of foster care (ACPFC, art 46). Foster care may be prolonged after the age of 18 if there are circumstances indicating that a prolongation of foster care is beneficial for the child. This is usually the case if the child is regularly attending school.

---

[14]   Uradni list SRS, no 15/1976; Uradni list RS, no 69/2004 (officially consolidated text).

[15]   Article 12 of the CRC: '1. States Parties shall assure to the child who is capable of forming his or her own views the right to express those views freely in all matters affecting the child, the views of the child being given due weight in accordance with the age and maturity of the child. 2. For this purpose, the child shall in particular be provided the opportunity to be heard in any judicial and administrative proceedings affecting the child, either directly, or through a representative or an appropriate body, in a manner consistent with the procedural rules of national law.'

[16]   Uradni list RS – MP, no 26/1999.

[17]   Article 3 of the ECECR (Right to be informed and to express his or her views in proceedings): '1. A child considered by internal law as having sufficient understanding, in the case of proceedings before a judicial authority affecting him or her, shall be granted, and shall be entitled to request, the following rights: a. to receive all relevant information; b. to be consulted and express his or her views; c. to be informed of the possible consequences of compliance with these views and the possible consequences of any decision.'

Foster care is established by a decision of the CSW and by agreement. The CSW proceeds according to the General Administrative Procedure Act (GAPA).[18] However, the administrative court decided in a conflict about a foster agreement that the conclusion of a foster agreement on the part of the CSW is not an administrative proceeding, but the regulation of a contractual relationship, and in cases of conflict, if the proceedings are not specially regulated within the ACPFC or standing orders, the general regulations on agreements according to the civil law apply. The plaintiff was sent to the court of justice having general jurisdiction. Even if it was an administrative proceeding, such a decision would be a violation of ECECR. The ECECR demands a decision of a judicial authority (ie the court) in decision making on the upbringing and protection of a child.[19] This was followed by the new FC that transferred jurisdiction to the courts of justice.

When the decision on the foster care for a child comes into force, the CSW concludes an agreement with the foster parent. The foster agreement is made only with the foster parent who actually does the caring, in spite of the fact that the foster child lives in the foster parent's family in a common household with other family members of the foster parent. The ACPFC determines in art 45 that foster agreements are written agreements and determines the range of care for a child in foster care, the rights and obligations of the parties to the agreement, the duration and the way of ending foster agreements. Furthermore, the concrete contents of a foster agreement are determined within the rules on conditions and procedures for the implementation of the Act concerning the pursuit of foster care (Rules of Foster Care).[20] Article 26 determines that in a foster agreement among other obligations and rights there are regulations also on fostering allowances including a maintenance allowance and payment for work, and for foster parents performing foster care as a profession, even on payment of contributions for social security. Parties to the agreement may conclude annexes to the foster agreement on changes of rights and obligations.

In a foster agreement the monthly fostering allowance is determined, including a maintenance allowance and payment for the work. The maintenance agreement is composed of material costs for the foster child and an amount of money for child support, defined as for the lowest income class for the first child, in accordance with special provisions regulating family incomes (this means the highest child support for the first child). The payment for material costs amount since 1 July 2011 to 272.74 EUR; the money amounting to child support is 114.85 EUR, and the maintenance allowance amount to a total of 387.59 EUR. Payment for work done by a foster parent amounts to 123.51 EUR. The maintenance allowance may be reduced or increased by 25% with regard to the child's needs, and in the same way payment of work might be increased by 25% or 50% due to the performance of foster care if the child

---

[18]   Uradni list RS, no 24/2006 (officially consolidated text).
[19]   Vida Berglez 'Rejniška pogodba ter razmerja in odnosi po sklenitvi pogodbe' (2007) 48 *Pravna praksa* 11, 12.
[20]   Uradni list RS, no 54/2003.

needs special care. Payments for the fostering allowance are guaranteed in the budget of the Republic of Slovenia and are not subject to the payment of income tax.

Table 1: Demonstration of fostering allowance for one foster child according to the norms for professional foster care

Fostering Allowance	*Amount in EUR*
Payment for material costs	272.74
Payment for child support	114.85
Maintenance allowance in total	387.59
Payment for foster parent's work	123.51
Fostering allowance in total	511.11

In spite of the undertaking of foster care, the child's original parents have a duty to maintain the child, manage the child's property and represent the child in property matters. A novelty here was brought in by the FC, determining that the court of justice can decide in cases of longer lasting placement of a child in foster care that the maintenance allowance, being the same or lower than the material costs, is transferred to the budget of the Republic of Slovenia. If maintenance is higher than these costs, the court of justice can decide that the difference is transferred to a special account for the child, opened by the child's guardian for this purpose (FC, art 188(3)).

A foster parent and child do not need to belong to the same religion. The CSW has to take care only that the wishes of the parents, the guardian and the child are respected. The foster agreement may also contain provisions on the religious upbringing of the child, that have to be respected by the foster parent accordingly.[21] An important role is played by the parents, if they still have parental rights. Parents have the right to request a religious matching placement for their children under the settlement. On the other hand, when parents have stated no religious preference, the CSW should put the child in the best available placement without regard to religion. Religion is also a field that deserves special attention in the training framework and in general, if the foster parent and child are members of different beliefs.

There is also the important question: how come parents, who are not capable, do not want or do not know how to take care of their child, are not deprived of the parental rights? What about parents who have one child in foster care, whilst they still take care of other children? As foster care is an individual relationship and since a foster agreement is made for every foster child individually, lack of correct treatment of one child cannot be applied automatically also for other children (eg a mother is physically and psychologically violent only against her first daughter conceived in an act of rape, while towards the other, she is an 'ideal mother'). As the basic purpose of

---

[21]   Geoffrey Shannon *Child Law* (Dublin: Thompson, 2005) 150.

foster care is the abolishing of the reasons leading to a placement in foster care, it is important that a child, if it is for the child's benefit, maintains contact with the parents. Therefore, among the important duties of the foster parent is the duty to enable contact by the foster child with the parents. A foster parent opposing this or even hindering contact may be forced to do so in accordance with the Enforcement and Securing of Civil Claims Act (ESCCA).[22]

A foster agreement ends if foster care ends, by erasing the foster parent from the register of filed permissions, by lapse of time if the foster agreement is made for a certain period, except if it is prolonged, by cancellation, and by death of the foster parent or child (ACPFC, art 47). Foster care ends when the reasons for the need for foster care end. These reasons mostly end by maturity, but also before that if the child is capable of independent living. Foster care may also end by adoption, if a child in foster care enters matrimony or if the child dies. Foster care can be ended by decision of the CSW in an administrative proceeding.

III TRAINING FOR THE PERFORMANCE OF FOSTER CARE

We have to divide training of candidates, who wish to do foster care, and training of foster parents. Foster parents often receive inadequate training and lack the support systems necessary to properly care for foster children, who are likely to experience unique developmental, behavioural and psychological problems due to previous abuse. State agencies fail to carefully screen and license foster parents and to sufficiently supervise them when children are placed in their homes.[23]

(a) Training of candidates wishing to perform foster care

Candidates wishing to perform foster care have to take part in obligatory training, the content, conductor and duration of which is determined by the minister (ACPFC, art 12). Only when this is successfully concluded can candidates obtain the permission to undertake foster care (Rules of Foster Care, art 41).

Training lasts between 10 and 12 hours and is performed by the Faculty of Social Work of the University of Ljubljana, in co-operation with the CSW. The training programme for foster care contains the following elements:

(a) the concept of foster care in social work; presentation of the foster care system and individual project groups; co-operation with the original family;

---

22   Uradni list RS, no 110/2006 (officially consolidated text).
23   Laura A Harper 'The State's Duty to Children in Foster Care – Bearing the Burden of Protecting Children' (2003) 51 Drake L Rev 793, 799.

(b)   chapters from developmental psychology; emotional needs of the child; emotional needs of the foster child; and

(c)   chapters from family psychology (Rules of Foster Care, art 43).

(b)   Training of foster parents

All foster parents having permission to do foster care have to take part in obligatory training once every 5 years, at least. After the training is finished, a foster parent obtains a confirmation of participation at the training (Rules of Foster Care, art 44). This training takes from 20 to 25 hours and contains lectures, workshops and group conversations on people's own experience. The training programme for foster parents is also performed by the Faculty of Social Work of University of Ljubljana in co-operation with the CSW (Rules of Foster Care, art 45). The training programme for foster parents contains the following elements:

(a)   the deepening of knowledge about a child and child development; chapters on special needs of a child; understanding of the special position of a foster child;

(b)   family psychology; family and upbringing; characteristics that have to be guaranteed in a family community in order for the child to have sufficiently good possibilities for development; foster family; co-operation between the foster family and the original family; and

(c)   education of foster parents as collaborators in social work aid projects; the concept of an individual project group; social work in a family and foster care system; new concepts in social work; meaning of groups for self-aid.

(c)   Criticism and proposals for improvement

In both cases of training, the necessity for changes has to be stressed. For example, lectures are the same for all candidates and foster parents, disregarding their education. Thus, 12 or 25 hours are sufficient for a butcher and a doctor of science. All listen to the same content and nobody ever asks whether the level is proper for all, and what, if somebody needs more hours. After the training, MLFSM files permission to undertake foster care, and then the foster parent obtains a foster child, usually with big traumas that cannot be handled by everybody.[24]

The main criticisms by authors on the training are:

---

[24]   Tina Recek 'Rejenec – otrok s težko prtljago' (18 May 2010) *Bonbon* 10, 12.

(a)   that an initial 12 hours training of candidates and a one-off 25 hours
       training of foster parents within 5 years obviously is too short. The range
       of both trainings needs to be widened;

(b)   that there is no express provision in any of the trainings that participants
       also get acquainted with the content of the law. That is, foster care is
       connected to many legal contents that should be expressly presented to the
       participants (eg the content of family law, social law, criminal law, etc);

(c)   that trainings have to be done only by foster parents, as the foster
       agreement is made with them. But, as already mentioned, a foster child, as
       a rule, is placed into a foster family. Especially in cases of children with
       special needs, it would be necessary to think of widening the training to
       adult family members (in the first instance to the partner of the foster
       parent);[25]

(d)   that different specialised training should be formed, as children with
       different needs are given into foster care (eg blind ones, physically,
       emotionally and sexually abused children, death of parents, etc). Each
       child, thus, is an individual and already due to this cannot be handled by a
       merely general training. Although all foster parents should attend the
       general training, specialised training is also needed, where certain sorts of
       problems that caused the placement of a child into a foster family should
       be emphasised; and

(e)   special attention during the education should also be paid to the
       preparation of foster parents taking siblings into foster care.[26]

IV   NORMS

The ACPFC determines that a foster family may have three children in their
care (ACPFC, art 23). But, in practice it is different, as 30% of children are
placed with a foster parent, who has more children in care than is determined
by ACPFC, which means that foster parents have more children in care than
allowed by the legislation. At the same time, there are foster parents without
any children in care. In May 2012 there were 770 foster parents with permission
to do foster care (691 women and 79 men) and 115 foster parents did not have

---

[25]   Austria demands that both parents deciding to undertake foster care participate in educational
        courses while in Slovenia it is sufficient that only the foster parent, ie one of the spouses, takes
        part, disregarding the fact that the child will live with both parents in foster care. Attendance at
        the education in Austria lasts, on average, 3 to 4 weeks – Gajšek Iva 'Primerjava pravne
        ureditve rejništva med Slovenijo in Avstrijo' (2011) 50(6) *Socialno delo letnik* 379–387.

[26]   In the USA there are individual agencies dealing with foster care, and they introduced special
        trainings and support for foster parents accepting brothers and sisters – see David J Herring
        'Foster Care Placement: Reducing the Risk of Sibling Incest' (2004) 37 U Mich J L Reform
        1145, 1166.

any children in foster care.[27] According to data from the Association MOČ in 2007 there were 53 foster carers with 4 or more foster children. These foster parents had 212 children out of 1214 in their foster care.[28]

We believe that, in families where there are more children than at the same time legally determined, foster parents, due to work overload, are not capable of intensively taking care of the needs of each child in foster care, but this care is what is urgently needed in the cases of children who experienced emotional and physical abuse or neglect.

As a rule (deviating from the norms) siblings should be placed in the same foster family. The common placement has many advantages, and they are:

(a)   siblings placed together are more emotionally stable and have fewer behavioural problems than children separated from siblings;

(b)   siblings placed together are more likely to stay in that first placement;

(c)   siblings benefit from reunification efforts that help them learn to function as a group and develop the same expectations about what family life is; and

(d)   consistent visitation is the single most important factor in getting children back with their biological families and visitation is easier if all the children are in one location.[29]

When this is not possible, it is the task of the CSW and also of the foster parents with siblings from the same family to enhance and enable contacts between the siblings.

V   AGE STRUCTURE OF FOSTER PARENTS

Before the adoption of the ACPFC, the MFRA determined an age limit for foster parents, ie 60 years. Today, there is no such age limit any more, and one of the reasons is 'professional' foster care, where the 'professional' foster parent's years of service are running and their contributions for social security, among which also belongs pension insurance, are paid for from the state budget. In Slovenia a woman retires at the age of 63, and a man at 65, if they have at least 15 years of service. Thus, a preservation of the age limit would be contrary to the legislation on retirement.

---

[27]   www.mddsz.gov.si/si/uveljavljanje_pravic/statistika/rejnistvo/ (accessed 21 May 2012).

[28]   Iva Gajšek 'Primerjava pravne ureditve rejništva med Slovenijo in Avstrijo' (2011) 50(6) *Socialno delo letnik* 379–387.

[29]   David J Herring 'Foster Care Placement: Reducing the Risk of Sibling Incest' (2004) 37 U Mich J L Reform 1145, 1165.

Table 2: Age structure of foster parents

Age	Number of foster parents
Up to 30 years	8
30–35 years	34
35–40 years	62
40–45 years	93
45–50 years	135
50–55 years	137
55–60 years	141
60–65 years	79
over 65 years	106

Most foster parents are within the age of 55–60 years, followed by foster parents from 50–55 years, after them those aged 45–50 years, and there are 106, who are older than 65 years. The smalllest category is foster parents aged up to 30 years, where there are only 8. We can conclude that mainly people over 45 years opt for foster care (75.2%).

VI   DURATION OF FOSTER CARE

The ACPFC has determined that foster care is just a short-term measure, and is for the time when the CSW tries to get rid of the reasons which caused a child to be placed into foster care. But, the position in practice is very different from the basic guideline of the ACPFC. According to data from the Directorate for families at the MLFSM, over the past few years foster care has lasted on average for 10.2 years. From 645 concluded foster cares since 2004, only 220 children returned to their original families. We can conclude that, of all children placed in foster families, one third returns to their original families. We ask ourselves what are the main reasons for such a situation? Maybe the reason is the low attention paid to overcoming the reasons why a child is separated from parents and is placed into foster care.

As mentioned, as a matter of fact, foster care is a long-term measure, in spite of the basic guideline of the ACPFC, ie the short-term measure of placement into foster care. Due to the long-term duration of foster care, problems appear mainly with small children being tied to two families. When a small child comes into a foster family and lives there for several years, the child totally gets used and affiliated to it. After living for many years with foster parents, they may later have to return to their original family, having lost any true contact or even not knowing them at all.

Following the ACPFC, foster care is a temporary solution, and it is necessary to keep that in practice. Because of this, on the one hand foster care should be limited in time, and on the other hand there should be a more intensive dealing with the reasons on the parents' side for the placement of a child into foster care. If dealing with the reasons does not run successfully within a certain time-limit, and also it is not possible to think, given the circumstances, that this could be achieved in the near future, the second stricter step should be taken. Here, adoption would be an ideal option, especially considering the fact that in Slovenia, in the last years there have been extraordinarily few adoptions (in 2007 in Slovenia there were only 14 adoptions).[30] By this, long-term foster care would be prevented, as the parents would be stimulated to strive for a short-term improvement of the reasons leading to the taking away of their child. Finally, by this the child would also be offered the possibility of integration into the adopters' family.

A problem with foster care is especially noted when the foster child changes families several times, because the child is not given the necessary stability. Joseph Goldstein, Anna Freud and Albert J Solnit thus developed the so-called 'psychological parent theory'. They argue that a child's healthy psychological development is contingent upon a stable and uninterrupted relationship with one caregiver – 'the psychological parent'.[31] The 'psychological parent' is not necessarily the biological parent, but it may be any person offering a secure and stable environment for the child's development – that means also the foster parent. And frequent change and movement of the foster child from one foster family to another does not offer or create a feeling of safety, belonging and stability. Therefore, one has to avoid too frequent shifts of foster parents or foster families, respectively. This could be avoided, for example, by a more intensive preparation in the framework of the obligatory starting training. Several candidates decide to do foster care based on the wish to help children, but we think that too few are aware of the meaning of taking over responsibility for another person's child and to face the child's needs (eg a child with Down Syndrome), problems and disappointments. The choice of a foster parent has to be adapted and directed to the needs of the foster child as much as possible. For each foster child, the best suitable foster parent should be found, as in this way it is possible to avoid eventual further changes of foster parents or families, respectively.

Further, long-term foster care may also be avoided by a more active effort in supporting the family or parent from whom the child is divided in the case of foster care. This means that in the case of the placement of a child into foster care, it is necessary to help the family to get rid of the reasons for the placement into foster care as soon as possible.

As stated, 1090 children are in foster care according to data from January 2012, and there were only 17 adoptions in 2007 (some of them were still one-sided, when the child was adopted by the partner of the parent). For the above-mentioned reasons, we notice an imbalance. According to the ACPFC, foster care should be a short-term measure, but this cannot be confirmed from

---

[30] www.stat.si/novica_prikazi.aspx?id=2343 (accessed 26 February 2012).
[31] Cheryl A DeMichele 'The Illinois Adoption Act: Should a Child's Length of Time in Foster Care Measure Parental Unfitness?' (1999) 30 Loy U Chi L J 727, 747.

the cited data. On the other hand, in the past years we have extraordinarily few adoptions, and in 2010, children in Slovenia were in foster care on average for 7.16 years.[32] If the parents are deprived of parental rights and the child is placed into foster care, the phenomenon of so-called 'legal orphans' may appear. This is a situation where the rights of parents are terminated, but the children are not waiting for adoption. They are in long-term foster care.[33] At the same time, there is the additional circumstance influencing long-term foster care, namely, the older the child, the harder it is to find an adopter for that child.

VII   FOSTER PARENT V CHILD'S PARENTS

A foster parent is required to deal with all important questions regarding the foster child's protection and upbringing (eg choice of kindergarten, medical actions, obtaining of documents, crossing of borders) in accordance with wishes of the parents or the guardian, respectively, and the CSW. Thus, the foster parent cannot raise a child according to his or her criteria, but only in accordance with the parents' and the CSW's. In practice, this represents a big problem, as the obtaining of the parents' consent is frequently almost impossible, as the parents of the foster child are not capable, do not want or cannot take care of their child who was placed into foster care due to this fact. In many cases, they also change their residence without informing the foster parent, who then try to establish their residence and obtain the consent.

Problems in the performance of foster care are also seen in the field of contacts of the foster child with parents, as there is no clear definition on how many contacts the foster child shall have with its parents and when. This matter is left to the discretion of the professionals at the individual CSW. Contact of the child with the parents is especially important in cases where the reasons leading to foster care can be removed. Frequently, contacts of the foster child with the parents are problematic when a child is given into the foster care of a relative. Here, personal hard feelings are frequently present, and the emotional involvement of all participants is higher than in cases where the child is given to a foster parent who did not know the child before. But, it is necessary to stress that, even in the latter cases, it happens that the foster child and the foster parent connect emotionally in a strong way, which creates problems in practice (eg especially in case of small children emotionally tied to the foster parent whom they take for their 'parent'. Frequently, foster children name their foster parents and members of their families 'mom', 'dad', 'sister').

If, in spite of the legal provisions that a foster parent has to enable and enhance contacts between the foster child and the parents (ACPFC, art 26), it happens that foster parents do not do this, that foster parent may be forced in line by the

---

[32]   Data on average duration of foster care are accessible at www.irssv.si (accessed 26 February 2012).
[33]   See also Cheryl A DeMichele 'The Illinois Adoption Act: Should a Child's Length of Time in Foster Care Measure Parental Unfitness?' (1999) 30 Loy U Chi L J 727, 756.

ESCCA (direct and indirect enforcement). The child might also be placed into another foster family, where the question of the child's benefit arises again. That is, the child has to again get used to a new foster parent and a new environment in such a case. Life for many youths in foster care is characterised by movement from placement to placement, disruption of schooling and the severing of ties with all that is familiar to the child, often including siblings and extended family.[34]

As a foster parent has the child at home and is also responsible for the child's safety and upbringing, it is necessary to think of a transfer of a higher authority in the field of decision making to the foster parent. The latter's status could be regulated in a similar way to guardianship, where, in the MFRA, it is determined that a guardian carries out his or her function independently, but for certain more important acts, he or she needs the consent of the CSW. The present situation is not appropriate, as the parents are still competent to decide on the safety and upbringing of their child, who does not live with them for certain reasons. In certain cases, the child was taken away from the parents due to irregularities or inadequacies shown in the custody and upbringing of their child.

VIII FINAL THOUGHTS

The purpose of the foster care system is to provide a temporary, safe haven for children whose parents are unable to care for them. The idealistic 'safe haven' envisioned for the rescued child, however, is often not the reality experienced by foster children. Many foster children suffer abuse and neglect in foster homes, in some cases much more severe than any they may have experienced in their own homes.[35] If there is abuse of the child within foster care, there is a so-called double abuse: the foster child is abused either physically, psychologically, or sexually in the foster family, and by the legal system, which should provide children with a safe, stable home environment or with adequate services to meet the child's medical, psychological and emotional needs.[36]

Therefore, the CSW has a duty to pay special attention to the choice of candidates for the performance of foster care. Children placed into foster care already have their own 'tragic story', due to which they do not live in their original family. And, if the present foster parent is not appropriate, the suffering is continued, instead of being finished or at least lowered. By the end of foster care itself, their suffering does not yet end, as such children frequently are 'marked' for all their lives. Data referred to by Aroni Krinsky on the destiny

---

[34] Miriam Aroni Krinsky 'Disrupting the Pathway from Foster Care to the Justice system – A Former Prosecutor's Perspectives on Reform' (2010) 48 Fam Ct Rev 322, 325.

[35] Laura A Harper 'The State's Duty to Children in Foster Care – Bearing the Burden of Protecting Children' (2003) 51 Drake L Rev 793, 797.

[36] Ibid 798.

of children in foster care in the United States are frightening (in Slovenia no such research has been done yet!). After the end of foster care, he lists the following data:

- 51% will be unemployed;

- one-third will be on public assistance;

- 25% become homeless; and

- 25% will be incarcerated.[37]

To be a foster parent is something special, as the responsibility for the protection and upbringing of another person's child, a child whose childhood usually is already marked with negative events, is taken on. It lies on the shoulders of the foster parent to prepare and enable such a child, if only possible, for living. Therefore, more attention should be paid to the training of foster parents. The present 12 and 25 hours training should be widened and also additional contents stressing individual needs of a child should be included. We may speak of successful foster care only when a former foster child starts an independent life and is included into the social environment where the child lives and works. But, these responsibilities are not born only by the foster parent, but also by the CSW being responsible for the choice of foster parents. Finally, the MLFSM, adopting and confirming, for example, the training programme, is also involved. In the future, the court of justice deciding on the placement of a child into foster care will also be included. Whether the transfer of jurisdiction will have brought changes in the field of foster care, maybe regarding the shortening of the duration of foster care, especially in cases where there are possibilities of a child being adopted, we will see only after several years.

---

[37] Miriam Aroni Krinsky 'Disrupting the Pathway from Foster Care to the Justice system – A Former Prosecutor's Perspectives on Reform' (2010) 48 Fam Ct Rev 322, 325.

South Africa

KINSHIP CARE AND CASH GRANTS: IN SEARCH OF SUSTAINABLE SOLUTIONS FOR CHILDREN LIVING WITH MEMBERS OF THEIR EXTENDED FAMILIES IN SOUTH AFRICA

Ann Skelton[*]

Résumé

En Afrique du Sud, de nombreux enfants vivent en présence de membres de la famille élargie. La nouvelle loi sur l'enfance ne reconnaît pas expressément ces relations personnelles et elle propose plutôt la famille d'accueil, désignée par le tribunal et supervisée par les services sociaux, comme modèle alternatif principal de prise en charge des enfants. Le présent article fait état des raisons qui ont motivé ce choix et il examine les changements qui ont été introduits par le gouvernement et le Parlement. La prise en charge des enfants est analysée dans le contexte du système d'assistance sociale qui favorise le modèle de la famille d'accueil en raison de la rémunération qui y est rattachée, alors que dans la prise en charge informelle des enfants, les parents d'accueil doivent se contenter de l'obligation alimentaire. Le fait d'avoir trop favorisé le modèle de la famille d'accueil a généré un état de crise perpétuel dont il sera fait état dans cet article qui propose également des pistes de solution.

I INTRODUCTION

A general household survey in 2009 counted approximately 18.6 million children under the age of 18 years living in South Africa, which amounts to 38% of the total population.[1] Further analysis of the data has indicated that approximately 6 million children live with both parents, 6.9 million live with the mother but not their father; and a startlingly high 5.6 million live with family members other than their biological parents.[2] In 2009 there were approximately

---

[*]   Associate Professor and Director of the Centre for Child Law, Faculty of Law, University of Pretoria. The research was supported by funds made available by the National Research Foundation.
[1]   The General Household Survey (2009) records the total population of South Africa as 49.4 million people.
[2]   K Hall and P Proudlock 'Orphaning and the foster child grant: A return to the "care or cash" debate' (2011) 29 (5&6) *Child and Youth Care Worker* 23.

1.5 million maternal orphans, but the analysis shows that 4.1 million of the children in care of extended families have mothers who are alive but for reasons that are partly historical, partly cultural and deeply linked to patterns of poverty, live apart from them.[3] A typical scenario is that children are left with grandmothers or aunts whilst mothers go to the city to find work.

This chapter considers the situation of children living with extended family members or 'kinship care' in South Africa. The law does not specifically recognise kinship care. Instead, the Children's Act has set up a complex and labour intensive court-ordered foster care system, which allows children to be fostered by a person who is or who is not a family member of the child.[4] The care of children must also be viewed against the fact that 11.3 million children (61% of the total number of children) are living in poverty.[5] South Africa has an ambitious social assistance system based on monthly payable cash grants, some of which are directly linked to childcare. This social assistance includes, first, the child support grant which, subject to a means test, is payable to any caregiver who is caring for a child, including a biological parent, and secondly, the foster child grant which is payable to a foster parent and is not subject to a means test.[6] Over and above the difference occasioned by the means test, the cash amounts for these two grants are considerably dissimilar, which causes caregivers to pursue the more lucrative foster child grant. Concerns are raised in this article about the efficacy of this approach, problems with implementation of the law, and a burgeoning systemic crisis. Sustainable solutions for the care of South Africa's children living in kinship care are proposed.

II SOCIAL ASSISTANCE AND CHILDCARE

South Africa has the most comprehensive social grant system in Southern Africa.[7] The legal impetus for social assistance to citizens by the state is provided by s 27 of the Bill of Rights in the Constitution which provides that everyone shall have the right to social security including, if they are unable to support themselves and their dependants, appropriate social assistance. The legal regulatory framework for social assistance is provided by the Social Assistance Act 13 of 2004 and the accompanying regulations. There are three social assistance grants that relate to the care of children, namely the child support grant, the foster child grant and the care dependency grant. The first

---

3   Children's Institute *Child Gauge 2010–2011* (2011) University of Cape Town 80.
4   Section 180 of Act 38 of 2005.
5   Children's Institute *Child Gauge* 2010–2011 (2011) University of Cape Town 85. The measure used is the 'ultra' poverty line of a household with a per capita income of R552 per month, which would be the equivalent of approximately 56 euros or 69 US dollars at February 2012 exchange rates.
6   The system includes the care dependency grant for parents caring for disabled children, but the recipients are a narrowly defined group and therefore this grant is not central to the general discussion in this article.
7   K Hall and P Proudlock 'Orphaning and the foster child grant: A return to the "care or cash" debate' (2011) 29 (5&6) *Child and Youth Care Worker* 23.

two are relevant to this chapter and will be discussed in some detail. The care dependency grant is payable to a caregiver who cares for a disabled child, and due to its specificity is not centrally relevant to the issues under discussion.

The child support grant was introduced in 1998.[8] Eligibility to receive the child support grant derives from being a 'primary caregiver' of a child. A primary caregiver is defined as a person, whether or not related to the child, who takes primary responsibility for meeting the daily care needs of the child. This definition moves away from definitions of care based on biological ties or common law relationships, and in doing so gives recognition to the many family forms and care arrangements that are commonplace in South Africa, most notably children being cared for by extended family members. The grant was originally targeted specifically to the poorest and youngest children, but has since been progressively increased both in terms of the amount and the eligibility age range and is now payable in relation to all children under the age of 18 years. It is means-tested on the basis of household income, but the threshold is relatively low. The grant currently reaches 10.6 million children through their primary caregivers. The amount is small in monetary terms, only R270 per child per month,[9] up to a maximum of six children per household.

The other important cash grant to be considered is the foster child grant. The term 'foster care' was first included in the law in the Children's Act of 1960.[10] Foster care as introduced at that time was, for the most part, a 'classic' foster care model in which children who were found to be in need of care were placed by a children's court into foster care with foster parents who were not related to them. This cost-effective form of alternative care was and is subsidised by the government through the monthly payment of a cash grant. This foster child grant is free from any means test. Apart from being cost effective when compared with residential alternative care options, foster care is viewed as a preferred form of alternative care for children who are not living with biological parents and for whom adoption is not appropriate.[11] This form of care was utilised in a stable manner over a number of decades from 1960 onwards and the numbers of children in foster care never rose above 40,000. However, in the last decade the situation has changed dramatically, with the numbers of children in foster care showing a marked increase from 2002 to 2012, tapering off in 2010 when the new Children's Act came into operation. These trends will be discussed in more detail later in the chapter.

---

[8]   Under the apartheid regime there was a state maintenance grant which excluded black families and children. In 1994 South Africa became a constitutional democracy and the new government was tasked with creating support systems for poor families. A committee was appointed, chaired by Professor Frances Lund, to investigate the various options. The Report of the Lund Committee on Child and Family Support (August 1996) recommended the child support grant.

[9]   Approximately 27 euros or 34 US dollars at February 2012 exchange rates.

[10] A Skelton A and P Proudlock 'Interpretation, objects, application and implementation of the Act' in CJ Davel and AM Skelton *Commentary on the Children's Act* (Claremont: Juta, Original Service 2007) 1–6.

[11] Gallinetti J and Loffell J 'Foster care' in CJ Davel and AM Skelton (eds) *Commentary on the Children's Act* (Clarement: Juta, Original Service 2007) 12–2.

The sudden rise in the number of children being fostered has its genesis in the HIV/AIDS pandemic that South Africa has experienced, and the concomitant rise in the number of orphans. As will be demonstrated later in this chapter, the rise in numbers was also driven by certain policy choices that were made by the executive and the legislature.

Apart from not being subjected to a means test, the value of the foster child grant in 2012 is R740 per child per month,[12] not a large amount in terms of its value, but considerably larger than the child support grant which stands at R270. This difference in amount understandably causes poor families caring for children who are not biologically their own to seek regularisation of their child care arrangements through the foster care system. This in turn places burdens on an over-stretched care and protection system. The child support grant can be relatively easily accessed by primary caregivers through an administrative application to the South African Social Assistance Agency.[13] There is no social work oversight or involvement after the grant is initially approved. By contrast, foster care is viewed as an alternative care placement and as part of the care and protection system.[14] A decision to place a child in foster care is made by a children's court which is satisfied, on the basis of a social worker's report and any other evidence it calls for, that the child is in need of care and protection, that the prospective foster parent is a fit and proper person and that the placement is in the best interests of the child. Once a child is placed in foster care, there must be ongoing social work oversight of the placement, and subsequent reports to court, usually every 2 years, to recommend whether the foster care placement should be extended or whether some other care arrangement is more appropriate.[15]

III   THE IMPETUS FOR THE NEW CHILDREN'S ACT

The Children's Act 38 of 2005 was born as a result of South Africa's transition to a constitutional democracy. The Child Care Act 74 of 1983 had been written during the apartheid regime and had failed to predict or provide for a number of social problems that South Africa was to face. Like much of the Apartheid legislation, it focused narrowly on the welfare needs of the white population group, and was an inappropriate vehicle for the social development policy that was to be implemented for the entire nation by the post-1994 democratically elected government. The drafting of the Children's Act was thus informed by a transformative impetus that aimed for inclusion of the most poor and

---

[12]   Approximately 74 euros or 92.5 US dollars at February 2012 exchange rates.

[13]   The Agency was established by government in terms of the South African Social Security Agency Act 9 of 2004 to administer and pay out social assistance payments.

[14]   A Skelton and M Carnelley (eds) *Family Law in South Africa* (Cape Town: Oxford University Press, 2010) 318.

[15]   Ibid 323. The court can order foster care for periods longer than 2 years in certain specified circumstances, which obviates the need for further court appearances, the supervision by a social service professional is still required for the duration of the foster care placement, as per s 186(3) of the Children's Act.

marginalised in society. The South African Law Reform Commission (SALRC) was tasked with its design.[16] A committee of experts was appointed to assist the Commission researchers in the task. The vision of the Act was to provide a single comprehensive children's statute for South Africa. The SALRC stated that this vision was based not only on the protection accorded to children's rights in the South African Constitution, the effect and interpretation given thereto by the courts, but also to the country's international obligations. The impact of HIV/AIDS was expressly stated as an underpinning feature of the vision, as well as a pragmatic approach that attempted to strike a balance between the available resources, their optimal use and application, and the realisation that social welfare and other services for children in South Africa would continue to need 'massive injections of resources in the foreseeable future in order to fulfil the basic needs of the most vulnerable members of society'.[17]

The SALRC brought out a Discussion Paper in 2001 as part of its consultative process of law reform.[18] The Discussion Paper observed that the foster care system was already being pursued by families providing kinship care, largely for the higher-in-value grant to which it provided access. The SALRC prophesied that the foster care system would lack sufficient capacity to absorb the numbers of children who were orphaned or were for other reasons living with members of their extended family. Accordingly, the SALRC proposed that the kinship care should be distinguished from foster care, and that special provision should be made for its recognition.[19]

The Children's Bill produced by the SALRC provided for three models of care, namely foster care, court-ordered kinship care and informal kinship care. Foster care was limited to children placed by the formal childcare and protection system in the care of persons unrelated to them. These foster carers would be screened and carefully selected, and the initial court order would be of limited duration, with the emphasis on family reunification services. Court-ordered kinship care would aim to provide care with relatives for children who were unable to remain in their own homes due to abuse or neglect. Although reunification services would often be appropriate in these cases, the court should also have a discretion to make a longer term order from the outset, and to dispense with social work supervision in appropriate cases. Informal kinship care was for the recognition of children being cared for by their families in situations where they did not need care and protection services, but needed social security to help the families financially.

---

[16] The South African Law Reform Commission was at that time called the South African Law Commission. The task was described as a Review of the Child Care Act, but it soon became apparent that the overhaul would require a new law rather than amendments to the existing one, and the SALRC viewed its mandate accordingly.

[17] SALRC Report on the Review of the Child Care Act, Project 110 (2002) 3.

[18] SALRC Discussion Paper on the Review of the Child Care Act, Project 110 (2001).

[19] SALRC Discussion Paper on the Review of the Child Care Act, Project 110 (2001) 17.2.2.

The SALRC's approach to social assistance was that a universal grant for children in need would assist in the prevention of children being drawn into the care and protection system. In relation to the specified forms of care, the SALRC recommended a non-means tested grant for foster care, a means tested grant for court-ordered kinship care and a grant payable through the social assistance system (following the method of the child support grant administration). Foster care grants should not be a vehicle for poverty alleviation, but rather be viewed as a mechanism for ensuring short-term support for the temporary care of children. Furthermore, the SALRC proposed an adoption grant to enable long-term foster care to be converted into adoption in appropriate cases. Other advantages for people caring for children were contemplated, such as access to free health care and education.

The overall effects intended by innovations proposed in the SALRC draft Children's Bill would be that only children who really needed services would come into the care and protection system, and that social work services would be used optimally for children most in need. Families whose main need was for financial assistance would be able to access it without engaging with the formal care and protection system.

IV   THE PARLIAMENTARY PROCESS

The far-sighted approach of the SALRC was to be minimised soon after the publication of their draft Children's Bill which, together with the Report explaining its rationale, was issued in December 2002. In the South African law-making process Bills from the SALRC are treated as recommendations, and are subject to changes by the executive and by Parliament. The draft Children's Bill was amended by the Department of Social Development and Cabinet before it was tabled in Parliament.[20] The chapter on social grants was removed. The distinction between foster care, court-ordered kinship care and informal kinship was retained, for the time being. Towards the end of 2003 the Cabinet-approved Bill began its slow journey through the parliamentary law-making process. One of the issues which thwarted its progress was a constitutional requirement that Bills must be divided for debate and passage through Parliament, depending on whether they deal with matters of national or provincial competency.[21] This technical hitch was to cause significant delay, but also required the Children's Bill to be split into two separate Bills, which were processed sequentially rather than simultaneously, resulting in the debates about the Bill becoming fractured. The South African law-making process is remarkably open and democratic,[22] and civil society was afforded opportunities to engage with the politicians about the Children's Bill. Johannesburg Child

---

[20]   A Skelton and P Proudlock 'Interpretation, objects, application and implementation of the Act' in CJ Davel and AM Skelton (eds) *Commentary on the Children's Act* (Claremont: Juta, Original Service 2007) 1–13.

[21]   Sections 77 and 78 of the Constitution of the Republic of South Africa (1996).

[22]   See further S de Villers *A people's government. The people's voice* (Cape Town: Parliamentary Support Programme, 2001).

Welfare was invited to make submissions on foster care at an Expert Policy Workshop in April 2005, and they used the opportunity to point out the problems in the foster care system and the importance of a differentiated model.[23] This must have alerted the Parliamentary Portfolio Committee about the risks of overloading the foster care system. On 14 June 2005 the Parliamentary Portfolio Committee passed an amendment to a clause in the Bill that dealt with the grounds for finding a child in need of care and protection. Such a finding is a precursor to placing a child in foster care. Clause 150 provided a list of grounds, the first of which read '[a] child is in need of care and protection if (a) the child has been abandoned or orphaned or is without any visible means of support'. The Portfolio Committee made a decision to delete the word 'or' that appears before 'is without visible means of support' and replace it with the word 'and'. This small change in wording has proved to be significant, because it has subsequently been interpreted by some children's courts to mean that a child who is being cared for by a family member has 'visible means of support' and that the child, whilst he or she may have been abandoned or orphaned, is thus not in need of care and protection.

In 2006 the second Children's Bill, dealing with matters of provincial competency, was tabled in Parliament. Civil society role-players were concerned about the fact that the sections relating to court order kinship care and informal kinship care had been removed.[24] Deliberations on the issue of foster care and kinship care took place on 11 October 2007. The Parliamentary Monitoring Group minutes record the chairperson of the Committee as having noted that there is a difference between family care and alternative care, and that kinship care should be resuscitated to solve the problem of the high uptake of foster care by caregivers related to children. Despite this discussion, no further changes were made to this Bill with regard to this issue. Elsewhere in the Bill, it was unequivocally stated that a child can be fostered by a suitable person who is not a relative, or who is a relative but not the biological parent of a child. This made it clear that foster care had eclipsed the concept of kinship care in the Children's Bill. According to Budlender, Proudlock and Jamieson, some of whom were present at the hearings, the chairperson of the Parliamentary Portfolio Committee explicitly stated that the Committee did not want to be the ones that prevented 'grannies and aunts' from accessing the foster child grant.[25] The authors go on to comment that, in the absence of a grant for kinship care of similar value to the foster care grant, the politicians could not face making an unpopular decision. It is of great interest, however, to note what the Parliamentary Portfolio Committee recorded in their Committee Report to the National Assembly. They stated that they were concerned about

---

[23] Johannesburg Child Welfare 'Conceptualisation of foster care' A workshop paper for the Portfolio Committee on Social Development (2005), presented to the Portfolio Committee on 13 April 2005.

[24] Submissions were made to the Social Development Parliamentary Portfolio Committee in August 2007 by ACESS and by the HIV/AIDS subgroup of the Children's Bill Working Group.

[25] D Budlender, P Proudlock and L Jamieson 'Developing social policy for children in the context of HIV/AIDS: A South African case study' A Children's Institute case study (2008) University of Cape Town 43.

the 'phenomenal growth in the uptake' of the foster child grant which, they noted, could place the long-term sustainability of the grant at risk. They requested the Department of Social Development to conduct an urgent comprehensive review of the social security policy for children and the foster care system. The review has never been carried out.

V SYSTEMIC CRISIS

The phenomenal growth in uptake of the foster care grant that the Committee referred to had begun some years earlier. Statistics demonstrate that the foster child grant had been fairly stable for many years at around 40,000 children, rising slightly to 49,843 by April 2000. From this time onward it showed a sharp increase which continued to rise exponentially until 2010 to over 500,000 in 2010, and then tapered off. The sudden sharp increase from the year 2000 may have been a reflection of the impact of HIV/AIDS-related orphanhood rates. Another possible explanation is that the Minister of Social Development delivered a public address in 2002 in which he stated that the foster child grant would be made available to relatives caring for children.[26] He was unwavering in his promotion of this idea: at the second reading of the Children's Bill in the National Assembly in 2007 he reiterated that relatives caring for orphaned children who were receiving the child support grant should rather be receiving the foster care grant. He noted that some magistrates were reluctant to place children with relatives, and he singled out three magistrates who were making foster care placements with relatives, and praised their approach.[27]

The system began to lurch in 2010. Over the previous decade the number of foster child grants had increased significantly every year, despite a drop off at the end of each year when children who had turned 18 during the year were discharged from the foster care system and their foster child grants lapsed.[28] Hall and Proudlock, using the South African Social Security Agency's own SOCPEN social grants database, have revealed that 129,500 foster care grants lapsed in the financial year April 2009 to March 2010, and that a further 164,900 lapsed in the year April 2010 to March 2011. Allowing for the fact that some of these lapses are as a result of the children turning 18 years, the beneficiary's death, or the child no longer being with the beneficiary, Hall and Proudlock come to the astonishing but irrefutable conclusion that 39,200 (April 2009–March 2010) and 74,200 (April 2010–March 2011) foster child grants had lapsed due to a failure to review the foster care placement, resulting in an expired court order.

---

[26]   Z Skweyiya, Keynote address at the conference on HIV/AIDS and the Education Section: Together the Education Coalition Against HIV/AIDS, ESKOM Conference Centre, Midrand, 30 May–I June 2002.

[27]   Budlender, Proudlock and Jamieson (2008) above n 25, 38.

[28]   K Hall and P Proudlock 'Orphaning and the foster child grant: A return to the "care or cash" debate' (2011) 9 *Child and Youth Care Work* 23 at 25.

Prior to the analysis by Hall and Proudlock, those working in the care and protection system were alerted to the crisis by the Department of Social Development. An official of the Department reported at a forum at which civil society partners were present, that 123,236 foster care grants had already lapsed by January 2011. Alarmed, civil society organisations Childline and Jo'burg Child Welfare approached the Centre for Child Law, a law clinic based at the University of Pretoria which undertakes litigation on children's rights. They called upon the Centre to bring an urgent application before the High Court in an attempt to resolve the crisis and prevent any further children from dropping out of the foster child grant system. The reason for the crisis as advanced in court papers was that under the new Children's Act foster care orders lapse after 2 years from the date on which the order was made (unless the court specified a shorter period) and had to be extended by the children's court.[29] This process had to be preceded by a social work investigation, and a social worker's report must be placed before the court. These requirements of the Children's Act marked a substantial departure from the previously applicable Child Care Act which had allowed foster care placements to be extended via an administrative process governed by the Department of Social Development. It was evident, the court papers averred, that the lapsing of such large numbers of foster care orders was due to systemic failure. This involved both social workers, who had failed to investigate and compile reports timeously, and the children's courts, which had failed to consider the extensions prior to the lapsing of the orders. The Department of Social Development did not oppose the application, and a draft order was presented to the North Gauteng High Court by agreement between the parties.[30] The court order provided that until such time as the foster care backlog could be resolved, but not later than the end of 2014, an administrative process similar to the one previously applicable under the Child Care Act must be utilised in respect of children whose foster care orders were due to lapse. The court order also provided that all orders that had already lapsed would be deemed not to have lapsed, and would be extended for a period of 6 months from the date of the order. The court order has provided a temporary 'band-aid' solution, but it is clear that law reform will be required to properly resolve the crisis. The Department of Social Development has already embarked on a consultative process towards amendments to the Children's Act. One of the issues that has been placed on the list of necessary amendments is the question of foster care, though the Department of Social Development has not yet indicated the precise form these amendments should take.

Hall and Proudlock question whether the lapsing of foster care orders can be fully laid at the door of the newly required procedures under the Children's Act. They acknowledge that the introduction of the Children's Act has exacerbated the problem of backlogs, but they point out that the problem pre-dates the Children's Act. They point to the fact that a total of 39,000 foster care grants had lapsed before the Act was put into operation. The authors

---

[29] *Centre for Child Law v Minister of Social Development and Others*, North Gauteng High Court, case no 21726/11, Founding Affidavit of the Applicant.

[30] The Court Order was granted on 7 April 2011.

therefore predict that, even if the temporary solution of administrative extension provided by the court order were to be made permanent, it would not in and of itself solve the problem of backlogs.[31] There are only 13,773 registered social workers in South Africa. The costing of the Children's Bill predicted that by 2010/2011 the system would require 16,504 social workers, assisted by 14,648 auxiliary social workers to run the services under the Children's Act, and this was on a 'low case scenario' developed by the costing team.[32] The concern is that social workers are currently spending an inordinate amount of their time servicing the foster care system, where they are dealing with children who are, for the most part, not in any danger. As a result, children who are more acutely in need of services, such as children who are abused or neglected, or orphaned and abandoned and have no one caring for them, are not receiving prompt services from social workers.[33] This is untenable, and calls out for a sustainable solution.

A second systemic trend has emerged since the implementation of the Children's Act, which is an important issue in itself, but may also be one of the factors for the decline in existing foster care orders not being extended, and a drop in the number of new applications. This centres around s 150(1)(a) of the Act, mentioned earlier in the article. It is the first in a list of grounds on which children may be found in need of care and protection, and states that a child may be orphaned or abandoned and without visible means of support. The reader will recall that this clause had originally read as 'orphaned or abandoned or without visible means of support', and this simple amendment of 'or' to 'and' was, in all probability, a purposeful attempt by the Parliamentary Portfolio Committee on Social Development to oust children already being cared for by their relatives from the care and protection system, thereby excluding them from foster care and the accompanying grant. However, in the foster care chapter of the Act, it was clear that children could be fostered by persons who were or were not related to them. This apparent contradiction left the law open to interpretation.

A matter came before the Krugersdorp Children's Court,[34] which highlighted this problem. A boy born to a single mother had lived with his mother and grandmother in the Eastern Cape for the first 2 years of his life. Details of the father are unknown. After the grandmother died, the boy's mother took the boy to her uncle and aunt who lived near Krugersdorp and asked them to care for him. After a period of sporadic contact, the mother died. When the boy had been living with his great uncle and aunt for 8 years they were advised by a social worker to approach the children's court so that the boy could be legally placed in their care and they would then be able to apply for the foster child grant which was more lucrative than the child support grant they were already

[31] Hall and Proudlock (2011) above n 28, 26.
[32] C Barberton *The cost of the Children's Bill* (Cape Town: Cornerstone Economic Research, 2006) 94.
[33] H Meintjies, L Johnson, D Budlender and S Giese 'Children "in need of care" or in need of cash? Social security in a time of AIDS' (2005) 36(2) *South African Review of Sociology* 238.
[34] Krugersdorp Children's Court, case no 14/1/4/-206/10.

receiving. This was important as they were a poor family and the additional funds would lessen the burden of caring for the child. Argument before the court turned on whether the phrase 'and without visible means of support' meant that the child could not be found in need of care and protection and therefore could not be placed in foster care. The child's legal representatives argued that the Children's Act allowed for foster care by relatives, and that it would be contrary to spirit of the Act to interpret the law so narrowly. They urged an interpretation that would be in keeping with the spirit, purport and objectives of the Bill of Rights in the Constitution, even if this meant reading the 'and' as an 'or'.[35] In his written judgment, the presiding officer in the Children's Court found that the Act had intended to preserve foster care for children who had no one caring for them. Furthermore, he said that it was clear that 'the main reason for this enquiry is to alleviate the parties' financial position by a foster care order'. This, he said, was not what the law intended, and that the country's foster care system had become an 'income maintenance system'. He found that the child was not in need of care and protection and refused to place the child in foster care.[36] The matter is being taken on appeal,[37] and until the matter is finalised it appears that the majority of presiding officers in the children's courts around the country will follow this approach, although they are not bound by the decision. Not all presiding officers in the children's courts agree, and this raises a further spectre of inconsistency and unequal application of the law. In fact, the system is currently very unequal, with some caregivers receiving the foster grants, and others only able to access the child support grant. As the foster care orders come up for review, some presiding officers in the children's courts are refusing to extend existing foster care orders on the grounds of s 150(1)(a) of the Children's Act.

VI SUSTAINABLE SOLUTIONS

The Appeal case arising from the Krugersdorp Children's Court matter, namely *SS v the Presiding Officer of the Children's Court and Others*, to be heard in the South Gauteng High Court may provide some interim solutions, but it is unlikely that the judiciary can provide comprehensive answers to the range of systemic difficulties raised in the case. The Department of Social Development's plan to draft amendments to the Children's Act provides a better opportunity to resolve the systemic crises that have arisen. However, tinkering with the existing provisions is unlikely to achieve what is required. The executive must adopt a clear and firm policy approach to the issue of children being cared for by relatives. To be sustainable, this approach will have to take into account the financial realities of extending the foster care grant or a grant of similar monetary value to the number of children living with extended family members. If the model of foster care is to be applied to family

---

[35] Head of Argument on behalf of the child filed in Krugersdorp Children's Court, case no 14/1/4/-206/10.

[36] Judgment, Krugersdorp Children's Court, case no 14/1/4/-206/10.

[37] *SS v The Presiding Officer of the Children's Court*, District of Krugersdorp and others, South Gauteng High Court, case no A 3056/11.

caregivers, the cost calculation must include not only the cost of the grant itself (which comes from the social security budget) but also the cost of social work hours that will be spent on oversight and, if a court order and extension system is retained, the costs related to that must also be factored in. The intractable hurdle that will face the proposition of a court-ordered and extended foster care system for all the children who will be eligible, including those living with families, is the shortage of social workers in South Africa.

It is submitted that a model similar to that proposed by the SALRC in the original draft Children's Bill that was published with their Report on the Child Care Act in 2002 is the most sustainable solution. That model limited foster care to placement with unrelated caregivers, and divided kinship care into two categories, court-ordered and informal. Court-ordered kinship care was required for children who were in fact abused or neglected and needed to be placed with social work oversight whilst informal kinship care was recognised and supported by the provision of a grant payable through the social assistance system, with no social work oversight.

Furthermore, the first 2 years of implementation of the Children's Act has raised questions about the viability of court-ordered extensions of foster care.[38] If foster care remains the central model of community-based care, it is apparent that the courts and the social workers providing support for the court processes will struggle to cope with the numbers of foster care orders that have to be processed. However, if the SALRC model or a variation thereof is adopted, the majority of kinship care cases will be informal ones, and court orders and extensions, as well as social work oversight, are not required. The number of foster care cases of children with non-related caregivers will in all probability be reduced back down to the levels in 2000 which was just under 50,000. The court-ordered kinship care will obviously add to this number for first-time court orders, but once in the system the orders can be made for longer than two years, so extensions will not need to be made by the court. Social work oversight will depend on the needs of the children. However, despite the fact that the numbers will be significantly reduced from the current foster care case loads, it is a moot question whether the courts and social workers will cope because South Africa has no experience of this. The pre-2000 foster care figures of just under 50,000 were court-ordered but administratively extended. The reason that the SALRC recommended that foster care orders should be determined by the courts rather than by an administrative process was driven by concerns that social workers were inclined to leave children in foster care for long periods, even where reunification services were indicated, and that problems experienced by biological parents in relation to access to their children who are in foster care were not always effectively managed by social workers.[39] These concerns remain valid, though they pertain most strongly to

---

[38]   K Hall and P Proudlock 'Orphaning and the foster child grant: A return to the "care or cash" debate' (2011) 29 *Child and Youth Care Work* 23 at 26.

[39]   For a discussion of these concerns see C Matthias and N Zaal 'Can we build a better children's court? Some recommendations for improving the processing of child-removal cases' (1996) 51 *Acta Juridica* 51 at 64–66.

the 'classic' foster care situation. Similar concerns also have application in court-ordered kinship care. Nevertheless, it is likely that the majority of placements in the proposed system will be informal kinship care placements which are purely administrative in nature.

VII CONCLUSION

The foster care system in South Africa is overburdened, and this in turn impacts on the entire childcare and protection system. Many South African children are orphans, and there are many others who live with related caregivers rather than with their biological parents. Sustainable solutions need to be found for these children. It is apparent that many children living with related caregivers are looked after very well, and are not in need of care and protection. Others, though, may be neglected or abused despite living with members of their extended family, and any proposed solution must be balanced in such a manner as to recognise these realities. The solution that has been proposed in this article is a multi-layered one which echoes the original intentions of the SALRC. Furthermore, it faces up to the reality that the care models are underpinned by social security arrangements, and that some families simply need the cash grant. The article thus proposed three models of care which can co-exist. The first is foster care, in which children who are found to be in need of care and protection are placed by way of a court order with foster parents who they do not know, and reintegration services are offered. The second option, kinship care, is divided into two streams: court-ordered kinship care for children who are in need of care and protection, and an administrative process, for those families who are caring adequately for children, but are in need of financial support. It is predicted that the latter option will be the one more commonly used, and that this will release social workers from the burden of foster care placements and extensions, and allow them to focus on the wide range of services they are required to perform. This will ensure that children who are abused or neglected receive the prompt and efficient services that they need.

Sri Lanka

THE SRI LANKAN GENERAL LAW OF MARRIAGE: DUTCH, VICTORIAN OR INDIGENOUS

*Sharya Scharenguivel**

Résumé

La loi sur le mariage du Sri-Lanka est largement tributaire du droit civil néerlandais et du droit anglais. Cette loi n'a pas beaucoup évolué et elle ne répond pas, pour l'essentiel, aux valeurs dominantes en matière de mariage et de dissolution du mariage. Le présent texte analyse certains aspects de la loi afin de vérifier si celle-ci relève avant tout du droit néerlandais, du droit anglais ou plutôt du droit local. Il faut également se demander si l'absence de mouvement en faveur d'une réforme ne s'explique pas tout simplement par le fait que le droit actuel reflète adéquatement les valeurs contemporaines du pays et qu'il serait donc authentiquement indigène. Le mariage est analysé tant toutes ses dimensions: sa célébration, ses effets litigieux et sa dissolution. Le divorce est basé sur la faute et la procédure est contentieuse, avec tout ce que cela implique de conflits potentiels. La question se pose donc de savoir si les règles coutumières qui réduisent l'importance de la faute et mettent l'accent sur la conciliation et la médiation peuvent représenter une meilleure avenue.

I ESSENTIAL CHARACTERISTICS OF CUSTOMARY MARRIAGES AND DIVORCES

In the customary laws of Sri Lanka, marriage was an informal union which could be better characterised as a union between two families. The main requirements of Sinhala marriage (now known as Kandyan law) were that the parties should have been of the same caste and rank, should not have been within the prohibited degrees of relationship, and the parents and respective heads of families and in some cases even the king should have consented to the marriage. Forms and ceremony although found amongst affluent persons were not observed by the ordinary people and were not an essential requirement of marriage.[1] Tamil customary marriage also had its requirement of parties not marrying within the prohibited degrees of relationship. Parental consent was an

---

* Professor of Law, Faculty of Law, University of Colombo.
[1] Many books discuss the requirements of a valid marriage in Sinhala law, now termed Kandyan law. Reliance has been placed on *Sawyers Digest* (1826); Davy *An Account of the Interior of Ceylon and its Inhabitants* (1821); HW Tambiah *Sinhala Law and Custom* (1968).

essential requirement. This was particularly important since child marriages were common in Tamil customary law (*Thesawalamai*). The consent of the parties, as in the Kandyan law, was not that important and particularly since the parties often being children did not have the capacity to consent. Thus parental consent was essential.[2] The concept of an age of marriage was known to the law since it appears to have been well recognised that a woman could marry without parental consent if she had reached the age of 13. In colonial times marriages amongst the Tamils were contracted according to Hindu rites. The Dutch considered such practices to be heathen ones and recognised only marriages registered in the church rolls. A relaxation of Dutch policy led to marriages celebrated by Hindu priests to be recognised.[3] Ritual or ceremony appeared to have been an essential element of a Tamil customary marriage. The rituals moreover varied depending on whether the parties were Vellalas, Koviars, Chandars, Nallavas or Pallars. What appears evident is that higher castes had more elaborate rituals while the supposed lower castes had less elaborate procedures.

Muslim law also lays down certain requirements in relation to marriage. Marriages could not be contracted between persons within prohibited degrees of relationship. Fosterage was a bar to a marriage. The intervention of a marriage guardian was necessary if the male party was below the age of puberty and in Shafei law, at least, continues to be a requirement as regards a female of whatever age if she is a virgin. Minority, unlike in the other systems does not appear to be a bar to marriage since Muslim law recognises that a guardian may give a minor child in marriage. It also recognises a concept of repudiation of a marriage by a girl who has reached puberty. The *nikah* ceremony appears to be the essence of a Muslim marriage and consists of an offer and acceptance before the required number of witnesses.[4]

Divorce in these systems was easily obtained. In Kandyan law it was effected by a mere separation with the requisite intent. There is no reference in the Thesawalamai Code as to how divorce was effected. Yet there are references to second marriages and the property consequences of second marriages. Thus one must assume that divorce was possible. Muslim law recognises unilateral repudiation of marriage for the male and both fault and non-fault grounds for the female. Both the Kandyan law and the Muslim law had inbuilt procedures for reconciliation and where reconciliation failed divorce was granted with no stigma.

---

[2]   See J de Krester in *Selvaratnam v Anandavelu* (1941) 42 NLR 487 at 491 where when describing the Tamil customary marriage he declared: 'The parents give their consent and so implement what was wanting in discretion on the part of the minors.'

[3]   See HW Tambiah *The Laws and Customs of the Tamils of Jaffna* (Times of Ceylon, 1955) 107 citing Mutukisna on *Thesawalamai* 18.

[4]   For further reading see Savitri Goonesekere *Muslim Personal Law in Sri Lanka* (Colombo: Muslim Women's Research and Action Forum, 2000); MS Jaldeen *The Muslim Law of Marriage Divorce and Maintenance in Sri Lanka* (Colombo: Haji Omar Foundation for Peace, Education and Research, 2nd edn, 2010); and Chulani Kodikara *Muslim Family Law in Sri Lanka* (Colombo: Muslim Women's Research and Action Forum, 1999).

II REQUIREMENTS OF A MARRIAGE IN THE GENERAL LAW OF SRI LANKA

These relatively simple unions with heavy family involvement have been replaced by a much more formalised marriage and a divorce law which embodies the Christian ethic of marriage which is based on the idea that it is a sacrament. The General law now applies to low country Sinhalese and Tamils including those governed by the Thesawalamai (with the exception of aspects of matrimonial property and succession). It also applies to Kandyans who wish to marry under the General law in preference to the Kandyan law. It also brings Kandyans who have married under the Kandyan law within its ambit in relation to some of the consequences of marriage. Excluded from the ambit of the law are marriages of two Muslims.[5]

The most significant requirements of a valid marriage in terms of the General law are that the parties should not be within the prohibited degrees of relationship, that they should not be under the prohibited age of marriage, that the marriage should not be polygamous and that the requirements in relation to notice, solemnisation and registration should be followed except where a customary marriage takes place. Each of these requirements is part of the received law of the country.

III PROHIBITED DEGREES OF RELATIONSHIP

The prohibited degrees of relationship are laid down in s 16 of the Marriage Registration Ordinance.[6] They cover both consanguinity and affinity and are clearly based on English law which in turn incorporated Christian notions of prohibited marriages. The Christian marriage is premised on the idea that on marriage husband and wife become one and thus it is wrong to marry anyone closely related to one's wife or one's ex-wife. To marry one's wife's sister even after the death of one's wife would be like marrying one's own sister and was thus prohibited. These prohibitions were codified in the time of Archbishop Parker (1559–1575) and were known as Archbishop Parker's Table of Kindred and Affinity and are still customarily found at the back of the Book of Common Prayer. Any marriage in breach of these rules is considered incestuous and unlawful and void ab initio.[7] Some amelioration of these rules has taken place in England. The Deceased Wife's Sister Marriage Act of 1907 and the Deceased Brothers Widow's Marriage Act 1921 are notable examples. The Sri Lankan law as it currently stands does not prohibit a marriage between a man and his wife's sister on the termination of the marriage or between a woman and her husband's brother on the termination of the marriage. Yet

---

[5] See Marriage Registration Ordinance no 19 of 2007, s 64 which defines marriage so as to exclude marriages of Muslims.

[6] No 19 of 1907 (as amended).

[7] For an excellent account of these prohibitions and the subsequent changes in the law governing the prohibitions based on affinity see S Cretney *Family Law in the Twentieth Century* (Oxford: Oxford University Press, 2003) 38–56.

other prohibitions based on affinity continue to be part of our law. Thus, a man is precluded forever from marrying his stepdaughter or his son's or grandson's widow. Equally a woman is prohibited from marrying the son of her husband by another woman or her deceased daughter's husband or granddaughter's husband.

The question that has to be posed is the relevance of prohibitions based on affinity in the Sri Lankan law of marriage. Do persons governed by the General law identify with these prohibitions? Has there been an indigenisation of the Christian norms relating to prohibited relationships?

Neither the Sinhala law nor the Thesawalamai saw affinity as resulting in a prohibited relationship. Sawyers writing of the Kandyan law says that:[8]

> '... marriage cannot be contracted between parties in any nearer degree of relationship than that of first cousins, being the children of a brother and sister. This, is the most becoming matrimonial union that can be made. But the children of two brothers cannot intermarry, nor can the children of two sisters, their offspring being considered respectively brothers and sisters to each other.'

Thesawalamai had a similar prohibition. The Thesawalamai Code is somewhat brief on the subject but states that persons who want to marry should not be blood relatives. Customary cross cousins, as in Kandyan law, were not prohibited from marrying each other. Parallel cousins by contrast were prohibited from marrying each other.[9]

The Muslim law does recognise affinity as a prohibition to contracting a marriage. Thus Goonesekere opines:[10]

> 'That the prohibited degrees of relationship which renders a marriage *batil* in Islamic law correspond in general with the prohibited degrees of consanguinity (blood relationship) and affinity (relationship by marriage) recognized in the Muslim Marriage and Divorce Act (1951).'

Thus it would seem that the Muslim law did encompass rules of affinity which even extended to marriage with step children and step grandchildren unless the marriage of the spouse was either *fasid* or *batil*.[11]

Relationships arising through fosterage also are a bar to marriage in Muslim law, a concept not found in any other system. Whilst the main Sunni and Shia Schools apply the same or similar prohibitions relating to consanguinity and affinity, they differ dramatically in their treatment of fosterage. Shias treat fosterage in the same way as they treat consanguineous relationships. Sunnis in contrast treat these relationships as prohibitions only if the mother had

---

8   *Sawyers' Digest on the Kandyan Law* (1826) 35.
9   HW Tambiah, above n 3, 105.
10   Goonesekere, above n 4, 20.
11   Goonesekere, above n 4, 21.

breastfed the foster child. Some schools look at the duration of the feeding in order to determine whether marriage is forbidden or not.

The affinity-based prohibitions in the General law have little to do with how the Sinhalese and Tamils view prohibited relationships. It is other relationships that are considered taboo. Thus parallel cousin marriages are still frowned on despite there being no legislative prohibition against first cousin marriages. Amongst the Kandyan Sinhala people one's father's brothers are still referred to as *loku appachi* and *kuda appachi* (big father and small father) and one's mother's sister as *loku amma* and *kudamma* (big mother and small mother) and the children of such persons are referred to as brother or sister. A marriage between such parties is viewed as incestuous and the parties would be treated as outcasts. The cross cousin marriage by contrast may still be viewed as a desirable marriage amongst some and could take place not so much because there is no current prohibition but because it is culturally acceptable. The same attitude prevails amongst the Tamils. Parallel cousin marriages are socially unacceptable and the cross cousin marriage is acceptable.[12] Raghavan writing originally in 1964 says that although under the Marriage Registration Ordinance the marriage between children of two brothers or two sisters is not illegal the social taboo remains as strong as ever.[13]

Since the prohibitions in Muslim law are derived from the Quran and Muslims cannot marry under the General law the General law prohibitions do not impact or affect the Muslim community.

Thus it would seem that by and large the major communities governed by the General law namely the Sinhala and the Tamil people will bring into marriage their own prohibitions based on custom irrespective of whether they have a legal base or not. A good example is the prohibition of marriages between parallel cousins amongst the Kandyan Sinhala people. This is not a statutory prohibition but scrupulously observed. A sample survey done by the author reveals that the Kandyans still view such a marriage as a taboo relationship although not a part of the legal framework. The reasons for the distinction between the parallel cousin and the cross cousin are not known although all parties questioned stated that they would not permit their children to marry a parallel cousin. They all stated that the cross cousin marriage was permissible but not common. Some stated that it was permissible in former times for a woman to marry her mother's youngest brother whilst others stated that it was prohibited. None of the parties made any reference to the modern codified law (both Kandyan and General) where such a relationship is prohibited.[14] The prohibitions in the General law which are also found in the customary laws would be scrupulously followed whilst there is a certain grey area about the other prohibitions found in the legislation. They may well have been absorbed

---

[12] See now MD Raghavan *India in Ceylonese History, Society and Culture* (Asia Publishing House, 2nd edn, 1969) 178–179.

[13] Ibid, 179.

[14] A random survey of those governed by the Kandyan law was conducted of Kandyans living in Colombo, Kandy and Kurunegale. A structured questionnaire was not used.

into the mindset of members of these communities and thus being indigenised. Or they may be peripheral to the thinking of the people and pass off undetected.

IV PROHIBITED AGE OF MARRIAGE

Section 15 of the Marriage Registration Ordinance,[15] until it was amended in 1995, incorporated a low age of marriage, 16 for boys and 12 for girls unless they were of European descent in which case the age was 14. Any marriage in breach of this requirement was treated as void.

England which inspired this statutory prohibition had no statute at the turn of the century which laid down a minimum age of marriage. The common law embodied a presumption that a boy under the age of 14 and a girl under the age of 12 were incapable of entering into a marriage. The rule however was not absolute and if the parties remained together after they reached the age of discretion the marriage would be treated as valid. In legal terms such a marriage may have been viewed as voidable rather than void. Another view that has been expressed is that such a marriage was capable of ratification.[16] It was only in 1929 that the English law brought in the concept of a prohibited marriage for those under the age of 16. The proponent of the new law, Lord Buckmaster, a Liberal Lord Chancellor, claimed inter alia that permitting a low age of marriage defeated the policy of the Criminal Law (Amendment Act) of 1885 which made it a criminal offence for a man to have intercourse with a female under 16. Buckmaster argued that it was meaningless to make a woman incapable of consenting to a single act of intercourse under the age of 16 whilst at the same time permitting her to marry under that age and thereby consent irrevocably to sexual intercourse with her husband. Although initially there was no great support for this legislation, in the Committee stage it appears to have mustered sufficient support. The work of the League of Nations towards better protection of children was also a reason for this legislation being carried. It would appear that the state of English law at the time prevented the United Kingdom from actively participating in these discussions and the stature of the UK was increased through the passing of the legislation.

V WHAT THEN WAS THE REASON FOR THE BRITISH TO BRING IN A CONCEPT OF AN ABSOLUTELY PROHIBITED MARRIAGE IN 1906?

This does not appear to have been well documented. There is no indication that low age marriage was practised in Sri Lanka extensively. Davy writing on the marriage customs of the Sinhala people states that a man is considered

---

[15] No 19 of 1907.
[16] Cretney, above n 7, 57–58.

marriageable when he reaches the age of 18 or 20.[17] There is no indication in his work or that of Knox that child marriages were a feature of Sinhala society. Knox writing in 1681 describes the marriage requirements and the customary rites associated with marriage but nowhere makes any reference to early marriage.[18] Amongst the northern Tamils clearly child marriage was commonly practised but there is no indication that there was any agitation about child marriages. One may also assume that it was known to the Muslim community which to date does not have a prohibited age of marriage. Yet this law does not impact on the Muslim community who as we have pointed out earlier are excluded from the purview of this Act. By contrast in India at about this time there was a widespread movement against child marriage which finally culminated in an Act commonly known as the Sarda Act in 1929, the same year as the Act restraining child marriage came into force in England. The British press claimed that with the passing of the Sarda Act Indian opinion had at last yielded to the reformist pressure exerted by the government. Yet it has been pointed out that the efforts to raise the age of marriage in India were entirely due to Indian initiative.[19] No such movement can be identified in Ceylon as it then was.

The stipulated age in the then Ceylon legislation moreover was not an age which corresponded to the common law presumption. There are some dicta which suggest that the codification was on the lines of the Roman Dutch law and not the English law.[20] However, the ages known to the Roman Dutch law were different to those embodied in the statute. Hahlo states that the earliest age at which a valid marriage could be contracted was 14 for boys and 12 for girls.[21] Moreover, the Roman Dutch law did not view such marriages as incapable of validation if the parties continued cohabitation after the minor had reached the required age subject to the condition that parents had the right to have the marriage set aside if they had not consented to it.[22] This goes back to the canon law where marriages could be informally contracted. Continued cohabitation reaffirmed their consent to be married. Hahlo proceeds to say that this same reasoning is not possible in the context of the statute law of South Africa where the Marriage Act is clearly an exhaustive regulation of the matter. Such a marriage today is null and void subject to the post facto ratification of the marriage by the minister.[23] Thus just as the prohibited degrees of relationship were based on a completely alien system, the prohibited age too

---

[17]   Davy *An account of the Interior of Ceylon and of its Inhabitants* (1821) 284.

[18]   Robert Knox *An Historical Relation of Ceylon* (Glasgow: J Maclehose, 1911) Part 3 chapter 7 pp 92–93.

[19]   M Basu *Hindu women and Marriage law From Sacrament to Contact* (Oxford University Press, 2001) 58–59.

[20]   See also p 49 for an example of a viewpoint against bringing such legislation. *Thiagaraja v Kurukkal* (1923) 25 NLR 89 at 92.

[21]   HR Hahlo *The South African Law of Husband and Wife* (Cape Town: Juta, 4th edn, 1975) 86.

[22]   Ibid, 87 citing Voet 23.2.39 (transl PC Cane *The Selective Voet*, 8 vols (Durban, 1955)) and Van Der Keessel Th 66 (transl CA Lorenz *Select Theses of the Laws of Holland and Zeeland* (Cape Town, 2nd edn, 1884)).

[23]   Ibid.

was introduced by the British more as a response to the prevalence of underage marriages in another part of the Empire namely, India.

Yet the requirement has been internalised and entered a new phase when the marriageable age was statutorily amended to the age of 18 by virtue of an amendment to the Marriage Registration Ordinance.[24] The amendment was as a consequence of considerable medical opinion to the effect that the Asian woman matures later physically and that childbearing was better undertaken at the age of 18 and above. Moreover, Sri Lanka's constitutional provisions on equality and her international obligations under the Convention on the Elimination of All Forms of Discrimination against Women required a re-examination of a statutory provision with different ages of marriage for males and females, thus the reason for introduction of a uniform age of marriage for both sexes.

VI   REQUIREMENTS RELATING TO NOTICE AND SOLEMNISATION OF MARRIAGE

The Ordinance prescribes preliminaries to be observed in relation to a purported marriage. Thus where both parties to the intended marriage are resident in the same division one of the parties is required to give notice of marriage.[25] Where they live in two different divisions each is required to give notice of marriage to the respective registrar of the division in which he or she lives.[26] The law stipulates a number of specifics that have to be included in the notice. These include the name in full, race, age, profession, civil condition and dwelling place of each of the parties and the name in full and rank or profession of the father of each of the parties.[27] Interestingly the party giving notice of the marriage shall make and sign a declaration that he or she believes that there is 'no impediment of kindred or alliance or lawful hindrance to the marriage'.[28] The requirement comes from the Book of Common Prayer where the parties are required to disclose any impediment why they may not be joined in matrimony.[29]

Every such notice shall be signed in the presence of an attesting officer and two witnesses. The witnesses should be personally acquainted with the party giving notice and their full names, rank or profession and place of abode is to be entered in the notice.[30] The Act also specifies that the registrar to whom notice of marriage is duly given shall enter all the particulars in a book called the Marriage Notice Book which shall be open at all reasonable times for

---

[24]   Marriage Registration Amendment Act No 18 of 1995.
[25]   Marriage Registration Ordinance, s 23(1).
[26]   Ibid, s 23(2).
[27]   Ibid, s 24(1).
[28]   Ibid, s 24(3)(a).
[29]   Book of Common Prayer (1660) 'The Form of Solemnization of Matrimony'.
[30]   Marriage Registration Ordinance, s 23(4).

inspection without fee.[31] Once again the requirement is an adaptation of the requirement in the prayer book which allows any man to show any just cause why the parties should not lawfully be joined together.[32] Whilst in church the minister after having detailed the purposes of matrimony would ask any person who knows of any impediment to 'now speak, or else hereafter forever hold his peace'. The civil form allows any person to communicate any known impediment to the registrar. Thus the Ordinance once again is an embodiment of the religious requirement contextualised into statutory form. After the giving of requisite notice and upon the expiry of the stipulated time period the registrar will issue a certificate and a licence of marriage which will then enable a marriage to be solemnised by a minister in a registered place of worship or by the registrar in his office station or other authorised place.[33]

Yet it is significant that the Marriage Registration Ordinance does not stipulate that these requirements relating to registration of the marriage are compulsory. The fact that the British after so many attempts at making solemnisation and registration compulsory chose not to do so in the Marriage Registration Ordinance of 1907 is a 'tacit acceptance of defeat' in implementing their official policy relating to requiring a formal celebration of marriage.[34] A comparison with the provisions of the 1822 Ordinance and later Ordinances shows the extent of the deviation. In 1822 reg 19 provided that no marriages contracted after 22 August 1822 were to be considered valid unless registered. Government schoolmasters were appointed as registrars to provide the necessary infrastructure for giving effect to this legislative intention. Furthermore, no marriage could be registered unless a proclamation of marriage had been given on three consecutive Sundays except in the case of Muslims.[35] Ordinance no 6 of 1847 retained the British policy of compulsory registration of marriage except where they were solemnised by Christian ministers under clause 4 of the Ordinance. One Registrar General of Marriage was appointed for the whole Island. All previous marriages invalidated for want of registration were validated. Ordinance no 13 of 1863 revealed a change of policy with regard to non-registration. The penal provisions of the 1847 legislation were withdrawn and the Ordinance was made applicable to all marriages except those contracted in the Kandyan provinces and between persons professing the Mohammedan faith. Ordinance no 8 of 1865 which amended Ordinance no 13 of 1863 brought further concessions. Registration was now possible in any place or at any time where the bride belonged to a community whose 'habits and feelings' did not allow their females 'to appear in public' prior to marriage. Death bed marriages were introduced. A few other Ordinances followed and then Ordinance no 2 of 1895 was enacted. This

---

[31] Ibid, s 25(1).
[32] 'The Form of Solemnization of Matrimony', above n 29.
[33] Marriage Registration Ordinance, s 26(1) and (2) and s 27(1), (2), (3), (4) and (5) and s 33.
[34] Savitri Goonesekere 'Some reflections on Solemnization of Marriage in the General law of Sri Lanka' citing TE Gooneratne Report of the Commission on Marriage and Divorce Appendix A (1984) *Moot Society Review* 24, 28.
[35] *Report of the Commission on Marriage and Divorce* Ceylon Sessional Paper 16 (Colombo: Government Press, 1959) 171.

consolidated and amended the law relating to registration of marriages other than those of Kandyans and Muslims. Once again s 15 brought about the requirement of compulsory registration. This section was repealed by amending Ordinance no 10 of 1896 and not reintroduced in the 1907 Ordinance.[36]

Nagendra presents an interesting viewpoint. In her view the statutory effect of making registration non-compulsory coupled with the definition of 'Marriage' as 'any marriage excepting marriages between Kandyans and those professing Islam' made it possible for the Sri Lankan courts to recognise a mode of solemnisation different from those specified in the statute. Thus, she says that a 'gateway' was created 'to bring within the Ordinance a marriage which did not fulfill the requirement of registration'.[37]

The 'gateway' that Nagendra refers to provided for the indigenisation of marriage. Thus, customary marriages continued to be recognised provided that the other requirements of the Ordinance were satisfied. The courts developed the concept of the minimum ritual. A customary marriage if it was to be recognised needed to satisfy the element of an acceptable ritual. The accepted ritual whether in a customary or a non-customary marriage continues to be a vital feature of marriage and brings the law closer to the people. The fact that it is not a requirement of marriage is lost sight of. The registration of a marriage often now takes place prior to the ceremony and the custom is for the couple to live with their respective families until the ceremony takes place. Ten interviews carried out by the author amongst a cross-section of persons reveal the following. In nine cases the persons felt that the ceremony was vital in the contraction of the marriage. In just one case was it stated that the valid marriage came about as a consequence of the registration.

Goonesekere points out that even after the enactment of the Marriage Registration Ordinance of 1907 those Sri Lankan cases requiring some public ceremony as a requirement of a valid marriage in relation to the application of the presumption of marriage by habit and repute may be cited in support of the view that there is no total dispensation of the requirement of form. Yet as she points out the courts are divided on this, the earlier cases being less concerned with the requirement of a public ceremony than the later cases.[38]

VII   CONSEQUENCES OF MARRIAGE

(a)   Support

Traditional Sinhala law was not premised on the idea of spousal support. It would appear that all persons who worked on the land had the right to support

---

[36]   Ibid, 172–174.
[37]   'Customary and Statutory marriages in Sri Lanka – A Hybrid Approach' (2009) *Neethi Murasu* (44th Issue of The Law Students Thamil Mantram) 86.
[38]   Goonesekere, above n 34, 31.

and sustenance from the land. Thus, the diga married daughter ceased to be entitled to support from her fathers *paraveni* (ancestral) land only because she ceased to live on the land and work on the land. Her entitlement took the form of the dowry that she got at the time of the marriage. Her unmarried sisters and binna married sisters continued to have a right to sustenance from the land because they were part of the economic unit that contributed to the working of the land. Thus, the concept of sharing produce or the fruits of the land was well known in Sinhala law.

Hayley makes the following observation:[39]

> 'Even at the present day the lands of a village community or family are frequently owned in common, and, although each member is well aware of the share to which he in law is entitled, the produce is divided by common consent until a quarrel leads to the institution of partition proceedings.'

Into this system the British imposed a family maintenance system whereby the support obligation was imposed on a husband to support his wife and a father to support his minor children. The early British legislation was modelled on the Poor Laws in England and imposed a criminal liability on a man who did not fulfil his obligations of support. The criminal liability had other ramifications. Proof of paternity in the case of an extramarital child was framed in the context of rules operating in the criminal justice system. Corroboration of the mother's evidence was required and strict rules of evidence were followed.[40] The husband was clearly seen as the provider and the wife as the recipient of support. The more enlightened Roman Dutch law principles based on a reciprocal duty of support had given way to a system where the husband was seen as the breadwinner and the wife as a passive recipient of support. The obligation of support was conditional on the woman living with the husband unless the woman could establish that the husband was living in adultery or was guilty of habitual cruelty. Non-habitual cruelty or occasional acts of adultery then did not suffice for a woman to refuse to live with the husband.[41]

This model of support had other ramifications. It reinforced the Roman Dutch law notion that the husband was the predominant partner in the marriage. This was particularly evident in relation to two aspects of the marriage: first the powers the husband had by virtue of the marital power over the wife and second the rights he had in relation to the children of the marriage as natural guardian of the children. The law by imposing the obligation of support almost exclusively on the husband justified his pre-eminent position in the marriage.

---

[39] Hayley *A treatise on the Laws and customs of The Sinhalese* (Colombo: Navrang Booksellers and Publishers, 1923) 166.

[40] See eg s 6 of Maintenance Ordinance No 19 of 1889 which mandated that an application relating to maintenance should be made within a 12 month period.

[41] See s 3 of the Maintenance Ordinance No 19 of 1889. For a detailed account, see Savitri Goonesekere 'Family Support and Maintenance: Emerging Issues in Some Developing Countries with Mixed jurisdictions' (2006) 44 Family Court Review 361–375.

A parallel development seems to have been the 'head of the household concept'. Widely used in administration it appears to have absorbed the idea that the male is the head of the household. The concept is used in relation to electoral registers, forms for collecting information on occupants in houses for security purposes, relief and construction programmes.[42]

1999 saw a more enlightened approach to support obligations which were now equally shared between husband and wife in relation to their marital children. Non-marital children had a right of support from both their mother and father provided paternity was established by cogent evidence. Husband and wife had reciprocal obligations of support towards each other. The reforms were clearly inspired by international conventions rather than the customary law.

(b)   Property consequences

Very evident in the Sri Lankan law is the influence of Victorian ideas in the law relating to matrimonial property. In the nineteenth century in England, a group of women comprising in the main of writers wanted to protect their earnings from their husbands. This was the beginning of a movement towards separate property. This movement had its desired impact not only in England but also in the colonies. In Sri Lanka the introduction of a separate property regime took place initially through the Matrimonial Rights and Inheritances Ordinance of 1876.[43] Yet the legislation must be viewed as a transitional piece of legislation since it did not bring about complete separation of property. It vested in the married woman complete property rights in relation to certain categories of movable property but restricted her rights in relation to immovable property by requiring her to obtain her husband's consent if she wished to alienate the property.[44] The consent of the husband was required to be given in writing and the case-law is divided on whether that consent was required in relation to every transaction or whether consent in a more general sense sufficed. In certain stipulated circumstances the husband's consent could be substituted by a court order. The court's order could be either unconditional or subject to such terms and conditions as the court considered necessary.[45] Importantly, the married woman was no longer liable for the debts or engagements of her husband unless the debt was incurred for or in respect of cultivation or upkeep of her property or for taxes imposed by law.[46] Community property which was part of the Roman Dutch law was expressly repealed.[47] The wages and earnings of the married woman were deemed to be her separate property and placed completely outside the control of the husband. Similarly full powers of dealing with such property were vested in the married woman. Other categories of

---

[42]   For a comprehensive analysis of the concept see Shyamala Gomez (ed) *A Socio Legal Study of The Head of the Household Concept* (Sri Lanka: Centre on Housing Rights and Evictions (COHRE), 2008).

[43]   No 15 of 1876.

[44]   Ibid, s 8.

[45]   Ibid, s 11.

[46]   Ibid.

[47]   Ibid, s 7.

movable property which vested in the married woman were her paraphernalia and implements for trade and agriculture.[48] Movable property not falling into these categories vested in the husband.[49]

This piece of legislation which drew its impetus from English legislation clearly did not meet the aspirations of married women even at that time. It gave married women rights over their earnings. The legislation was drafted in England so as to exclude 'alien connotations of community property regimes in force in most of the continental regimes'.[50] It has been pointed out that it did no more than what English gentlemen had secured for their daughters by marriage settlements, namely putting some property out of the clutches of avaricious husbands, picturesquely described by Kenny as affording to the 'mangle, the teapot and the sewing machine the same protection which diamonds and consols had always purchased for themselves in the teeth of the law'.[51] 1923 saw a more substantial reform. A complete separate property regime was brought about. The married woman was equated to a femme sole and given complete control and management of her property.[52]

The issue that faces Sri Lankan women today is whether they are better protected by the separate property regime or a community property regime. The separate property regime clearly helps the professional or high earning wife. Once her maintenance obligations are discharged her savings are beyond the reach of the other spouse. Acquisition of assets becomes a distinct possibility and in the event of marriage breakdown such a woman would leave the marriage with considerable assets. But what of the majority of married women who have to sacrifice career for being the primary caregivers of the children of the marriage or at least settle for jobs or careers that allow them to combine the dual role that they have to play. The separate property regime does not really provide the protective framework for such a woman. Nor does it take sufficient note of her non-financial contribution to the marriage which if quantified could be significant except where there is specific legislation which provides for such a contribution to be taken into account.

The matrimonial property regime in South Africa, the other Roman Dutch jurisdiction apart from Sri Lanka, took a completely different direction. Community of property was retained although it could be excluded by antenuptial contract. Yet the current regime is a vastly modified community property regime. The Roman Dutch community was an unequal partnership with husband having complete administrative powers over the property. Fraudulent dispositions could be set aside,[53] and remedies were available in

---

48   Ibid, s 10.
49   Ibid, s 17.
50   Cretney, above n 7, 97.
51   CS Kenny *History of the Law of England as to the effects of Marriage on Property and on the Wife's legal capacity* (London, 1879) 16 cited by Cretney, above n 7, 97 fn 43.
52   Married Women's Property Ordinance No 19 0f 1923.
53   Voet 23.2.54, above n 22, Van der Linden *Institutes of Holland* 1.15.1 (transl H Juta, Cape Town, 1897), Schorer *Notes on H Grotius Inleiding* (transl AFS Maasdorp, Cape Town, 1903).

relation to a wife who could satisfy the court that the husband was maladministering the property. The most drastic remedy was the *boedescheiding* or the decree for separation of goods.[54] Less drastic and more commonly used was the suspension of the marital power and the appointment of a curator.[55] The South African courts had also exercised the power of making specific orders in relation to a particular transaction.[56]

The new community regime in South Africa is of a very different ilk. Both spouses have equal powers of administration[57] and may perform any juristic act with regard to the joint estate without the consent of the other spouse.[58] Important transactions that may impact on the corpus of the community, however, require joint written consent.[59] Transactions in relation to certain other properties in the joint estate require the consent of the other spouse but not the written consent.[60] These properties include furniture and other effects of the common household.[61] A spouse is also precluded from receiving any employment related payments, professional income or business income accruing to the other spouse or the joint estate without the consent of the other spouse. This requirement also attaches to inheritances, legacies, donations, etc awarded to the other spouse or dividends or interest on the proceeds of shares or investments in the name of the other spouse.[62] Proceeds from an insurance policy are dealt with in the same way.[63]

In England, the separate property regime continues but is today combined with wide powers in the court to reallocate property on divorce. Settlements and conveyances can be ordered to ensure that the economically vulnerable spouse is protected at the point of divorce. Settlements are particularly attractive since the property can be earmarked for a particular use which could be time-bound whilst preserving the party's financial interests in the property. Thus the matrimonial home could be settled on the wife until the children cease to be dependants or until they cease to be minors. Pension sharing orders are also now possible in terms of English law. The court may also order a sale of property.[64] The wide discretionary powers conferred on the English courts came about as a consequence of a realisation that an unmitigated separate property regime could not be justified. With the influence of human rights jurisprudence and the equality concepts, reasonable requirements of the more

---

[54]   Grotius 1.5.24 *Jurisprudence of Holland* (transl RW Lee, London, 1926), Voet 23.3.52, above n 22, Van Leeuwen 1.6.7. *Commentaries on Roman Dutch Law* (transl JG Kotze, London, 1921), Schorer, above n 53.

[55]   *Naude v Norwich Union Fire Insurance Co Ltd* 1913 WLD 207 at 211.

[56]   *Venter v Venter and Registrar of Deeds* (1892) 9 SC 381.

[57]   Matrimonial Property Act No 88 of 1984 (as amended), s 14.

[58]   Ibid, s 15.

[59]   Ibid.

[60]   Ibid, s 15(3).

[61]   Ibid, s 15(3)a.

[62]   Ibid, s 15(3)b.

[63]   Ibid.

[64]   See further Cretney and Proberts *Family law* (London: Sweet & Maxwell, 9th edn, 2009) 168–199.

vulnerable spouse no longer seem to be the yardstick of the English courts. In *White v White*[65] Lord Nicholls posed the question:[66]

> 'If a husband and wife by their joint efforts over many years, his direct in the business and hers indirectly at home have built up a valuable business from scratch why should the claimant wife be confined to the court's assessment of her reasonable requirements, and the husband be left with a much larger share.'

More recent cases have identified relationship-generated needs, compensation for relationship-generated disadvantages and sharing of the fruits of the partnership as the ingredients that should be taken into account by an English court[67] in the exercise of their discretionary powers under the Matrimonial Causes Act.[68] In *K v L*[69] much of the wealth of the family was generated by shares which the wife brought into the marriage. Despite their assets the couple lived very modestly on the dividends from the shares and occasional sales of shares. Neither party worked during the marriage. Indeed there was no need for them to do so given the wealth of the wife. Both had contributed to the family. Yet here the Court of Appeal whilst endorsing the principle in *White v White* stated that whilst a court cannot differentiate between spouses on the basis of the division of labour in the marriage nevertheless one could take into account a substantial contribution made by one of the parties. In this case that contribution came from the wife and took the form of inherited property. In ordering a division of the assets the English courts have also departed from the principle of equal division where much of the assets were acquired prior to the marriage.[70] Thus, in *Charman v Charman*[71] the Court of Appeal stated that there was is no rigid distinction drawn between matrimonial and non-matrimonial assets and that the sharing principle applies to all the property of the parties but in the case of non-matrimonial property there is likely to be a better reason for departure from the equality principle.

It is hard to rationalise the unmitigated separate property regime that remains a feature of the General law in Sri Lanka, particularly since both the Kandyan law and the *Thesawalamai* have elements of the concept of marital property. In the Thesawalamai it is more developed with property acquired during the marriage being designated *Thediathettam* over which both spouses had equal rights of ownership. The administration of the property, however, remains with the husband with certain inbuilt restrictions on donations.[72] In Kandyan law the concept of marital property can be seen in the widow's rights in relation to the acquired property of the husband which took the form of a life interest.[73]

---

[65] [2000] 1AC 596 (HL).
[66] At p 608.
[67] *Miller v Miller* [2006] UKHL 24, [2006] 2 AC 618 per Justice Hale [138]–[144].
[68] Section 25.
[69] [2011] All ER 124.
[70] See *McCartney v Mills McCartney* [2008] EWHC 401.
[71] [2007] EWCA Civ 503.
[72] For a detailed consideration of the subject see Kamala Nagendra *Matrimonial Property and Gender Inequality : A Study of Thesawalamai* (Colombo: Stamford Lake, 2008).
[73] HW Tambiah *Sinhala Laws and Customs* (Colombo, 1968) 229.

In relation to *paraveni* or ancestral property her rights were more circumscribed and never extended to more than a right to support from such property in a situation where the acquired property was insufficient for her maintenance.[74] The widower's rights were less well defined but there is some indication that he too had rights in relation to the wife's movable property.

The Family Law Committee in 2010 addressed the issue of changing the matrimonial property regime of the General law but could not reach a consensus. Most members agreed that the General law should draw its inspiration from the personal laws and combine a concept of separate property and shared matrimonial property rights in property acquired after the marriage. Some members supported the concept of deferred community of gains. Some members were of the opinion that needs-based family provision should be combined with a concept of deferred community of gains.[75] Yet there is no indication that any of these proposals is receiving the attention of the legislature. A much earlier initiative of the Law Commission in the form of a proposed Matrimonial Causes Act appears to have been relegated into the lumber room. The Matrimonial Causes Act also proposed a reform of the General law. The Law Commission draft proposed the replacement of the current fault system with a system of matrimonial breakdown. It also dealt with property orders that could be made. Whilst the proposed law did not bring about a radical change in the matrimonial property regime, it did envisage greater discretionary powers being exercised by the court. Thus the court was empowered to make orders relating to the occupation of any residential premises, the provision of a dwelling house or accommodation and to make any settlement or conveyance of any property that either the spouses was entitled to.[76] A feature of the proposed reform was that it laid down guidelines in relation to the making of such orders.[77] A needs-oriented approach was recommended by the Commission as opposed to an entitlement approach although contributions, including contributions towards the care and welfare of the family and the matrimonial home, were included in the criteria stipulated in the draft Act.

Thus the separate property approach continues to be the basis of the General law with some discretionary powers vested in the court at the point of divorce. These discretionary powers are found in the Civil Procedure Code, an 1889 Ordinance which has been subject to many amendments. In 1977 some amendments were made in relation to the chapter relating to matrimonial actions.

---

[74]   Ibid, 223–224.
[75]   Family Law Committee *Proposed Reform on Family Law* (unpublished, Colombo, 2010) 16–18 (Ministerial Committee reports are seldom published in Sri Lanka unlike parliamentary committee reports).
[76]   Draft Matrimonial Causes Act, s 13(e), (f) and (h).
[77]   Draft Matrimonial Causes Act, Sch 3.

In essence the court upon pronouncing a decree of separation or divorce could make any conveyance or settlement as the court 'thinks fit'.[78] Yet there is no indication that this power is exercised by the court to make any far ranging decisions in relation to property at the point of divorce or separation. The usual award is gross, annual, or monthly sums of money. Where the parties are well off, however, it is usual for the parties to come to court with a negotiated settlement that could include property settlements. The problem with this kind of approach is that it is highly individualistic and depends in essence on the negotiating power of the lawyers. No clear guidelines have emerged on how property is to be distributed in short-term, medium-term or long-term marriages. Some rules of thumb have emerged on how financial provisions will be made. A one fifth rule is statutorily embodied as the starting point of alimony pendente lite.[79]

VIII   DIVORCE

The General law of divorce remains largely fault-based. Adultery, desertion and impotency remain the principal grounds of divorce.[80] An attempt to bring in a somewhat misconceived breakdown ground in 1977 failed first, because the statutory provision was ambiguous and secondly, because it was sought to be introduced through the Civil Procedure Code which regulates procedure rather than substantive law.[81] The Law Commission draft Matrimonial Causes Act as we have noted recommended a single ground of divorce based on the principle of irretrievable breakdown.[82]

The Family Law Committee of 2010 also recommended a single ground of divorce and went further than the Law Commission by also advocating that judicial separation which had been a part of the law of the country as a result of the influence of both the Roman Dutch law and the English law should be abolished since it was inconsistent with the breakdown premise.[83] The Committee also recommended that the concept of annulment of voidable marriages be eliminated from the law. In a system which recognises only fault-based voidable marriages on grounds such as antenuptial stuprum (pregnancy by a man other than the husband at the point of marriage), lack of consent, fraud, non-consummation, etc had to be accommodated since these grounds did not come within the scope of a divorce law based on fault. However, these grounds can clearly be encompassed within a divorce law based on the premise of irretrievable breakdown. Marriages which are void ab initio in terms of the Family Law Committee report entail no legal consequences and no court decrees are therefore necessary in relation to them.[84]

---

[78]   Civil Procedure Code No 2 of 1889 (as amended), s 615.
[79]   Ibid, s 614.
[80]   Marriage Registration Ordinance No 19 of 1907, s 19(2).
[81]   Civil Procedure Code No 2 of 1889, s 608(2)(a) and (b).
[82]   Matrimonial Causes Bill (Law Commission 2006), s 3(1).
[83]   Family Law Committee report, 6–7.
[84]   Ibid, 8.

Despite the fault-based framework of the General law of divorce the Family Law Committee found that the fault-based ground of malicious desertion was being interpreted to accommodate irretrievable breakdown of marriage. It is well accepted that the uncontested divorce is now used to deal with cases of irretrievable breakdown. The only situation in which one sees the application of the fault-based divorce is where one party does not wish to obtain a divorce or where a negotiated 'deal' cannot be worked out.

Given this scenario the Family Law Committee concluded that the new ground of irretrievable breakdown will not result in a dramatic change from current practice. The proposed divorce law will, however, have the salutary effect of bringing the process into the court rather than the now prevalent mechanism of out of court settlements. Currently in the absence of a provision which provides for parties to enter into a settlement which then can be scrutinised by the courts the parties and their lawyers negotiate a settlement and one of the parties agrees not to contest the divorce. The divorce then is secured ex parte and the negotiated settlement forms the basis of a court decree without any examination as to the terms of the agreement. Whether the financially vulnerable spouse is adequately safeguarded in this scenario is doubtful. The more prominent lawyer (invariably representing the financially stronger spouse) may well have an edge in this process. There is moreover the strong possibility that even child custody issues do not receive adequate attention in the ex parte or uncontested cases. In the Law Commission draft Bill, however, the court will have a role in seeing whether the marriage has in fact broken down or in the terminology of the Bill to ascertain whether the 'relationship between the parties has reached such a state of disintegration that there is no reasonable prospect of the restoration of a normal marriage relationship between them'.[85] Where it appears to the court that there is 'a reasonable possibility that the parties may become reconciled through counselling, treatment or reflection the court may, after recording its reasons' postpone proceedings for a period not exceeding 6 months.[86]

Divorce in the special laws is different both in relation to the grounds of divorce and the procedures governing divorce. In Kandyan law the process is administrative rather than judicial with the Kandyan Marriage Registrar being vested with the power to dissolve Kandyan marriages.[87] Whilst he is expected to hold an inquiry prior to dissolving the marriage the law does not specify what the nature of this inquiry is. The only requirement is that he should hear both parties.[88] The grounds of divorce are a curious mixture of old English law and Kandyan law as understood through the eyes of legislators who were trained in another system. Thus, adultery is a ground of divorce for the male spouse without any additional requirement.[89] The female spouse is required to prove

---

[85]   Matrimonial Causes Bill (Law Commission), s 3(2).
[86]   Ibid, s 3(3).
[87]   Kandyan Marriage and Divorce Act No 44 of 1952, s 33(5), (6) and (7).
[88]   Ibid, s 33(8).
[89]   Kandyan Marriage and Divorce Act, s 32(a).

gross cruelty in addition to adultery.[90] The non-fault based premises of the Kandyan law are retained in the grounds that permit divorce on the ground of inability to live happily together which the law requires to be manifested by separation from bed and board for a period of one year and mutual consent.[91] The section is an amalgamation of the English law of the time which saw judicial separation as one that permitted a separation from bed and board and the Kandyan law which allowed parties to set aside a marriage where the parties could not live together amicably.

The Muslim law codified by the Dutch and given statutory recognition by the British now finds expression in a post-colonial statute.[92] Unlike the Kandyan Marriage and Divorce Act which attempts to codify the Kandyan law and which has consequently incorporated many non-Kandyan elements into the law, the Muslim Marriage and Divorce Act preserves the Islamic law by expressly stating that 'in all matters relating to any Muslim marriage or divorce the mutual rights and obligations of the parties shall be determined according to the Muslim law of the sect to which the parties belong'.[93] The Act therefore deals more with the procedural aspects although there are a few clauses which are essentially restatements of Shafei law.[94] What would be of interest to law reformers would be the schedules of the Act which deal in depth with conciliation measures that a *quazi*[95] is required to engage in a situation where a husband intends to divorce the wife or a wife intends to divorce a husband. Goonesekere commending the non-adversarial approach to dispute settlement in family disputes is critical of recent cases in which the Supreme Court attempted to reduce the significance of reconciliation measures in the Muslim law and states that the experience of the Muslim personal law should be strengthened rather than undermined.[96] She also expresses the view that the processes in the Muslim law should be used to change the General law.[97]

Despite more enlightened concepts and procedures in the customary laws and recommendations of successive committees appointed to look into reforming the marriage laws, the Sri Lankan General law remains firmly rooted in the Roman Dutch law and unreformed English law. Goonesekere observes that 'the apathy in regard to initiating legislative changes contrasts sharply with the rhetoric on women's rights and frequent discussion and debate on women's issues in the press and public fora'.[98] Yet, is it apathy or indigenisation of these concepts with marriage and divorce taking on a colonial identity? The writer is reminded of a meeting that took place with women lawyers after a committee

---

[90] Ibid, s 32(b).

[91] Ibid, s 32(e) and (f).

[92] Muslim Marriage and Divorce Act No 13 of 1951.

[93] Section 98(2).

[94] See s 25(1) which restates the requirement that a woman of the Shafei sect must have a *wali* or a marriage guardian.

[95] A Muslim judge.

[96] Goonesekere, above n 4, 106.

[97] Ibid.

[98] Savitri Goonesekere *Realizing Gender Equity through Law; Sri Lanka's Experience in the Post Nairobi Decade* (Colombo: Centre for Women's Research, 1995) 31.

appointed by the Minister of Legal and Prisons Reform made their recommendations public. The Committee had recommended that the sole ground of divorce should be irretrievable breakdown evidenced by adultery, malicious desertion, 2 years continuous separation with mutual consent to dissolve the marital relationship, or 5 year's separation.[99] The recommendations were clearly inspired by the English legislation prevalent at the time.[100] The recommendations included a mandatory distribution of matrimonial property and also a recommendation that the matrimonial home should be treated as matrimonial property if it satisfied certain conditions. Reforms in the law relating to financial provision on divorce were also recommended. These recommendations were made so as to cushion the effects of divorce particularly since, during the course of the Committee's deliberations, the view had been expressed that women preferred not to terminate a dead marriage because of the financial implications of divorce. The response to the Committee's report by women lawyers and women's groups revealed hostility towards the reforms. They were seen as facilitating divorce and allowing men to escape from their matrimonial obligations. Women expressed the view that the proposed reforms would result in their losing their status as married women. Clearly they felt that there was a stigma attached to the status of a divorced woman. The response was unexpected and a senior male lawyer expressed the view that the reforms would endanger the stability of family life. In essence the response was not very different to some views that had been articulated by a minority of members in 1956 when a Commission had been appointed to look into marriage and divorce.[101] The Commission was unable to reach a consensus but recorded in detail the different views of the members. There were those who felt that a marriage should be terminated if it was found to have been broken down irretrievably. There were others who felt that marriage could not be reduced to the status of any other contract. These persons advocated the retention of the fault-based divorce grounds. Four of the members who advocated irretrievable breakdown of marriage as the basis of divorce felt that there should be a judicial inquiry as to whether the marriage had broken down or not. The other four members of the Commission who advocated irretrievable breakdown of the marriage as the basis of the divorce law felt that it was damaging to have an inquiry as to whether the marriage had broken down. Instead they recommended that the principle of mutual consent which was found in the Kandyan law be used to permit a joint application for divorce. It is clear that the division that prevailed in 1959 was on religious lines with the Christian members holding out against any liberalization of divorce. Whilst such polarization was not evident in the later Committees it is clear that the government has not acted on the recommendations of the later Committees since it is unclear what the response to changing the General law relating to marriage and divorce will be. It seems clear that in the near future at least Sri Lanka will not have any changes in the General laws relating to marriage and

---

[99]   *Report of Ministerial Committee on Reform of the Divorce Laws* (Colombo, November 1990) (see explanation, above n 75).

[100] Matrimonial Causes Act 1973, c 18.

[101] *Report of the Commission on Marriage and Divorce 1956–1959* Sessional Paper 16 (Colombo: Government Press, 1959).

divorce law unless it becomes evident to the government that there is mass support for such change. There is no evidence of such a ground swell movement.

Sweden

PARENTAL INFLUENCE – MORE AND LESS

*Anna Singer**

Résumé

Le droit de la famille suédois a été continuellement réformé et adapté en fonction de l'évolution de la famille et des relations familiales. Petit à petit, les relations parents/enfants ont été modifiées. Ceci est la marque d'un développement progressif des droits de l'enfant et de la reconnaissance de son autonomie, de son indépendance. Ainsi, les parents ont vu leurs pouvoirs diminuer dans les questions strictement relatives à la personne de l'enfant. A l'opposé, les relations parentales ont évolué vers une plus grande responsabilisation des père et mère, pour les faits commis par leurs enfants. Il s'agit de responsabiliser les parents dans le but de protéger les tiers.

I INTRODUCTION – INCREASING INDEPENDENCE FOR CHILDREN

During the past 2 years there have been no major reforms of family law in Sweden. But there are continuously small, but not unimportant, adjustments in the law worth noticing. One topic that is given continuous attention is the one concerning the relationship between parents and children and more specifically, the question of the nature and limits of parental responsibility and rights in relation to the child. Looking at the matter from a different perspective the reforms concern the child's right to independence from the parents as custodians. The changes of the law reflect a slow but steady development towards the recognition of the child as an independent, even autonomous, individual. Parents' right to decide in personal matters for the child is questioned.

Three recent changes in the law can be given as an illustration of this.

In 2010 a new paragraph was introduced in the Social Services Act, ch 11, s 10, that gives the Social Welfare Committee the right to talk to children without the consent of the custodial parents when investigating if the social authorities

---

* Professor of Private Law, Faculty of Law, Uppsala University.

should act in order to protect a child.[1] When the child is mature enough to consent on his or her own behalf to be interviewed no permission from the custodians is necessary. But when the child is considered too young to consent, the custodial parents have to give their permission. If they did not agree, which did happen, the social authorities could not talk to the child and their investigation, and thus the child's right to protection, was thwarted. This new provision makes it possible to talk to younger children if such talks are considered useful in order to obtain a complete picture of the child's situation.

The child's independent right to protection, regardless of the parents' interests, was also strengthened in 2010 by a new provision in the Parents and Children Code, ch 6, s 15(c).[2] In cases concerning the child's visitation with a parent not living with the child the court now has the option of stipulating that the Social Welfare Committee must provide a person to accompany the child.

It is solely the child's need for a sense of security that is to be considered when deciding on visitation support. Such a need might be present in order to avoid conflict or confrontation between the parents when the child is picked up or brought back from visitation or if the child feels worried about meeting a parent, for example if the child has not met the parent for a long time or if the parent whom the child is living with has given the child an unfounded fear of the other parent. If there is an actual risk for the child in meeting the parent, for example a risk that the parent could abduct the child or cause the child harm, no visitation should be granted.

The most recent change in the law reflecting a view of the child as an individual independent from the parents was decided in March 2012 and concerns the child's right to, for example health care. The background is the following:

Joint custody for parents not living together has for a long time been a general aim behind the Swedish legislation regarding parental responsibility. Joint custody means that all decisions concerning the child's personal matters have to be made by the parents together. Not all separated parents have the capacity to co-operate to the degree required in order to manage all these decisions by agreement. Considering that Swedish law gives the court an option to decide on joint custody even if one of the parents is opposed to this, the problems that can arise from the joint right to decide become obvious.

In some cases the necessity of a joint decision by the parents has, for example resulted in an inability to give the child needed medical care since this requires the consent of both parents. One could probably question whether the parents should have joint custody if they cannot reach a joint decision on the child's

---

[1] Government Bill 2009/10:192 Visitation support and conditions for the Social Services to talk to children [Prop 2009/10:192 Umgängesstöd och socialtjänstens förutsättningar att tala med barn].

[2] Government Bill 2009/10:192 Visitation support and conditions for the Social Services to talk to children [Prop. 2009/10:192 Umgängesstöd och socialtjänstens förutsättningar att tala med barn].

right to health care. The Swedish legislator has, however, chosen another solution by accepting a government Bill through parliamentary decision in March 2012.[3] The new law states that, if one of the child's guardians does not agree to non-somatic treatment of the child by the health services or that the child be given certain support measures according to the Social Services Act, the Social Welfare Committee will be able to decide that treatment or another measure can be given. This reform came into force 1 May 2012.

This recent development in the legislation concerning the role of parents in the lives of their children reflects a growing awareness of children as independent rights holders. The Convention on the Rights of the Child has no doubt contributed to this changing view of children and the right of parents to decide on the child's personal matters.

Against this background it is interesting to notice another change in the law concerning the relationship between children and parents, but this time not in family law legislation but in the Tort Liability Act. In the fall of 2010 a change in the Tort Liability Act was introduced concerning the responsibility of parents for damages caused by their children.[4] Swedish tort law is thereby brought into line with many other European jurisdictions concerning parents' liability.[5] From a liability point of view this reform is of great interest as a matter of principle since it, for example entails a step away from the previous position concerning limited vicarious liability. But also from a family law perspective the reform is of interest. Despite being in tort law the change concerns the very core of parental responsibility and therefore should be mentioned here. The message is that parents have to be more involved in their children's lives and that if they are not they might be made economically accountable!

II CHILDREN IN TORT LAW

(a) Liability of the child

According to the Swedish Tort Liability Act (*skadeståndslagen* (SkL)) and its application, children are basically deemed to be liable to the same extent as adults, with the exception of very young children. Children under the age of 4 or 5 would probably not be found liable since they are considered to be too young to be legally responsible for their acts.

---

[3] Government Bill 2011/12:53 Children's possibilities of treatment [Prop 2011/12:53 Barns möjligheter att få vård].

[4] Ministry Publication Series 2009:42 Increased Liability for Parents [Ds 2009:42 Ett skärpt skadeståndsansvar för föräldrar]; Government Bill 2009/10:142 Increased Liability for Custodians [Ett skärpt vårdnadsansvar för vårdnadshavare].

[5] See M Martín-Casals (ed) *Children in Tort Law. Part I: Children as Tortfeasors. Tort and Insurance Law* Vol 17 (New York: Springer Wien, 2006).

When a child has caused damage the behaviour of the child is judged in the same way as the behaviour of an adult person in the same situation. In other words, if a 6-year-old causes a traffic accident because of reckless behaviour and thereby causes damages, the child will be considered responsible if the behaviour could not be expected from an adult in the same situation. That the behaviour can be considered reasonable for an average 6-year-old child is of no importance. The child is instead protected by the possibility of the court mitigating the amount of damages to be paid according to reasonableness. Factors that are considered are the age and maturity of the child, the character of the damaging act, insurance on the side of the tortfeasor and the victim, the economic situation of the parties and other circumstances. This possibility of mitigating the damages is of most importance when the child is under 15 years of age but can be applied if the tortfeasor is under 18 years even though the main rule is that a tortfeasor above 15 years of age should pay full damages.

The reasoning behind this rather strict view of children's liability is explained by the aim of attaining loss distribution by insurance and the related frequency of liability insurance in Sweden. It is estimated that approximately 95% of all households have liability insurance as part of the home insurance. Liability insurance will normally cover all damages caused by children under the age of 12, probably even if the child is less than 4 years old and therefore most likely not liable. If the damages are covered by insurance it has been considered reasonable not to adjust the liability of the child since that would not give the victim full compensation and only benefit the insurance company.

However, most liability insurances exclude intentional damaging acts by children above 12 years of age. In other words, damage caused by teenagers should be covered by the tortfeasor. In cases where the damages are high the possibility of determining liability according to reasonableness is of great practical importance for the child.

In view of the fact that many children lack the economic resources to pay damages, even when the damages have been reduced according to reasonableness, the liability of parents comes into focus.

(b) Liability of parents

A child's custodians, usually the parents, can according to the Swedish law be liable for damage caused by the child but only if fault on their part can be shown. This follows from the general rule in the Tort Liability Act, ch 2, s 1, stating that anyone who intentionally or by negligence causes damage should indemnify the damage. Guidance when considering the liability of a parent can be sought in the Children and Parents Code, ch 6, s 2, where it says that the person having custody over a child has a duty to make sure that the child is under supervision, or that other appropriate measures are taken, in order to prevent the child from causing damage to others. A custodian can consequently be found liable for damage the child has caused if it can be shown that the custodian intentionally or negligently failed in the duty to supervise the child in the way that is stipulated and thereby can be said to have caused the damage.

It is obviously very difficult to show that the parent has not supervised the child in the required way and furthermore through this lack of supervision also (indirectly) caused the damage. There are consequently very few court decisions concerning parents' liability and even fewer where liability has been established.

(c) Increased liability for parents

The lack of legal grounds for making custodial parents liable for the damage their child causes has been a recurring topic for debate in Sweden during the past decades. Different solutions have been considered. One proposal has been to increase the liability for negligent supervision of the child, another strict liability for parents of children up to a certain age, and a third alternative has been a limited vicarious liability. These suggestions have been rejected on the grounds that increased liability for parents does not harmonise with the basic principles of fault in Swedish tort law. Other arguments against an increase in parental liability is that such a solution would go against the tendency to stress the value of loss distribution by insurance and, maybe the most convincing argument in the Swedish debate, that increased liability of parents would only very marginally influence the extent of damaging acts by children. Furthermore, an increased liability for parents would most likely strike very hard on parents who are already economically vulnerable.

However, in 2010 all these objections were rejected when Parliament adopted an amendment to the Tort Liability Act. In ch 3, s 5 it is now stated that a parent with custody of a child is liable for personal injury, material damage and aggravated non-pecuniary harm through a criminal act by the child. The liability is however limited to one fifth of the Price Base Amount for damage caused on one occasion.[6] Consequently, a parent with custody over the child can be obliged to pay approximately €1,000 every time the child commits what would be considered a crime, regardless of whether the child is actually held criminally responsible or not. If the child has two custodial parents this limitation of liability applies to both of them together.

The change in the law concerning the parents' liability has been widely criticised, not only because the effects are doubtful or at least unclear but also because it causes procedural problems. Questions that remain to be answered include: whether the parents should always be sued along with the children and how a victim can show that the damaging act would constitute a crime when the child is under 15 years of age and therefore not prosecuted.

---

[6]   The Price Base Amount [prisbasbelopp] is calculated based on changes in the general price level in accordance with the Social Insurance Code [Socialförsäkringsbalken]. The Price Base Amount for 2012 is 44,000 SEK, approximately €5,000.

These problems have nevertheless been considered tolerable considering the intentions of this, in a sense radical, change in tort law – to prevent youth crime. The message is that parents have the main responsibility for their children and, by reinforcing the liability, signals are sent to the parents that they are responsible for their children. A limited vicarious liability is perceived as an incitement for parents to make sure they have insights into the lives of their children and a reason to react when the child shows signs of unwanted and damaging behaviour. In other words, stricter liability for parents underlines the parents' responsibility to guide their children.[7]

The parents' liability is not unconditional though. It can be reduced according to the Tort Liability Act, ch 3, s 6, if it would be evidently unreasonable to oblige the parent to pay the (albeit limited) damages considering the relationship between the parent and the child or the steps the parent has taken in order to prevent the child from committing the criminal act causing the damage. It is said in the travaux préparatoires that the possibility of reducing damages should be used restrictively if the preventive effect sought with the provision is to be achieved. The fact that the parent in reality had no possibility to actually control the child's actions, for example if the child is living with the other parent in a different city, should not be taken into consideration, neither should the economic consequences for the parent.

It has been feared that the increased liability for parents will strike very hard on some parents without any preventive effects being gained. The liability for custodial parents risks in reality becoming a punishment for bad upbringing of the children. Of interest therefore is to look at what circumstances can be considered when reducing or altogether eradicating parents' liability. How active must a parent be in order to avoid paying damages?

The law has been in force only a limited time and there are not yet any precedents from the Supreme Court. There has, however, been one case from one of the Courts of Appeal where the parents were relieved of the obligation to pay damages.[8] The case concerned a 16–year-old girl who had been found guilty of robbery and assault. The victims of her crime had sued the girl and her parents for damages. The Court of Appeal had to decide if it would be evidently unreasonable to oblige the parents to pay damages. The key questions was how much must a parent do to prevent a child from causing damages in order to avoid liability. The court found that the parents in this case repeatedly had sought the help of social authorities and the school during the years preceding the criminal acts of the girl. They had also on their own to a large extent arranged measures that could reasonably be expected of parents towards a child with the problems the girl had. Because of this the parents did not have to pay damages.

---

[7] Ministry Publication Series 2009:42 Increased Liability for Parents [Ds 2009:42 Ett skärpt skadeståndsansvar för föräldrar] 39–61; Government Bill 2009/10:142 Increased Liability for Custodians [Ett skärpt vårdnadsansvar för vårdnadshavare] 19–37.

[8] The Court of Appeal for Western Sweden, Gothenburg, (verdict 2012–02–15, Case T 4008–11) [Hovrätten för Västra Sverige, dom 2012–02–15, mål T 4008–11].

The verdict seems reasonable. It has to be possible for a parent to avoid liability if it can be shown that the parent has acted in a way the legislator envisaged. Very strict demands on a parent in order to avoid liability could cause parents with children at risk to consider it meaningless to act; they would be liable in any case. That way the law would lead to a result contrary to the one intended. The question concerning exactly what a parent must do in order to avoid liability still needs further clarification. Is it reasonable to demand that a parent repeatedly calls for assistance from the social authorities for help in the supervision of a child? What other measures, apart from 'normal' parental guidance, will be considered relevant when judging the parents' liability. And how are the rights of the child protected?

It can be questioned whether tort law should, or even can, be used as an instrument to underline the role of parents and the family in the normative content of children's upbringing. If the answer is yes it is important to also reflect on the impact on children's rights. Children's rights are in a sense absolute, and should not be made relative. The child's right to protection but also autonomy must be considered in a consistent way regardless of whose interest legal reform is for. Varying respect for children's rights depending on legal context risks undermining the work that so far has been done to give children a stronger position as legal subjects and citizens.

Switzerland

NEW SWISS CODE OF CIVIL PROCEDURE: SPECIAL PROCEEDINGS IN MATRIMONIAL AND FAMILY LAW MATTERS

*Ingeborg Schwenzer and Tomie Keller**

Résumé

Le Code de procédure civil suisse est entré en vigueur le 1er janvier 2011. Le nouveau Code uniformise le droit judiciaire à travers la Suisse, faisant de celle-ci le dernier pays européen à effectuer une telle opération. Il remplace les 26 différentes lois cantonales en la matière. Il faut dire qu'en ce qui concerne la procédure en matières familiales, le Code civil suisse contenait déjà un certain nombre de règles de procédure qui garantissaient un minimum d'uniformité au sein des cantons. Ces règles ont été abrogées pour être incorporées, parfois avec quelques modifications, dans le Code de procédure civile. Après un survol de quelques-unes des règles générales du Code de procédure civile, le présent texte expose les différentes procédures familiales qu'on y retrouve et il conclut en s'intéressant à la médiation et à l'absence de tribunal spécialisé en matières familiales en Suisse. Les changements sont mineurs et n'innovent pas vraiment. Malheureusement, la Suisse a manqué l'occasion de se montrer plus progressiste.

I   INTRODUCTION

On 1 January 2011 the Swiss Code of Civil Procedure (CCP) entered into force.[1] The new code unified civil procedure throughout Switzerland, by replacing the 26 different cantonal statutes on civil procedure. Primarily, the

---

*   Ingeborg Schwenzer, Prof Dr iur, LLM (UC Berkeley), Professor of Private Law, University of Basel, Switzerland.
    Tomie Keller, Bachelor of Law, Research and Teaching Assistant, University of Basel, Switzerland.
1   Swiss Code on Civil Procedure of 19 December 2008 (Schweizerische Zivilprozessordnung (ZPO), SR 272, cited as CCP; c f Message of the Federal Council of 28 June 2006 on the CCP (Botschaft zur Schweizerischen Zivilprozessordnung), Bundesblatt 2006, 7221 et seq, cited as Msg CCP. For the translation of the provisions of the Swiss Code of Civil Procedure the authors relied on: Gehri and Walther *Swiss Laws on Civil Procedure* (English Version) (Zurich: Orell Füssli, 2010); and Valloni and Bloch *Swiss Civil Procedure Code* (CPC) (Zurich: Dike, 2010).

new code governs proceedings of litigious civil cases before cantonal courts,[2] whereas for proceedings before the Swiss Supreme Court the Federal Supreme Court Act (FSCA)[3] still applies.

One of the main purposes of the new Code of Civil Procedure was to consolidate the existing procedural law provisions that were scattered throughout various federal statutes, by integrating them into the new code.[4] In regard to procedural family law, the substantive family law in the Swiss Civil Code (CC)[5] already contained several procedural provisions, to guarantee at least a minimum of uniformity amongst the different cantons. These procedural provisions have now been deleted from the Swiss Civil Code and been integrated – to some extent with certain modifications – in the Swiss Code of Civil Procedure.[6]

After giving a short overview of some general provisions of the Swiss Code of Civil Procedure, this chapter will outline the different family law procedures regulated in the new code and close with a look at the mediation and the (missing) specialised family courts in Switzerland.

II GENERAL PROVISIONS OF THE SWISS CODE OF CIVIL PROCEDURE

The Swiss Code of Civil Procedure is divided into four different parts: general provisions, special provisions, arbitration and final provisions. The second part of the code regulates the special proceedings in matrimonial and family law matters. Among these are the special proceedings regarding matrimonial law (CCP, arts 271–294), which include the proceeding of the protection of the marital union (CCP, art 271(a)) and divorce proceedings (CCP, arts 274–294), children's interest in family law matters (CCP, arts 295–304) and registered-partnership proceedings (CCP, arts 305–307). In addition to these specific provisions several other provisions have to be observed.

Procedural principles regulate the division of work between the court and the parties.[7] There are two pairs of procedural principles: first, the principle of party disposition[8] leaves it to the parties to decide whether and to what extent they want to claim something before a court, while its counterpart, the

---

2   CCP, art 1(a).
3   Federal Supreme Court Act of 17 June 2005 (Bundesgesetz über das Bundesgericht (BGG)), SR 173.110, cited as FSCA.
4   Msg CCP, above n 1, 7237; Valloni and Bloch, above n 1, 2 et seq.
5   Swiss Civil Code of 10 December 1907 (Schweizerisches Zivilgesetzbuch (ZGB)), SR 210, cited as CC.
6   Msg CCP, above n 1, 7359.
7   Vetterli 'Das Eheschutzverfahren nach der schweizerischen Zivilprozessordnung' *Die Praxis des Familienrechts* (FamPra.ch 2010) 785, 790.
8   CCP, art 58(1).

principle of official disposition,[9] restricts the parties' power of disposition. And second, the principle of party presentation[10] cedes the presentation of the facts and submission of the evidence thereof to the parties. The principle of judicial investigation,[11] however, obligates the court to contribute to the finding of the facts and the taking of evidence. The principles of party disposition and party presentation are the rule, whereas their counterparts apply only if the law explicitly so provides. Such deviation can especially be the case in matrimonial and family law matters. The different applications of the principles will be described in detail below.

Generally in civil proceedings the costs are charged to the losing party.[12] This can seem unfair. In cases such as divorce by mutual consent, it is not possible to discern between the winning or losing party.[13] With regard to the costs of family law proceedings art 107(1)(c) of the CCP thus specifies that 'the court can deviate from the allocation principles and allocate the costs at its own discretion'.[14] It is not clear, however, which criteria should be applied pursuant to this discretion. The views in doctrine differ. It is suggested dividing the costs equally[15] or according to financial means.[16] It seems, however, that flexibility with regard to the special circumstances is preferred rather than a strict rule.[17]

Furthermore, in Switzerland there is no statutory requirement to be represented by a lawyer in family law proceedings[18] such as in Germany.[19] Hence, anybody can in principle submit his or her own case before the court. Only if a party is obviously incapable of handling the proceedings independently can the court ask him or her to appoint a representative or appoint a representative itself.[20]

---

[9]   CCP, art 58(2).
[10] CCP, art 55(1).
[11] CCP, art 55(2).
[12] CCP, art 106(1).
[13] Msg CCP, above n 1, 7297.
[14] Fankhauser 'Das Scheidungsverfahren nach neuer ZPO' *Die Praxis des Familienrechts* (FamPra.ch 2010) 753, 754 et seq and especially note 7. For proceedings in family law matters art 107 of the CCP is always the rule; different opinion Jenny in Sutter-Somm, Hasenböhler and Leuenberger (eds) *Kommentar zur Schweizerischen Zivilprozessordnung* (ZPO) (Zurich: Schulthess Verlag, 2010), cited as ZPO Komm, art 107 para 12, art 106 of the CCP is the rule, whereas art 107 of the CCP is the exception and only applies if there are special circumstances.
[15] Leuenberg and Uffer-Tobler *Schweizerisches Zivilprozessrecht* (Berne: Stämpfli Verlag, 2010) para 10.40; Vetterli, above n 7, 785, 794, for the costs of proceedings of protection of the marital union.
[16] Staehelin, Staehelin and Grolimund *Zivilprozessrecht* (Zurich: Schulthess, 2008), § 16 para 36.
[17] Vetterli, above n 7, 785, 794 et seq; Fankhauser, above n 14, 753 et seq.
[18] FamFG, § 114. Act on Proceedings in Family Cases and in Matters of Non-Contentious Litigation of 17 December 2008 (Gesetz über das Verfahren in Familiensachen und in den Angelegenheiten der freiwilligen Gerichtsbarkeit (FamFG)), cited as FamFG.
[19] E Staehelin and Schweizer, ZPO Komm, above n 14, art 68 para 1.
[20] CCP, art 69(1).

III   PROCEEDING OF THE PROTECTION OF THE MARITAL UNION

The purpose of the protection of the marital union is to find solutions in cases of marital problems. Although not conforming with today's reality, protection of the marital union originally had been established to support endangered marriage.[21] Influenced by the ideal of a marriage 'till death do us part', a divorce or even separation had been seen as ultima ratio.[22] Today's provisions on 'marriage protection' in the Swiss Civil Code (CC, arts 172–179) are therefore based on the idea of reconciliation of a marriage and elimination of rash divorces.[23] Nowadays, however, such reconciliation is rare and measures ordered for the protection of the marital union are rather a preparation for divorce.[24] This difficult and delicate situation of reorganising a relationship between the spouses requires a considerate procedural approach. Written arguments should – whenever possible – be avoided in order to facilitate the access to the court and further to prevent the hardening of the situation.[25] Marriage protection proceedings typically aim at injunctive relief relating to child and spousal support, child custody and allocation of the family home.

The protection of the marital union is regulated as a summary proceeding[26] with some special provisions.[27] The summary proceeding is characterised by two aspects: first, flexibility, by allowing different forms of proceedings (oral or written) and second, rapidity, by limiting evidence.[28] The summary proceeding is therefore not an ordinary civil proceeding but a special, relatively informal type of proceeding.[29] It is the aim of the summary proceeding to consider every individual case in detail whilst obtaining a satisfying result as quickly as possible. In other words, the proceeding should be held as thoroughly and as fast as possible.[30] One of the special provisions concerning the protection of the marital union is the application of an alleviated principle of judicial investigation (CCP, art 272).[31] The court establishes the facts on its own accord. This, however, primarily encompasses an increased duty to interrogate and to thereby balance the disparity of unequal power or information of the parties.[32]

---

[21]   Sutter-Somm and Lazic, ZPO Komm, above n 14, art 271 para 7.
[22]   For more details on the historical background of protection of the marital union cf Bräm 'Der Schutz der ehelichen Gemeinschaft: Besonderheiten, Tendenzen, Widersprüche' *Die Praxis des Familienrechts* (FamPra.ch 2006) 519, 523 et seq.
[23]   Bräm, ibid 519, 523 et seq; Büchler and Vetterli *Ehe Partnerschaft Kinder* (Basel: Helbing Lichtenhahn, 2011) 84.
[24]   Vetterli, above n 7, 785, 786; Sutter-Somm and Lazic, ZPO Komm, above n 14, art 271 para 7.
[25]   Vetterli, above n 7, 785, 786.
[26]   CCP, art 271(a); for the summary proceeding see CCP, arts 248 et seq.
[27]   Msg CCP, above n 1, 7358; Büchler and Vetterli, above n 23, 97.
[28]   Msg CCP, above n 1, 7349; Vetterli, above n 7, 785, 787 et seq.
[29]   Sutter-Somm and Kobel *Familienrecht* (Zurich: Schulthess, 2009), para 205
[30]   Vetterli, above n 7, 785, 787.
[31]   Also known as 'social principle of judicial investigation', cf Msg CCP, above n 1, 7348; Büchler and Vetterli, above n 23, 98; Vetterli, above n 7, 785, 790; Sutter-Somm and Lazic, ZPO Komm, above n 14, art 272 para 12.
[32]   Msg CCP, above n 1, 7348; Vetterli, above n 7, 785, 790 et seq; Sutter-Somm and Lazic, ZPO Komm, above n 14, art 272 para 12.

The proceeding of protective measures commences with a request addressed to the court.[33] The request can be provided in written form; in simple or urgent cases it can be declared orally for recording by the court.[34] There is no need for a prayer for relief; it suffices if the request defines the concerning matter.[35] Article 273 of the CCP regulates the further proceeding in detail. Generally, the court conducts a hearing,[36] in which it attempts to find an agreement between the parties.[37] It can waive a hearing only if the facts are clear from the pleadings submitted by the parties or if the facts are undisputed.[38] Furthermore, the parties must appear in person.[39] Since they are the 'actors of their dispute' they should not leave the discussion of their problems up to their counsel and the court.[40] Rather, the proceeding should allow the spouses to continue their interrupted dialogue with the assistance of the court.[41] Hence, the court excuses them only on the grounds of illness, old age or for other good reasons,[42] such as permanent stays abroad.[43]

Sometimes, however, if a matter is particularly urgent the court can immediately order temporary measures without hearing the opposing party (CCP, art 265(1)). Such measures can for instance be required in cases of domestic violence. In essence, the court must balance the pros and cons of the requested measure and evaluate whether it is particularly urgent.[44] The omitted hearing then has to be conducted as soon as possible. Thereafter the court decides on the application by upholding, modifying, or suspending the temporary measure.[45]

IV DIVORCE PROCEEDINGS

Over the past years the divorce rate in Switzerland has been around 50%, with a peak of 54.4% of divorces in 2010.[46] If the currently observed trend lasts, it would mean that more than every second marriage will end in divorce. By

---

33 CCP, art 252(1); Tappy 'La procédure de mesures protectrices de l'union conjugale selon le nouveau Code de procédure civile suisse: constantes et nouveautés' in Büchler and Müller-Chen (eds) *Festschrift für Ingeborg Schwenzer zum 60. Geburtstag* (Berne: Stämpfli Verlag, 2011), cited as FS Schwenzer, 1699, 1704; Vetterli, above n 7, 785, 789.
34 CCP, art 252(2).
35 Vetterli, above n 7, 785, 789.
36 CCP, art 273(1); Tappy, FS Schwenzer, above n 33, 1699, 1710; Vetterli in Schwenzer (ed) *Fam Kommentar Scheidung* (Berne: Stämpfli Verlag, 2011), cited as FamKomm, Anh ZPO art 273 para 1.
37 CCP, art 273(3); Büchler and Vetterli, above n 23, 97.
38 CCP, art 273(1).
39 CCP, art 273(2); Tappy, FS Schwenzer, above n 33, 1699, 1712.
40 Vetterli, FamKomm, above n 36, art 273 para 3.
41 Vetterli, above n 7, 785, 786.
42 CCP, art 273(2).
43 Vetterli, FamKomm, above n 36, art 273 para 3.
44 Büchler and Vetterli, above n 23, 98.
45 CCP, art 265(2).
46 BFS, www.bfs.admin.ch/bfs/portal/en/index/themen/01/06/blank/key/06/03.html (accessed 20 December 2011).

comparison to other European countries, Switzerland thus is among those with the highest divorce rates. An even higher divorce rate is found only in Belgium, the Czech Republic and Lithuania.[47]

Swiss law distinguishes between two kinds of divorce: divorce by mutual consent (CC, arts 111, 112) and divorce without the consent of one of the spouses. The latter can be decreed either after a certain period of factual separation (CC, art 114) or because the upholding of the marriage appears to be unacceptable for the claimant (CC, art 115). Most of the divorces in Switzerland are divorces by mutual consent. In 2010 almost 95% of the divorces were by mutual consent (89.1% in cases of CC, art 111; 5.0% in cases of CC, art 112). Only 5.6% were divorces according to art 114 of the CC, which leaves a mere 0.3% for the cases of art 115 of the CC.[48] Nevertheless, in Switzerland divorce is only possible by decree of a court (although marriage takes place before a civil registry office), which still safeguards the belief of the institutional character of marriage.[49]

Under the old law numerous provisions regarding the divorce proceeding already existed in the (substantive) family law in the Swiss Civil Code. These provisions (old CC, arts 135–149) have mostly been integrated into the new code.[50] The divorce proceeding is now comprehensively dealt with in arts 274–293 of the CCP with the provisions for the ordinary proceeding applying supplementary.[51] The divorce proceeding is thus a 'special ordinary proceeding'.[52]

Articles 274–284 of the CCP regulate the general provisions, which are applicable for all divorce proceedings.[53] Generally, the parties have to appear personally at the hearings.[54] Furthermore, an alleviated principle of judicial investigation is applicable for divorce proceedings according to art 277(3) of the CCP. The court therefore has an increased duty to interrogate.[55] However, for the division of matrimonial property and spousal support art 277(1) of the CCP defines the application of the principle of party presentation. This leads to the peculiarity that in proceedings of protection of marital union the principle of an alleviated judicial investigation always applies,[56] whereas for

---

[47]   Eurostat,   http://epp.eurostat.ec.europa.eu/tgm/table.do?tab=table&init=1&language= en&pcode=tps00013&plugin=1 (accessed 20 December 2011).

[48]   BFS, www.bfs.admin.ch/bfs/portal/de/index/themen/01/06/blank/data/03.Document.97676.xls (accessed 20 December 2011).

[49]   Sutter and Freiburghaus *Kommentar zum neuen Scheidungsrecht* (Zurich: Schulthess, 1999) Vorbemerkungen zu arts 111–118 para 5.

[50]   Msg CCP, above n 1, 7359.

[51]   CCP, art 219.

[52]   Kobel, ZPO Komm, above n 14, art 274 N 5; Sutter-Somm 'Das familienrechtliche Verfahren nach der Schweizerischen Zivilprozessordnung' in *Vierte Schweizerische Familienrecht§tage* (Zurich: Stämpfli Verlag, 2008) 79, 82 et seq.

[53]   Sutter-Somm, ibid 79, 85.

[54]   CCP, art 287.

[55]   Meyer, FamKomm, above n 36, Anh ZPO art 277 para 14.

[56]   CCP, art 272.

divorce proceedings in financial matters the principle of party presentation applies.[57] Although no reasonable explanation exists, this difference should not be overrated.[58]

(a) Divorce by mutual consent

The proceeding of divorce by mutual consent[59] can be requested in cases where the spouses have agreed upon divorce and on the consequences thereof (CC, art 111). The proceeding commences by the spouses filing a joint petition directly with the court.[60] Article 285 of the CCP now further specifies the formal requirements and thereby completes art 111 of the CC. The petition must contain the names and addresses of the spouses as well as the names of any representatives. Moreover, a comprehensive agreement regarding the consequences of the divorce, along with any necessary documents and with joint applications in relation to the children, as well as the date and signatures are required. If the spouses agree only on the divorce but not on (all) consequences thereof (CC, art 112), art 286 of the CCP further requires them to specify those matters which they want to delegate to the court.

If the petition is complete, the court has to hear the spouses both jointly and separately in order to make sure that both parties agree on the divorce as well as on the divorce settlement.[61] The hearing can be seen as a counterpart of the wedding. Only now, the parties have to confirm their 'no' to the marriage.[62] The court, however, does not have to determine the 'whether and why' of the breakup of the marriage.[63] Hence, the court issues the divorce decree if it is convinced that the willingness for divorce and the settlement are the 'product of free will and careful reflection'[64] and that the settlement is 'clear, complete and not obviously inappropriate'.[65]

The degree of judicial review varies in regard to the different matters contained in the settlement. At first, child issues are not within the parties' disposition and the court is obliged to investigate the facts on its own accord (CCP, art 296). Also, the division of occupational pensions (CC, art 122) is not within the parties' disposition.[66] Any deviating agreement (CC, art 123) is only approved by the court if it complies with the law.[67] In regard to the financial consequences of the divorce (matrimonial property and spousal support),

---

[57] Fankhauser (above n 14) note 20; Vetterli, above n 7, 785, 790.
[58] Vetterli, above n 7, 785, 790.
[59] CCP, arts 285–289.
[60] CCP, art 274; CC, art 111.
[61] CCP, art 287; Fankhauser, FamKomm, above n 36, Anh ZPO art 287 para 1, for the hearing CCP, art 287 refers to CC, arts 111(1) and 112(2).
[62] Büchler and Vetterli, above n 23, 110.
[63] Büchler and Vetterli, above n 23, 110; Fankhauser, FamKomm, above n 36, art 111 para 10; Sutter and Freiburghaus, above n 49, Vorbemerkungen zu arts 111–118 para 5.
[64] CC, art 111(2).
[65] CCP, art 279(1).
[66] Baumann K Lauterburg, FamKomm, above n 36, art 123 para 2.
[67] CCP, art 280(3).

however, it is controversial as to what extent the judge is allowed or obliged to control the agreement. The Swiss Supreme Court generally does not interfere with the parties' will.[68] The judicial review with regards to the contents of the divorce settlement, however, should protect the weaker spouse – which in most cases is the wife.[69] It is thus questionable as to what extent party autonomy should be respected in such a situation.[70]

The judgment follows right after the hearing.[71] The court grants the divorce and ratifies the settlement.[72] The divorce decree can only be appealed on the grounds of defects in consent.[73] If, however, the consequences of the divorce remain disputed (primarily in cases of CC, art 112), the proceedings are continued contradictorily.[74] For this part of the proceedings the provisions for unilateral divorce and the ordinary proceedings apply.[75]

(b)   Unilateral divorce

In cases of unilateral divorce the proceeding commences with a request for divorce.[76] The unilateral divorce can be filed without written arguments. It is sufficient if the particular ground for divorce is specified (CC, art 114 or 115) and the request contains the prayers for the consequences of the divorce as well as the required documents.[77]

After filing the request for divorce, the court summons the spouses to a settlement hearing and enquires whether there are grounds for divorce.[78] Such a reason is given if the factual separation has lasted for 2 years (CC, art 114). If the spouses do not agree on divorce, the court can hardly judge whether or not a marriage has failed. The time of separation demanded by the legislator is therefore an irrefutable presumption of the irretrievable breakdown of the marriage[79] – but certainly also a threshold for the claimant in order to safeguard the institutional character of marriage.[80] The court, however, only has to establish if the 2-year period has elapsed.

---

[68]   Stein-Wigger, FamKomm, above n 36, Anh ZPO art 279 para 23.

[69]   Schwenzer 'Vertragsfreiheit im Ehevermögens- und Scheidungsfolgerecht' (1996) 196 *Archiv für die civilistische Praxis* (AcP) 88, 108 et seq.

[70]   Schwenzer 'Grenzen der Vertragsfreiheit in Scheidungskonventionen und Eheverträgen' *Die Praxis des Familienrechts* (FamPra.ch 2005) 1 et seq.

[71]   There is no reflection period as formerly required by art 111 of the old CC, cf Schwenzer 'Ten Years of Divorce Reform' in Bill Atkin (ed) *International Survey of Family Law, 2011 Edition* (Jordan Publishing Limited, 2011), 397, 400.

[72]   CCP, art 288(1).

[73]   CCP, art 289.

[74]   CCP, art 288(2).

[75]   Fankhauser, FamKomm, above n 36, Anh ZPO art 288 N 13.

[76]   CCP, art 274.

[77]   CCP, art 290; Büchler and Vetterli, above n 23, 111.

[78]   CCP, art 292(1).

[79]   Fankhauser, FamKomm, above n 36, art 114 para 3.

[80]   Büchler and Vetterli, above n 23, 102.

If the grounds for divorce have been established, the court attempts an agreement between the spouses with regard to the effects of the divorce.[81] In difficult cases more than one hearing may be necessary.[82] If the grounds for divorce have not been established or if the spouses cannot reach an agreement, the court grants the claimant a certain period of time to submit written arguments.[83] For further proceedings arts 274–284 of the CCP as well as the provisions for the ordinary proceedings pursuant to arts 219 et seq of the CCP apply.

In any case, however, the divorce decree should be scrutinised as to its appropriateness. Unfortunately, neither the Code on Civil Procedure nor the Civil Code contains a rule similar to art 279 of the CCP, which would allow the court to review the decree with regard to its contents. If such a review is not undertaken it may yield inadequate results:[84] a divorce decree could be rendered which – under judicial review according to art 279 of the CCP – would not have been approved in a divorce settlement. In a divorce settlement, for example, a waiver of spousal support can be approved by the court only if it is not 'obviously inappropriate'. In unilateral divorce, however, the court is not obliged to question missing requests since the consequences of the divorce (such as spousal support) are within the parties' disposition.[85]

V CHILD ISSUES

In many divorces (43.5%)[86] minor children are affected, in 2010 all in all a total of 15,374 children.[87] Although most births still take place within marriage, the proportion of births out of wedlock has quadrupled since 1970. Last year a total of 18.6% of the births in Switzerland were outside marriage.[88] Still, in comparison with Europe (EU 2009: 37%) this figure is very low.[89] Simultaneously with the increase of births out of wedlock the number of recognitions of paternity has increased. In 2010 about 15,000 recognitions have

---

[81] CCP, art 291(2).
[82] Fankhauser, FamKomm, above n 36, Anh ZPO art 291 para 5.
[83] CCP, art 291(3).
[84] Entscheid Appellationsgericht Basel-Stadt (Appellate Court Decision), 16 January 2004 – *Die Praxis des Familienrechts* (FamPra.ch 2006) 454 et seq; cf Schwenzer 'Urteilsanmerkung' *Die Praxis des Familienrechts* (FamPra.ch 2006) 458 et seq.
[85] Stein-Wigger, Inhaltskontrolle von Scheidungsurteilen, FS Schwenzer, above n 33, 1637 et seq.
[86] BFS, www.bfs.admin.ch/bfs/portal/de/index/news/publikationen.Document.149588.pdf (see page 12, G11) (accessed 20 December 2011).
[87] BFS, www.bfs.admin.ch/bfs/portal/en/index/themen/01/06/blank/key/06/06.html (accessed 20 December 2011).
[88] BFS, www.bfs.admin.ch/bfs/portal/en/index/themen/01/06/blank/key/02/03.html (accessed 20 December 2011).
[89] Eurostat, http://epp.eurostat.ec.europa.eu/tgm/table.do?tab=table&init=1&language=en&pcode=tps00018&plugin=1 (accessed 20 December 2011).

been registered, while the number in the year before was only about 14,000.[90] In most of the cases (98.5%) the recognition of paternity was voluntary.[91]

On grounds of Art 12 of the United Nations Convention on the Rights of the Child, Switzerland implemented certain provisions regarding the child's position in proceedings. These provisions, such as the child's right to be heard (old CC, art 144) or representation of the child (old CC, art 146), were regulated under divorce proceedings.[92] The provisions on child issues before civil courts are now governed in a separate heading (CCP, arts 295–304) and therefore not restricted to divorce proceedings any more.[93] The first two articles apply to all child issues (CCP, arts 295 and 296) whereas arts 297–301 of the CCP are restricted to the proceedings in matrimonial law matters. This includes proceedings of the protection of the marital union, divorce, separation and annulment of marriage.[94] Article 302 of the CCP enumerates the matters submitted to summary proceeding, and finally, arts 303 and 304 of the CCP regulate the claims for child support and paternity.

As a general provision art 295 of the CCP determines that independent actions such as actions for child support (CC, arts 276 et seq), duty of support by relatives (CC, art 329(3)) and also actions to determine or challenge paternity (CC, arts 252 et seq), are decided in simplified proceedings.[95] If child issues, however, have to be decided in the course of matrimonial proceedings the special provisions (CCP, arts 297–301) apply. Furthermore, art 296 of the CCP specifies that the (absolute) principle of judicial investigation and the principle of official disposition apply to all cases of child issues. The court therefore has to investigate the facts of the case and is not bound by the prayers for relief of the parties. This provision is mandatory for all proceedings regarding child issues. This means that: for instance in proceedings of the protection of the marital union, art 296 of the CCP applies with regard to child issues, while for all other matters the alleviated principle of judicial investigation (CCP, art 272) is decisive.[96] Finally, art 296(2) of the CCP obliges the parties and third parties to co-operate in the necessary investigations to determine paternity to the extent that their health is not threatened.[97]

In cases of matrimonial proceedings there are three ways of 'integrating a child': first, virtually in dialogue with the parents (CCP, art 297), second by

---

[90]   BFS, www.bfs.admin.ch/bfs/portal/en/index/themen/01/06/blank/key/10.html (accessed 20 December 2011).

[91]   BFS, www.bfs.admin.ch/bfs/portal/de/index/themen/01/22/press.Document.145036.pdf (see page 2) (accessed 20 December 2011).

[92]   Sutter-Somm, above n 36, 79, 83; Schweighauser, FamKomm, above n 36, Anh ZPO Vorbem zu arts 295–302 para 2.

[93]   Schweighauser, FamKomm, above n 36, Anh ZPO Vorbem zu arts 295–302 para 2.

[94]   Schweighauser, FamKomm, above n 36, Anh ZPO Vorbem zu arts 295–302 para 5.

[95]   CCP, arts 243 et seq.

[96]   Steck and Schweighauser 'Die Kinderbelange in der Schweizerischen Zivilprozessordnung' *Die Praxis des Familienrechts* (FamPra.ch 2010) 800, 801 et seq.

[97]   Accordingly the provisions on the rights of parties and third parties to refuse (CCP, arts 160 et seq) do not apply (CCP, art 296(2)).

hearing the child (CCP, art 298), and finally, by representation of the child (CCP, arts 299 and 300).[98] This reflects the idea of the child not only being present once but rather throughout the proceedings.[99]

If the court has to issue orders regarding a child, it has to hear the parents in person. Moreover, the court is now authorised to order the parents to submit to mediation proceedings.[100] Already before this new provision, however, the Swiss Supreme Court had taken one step further by permitting an authority to oblige the parties to mediate in order to protect the child's welfare.[101] Such a duty of mediation should confront the parents with the needs of the child and rather has to be seen as an obligation to reflect the child's interest.[102] The legislator acknowledges the importance of communication between the parents in such cases by allowing free mediation under certain circumstances.[103] Any agreements reached by the parents in mediation have to be comprehensively reviewed and approved by the court as child issues are not within the parties' disposition (CCP, art 296).[104]

The child's right to be heard had been introduced in Switzerland in the course of the divorce reform in 2000.[105] With the new code, however, the child hearing is now no longer restricted to divorce proceedings and has to be granted in all matrimonial proceedings.[106] According to art 298(1) of the CCP the court, itself or via a third person, has to hear the child. The realisation of child hearings in practice is, though, hesitant. It is not clear how many children actually get invited to a hearing. An analysis of three cantons[107] in 2002–2003 showed that only a third of the minor children affected by divorce had been invited to such a hearing.[108] Of these invited children another third (approximately 11% of all minor children affected by divorce) have actually

---

[98] Vetterli, above n 7, 785, 796.

[99] Büchler and Vetterli, above n 23, 259; Schreiner 'Einbezug von Kindern und Jugendlichen in die Regelung von (gerichtlichen) Trennungs- und Scheidungsangelegenheiten: Überlegungen aus der Praxis' in Büchler and Simoni (eds) *Kinder und Scheidung: Der Einfluss der Rechtspraxis auf familiale Übergänge* (Zurich: Rüegger, 2009) 362, 367 et seq.

[100] CCP, art 297(2).

[101] BGer, 9 December 2009, 5A_457/2009, E.4.1–4.3 – *Die Praxis des Familienrechts* (FamPra.ch) 2010, 474 et seq; cf Gloor and Umbricht 'Urteilsanmerkung' *Die Praxis des Familienrechts* (FamPra.ch) 2010, 478 et seq.

[102] Vetterli, above n 7, 785, 796 et seq.

[103] CCP, art 218(2), free mediation in non-pecuniary children's rights cases if the parties do not have the necessary resources; Msg CCP, above n 1, 7337 et seq; Steck and Schweighauser, above n 96, 800, 804.

[104] Steck and Schweighauser, above n 96, 800, 803 et seq.

[105] CC, arts 111–149; cf Message of the Federal Council of 15 November 1995 on amendments to the CC (divorce law) (Botschaft über die Änderung des Schweizerischen Zivilgesetzbuches (Personenstand, Eheschliessung, Scheidung, Kindesrecht, Verwandtenunterstützungspflicht, Heimstätten, Vormundschaft und Ehevermittlung), Bundesblatt 1996 I, 1 et seq, cited as Msg Divorce.

[106] Schweighauser, FamKomm, above n 36, art 298 para 9, 24.

[107] Basel-Stadt, Basel-Land and Zurich.

[108] Simoni and Trost-Melchert 'Partizipation der Kinder im Scheidungsprozess – Ergebnisse der Untersuchung' in Büchler and Simoni (eds) *Kinder und Scheidung: Der Einfluss der Rechtspraxis auf familiale Übergänge* (Zurich: Rüegger, 2009) 52, 54, 78.

been heard.[109] Furthermore, the results clearly showed that age is a very important factor. The older a child the more likely it becomes that the child will be invited and therefore will be heard.[110] In 2005, the Swiss Supreme Court[111] held that in principle children from the age of 6 should be heard. Although this threshold is still rather high in comparison with other countries such as Germany, where children are already heard from the age of 3,[112] judges question the practicability of this age for different reasons.[113] Overall, judges have an ambivalent attitude towards child hearings. A general belief that the child is entitled to be heard has not yet been achieved.[114]

To an even lesser extent courts order the separate representation of the child (CCP, art 299(1)). In the above-mentioned analysis a representative had been appointed only once. One of the main reasons for the lack of child representation is the judicial discretion.[115] The court orders the representation of the child if it is 'necessary'. Although art 299(2) of the CCP defines situations in which necessity especially can be presumed, such a situation does not give the right to mandatory representation.[116] Only if a child requests representation is the court legally obligated to issue such an order (CCP, art 299(3)).[117] A child will obviously only know about this possibility if the child had been told about it (probably in a previous child hearing). This leads to the conclusion that the court is hardly ever obligated to order representation.

VI   MEDIATION AND THE FAMILY COURT

The Swiss Code on Civil Procedure for the first time establishes certain rules on mediation. Although mediation had been nearly absent in Swiss law,[118] it has steadily developed on a private basis and is now better known by the public and respected among professionals.[119] Many lawyers as well as judges have

---

[109] Simoni and Trost-Melchert, ibid 52, 56, 78.

[110] Simoni and Trost-Melchert, ibid 52, 64.

[111] BGE 131 III 553 – *Die Praxis des Familienrechts* (FamPra.ch) 2005, 958 et seq.

[112] Karle 'Die Praxis der Kindesanhörung in Deutschland unter besonderer Berücksichtigung der Frage einer Be- oder Entlastung der Kinder' *Die Praxis des Familienrechts* (FamPra.ch) 2011, 651, 656.

[113] Simoni, Büchler and Baumgarten 'Interviews mit den Richterinnen und Richtern' in Büchler and Simoni (eds) *Kinder und Scheidung: Der Einfluss der Rechtspraxis auf familiale Übergänge* (Zürich; Rüegger, 2009) 107, 108, 114.

[114] Simoni, Büchler and Baumgarten, ibid 107, 115.

[115] Schweighauser 'Warum gibt es keine Kindesvertretungen in Scheidungsverfahren?' in Büchler and Simoni (eds) *Kinder und Scheidung: Der Einfluss der Rechtspraxis auf familiale Übergänge* (Zurich: Rüegger, 2009) 372 et seq.

[116] BGer, 28 August 2001, 5P.173/2001, E.2 – *Die Praxis des Familienrechts* (FamPra.ch) 2002, 163 et seq; BGer, 27 October 2000, 5C.210/2000, E.2.b – *Die Praxis des Familienrechts* (FamPra.ch) 2001, 606, 607 et seq.

[117] Ibid.

[118] Gloor and Umbricht Lukas 'Die Mediation in der Zivilprozessordnung' *Die Praxis des Familienrechts* (FamPra.ch) 2010, 818, 819.

[119] Liatowitsch 'Was das Familienrecht von der Mediation erwartet und (noch) nicht für sie tut' in FS Schwenzer, above n 33, 1069, 1074.

undergone intensive training in mediation. The new provisions in the code in particular clarify the relationship between mediation and court proceedings: mediation as an equal alternative to conciliation proceedings (CCP, art 213) or as an instrument during proceedings that are already pending (CCP, art 214). The latter can be suspended at all times in favour of mediation if either recommended by the court or jointly requested by the parties. Moreover, the parties can request approval of an agreement reached in a mediation process – which then has the same effect as a final court decision (CCP, art 217). In comparison with other countries,[120] however, the new code still lacks important regulations on requirements, duties, education and registration of approved mediators. Nevertheless, with the possibility of an 'anytime recommendation of mediation' by the court, an important step has been made towards further establishing mediation in Switzerland.[121]

With regard to family law proceedings, mediation is more emphasised in regard to child issues. As already seen, the court is authorised to order the parents to submit to mediation proceedings. Special importance is further attached to mediation in cases of international child abduction.[122] There, mediation is explicitly provided for in order to accomplish the voluntary return of the child or an amicable settlement of the case.[123] The parties therefore can be induced in a proper way to engage in mediation.[124] Regrettably, the legislator imposes the costs of the mediation on the parties (CCP, art 218). As already mentioned, an exception may be made only in children's rights cases. Hence, for financially weak parties the free choice between mediation and litigation is narrowed.[125]

With regard to establishing specialised family courts in Switzerland unfortunately again the time seemed not to be ripe.[126] Although most of the proceedings in civil law matters brought before courts of first instance are family law matters and the positive aspects are unquestioned, it seems that Switzerland is somehow reluctant to have specialised family courts.[127] Several attempts failed: the draft of the divorce law in 1995[128] contained a

---

[120] Cf the comparison with Austria and Liechtenstein in Gloor and Umbricht Lukas, above n 118, 818, 820 et seq.

[121] Gloor and Umbricht Lukas, above n 118, 818, 823.

[122] Already mentioned in: Schwenzer, above n 71, 397, 407.

[123] Article 3(1) of the Statute on International Child Abduction of 21 December 2007 (Bundesgesetz über internationale Kindesentführung und die Haager Übereinkommen zum Schutz von Kindern und Erwachsenen (BG-KKE)), SR 211.222.32, cited as SICA, in force since 1 July 2009; cf Message of the Federal Council on the SICA (Botschaft zur Umsetzung der Übereinkommen über internationale Kindesentführung sowie zur Genehmigung und Umsetzung der Haager Übereinkommen über den Schutz von Kindern und Erwachsenen), Bundesblatt 2007, 2595.

[124] SICA, arts 4(2), 8(1) (above n 123).

[125] Gloor and Umbricht Lukas, above n 118, 818, 828.

[126] Already discussed in: Schwenzer, above n 71, 397, 406.

[127] Aeschlimann *Familiengerichtsbarkeit im internationalen Vergleich* (Berne, 2009) 104 et seq; Häfeli 'Familiengerichte in der Schweiz – eine ungeliebte Institution mit Zukunft' *Die Praxis des Familienrechts* (FamPra.ch) 2010, 34, 42, 54.

[128] Cf Divorce Reform (above n 105).

recommendation for introducing specialised family courts in Switzerland.[129] Parliament, however, rejected this proposal.[130] Despite numerous requests from scholars and practitioners[131] specialised family courts did not find their way into the new code.[132] The last attempt at introducing family courts in the course of the reform of child protection and tutelage[133] did not succeed either. The only leftover of this approach is that with the future amendment of the Civil Code the cantons will be ordered to organise specialised authorities for child and adult protection until 2013.[134] This leads to somewhat absurd results:[135] in case of children whose parents are not married child protection measures have to be dealt with by the specialised authority; if, however, the same question comes up within divorce proceedings concerning a child of married parents a non-specialised court – usually a sole judge – will have jurisdiction.

Even more unfortunate is that with this last approach the discussion of introducing specialised family courts in Switzerland seems to have settled at least for the foreseeable future.[136] The lack of specialised family courts will become even more obvious as more and more lawyers specialise in family law. Since 2006 for instance a lawyer can become a 'specialist in family law' (*Fachanwalt Familienrecht*) by undergoing further intensive education with practical training as well as passing an exam.[137]

VII SUMMARY

Switzerland was the last country in Europe to unify its civil procedure.[138] With this step it harmonised the different cantonal procedures and thereby facilitated the understanding and application of Swiss procedural law. By introducing conciliation and mediation proceedings, the new code encourages settlement of disputes out of court.

---

[129] Msg Divorce, above n 105, 154 et seq; Aeschlimann, above n 127, 103.

[130] Aeschlimann, above n 127, 103.

[131] Schwenzer 'Braucht die Schweiz Familiengerichte' in Vetterli (ed) *Auf dem Weg zum Familiengericht* (Berne, 2004) 89 et seq; Aeschlimann, above n 127, 133 et seq; Häfeli, above n 127, 34 et seq.

[132] Schweizerische Zivilprozessordnung: Bericht zum Vorentwurf der Expertenkommission Juni 2003, 16 et seq.

[133] Articles 360–454 of the Draft CC (entering into force on 1 January 2013); cf Message of the Federal Council of 28 June 2006 on amendments to the CC (adult protection, law of persons, child law) ((Botschaft zur Änderung des Schweizerischen Zivilgesetzbuches (Erwachsenenschutz, Personenrecht und Kindesrecht)), Bundesblatt 2006, 7001 et seq.

[134] Draft CC, art 220, Bundesblatt 2009, 141, 164; Aeschlimann, above n 127, 103 et seq; Häfeli, Familiengerichte, above n 127, 34 et seq.

[135] Problem already addressed in: Schwenzer, above n 71, 397, 406; see also Büchler and Vetterli, above n 23, 113.

[136] Aeschlimann, above n 127, 104; Fassbind 'Die Organisation des Kindes- und Erwachsenenschutzes nach neuem Erwachsenenschutzrecht' Die Praxis des Familienrechts (FamPra.ch) 2011, 553, 584 et seq.

[137] For further details see http://fachanwalt.sav-fsa.ch/UEber-den-Fachanwalt.239.0.html (accessed 20 December 2011).

[138] Msg CCP, above n 1, 7228.

In regard to matrimonial and family law proceedings, however, the new code adopted mainly the benchmarks already set up in the (substantive) family law in the Swiss Civil Code. The changes are minor and not particularly innovative. Unfortunately, in many points Switzerland missed out on the opportunity of being more progressive.

Uganda

WIDOW INHERITANCE IN UGANDA

Jamil Ddamulira Mujuzi[*]

Résumé

La constitution de l'Ouganda et les instruments internationaux et régionaux sur les droits de la personne que l'Ouganda a ratifiés ou auxquels le pays a adhéré, tels le Protocol sur les droits de la femme en Afrique de la Charte Africaine des droits de l'homme et des peuples, la Convention sur l'élimination de toutes les formes de discrimination à l'égard des femmes et le Pacte international sur les droits civils et politiques, prévoient que le femmes ne peuvent être obligées de se marier sans leur consentement. Pourtant la tradition du legs de la veuve est toujours vivante dans certaines communautés ougandaises. Plusieurs tentatives ont été faites pour éliminer cette pratique. Ce texte en fait la description, en partant de la Commission constitutionnelle de 1988 jusqu'au projet de loi de 2009 sur le mariage et le divorce.

I   INTRODUCTION

Although the Constitution of Uganda[1] and the regional and international human rights instruments that Uganda has ratified or acceded to such as the Protocol to the African Charter on Human and Peoples' Rights on the Rights of Women in African,[2] the Convention on the Elimination of All Forms of Discrimination against Women[3] and the International Covenant on Civil and Political Rights[4] specifically provide that marriage should be entered into only with the free and full consent of both parties, widow inheritance is reportedly 'a

---

[*]   Senior Lecturer, Faculty of Law, University of the Western Cape (UWC); LLD (UWC); LLM (Pretoria); LLM (Free State); LLB (Makerere). I am grateful to the National Research Foundation for making the funds available for me to conduct research in Uganda for the purpose of writing this paper. I am also grateful to Mr Khaukha Andrew of the Uganda Law Reform Commission and to Mr Andrew Abayunga of the Parliament of Uganda for availing me some of the materials used in this paper during my visit to Uganda.
[1]   Article 31(3).
[2]   Article 6(a) of the Protocol to the African Charter on Human and Peoples' Rights on the Rights of Women in Africa provides that 'no marriage shall take place without the free and full consent of both parties'.
[3]   Article 16(1)(b) of the Convention on the Elimination of All Forms of Discrimination against Women.
[4]   Article 23(3).

common practice in Uganda'[5] with recent cases reported in some areas.[6] Dr Florence Ebanyat, an assistant commissioner in the Uganda Ministry of Health, reportedly said that widow inheritance has 'immensely' contributed to the spread of HIV in Uganda.[7] Traditional and cultural leaders are also of the view that widow inheritance is one of the practices that 'fuel HIV transmission'.[8] A High Court judge reportedly said that the custom of widow inheritance 'does not recognise the widow as a human being with a mind and conscience'.[9] Commenting on the Marriage and Divorce Bill, one commentator said that '[w]idow inheritance is there because of lack of social security for women and an alternative has to be found to this practice'.[10] This chapter highlights the steps taken to eliminate widow inheritance in Uganda. It is divided into five parts: Part I is the introduction; Part II highlights the views that Ugandans expressed on the issue of widow inheritance before the Constitutional Commission which gathered the views of Ugandans on what should be included in the Constitution; Part III deals with the Constituent Assembly debates in which the delegates who debated the Constitutional Commission recommendations expressed their views on the issue of widow inheritance; Part IV looks at the legislative steps taken by the Ugandan government to abolish widow inheritance; and Part V is the conclusion.

II THE UGANDA CONSTITUTIONAL COMMISSION (THE ODOKI COMMISSION)

Before the Ugandan Constitution was drafted, the Ugandan government established the Uganda Constitutional Commission (popularly known as the Odoki Commission because it was chaired by Justice Benjamin Odoki) to gather the views of all Ugandans on what they thought should be included in the Constitution. Ugandans informed the Odoki Commission that women's right to equality was one of the most violated rights in pre-colonial Uganda.[11] The right to equality was also highlighted as one of the most violated rights

---

[5] M Tebajjukira 'Widow inheritance to be banned' *The New Vision* (28 September 2009) available at www.newvision.co.ug/D/8/12/696002 (accessed 18 January 2012).

[6] A Ondoga and B Okethwengu 'Alur King warns against domestic violence' *The New Vision* (15 December 2010) available at www.newvision.co.ug/PA/8/16/741265 (where it is reported that the king said that the practice of widow inheritance contributed to the spread of HIV); F Mugabi 'Arua HIV rate high' *The New Vision* (8 July 2007) available at www.newvision.co.ug/D/8/16/574825 (where it is reported that widow inheritance was on the increase in Arua) (both accessed 18 January 2012).

[7] M Nampala 'Widow Inheritance Escalates HIV/AIDS' *The New Vision* (9 February 2003) available at www.newvision.co.ug/PA/8/17/114867 (accessed 18 January 2012).

[8] R Baguma and P Kwesiga 'Traditional leaders join HIV fight' *The New Vision* (7 March 2010) available at www.newvision.co.ug/D/8/13/712231 (accessed 23 January 2012).

[9] Vision Reporter 'Judge calls for tough law on HIV/AIDS' *The New Vision* (29 June 2008) available at www.newvision.co.ug/PA/8/16/636217 (accessed 23 January 2012) (comments by Justice David Wangutusi at a workshop for judges and magistrates).

[10] J Jagire 'Marriage Bill is still oppressive' *The New Vision* (4 October 2009) available at www.newvision.co.ug/PA/8/21/696723 (accessed 23 January 2012).

[11] *The Report of the Uganda Constitutional Commission: Analysis and Recommendations* (1992) para 7.19(a).

since Uganda attained independence as laws and cultural practices denied women their right to equality.[12] Women's groups criticised cultural practices that discriminated against women and those that violated women's right to human dignity.[13] The Odoki Commission wrote that:[14]

'The tradition of widow inheritance which still exists in some societies was very hotly discussed. The practice offends against the definition of marriage in our laws, since often the free consent of the widow is not considered. The possibility of spread of AIDS was also seen as an issue connected with the practice. It appeared to most people that the practice has outlived its originally intended purpose and should be abolished either by law or by the communal decision of societies concerned.'

The Odoki Commission recommended that the new Constitution should recognise the right of everyone to practise his or her culture but[15] added that '[l]aws, cultural practices and customs which are against the dignity, equality, welfare or interests of women should be prohibited by the new Constitution, the laws of the country and the relevant cultural groups in the country'.[16] The recommendations that were contained in the Odoki Commission report were discussed by the Constituent Assembly which was made up of delegates from all parts of Uganda. Three points should be noted at this stage with regards to the Odoki Commission report: (i) most Ugandans were of the view that widow inheritance should be abolished; (ii) the abolition of widow inheritance could be done either through a piece of legislation or by the communities themselves; and (iii) the right to culture has to be compatible with Uganda's human rights obligations.

III THE CONSTITUENT ASSEMBLY PROCEEDINGS

During the Constituent Assembly (CA) debates, the CA[17] delegates expressed views on the issue of widow inheritance. One delegate submitted that:

'Customs like wife inheritance, which [members of her constituency] say is purely to benefit the inheritor, who squanders what he never sweated for and abandons the woman with the responsibility of looking after the orphans alone, must be done away with, not to mention the scourge of the AIDS. The Constitution we are

---

[12] *The Report of the Uganda Constitutional Commission: Analysis and Recommendations* (1992) para 7.59.

[13] *The Report of the Uganda Constitutional Commission: Analysis and Recommendations* (1992) para 7.64.

[14] *The Report of the Uganda Constitutional Commission: Analysis and Recommendations* (1992) para 7.69(c).

[15] *The Report of the Uganda Constitutional Commission: Analysis and Recommendations* (1992) paras 7.132–7.140.

[16] *The Report of the Uganda Constitutional Commission: Analysis and Recommendations* (1992) para 7.141(e).

[17] *Proceedings of the Constituent Assembly (Official Report)*, submissions by Mrs Lagada, 1 August 1994, p 1423.

making should protect widows and orphans ... [T]he eradication of negative cultural practices will only come with massive and patient education of the masses, both men and women.'

Another CA delegate submitted that, although the right to culture had to be protected in the Constitution, 'customs such as widow inheritance ... which treat a woman like property which belongs to one man, when he dies it goes to another man ... really subordinate us to hysteria and low status'.[18] Another CA delegate submitted that succession laws discriminated against women and especially widows and that '[i]t is even worse when the Law of succession is exercised, in which a woman is in most cases forced to remarry or be inherited by a man of the clan's choice and not the woman's choice. So this Constitution should ensure that women have ... [the right] to choose which man to stay with when the husband dies'.[19] Another delegate submitted that his constituents had urged him to submit that the cultural practice of a 'widow being inherited by the brother of the deceased' 'should be done way with' because it was 'out modelled and inflict[s] injustice' on women.[20] One delegate appealed to others that in the making of the Constitution and in particular the relevant provisions on women's rights they should '[t]hink about those widows who continue to be inherited by force as part of their husbands' estate, irrespective of whether the inheritor or inherited has [the] HIV Virus'.[21] One delegate submitted that in some communities women did not inherit any property at their husbands' death and that 'some men even try to inherit women as if they are properties'.[22] Another delegate linked bride price with widow inheritance by arguing that '[t]he tradition of inheriting widows is a result of bride price' because '[a] woman is considered bought and therefore can be ... mistreated at will'.[23] In

---

[18] *Proceedings of the Constituent Assembly (Official Report)*, submissions by Mrs Matembe, 23 August 1995, p 5840.

[19] *Proceedings of the Constituent Assembly (Official Report)*, submissions by Mrs Okorimoe, 15 July 1994, p 906.

[20] *Proceedings of the Constituent Assembly (Official Report)*, submissions by Mr Kitaka-Gawera, 21 July 1994, p 1084.

[21] *Proceedings of the Constituent Assembly (Official Report)*, submissions by Mrs Matembe, 22 July 1994, p 1148.

[22] *Proceedings of the Constituent Assembly (Official Report)*, submissions by Mrs Oryem, 25 July 1994, p 1174. See also submissions by Miss Nankabirwa, 27 June 1994, p 348, where its argued that widows are not only deprived of the right to inherit their deceased husbands' property but that '[i]n some tribes, the poor widow is regarded as property herself, able to be inherited as part of the estate'; submission by Mrs Rhoda Kalema 2003, 9 September 1994, who argued that 'unfortunately, in quite a number of our cultures, women, I understand, are shared by families, women are not married to one man. They are married to the families and unfortunately this makes it easy for the women to be inherited themselves as property. And once they inherit the widows it is even more easy for the property to be taken away from them'.

[23] *Proceedings of the Constituent Assembly (Official Report)*, submissions by Mrs Dominica Abu, 28 July 1994, p 1290.

some societies 'if a widow refuses to be inherited' her children are removed from her by her deceased husband's relatives.[24] One delegate compellingly submitted that:[25]

> '[S]ometimes a woman is forced even to re-marry a young boy she has helped to look after in her home. Somebody who stayed with you as a student you are forced to marry him because you are supposed to remain in that home. If you cannot marry that boy, then you must leave your children, and you must leave your property too if you want to marry outside of the clan. So, if these rights can be protected and we women are given the freedom to choose whatever partners we want after the death of our husbands, I think then, our rights will have been protected. We feel that here, the State could help so that we are not property which is inherited by anybody who wishes to inherit us.'

The above extracts from the Constituent Assembly proceedings show that all those who made submissions on the question of widow inheritance were of the view that the practice violated the rights of women and should be abolished. The submissions by the CA delegates were of two categories: those based on the personal views of the CA delegates and those based on the views of the delegates' constituents. Although the delegates were opposed to the practice of widow inheritance and highlighted its human rights implications and the dangers associated with, they did not suggest concrete measures that should be taken to eliminate it. All they called for was for its abolition. The Constitution that the CA delegates produced does not expressly prohibit the custom of widow inheritance. It does, however, contain at least two provisions that could be interpreted as making the custom of widow inheritance unconstitutional. The first provision is art 31(3) which provides that '[m]arriage shall be entered into with the free consent of the man and woman intending to marry'. Because of the fact that a widow who has been inherited does not have to consent to such inheritance, such a marriage would be contrary to art 31(3) of the Constitution. The second provision is art 33(6) of the Constitution which provides that '[l]aws, cultures, customs or traditions which are against the dignity, welfare or interest of women or which undermine their status, are prohibited by this Constitution'. There is no doubt that widow inheritance is a cultural practice that is against the dignity, welfare or interest of women and that it undermines their status and is thus prohibited by art 33(6) of the Constitution. The submissions before the Odoki Commission and during the Constituent Assembly proceedings that have been illustrated above clearly demonstrate this.

---

24   *Proceedings of the Constituent Assembly (Official Report)*, submissions by Ms Akello, 27 June 1994, p 337.
25   *Proceedings of the Constituent Assembly (Official Report)*, submission by Mrs Akech Okullu, 9 September 1994, p 2007.

IV   THE ISSUE OF WIDOW INHERITANCE BEFORE THE CONSTITUTIONAL COURT

As indicated earlier, one CA delegate submitted that there was a link between bride wealth and widow inheritance. The delegate, Mrs Abu, argued that because of bride wealth '[a] woman is considered bought and therefore can be ... mistreated at will'.[26] One of the grounds on which the constitutionality of the practice of bride wealth was unsuccessfully challenged in Uganda was that the 'payment of bride price reduces women to the status of chattel or property and exposes them to all sorts of abuse, [such as] widow inheritance and the risk of HIV infection'.[27] The Constitutional Court, in holding, by majority, that the practice of bride wealth was not contrary to Uganda's Constitution, did not express its view on the question of whether the practice of widow inheritance was unconstitutional. But in the light of art 31(3) of the Constitution which provides that marriage shall be entered into with the free consent of both parties and art 33(6) which prohibits customs and traditions that violate the dignity and welfare of women, it can be compellingly argued that the practice of widow inheritance is unconstitutional and that, had the Constitutional Court considered that issue, one might optimistically have expected it to have reached the same conclusion.

The fact that the custom of widow inheritance is against Uganda's national and international human rights obligations has also been mentioned at the international level. The Committee on the Elimination of Discrimination against Women noted with satisfaction the existence of art 36(6) in the Ugandan Constitution but noted with concern 'the continued existence of ... customary laws and practices on ... widow inheritance ... that ... conflict with the Constitution and the Convention'.[28] The Committee urged Uganda to prohibit widow inheritance and requested the government 'to work with the relevant ministries and nongovernmental organizations, including lawyers' associations and women's groups, to create an enabling environment for legal reform and effective law enforcement and legal literacy'.[29] The above discussion shows that it was a matter of time before Uganda enacted a specific legislative provision that would deal with the issue of widow inheritance.

---

[26]   *Proceedings of the Constituent Assembly (Official Report)*, submissions by Mrs Dominica Abu, 28 July 1994, p 1290.

[27]   *Mifumi(U) Ltd & 12 others v Attorney General, Kenneth Kakuru* (Constitutional Petition No 12 of 2007) [2010] UGCC 2 (26 March 2010).

[28]   Report of the Committee on the Elimination of Discrimination against Women, A/57/38 (2002) para 153.

[29]   Report of the Committee on the Elimination of Discrimination against Women, A/57/38 (2002) para 154.

V   LEGISLATIVE REFORMS

The Uganda Law Reform Commission[30] embarked on the process of putting in place a legislative provision that would deal with the issue of widow inheritance. The Uganda Law Reform Commission undertook field studies in different parts of Uganda on the question of widow inheritance in order to devise appropriate measures for its abolition. In its report that preceded the drafting of the Domestic Relations Bill, the Uganda Law Reform Commission wrote that:[31]

> 'The customary studies found that in some communities, widow inheritance is still practiced. Among the Alur, the widow has a right to select which of the deceased should inherit her; among the Banyankole a young widow is inherited by a step son, while among the Iteso the younger brother, or a clans mate, usually inherits the widow. In fact a widow who refuses to be inherited may be evicted from the clan land and a refund of bride-wealth paid to marry her demanded. However, AIDS and changing socio-economic relations has [sic] led to a decline in the practice ... All studies agreed that widow inheritance should cease and where it occurs, the refund of bride-wealth upon refusal to be inherited should be prevented.'

Based on those findings the Uganda Law Reform Commission recommended that '[c]onsidering the current social realities, the practice of widow inheritance should be prohibited'.[32] It is against that background that the Domestic Relations Bill[33] expressly prohibited widow inheritance,[34] and provided that 'a man shall not marry a widow through the custom or practice of widow inheritance'[35] and that 'a man may marry his relative's widow where both the man and the widow' freely consent to such a marriage.[36] The Domestic Relations Bill thus dealt with two forms of widow inheritance. The first form, which was prohibited, was the one in which the widow's consent was not necessary for her to be inherited by her deceased husband's relative. This was punishable by a fine and imprisonment not exceeding one year or both.[37] The second form of widow inheritance is not actually widow inheritance in the true sense of the word. In this case the widow's consent is needed for her to marry any of her deceased husband's relatives. The widow cannot be compelled to marry any of her husband's relatives.

---

[30]   The Uganda Law Reform Commission has the mandate to 'study and keep under constant review the Acts and other laws comprising the laws of Uganda with a view to making recommendations for their systematic, development, modernisation and reform' in line with Uganda's national, regional and international human rights obligations. See s 10 of the Uganda Law Reform Commission Act, Chapter 25 of the Law of Uganda.

[31]   *Uganda Law Reform Commission, Study Report on Marriage and Divorce in Uganda* (Publication No 2 of 2002, revised 2010) 174.

[32]   *Uganda Law Reform Commission, Study Report on Marriage and Divorce in Uganda* (Publication No 2 of 2002, revised 2010) 174.

[33]   Domestic Relations Bill, Bill No 21 of 2003.

[34]   Clause 16(3).

[35]   Clause 16(1).

[36]   Clause 16(2).

[37]   Clause 16(4).

The Uganda Law Reform Commission also points out the relationship between widow inheritance and bride-wealth. Its report shows that one of the factors that contributes to widow inheritance is bride-wealth. In some communities a widow has to 'consent' to be inherited because failure to do so would force her to refund the bride-wealth that her deceased husband would have paid at the time of marrying her. It has to be recalled that some of the said bride-wealth might have been 'eaten' by some of the widow's relatives years before the husband's death, thus making it impossible for such a woman to refund it especially if she has not been working. Therefore, the issue of poverty is a very important factor contributing to widow inheritance. A woman who can afford to refund the bride-wealth and who can afford to sustain herself and her children, including paying for her own accommodation and food, without relying on her deceased husband's clan members, cannot be forced to be inherited. If she chooses to remarry, she can freely and fully consent to remarrying one of her husband's relatives of her choice or she can choose to marry someone else.

After drafting the Bill, the Uganda Law Reform Commission presented it to the relevant parliamentary committee for its comments. In its report on the Domestic Relations Bill, Parliament's Committee on Legal and Parliamentary Affairs was of the view that the provision on widow inheritance should be deleted from the Bill. The Committee was of the view that:[38]

> 'The use of the phrase "widow inheritance" is a deliberate coining to make this cultural form of marriage derogatory. For as long as there is free consent of the widow this should be a form of recognised marriage. The reason for supporting this is that it gives protection and dignity to the widow and the orphans to remain in the home of the deceased and bring up the children according to customs of the clan. As long as we have patrimonial system, re-marriage within the clan provides a way of maintaining the lineage.'

This statement shows that the Committee was opposed to widow inheritance if it meant that the widow will have to marry her deceased husband's relative without her consent. However, in a case where such a widow with her consent remarried one of her deceased husband's relatives, the Committee argued that it is wrong to refer to this as widow inheritance. It should be called remarriage. Although the Committee highlights its reasons for the support of the remarriage of a widow to a clan member of her deceased husband, it could be argued that a poor woman may not be able to freely and fully give her consent to such a marriage if she knows that the refusal to marry a clan member of her deceased husband's clan will result in her children being removed from her and also being 'kicked out' of the matrimonial house. There is nothing that prevents a widow from bringing up her children according to her deceased husband's clan custom if she chooses not to remarry one of the clan members of her deceased husband's clan. Arguing that by remarrying a member of her deceased husband's clan the widow will be able to retain the matrimonial house

---

[38] *Report of the Committee on Legal and Parliamentary Affairs on the Domestic Relations Bill,* 2003, March 2005 para 13.

and also to bring up children in accordance with the deceased husband's custom is an indirect way of forcing poor women to marry within their deceased husband's clans. The Committee's report seems to have ignored s 39 of the Land Act which protects the rights of orphans and spouses to property[39] and Art 20 of the Protocol to the African Charter on Human and Peoples' Rights on the Rights of Women in Africa which protects widows' rights such as the right to own property, the right to custody of the children and the right to marry men of their choice.[40] The Committee's reasoning also seems to be contrary to Art 21(1) of the Protocol to the African Charter on Human and Peoples' Rights on the Rights of Women in Africa.[41]

As a result of the strong opposition to the Domestic Relations Bill,[42] it was split into the Marriage and Divorce Bill[43] and the Administration of Muslim Personal Law Bill.[44] The Marriage and Divorce Bill, like its predecessor the Domestic Relations Bill, prohibits widow inheritance,[45] provides that 'a man shall not marry a widow through the custom or practice of widow practice'[46] but adds that 'a man may marry his relative's widow where both the man and the widow, with their free consent, adopt any form of marriage provided for under this Act'.[47] A man who marries his relative's widow without her consent commits an offence and is liable to a fine or to imprisonment not exceeding one

---

[39] The Land Act, Chapter 227, 1998. Parliament is yet to enact a law to put into effect art 31(2) of the Constitution which provides that 'Parliament shall make appropriate laws for the protection of the widows and widowers to inherit the property of the deceased spouses and enjoy parental rights over their children'.

[40] Article 20 provides that: 'States Parties shall take appropriate legal measures to ensure that widows enjoy all human rights through the implementation of the following provisions:
(a) The widows are not subjected to inhuman, humiliating or degrading treatment;
(b) That a widow shall automatically become the guardian and custodian of her children, after the death of her husband, unless this is contrary to the interests and the welfare of the children;
(c) That a widow shall have the right to remarry, and in that event to marry the person of her choice.'

[41] Article 21(1) provides that '[a] widow shall have the right to an equitable share in the inheritance of the property of her husband. A widow shall have the right to continue to live in the matrimonial house. In the case of remarriage, she shall retain this right if the house belongs to her or she had inherited it'.

[42] See e g Hansard of the Parliament of the Republic of Uganda, Second Reading, The Domestic Relations Bill, 2 May 2006, pp 17182–17187, where members of Parliament highlight the fact that the Muslim community was opposed to the Bill. As a result of the Muslim community's opposition to the Domestic Relations Bill, in 2008 the Uganda Law Reform Commission drafted the Administration of Muslim Personal Law Bill, 2008 which provides, in clause 11(2), that Qadhi courts shall have jurisdiction over: marriage; divorce; nullity of marriage; the disposition of property on divorce or nullification of marriage; the maintenance of dependants, guardianship or custody of children; wakfu; division and inheritance of property of a person who has died testate or intestate; the determination of persons entitled to share in the estate of a deceased or of the shares to which such person is respectively entitled; other matters in respect of which jurisdiction is conferred by any written law.

[43] Marriage and Divorce Bill, No 19 of 2009.

[44] Administration of Muslim Personal Law Bill, 2008.

[45] Clause 13(1).

[46] Clause 13(2).

[47] Clause 13(3). The Bill provides for the following types of marriage: civil marriage; Christian marriage; customary marriage; Hindu marriage; and Baha'i marriage.

year or both.[48] Many members of Parliament support the Bill with one arguing that 'widow inheritance was primitive and should be abandoned'.[49]

The drafters of the Marriage and Divorce Bill seem to have ignored one important aspect that could have been essential in the elimination of widow inheritance in Uganda – education or sensitisation. It is unlikely that criminalisation and the threat of punishment will be sufficient to eliminate widow inheritance. In 2001 the government established the Constitutional Review Commission[50] which traversed the whole country soliciting peoples' views on the amendments that should be made to the Constitution. In their submissions to the Constitutional Review Commission women's groups were 'concerned about the discriminative cultural practices' that continued 'unchecked and which pervade social relations'.[51] Dispossessing women of property at the death of their husbands was one of the practices which women's groups were concerned about.[52] The Constitutional Review Commission, although recognising the fact that strict laws were needed to curb such practices, recommended that '[t]he lasting solution lies in changing the attitudes of the people through continuous education and sensitisation'.[53] As illustrated earlier, the Odoki Commission report and the submissions before the Constituent Assembly directly or indirectly recognise the importance of education and sensitisation in the fight against widow inheritance. The sensitisation of people, especially on human rights and the dangers associated with widow inheritance such as HIV infection, could be an effective way in fighting widow inheritance in addition to criminalisation. Experience has shown that the threat of punishment has not deterred some Ugandans from practising cultural practices that are against the rights and dignity of women. On 9 April 2010 the Prohibition of Female Genital Mutilation Act,[54] which criminalises female general mutilation (FGM),[55] came into force but a few months after that hundreds of girls had their genitals mutilated.[56]

---

[48]   Clause 13(4).
[49]   M Karugaba and C Bekunda 'Legislators back new marriage Bill' *The New Vision* (28 September 2009) available at www.newvision.co.ug/PA/8/13/696155 (accessed 18 January 2012) comments by Agriculture and Animal Industry State Minister, Bright Rwamirama.
[50]   See Commission of Inquiry (Constitutional Review) Legal Notice No 1 of 2001.
[51]   *The Report of the Commission of Inquiry (Constitutional Review): Findings and Recommendations* (2003) Makerere University Printery, 10–140.
[52]   *The Report of the Commission of Inquiry (Constitutional Review): Findings and Recommendations* (2003) Makerere University Printery, 10–140.
[53]   *The Report of the Commission of Inquiry (Constitutional Review): Findings and Recommendations* (2003) Makerere University Printery, 10–141.
[54]   The Prohibition of Female Genital Mutilation Act 5 of 2010.
[55]   Sections 2 (creates the offence of carrying out FGM); 3(1) (creates the offence of aggravated FGM); 4 (creates the offence of carrying out FGM on oneself); 5 (creates the offence of attempting to commit FGM); and 6 (creates the offence of aiding and abetting FGM). For a detailed discussion of the different provisions of the FGM Act and the steps taken in Uganda to abolish FGM see JD Mujuzi 'Female genital mutilation in Uganda: A glimpse at the abolition process' (2012) 56(1) *Journal of African Law* 139–150 available at http://journals.cambridge.org/action/displayJournal?jid=JAL (accessed June 2012).
[56]   See F Womakuyu 'To hell with the law! We shall circumcise the girls' *The New Vision* (5 November 2010) available at www.newvision.co.ug/PA/9/183/737167 (accessed 23 January 2012) where its reported that some community members made it clear that they were preparing

VI CONCLUSION

This chapter has shown that, although the Constitution of Uganda and international and regional human rights instruments that Uganda has ratified or acceded to such as the Protocol to the African Charter on Human and Peoples' Rights on the Rights of Women in African, the Convention on the Elimination of All Forms of Discrimination against Women and the International Covenant on Civil and Political Rights specifically provide that women should marry only after having freely consented to such marriages, widow inheritance is still practised in some communities in Uganda. This chapter has shown the steps taken to abolish this practice and has argued that in the face of poverty many widows may not be able to resist being inherited by their husbands' relatives. Even where such consent is ostensibly given, it cannot be called free and full consent where a widow knows that her refusal to be inherited by one of her husband's relatives will result in her dismissal from her deceased husband's house or her children being taken away by her husband's family members. Women's economic empowerment will go a long way to making women financially independent and ultimately making it possible for them to meaningfully resist being inherited on the death of their husbands. It has been argued that the criminalisation of widow inheritance, although a positive development in the process of the abolition of this practice, may not be sufficient to eradicate it. Education and sensitisation should also be streamlined with the objective of changing people's mindsets and also highlighting the human rights and health implications of this practice.

---

to circumcise over 200 girls although the law banned female genital circumcision; see also S Ariong 'Pokot circumcise 200 girls in a month' *Daily Monitor* (23 June 2011) available at www.monitor.co.ug/News/National/-/688334/1187638/-/c07v60z/-/index.html (accessed 23 January 2012) where it is reported that at least 200 girls aged between 8 and 14 were forced by their parents to undergo female genital mutilation.

United States

PREMARITAL AGREEMENTS IN THE UNITED STATES

*J Thomas Oldham**

Résumé

Au cours des quarante dernières années, les tribunaux américains ont accepté que les conjoints puissent, dans le cadre de contrats prénuptiaux, modifier les règles de partage en cas de divorce. Il n'existe cependant pas de consensus sur la question de savoir si le droit commun des contrats s'y applique ou si des protections particulières devraient pouvoir jouer. Dans le présent texte, les auteurs proposent deux importants changements. Le premier obligerait les parties à négocier et à signer ce type d'entente avant la célébration du mariage, ce qui leur donnerait plus de temps pour réfléchir à l'opportunité de s'engager dans ce genre de contrat. Cette nouvelle exigence représenterait un changement considérable du droit actuel; en effet, dans de nombreux états les contrats prénuptiaux sont exécutoires, même s'ils ont été envisagés pour la première fois à peine un ou deux jours avant le mariage. Le deuxième changement consisterait à interdire aux époux de renoncer mutuellement au droit alimentaire entre conjoints, s'ils ont eu un enfant commun à charge pendant le mariage. Une telle restriction garantirait au conjoint dont la capacité à générer des revenus a été considérablement affectée en raison du fait qu'il s'est occupé des enfants, de pouvoir faire valoir son droit alimentaire, quels que soient les termes du contrat de mariage.

I INTRODUCTION

The economic consequences of divorce in the United States are governed by the law of the state where parties divorce. State laws vary to some degree, but in many states the norm is that property accumulated during marriage (except gifts or inheritances) is divided approximately equally, while premarital acquisitions and gifts and inheritances received during marriage are retained by the recorded owner. In addition, if the parties' earnings vary greatly at divorce and the marriage lasted for a substantial period, there is also a possibility that the party with higher earnings will have to pay post-divorce support to the other.

---

* John Freeman Professor of Law, University of Houston. I would like to thank Jessica Eberle for her word processing assistance.

During the past 40 years, all states have accepted that the economic rights of the parties if they divorce can be altered via a premarital agreement. There are conflicting views regarding the rights that can be modified or eliminated via a premarital agreement, as well as when courts should refuse to enforce the agreement.

I will summarise below the various approaches taken by United States courts and legislatures and propose what I believe would be the optimal set of rules.

II CURRENT UNITED STATES RULES TOWARD PREMARITAL AGREEMENTS

(a) Rules relating to the circumstances surrounding execution

(i) The contract must be voluntarily signed

All states agree that a premarital agreement must be voluntarily signed without duress, but there is no agreement on what this requires. In New Zealand and Australia, voluntary execution is made more likely by the requirement that both parties have independent counsel.[1] In the United States, while independent counsel is considered a factor relevant to the issue of voluntary execution, in no state is it a requirement.[2]

The most common scenario presenting the issue of voluntary execution arises when the wealthier prospective spouse presents a draft agreement to the less wealthy party a day or two before the wedding date, and states that there will be no wedding unless the agreement is signed. Such agreements frequently limit the rights of the less wealthy party significantly if the marriage ends in divorce. This obviously places the less wealthy party in a difficult position. He or she must decide on quite short notice whether to retain a lawyer and, if legal advice is desired, a lawyer must be identified and an appointment obtained. In addition, while the parties are discussing the prenuptial agreement a variety of other activities associated with the wedding may also be taking place and guests from out of town may be arriving, thus making it difficult to focus on the agreement and digest any legal advice obtained.

---

[1] See Bill Atkin and Wendy Parker *Relationship Property in New Zealand* (Wellington: LexisNexis, 2nd edn, 2009) 193; Belinda Fehlberg and Bruce Smyth 'Binding Prenuptial Agreements in Australia: The First Year' (2002) 16 Int J Law, Policy & Fam 127, 128, 130–31.

[2] See *Randolph v Randolph*, 937 SW2d 815 (Tenn 1996); *In re Estate of Smid*, 756 NW2d 1 (SD 2008); *In re Estate of Lutz*, 563 NW2d 90 (ND 1997); *Fletcher v Fletcher*, 68 Ohio St3d 464, 628 NE2d 1343 (1994); *Holler v Holler*, 364 SC 256, 612 SE2d 469 (SC App 2005); *Edwards v Edwards*, 744 NW2d 243 (Neb 2008); JT Oldham *Divorce Separation and the Distribution of Property* (New York: Law Journal Press, 2011) § 4.03[5]. In California it is required if the contract restricts the right to spousal support. See California Family Code, § 1612. If a California contract does not impact spousal support and a party does not want to consult a lawyer, the agreement will be enforced over that party's objection only if the party, before the premarital agreement was signed, signed a written waiver of the right to consult with a lawyer. Cal Fam Code, § 1615(c).

United States courts disagree regarding whether a premarital agreement should be considered voluntarily signed if a draft is presented a day or two before the wedding and the other party signs the agreement without consulting a lawyer. Some courts have not enforced such agreements.[3] If the proponent of the agreement discouraged the other party from consulting a lawyer, this may make it more likely the court will not enforce the agreement.[4]

In contrast, a number of other courts have enforced agreements first presented a day or two before the wedding.[5] These courts appear to believe that 'two days ... provided [the party] ample opportunity to seek advice of counsel before signing'.[6] Another court held that 'the mere shortness of time ... between presentation of the premarital agreement and the wedding is insufficient alone to permit a finding of duress'.[7] It has not been considered relevant that the party tried to contact a lawyer but due to time constraints could not talk to him before the agreement was signed.[8] If the objecting party was represented by counsel it is more likely that an agreement negotiated at the last minute will be considered voluntarily signed.[9] Another court commented:[10]

> 'For [the male] to trick [the female] into going to [the lawyer's] office just days before their marriage, and then condition the marriage on her signature [of the premarital agreement], was certainly not laudatory. However, while these actions may be fairly characterized as surprise pressure tactics, they do not negate the knowing and voluntary nature of the execution.'

These courts treat a premarital agreement like any other commercial contract. The prospective spouses are treated as unrelated third parties with no special or fiduciary relationship. An agreement is considered enforceable even if one party engages in 'surprise pressure tactics' at the last minute.

In most states, agreements first presented more than a few days before the wedding have been considered voluntarily signed.[11] In California, if the party is not represented by a lawyer, the person must be given at least 7 days to decide

---

3   See *Pember v Shapiro*, 794 NW2d 435 (ND 2011); *Hoag v Dick*, 799 A2d 391 (Me 2002); *Bakos v Bakos*, 450 So2d 1257 (Fla App 2007); *Hjortas v McCabe*, 656 So2d 168 (Fla App 1995); Estate of Hollett, 834 A2d 348 (NH 2003).

4   See Marriage of Rudder, 217 P3d 183 (Ore App 2009).

5   See *DeLorean v DeLorean*, 511 A2d 1257 (NJ Ch Div 1986); *In re Yannalfo*, 147 NH 597, 794 A2d 795 (2002); *Fletcher v Fletcher*, 628 NE2d 1343 (Ohio 1994); *Ware v Ware*, 7 So3d 271 (Miss App 2008); *Pajak v Pajak*, 385 SE2d 384 (W Va 1989); *Mann v Mann*, 36 Fam L Rep (BNA) 1262 (Ohio App 2010); *Simeone v Simeone*, 581 A2d 162 (Pa 1990); *Panossian v Panossian*, 172 AD2d 811, 569 NY S2d 182 (1991).

6   *Wiethe v Beaty*, 1999 WL 74595 (Ohio App).

7   See *Howell v Landry*, 96 NC App 516, 386 SE2d 610 (1989).

8   See *Brown v Brown*, 26 So3d 1210 (Ala App 2007).

9   See Marriage of Murphy, 359 Ill App 3d 289, 834 NE2d 56 (2005).

10 Estate of Ingmand, 2001 WL 855406 (Iowa App).

11 See *Biliouris v Biliouris*, 852 NE2d 687 (Mass App 2006) (one week before the wedding); *Gordon v Gordon*, 25 So3d 615 (Fla App 2009) (10 days before); *Millstein v Millstein*, 2002 WL 31031676 (Ohio App) (8 days before).

whether to sign.[12] A Washington court held that an agreement was not voluntarily signed when a draft of the agreement was given by a very rich man to his poor prospective bride 2 weeks before the wedding, but negotiations regarding the terms of the agreement did not begin until a few days before the wedding.[13]

(ii)   Exchange of financial information

In a majority of states, an agreement may be successfully challenged if the objecting party did not have adequate information about the finances of the other party at the time of signing.[14] States disagree about the amount of information the objecting party must have received. Some require only very general information, while others require more specific information about the party's property, debts and income.

This distinction is highlighted in the divorce case of the auto executive John DeLorean. The parties signed a premarital agreement in California and divorced in New Jersey. Pursuant to the agreement, Mrs DeLorean waived any rights she would otherwise have if the parties divorced. Mrs DeLorean at the time of the wedding knew only that Mr DeLorean owned certain properties; she did not know of all the properties he owned or their value. The New Jersey court noted that this level of financial disclosure did not satisfy New Jersey law and would be grounds for not enforcing the agreement if New Jersey law would be applied. In contrast, California did not require extensive financial disclosure. Because the parties signed the agreement in California and because the agreement stated that it was to be governed by California law, the court applied California law and concluded that Mr DeLorean had satisfied the lower California standard of financial disclosure.[15]

Many courts have ruled that, if a party has a general idea of the financial condition of the other, this is adequate financial information.[16] For example, if the parties lived together or dated for a substantial period before the contract was signed, this can lead a court to conclude that the party was generally aware of the other's financial condition, and that this general awareness was sufficient, even if no financial disclosure was received when the agreement was signed.[17] If a party is represented by counsel, it is more likely the court will find

---

[12]   See Marriage of Cadwell-Faso and Faso, 2011 WL 72179 (Cal App); Cal Fam Code, § 1615(c).
[13]   See Marriage of Bernard, 204 P3d 90 (Wash 2009).
[14]   See e g Iowa Code, § 596.8(3); Nev Rev Stat, § 123A.080; NJ Stat Ann, § 37.2–36(c); Conn Stat, § 46b-36g; Marriage of Seewald, 22 P3d 580 (Colo App 2001); *DeMatteo v DeMatteo*, 436 Mass 18, 762 NE2d 797 (Mass 2002); Estate of Benker, 416 Mich 681, 331 NW2d 193 (1982).
[15]   See *DeLorean v DeLorean*, 511 A2d 1257 (NJ Ch Div 1986).
[16]   See *Robinson v Robinson*, 2010 WL 5030120 (Ala App); *Gordon v Gordon*, 25 So3d 615 (Fla App 2009); *Brown v Brown*, 26 So3d 1210 (Ala App 2007); Estate of Davis, 213 SW3d 288 (Tenn App 2006); *Cannon v Cannon*, 865 A2d 563 (Md 2005); *Millstein v Millstein*, 2002 WL 310311676 (Ohio App); *Griffin v Griffin*, 94 P3d 96 (Okla App 2004); *Binek v Binek*, 673 NW2d 594 (ND 2004).
[17]   See *Donovan v Donovan*, 1999 WL 1499141 (Va Cir Ct); *Dove v Dove*, 680 SE2d 839 (Ga 2009).

the party had an adequate opportunity to obtain financial information.[18] If one party materially misrepresents to the other prospective spouse the nature or value of his property, however, this can result in a court invalidating the agreement.[19]

Some courts have required more detailed disclosure. For example, some have invalidated an agreement where the objecting party did not know the income of the other party.[20] In New Jersey, before the agreement was signed each party must have 'full awareness' of the other's income and assets.[21] In Minnesota there must be 'full disclosure of the earnings and property' of each party.[22]

(iii) Understanding the effect of the agreement

It was mentioned above that, under United States law, independent counsel is not required in order to have an enforceable agreement. Some have proposed that, if one party is represented by a lawyer and the other is not, the agreement should not be enforced unless the unrepresented party received a written summary of the effect of the agreement before the agreement was signed.[23] To date only California has adopted this requirement.[24]

(b) Reviewing the agreement for substantive fairness

When parties sign premarital agreements in the United States, frequently one party has substantially more property than the other. In this situation, the wealthier party often seeks, via the premarital agreement, to restrict the economic rights the other party would normally have if the parties divorce. This can leave the parties in very different economic circumstances if they divorce and the agreement is enforced. American courts and legislatures have not reached a consensus regarding the extent to which a divorce court should review a premarital agreement for substantive fairness before enforcing it. At one extreme are states that have enacted a rule that an agreement should not be enforced only if (i) it was unconscionable when signed and (ii) the objecting party did not receive adequate financial information regarding the other party.[25] In other words, even if an agreement was unconscionable when signed it should be enforced if there was adequate disclosure of financial information.

---

[18] See *Reece v Elliott*, 208 SW3d 419 (Tenn App 2006); *Winchester v McCue*, 91 Conn App 721, 882 A2d 143 (2005); *Gardner v Gardner*, 527 NW2d 701 (Wis App 1994).

[19] See *Peters-Riemers v Riemers*, 644 NW2d 197 (ND 2002).

[20] See *Corbett v Corbett*, 628 SE2d 585 (Ga 2006). See also *Casto v Casto*, 508 So2d 330 (Fla 1987); *Stemler v Stemler*, 36 So3d 54 (Ala App 2009) (applying Florida law).

[21] See *Marschall v Marschall*, 195 NJ Super 16, 477 A2d 833 (Ch Div 1984).

[22] See Minn Stat, § 519.11.

[23] The American Law Institute's Principles of the Law of Family Dissolution has made this recommendation. See American Law Institute *Principles of the Law of Family Dissolutions: Analysis and Recommendations* (Newark: LexisNexis, 2002) § 7.05.

[24] See Cal Fam Code, § 1615(c).

[25] See Ariz Rev Code, § 25–201 et seq; Ark Rev Stat, § 9–11–401 et seq; Del Code Ann Tit 13, § 321 et seq; Hawaii Code, § 572D-1 et seq; Idaho Code, § 32–921 et seq; 750 Ill Cons Stats, ch 40, para 2601 et seq; Kan Stat, § 23–801 et seq; Mont Code Ann, § 40-2-601 et seq; Neb Stats,

Some other states do not enforce the agreement if it is shown to be unconscionable at the time of execution regardless of the amount of financial information disclosed.[26]

In these states, changes in the parties' circumstances during marriage are not considered. Some states have concluded that this is unfair, and that the agreement should not be enforced if it would be unconscionable at the time of divorce to do so.[27]

In many states, if an agreement is found to be unconscionable (either at the time of signing or at divorce, depending on the state's law) the agreement will be considered void. In North Dakota, if an agreement is found to be unconscionable the court is given the discretion to (i) refuse to enforce the entire agreement, (ii) enforce a severable portion of the agreement and (iii) limit the application of the unconscionable provisions to avoid an unconscionable result.[28]

States are still clarifying how to determine whether an agreement is unconscionable. A New Jersey statute defines an unconscionable agreement as one that leaves a party without a means of reasonable support or would provide a standard of living for a party far below what the party enjoyed before the marriage.[29] One court has suggested that, when reviewing an agreement for unconscionability, courts should consider factors of unfair surprise, disparity of bargaining power and substantive unfairness.[30] Another has suggested the primary focus should be to determine whether there was unfair surprise and the extent to which the agreement is one-sided.[31] Other descriptions offered have been that an unconscionable agreement is one where the terms are 'manifestly unfair and unreasonable'[32] or that enforcement would 'work an injustice'.[33] Another perspective is that an agreement is unconscionable if a party would be left a public charge,[34] or would not be able to be self-supporting.[35] One court proposed that courts should be more willing to enforce agreements involving spouses who married later in life as opposed to spouses who married while relatively young and raised children.[36] Some have suggested that the relevant

---

§ 42.1001 et seq; NC Code, § 52B-1 et seq; Ore Stats, § 108.700 et seq; Tex Fam Code, § 4.001 et seq; Va Code, § 20–147 et seq; DC Code, § 46–501 et seq.

[26] See Wis Stat Ann, § 766.58(6); Ind Code 31–11–1-8; Nev Rev Stat, § 123 A.080.

[27] See *Blue v Blue*, 60 SW3d 585 (Ky App 2001). See also Conn Stat, § 46b-36g; NJ Stat Ann, § 37:2–37; ND Code, § 14–03.1–07; *DeMatteo v DeMatteo*, 436 Mass 18, 762 NE2d 797 (2002).

[28] See ND Code, § 14–03.1–07.

[29] NJ Stat Ann, § 37: 2–32.

[30] Marriage of Shanks, 758 NW2d 506 (Iowa 2008).

[31] *Lewis v Lewis*, 69 Haw 497, 748 P2d 1362 (1988).

[32] *Blue v Blue*, 60 SW3d 585 (Ky App 2001).

[33] *Bedrick v Bedrick*, 300 Conn 691, 17 A3d 17 (2011).

[34] See *Bassler v Bassler*, 593 A2d 82 (Vt 1991); *Osborne v Osborne*, 428 NE2d 810 (Mass 1981); *McFarlane v Rich*, 567 A2d 585 (NH 1985).

[35] See *Gentry v Gentry*, 798 SW2d 928 (Ky 1990); *Justus v Justus*, 581 NE2d 1265 (Ind App 1991).

[36] See *Lane v Lane*, 202 SW3d 577 (Ky 2006).

inquiry for determining whether an agreement is unconscionable should be whether one or both party's circumstances have changed in an unforeseeable way during marriage.[37]

Other courts have not applied a standard of unconscionability; instead, they have applied a standard that a premarital agreement should not be enforced if the circumstances of the parties changed during marriage in ways that were unforeseeable when they married.[38] When applying this standard, a number of courts have found the changes in circumstances were foreseeable, so the agreement was enforced. For example, in a few cases a spouse who had significant assets at the time of marriage had become substantially more wealthy at the time of divorce.[39] Substantial changes in the parties' financial circumstances over a marriage lasting 26 years have been considered foreseeable.[40] In another case, a spouse had a number of health problems when the marriage began. These became more severe and she was totally disabled at the time of divorce.[41] All of these changes in circumstances were considered foreseeable.

Some courts have found the changes to be unforeseeable. In one case, a woman argued that she had imagined she would take a short break from her career to have a child and then quickly resume working. Instead, she spent 10 years at home as a caretaker of the children. This impact on her career prospects was considered unforeseen.[42] In addition, the Wisconsin Supreme Court has suggested that an unplanned pregnancy or an unforeseen medical problem could be an unforeseen change in circumstances that would justify not enforcing a premarital agreement.[43]

In the United States, courts sometimes choose an option other than either fully enforcing or totally invalidating the agreement. They might choose to enforce a portion and invalidate another. In most states, it is possible to restrict or eliminate both the right to receive a distribution of marital property as well as the right to post-dissolution support. Still, a number of courts have more aggressively reviewed for fairness agreements that purport to limit both. They have been willing to enforce the portion of the agreement that limits the right to

---

[37] See *Blue v Blue*, 60 SW3d 585 (Ky 2006).

[38] See *Woodington v Shokoohi*, 792 NW2d 63 (Mich App 2010); *Mazzitelli v Mazzitelli*, 2005 WL 221683 (Minn App); *Warren v Warren*, 147 Wis2d 704, 433 NW2d 295 (1988); *Gant v Gant*, 329 SE2d 106 (W Va 1985); *Winchester v McCue*, 91 Conn App 721, 882 A2d 143 (2005); *Crews v Crews*, 36 Fam L Rep (BNA) (Conn 2010); *Mallen v Mallen*, 622 SE2d 812 (Ga 2005) *Hardee v Hardee*, 585 SE2d 501 (SC 2003).

[39] See *Winchester v McCue*, 91 Conn App 721, 882 A2d 143(2005); *Crews v Crews*, 36 Fam L Rep (BNA) 1267 (Conn 2010); *Mallen v Mallen*, 622 SE2d 812 (Ga 2005).

[40] See *Reed v Reed*, 265 Mich App 131, 693 NW2d 825 (2005).

[41] *Hardee v Hardee*, 585 SE2d 501 (SC 2003).

[42] See *Mazzitelli v Mazzitelli*, 2005 WL 221683 (Minn App).

[43] See *Warren v Warren*, 147 Wis2d 704, 433 NW2d 295 (1988).

property division, but have not enforced spousal support restrictions, at least in marriages of some duration where the circumstances of the parties have changed during marriage.[44]

The American Law Institute has proposed, in its re-evaluation of the principles of US divorce law, that a divorce court should review the fairness of a premarital agreement at divorce before enforcing it. If enforcement of the agreement would 'work a substantial injustice', it should not be enforced.[45] This suggested approach has yet to be adopted by a US state.

(c) Restricting the right to post-divorce spousal support

In a few states, the right to post-divorce support may not be restricted in a premarital agreement.[46] In addition, spousal support restrictions are not enforceable in Colorado if as a result a spouse would not be able to provide for his or her reasonable post-divorce needs.[47] In Illinois, if a provision restricting spousal support would cause 'undue hardship in light of circumstances ... not reasonably foreseeable at the time of execution ... a court ... may require the other to provide support to the extent necessary to avoid such hardship'.[48] Similarly, under Indiana law if a restriction on the right for spousal support would cause 'extreme hardship under circumstances not reasonably foreseeable at the time of execution ... a court ... may require the other party to provide spousal maintenance to the extent necessary to avoid extreme hardship'.[49]

A number of other states generally enforce contractual restrictions on the right to spousal support. If enforcement of the waiver would result in a party qualifying for state benefits, the court in such states is authorised to award sufficient support to avoid this result.[50]

III IMPROVING THE APPROACH IN THE UNITED STATES

(a) Clarifying voluntary execution

The most surprising aspect of the rules governing the enforcement of premarital agreements in the United States is the extent to which many courts let the more wealthy prospective spouse wait until the very last minute to notify

---

[44] See *Lane v Lane*, 202 SW3d 577 (Ky 2006); *Newman v Newman*, 653 P2d 728 (Colo. 1982); *Rogers v Gordon*, 404 NJ Super 213, 961 A2d 11 (2008); *Gross v Gross*, 11 Ohio St3d 99, 464 NE2d 500 (1984).
[45] See American Law Institute *Principles of the Law of Family Dissolution: Analysis and Recommendations* (Newark: LexisNexis, 2002) § 7.05.
[46] See Iowa Code, § 596.5; N Mex Code, § 40–3A-4; *Sanford v Sanford*, 694 NW2d 283 (SD 2005).
[47] See Marriage of Dechant, 867 P2d 193 (Colo App 1993).
[48] 750 Ill Comp Stat, § 10/7(b).
[49] Ind Code, § 31–11–3-8(b).
[50] See statutes cited in n 25 above.

the other party that, unless the parties sign a premarital agreement that substantially changes the parties' rights upon divorce, the wedding will be called off. Such bargaining should not be permitted. If a draft agreement is first presented a few days before the wedding, this does not give a party adequate time to consider whether to retain a lawyer, to identify a lawyer, to make an appointment and obtain advice, and to negotiate changes in the agreement and decide whether to sign it. People engaged to be married have a special confidential relationship, and it is fair to hold an engaged couple to a higher standard than would normally apply when unrelated third parties negotiate an agreement.

For a premarital agreement to be considered enforceable, the law should require that a draft is presented an adequate amount of time before the wedding, so the party can decide, before the frenzy of the wedding festivities begins, whether to retain a lawyer, obtain legal advice if desired, negotiate changes and decide whether to sign the agreement. One approach would be merely to state a general standard of this type. For example, a rule could be established that, for a premarital agreement to be enforceable, drafts need to be exchanged a sufficient time before the wedding day so that the parties can decide whether to retain independent counsel, consult with a lawyer, if desired, attempt to negotiate revisions, and have adequate time to decide whether to sign the agreement. Alternatively, the standard could set forth a specific minimum amount of time. For example, in California the party needs to be given 7 days to decide whether to sign the agreement.[51] Similarly, the American Law Institute has proposed that a presumption should arise that a premarital agreement was voluntarily signed only if the agreement was signed 30 days before the wedding.[52]

A general non-specific standard would allow each state to develop its own construction of the general standard. Until such a construction is clarified, however, it could be unclear to contracting parties what is required. So, a more specific standard seems desirable. One possible standard, which would combine elements of the American Law Institute and California approaches, would be that a draft of the agreement needs to be exchanged at least 14 days before the wedding, and the agreement needs to be signed at least 7 days before the wedding.

(b)   Limits upon the right to restrict spousal support

In most states today, the right to distribution of property at divorce may be limited or eliminated via a premarital agreement. There is less agreement regarding the extent to which post-divorce spousal support may be impacted.

---

[51]   See Cal Fam Code, § 1615(c).
[52]   See American Law Institute *Principles of the Law of Family Dissolutions: Analysis and Recommendations* (Newark: LexisNexis, 2002) § 7.04(3).

If parties restrict only the right to a division of property in a premarital agreement, if the parties divorce after being married for a substantial period and the financial situations of the parties vary greatly, the court could still award spousal support to assure that each party will have reasonable support post-divorce. In contrast, if parties are also able to eliminate spousal support via a premarital agreement, this could leave one of the parties in quite precarious financial circumstance, even if the marriage lasted a fairly long time and the other spouse has substantial resources.

I propose that, if the parties raised a common child together during marriage, they should not be able to restrict a court's power to award post-divorce support. In marriages where the parties raise a child it is common for one party to incur substantial 'career damage' due to childcare duties.[53] In such situations, the primary caregiver's claim for post-divorce support is particularly compelling if the parties divorce after a marriage of significant duration. When such marriages end in divorce it would be fair to clarify that, regardless of the terms of any premarital agreement, spousal support will be possible where circumstances warrant it. This proposed limit upon premarital agreements would be consistent with the law of many countries of Western Europe, where parties cannot by premarital agreement limit the right to post-divorce maintenance.[54]

IV CONCLUSION

During the past 40 years United States courts have accepted that parties can, via a premarital agreement, change the rules governing the economic rights of the parties if they divorce. There is as yet no consensus regarding the extent to which contract rules normally applied to agreements between unrelated third parties should govern, or whether additional safeguards are needed.

I have suggested above two major changes in United States rules. The first attempts to assure that parties will negotiate the terms of such agreements and sign the agreement before the wedding festivities begin. This should give parties more time to intelligently consider whether to sign the agreement. Such a change would be a substantial improvement over current law; in many states, a premarital agreement will be enforced even if it is first presented a day or two before the wedding.

The second proposed change would bar parties from impacting the right to spousal support if the parties raised a common child during marriage. Such a limit would ensure that, if one party's earning capacity is significantly reduced

---

[53] See generally Cynthia Lee Starnes 'Mothers As Suckers: Pity, Partnership, and Divorce Discourse' (2005) 90 Iowa L Rev 1513, 1519–1527; J Thomas Oldham 'Book Review' (1992) 80 Calif L Rev 1091.

[54] See Walter Pintens 'Matrimonial Property Law in Europe' in Katharina Boele-Woelki, Jo Miles and Jens M Sherpe (eds) *The Future of Family Property in Europe* (Cambridge: Intersentia, 2011) 37.

due to childcare responsibilities during marriage, spousal support would potentially be available regardless of the terms of a premarital agreement.